D1614402

003322

Central Banks in the Age of the Euro

Central Banks in the Age of the Euro

Europeanization, Convergence, and Power

Edited by
Kenneth Dyson and Martin Marcussen

OXFORD

UNIVERSITY PRESS

Great Clarendon Street, Oxford OX2 6DP

Oxford University Press is a department of the University of Oxford.
It furthers the University's objective of excellence in research, scholarship,
and education by publishing worldwide in

Oxford New York

Auckland Cape Town Dar es Salaam Hong Kong Karachi
Kuala Lumpur Madrid Melbourne Mexico City Nairobi
New Delhi Shanghai Taipei Toronto

With offices in

Argentina Austria Brazil Chile Czech Republic France Greece
Guatemala Hungary Italy Japan Poland Portugal Singapore
South Korea Switzerland Thailand Turkey Ukraine Vietnam

Oxford is a registered trade mark of Oxford University Press
in the UK and in certain other countries

Published in the United States
by Oxford University Press Inc., New York

British Library Cataloguing in Publication Data

Data available

Library of Congress Cataloging in Publication Data

Data available

Library of Congress Control Number: 2009924588

Typeset by SPI Publisher Services, Pondicherry, India
Printed in Great Britain
on acid-free paper by the
CPI Antony Rowe, Chippenham, Wiltshire

ISBN 978–0–19–921823–3

1 3 5 7 9 10 8 6 4 2

Acknowledgements and Preface

By general consent European monetary union represents an historic event for European unification and for European Union (EU) member states. Manifestly, it is also historic in central banking: A new 'stateless' central bank managing a single currency, the euro, for (by 2009) sixteen EU member states, which voluntarily delegated their sovereignty over monetary policy.

This book examines the effects of this new 'age of the euro' on European central banks: Euro Area 'insiders', temporary 'outsiders', and semi-permanent 'outsiders'. These effects are matters of great topical and academic interest. They provide insights into the complex relations between Europeanization, power, and convergence in European central banking and into how international, European, and domestic factors shape these relations into different configurations.

The book is a companion to *The Euro At 10* (OUP) in addressing the same questions but with a narrower focus. Central banking provides an opportunity to explore a paradox. On the one hand, it has been subjected to major European-level institution building with the creation of the 'Eurosystem', which brings together the European Central Bank (ECB) and its national central banks (NCBs). Europeanization processes have in consequence, been unusually powerful. On the other hand, central banking is deeply and exceptionally embedded in an internationalized professional community, in globalized financial markets, and in academic macroeconomic debates. These three characteristics shape its contemporary professional character: cosmopolitan, market-oriented, and technocratic. Consequently, the independent impact of European monetary union (EMU) on central banking is limited. Europeanization reinforces central banking policy beliefs and practices that have their roots in wider processes of international diffusion. As will also become clear, the limitations of Europeanization also stem from the significance of domestic political contexts and historical legacies, most evidently in 'semi-permanent' outsiders like Britain and Sweden. Nevertheless, Europeanization has never before been so potent a force in European central banking; this process has accompanied the empowerment of central banks in macroeconomic discourse and management; whilst convergence pressures in central banking have strengthened. This book maps these three interconnected phenomena.

The book's distinctive character derives from the focus, questions, and approaches typical of political science in addressing comparative political economy. It deals with Europeanization, power, and convergence in institutions and policy processes. It focuses on ideas, institutions, discourse, and strategies in central banking; asks questions about how they mediate the effects of the euro on states (Europeanization) and about what they tell us about power and convergence. At the same time a key theme is the limits of Europeanization as a concept for capturing processes of change in central banking and differences in reform trajectories.

The book benefited from two major opportunities to bring together contributors in research workshops. The EU-CONSENT Network of Excellence supported a first workshop in Cardiff University in May 2007. Special thanks are due to the British Academy for co-funding a second research workshop in November 2007 with the EU-CONSENT Network. These workshops provided invaluable opportunities for authors to present drafts of their chapters for discussion. In particular, Angela Pusey at the British Academy displayed great courtesy, patience, and efficiency in ensuring the smooth running of the British Academy workshop.

In addition, the final revision of chapters benefited greatly from the comments of all contributors, who served as discussants on each other's papers at the two workshops. Particular debts of gratitude are owed to Professor Charles Goodhart (LSE) and to Professor Ivo Maes (Catholic University of Louvain) for their trenchant advice.

Dominic Byatt and his team at Oxford University Press have offered unfailing encouragement and support at every stage. Through their commitment, willingness to work as a team, and patience with our efforts at guidance, the contributors have made our task pleasant and rewarding in personal as well as in academic terms. The combination of OUP's professionalism with the dedication of contributors lightened the editorial load. Nevertheless, as ever, any shortcomings in the final product remain the responsibility of the editors.

Finally, a few words are needed about the immediate context of the book. It was written as the dramatic events associated with the financial crisis of 2007–8 began to unfold. The US sub-prime mortgage crisis and the crisis in the interbank money markets had occurred. However, the US rescues of the mortgage financing giants Fannie Mae and Freddie Mac and the insurance giant AIG, the bankruptcy of Lehman Brothers, and the spread of bank solvency crises to the EU and Euro Area lay ahead. By September 2008, the three Benelux governments were rescuing Fortis bank; the German government and Bundesbank were bailing out Hypo Real Estate; a number of German states were rescuing their state banks; whilst EU governments were offering guarantees for bank deposits in an ad hoc, initially uncoordinated manner. Central banks were drawn into liquidity support operations and into bank rescue operations on a massive scale, rediscovering their role as banker to the banks; huge public stakes were taken in banking systems, not least in the United States and Britain, the homes of archetypal 'Anglo-American free market capitalism'; the regulation and supervision of financial markets became a high-profile political issue; whilst monetary policy stood uneasily poised between the challenge of inflation and threats from the financial crisis to the real economy of output and jobs. The economic and political world of central banking was in transformation: A favourable tailwind for monetary policy had been replaced by strong, volatile headwinds. Clearly, this book does not have the benefits of being able to look back on this crisis and assess its historical scale and long-term effects on central banking, an exercise that will be possible in a few years time, though some points are fairly safe to establish even at this early stage. We can only take note of events up to spring 2008. This problem is not, however, central to the book. The first chapter recognizes that since 1999 the age of the euro has been embedded in a political economy of (in historical terms) good times. This era is closing. Central banks, financial markets, politicians, and officials will be making history in a very different context of hard times. Just how different that context will be, and what effects their actions will have, we do not yet fully know.

Kenneth Dyson
Cardiff University, Wales

Martin Marcussen
Copenhagen University, Denmark

June 2008

Contents

Contents

List of Figures

List of Tables

Abbreviations

AMLF	Asset Backed Commercial Paper Money Market Mutual Fund Liquidity Facility
APRA	Australian Prudential Regulation Authority
ASIC	Australian Securities and Investments Commission
BCBS	Basel Committee on Banking Supervision
BEPG	Broad Economic Policy Guidelines
BFIC	Banking, Finance and Insurance Commission
BIS	Bank for International Settlements
BoG	Bank of Greece
BSC	Banking Supervision Committee
CBI	Central Bank Independence
CCBM	Correspondent Central Banking Model
CEBS	Committee of European Banking Supervisors
CECEI	Comité des établissements de crédit et des entreprises d'investissement
CEE	Central and Eastern Europe
CEG	City Euro Group
CFR	Code of Federal Regulations
CNB	Czech National Bank
CP	Core Purposes
CPFF	Commercial Paper Funding Facility
CSSB	Czechoslovak State Bank
DNB	De Nederlandsche Bank
EBRD	European Bank for Reconstruction and Development
ECB	European Central Bank
ECMS	Euro Collateral Management System
EFSAL	Enterprise and Financial Sector Adjustment Loan
ERM	Exchange-Rate Mechanism
EMI	European Monetary Institute
CPM	Conseil de la Politique Monétaire

Abbreviations

EMS	European Monetary System
EMU	Economic and Monetary Union
EP	European Parliament
ESCB	European System of Central Banks
FFIEC	Federal Financial Institutions Examination Council
FFR	Federal Funds Rate
FIDL	Financial Institutions Development Loan
FOMC	Federal Open Market Committee
FRB	Federal Reserve Board
FSA	Financial Services Authority
FTE	Full-Time Equivalent
GDP	Gross Domestic Product
HFC	Holland Financial Centre
IGC	Intergovernmental Conference
IMF	International Monetary Fund
IT	Inflation Target
JVI	Joint Vienna Institute
MMIFF	Money Market Investor Funding Facility
NBB	National Bank of Belgium
NBP	National Bank of Poland
NCB	National Central Banks
NCP	National Convergence Program
NSP	National Stability Program
OCR	Official Cash Rate
OECD	Organization for Economic Cooperation and Development
OEEC	Organization for European Economic Cooperation
OFS	Overview of Financial Stability
PDCF	Primary Dealer Credit Facility
QMA	Quarterly Monetary Assessment
ROW	Rest of the World
SDP	Social Democratic Party
SEPA	Single Euro Payment Area
SGP	Stability and Growth Pact
SNB	Swiss National Bank
TAF	Term Auction Facility
TARGET	Trans-European Automated Real-time Gross Settlement Express Transfer

TEU	Treaty on European Union
TSLF	Term Securities Lending Facility
USAID	US Agency for International Development
WP	Working Party

Notes on Contributors

Iain Begg is a Professorial Fellow in the European Institute at the London School of Economics and Political Science. His research focuses on the political economy of European integration and on EU economic policy, on which he has published numerous co-authored, edited, and co-edited books. He was a co-editor of the *Journal of Common Market Studies* from 1998 to 2003.

Kenneth Dyson is a Research Professor in European Politics at Cardiff University, Wales. He is a Fellow of the British Academy and an Academician of the Learned Society of the Social Sciences. His books on EMU include *Elusive Union: The Process of Economic and Monetary Union* (Longman 1994); *The Road to Maastricht: Negotiating Economic and Monetary Union* (with Kevin Featherstone, Oxford University Press 1999); *The Politics of the Euro-Zone: Stability or Breakdown?* (Oxford University Press 2000); *European States and the Euro* (Oxford University Press 2002); *Enlarging the Euro Area: External Empowerment and Domestic Transformation in East Central Europe* (Oxford University Press 2006); and *The Euro At 10: Europeanization, Convergence and Power* (Oxford University Press 2008). He was an adviser to the BBC2 series 'The Money Changers' on the making of EMU. His main research interests are in German policy and politics, European economic policies and politics, and the EU. He is the co-editor of the journal *German Politics*.

Chris Eichbaum is a Senior Lecturer in Public Policy in the School of Government at Victoria University of Wellington New Zealand. His doctoral research entailed a comparative study of the shaping of the institutions of central banking in Australia and New Zealand. His current research interests are in the institutions of central banking, governance and public administration, and political and bureaucratic actors in executive government.

Rachel Epstein is an Assistant Professor at the Graduate School of International Studies at the University of Denver. She is the author of *In Pursuit of Liberalism: International Institutions in Postcommunist Europe* (Johns Hopkins University Press 2008) and has written widely on NATO and EU enlargement as well as on the effects of the International Monetary Fund and World Bank in the post-communist transition. She was a Jean Monnet postdoctoral fellow at the European University Institute in 2001 and 2002 and returned to EUI in

2004 to serve as the Robert Schuman Centre's Transatlantic Research Fellow. She received her PhD in the Department of Government at Cornell University in 2001.

Charles Goodhart, CBE, FBA is a member of the Financial Markets Group at the London School of Economics (LSE), having previously, 1987–2005, been its Deputy Director. Until his retirement in 2002, he had been the Norman Sosnow Professor of Banking and Finance at LSE since 1985. Before then, he had worked at the Bank of England for seventeen years as a monetary adviser, becoming a Chief Adviser in 1980. In 1997, he was appointed one of the outside independent members of the Bank of England's new Monetary Policy Committee until May 2000. Besides numerous articles, he has written a couple of books on monetary history; a graduate monetary textbook, *Money, Information and Uncertainty* (2nd edn, 1989); two collections of papers on monetary policy, *Monetary Theory and Practice* (1984) and *The Central Bank and The Financial System* (1995); and a number of books and articles on financial stability, on which subject he was Adviser to the Governor of the Bank of England, 2002–4, and numerous other studies relating to financial markets and to monetary policy and history.

Béla Greskovits is a Professor of International Relations and European Studies at the Central European University, Budapest. He is the author of *The Political Economy of Protest and Patience. East European and Latin American Transformations Compared* (Central European University Press 1998). His most recent articles on the political economy of policy reform and the diversity of post-socialist capitalism have appeared in *Studies in Comparative and International Development*; *Labor History*; *Orbis*; *West European Politics*; *Competition and Change*; and *Journal of Democracy*.

David Howarth is a Senior Lecturer in Politics at the University of Edinburgh. He is the author of the *French Road to European Monetary Union* (Palgrave 2001); (with Peter Loedel) *The European Central Bank* (Palgrave 2003 and 2005); and (with Georgios Varouxakis) *Contemporary France* (London: Edward Arnold 2003). He has written several articles and book chapters on French economic policy and policy-making and Economic and Monetary Union.

Nicolas Jabko is a research director at the Centre d'Etudes et de Recherches Internationales (CERI) of SciencesPo in Paris. He is the author of *Playing the Market: A Political Strategy for Uniting Europe, 1985–2005* (Cornell University Press 2006) and the co-editor of the eighth volume of the *State of the European Union* (Oxford University Press 2005).

Juliet Johnson is an Associate Professor of Political Science at McGill University. She is the author of *A Fistful of Rubles: The Rise and Fall of the Russian Banking System* (Cornell 2000) and the co-editor of *Religion and Identity in Modern Russia: The Revival of Orthodoxy and Islam* (Ashgate 2005). She is also the co-editor of the *Review of International Political Economy* and has published numerous articles and book chapters on post-communist political economy and identity politics. She has served as both a Research Fellow in Foreign Policy Studies at the Brookings Institution (1995–6) and the A. John Bittson National Fellow at the Hoover Institution (2001–2). She is currently finishing a book entitled *Priests of Prosperity: The Transnational Central Banking Community and Post-Communist Transformation*. She received her PhD in Politics from Princeton University in 1997.

Huw Macartney is an ESRC Postdoctoral Fellow at Nottingham University. He has recently completed his PhD, *Transnational Social Forces, Variegated Neo-liberalism and Financial Market Integration in the EU*, at the University of Manchester and has a forthcoming article in the *British Journal of Politics and International Relations*.

Ivo Maes is a Deputy Head of the Research Department of the National Bank of Belgium and holds the Robert Triffin Chair at the Institut d'études Européennes of the Université Catholique de Louvain. His current research focuses on the history of central banking and European monetary and financial integration. His recent publications comprise *Economic Thought and the Making of European Monetary Union* (Edward Elgar 2002); *The Bank, the Franc and the Euro, A History of the National Bank of Belgium* (Lannoo 2005, co-author); and *Half a Century of European Financial Integration. From the Rome Treaty to the 21st Century* (Mercatorfonds 2007). He has been a visiting professor at Duke University (USA) and at the Université de Paris-Sorbonne.

Martin Marcussen is an Associate Professor of Politics at the University of Copenhagen. He specializes in global governance, European integration, and the role of ideas in public policy. He is the author of *Ideas and Elites: The Social Construction of Economic and Monetary Union* (Aalborg University Press 2000).

Michael Moran is WJM Mackenzie Professor of Government at Manchester University and a Fellow of the British Academy. His most recent book is *The British Regulatory State: High Modernism and Hyper-Innovation* (Oxford University Press, 2nd edn, 2007).

George Pagoulatos is an Associate Professor of Politics at the Department of International and European Economic Studies, Athens University of Economics and Business, and Visiting Professor at the College of Europe in Bruges. He was a member of the Greek government's Council of Economic Advisors (2002–4). He has published extensively in journals such as *West European Politics*; *Journal of Common Market Studies*; *Journal of Public Policy*; *Public Administration*; and *European Journal of Political Research*. His book *Greece's New Political Economy: State, Finance and Growth from Post-war to EMU* (Oxford St. Antony's Series, Palgrave Macmillan 2003) received the Academy of Athens award for best book in economics.

Lucia Quaglia is a Senior Lecturer in Politics and Contemporary European Studies at Sussex University. In addition to numerous articles in journals and chapters in edited volumes, she has published *Central Bank Governance in the EU: A Comparative Analysis* (Routledge 2008).

Gaby Umbach is a research associate at the Jean-Monnet Chair for Political Science, University of Cologne. Her main field of research and expertise includes European integration and governance and Europeanization studies. Her doctoral thesis is on the Europeanization of British and German employment policies and policy-making structures.

Amy Verdun is a Professor of Political Science, Jean Monnet Chair and Director of the Jean Monnet Centre of Excellence at the University of Victoria, Canada. She is the author or editor of nine books and has served as guest editor of five special issues of peer-reviewed journals. She has published in peer-reviewed journals such as *British Journal of Politics and International Relations*; *Journal of Common Market Studies*; *Journal of European Public Policy*; *Journal of Public Policy*; and *Review of International Political Economy*.

Wolfgang Wessels holds the Jean Monnet Chair for Political Science at the University of Cologne. In 2007, he received the European Award 'Jean Monnet' in Gold. He is chair of the Executive Board of the Institut für Europäische Politik (Berlin) and of the Trans European Policy Studies Association (Brussels), as well as coordinator of the EU-CONSENT Network of Excellence. Recent publications include *Economic Government of the EU. A Balance Sheet of New Modes of Policy Coordination* (ed. Ingo Linsenmann and Christoph O. Meyer, 2007).

John T. Woolley is a Professor of Political Science and Chair of the Political Science Department at the University of California, Santa Barbara. Starting with *Monetary Politics* (Cambridge 1984), he has published extensively on the politics of monetary policy and European monetary integration. He has studied the politics of environmental politics and is co-founder of a well-known web site, *The American Presidency Project* www.americanpresidency.org

1

The Age of the Euro: A Structural Break? Europeanization, Convergence, and Power in Central Banking

Kenneth Dyson

The coming of the age of the euro, signalled by the establishment of the European Central Bank (ECB) in 1998, represented a bold novelty in the history of central banking. It involved the birth of a small, untested, supra-national central bank, which was cast directly into the role of the second most powerful in the world, only half a decade after the European Exchange-Rate Mechanism (ERM) had been convulsed by crises in 1992–3 (on which Dyson 1994). The unprepossessing context was an institutionally weak European polity, without independent fiscal competence, not least to bail out cross-nationally active banks, and without a centralized European banking supervisory structure (Dyson 2008*b*). A lonely 'institution-in-the-making', the ECB was responsible for managing a new single currency, the euro, for over 300 million Europeans in, initially, 11 of 15 European Union (EU) member states. As one of its first Executive Board members noted, its youth, its distinctive institutional loneliness, and its lack of the attributes of a fully integrated central bank—notably in banking supervision—left it exposed (Padoa-Schioppa 2000, 2005). Second, the age of the euro involved a core grouping of European states, which incorporated a mosaic of historically formed identities, voluntarily merging their currencies in a time of peace. In consequence, the ECB was formed in elite consensus but had weak resources of European identity and solidarity on which to draw.

Unsurprisingly, given these two aspects of its context, its first Chief Economist, Otmar Issing (2008) stresses the scepticism that prevailed initially, not just amongst characteristically cautious central bankers but also in the financial markets and amongst financial journalists (cf. Woolley's chapter on the US Fed in this volume). Structural rigidities, not least in financial, services, and labour markets, suggested the danger of persisting and economically and politically

1

problematic differentials in output growth; there was high uncertainty about whether monetary union would disrupt economic relationships and regularities; institutional arrangements for cross-national banking supervision were weakly developed; procedures for cross-national bank bail outs remained uncertain; whilst member-state governments were often reluctant to 'own' the importance of compliance with stability-oriented fiscal policy rules and structural reforms (Weber 2008*a*).

Finally, in a post-war European integration process that had had containment of German power as one of its central motifs, the age of the euro represented the most explicit example of Europeanization on the basis of a German central banking template (Dyson and Featherstone 1999). It embodied German 'soft' power in the most vivid structural terms. This power was evident in the ECB's institutional modelling on the Bundesbank; in the role accorded to monetary and credit analysis and long-term time horizons in monetary policy; and in historical lesson drawing from the Bundesbank's relative success in the 1970s–80s in forging a powerful reputation for fighting inflation by pre-emptive action to shape expectations and by its belief that 'stability begins at home'.

The Birth of the Euro

The idea of the age of the euro as a structural break was blunted by the reality of its smooth birth. The ECB's early success owed much to its careful, meticulous technical preparation by EU central bankers in the decade before its launch. More specifically, it derived from 'borrowing credibility' by its institutional modelling on the foremost and most-admired EU central bank, the German Bundesbank. In particular, from 1 January 1994 the new European Monetary Institute (EMI), composed of EU central bankers, prepared this final stage three of Economic and Monetary Union (EMU) (on which Dyson 2000; Dyson and Featherstone 1999). This period offered an opportunity to build a team approach to monetary policy and for many national central banks to begin upgrading their analytical capacity to contribute to this process. In fact, the post-1979 ERM had served as an even longer training ground in monetary policy coordination and in learning through crisis management, on which many of the founding central banks could draw (Dyson 2000).

The EMI period also clarified the centrality of the principle of decentralization in the design of the Eurosystem. Its justification depended on the role of the national central banks in cultivating public confidence by maintaining the quality of banknotes in circulation. It also recognized the historically different functions of national central banks in their own societies (on which see pp. 19–28 below). Finally, given the association of national central banks with a state-based EU, they were essential for communicating monetary policy to different domestic audiences. At the same time, the EMI period manifested a concern of national central banks—cloaked behind the principle of decentralization in designing the new central banking system—to find a new mission for themselves, protect their activities, and thereby secure jobs. This concern focused on ensuring their role in monetary policy implementation and on designing an appropriate formula-based approach to the allocation of monetary income in the Eurosystem. Against this background EMI 'staffers' sought successfully to ensure that adequate resources were made available for the new ECB to discharge its functions effectively. The results of the ERM experience and of the EMI period supported a seamless transition, first to monetary union in 1999 and then to currency union. It was the culmination of the technically demanding transition to euro notes and coins in January 2002 that intensified domestic questioning of national central banks' inherited structures and staffing levels, even rhetorical questions about their very rationale to exist.

The euro evoked expectations of a structural break that went beyond just locking in a cross-national 'stability culture' across its member states by means of a radically independent ECB. It represented the promise of a new symbol of European identity and unity, of a political catalyst for closer European integration, of an economic stimulant to increased trade and financial integration, and of a new rival international currency to the US dollar (on its performance in these respects, see Dyson 2008*b*). At the same time, however, echoing the EU into which it was born, the Euro Area remained a political pygmy on the international stage, unable to speak with a single authoritative voice in international economic diplomacy (cf. European Commission 2008). It also failed, at least in its first decade, to become 'loved' by the citizens of the Euro Area (on which in detail Dyson 2008*b*). Not least, three Euro Area states rejected further EU treaty-making exercises in deepening political union: France and the Netherlands in 2005, and Ireland in 2001 and 2008. Paradoxically, Irish rejection took place in the context of Eurobarometer data suggesting that the euro had led to a greater increase in European identity than in any other Euro Area state (ibid.).

The distinctiveness of the age of the euro lies in a paradox. On the one hand, the ECB is a supra-national central bank, which by 2009 covered 16 out of 27 EU member states. It possesses a radical form of Treaty-based independence, including the capacity to define what its strictly limited Treaty mandate of securing price stability means: the so-called 'goal' independence. In addition, the ECB, and the wider Eurosystem of central banks of which it is part, constitutes a 'missionary' institution. It is unified around a coherent, intellectually robust body of macro-economic knowledge about the normative basis of, and causal mechanisms at work in, monetary policy. In addition, the ECB is held together by a sense of 'making history'. This combination of radical supranational independence with epistemic consensus and missionary character makes it more akin to the European Court of Justice than to the European Commission in its unity, self-confidence, and didacticism.

On the other hand, the ECB lacks the traditional central banking advantage of being able to take shelter, as a technocratic entity, beneath the protective umbrella of a unified political authority that supports its mandate. It lacks the supportive political context of a federal European fiscal stabilizing mechanism to cushion and smooth adjustment to asymmetric economic shocks. Perhaps more ominously, in light of the traditional function of central banking in safeguarding financial stability, the ECB cannot confidently rely on a federal 'bail-out' mechanism in case of contagious, systemic cross-national banking and financial crisis. The EU-level Memorandum of Understanding in April 2008 represented progress in organizing cross-national 'stability groups' of supervisors for some 20 to 30 cross-border banks. Nevertheless, the Euro Area had a weakly developed and, up to the 2008 financial crisis, untested institutional capacity for cross-national crisis management and is deficient in traditional symbols of collective solidarity in dealing with future configurations of the political economy of 'hard times' (Dyson 2008*a*). The ECB is a 'stateless', isolated central bank in an 'institutionally fuzzy' polity (on which Dyson 2008*b*).

The age of the euro combines sharply defined central bank independence in monetary policy with institutional 'fuzziness' in the key functions of financial stability and fiscal compensation. It represents a form of hybrid central banking. The Euro Area is both located 'beyond the state' in monetary policy and yet constrained by member states' willingness to 'own' the euro in their domestic fiscal, economic reform, and banking and financial market supervisory policies and in coordinating nationally organized bank bail outs. At the same time, in involving the most radical Europeanization of its member states through delegation of sovereignty in monetary policy, the age of the euro highlights even further the domestic distinctiveness of the constituent national central banks of the Eurosystem. These national central banks are the most 'Europeanized' of domestic institutions. In consequence, they are particularly interesting cases for Europeanization research.

This institutionally lonely and exposed position of the ECB and of the national central banks of the Eurosystem induces tension. In this context the striking, even radical accentuation of the principle of central bank independence is functional. It acts as collective insurance for a new untried currency against the heightened risks to credibility from its political dependence on problematic domestic 'ownership' and loyalty by member-state political and economic elites. It relies on them to expedite reforms to make adjustment processes more speedy and efficient and to lower the costs of disinflation. In this paradox, we encounter the elusiveness of Eurosystem central bank power in the age of the euro: the combination of strong institutional profiling and discursive confidence in monetary policy with problematic domestic political ownership in fiscal and economic reform policies and weak institutional capacity in cross-national financial market crisis management and bank bail outs.

Institutional and policy privileging of the ECB in an 'ECB-centric' Euro Area (Dyson 2000) and its bias to anti-inflation 'vigilance' in monetary policy are the counterweight to the distinctive set of political and economic uncertainties that it faces in attempting to deliver its Treaty mandates of price stability and promoting financial stability. The euro was born against the historic background of deep scepticism in international banking and monetary policy circles, notably in the United States, that European monetary union would go ahead and, if so, could prove feasible. The scepticism was in part technical, notably related to the gigantic scale of the problems in conversion to the new currency across 11 member states, to the paucity of relevant, reliable economic and monetary statistics for the Euro Area, and to incomplete institution building notably in macro-economic coordination of domestic fiscal policies and economic reforms and in banking supervision and crisis management. Above all, there were the political as well as economic uncertainties associated with a 'one-size-fits-all' monetary policy for an economically heterogeneous group of states, lacking the attributes of an 'Optimum Currency Area'. There was also uncertain knowledge about how monetary policy transmission mechanisms would work. In confronting these, and other more widely shared, sources of uncertainty in central banking, the ECB had to rely on 'borrowing' credibility from the German Bundesbank. Above all, the ECB faced uncertainties about the collective action capacity of the Euro Area and the wider EU and about domestic ownership by political elites. Domestic political elites faced temptations to play a 'blame-shifting' populist politics, in which the ECB would emerge as a scapegoat for domestic failures to tackle problems of economic growth, employment, and unsustainable public finances.

Populist incentives to shift blame to the ECB materialized in the French Presidential elections of 2002 and 2007 and the Italian elections of 2006 and 2008. National central banks, for instance in Greece, were drawn into domestic political controversy as they argued for more comprehensive and faster domestic economic reforms. Central banking in the age of the euro was a story of stronger independence and a more central role in domestic macro-economic policy coexisting in tension, and potentially in conflict, with politicization. Europeanization of central banking involved simultaneous de-politicization and politicization as the domestic reform implications of the age of the euro, above all market liberalization, made institutional veto points and partisan veto players more transparent, mobilized losers, and raised politically difficult problems of their compensation in exchange for reforms, especially when public finances were already 'unsound'.

In another sense, however, the combination of Treaty-based independence, creating a very high legal hurdle for collective political action to curb the ECB, with the sheer number of veto points and partisan veto players increased the credibility of central bank independence (cf. Keefer and Stasavage 2003). The decentralized structure of the Euro Area helps insulate the ECB from political interference, in a way that further mimics earlier German experience (cf. Hallerberg 2002; Lohmann 1998). As French President Nicolas Sarkozy and Italian Prime Minister Silvio Berlusconi discovered, organizing an EU-wide unity of purpose to curb the ECB is highly problematic, not least faced with resolute German attachment to the principle of its independence. In the context of partisan veto players and high Treaty-based hurdles, the ECB could take a fairly relaxed view of its independence.

Key Questions

As an exercise in comparative political economy this volume seeks to avoid idiosyncratic, detailed accounts of changes in European central banks and central banking (and in their non-European equivalents). It seeks to address a set of common questions within a shared framework of concepts—'Europeanization', 'power', and 'convergence'. These three questions focus on the issue of what, if anything, is distinctive about European central banks and banking.

To what extent, in what ways, how, and with what effects, have European central banks changed within the framework of European monetary integration, pre- and post-euro, and whether as euro-insiders or euro-outsiders?

The volume examines different dimensions of change in European central banking—in scope, content, process, and outcomes. What changes can we identify in the functions, structures, instruments, styles, and cultures of central banking? Can they be attributed to European integration? In answering these *Europeanization* questions, we need to be sensitive to the domestic and the international embeddedness of central banking and banks. The danger is attribution bias: presuming the significance of European integration. It can be reduced by contextualizing and problematizing Europeanization. Changes in European central banking reflect different *domestic* historical legacies from individually distinctive 'defining moments', different domestic political opportunity structures, and varying attitudes to monetary 'sovereignty' and how it relates to national identity. These changes also respond to *international* developments in financial markets and asymmetries in exposure to financial crises, to pressures from international institutions (and how they relate to the timing of development of national central banking), to new ideas about monetary policy and about public management that are trans-national, and to new information and communication technologies.

There is, in addition, the dimension of time. The *longue durée* invites us to reflect on different 'ages' of central banking: how, over time, the characteristic functions, styles, and cultures of central banking have evolved. These 'ages' have in turn a quality of myth in that they are idealized representations of a much more complex reality. They include the 'classic' pre-1914 Gold Standard era and the post-1945 'US-dollar-backed' Bretton Woods era till 1973. They provided a set of international rules in which central banks were embedded. Correspondingly, the contexts and experiences of globalization differed across these ages of central banking, in ways that profoundly affected their functions and organizational cultures.

What do these changes consequent on European monetary integration reveal about the power of central banks?

There are two senses of power: 'power over' and 'power to' (cf. Morriss 2002). In its first, most frequently used sense, the power of central banks rests in their power *over* other actors, in its being asymmetric. This power describes their capacity to make others comply with their distinctive preferences: for instance, to gain or retain functions and legal competences; to align market and political expectations with their mandate for price stability; to increase their monetary income in the Eurosystem; or to gain longer periods of exercising voting rights in reform of the ECB Governing Council. Perhaps most strikingly in this respect, the age of the euro disempowered the Bundesbank and empowered other central banks in monetary policy.

Conventionally, this perspective sees power in '*relational*' terms. It imputes to central banks self-interested motives of 'bureau' expansion of functions, career opportunities, and budgets: for instance, in developing and managing euro payment and settlement systems, in centralizing banking supervision, or in maximizing their monetary income. The question is whether in practice they make effective use of the various resources of power on which they can draw to enhance their relative power at domestic, European, and international levels. These resources include their legal authority to act; professional expertise and ideas; experience and reputation; information about markets and probable effects of policy actions; the scale of the economy (defined by GDP size and financial assets); and the weight of the currency in international markets and in central bank reserves. Because of varying resources, some central banks are relatively more powerful (at least potentially) than others, the US Fed internationally and traditionally the Bundesbank in Europe. In reallocating these resources of power EMU has transformed relative power in European central banking.

'Power over' also has a *structural* element, which expresses itself in the two less visible dimensions of central bank power: the power to frame and shape how other actors define their economic interests (what is seen as appropriate behaviour), and the power of agenda setting in economic policy (including keeping certain issues off the agenda) (cf. Lukes 2005). Seen in these terms, EMU 'uploaded' to the Euro Area the structural power of the Bundesbank and its distinctive Ordo-liberal ideas as well as ratified a more general international structural shift to 'stability-oriented' policies (see Dyson's chapter). By this mechanism of 'Europeanization as Germanization' it reframed domestic debates about macro-economic policy interests across the Euro Area towards

7

'stability' and shifted agenda setting to issues of 'competitiveness' and 'fiscal discipline'. Central bank power is at work even when there is no overt conflict.

In its second sense, the power of central banks refers to their capacity to shape outcomes in areas where they have a function, notably to safeguard price stability and to promote financial stability. This power rests on their functions being widely socially valued and supported by a public 'permissive' consensus (a long-term 'stability culture' of the kind enjoyed by the Bundesbank); on their professional capacity and reputation especially with markets, at a time when the shift to financial intermediation and 'shadow' banking, new complex and opaque forms of structured finance, and internationalization meant that they had lost power to markets; and, not least, on them having policy instruments fit for purpose. 'Fitness for purpose' is clearer in the case of interest-rate policy and fighting inflation than of banking supervisory policy and financial stability (cf. Tinbergen 1952). The power 'to' pursue their price stability mandate has been enhanced by an emerging consensus around an ascendant 'stability-oriented' economic paradigm that has empowered central banks. It assigns special knowledge, purpose, and significance to their activities and pronouncements. In monetary policy, central banking had renewed its intellectual capital, from which it gained increased professional self-confidence and credibility: namely, a set of theoretically validated beliefs in stability-oriented policies. In the process an imbalance emerged between its two functions of macro-economic stability and financial stability. This process was reflected in internal central bank power, which shifted from the experiential realm of financial stability, involving detailed, hands-on supervision, to the more intellectual realm of macro-economic competence in inflation fighting.

A key dimension of the dramatic financial crisis of 2007–8 was the shock to the money markets, where banks' confidence in each other's solvency evaporated and liquidity tensions proved persisting. It exposed just how dependent macro-economic stability was on financial stability and highlighted the significance of the traditional, and more recently, neglected role of central banks as banker to the banks. It showed how weakly positioned central banks were vis-à-vis the financial markets, whose convulsive transformations in the wake of the pace of innovation, the amount of embedded leverage in the system, and more interconnected markets had implications for monetary policy that had not been fully appreciated. Central banks were vulnerable to claims that their monetary policies had been too accommodative in the face of asset price bubbles, in short been pro-cyclical and asymmetrical across the financial cycle, and had encouraged excessive risk taking, laying the ground for crisis (Draghi 2008). They had been too disposed to trust in the superior knowledge of the private sector in asset pricing.

More generally, central banks are faced with the acute recurring fragility of a market-based financial system whose lifeblood is trust. The events of 2007–8 were a lesson in how a confident discourse of stability, competitiveness, and fiscal discipline, rooted in the less visible structural dimensions of central bank power, can mask the highly contingent nature of this trust, the problematic relationship of instruments to goals, and a vulnerability to market complexity, opacity, and volatility. In addition, it highlighted the continuing openness of structural power in banking and financial markets to political contest, especially once banking 'originate-and-distribute' business models proved reckless, reward structures were vulnerable to charges of being iniquitous, and the state was drawn into multiple bank rescues and sought to impose new regulatory conditions. As we see below, persisting national variability in political constellations of ideologies and interests, in 'path dependence' and in state traditions of thought define the varying limits of central bank power to frame how interests are conceived and to keep certain issues off the agenda.

In banking supervisory policies and financial stability the relationship of instruments to goals is more problematic and vulnerability to markets most acute. Analytical models are less robust in the face of the fast pace of financial market innovation and multiple hidden potential sources of shocks, rules fail to give strong backbone to supervisors, regulatory self-confidence is more brittle, and central bank policy instruments are less clearly fit for purpose. Examples were plentiful in 2007–8 with the manifest failures to regulate the 'shadow' banking system, the ongoing uncertainties about who owned securitized loans and about what they were worth, the muddled rescues of Bear Stearns and of Northern Rock, the systemic aftershocks of the collapse of Lehman, the massive governmental interventions to recapitalize banks, buy up toxic assets and guarantee credits, and central bank engagements in providing liquidity to credit-starved banks. Policy was torn between the poles of avoidance of 'moral hazard' associated with banking bail outs (thereby giving an incentive to reckless lending) and preventing systemic crisis, which feeds into the 'real' economy of output and jobs. The central, blunt central bank policy instrument of interest-rate changes cannot alone deliver both price and financial stability (Draghi 2008). The use of interest-rate hikes to prick specific asset price 'bubbles', say in housing, risks broad damage to macro-economic growth and employment. Conversely, problems of locking in price stability have been historically linked to asset 'bubbles': note the United States in 1929, Japan in the 1990s, Asia in 1997–8, and sub-prime mortgages in 2007–8. By mid-2008 the international central bank community had yet to devise simple, transparent supervisory rules that would enable supervisors to play a credible counter-cyclical role in moderating excessive bank lending and accumulating bank capital reserves during booms (cf. Goodhart and Persaud 2008). In their absence, there was a plausible case for making greater use of monetary policy for macro-prudential purposes (cf. Bank for International Settlements 2008).

A number of hypotheses about central bank power seem well supported by the evidence in this volume. First, a complex combination of European with domestic and international factors has strengthened central bank power. In particular, their structural power has grown in the form of a cross-national convergence in general political support for price stability, central bank independence, tighter internal management efficiency, and strengthened accountability and transparency.

Second, this strengthening of central bank power has been dwarfed by the growth of the structural power of the global financial markets, in relation to which central banks have been spectators rather than independently active regulatory players. In consequence, central banks sought to play a difficult balancing game. On the one hand, they attempted to work *with* the markets to ensure their continuing efficiency, creativity, and dynamism in providing liquidity. Central banks had also to recognize that financial and asset markets were of increasing importance for monetary policy transmission, making financial stability of growing importance in monetary policy formation (Weber 2008). On the other hand, central banks have to ensure that they are not captured *by* the markets, that they exercise independent professional judgement, and take a system-wide independent perspective. Consistent with this view, they distrust signals of readiness to bail out troubled banks as creating potential moral hazard, providing incentives to reckless risk taking, and jeopardizing financial stability and their own professional reputation. The acute difficulties of this balancing game came to the fore in the credit crunch and financial crisis of 2007–8.

Third, the growth of the power of the global financial markets simultaneously empowers and threatens to disempower central banks. They are empowered as political elites come to rely on central banks as professional 'gate keepers' to complex, volatile, interconnected, and opaque markets. Central bank independence and the appointment of 'hawkish' central bankers act as a form of political insurance. Conversely, the sheer scale, creativity, and proneness of the global markets to excess threaten to disempower central banks through new sources of systemic risk and crisis. Once, as in 2008, financial crisis spills over into acute threat to the 'real' economy, the issue of confidence shifts from financial markets and central banks to governments, which became massively active on a scale designed to ward off risks of any repeat of the Great Depression of the 1930s. Keynesian ideas of counter-cyclical, government-led fiscal policies enjoyed an intellectual renaissance that suggested a shift in structural power away from central banks towards elected governments.

Fourth, at least in the period till the financial crisis of 2008, EMU had served to shore up the structural power of European central banking via an 'ECB-centric' Euro Area and by EU accession and Maastricht conditionality criteria for Euro Area accession. At the same time EMU led to divergent changes in the relative power of different European central banks. In the case of Euro-insiders, the Bundesbank was the big net loser; others, especially the central banks of smaller states, were net gainers. Diminished relative power in Europe for the Bundesbank translates into new domestic weakness and vulnerability.

Conversely, increased relative power in Europe for many small state central banks creates potentially enhanced domestic leverage over policy, a more authoritative role in domestic policy debate, and—as in Greece—new exposure as a focal point in domestic political opposition to a 'neo-liberal' agenda of reform. Domestic leverage is increased when national central banks retain a wide range of national functions that predate the Eurosystem (e.g. the National Bank of Belgium). However, this outcome does not hold when these functions—like protecting a weak domestic banking sector in the case of the Bank of Italy—involve 'misfit' with EMU and EU templates.

Fifth, for euro-outsiders the international sources of a strengthening of structural power of central banking remain similar, notably in the impacts of global financial markets and of ascendant trans-national policy ideas that privilege stability-oriented policies and a set of shared understandings about their institutional, procedural, and policy preconditions. However, in these cases domestic variegation in Europeanization is even more pronounced. This variegation reflects contrasts in attitudes to monetary 'sovereignty' and how it relates to national identity; the timing of central bank development in relation to international financial market liberalization; the character of the economic and financial structures in which central banks are embedded; how domestic political parties use the processes of granting central bank independence and of appointments to top posts; and whether, in consequence, central bank governors are seen to be personally politically independent and thus reliable authoritative professional figures. These factors are explored in the volume.

To what extent, and in what ways, is EMU producing convergence across these various dimensions and across functions?

'Europeanization' begs the question of whether it is associated with *convergence*, with central banks coming to resemble each other. This resemblance can take different forms: resemblance in agenda stemming from increasingly shared pressures; in ideas and functions; in instruments and structures; in cultures; and in outcomes. Hence convergence is a multi-dimensional concept. The question produces, in consequence, differentiated answers depending on precisely what we are talking about.

Convergence exhibits *functional specificity*. Patterns of convergence/divergence vary across monetary policy, transparency and accountability, financial market supervision, and research. In this volume, Marcussen outlines a convergence around a new age of the 'scientization' of central banking, exemplified in the new prestige to research and 'knowledge-based' policies in legitimating their power. Macartney and Moran identify simultaneous epistemic convergence and institutional divergence even within the same functional area of financial market supervision: whilst Jabko points out that policies on transparency are very different in financial market supervision from monetary policy. Begg sees an international process of convergence in monetary policy strategy towards inflation targeting, though one in which the ECB remains an outsider.

However, convergence in central banking is often superficial. On closer examination it turns out to be more variegated and to involve multiple equilibria. The dynamic nature of convergence highlights, in part, the 'path-dependent' specificities of historical and institutional contexts. These specificities shape the differential reception of ideas (Hay 2000). However, they also illustrate the sheer randomness in market and political developments. The incidence and particularities of crises in central banking vary and have the potential to shift central banks off their trajectory of development. These crises become in turn embedded in different institutional memories, for instance about the dangers of exchange-rate fixing in the Bank of England and of 'hyper-inflation' in the Bundesbank.

In consequence, convergence displays not just functional specificity but also *temporality*. It exhibits historical contingency. The preparatory phase of the age of the euro was associated with convergence in inflation rates. Since European monetary union, however, differences in inflation have proved persistent. This persistence threatens longer-term strains through consequent loss of competitiveness and serious protracted adjustment problems that could lead to divergences in wider macro-economic performance, especially output growth and employment. Outcomes can, in short, move in different directions over time, again reflecting contingency. Similarly, the national banking systems in which European central banks are embedded display strong historical path dependence so that institutional arrangements for supervision are resistant to convergence. As we see below, 'New Public Management' ideas have also been adopted variably: amongst euro insiders more by the Bundesbank than the Banque de France, and amongst outsiders more by the Swedish than the Danish central bank.

In addressing these questions about Europeanization, power, and convergence, the volume retains a strong sense of varying historical, international, and domestic contexts. Weighing these contextual factors raises perennially problematic issues of scholarly judgement about the appropriate 'level of analysis'. The editors have not sought to 'resolve' these issues. In fact, we have encouraged pluralism by juxtaposing European country case studies with Euro Area-level chapters, functionally specific chapters, and non-European 'control' cases.

In a comparative and international context, is what is happening in European central banking distinctive?

The issue of distinctiveness is raised in asking the questions about Europeanization, power, and convergence. The specific EU context—its institutional 'fuzziness', its lack of unified political authority, and its historically varied states with their varying identities voluntarily ceding monetary sovereignty but retaining fiscal, economic policy, and banking supervision sovereignty—imparts a specificity and originality to the Eurosystem. In addition, the distribution of power in the negotiation of EMU meant that the German Bundesbank 'uploaded' many of its core Ordo-liberal ideas into the design of the ECB and the Euro Area: the strictly defined Treaty mandate of price stability, a radical version of central bank independence, a 'principles-based' approach to monetary policy, the stress on long-term, multi-dimensional 'monetary analysis', and scepticism about analytical modelling based on 'real' time economic data and forecasting in monetary policy strategy (Weber 2006*b*). In these terms, Europeanization served as 'Germanization' of European central banking (see Dyson's chapter). The Treaty entrenchment of central bank independence meant that the ECB was in fact a more institutionalized form of the Ordo-liberal model than the Bundesbank; whilst the principle of decentralization in the Eurosystem was more akin to the earlier Bank deutscher Länder than to the Bundesbank. Finally, though differentiated integration is not unusual in the EU, the Euro Area represents its most distinctive institutional development both in supranational design and in the toughest and most wide-ranging entry criteria.

At the same time, the larger historical context of post-Bretton Woods, global, volatile, and opaque financial markets, and US economic hegemony, however variable and threatened its fortunes, means that European central banking—whether for euro insiders or outsiders—cannot escape its historical and international embeddedness. In terms of financial markets the pacesetter has been the United States, with the United Kingdom taking up this role in Europe in the 1980s. This UK role was further evident in the EU organization of a coordinated set of principles for bank bail outs in October 2008. The British Prime Minister was invited to the first meeting of Euro Area heads of government to present British plans as a model for the wider EU.

In terms of power to effect international financial markets and monetary policies the US Fed remained unrivalled in the first decade of the euro. If the earlier collapse of the US-centred Bretton Woods system had provided the catalyst for EMU, the continuing reputation of the US Fed (a reputation that grew in the Volcker-Greenspan years) remained a constraint on the ECB's capacity to play an independent and distinctive international role. In its inevitably protracted birth—unlike the US Fed it must anticipate continuing Euro Area enlargement and thus spatial incompleteness and it must build its own identity—the ECB had less incentive to be forced prematurely into a role of international leadership. European leadership is a sufficient challenge. Behind the US Fed stood a formidable intellectual armoury both in monetary policy and in financial market supervision (though even its weaknesses were manifest in 2007–8), with the ECB playing 'catch up'. However, the events of early 2008 suggested that divergence of interests and outlooks could lead the ECB to attempt at least initially to decouple its monetary policy direction from the US Fed in order to emphasize its strict price stability mandate and 'hawkish' attitudes. This decoupling became more problematic as the financial crisis proved systemic and required cross-national coordination.

Meanwhile, in a world of two big central banks—asymmetric in their power—small central banks have opportunities and incentives to carve out niches of creativity in central banking. This process is apparent in monetary policy—New Zealand, for instance, in inflation targeting; Sweden in the New Public Management and in transparency; and, inside the Eurosystem, small central banks in cash management and in exchange of credit information.

The Eurosystem creates an intense institutional context in which through technical harmonization and benchmarking there is a high degree of self-referential behaviour in European central banking. In contrast, European central banks in states that have opted for 'semi-permanent' euro outsider status are much more catholic in their pursuit of independent profiles. In compensation, they focus more intensively on building their individual international networks and on extracting policy lessons from a wider international central banking milieu. As Umbach and Wessels show, differentiation in European central banking has grown. However, this differentiation has not been just a formal matter of membership. It reaches deep down into international policies and what are judged to be the appropriate role models for lesson drawing. In designing independence for the Bank of England, overhauling financial market supervision, elaborating fiscal rules, even producing tests for euro entry, the British Treasury studiously ignored European templates.

Europeanization, Power, and Convergence

The questions that animate this volume, and its core organizing concepts and approaches, reflect its intellectual origins in comparative political economy, notably the study of the institutional basis of macro-economic policies. 'Europeanization', 'power', and 'convergence' offer a cluster of interrelated concepts with which to examine change in central banking.

Europeanization

Europeanization refers to the domestic effects of European integration on policies, polities, and politics and characteristically focuses on mechanisms and the qualitative aspects of time (Dyson and Goetz 2003; Featherstone and Radaelli 2003). This volume examines the effects of the creation of the Euro Area on national central banks: their competences, their structures and functioning, and how they relate to their political and policy contexts. We are interested in how they respond to European-level requirements and in how they make strategic use of the creation of the Euro Area. In the first sense, Europeanization functions as a 'top–down' mechanism. It provides strongly

Germanic institutional templates that highlight 'misfit' and need to adapt at the domestic level by 'downloading' EU requirements (cf. Green Cowles, Caporaso, and Risse 2001). For instance, EU accession requires the abolition of monetary financing of government deficits and domestic central bank independence. 'Top–down' Europeanization increases in potency once states enter ERM II, thereby subordinating domestic policies to the stable exchange rate with the euro, and directly target compliance with the Maastricht convergence criteria for euro entry (covering inflation, long-term interest rates, fiscal deficit and public debt, as well as the exchange rate).

In the second sense, Europeanization operates as a 'bottom–up' process (cf. Dyson and Goetz 2003). Domestic central banks seek to seize the new opportunities offered by political commitment to EU accession and later euro entry to augment their status and power. Central bankers in Greece, for instance, defined euro entry as a 'modernization' process that involves a comprehensive range of reforms and through which the central bank carves out a strong leading domestic role. With more mixed success, the Bundesbank sought new domestic roles to compensate for its lost monetary policy-making function, invoking European models like the Dutch model of banking supervision. With euro entry, NCBs play a new role in communicating ECB monetary policy to domestic audiences and the 'logic' of monetary union for structural economic reforms.

The effects of 'Europeanization as Germanization' on central banks are by no means uniform. They range from ready accommodation, where there is substantial domestic 'fit' with the European template; through substantial transformation where 'misfit' coincides with domestic political will and capability to reform; to inertia and even resistance. Respective examples are the German Bundesbank (in monetary policy accommodation), the Greek central bank (in leading debate on domestic economic policy transformation), and the Bank of France (in inertia on internal structural reforms) and the Bank of Italy (in resistance to opening Italian financial markets to competition). Europeanization is a variegated experience. However, its result is to turn the NCBs of the Eurosystem into the most Europeanized domestic institutions. The paradoxical result is their empowerment and heightened vulnerability to domestic critique.

Power

Europeanization of central banks and banking is bound up with power. Power remains a complex and elusive concept with many facets. It sources are varied: moral authority, legal competence, position in domestic economic governance, expertise, financial resources, performance, even personal attributes of central bankers. Central bank power is relative to, and contingent on, possession of these various resources, which are distributed unevenly across space and over time. It is, in consequence, fragile and mutates.

Potential to exercise central bank power, above all to rely on suasion, is related to several variables: the legacy of its role in state and nation building and in historical memory, shaping whether its central purpose is endowed with popular support; its historically acquired range of competences and degree of independence; the range of domestic veto players that it faces and whether there is a unity of purpose amongst them in support of its mandate; its capacity to attract and retain highly rated expert staff; the role of its currency in international financial markets and in central bank reserves; whether it has been effective in delivering price stability and handling banking and financial crises ('matching words to deeds'); and the status and respect in which its governor and senior officials are held amongst peers and in the markets (including the mythology of central bankers). On these indicators, the Bank of England had relative power in the age of the classical Gold Standard; the Bundesbank in the post-Bretton Woods age in Europe; and the US Fed in the post-Volcker period. The differences within the Eurosystem are examined in this volume.

The power of central banks is an enduring and controversial theme in the history of international political economy. Sometimes it is reduced to individual central bankers like Montague Norman, governor of the Bank of England or Alan Greenspan at the US Fed. Conversely, their power is seen as an epiphenomenon of structural changes: in ascendant notions of domestic governance, in a wider shift to 'scientization' in contemporary society, or in the growing power of the international financial markets (which they 'ratify'). Underpinning these debates are alternative understandings about power. For some, central bank power is relational. It depends, for instance, on the persuasiveness of individual central bankers or a favourable constellation of actors and circumstances, which help them to win arguments. For others, power is structural: rooted, for instance, in whether central banks are central in dominant economic policy beliefs, and in whether political elites are dependent on them to 'control' dominant market player. In short, power rests in intellectual ascendancy in macro-economic policy through the prestige of monetary economics and expertise in dealing with complex, opaque, and volatile markets. Structural power helps them both to act as agenda-setters on behalf of price stability and to shape how other actors—governments, financial institutions, firms, trade unions—perceive and reframe their own interests (cf. Lukes 2005). In this narrative, the age of the euro, at least up the financial crisis of 2008, has been characterized by both the relational and the structural power of the ECB.

Europeanization provided central bankers with enhanced resources of legal authority, especially in monetary policy independence, and thereby augmented their structural and agenda-setting power. This increased potential to exercise power had its roots, however, in global-level developments. The research and 'knowledge base' of central banking has been transformed by monetary economics (see pp. XX). Following the 'stagflation' of the 1970s and the eclipse of Keynesianism, central banking acquired a powerful intellectual armoury, which in turn strengthened its agenda-setting role in macro-economic policy. Growth and employment problems were 'assigned' to governments and to employers and trade unions; their solution resided not in monetary policy or fiscal activism and 'fine-tuning' but in structural reforms to the supply side. In short, central banks promoted an agenda of product, services, labour, and financial market liberalization: in 2008, for example, the ECB Governing Council called for the end of wage indexation policies in seven Euro Area states as inimical to price stability. The age of the euro strengthened this agenda-setting role by removing the alternative policy options of exchange-rate and interest-rate adjustment. 'Structural reform' was the mantra of European central banking and a matter of broad consensus in the economics profession; embodied in and articulated by international institutions like the Organization for Economic Cooperation and Development (OECD) and the International Monetary Fund (IMF); and the benchmark for measuring the success of governments and states.

The potential of NCBs in the Eurosystem to exercise domestic power increased in three ways. First, they have a new incentive to use their enhanced reputation for objectivity by seeking a stronger shaping role in domestic economic policy debate, for instance by publishing their economic forecasts. Second, NCBs have an incentive to carve out a role as domestic pacesetters in public-sector reforms by adopting the efficiency-oriented agenda of the New Public Management with its target setting, performance indicators and monitoring, and 'outsourcing'. This agenda had an external function in protecting NCBs against political charges of hypocrisy in calling for domestic structural reforms and an internal function in strengthening centralized management. Third, NCBs have a new incentive to seek out domestic political support for enhancing their legal competences, for instance in banking and financial market supervision, so that they can compete more effectively in the competition of ideas in the Eurosystem.

However, there are also aspects of new vulnerability. In particular, 'the brightest and the best' tend to move 'upwards' in career terms to the ECB, which has steadily strengthened its research and monetary policy armoury. The NCBs have little leverage to halt this process. Second, NCBs face domestic challenge on 'overstaffing' and internal delays in their own structural reforms. At one level, they face increasing domestic questioning about the efficiency of their operations; at another, the ECB has been increasingly active in setting performance indicators for the Eurosystem and adding to internal pressures through systematic comparisons. Rationalization has proved internally contentious and typically protracted. In its absence, it has been difficult to release extra resources to strengthen internal expert research to strengthen profile in the Eurosystem. The French central bank exemplifies this difficulty. In general, the smaller NCBs have had an easier time in sustaining domestic coalitions of support, notably for their role in banking and financial market supervision (e.g. the Dutch and Irish central banks). However, this role also highlighted their vulnerabilities as the financial shock of 2008 gathered pace, especially as the scale of their national commercial banks potentially eclipsed the domestic capacity to bail them out.

The varied sources, different manifestations, and discrepancies between potential and actual power underline the continuing difficulty of pinning down power, not just in the Eurosystem, but even in the financial markets. At least up to the financial crisis of 2008, financial institutions seemed to exude vast power. However, much of this power depended on their creativity in inventing new complex products, like various forms of derivative, and more problematically on their capacity to retain market confidence in these products. Moreover, these ideas were hard to patent, could be easily copied, and soon became low-margin widely available products. Hence they were in practice vulnerable to rapid loss of competitive advantage. The result was an enormous incentive to permanent creativity that briefly marked out certain key individuals and companies as powerful. In short, creativity took its place, alongside capital and financial leverage, as a key source of market power. Financial market players, as well as central bankers, proved acutely vulnerable to the complexity and opacity that followed from this creativity and the 'herd' instincts in search of higher yield, as the crisis of 2008 revealed. The paradox of central bank power was that, in successful delivering low real interest rates and in neglecting the mundane world of financial stability for the intellectually exciting world of monetary policy strategy, they increased incentives to the markets to be more creative and take higher risks in search of yield.

The complexities and paradoxes of central bank power are highlighted in part by the above focus on the political criterion of their capacity to make a difference to outcomes. They also surface in the use of the moral criterion of praise or blame in evaluating the responsibility of central bankers for outcomes. Here a tension opens between 'power to' and 'power over'. Providing central bankers with the 'power to' deliver outcomes, whether to entrench low inflation or promote financial stability, is a matter of endowing them with appropriate instruments. However, the possession and, above all, use of these instruments open central bankers to the moral paradox of praise for delivering socially desired outcomes like price stability and blame for exercising excessive power over others (domination) without sufficient democratic accountability and transparency. This moral conundrum bedevils the debate about central bank power.

Convergence

The creation of the Euro Area was notable in both expressing and reinforcing a broader international and historical trend to enhanced central bank power in macro-economic policy. In other words, Europeanization is bound up with international convergence, especially in common pressures. Central banks look more alike—even if not exactly the same—on such dimensions as their independence, collective internal decision-making structures, monetary policy strategies that target inflation, stress on transparency, and 'knowledge-based' operation.

In empowering central banks and banking, Europeanization acts as a catalyst for convergence around German templates in the organization and making of macro-economic policies. However, as we shall see, its domestic effects—on both the power of European central banks and their convergence—have been more complex, variegated, and contingent. Continuing divergence reflects in part their hybrid characters in combining European with varying national competences, domestic path dependency in development, and economic and political contingencies. National central banks have different institutional relationships to social partnership (note Maes and Verdun's chapter on the Belgian and Dutch central banks). Moreover, both the EU and the Eurosystem lack a single authoritative institutional model in banking supervision so that the role of national central banks in this area varies widely. Central banks in smaller states tend to be more involved not just in supporting domestic adjustment through social partnership but also in operational banking supervision, reflecting the less complex domestic banking structures. Finally, national central banks demonstrate internal differences and differences in domestic support for playing effective roles in the new dynamics of the competition of ideas inside the Eurosystem. In particular, they exhibit different trajectories in internal reforms.

Historic Commonalities and Variations Amongst Central Banks

On both the international and the European levels, central banks perform broadly similar core functions in delivering price and financial stability. They are embedded interdependently in international and interconnected financial markets, characterized by complex opaque forms of intermediation, and hence have a common vulnerability to contagious financial crises. In the face of a market context driven by greed and fear, central bankers share common professional attributes, ranging from an ingrained caution and risk aversion, through a 'stability-oriented' conception of macro-economic policy, to a focus on capacity to communicate in suitably coded terms with financial markets. Not least, central banks interact cross-nationally to an unusual extent in a variety of international forums. In consequence, they represent an 'epistemic community' with a high degree of readiness to engage in cross-national policy coordination (cf. Haas 1992). Central bankers' professional beliefs also dispose them to seek to build effective cross-national policy coordination on the solid foundations of credible domestic commitment and capability to build stability 'at home'. In short, their attitudes to international coordination tend to be similarly conditional. These factors suggest a potentially relatively high level of convergence amongst central banks in professional beliefs, in functions, and in pressures.

Historically speaking too, central banking is two shared stories of transition. The first is from an early phase of central banks as primarily banks financing wars, dispensing short-term commercial credits and emerging as banker to the banks, ensuring efficient and secure payment systems, and lenders of last resort, to a central macro-economic role for monetary policy. This story is one of the displacement of an image of professionally 'boring' work, requiring tacit knowledge and practical career experience, to an image of intellectual 'fire-power'. The second is the story of the 'de-territorialization' of certain national currencies—notably the pound sterling, the US dollar, and the former D-Mark—as they become dissociated from state boundaries, making more pivotal the role of market forces (Cohen 1998). At the same time, this second story is more Anglo-American. Most continental European central banks retained the historic imprint of their origins in unifying banknote circulation in the context of convertibility crises associated with several issuing banks. Maintaining public confidence by guaranteeing the quality of banknotes in circulation was more fundamental to their identity. Notwithstanding this variation, these two stories are linked to internal changes in central bank career structures and socialization processes that reflect wider structural changes. They opened up central banks to academic economics and to international financial market experience, at a cost to their traditional, more practical work as bankers to the bank that was highlighted with the financial crisis of 2007–8.

At the same time central banks remain context-specific, exhibiting a high degree of historical path dependency and persisting national variation. National variation is evident even within the Eurosystem and can be traced to five main sources. The first is dealt with elsewhere in this chapter (pp. 20–23). Their relationship to international financial markets and the strength/weakness and organization of their domestic financial sectors help distinguish 'core' and 'periphery' central banks. *Ceteris paribus* 'core' central banks in the international financial system are more likely to be able to exert domestic as well as international power. Outside the Eurosystem the Bank of England and the Swiss central bank have benefited in this way. This section focuses on the other four factors.

'Path Dependence' and State Traditions: Institutional Legitimacy

Central banks have different relationships to historical processes of European state building and nation building and to the consequent character of the states in which they are embedded. Generally, this association endows them with dignity and status in embodying some conception of highly valued public interest and with symbolism in representing shared identity. However, 'path dependence', in the form of differences in starting points in state building, shape and constrain the limits of change in central banks. It also affects notions of institutional legitimacy.

In certain cases central banks acquire a heroic role, as with the Baltic State central banks in the post-1991 process of independence from the Soviet Union. Intimate association with independence means that they, and the currencies that they manage, become bound up in images of national identity and state sovereignty. This factor distinguishes the central banks in the Baltic States—where there is substantial public (though not elite) reluctance to give up national currencies—from that in Hungary (cf. Greskovits chapter). They are key arbiters of national economic policy debate and enjoy high levels of trust. In other cases, like France and the German Second Reich (1871–1918), central banks had a more 'humdrum' role in national debates. Although part of state building, they were not so intimately linked to national independence, compared for instance to the government bureaucracy and the army.

An aspect of 'path dependence' is the timing of state and nation building—and hence central bank formation—in relation to the development of the international political economy. Notably, the east central European central banks were reconstituted after the end of the Cold War in an international context of consensus about freedom of capital movement, central bank independence, and 'stability-oriented' policies (cf. Epstein and Johnson chapter). This timing empowered them domestically as 'liberalizers' and 'modernizers' and powerfully shaped their identity.

In addition to 'path dependence', state traditions of thought about the role of public authority in economic development matter (Armstrong 1973; Dyson 1980). Association with state building highlights the particularities of state traditions in economic development, which in turn help forge role conceptions of central banks and leave their own distinct genetic footprints. The French central bank, for instance, retains an image and style of *'interventionism'*, of embodying certain state purposes. This style was evident in a 'developmental' role in the early post-1945 period in implementing economic priorities in national plans through its credit policies; in its role with government in seeking consolidation of the French banking sector (e.g. the BNP, Paribas, and the Societe Generale in 1999); or, since 2006, in assuming a 'social' role in personal debt management (cf. Howarth's chapter). The image of the Bank of England is bound up in a very different relationship of state building to the economy. Its traditional *'hands-off' approach* centred on supporting the international role of the City of London. The Bank was embedded in the 'club-like' social networks of the City that were premised on a gentlemanly code of trust and informally held together government, central banks, and finance, at least till the 1980s (Kynaston 2002; Roberts and Kynaston 1995).

In Belgium, the Netherlands, and Sweden, by contrast, the imprints of social partnership find their expression in a role in *supporting 'concertation'* amongst employers and trade unions. In reaction to the cataclysm of the collapse of the Weimar Republic and the Third Reich, the Bundesbank embodies the post-war Ordo-liberal conception of a new German state bound by clear principles and

21

firm rules to safeguard long-term stability. Hence it espoused a *'public trustee'* role on behalf of price stability that made it more distant from the 'short-termism' of financial markets (than the Bank of England), government (than the French central bank), and the social partners (than the Belgian or Dutch central banks).

'Path dependence' in state building also deeply shaped notions of institutional legitimacy in central banking, especially conceptions of accountability. The chapter by Eichbaum on Australasian central bank illustrates the background role of the British *Westminster political model* in the development of ideas on central bank independence and inflation targeting. This constitutional model, which focuses on ministerial responsibility to Parliament, has a 'misfit' with ideas of 'goal' independence (as opposed to 'instrument' independence) in central banking. Conversely, it fits with the idea of political determination of the inflation target and central bank accountability for meeting this target. However, as the chapters on the US Fed and the ECB and Jabko's chapter show, these ideas flow less easily into different constitutional frameworks. The US separation of powers model involves more complex accountability relationships to Congress and the federal executive. In the Euro Area context two different constitutional models have competed, though very asymmetric in terms of their power over central bank design. The French *republican model* focuses on accountability to the nation, whose will is delegated to the sovereign political institutions of the Republic. Hence it fits badly with 'goal' independence in central banking and advocates European-level 'economic government', to which the ECB should be accountable and which should coordinate economic and monetary policies (see Howarth's chapters). Far more powerful in shaping the institutional design of independence and accountability of the ECB have been *German Ordo-liberal ideas of trusteeship* (see Dyson's chapter on the Bundesbank; also Dyson and Featherstone 1999 for the reasons). These ideas focus on a strong institution with a narrowly defined mandate for price stability, on behalf of which the central bank acts as public trustee.

Domestic Governance Patterns: 'Strong' and 'Weak' States

Central bank power also varies in relation to the institutional characteristics of domestic economic governance and the wider politico-administrative systems in which they are embedded. This factor highlights distinctive domestic political constellations and interests, like intra-governmental pattern of power, party ideologies and strength, party factionalism, and cohesion or fragmentation in party systems. They affect the balance in the relationships to finance ministries and more widely to governments. Although there are patterns, their precision should not be exaggerated. In analysing 'path dependence', we have noted different types of state tradition in terms of their distinctive preferences. Simplistically, on the measure of their historical capacities to act on behalf of these preferences, there are 'strong' and 'weak' states and 'strong' and 'weak' central banks.

'Weak' states lack the unity of purpose amongst domestic veto players to pursue consistent economic policies and suffer from a plethora of veto points on change. In short, they lack institutional capacity to deliver their preferences. These veto points are to be found in party system fragmentation and party factionalism, in ministerial 'fiefdoms' within coalition governments, in potentially competing legislative majorities in lower and upper houses, in various organized groups, and in structures of territorial interest. As the Italian case demonstrates, they can be associated with (relatively) 'strong' central banks, providing an opportunity to carve out a niche of power: a case of a 'strong' central bank in a 'weak' state. Conversely, 'weak' states do not guarantee central bank power: the Greek central bank was a 'weak' central bank in a 'weak' state. 'Weak' states can erode the authority of central banks, whether by enmeshing them in clientele relationships for rewarding supporters or by politically motivated processes of partisan advantage through appointments to top posts. In consequence, their authority is eroded (see Greskovits' chapter on east central Europe). If state capacity to act matters for central banks, so too does whether state actors share or subvert their core purposes.

Conversely, 'strong' states embody a greater unity of purpose that enables coordinated action amongst various veto players. Again, there is no single pattern. Where state capacity to deliver is linked to a shared social purpose with the central banks, a 'strong' state is consistent with a 'strong' central bank. An example is Sweden, where the central bank has been supported by the capacity of the state to deliver a context for neo-corporatist forms of responsible, macro-economic–focused collective bargaining. The Bank of England has similarly benefited from the capacity of the British state to deliver on fiscal discipline and market liberalization (when governments are so inclined). In contrast, the French central bank has been a 'weak' central bank in a 'strong' state. In this case, domestic political ideology has proved less supportive of fiscal consolidation and structural reforms to liberalize markets.

In consequence, there are cross-national variations in the institutional capacity of states to support central banks by delivering domestic stability-oriented fiscal policies and wage bargaining. There are also variations in the vulnerability of central banks to the political use of the appointments process to their top posts, notably in undermining their reputation for objectivity (see Greskovits's chapter).

'Output' Legitimacy; 'Matching Words to Deeds'

Central banks vary in their image for professional competence and objectivity according to their effectiveness in performing their functions. Some central banks are more trusted than others to match 'words to deeds'. Most notably, the Bundesbank gained from its perceived, though hard-fought, success in delivering price stability in Germany, in the context of growth and high employment. Central banks are, in short, dependent on 'output' legitimacy.

The 'output' legitimacy of the Bundesbank made it the model for the design of the ECB. In gaining 'output' legitimacy in its first decade the relative power of the ECB within the Eurosystem was strengthened. However, this legitimacy is contingent on performance.

The Eurosystem provided a new challenge of 'output' legitimacy for constituent national central banks: their capacity to pursue internal efficiency-oriented reforms, like tighter strategic control, 'de-layering' of structures, 'outsourcing', and performance measurement. Here again contrasting trajectories of reform were evident, with different emphases in individual cases (cf. Pollitt and Bouckaert 2000). The French and the Greek central banks adapted to *maintain the status quo*. Rationalizing measures were introduced without recourse to the legitimating discourse of the New Public Management. 'Outsourcing' initiatives were limited. Strong internal trade-union presence proved a key constraint. Thus in 2008 the union's forceful demonstration led to an exemption of Bank of Greece staff from the pension system reform. In the Banque de France internal vested interests blocked major strengthening of macro-economic research capacity. A different emphasis was apparent in the Danish central bank, which also eschewed a pace-setting role in public-sector reforms. A key reason was that it experienced little external pressure for reform because of the continuity in making monetary policy from the 'old' ERM to the 'new' ERM II.

More characteristic of Eurosystem central banks was *modernization through transformation* of existing structures. These central banks sought to be pacesetters in domestic public-sector reform and included Germany and the Netherlands. The 'outsider' Swedish central bank became a key benchmark. In these cases the New Public Management was a legitimating discourse. The third reform trajectory—*'marketizing'* central banks by introducing private-sector practices—was pursued much more cautiously and characteristically in the function of cash management.

Central Banker Preferences

A final source of variation lies in the preferences of central bankers themselves in a context of discretion, however constrained. At this more individual level, factors of socialization and career ambitions and incentives play a role (cf. Adolph 2003). Recruitment to top central bank posts from government service or from the financial sector seems to have implications for whether monetary policy preferences are 'dovish' or 'hawkish' (Adolph 2005 and p. 32 above). There are also different positions on the appropriate trade-off between risks of damaging market efficiency and innovation through tight supervision (stressed notably by Greenspan) and risks to systemic financial stability from the misalignment of private incentives through lax supervision (highlighted by the Bank for International Settlements). Here again socialization and career incentives seem relevant.

In addition, though there may be broad general shifts in central banking and evidence of epistemic convergence, there is room for differences of view on a range of issues. For instance, views on how random and unpredictable are financial markets feed into different assessments of the value of formal macro-economic modelling in monetary policy and of how much reliance to place in an individual 'anchor' like money supply growth, exchange-rate targeting, or inflation targeting. The view that markets are random and unpredictable translates into the belief in the primacy of expertise in the form of tacit knowledge, grounded in the value of long experience of managing crises, in the cultivation of a certain mystique in central banking, and in personal trust as vital to the transfer of this tacit knowledge (cf. Collins 2007). There are also differences of view on whether central banks should ignore asset prices and deal only with the economic consequences of an asset price bust the 'mop-up-after' policy (cf. Greenspan 2007) or be more proactive and 'lean against the wind' (e.g. the Bank for International Settlements 2008; Bordo 2007; Draghi 2008; Weber 2008). Similarly, transparency can be regarded as potentially subversive, to be conceded in response to demands from political institutions (see Woolley's chapter on the US Fed), or as an instrument for making monetary policy more effective and hence to be embraced pro-actively (see Marcussen's chapter on Sweden).

Central banker preferences are typically linked to domestic state traditions. In accountability, for example, two positions can be identified. Central banks can be seen as embedded in principal/agency relations, in which the governing majority delegates and in turn demands accountability. This notion fits closely with states that emphasize Parliamentary sovereignty (as in the 'Westminster' model) and with inflation targeting as a device for holding central banks to account. Conversely, central banks can be seen as 'disinterested' trustees for a specific public interest. This notion is very strong in the post-war German tradition and has been uploaded into the ECB. The ECB is accountable to the public of the Euro Area to deliver its Treaty mandate of price stability.

Within the shared context of the Eurosystem, these four factors—alongside the international strength of the domestic financial sector—provide different opportunity structures and constraints for central banks. They account for persisting variations in their potential to project and exercise power. The presence and effect of these factors is even more evident outside the Eurosystem. Persisting national preferences in key areas like accountability and transparency keep the Bank of England and the Swedish Riksbank at an intellectual distance from the Eurosystem.

History-Making: From State Building to Europe Building

The age of the euro suggests an inversion of the historic relationship between central banks and the state. The mechanisms are twofold: a collective empowerment of Eurosystem central banks vis-à-vis states through explicit and clear Treaty mandate; and their focus, for monetary and closely associated policies, on Euro Area identity and loyalty. In the process, the age of the euro has made more transparent the weaknesses in institutional capacities of states in fiscal and economic reform policies and in financial crisis management. This new capacity of central banks to transform European states does not amount to the end of the state nor of their distinctive, dissimilar characters. It means that the Eurosystem has become an agency of Europe building and of state transformation.

The novelty of the age of the euro stems from the breaking of this historical association of the creation of European central banks with 'state building' and 'nation building'—even if this association continued to be exemplified post-1991 in the Baltic States and post-1993 in Slovakia. The previous section showed how varying roles in state- and nation-building processes have given central banks distinctive characters and shaped how their functions have evolved. For instance, the Bundesbank's role in stabilizing post-war German democracy and differentiating it from the 'failed' Weimar Republic (and the hyper-inflation of 1923) involved a one-dimensional focus on price stability. It also highlighted the importance of the timing of their creation and entry into the modern state system. The development of the British and Dutch central banks in the seventeenth century had its rationale in providing a key driver of state building, namely, financing expensive wars without recourse to punitive and unpopular taxation (Roberts and Kynaston 1995; Tilly 1975). In consequence, the early central banks acquired the privileged functions of banker and advisor to governments. This war-fighting context of geo-military competition in the European state system was the antithesis of the context of central bank re-formation in the modern EU.

In later post–nineteenth-century stages of state and nation building, the changed political economy backgrounds of more developed international financial markets, combined with greater relative economic backwardness, meant that central banks were designed with other functions in mind, not least to provide monetary guarantees in order to safeguard the interests of international creditors (Gerschenkron 1965). Their evolution reflected the ambitions of states to strengthen their power through supporting the secure long-term financing of increasingly costly—because technologically more sophisticated—industrial development by mobilizing large sums of capital. In this context, central banks assumed functions as credit providers, using direct methods of intervention, and as 'bankers of last resort', offering safety nets to private banks (Broz 1997; Epstein 2005). Central bankers became pre-eminently 'banker to the banks'. Where liquidity was limited and the private sector undeveloped, the state supported extensive financial intervention by the central bank, which targeted credit to particular sectors and activities judged conducive to economic development. Examples of this interventionist role included the central banks of France, Italy, Prussia, and Spain. This interventionist historical context of much continental European central banking contrasts with the market-based financial system into which the age of the euro was born.

Despite these marked historical contrasts in the European state system and in relations between states and markets, central banks bear the imprint of this past. In their origins central banks served to augment the power of European states. They attained, in consequence, as we saw above, a status of dignity and high social prestige. This status expressed either the ethic of public service, which was imputed to a social class that embodied the civic virtues (characteristic of the Bank of England), or their embodiment of the authority of the state and its purposes (as in the German Reichsbank). Equally, central banks reflected the historical variability in state- and nation-building experiences and—in the case of the Bundesbank—historical ruptures.

This historical context means that central banks articulated the financial and monetary dimensions of sovereignty. Just as it had armed forces and police to protect its subjects and its borders, so the state had its own money. The central bank was there to safeguard the value of the national currency. It had, accordingly, a symbolic power. It represented the nation. Central banks were bound up with nation building as well as state building. In the process their individual definitions of their common functions took on the attributes of distinct conceptions of statehood and nationhood.

This role of central banks in state and in nation building was articulated in their architecture, characteristically austere, classical, dignified, and imposing, and in the formality of their rituals and traditions. The imposing edifices of the Bank of England and the Bank of France convey powerful images of historic grandeur and solemnity. In contrast, the German Bundesbank's modernist architecture symbolizes a ruptured tradition after 1933–45, a new central bank for a new state, and a redefined nation. Even so, the traditional central bank images remain: calm solemnity and the 'private' government of public money.

The striking feature of the age of the euro is the historic attenuation of this association of European central banking with state, sovereignty, and national identity. Architecturally, it is the post-modern age of central banking, symbolizing a hybrid of European cross-national identity building with national particularities. The futuristic design of the ECB tower in Frankfurt expresses this spirit. Socially and culturally, the ECB brings together seconded officials from national central banks with permanent officials from a range of European states. Their commonality resides in shared central banking professionalism, in cultivating a Euro Area identity in policy formation that is non-national, and in the exclusive use of the English language. In short, the ECB represents a highly cosmopolitan expert elite, a trans-national 'epistemic community' united by shared beliefs and policy projects (on which Haas 1992).

The distinctiveness of the ECB resides in its 'stateless', 'supra-national' character, which is expressed in the non-national symbols on euro notes (the main motifs being bridges and gateways). Simultaneously, it remains embedded in enduring European states and in national identities. These identities are still reflected in the motifs chosen for the euro coins. For instance, Slovakia adopted three motifs: the first represented a national cultural monument (Bratislava Castle), the second expressed the permanency and firmness of the state (the double cross on three hills), and the third was a symbol of the protection of Slovak independence and historical territory (Krivan peak).

The next two sections deal with the determinants of the substance and the process of European monetary integration, highlighting, respectively, international dynamics of convergence and intra-European dynamics.

The International Context of the Age of the Euro

In contrast to the internal European processes leading to its birth and evolution, the age of the euro is defined in substance by the larger spatial and historical framework of the international political economy.

Historical Legacy: Core and Periphery Central Banks

Historically, power to shape monetary and financial stability policies migrates to the central bank or banks in the major international financial centre or centres, creating 'core' and 'periphery' central banks. These centres are defined by the size, depth, and liquidity of their financial markets and by the significance of their domestic currencies in financial market trading and in central bank reserves. Central banks in these locations gain status and power over international capital flows and over the politics of international coordination denied to others. This advantage is enhanced when they are able to accumulate their own large reserves and to avoid unsustainable external imbalances that threaten to unwind. Even under a 'managed' system like the classical Gold Standard (1880–1914), these 'core' central banks have greater discretion about whether, when, and how to act and not least about whether to engage in central bank cooperation (Eichengreen 1985). Whether with or without explicit rule-based international coordination, 'periphery' central banks adjust to the actions of 'core' central banks and the expectations that they generate. They fear capital flight to the financial 'core' at times of strain. The result is an asymmetric central bank experience of the realities of international coordination. Coordination looks less smooth from the perspective of the periphery, where crises tend to concentrate. Of course, financial crisis management takes on a different character when it originates in and strikes at the 'centre', as in 1929–31, 1987, and 2007–8, compared to its origination in the periphery, as in 1997–8.

The big international central banking story of the first part of the twentieth century was the protracted power shift from the Bank of England, the putative fulcrum of the classical Gold Standard, to the US Fed. The 'gold-backed' age of globalization witnessed even higher levels of trade and financial integration than in the 'US-dollar-backed' Bretton Woods age of globalization. It rested on the credible commitment of the Bank of England to convertibility of the pound sterling to gold. Given this external discipline and the associated notion of 'automaticity' in adjustment, there was little incentive to develop national central banking. Its emergence in the period 1870s–1914 owed more to a new and growing emphasis on 'monetary sovereignty' associated with newly emergent 'nation' states, a process that gathered pace in the interwar period. The shift to the post-1945 'US-dollar-backed' age of globalization reflected a rebalancing of financial and economic power within the North Atlantic–centred world economy away from London to New York and a new willingness of the United States, not apparent in the 1930s, to assume the leadership role in international stabilization.

Central banking in the age of the euro reflected this legacy of international economic history. Historical legacy, notably associated 'agglomeration' effects, along with its favourable location between international time zones, meant that London remained the core European financial centre. This comparative advantage was reinforced by the pioneering role of the British government in deregulating the financial sector in the 1980s and in benefiting from the financial services revolution; it was seen again in October 2008 in the model character of the British banking bail out for the EU. The City was the main global centre for *international* business. Hence a further distinctive feature of the age of the euro has been the separation of 'financial' Europe (centred on London and firmly global and US-centric in outlook) and 'monetary' Europe (focused on the ECB in Frankfurt). In consequence, the Euro Area lacks the core European financial centre.

More fundamentally, however, the post-1945 period has been characterized by the financial and monetary ascendancy of the United States, represented by New York and Chicago, the US Fed, and the US dollar. Despite recurrent and often sharp volatility, the US dollar remains the core international currency in foreign-exchange trading, the main denominator in world trade, the main 'anchor' currency for states pursuing explicit exchange-rate policies (leading to talk of an informal 'Bretton Woods II'), and the dominant reserve currency for other central banks. Financial and monetary crises transmit more forcefully outwards from the United States than into the United States. Post-1973, the leadership role of the US Fed survived the end of the Bretton Woods system, which had been in effect a US dollar-based international exchange-rate system, and the tribulations of the US dollar in the late 1970s and beyond. Drawing on memories of the disruptive effects of US-based market excesses and benign neglect of international responsibilities, the age of the euro was in part designed to better insulate Europe in this new era of market-led globalization. Although this aim could in part be realized in terms of the reduced external trade dependence of a large currency union, global financial market integration continued to provide powerful transmission mechanisms through which US power was manifested.

In this context of a 'financial' Europe centred on London and of US-centred global financial and monetary power, the ECB had limited scope to carve out an international role. This constraint offered an extra incentive to focus on establishing credibility through fulfilling its Treaty mandate of price stability and through encouragement of member-state governments to increase the output growth potential of the Euro Area by domestic economic reforms. Performance—'output' legitimacy—was the key to international credibility but ran into the paradox and uncertainties outlined at the outset of this chapter.

Market-Driven Globalization Post-1973: Ideational and Socio-Cultural Change in Central Banking

No less fundamentally, the context of the international political economy into which the age of the euro was born was the newly established centrality of central banks in domestic macro-economic policy. This centrality was established either *de facto*, as with the US Fed under powerful chairs like Paul Volcker and Alan Greenspan, or *de jure*, most notably in Germany. The substantive content of the negotiations on EMU in 1988–91 reflected an underlying, pre-existing structural shift in economic policy ideas, usually described simplistically as the shift from Keynesianism to monetarism, from discretionary demand management based on fiscal policy activism to rule-based stability-oriented policies (Dyson 2000; cf. Kydland and Prescott 1977). Discretion favoured the role of political elites in monetary policy and using central banks to complement fiscal policy. Rules favoured policy commitment by delegation to expert central bankers.

This characterization of the ideational shift from fiscal discretion to monetary rules, from Keynesianism to monetarism, can be overstated. It underestimates the ongoing nature of contest within the new consensus about stability-oriented policies, central bank independence, and rules, exemplified in the 'uploading' of German Ordo-liberal ideas into ECB monetary policy strategy. It also fails to recognize the development of New Keynesian models and their particular appeal to central bankers as arguably the most influential macro-economic theory. The Bundesbank continued to offer a critique of New Keynesian models of monetary policy for their excessive stress on short-term 'real' economic data, at the expense of nominal indicators, and for their reliance on economic forecasts which were exposed to high uncertainty. Above all, it advocated a 'principles-based' approach over reliance on the so-called dynamic stochastic general equilibrium model and stressed the virtues of longer-term 'monetary analysis' and the high risks in ignoring asset price bubbles models.

New Keynesian models were seen as weak in spotting asset price developments, notably 'bubbles', through longer-term analysis of money and credit and too prone to 'real-time' data problems and estimation errors that could lead to destabilizing effects from monetary policy (Weber 2006*b*). The Bundesbank saw its views on the importance of money and credit analysis as confirmed and strengthened by the 2007–8 financial crisis and as the indispensable stabilizing element in a more symmetric long-term monetary policy across the financial cycle that could dampen fluctuations (Weber 2008).

At the same time the Bundesbank accepted that New Keynesian models were useful in highlighting the concept of 'staggered' prices and the role of 'friction' in the real, imperfect world of wage and price adjustment and in picking up cost-push factors like productivity growth, regulatory and competition policies, wage indexation formulas, labour-force developments, fiscal policy shifts, and tax structure (classically Woodford 2003). The real-world problems of insufficiently rapid adjustment of wages and prices, compared to the United States (notably in services), meant that New Keynesian models retained a strong appeal to EU central bankers. In consequence, the ECB sought to reconcile New Keynesianism and German 'money growth' models in its two-pillar monetary policy strategy, though in the process retaining a critical distancing from the US-centred, New Keynesian consensus.

In particular, within the consensus on stability-oriented monetary policies, contest focused on asset price 'bubbles' like the bursting of the Internet bubble in 2000 and of the credit and house price bubble that burst in 2007. Given two key problems—that bubbles can be hard to identify until they burst and hard to prick without collateral damage to other activities, there were differences of view about whether monetary policy could, and should be used to counter them or whether it was better to rely on regulation of capital requirements and lending standards. Recurrent bubbles prevailed over regulatory quality and, above all in 2008, exposed an Achilles heel of central banking. In the wake of the credit crisis of 2007–8 the Bank for International Settlements (2008) stressed the need for greater use of monetary policy for macro-prudential purposes. The frequency and severity of crises could be reduced by a more symmetrical use of monetary policy: by tightening it when credit growth soars and asset prices explode, even if it temporarily reduces inflation below target levels. This assessment rested on the attribution of a sizeable portion of blame for the 2007–8 crisis to the central banks, led by the US Fed, for tolerating a long period of easy money and rapid asset price inflation.

Academic monetary economists were in general powerful advocates of rules, though their advocacy varied from money supply growth, exchange-rate targeting, to direct inflation targeting. Central bankers were also attracted to rules as insurance to protect against political incursions on their independence and, not least, as an anchor to entrench market expectations of inflation consistent with their objectives. However, they were most directly exposed to the volatility and random character of increasingly large, fast-changing, interconnected, and opaque financial markets. In consequence, they were both unsure what constituted the appropriate rule and cautious about using simple rules. They differed on how much insurance they were prepared to pay to protect themselves against failure to meet their target. Central bank career officials ('lifers'), as well as academic economists and government officials after appointment to top central bank posts, were typically more disposed to the pragmatism of 'rule-bound' discretion. This underlying professional pragmatism was apparent in how the Bundesbank actually used its monetary targeting, 1974–98, and in the ECB's design of a 'two-pillar' monetary policy strategy. It was evident in its decision in December 2003 to stop publishing a reference value for growth of money supply in favour of more detailed, multi-dimensional 'monetary analysis' to cross-check 'economic analysis'.

The diffusion of this ideational shift to rules and institutional independence was reinforced by a change in the career backgrounds and incentives of top central bankers from the late 1970s and thus a strengthened disposition to 'hawkish' attitudes to inflation. This preference shift was independent of institutional independence and reflected the role of central banks as 'revolving doors' in careers. Internationally, though the mixture of career types varied between central banks, the trend was away from appointing those with non-specialist bureaucratic experience in government to top central bank positions; they were associated with a more 'dovish' attitude to inflation (Adolph 2003: 24). There was a stronger representation from the private banking and financial sectors, which were more closely linked to 'hawkish' attitudes to inflation and which acted as a 'shadow principal' of central banks and incentivized inflation-aversion (Posen 1995). Similarly, the career inducements of the financial sector to central bank 'lifers' and to those from finance ministry backgrounds offered an incentive for them to be 'hawkish'. The second shift was to a greater presence of academic economists in top posts; they were often, if less frequently, 'hawkish' in views (Adolph 2003, 2005). In short, career socialization and incentive patterns changed, privileging 'conservatism' in monetary policy preferences. However, these same career and socialization factors produced a disincentive to pay attention to financial stability issues and to asset price bubbles from which market participants made major financial gains. The effects of this disincentive were demonstrated in 2007–8 and raised questions about the *de facto* relationship of central bankers to financial markets.

Moreover, at least amongst 'outsider' EU central banks, there is some limited evidence that the appointment process to top posts is used as a channel for political influence by trying to entrench attitudes to monetary policy that complement the stance of fiscal policies: respectively, favouring 'dovish' attitudes in appointees when fiscal policy is tight and 'hawkish' when it is relaxed (Hix, Hoyland, and Vivyan 2007). It is precisely the element of discretion in monetary policy that makes the preferences of central bankers—and their socialization and career inducements—important and that offers an incentive to use this political channel of influence.

In acting as a catalyst for a new 'market-driven' age of globalization, the post-1973 period represented a more definitive structural break with the legacy of 'gold-backed' globalization. Against this international background, the new centrality of central banks in macro-economic policy making evolved gradually and at different speeds. It responded to the new post-Bretton Woods context of floating exchange rates amongst the leading currencies, US-led (and in Europe UK-led) capital liberalization, and increasingly powerful, internationally integrated, and institutionally more complex and interconnected financial markets.

Market-driven banking and financial crises increased substantially, alongside the liberalization of capital flows, becoming as high since 1980 as in any period since 1800 (Reinhart and Rogoff 2008; also Kindleberger and Aliber 2005). They were the trigger for domestic political elites to absorb two painful lessons. First, in the absence of a formal international 'anchor', backed by a leader willing and capable of leading international stabilization, and given the sheer scale and speed of capital movements, pegging the exchange rate was hazardous. In this respect, the notion of a 'Bretton Woods II', in effect an informal 'dollar zone' as states like China pegged to the US dollar and became 'takers' of US monetary policy, lacked traction. It was a subtext in the international monetary history of the period, though one that spoke to ongoing US monetary power. The most credible choices were 'floating'—with a credible domestic monetary policy, a 'hard peg' (like currency boards) or a monetary union (Fischer 2001). Floating appealed particularly to believers in national monetary sovereignty and to those who saw devaluation as a speedier means for regaining lost competitiveness.

Second, domestic political elites came to see that central bank empowerment through independence offered valuable institutional insurance against the heightened risks of exchange-rate volatility and 'overshoots' at costs to the real economy, of inflation, and of banking and financial crises. These risks increased once external constraints, like exchange controls, were relaxed and once complex financial market intermediation made supervision of markets more difficult. Governments recognized their increased vulnerability to domestic pressures for politically motivated loose monetary (and fiscal) policies, to consequent electoral 'boom' and 'bust' cycles, and to episodic exchange-rate crisis. Empowerment of central bakers reflected a series of painful political experiences: the Great Inflation of the 1970s, fuelled by trade-union power over wage setting; exchange-rate crises that threatened to disrupt European integration and reduce trade (like the ERM crises of 1983, 1987, and 1992–3); and periodic contagious banking and financial crises, even if chiefly originated outside Europe.

This changed international context led to major conceptual and theoretical innovations in monetary economics, which in turn legitimated a stronger role for central banks in macro-economic policy. Inflationary and financial crises provided a receptive context for the international diffusion of new policy ideas. Monetary economics constructed an impressive technical edifice of ideas that buttressed the assignment of an explicit mandate of price stability to independent central banks. They centred on the restoration of the traditional belief in the neutrality of money in the late 1960s to early 1970s (arguing that, in the long term, monetary policy does not affect 'real' variables like growth and employment) and an emerging consensus that high and variable inflation has detrimental effects on macro-economic performance, job creation, and social stability (on which the European Central Bank 2008). In short, inflation is a monetary phenomenon; and effective monetary policy helps maximize the long-term productive potential of the economy.

In further refinements inflation was recast as a phenomenon of private-sector expectations, whose management required policy credibility; and macro-economic policy was viewed as confronting a 'time inconsistency' problem. This problem was created by political intervention to boost economies prior to elections, destabilizing expectations, and undermining policy credibility. The consequence was a new emphasis on the policy solutions of non-monetary financing of fiscal deficits, central bank independence and transparency in monetary policy, 'rule-based' fiscal and monetary policies as the embodiment of commitment to deliver stability, and 'supply-side' reforms of market liberalization to generate growth and employment.

Hence the birth of the age of the euro was encapsulated within, and substantively defined by, the longer age of post-Bretton Woods. Central banks gained new political power by offering improved insurance to states against volatile international financial markets. In turn, by the 1980s market players were being creative in offering investors new insurance against heightened risks from currency and interest-rate movements through the new instrument of derivatives and credit default swaps in particular. These instruments, in turn, could be used to speculate. The result was a bitter irony: whilst central banks gained political power, they were more vulnerable to market players' self-interest in generating complexity and opacity to create commercial advantage in offering innovative forms of high-yield risk insurance. Indeed, as by the 1990s central banks succeeded in bringing down interest rates, they encouraged financial market players to be even more creative in helping investors achieve good returns—for instance, credit default swaps and collateralized debt obligations.

Stability and Change in Domestic Political Incentives

Above all, the age of the euro helped not only to accelerate the timing and tempo of central bank independence but also to shape its distinctive details on German Ordo-liberal lines, most notably in a critical distancing from New Keynesian models in monetary policy (Weber 2006b). Domestic political elites learnt from painful experience that they were acutely vulnerable to the massive size, global scale, speed, and random behaviour—in short, power—of highly complex, interconnected and opaque financial markets. European monetary union provided collective insurance, above all to small and medium-sized states, by safeguarding the trade and investment gains of the post-war European integration process, not least the single European market. In addition, it offered higher trade and investment gains through the elimination of exchange-rate risks and reduction of transaction costs.

The age of the euro helped to speed and consolidate the macro-economic power of central banking in Europe by overcoming vestigial domestic resistance to the idea and practices of central bank independence. This resistance reflected an enduring political incentive to try to control the business cycle for political reasons, not least by relaxing policies to gain electoral support. It was strengthened in 2008 as financial crisis in money and other markets and implosion of leading banks threatened recession. Bank bail outs were associated with a new loosening of fiscal rules in favour of counter-cyclical action. The political and intellectual context of central banks changed.

Incentives to control the political business cycle were stronger under two conditions. First, where domestic institutional rules established fixed electoral terms, as in France and Germany, governments lacked the discretion to time elections during a favourable period of economic expansion or in order to pre-empt a pending economic downturn. Hence they had a stronger incentive to manipulate the economy (Kayser 2005). Second, where governments were locked into long cycles of economic stagnation and weak wage growth (as in Germany in 1993–2005 and in Italy), they had an incentive to seek to manipulate economic conditions to favour re-election, irrespective of whether they had fixed or discretionary electoral terms. Deprived of monetary policy, the emphasis shifted to fiscal policies. In turn, politically opportunistic fiscal policies—and the credibility of the Stability and Growth Pact—became a major source of uncertainty and vulnerability to the ECB (Issing 2008).

In addition, many European states had an historic legacy of ideas favouring political intervention in the economy. These ideas were variously rooted in Catholic social teaching, social democratic ideas, 'realist' views of the state and markets, and not least dominant domestic political memories where they associated financial market power with unemployment. French *dirigisme* rests on the idea that elected governments, not least the President under the Fifth Republic, embody the superior republican legitimacy of the will of the nation. In Hungary and Poland, strongly entrenched ideas of social solidarity underpin a distrust of independent central bankers. In Italy, the state functions in a way that offers political elites scope to reward and protect their clienteles, not least subverting domestic structural reforms. Hence, central banking is exposed to varying European attitudes to the legitimacy of technocratic power in economic policy.

The paradox of the age of the euro was that, in a project constructed around Franco-German political leadership in European integration, French and German ideas about the relationship of central banks to the state were least easy to reconcile. Although the Treaty was firm on central bank independence, the ECB remained politically exposed to this paradox. Its capacity to endure this exposure reflected in part the tough Treaty provisions and high hurdles to amendment (unanimity in domestic ratification) and in part firm German support for central bank independence, grounded in bitter historical memories of interwar and post-war hyperinflation. The motto that 'the euro must be at least as strong as the D-Mark' overshadowed German policy towards the ECB.

Other than Germany, European states had two main incentives to renounce their residual sovereign powers over monetary policy, as well as the symbolism of their national currencies for identity: removing the capacity of the financial markets to directly punish and humiliate elected governments through exchange-rate crisis; and neutralizing German power over European monetary policies. A single currency and a single monetary policy eliminated a key international vulnerability of post-war European states and were consistent with an enduring post-war motive of power balancing, notably against Germany, in the European integration process. These incentives were especially strong for the smaller European states. They stood to gain disproportionately from the end of exchange-rate risk and the reduction of transaction costs in both trade and investment and from having formally equal 'voice' in monetary policy.

Changing International Vulnerabilities: From Exchange Rates to Financial Stability

In the process, however, the axis of vulnerability for European states in the age of the euro shifted from the exchange-rate crisis to contagious cross-national banking and financial crisis. Although this vulnerability was increased by strengthened incentives to trans-national European banking with the euro, it was more deeply rooted in the interconnectedness and opacity of global financial markets. Even if US-centred, the 2007–8 liquidity and solvency crisis highlighted the ongoing vulnerability of European states to excesses in financial market risk taking and the deficiencies of fragmented European regulatory systems in an age of interconnected financial markets. The age of the euro, and the financial crisis of 2008, challenged European central banks to refocus priorities around the financial stability function. The issues extended beyond their involvement in macro-level financial market risk analysis and stress testing; through the problem of their frequent exclusion from the micro-level, operational aspects of banking and financial market supervision; to questions about the adequacy of the rules underpinning banking supervision. In consequence, they lacked early warning of threats to financial stability and of pressures on their monetary policies from crisis in monetary market operations.

As the financial crisis of 2008 showed, the problems were exacerbated by the breaking down of the distinction between 'regulated' commercial banks and other lightly, even non-regulated financial actors—notably investment banks, hedge funds, private equity companies. Crisis overwhelmed this latter sector. Moreover, commercial banks were exposed to new 'off-balance-sheet' risks through creating new 'structured investment vehicles'. Central banks faced a new 'shadow' banking system, endogenously creating credit. As the US-Fed orchestrated Bear Stearns rescue in 2008 and later systemic rescue package revealed, other financial entities were becoming 'too interconnected to fail' and drawing central banks into crisis management. In exchange, central banks shifted their focus to designing more intelligent rules to align private incentives to make markets efficient and innovatory with the public good of financial stability: interesting themselves in counter-cyclical capital requirements to offset asset bubbles and bursts and in increased capitalization over the cycle. However, the initial focus of this shift was primarily global, focused on the Financial Stability Forum, the IMF, the G7/8, and the Bank for International Settlements, rather than on redesign of the Euro Area.

This shift towards financial stability was made difficult by several factors. The general central banking problem was 'moral hazard': their policies should not encourage financial institutions to take reckless risks, secure in the knowledge that they are too 'systemically important' to be allowed to fail. Policies that offer inducements to reckless behaviour threaten to create future financial crises. A further general factor was 'turf wars' within complex, multi-layered, often segmented regulatory bodies: for instance, in the United States. The Euro Area encountered its own problems in promoting financial stability. They included varied, historically distinctive domestic banking and financial structures, for instance, the 'three-pillar' structure in Germany and a traditionally highly protective, interconnected Italian banking structure; the incentive for national central banks, once deprived of monetary policy, to seek to carve out a niche in financial stability and in banking supervision and in the process to delimit the role of the ECB; the failure of non-central bank national financial market regulators to share information about bank exposures in a timely way with the ECB; and, most fundamental of all, the problem that states were even more hesitant to pool sovereignty in this area than monetary policy and that a Treaty basis did not exist to establish a European banking supervisory authority. Ultimately taxpayer money was required to act as lender of last resort to the banking system in a trans-national solvency crisis. Governments were unwilling to make their publics hostage to bailing out banking failures elsewhere in the Euro Area. In this context, the technocratic rationale for central bank

independence in monetary policy was less credible in financial stability policies. Hence the age of the euro represented a shift in vulnerabilities for European states and central banks. The threat of a Euro Area power vacuum was
higher in financial stability than in monetary policies and was exhibited in the
uncoordinated nature of Irish and other interventions as the 2008 financial
crisis unfolded.

The Changing Global Context of Monetary Policy

Additionally, the ECB had to cope with new vulnerability in monetary policy
from two shocks: international energy and commodity price shocks and
imported inflation from emerging markets; and the deflationary effects
from the credit crunch and financial crisis of 2008. The ECB benefited in its
early years (1999–2005) from the historical accident of a relatively 'good
birth'. The international political economy offered a context of 'good times'
for monetary policy. The global economy grew at an unprecedented rate,
even if the Euro Area economy exhibited symptoms of anaemic overall GDP
growth, productivity growth and high structural unemployment, largely
consequent on the weak performance of its core former 'D-Mark-Zone' economies. Its locomotives lay outside Europe in US consumer-led growth and in
the powerful entry of China and India into the international economy as
exporters of cheap manufactures (with by 2007 China accounting for just
over 25% of world economic growth at purchasing power parity). Above all,
'globalization' became associated for a period with the magic reconciliation
of the so-called 'Great Moderation' in low inflation, low short-term real
interest rates, and high growth (christened by the governor of the Bank of
England the 'NICE' decade of 'non-accelerating inflation and continuous
expansion'). In this benign context, like other central banks, the ECB was
able to pursue an 'accommodative' monetary policy without endangering its
strict price stability mandate, which it redefined in 2003 as 'below but close
to' 2 per cent. Above all, it succeeded in locking in long-term market expectations of inflation broadly consistent with this definition at historically low
real interest rates. The age of the euro benefited from this historical accident
of a good birth.

In contrast to the greater complacency about inflationary pressures exhibited
by some other leading central banks, from 2005 this 'accommodative' ECB
monetary policy was gradually reduced. Its 'monetary' pillar identified mounting inflationary risks in the context of continuing low output growth potential.
Even so, by late 2007, Euro Area inflation was accelerating well above target.
'Globalization' had ceased to function as a one-way inflation dampener. Food,
commodity, and energy prices rose sharply, reflecting partly supply problems
and partly new demand from rapidly growing economies like China and India;

subsequent falling real wages meant falling disposable income; whilst financial crisis intensified as the effects of the US sub-prime debacle spread across markets and, through tightening credit policies, into the real economy. Even if the threat of 'second-round' effects in wage settlements on the 1970s pattern was ameliorated by subsequent product, trade, and labour-market deregulations, as well as higher immigration, a global inflationary process threatened.

Hence, the ECB faced new challenges in monetary policy. The accommodation of new threats to the real economy of growth and employment from financial crisis proved more difficult to reconcile with the threats to the price stability mandate from imported global inflation. These 'globalization' challenges opened up new political space for tensions and conflicts about 'winners' and 'losers' and between supra-national central bankers, loyal to the Treaty mandate of price stability, and European governments, anxious about their electorates' tolerance for cuts in real incomes and determined to protect their national banks and depositors from banking failures. This changing environment offered new incentives to form coalitions of 'losers', altering the axis of political debate about globalization, financial markets, and central banks.

The potential for tension and conflict was already apparent in that the age of the euro had provided stark domestic challenges of economic and institutional reforms in Euro Area member states. In the process, it made more transparent both the weaknesses and failures of domestic political leadership and the deeper institutional, political, and cultural problems of managing economic change in the political and the corporate spheres. Euro Area member states had lost two traditional core mechanisms to speed adjustment to asymmetric shocks: the exchange rate, notably devaluation to regain lost competitiveness (in short, exporting adjustment problems to others); and the interest rate.

The age of the euro meant a 'one-size-fits-all' monetary policy that, in some cases, fuelled credit booms notably in residential investment through low, even negative real interest rates (as in Ireland and Spain up to 2007) and, in others, acted as a constraint through higher real interest rates (as in Germany till 2005–6). In consequence, there was a divergence in credit cycles between Germany and these states. Moreover, persisting inflation differentials and differentials in productivity growth led to changes in relative unit labour costs and 'real' exchange-rate changes inside the Euro Area. Firms in some states, notably Ireland, Portugal, Greece, Spain, and Italy, became less competitive and their current account deficits widened. In contrast, Germany, Austria, Finland, and Belgium gained competitiveness. In order to deal with asymmetric shocks in this altered policy framework, Euro Area states had to rely more on regaining budgetary room for manoeuvre through sound sustainable fiscal policies, on disciplined wage policies to enhance competitiveness, and on labour-market, employment, and product and service market policies to encourage flexibility. Domestic reform pressures mounted and were articulated not least by national central banks. In the process they were drawn into domestic political contest.

The combination of this gradual build up of differentials in competitiveness through contrasting unit labour cost development with political failures to expedite domestic structural reforms threatened to lock Euro Area states into long cycles of growth and stagnation. The German long cycle of painful adjustment, first to German unification and then to over-valuation of the D-Mark on conversion to the euro, is exemplary, above all for the timescale and pain in 'bottom–up' corporate-led change in the context of a domestic credit crunch. States that become locked into protracted periods of painful structural adjustment are at greater risk from random political outcomes from opportunist populist mobilization. For a variety of historical and institutional reasons Germany was relatively resistant to these domestic risks. The German pattern was unlikely to prove general.

The age of the euro is one in which the power of central bankers is vulnerable to the lack of domestic ownership for the euro's implications. This lack of ownership derives not just from political elites in fiscal and structural reform policies—witness the crisis of the Stability and Growth Pact in November 2003 and the failures of the Lisbon process of economic reforms. It depends also on the dynamics of wage bargaining by employers and trade unions and on the behaviour of corporate elites in restructuring their activities to capture the potential gains of a single currency. Consequently, however, it may have empowered central bankers, the age of the euro remains an uncertain venture in central banking. Adjustments are likely to be long-term, painful, and contested, testing domestic political will and the institutional capacity to reform and potentially making monetary policy more difficult to conduct. Although central banks are formally independent, they cannot be indifferent to the distribution and intensity of domestic political preferences. The multiplicity of domestic institutional and political veto points and of partisan veto players implies adverse conditions for unity of purpose in European macro-economic policies. This point applies not least to the independent central banks in east central Europe in the context of euro entry strategies.

States, Central Banks, and the Internal Governance of the Eurosystem

At the level of process the age of the euro was above all a European affair, bound up in the economic and political dynamics of European integration. It was part and parcel of various pro-integration arguments: about completing the 'logic' of European customs union and the single market ('one market, one money'); about trade and investment gains from eliminating exchange-rate risk and reducing transaction costs; and about making European integration, in German Chancellor Helmut Kohl's words, 'irreversible' and ensuring no future wars in Europe. Historical memory of catastrophic twentieth-century European wars and the failure of traditional faith in the 'balance of power' hung heavily over the politics of the process (Dyson and Featherstone 1999).

Central Banks, State Power, and Differentiated Integration

The euro raised in a highly focused manner the question of the relationship of European integration to state power. At its heart was a trade-off that invited different political choices based on contrasting domestic structures of preference. On the one hand, loss of state power was implicit in the formal renunciation of 'monetary sovereignty', both in its symbolic trappings especially of 'identity' and in the nominal form of the interest rate and the exchange rate as domestic policy instruments for cushioning asymmetric shocks. Domestic contests were sharpened: over implications for different national economic and social models, for who wins and who loses, and for whether 'real' convergence in living standards represented by GDP per capita was being sacrificed to 'nominal' convergence.

On the other hand, euro entry offered the gains of currency and monetary union. These gains in state power included the elimination of increased vulnerability to domestic exchange-rate crises in the post-Bretton Woods age of floating exchange rates and volatile global financial markets; sharing in European monetary policy rather than being a passive 'policy taker' from the Bundesbank in the Exchange-Rate Mechanism (ERM); as well as increasing growth and employment through trade effects from reduced transaction costs and reducing risk through access to much larger, more liquid financial markets

The complex trade-offs were evaluated differently by domestic elites. Amongst the 'old' 15 EU member states in 1998–9 Britain, Denmark, and Sweden chose to remain 'outsiders'; whilst newer EU member states divided between 'leaders' and 'laggards' on euro entry and shifted their positions on this spectrum (on which Dyson 2006, 2008).

Above all, the age of the euro represented the most advanced example of differentiated European integration. In contrast to full integration of all EU member states, it produced a radical restructuring of European central banking into the 'Eurosystem' and 'outsiders'. The Eurosystem comprised the ECB and the national central banks of those EU member states whose currency was the euro. In this new context, the formal conditionality attached to EU accession, and later to entry into monetary union, acted as powerful, top–down, European-level pressures for convergence around a clear, specific and detailed institutional template of central bank independence, prohibition of monetary financing of deficits, and strengthened incentives to pursue disinflation and fiscal discipline.

At the same time, as this volume shows, in the context of contrasting political choices, and not least underlying economic structures, national central banks behaved differently. The Bank of England, an 'outsider', focused very successfully on preparing the City of London wholesale markets so that London would become the major centre for euro-denominated financial business (Goodhart's chapter). Two Nordic 'outsiders', the central banks of Denmark and Sweden, pursued contrasting strategies; Sweden led in the practices of the New Public Management and transparency; whilst both compensated by more active international networking (Marcussen's chapter). The German Bundesbank, an 'insider', had to radically reconfigure strategy and structures to cope with monetary policy 'disempowerment' (Dyson's chapter). Another 'insider', the Bank of Italy, suffered a profound crisis of its centralized corporate governance in 2005, consequent on the failed attempt to act as champion of a protectionist approach to domestic banking consolidation (Quaglia's chapter). In east central Europe the domestic political complexities of euro entry, and often of partisan appointments to senior posts, exposed central banks to frequent challenges to their independence (Epstein and Johnson's chapter; Greskovits's chapter). These and other experiences of central banks in the age of the euro are examined in this volume.

Competing in Ideas; Seeking Niches: Developing Cooperation

More generally, the NCBs in the Eurosystem sought to occupy different specialized niches in the new more competitive environment of ideas. This pursuit of specialization within the Eurosystem was visible in contributing ideas to monetary policy, financial stability, new research networks, the euro payment and settlement system, the agenda of the New Public Management, and EU/Euro Area enlargement and transition economies. NCBs were forced to consider their comparative advantage and build their own niches as the basis for leadership roles in pooling services through specialized cooperation activities in the Eurosystem. How they developed specialization, and responded to wider Eurosystem pressures, reflected the historical accidents of their competences and strengths; the constraints of their size; and their geographical location. In competences, for instance, the Belgian and French central banks had traditionally strong roles in national accounting and in collecting data about firms, giving statistics a strong profile in their work. The Belgian and Dutch central banks had particular strengths in developing collateral central bank management systems that they could transfer to the Eurosystem. In general, smaller NCBs had a greater incentive to seek out cooperation. For instance, two systems of cooperative pooling of the operational management of the ECB's foreign reserve assets were established in 2007: between the Luxembourg and Slovenian central banks; and between the Cypriot, Greek, Irish, and Maltese central banks. Although small NCBs had a new incentive to engage in monetary policy analysis, they could not hope to match the ECB. In contrast, as a large central bank with an eminent reputation in monetary policy performance, the Bundesbank had a strong incentive to maintain both its traditional role in this policy area through its advocacy of a principles-based approach and its high international profile in various Eurosystem cooperative ventures to provide technical advice to states outside the EU, including Russia, the Gulf Cooperation Council, and the western Balkans. Geographic location led the Austrian and Finnish central banks to focus, respectively, on the Balkans and the Baltic States.

Contest emerged about different forms of cooperation, part of a larger debate about operating modalities in the Eurosystem, on which the Governing Council set up a Task Force. Examples of 'bottom–up' cooperation included the leading role of the Belgian National Bank in developing harmonized, efficient, and secure IT-based management of cash flows with the cash single shared platform (Cash SSP in 2006) as the model for a future Single Euro Cash Area; and, building on their geographic locations, the Austrian and the Finnish national banks in fostering privileged relations with post-communist transition economies in Euro Area enlargement. A more 'top–down' cooperation, negotiated in the ECB General Council, was the German Bundesbank, the Banque de France, and the Banca d'Italia leadership in the shared computer platform for the TARGET 2 electronic euro payment and settlement system. This leadership group was extended to the Spanish central bank in developing the proposal for TARGET2-Securities (T2S) for settlement of securities transactions using this shared platform. On issues like cross-border collateral management and statistics a tussle was apparent over the form that cooperation was to take. The new Collateral Central Bank Management (CCBM2)—endorsed by the ECB Governing Council in 2007—was modelled on the Belgian and Dutch central banks, but participation remained voluntary pending consultation on its further development.

The less central a function was to monetary policy, the greater was the scope to develop flexible, 'bottom–up' cooperation. Alongside the Cash SSP in cash management (by 2008 the Belgian, Dutch, Luxembourg, and Finnish central banks), an example of 'bottom–up' cooperation in banking supervision was the 2003 Memorandum of Understanding on the exchange of data in national central registers. This cooperation allowed better evaluation of credit risk in cross-border lending and involved a consortium of the central banks in Austria, Belgium, France, Germany, Italy, Portugal, and Spain. Membership was necessarily limited to those states with national credit registers and—given the focus of banking supervision on the EU level—not in principle limited to Eurosystem central banks.

Agendas and Processes of Change: Benchmarking and Binding Rules

'Analysis/research', 'efficiency', and 'specialization' gained a new status in the internal vocabulary of NCBs. In particular, the Eurosystem stimulated two agendas of change. First, NCBs were under increased pressure to stake out leadership in promoting internal efficiency through the techniques of 'New Public Management'. This pressure derived from their vulnerability to two arguments: that with centralized monetary policy making they were 'over-staffed' in relation to functions, bloated self-serving bureaucracies; and that they were hypocritical in calling for structural reforms when they were unwilling to bear the pain of reform themselves in the face of major structural change. Here the main model was a Eurosystem 'outsider', the Swedish central bank. Under Axel Weber the Bundesbank sought to carve out a leadership role on New Public Management; whereas the Banque de France, caught up in more difficult public-sector trade union problems, proved a laggard. The New Public Management was attractive to the new ECB because it combined an association with 'modernization' with centralizing implications and legitimated transformation in central banking.

Second, NCBs were under pressure to upgrade their applied research, consequent on the need to mount persuasive arguments in a new context in which they were no longer 'monopolists'. Quality of analysis was exposed when they had to share in debates in a large number of Eurosystem committees and working groups and, above all, to ensure that their governors were well-briefed for Governing Council meetings on both monetary and non-monetary matters. The Bundesbank's focus on developing its niche in the 'monetary analysis' pillar of ECB monetary policy strategy represented an attempt to directly shape centralized policy and to give more analytical clout to its traditional 'principles-based' approach. Similarly, building on its advantage in competence in banking supervision, the Dutch National Bank sought out a niche in the financial stability function. Overall, however, even for the top performers in quality research performance like the Dutch and Finnish central banks, it proved difficult to match the growing scale of research capacity in the ECB. In the three Eurosystem research networks—on monetary transmission (1999–2002), inflation persistence, and wage dynamics (2006–8)—ECB researchers played key roles. In cooperation with NCB research directors, the ECB also developed benchmarks for assessing research quality, ranking key policy-oriented academic journals. This new, intensifying benchmarking process in turn increased internal pressures to invest in research, as well as controversy about the appropriateness of benchmarking English-language journals when NCBs should be communicating more actively with domestic audiences.

Above all, the age of the euro witnessed the evolution of a body of principles, rules, and practices of cooperation and teamwork within the Eurosystem. In addition to the intense benchmarking described above, the Eurosystem spawned a body of binding rules. At the heart of this evolution was the search to marry common goals with the principle of decentralization that had been established in the preparatory work of the EMI. Centralization was in principle confined to monetary policy making; though its implementation was a matter for the NCBs. Nevertheless, the monetary policy function spawned the need to extend binding rules to ensure both consistent implementation and that related functions, like payment and settlement systems, were supportive.

This body of binding rules can be accessed elsewhere (see Dyson and Quaglia 2009). They include the following:

- Treaty articles, notably 4, 105, and 106
- The Statute of the European System of Central Banks (ESCB), especially articles 3, 12, 17–20
- The ECB regulation on the application of minimum reserves, December 1998 and subsequent amendments
- The ECB decision of 1998 (and subsequent amendments) on the key to subscriptions of NCBs to the capital of the ECB
- The decision on the rules of procedure of the ECB, February 2004
- The ECB monetary policy rules as laid down in October 1998 and 'clarified' in May 2003
- The ECB guidelines on monetary policy instruments and procedures of the Eurosystem, with various amendments
- The evolution from a two-tier to a single list in the collateral framework
- The correspondent central banking model
- The Council regulation of May 2000 on further calls of foreign reserve assets by the ECB
- The ECB guidelines of October 2003 on the management of foreign exchange reserves and operations
- The standards in the EU securities settlement systems
- The Council regulation of November 1998 on collection of statistical information and the ECB guidelines of November 2000 on statistical reporting requirements by the NCBs

Binding rules went along with the evolution of a body of principles about the organization of cooperation, which reflected the practices that had grown up in the various committees and working groups of the Eurosystem. They were articulated in the Eurosystem Mission Statement of 2005. The focus in the Mission Statement was on ensuring the effectiveness of the Eurosystem as a 'team of central banks', able to 'speak with one voice' and 'exploit synergies'.

Is the Age of the Euro a 'Structural Break'?

Prima facie the age of the euro suggests a 'structural break' in European central banking. The arrival of the euro as the second world currency after the US dollar is clearly an important moment in international monetary history. It is synonymous with a new, potentially powerful actor in international central banking: the ECB in Frankfurt. The possibility of the long-term displacement of the dollar by the euro, and of a multiple currency world, suggests a new era in central banking. However, one needs to be more precise in claiming that the age of the euro is a 'structural break'. To what extent is it a structural break in European integration, to what extent in central banking?

The most obvious sense in which the age of the euro is a structural break is in terms of the EU. The euro and the ECB have generated a set of institutional innovations, for instance, in EU financial market integration, and—in insuring Euro Area states against global financial market power—helped to rescue them. At the same time, it has been of limited significance in accelerating political union and shared identity (witness the Dutch and French 'no' votes on the Constitutional Treaty in 2005 and the Irish 'no' to the Lisbon Treaty in 2008) and has done nothing to reinforce the fiscal capacity of the EU (Dyson 2008*b*). More pertinently, the euro and the ECB are less central to the development of the political capacity of the EU than the EU's ability to extract revenue, acquire an independent fiscal competence, and engage in debt financing (cf. McNamara 2002*b*). Faced with the de-territorialization of money, EU member states have proved more jealous of their fiscal than their monetary sovereignty. The result is an imbalanced development in European economic governance and policies—between fiscal and monetary policies—and in the ECB—between its monetary and its financial stability/banking supervisory functions (Dyson 2008*b*).

In terms of structural power, the age of the euro embodies a 'Germanization' of central banking in institutional design and monetary policy development. Above all, it represents a structural break for the central banking system of the Euro Area. The chapters by Dyson on the German Bundesbank and Pagoulatos on the Bank of Greece suggest a real sense of structural break at the micro-level. These cases of Europeanization of national central banks point in different directions of 'disempowerment' and 'empowerment'.

The age of the euro may also serve as a structural break in the sense of producing more than 'one Europe' inside the EU. The Euro Area is the most potent expression of formally differentiated European integration: not all national central banks share the same rights and obligations. Just as some are Euro Area 'insiders', other national central banks are 'outsiders'. 'Insiders' themselves exhibit differentiation into 'core' and 'non-core' (see Umbach and Wessels' chapter). Only two EU states (Britain and Denmark) have an 'opt out' from the euro and thus are not obliged by treaty to seek euro entry. Given that they also lack euro entry plans with timetables they must be seen as 'semi-permanent' outsiders. In their cases, we would expect very different central bank trajectories in the age of the euro, plotted in the chapters by Goodhart on the Bank of England and Marcussen on the central banks of Denmark and Sweden. Sweden highlights how even a state with an obligation to seek entry can behave as a 'semi-permanent' outsider; whilst Denmark shows that, even with a formal 'opt out', a central bank can be bound by the constraints of linking its exchange rate to the euro through membership of the ERM II.

In addition, there is a large group of EU states, notably in the Baltic, east central Europe, and the east Balkans, which are formally 'temporary' outsiders. This status of derogation involves having euro entry plans with dates. Here the force of EU formal 'conditionality' operates on national central banks: in formalizing central bank independence and in meeting the so-called Maastricht convergence criteria. The chapters by Epstein and Johnson and by Greskovits explore Europeanization in relation to Baltic and east central European central banks. Their effects appear as variegated. In this case, as well as the 'semi-permanent' outsiders, the age of the euro does not suggest a structural break in central banking, rather a point in a well-defined trend line. The structural break is nationally diverse processes of post-communist transition that predate EU, let alone Euro Area entry. Moreover, some of these states may repeatedly defer euro entry to a degree that suggests 'semi-permanent' outsider status.

Hence, seen in terms of the European integration, the age of the euro is by no means destined to shift from short-term differentiation in national central banks and banking to longer-term integration of all in the Eurosystem. For some, possibly a good number of, EU central banks the age of the euro will not operate as a structural break.

To what extent is the age of the euro a structural break in central banking? The euro is not a new 'age' in central banking. Ages of central banking have typically been defined either in terms of central bank functions and styles of operation (see Marcussen's chapter on 'scientization') or in terms of changes in the underlying balance of power (hegemony) in the international monetary system (as in this chapter).

In functions and style, the age of the euro has not involved Europe-centred innovation. It reflects a 'global sea change' (Epstein 2005: 3) or 'quiet revolution' (Blinder 2004) in central banking, whose origins lie in the power and complexity of global financial markets, in monetary economics, and in changing ideas of democratic governance (Siklos 2002). Traditionally, central bankers were conservative, cautious and remote, addicted to opaque, circumspect and coded Delphic utterance, the cultivation of monetary mystique and a professional image of boredom, and the notion that central banking was pre-eminently an art, whose practice depends on tacit knowledge and experience (Hawtrey 1932). In turn, personal trust was vital to the transfer of this tacit knowledge (cf. Collins 2007). They represented a relatively closed gentlemanly world of expertise grounded in values of personal integrity and trust. This world was symbolized in Montagu Norman at the Bank of England and in William McChesney Martin at the US Fed, the latter famously describing the stern duty of central banks as to 'remove the punch bowl before the party gets going'.

Although it has by no means disappeared in central banking, the financial crisis of 2007–8 suggested that it had become in short supply.

In the post-1973 world of market-led financial globalization, central bankers are expected to engage in a subtler more Socratic—though still coded and esoteric—dialogue with powerful financial market actors. Securing and retaining credibility in this context meant possessing the authority of macroeconomic expertise, the capacity to communicate with markets that are themselves driven by new complex products and processes, and the possession of a feel for the markets (Bernanke 2004a; Blinder and Wyplocz 2004; Woodford 2005). In consequence, the career boundaries to academic economics and to financial markets were significantly opened. The effects of this opening were felt not just in socialization and in career incentives of central bankers (cf. Adolph 2003), underpinning a shift to more 'hawkish' attitudes to inflation. They also highlighted a new tension between macro-economists, who took a more remote view of markets, and those who had been closer to the minutiae of financial markets, especially the sensitive interbank market. This tension fed in turn into the politics around top central bank appointments, as in the case of the deputy governorship of the Bank of England in 2008. More seriously, it raised the question of whether central banks had too passive vis-à-vis the markets, in effect 'moping up' after bust and increasing moral hazard in the process.

In terms of balance of power in the international monetary system, the age of the euro raises the question about whether the ECB can decouple monetary policy from the US Fed and whether the euro could over the longer-term displace the US dollar as the pivot of the international monetary system. Far more powerful than the age of the euro has been the structural break in central banking associated with the birth of the 'post-Bretton Woods' system, post-1973. The collapse of the short-lived Bretton Woods system ushered in a new age of floating exchange rates, capital liberalization, and the exponential growth of a market-driven, Anglo-American, transaction-based global financial system. The 'post-Bretton Woods' age of market-led globalization overshadowed the birth of the age of the euro and more generally delimited the scope and reach of central bank power. Its globalizing financial markets—their scale, complexity, creativity, risk-taking, and opacity—defined the context in which central banking redefined its functions, recruitment, and styles of operation. This point comes out in both the non-European 'control' cases (the chapters by Eichbaum and by Woolley) and the chapters dealing with central bank functions. Where an element of central bank distinctiveness arises is in the stronger influence of German Ordo-liberal thought on money growth models in ECB monetary policy, its more critical distance from New Keynesian models, and in the 2008 financial crisis the ECB's stricter separation of its monetary policy from its liquidity operations than the US Fed.

Seen in a macro-historical context, the age of the euro is more a point in a well-defined 'trend line' that goes back to the ERM (1979–99) and the European

'Snake' (1973–9). Both these mechanisms—leading up to the euro—were part of a long-term process of trying to protect the trade gains of European integration, to reduce the vulnerability of European governments to the high randomness of global financial markets, and to centre money and credit growth in monetary policy. The unwinding of the Bretton Woods system in 1971–3 was the key structural break; whilst the 'trend line' exhibited abiding German Bundesbank influence.

Some Final Reflections: Central Banks and 'Europe Building'

Despite the qualified conclusion that it is more of a structural break in European integration than in central banking, the age of the euro involves an inversion of the historic power relationship between central banks of the Eurosystem and states. Principally in monetary policy (and related policies like financial market infrastructure including TARGET 2 and SEPA), central banks have carved out a historically new role and identity in 'Europe building'. However, this new role and identity of central banks as the most Europeanized domestic institutions does not imply 'Europeanization as homogenization' of European central banking on German Ordo-liberal terms. It means even less 'the end of the state' or that member states are becoming convergent. Europeanization of central banks involves different trajectories of domestic reform. These trajectories range from adapting to maintain the status quo, through modernizing by large-scale internal transformation, to 'marketizing' functions through private-sector techniques and involvement (cf. Pollitt and Bouckaert 2000). They represent contrasting ways, often mixed together in individual central banks in different forms, through which the age of the euro is rescuing European states. Central banks that seek a reform strategy of modernization through transformation carve out a role as pacesetters. In contrast, those adapting to maintain the status quo tend to remain laggards. The choice of central bank reform strategies is both structurally constrained and strategic, variable in nature, and designed with reference to 'path dependence', state traditions, domestic governance mechanisms, and domestic political constellations.

In this new age of the euro the most interesting aspects of central bank power have been its least visible dimensions in reframing and shaping how macro-economic policy interests are conceived and in agenda setting on behalf of competitiveness, stability, and fiscal discipline (cf. Lukes 2005). Its mechanisms are in part Europeanization, notably consequent on 'uploading' German Ordo-liberal ideas into Eurosystem design, and in part wider international diffusion of central bank best practices. However, this structural power is more evident in monetary policies than in financial stability policies, highlighting the shift of internal power within central banks and the problematic imbalance between these two core functions. Even in monetary policy it is open to domestic and

European contest. Central bank power is vulnerable to the potential for political mobilization of collective action on behalf of losers (putative or real) and to the association of central bank power with 'neo-liberal' Europeanization and globalization (and their conflation). Its Ordo-liberal variant is also subject to the contesting legitimacies of the republican and (should the UK ever enter) the Westminster models of institutional legitimacy and accountability.

Continuing broad political support for the high collective action capacity of central banks in safeguarding price and financial stability depends on their dissociation from the 'excesses' of financial market power and their avoidance of 'moral hazard'. The banking excesses revealed in the 2007–8 financial crisis and the systemic bail outs of the banking sector brought home this point. 'Working with the market' could be reconstructed as 'being captured by the market', as being over-accommodating to reckless risk taking and unjust private gains at huge cost to the public interest. Broadly held social norms of what constitutes appropriate behaviour in markets and in central banks are themselves a form of structural power that constrain central banks. Central banks have to be seen to be ensuring compliance with these socially valued norms, not just facilitating narrower standards of utility maximization by financial market actors. In this respect, public opinion, as mediated by political elites and given voice in the media, continues to matter in central banking. Central banks cannot rely for power on their institutional independence, their closeness to and understanding of the markets, or their macro-economic expertise. As the events of 2007–8 highlighted, they are caught up in larger political processes of (re)definition of norms of acceptable behaviour, whose neglect— benign or not—can only undermine popular support for central bank power.

Part I

The Changing Context of Central Banking

2

Differentiation in the European System of Central Banks: Circles, Core, and *Directoire*

Gaby Umbach and Wolfgang Wessels

In officially launching the euro with only a limited number of EU Member States partaking in the Eurosystem, the third stage of Economic and Monetary Union (EMU) intensified trends to the differentiated integration of Member States in tasks and competences within the EU system (Giering 2007; Janning 1997; Junge 2006; Tekin and Wessels 2008). The *ex ante* limitation of membership, as defined by the Maastricht convergence criteria, consolidated differentiated integration within monetary policy and the European System of Central Banks (ESCB). So, viewed from a systemic perspective on European integration, out of 'all the current activities of the European Union in which flexible integration plays or may play a role, the single European currency is undoubtedly the most important' (Federal Trust 2005: 23).

Institutionally dominated by the European Central Bank (ECB) both the ESCB and EMU show different patterns of differentiated integration. The major argument of this chapter is that EMU, and also the ESCB, can be characterized by the dynamic co-existence of a '*directoire*' of 'core insiders', which seeks to steer a 'core Europe' group of Eurosystem 'insiders', that is surrounded by several 'circles' of Eurosystem 'outsiders'. The logics and dynamics of the co-existence of these three differentiation patterns are assessed to lead to their co-evolution over time.

This differentiation is mirrored in different groups of ESCB membership. It is not only relevant for the ESCB and its decision-making processes. It is also politically relevant as it influences, and to a degree 'pre-defines', the future development of the ESCB, of EMU, and, most probably, of the overall political system of the EU. It does so by creating different starting conditions and opportunity structures for EU Member States to influence and shape the system from within.

As a starting point, it is necessary to examine the ESCB as an arena in which functional and institutional treaty-based, as well as 'real world', differentiation play a central role. This analytical focus provides the basis for more precise conclusions on the ESCB as well as on implications for 'insiders' and 'outsiders'. The key questions are whether the ESCB is moving towards a 'core of able and/ or willing' or even a *'directoire* of the powerful', that is, a *de facto* steering group, with smaller and/or weaker members surrounding the core in concentric circles; and whether the institutional set up of ESCB governing bodies supports or suppresses such forces within the 'living ESCB'.

The chapter starts with a tentative typology of different groups of 'insiders' and 'outsiders', which are defined by their (non-)membership in the Eurosystem and form the building blocks of institutional EMU/ESCB differentiation characterized by the distinct patterns identified above. Together with the most relevant areas of functional differentiation presented below, this typology forms the reference point for the analysis of ESCB differentiation. Throughout its analysis, the chapter draws on the examination of the ESCB's treaty-based foundations ('legal/formal ESCB') and gives examples of its institutional and functional elements in practice ('living ESCB'). Finally, the chapter's conclusions summarize the results and elaborate further on differentiation within the ESCB.[1]

Differentiation within the ESCB: A Typology of Facets, Groups, and Patterns

This section is based on the analysis of the two most relevant dimensions of differentiation of the ESCB, institutional and functional. With reference to institutional differentiation, the two groups of 'insiders' and 'outsiders' form the main point of reference. The second section of this part of the chapter analyses the functional dimension of ESCB differentiation.

Groups of ESCB Membership

The two *formal* groups of 'insiders' and 'outsiders' can be identified on the structural basis of Eurosystem membership. These two groups can each be further divided into informal (conceptual) sub-groups (Figure 2.1).

INSIDERS OF THE EUROSYSTEM (MATRIX: BOX 1)
The first formal group of the 'willing and able' forms the core of the ESCB as it combines ESCB and Eurosystem membership, given that they comply with the Maastricht criteria and chose to become members of the European currency union. The 16 members of this group are not only represented in the ESCB's General Council. More importantly, they form the ESCB's institutional core,

Willing

		Yes	No
Able (*Maastricht Convergence Criteria*)	**Yes**	**Core insiders** (*France, Germany, Italy, Spain*) **Normal insiders** (*Austria, Belgium, Finland, Greece, Ireland, Luxembourg, the Netherlands, Portugal*) **New insiders** (*Cyprus, Malta, Slovenia, Slovakia*)	**Semi-permanent outsiders with and without treaty-based opt outs** (*Denmark, Sweden, United Kingdom*)
	No	**Temporary outsiders keen to join** (*Bulgaria, Czech Republic, Estonia, Hungary, Latvia, Lithuania, Poland, Romania*) **Candidate countries as (potential) future outsiders** (*Croatia, Turkey, Former Yugoslav Republic of Macedonia*)	

Figure 2.1. Groups of ESCB membership

Source: Own design.

which is responsible for governing the Eurosystem through the ECB's Governing Council and its Executive Board. The 2004–7 EU enlargement boosted a further sub-division of this first formal group as it created the new informal (conceptual) sub-group of 'new insiders'.

'*Core insiders*'. The first informal (conceptual) sub-group of 'core insiders' is made up of (old and large) EU Member States (Germany, France, Italy, Spain) that are powerful enough to seek some kind of political leadership within EMU and the ESCB and, thus, to construct some sort of *de facto* differentiation amongst the 'insiders' (see chapters by Dyson, Howarth, and Quaglia). This sub-group could be eager to advance as a possible *directoire* (cf. below) of the 'core' Europe group of 'insiders'. 'Core insiders' long for a more stable and permanent institutional representation and influence within Eurosystem institutions and the ESCB in general, 'hoisting their national flags' within the ECB's Executive Board in terms of continuing occupancy of seats. During the first decade, France, Germany, Italy, and Spain are examples for 'core insiders'. Treaty provisions on the governing bodies of the ESCB seem to support this development as they provide opportunity structures for differentiation. 'Core insiders' might use these treaty provisions on the functions of the ESCB according to their national interests and monetary policy priorities to steer the ESCB.

'Normal insiders'. This second informal (conceptual) sub-group consists of Eurosystem members that are not powerful enough to secure strong, sustained representation within ESCB and Eurosystem institutions. Their relative position within both the ESCB and European economic governance is based on their national size and economic relevance. This sub-group is made up of smaller old Eurosystem members, notably Austria, Belgium, the Netherlands, and Portugal, which, due to more limited economic and political weight, do not belong to the sub-group of 'core insiders' (see chapter by Maes and Verdun).

'New insiders'. This third informal (conceptual) sub-group is composed of new and comparatively small EU Member States that only recently became Eurosystem members, namely, Cyprus, Malta, Slovenia, and Slovakia. Members of this sub-group are assumed to be inexperienced in the institutional, political, and economic logics of the ESCB and the Eurosystem and, hence, as needing a period to get acquainted with the system and its rules to become 'normal insiders'. Moreover, they are in part less advanced in domestic economic performance, *de facto* limiting their influence within the system, although no treaty-based barriers exist to their integration into the two other sub-groups of 'insiders'.

OUTSIDERS OF THE EUROSYSTEM (MATRIX: BOXES 2 AND 3)

The second formal group of the 'willing, but not able' and the 'able, but not willing' is composed of EU Member States that are not (yet) Eurosystem members. The 11 members of this group are represented only in the ESCB's General Council, not within the ESCB's institutional core responsible for governing the Eurosystem. Depending on their (economic) distance from the Maastricht convergence criteria or on their (un-)willingness to join the Eurosystem, these 'outsiders' can be arranged in different informal (conceptual) sub-groups. As with the 'insiders', the formal group of 'outsiders' was affected by the 2004–7 enlargement that initiated further differentiation by the creation of the new sub-group of 'temporary outsiders keen to join'.

Additional to this group are two informal (conceptual) sub-groups of states that are not members of the EU but that are influenced by ESCB decisions.

'Temporary Outsiders Keen to Join' (Matrix: Box 2). This first informal (conceptual) sub-group is made up of two clusters. The first cluster is constituted by new EU Member States, such as Lithuania, that are not yet economically advanced enough to become Eurosystem members. They are, however, on their way to fulfil the Maastricht convergence criteria with target dates for euro entry from 2010 onwards. The second cluster consists of new EU Member States like the Czech Republic, Estonia, Hungary, Latvia, Poland, and Romania that are in need of more substantial reforms to comply with the Maastricht criteria and to align with the ESCB and Eurosystem institutions (see chapters by Greskovits and by Epstein and Johnson). Dates for the

adoption of the euro have been self-set to 2012 onwards (European Commission 2007).

'Temporary outsiders keen to join' still have to adapt to the ESCB's institutional architecture. Moreover, they need to put noticeable efforts into domestic reforms to stabilize national economic performance in order to meet the Maastricht criteria and to become 'insiders'.

'Semi-permanent Outsiders Without a Treaty-based Opt Out' (Matrix: Box 3). This informal (conceptual) sub-group comprises EU Member States that are not Exchange Rate Mechanism II (ERM II) members, are not attempting to fulfil the Maastricht criteria, have not obtained any derogation in the treaties, and are not pushed towards Eurosystem membership by the EU. Currently, Sweden alone forms this sub-group that *de facto* does not have to fulfil the Maastricht criteria. Yet, in case of tedious and problematic accession processes amongst 'temporary outsiders' to the Eurosystem, this sub-group could serve to pool those frustrated with accession preparation.

'Semi-permanent Outsiders With a Treaty-based Opt Out' (Matrix: Box 3). This last informal (conceptual) sub-group is made up of EU Member States, like Denmark (ERM II member) and the United Kingdom (non-ERM II member) that are not required to join the Eurosystem and that have officially negotiated Treaty opt outs (see chapters by Marcussen and Goodhart). So, *de jure*, members of this sub-group do not have to fulfil the Maastricht convergence criteria. Accession to the Eurosystem strongly depends on domestic political constellations and priorities. Due to their strong economic performance, these EU Member States potentially act as role models for non-Eurosystem membership, establishing feasible reasons for 'temporary outsiders' to remain 'semi-permanent outsiders without a treaty-based opt out', that is, following the example of Sweden.

Additionally, two more informal (conceptual) sub-groups of 'outsiders' can be identified. They will, however, not form focus of the analysis in this chapter. These two sub-groups are constituted by states that are neither EU nor ESCB or Eurosystem members. They, nevertheless, have institutional links to the ESCB and are affected by Eurosystem and ESCB decisions as, for example, they are candidate states to become EU members or partners of international economic interaction, such as global economic players or international economic and financial fora.

'Candidate Countries as (Potential) Future Outsiders' (Matrix: Box 2). This informal (conceptual) sub-group consists of states that officially applied for EU membership like Croatia, Turkey, and the Former Yugoslav Republic of Macedonia. They are or might be on their way to (sooner or later) becoming EU members and are, hence, also affected by Eurosystem and ESCB decisions as well as by the Maastricht convergence criteria. Additionally, they have to adapt their national political and economic systems to become ESCB members by the

date of their (potential) accession to the EU. Thus they have to adapt *ex ante* to the ESCB's institutional architecture and functional particularities.

'Global Players'. Global economic players, such as Brazil, China, India, Japan, and the United States (including international fora such as G7/8, G8+, and the IMF), which have a substantial impact on global economic development, make up this final informal (conceptual) sub-group (see chapter by Woolley). They also affect and are affected by a strong/weak euro as part of the global economy and, thus, also by Eurosystem and ESCB decisions strengthening or weakening the euro. Their relation to the Eurosystem especially influences foreign-exchange operations and the external representation of the EU on the international arena.

Patterns of Institutional Differentiation: Relations of 'Insiders' and 'Outsiders'

Patterns of institutional differentiation in the ESCB reflect this structural differentiation amongst formal and informal (sub-)groups of 'insiders' and 'outsiders'. The ESCB's institutional differentiation not only creates 'insiders' and 'outsiders', it also tends to empower different sub-groups of 'insiders' differently in its political practice.

The ESCB is assumed to stimulate institutional differentiation between the two formal groups of 'insiders' and 'outsiders', resulting in different patterns of differentiation co-existing within the system. These patterns of institutional differentiation find further expression in the informal (conceptual) sub-groups of 'insiders' and 'outsiders'.

This sub-division of 'insiders' and 'outsiders' causes a substantial degree of institutional differentiation in the ESCB in the form of a 'Europe of concentric circles', as 'insiders' and 'outsiders' are represented differently in the ESCB's governing bodies, in other words are differently empowered to govern and influence ESCB decisions. The need and search for institutional leadership within a 'core Europe group of the able insiders' suggest the possibility of a *de facto* steering group, that is, a *'directoire'* of the powerful 'insiders', enforcing, stabilizing, and trying to steer the decision-making capacity of the system (Figure 2.2). This chapter argues that the logics and dynamics of the co-existence of these three patterns of institutional differentiation in the ESCB encourage this development.

EUROPE OF CONCENTRIC CIRCLES OF 'INSIDERS' AND 'OUTSIDERS'

The two formal groups of Eurosystem 'insiders' and 'outsiders' ensure a pattern of a *Europe of concentric circles* in the ESCB, involving an institutional hierarchy in participation rights within the governing bodies of the system (Art. 10–12

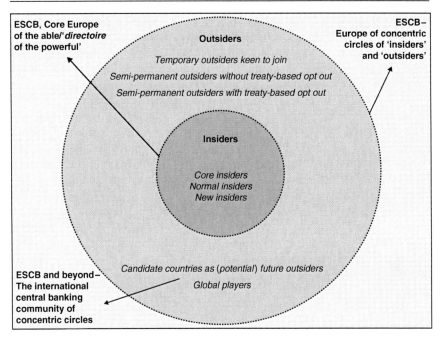

Figure 2.2. The ESCB—'Europe of concentric circles' led by a 'core Europe of the able' with traces of a *'directoire* of the powerful'

Source: Own design.

Protocol No. 18 TEC) Above, this pattern was further elaborated by the definition of different informal sub-groups of 'insiders' and 'outsiders'. A differentiation in terms of power and influence follows. At the same time, the boundaries of the 'insider' and 'outsider' groups are 'permeable' through EU accession and the adoption of the entire EU *acquis* by acceding states.

Within the treaties, this differentiation is formally enshrined in the separation between 'Member States without a derogation' and 'Member States with a derogation' (Art. 122 TEC). The provisions of the Lisbon Treaty were designed to make more visible the treaty-based opportunity structure for a *Europe of concentric circles*, that is, differentiation between 'insiders' and 'outsiders', by explicit legal provisions. It differentiates explicitly between 'countries whose currency is the euro' ('insiders') and those 'Member States with a derogation' ('outsiders'). It will insert new articles on both country groups into the treaties to ensure the proper functioning of EMU (Art. 136–138 TFEU). The Treaty amendments related to 'countries whose currency is the euro' refer to the Stability and Growth Pact (SGP), the Broad Economic Policy Guidelines (BEPG), and the Euro Group (cf. below), enhancing their visibility. In the case of 'Member States with a derogation', the new provisions (Art. 139–144 TFEU) include a precise list of elements that shall not apply to this group, enumerating them more explicitly and in more detail than Art. 122(3) TEC of the Nice Treaty. This development seems to point to a strengthening of treaty-based opportunity structures for a Europe of concentric circles.

'Core Europe of the able'

With the group of 'insiders', the ESCB carries traces of a *core Europe* (Schäuble and Lamers 1994; other labels are '*Avantgarde*', Chirac 2000; '*L'Europe pionnier*', Juppé 2000; and '*Centre of Gravity*', Fischer 2000). It shows signs of institutional and constitutional deepening by a group of 'willing and able' Eurosystem members. Although, from the start of EMU, they were supposed to attract 'outsiders' to follow, some semi-permanent outsiders like Denmark, Sweden, and the United Kingdom officially declined from doing so.

Analysis of the ESCB's institutional architecture seems to support this conclusion. The institutional centre of this ESCB core Europe group is provided by the ECB. To carry out the tasks of the ESCB, the ECB is equipped with quasi-legislative (Art. 110(1, 2) TEC) and regulatory/control powers (Art. 110(3) TEC) whose execution and implementation is strongly influenced by the ECB Executive Board's power to shape Governing Council decision-making (McNamara 2006: 177). The treaties provide the ECB with the means to make binding and directly applicable regulations and to take decisions (binding to those whom they address) necessary to carry out the tasks entrusted to the ESCB under the TEC and the Protocol No. 18, as well as to make recommendations and to deliver opinions (both instruments being non-binding) (Art. 110(1, 2) TEC). Related decision-making and decisions are prepared by the ECB's Executive Board. Underlining its dominant position are the additional competences of the ECB 'to impose fines or periodic penalty payments on undertakings for failure to comply with obligations under its regulations and decisions' (Art. 110(3) TEC), to 'require credit institutions established in Member States to hold minimum reserve on accounts with the ECB and national central banks in pursuance of monetary policy objectives' (Art. 19 Protocol No. 18 TEC).

Within the ESCB's institutional architecture, the core Europe element is already in the treaties, given that only 'insiders' are represented within the two central ESCB governing bodies, the ECB's Governing Council and the Executive Board (Art. 107(3) TEC, Art. 10 and 11 Protocol No. 18 TEC). Due to its responsibility for the implementation of the Euro Area's monetary policy, as well as its competence to give necessary instructions to national central banks (NCBs) and to prepare the meetings of the Governing Council (Art. 12 Protocol No. 18 TEC), the Executive Board is the key guarantor of the implementation of the system's tasks (Issing 2008: 62). This dominant position as the central decision-shaping body of the ESCB derives from the fact that it not only implements monetary policy decisions but also exercises considerable agenda-setting power, is involved in policy formulation (McNamara 2006: 175 and 177) and is given a high degree of authority amongst the ESCB governing bodies.

Underlining the assumption of existence of an ESCB core Europe group, 'outsiders' are represented only in the ECB's General Council (Art. 45 Protocol No. 18 TEC). It disposes of fewer powers and contributes 'merely' to statistical data collection, reporting activities of the ECB, establishing necessary rules for standardizing the accounting and reporting of operations undertaken by the NCBs, laying down the conditions of employment of ECB staff, and performing advisory functions (Art. 47 Protocol No. 18 TEC).

So, 'insiders' and 'outsiders' are represented differently, potentially resulting in a differentiated participation within the ESCB's governing bodies: 'insiders' are represented and involved in the Executive Board/Governing Council/General Council, while 'outsiders' partake only in the General Council. Yet, due to the supranational character of the body, the 'insiders'/'core insiders' representation within the Executive Board seems to be more supranational than national in character. Moreover, as a majority of ECB expert subcommittees also convene in EU-27 composition[2] (even though two compositions, Euro Group and EU-27, are possible), this effect, however, can be assumed to be partially counterbalanced in working-level practice.[3]

In EMU's 'living practice', the Euro Group (comprising Eurosystem members' finance ministers, the European Commission, and the ECB) formed the central Eurosystem body for informal exchange amongst 'insiders' as well as for Euro Area decision-shaping over the first decade of the euro. As such, it provided 'insiders' with an additional opportunity structure to strengthen core Europe patterns within EMU. The 2004–5 newly established Euro Group presidency offers the impression to, hence, be a sign for this pattern of institutional differentiation within the political practice. The turn of the 'living practice' into an element of the system's 'legal architecture' is exemplified in the Lisbon Treaty, which establishes a new protocol in order to 'lay down special provisions for enhanced dialogue between the Member States whose currency is the euro' (Protocol No. 3 TEU/TFEU). By doing so, it is to establish a formal treaty basis for the institutional aspects of the Euro Group's informal meetings, including the participation of the European Commission and the ECB as well as the election of a president of the Euro Group for two-and-a-half-year term. As a consequence, the treaty-based differentiation between 'insiders' and 'outsiders', that is, the Europe of concentric circles, can become more visible in EMU, potentially transforming the Euro Group into an institutional indication of the core Europe group of 'insiders' in supranational monetary policy-making. Yet, given the size of the Euro Group and its foreseeable enlargement in the future, it remains open whether it will evolve as quickly as the ECB's Executive Board into the key constitutional or institutional nucleus for the evolution of Euro Area decision-shaping and -making.

'Directoire of the powerful'

Over the first decade of the euro, the ESCB informal (conceptual) sub-group of 'core insiders' seems to have sought more permanent institutional influence within the ESCB's governing bodies (including more power over appointments to the ECB's Executive Board) in order to shape the ESCB's development on their own terms. This pattern can be perceived to have led to a certain element of guidance of the ESCB by 'core insiders', suggesting a '*directoire* of the powerful' within the core Europe group in conceptual terms. Such a *directoire* (Hill 2006) is defined by stronger intergovernmental cooperation between a few large and powerful 'core insiders' (EU-3, EU-5), excluding smaller 'insider'-states by definition.

The ESCB's treaty foundations create the opportunity for this '*directoire* of the powerful' in the institutional representation of certain 'insiders', for a long period predominantly 'core insiders', simultaneously within the ECB's Executive Board (Art. 11 Protocol No. 18 TEC), and the Governing Council. Via the six members of the Executive Board, certain '(core) insiders' were to a certain extent *de facto* 'double represented' in the ECB Governing Council. In analytical terms, the practice of the same four states (Germany, France, Italy, and Spain) retaining seats in the Executive Board over the years suggests such an element of a *directoire*. However, this national 'capture' of the ECB's Executive Board has been balanced by the fact that Executive Board members, regardless of her or his national socialization, have acted as supranational ECB actors rather than as national representatives. So, features of national 'capture' seem to be noticeable, yet, further empirical research concerning the 'living' ESCB still has to uncover whether these features constitute such a *de facto directoire* trend within the Executive Board.

Institutionally counterbalancing the influence of 'core insiders' vis-à-vis other sub-groups of 'insiders'—hence, counterbalancing the trend towards a *directoire* element within the ESCB's institutional architecture—is, moreover, the fact that within both the Executive Board and the Governing Council the personality and expertise of members is perceived to be more decisive for exerting influence than their respective country affiliation.[4] Nevertheless, particularly due to its agenda-setting power, and given that other bodies and actors followed its decisions on the implementation of the ECB monetary policy, the Executive Board turned out to be a prominent target for 'core insiders' to institutionally anchor a *directoire* element within ESCB decision-shaping. It can be assessed to have formed a central target for the institutional covetousness of 'core insiders' within the ESCB.

In relation to the ECB's Governing Council another element of an ESCB '*directoire* of the powerful', based on differentiation according to economic performance, can be found within the 'legal/formal' ESCB. This trend is exemplified in the reform of voting rules before formal accession of new members (Berger 2006; Eijffinger 2006). The treaty-based principle of 'one member, one vote' is kept only until the point in Eurosystem 'widening', when the Governing Council consists of more than 21 members (Art. 10(2) Protocol No. 18 TEC), that means until the entry of Slovakia in 2009. Thereafter, only 15 voting rights are attributed to the NCB governors, who are members of the Governing Council. The six members of the Executive Board keep one vote each. Special rotation rules are applied to the exercise of the voting rights by the NCB governors, who are divided into two/three groups (Art. 10 Protocol No. 18 TEC). From more than 15 to 22 governors, they will be allocated to two groups (ibid.). From 22 governors onwards, three groups will be established (ibid.). These different groups are defined 'according to a ranking of the size of the share of their [the governors'] national central bank's Member State in the aggregate gross domestic product at market prices and in the total aggregated balance sheet of the monetary financial institutions of the Member States which have adopted the euro' (ibid.). Acting by a two-thirds majority of all members, the Governing Council can, however, 'decide to postpone the start of the rotation system until the date on which the number of governors exceeds 18' (ibid.). With this treaty-based pre-definition of voting rule adaptation, differentiation is, hence, already introduced by the treaties, pointing at a treaty-based opportunity structure for the development of a *directoire* based on economic indicators and performance.

Functional Differentiation

The functional dimension of differentiation ties in with the basic institutional differentiation between 'insiders' and 'outsiders'. Within the ESCB, 'insiders' take on different functions from 'outsiders', especially in the implementation of ESCB decisions. As a consequence, 'insider' NCBs are affected differently by the ESCB than those of 'outsiders' in terms of obligation to take part in supranational policy-making and implementation.

MONETARY POLICY-MAKING

The core function of the ESCB is European monetary policy-making. Art. 105 to 124 TEC lay down the treaty foundation of monetary policy and the role of the ESCB in it. The core objective of the ESCB is to 'maintain price stability' and to 'support the general economic policies in the Community', while not losing sight of its aforementioned core objective (Art. 105(1) TEC). In the light of this priority and 'the principle of an open market economy with free competition, favouring an efficient allocation of resources' (ibid.), the main tasks of the ESCB are (1) the definition and implementation of the European monetary policy, (2) the conduct of foreign-exchange operations, and (3) the holding and management of the EU Member States' official foreign reserves

(Art. 105(2) TEC). Within the ESCB, the ECB is the predominant institution to safeguard this particular European monetary policy-making paradigm (Issing 2008: 85 *ff.*). It is exclusively and independently responsible for monetary policy decisions (Art. 105(2) TEC; Begg 2007: 36; Issing 2008: 115 *ff.*) and, hence, symbolizes 'the institutionalization of a monetary sovereignty' (Le Heron 2007: 11) within EMU. The main instruments of the ECB in this context are guidelines, recommendations, and opinions at the request of EU institutions, as well as decisions and regulations on European monetary policy. The Lisbon Treaty groups monetary policy-making for Member States whose currency is the euro under the 'exclusive competences' of the Union (Art. 3 TFEU) and formally integrates the ECB into the EU's institutional framework (Art. 13 TEU).

The ESCB's monetary policy function exerts strong implementation pressure on 'insiders', while 'outsiders' are affected to a lesser degree and more indirectly (especially via markets). ESCB monetary policy decisions, taken by 'insiders' within the Governing Council, are directly binding for 'insiders' who have to implement them on behalf of the ESCB. 'Outsiders' influence European monetary policy-making via their integration into the General Council (Art. 45 Protocol No. 18 TEC), focusing on advisory functions, statistical data collection, reporting activities of the ECB, etc. (Art. 47 Protocol No. 18 TEC).

FISCAL POLICY-MAKING

The ESCB is characterized and affected by the 'asymmetry between monetary and fiscal policy in the Euro Area ..., with the ECB setting a predictable policy based on price stability in the area as a whole and the member states setting fiscal policy individually subject to the joint arrangements of the Broad Macroeconomic Guidelines and the SGP processes' (Mayes and Virén 2007: 172). Under the SGP (Art. 104 TEC), both 'insiders' and 'outsiders' have to keep their national fiscal policies in line with the provisions of the pact to avoid violations through excessive deficit spending in order to lower the costs of supranational monetary policy-making by maintaining fiscal stability (Mayes and Virén 2007: 160). In case of non-compliances or breaches, however, only 'insiders' face the risk of financial sanctions, given that special rules apply to 'outsiders' (Art. 122(3) TEC). Under the pact, 'insiders' have to prepare annual National Stability Programs (NSPs), outlining their efforts to comply with the pact, such as a budgetary policy that guarantees sustainability of public finances and adheres to the treaty-based GDP threshold, policies to implement the objectives of the NSP, and main underlying economic ideas. These NSPs form the basis for the supranational surveillance process, for recommendations that aim at bringing excessive deficits to an end within a given period, and for possible sanctions in case of failure to do so.

In contrast to this strong 'hand-tying' impact on 'insider' budgetary policies, 'outsiders' are less strongly affected. They do not face financial sanctions in case of non-compliance with the SGP (Art. 122(3) TEC). They are, however, required to meet the convergence criteria, to generally follow the rules of the SGP and to prepare annual National Convergence Programs (NCP), outlining the same aspects as 'insider' NSPs. 'Outsider' NCPs form the basis for possible recommendations in case of breaches of the pact, obliging them to end excessive deficits as in the case of the United Kingdom in January 2006 (Council of the EU 2006: 6). As a consequence of the requirement to comply with the pact, even 'outsiders' are thus no longer entirely free to pursue their own budgetary and fiscal policy preferences.

PAYMENT SYSTEM OVERSIGHT

Another function of the ESCB is the promotion of a smooth operation of euro payment systems (Art. 105(2) TEC). This function aims at stabilizing euro payment systems to prevent systemic risks and the transmission of shocks, at maintaining and increasing payment systems' efficiency, at ensuring security of the payment instruments, and at supporting the implementation of supranational monetary policy.

To fulfil these ESCB objectives, the ECB and NCBs are competent to 'provide facilities … to ensure efficient and sound clearing and payment systems within the Community and with other countries' (Art. 22 Protocol No. 18 TEC) and 'operate in the financial markets by buying and selling outright (spot and forward) or under repurchase agreement and by lending or borrowing claims and marketable instruments, … [and to] conduct credit operations with credit institutions and other market participants' (Art. 18 Protocol No. 18 TEC). Additionally, the ECB and the NCBs have the 'power to give advice and deliver opinion, pursuant to Articles 4 and 34.1, third indent, ESCB Statute can also be employed to this end' (Smits 1997: 297). Moreover, the competence to open accounts and the ESCB's external competences are assessed to add to the competences within this sector of payment system control (ibid.). The ECB is competent to make regulations in this sector.

As the exercise of payment system oversight influences the stability of the Eurosystem and the implementation of supranational monetary policy, the institutional differentiation along the lines of 'insiders' and 'outsiders' follows from the way in which 'insiders' are affected more strongly by cross-border payment activities within the Eurosystem than 'outsiders'. While 'core insiders' within the Executive Board shape the area by developing and preparing policies and decisions—such as related to the Trans-European Automated Real-time Gross settlement Express Transfer (TARGET) System, the Single Euro Payments Area (SEPA), or the Correspondent Central Banking Model (CCBM)—'insiders' take the decisions within the Governing Council. ESCB members—regardless of their status as 'insiders' and 'outsiders'—are free to participate.

BANKING SUPERVISION

The ESCB is also responsible for 'the prudential supervision of credit institutions and the stability of the financial system' (Art. 105(5) TEC). However, this function is assessed not to belong to the core tasks of the ESCB (Smits 1997: 319) and of central banking in general (Stadler 1996: 118). The ESCB's and its Banking Supervision Committee's role within the sector is of mainly coordinative and consultative character (Schüler 2003: 4). National institutions responsible for banking supervision, thus, co-exist with the ESCB in this functional sector and partake in the ECB's Banking Supervision Committee. Based on Art. 14(4) Protocol No. 18 TEC, NCBs that were in charge of this function before EMU continue performing it also within the ESCB. Via the ECB, the ESCB is, moreover, integrated into international activities in the field, such as the Basel Committee on Banking Supervision, the European Securities Committee, or Committee of European Banking Supervisors (see Moran and Macartney's chapter).

From 'a financial integration perspective, the main priority [of this area] is to remove any supervisory obstacles to cross-border finance, notably via enhanced supervisory cooperation and convergence' (Papademos 2005). The ECB advises and is consulted by the European Commission, the Council, or institutions of EU Member States concerning the focus and 'implementation of Community legislation relating to the prudential supervision of credit institutions and to the stability of the financial system' (Art. 25(1) Protocol No. 18 TEC). If so decided by the Council (Art. 105(6) TEC), the ECB may take over particular tasks related to banking and financial supervision except for insurance undertaking. So, the competences and powers of the ECB and the ESCB depend on the Council. Thus, in this functional area, the ECB holds a weaker position than in supranational monetary policy-making.

Within this area of functional differentiation, the institutional differentiation alongside 'insiders' and 'outsiders' is relevant only insofar as the ECB's tasks related to banking supervision formally concentrate on credit and other financial institutions within the Eurosystem. Yet, in practice, 'the financial integration process ... has involved a substantial increase in cross-border banking' (Papademos 2005). As a result, 'cross-border banking broadens and deepens banking markets, increases liquidity and risk sharing and thus strengthens the overall resilience of the European financial system' (ibid.). Hence, also 'outsiders' are integrated into banking supervision activities of the ECB given that economic risks are spread across the different groups of Eurosystem members. As a result, the formal differentiation within the Eurosystem according to its legal basis—alongside the lines of 'insiders' and 'outsiders'—seems to a certain extent to be compensated, given that not only 'insiders" banking systems are exposed to such risks due to increased cross-border activities at many levels of the economic system.

FOREIGN-EXCHANGE OPERATIONS AND EXTERNAL REPRESENTATION

Based on Art. 105(2) TEC, the ESCB is responsible for the conduct of 'foreign-exchange operations consistent with the provisions of Article 111'. This 'task concerns intervention in the foreign exchange markets and the other operations which may be necessary for or conducive to the primary objective of price stability' (Smits 1997: 197). In contrast to its strong position in supranational monetary policy-making, where final decision-making powers lie with ESCB governing bodies, its powers to make decisions in foreign-exchange operations are more limited and shared with the Council. Based on Art. 111(1, 2, and 3) TEC, the ECOFIN Council holds the power to conclude formal agreements on an exchange-rate system in relation to non-Community currencies, to formulate general orientations for exchange-rate policy in relation to non-Community currencies, and to decide on arrangements for the negotiation and conclusion of formal agreements on monetary or foreign-exchange regime matters. Exercising these competences, the Council can act on a recommendation from the Commission and after consulting the ECB or on a recommendation from the ECB. So, in this area, the ESCB takes over a more operative function (Stadler 1996: 116), although the ECB is assessed to have 'a large measure of discretion within general orientations for exchange rate policy to be issued by the Ecofin Council' (Smits 1997: 197).

Adding to its tasks in foreign-exchange operations is the ESCB's competence to 'hold and manage the official foreign reserves of the Member States' (Art. 105 (2) TEC; Art. 30 and 31 Protocol No. 18 TEC). The NCB contribute to this function of the ESCB not only because they are 'allowed to perform transactions in fulfillment of their obligations towards international organizations' (Art. 31(1) Protocol No. 18 TEC). At the same time, if their transactions exceed certain limits to be established by the Governing Council, they are subject to approval by the ECB 'in order to ensure consistency with the exchange rate and monetary policies of the Community' (Art. 31(2) Protocol No. 18 TEC). Moreover, the 'contributions of each national central bank shall be fixed in proportion to its share in the subscribed capital of the ECB' (Art. 30(2), 31 Protocol No. 18 TEC). Furthermore, each 'national central bank shall be credited by the ECB with a claim equivalent to its contribution' (Art. 30(3), 31 Protocol No. 18 TEC).

Adding to its outreach into the international arena is the ESCB's (external) representation within the international (financial) system (Art. 6 Protocol

No. 18 TEC), which is taken over by the ECB President or his nominee (Art. 13 (2) Protocol No. 18 TEC). Based on this competence, the ECB 'and, subject to its approval, the national central banks [without prejudice to Art. 111(4) TEC] may participate in international monetary institutions' (Art. 6, 23, and 31 Protocol No. 18 TEC). NCBs may join these efforts (Art. 23 and 31 Protocol No. 18 TEC). In external representation, opportunity structures offered by the treaties open a certain area of potential conflict. According to Art. 111(4) TEC, positions 'of the Community at international level as regards issues of particular relevance to economic and monetary union and on its representation' are decided upon by the ECOFIN Council by qualified majority. In the past, this allocation of competences to different institutions in the field, that is, the Commissioner for economic and monetary affairs, the Euro Group president, and the ECB president, partially resulted in the EU having to orchestrate a chorus of several voices within its external representation in financial matters (DIE ZEIT 2007).

Changes regarding the procedure to establish and decide upon the EU's external representation introduced by the Lisbon Treaty (Art. 115a TFEU) might rebalance the weight of the EU institutions in external representation in financial matters. The new articles of the Lisbon Treaty seek to ensure a more uniform external representation by stating that the 'Council, on a proposal from the Commission, may adopt appropriate measures to ensure unified representation within the international financial institutions and conferences. The Council shall act after consulting the European Central Bank' (Art. 115a(2) TFEU). In decision-taking on these issues only members whose currency is the euro, that is, 'insiders' may partake in voting. So these provisions create a new opportunity structure for further institutional differentiation within the ESCB, favouring 'insiders'.

More specific forms of bi-/multilateral international relations are established through a number of regular and ad hoc high-level, 'closed-door' seminars, including members of the ESCB Governing Council and their respective national counterparts. By these means, the ESCB establishes direct contacts between 'insiders', 'outsiders', and international financial actors. Regular high-level seminars are held with representatives of Russia, the Barcelona Process countries, accession countries, Latin America, and South-East Asia. Ad hoc seminars link the ESCB with their counterparts in West Africa/South Africa and Gulf Group countries. Moreover, contacts are established with countries of the Middle East, neighbouring countries, emerging economies in Asia, the IMF, G7/8, as well as G8+ (i.e. 'Global Players'). Contacts to European non-EU Member States, that is, Norway and Switzerland, are held via other international fora, given that they, especially Switzerland, have long before EMU been 'part of the club' through their membership of the Bank for International Settlements (BIS). Contacts with Norway, on the other hand, are said to be not as close and less frequent.

Conclusion: Co-Existence and Co-Evolution of Three Distinct Patterns of Differentiation

Apart from its structural differentiation into Eurosystem 'insiders' and 'outsiders', the ESCB is characterized by two key dimensions of differentiated integration: functional and institutional. The functional dimension comprises different policy areas, in which the ESCB performs different functions and holds different decision-making competences vis-à-vis other supranational and national institutions. The ESCB holds strongest competences in supranational monetary policy-making. In the external representation of the Eurosystem in international organizations, the authority of the ECB to decide on the representation of the ESCB within international cooperation (Art. 6 Protocol No. 18 TEC) partially interferes with the external representation of the EU in financial matters by the European Commission and the Council of the EU. Here the Lisbon Treaty, if adopted and implemented to the letter, might lay the ground for a more uniform representation of the EU. In payment system oversight and banking supervision, in which the Council holds a more powerful position, ESCB competences strongly focus on the practical conduct of policies as well as on the operation of policies.

The institutional dimension of differentiation seems to display a dynamic co-existence and co-evolution of three different patterns over the first decade of the euro: a Europe of concentric circles ('insiders' and 'outsiders'), a 'core Europe group of the able' ('insiders'), and a *directoire* of the powerful' ('core insiders').

The legal basis of the ESCB stimulated both 'insiders' and 'outsiders' to engage in institution building and shaping. It motivated both groups to adapt to supranational monetary policy-making and to follow the implications of the ESCB. In consequence, a scenario of 'outsiders' steadily moving towards the centre of the ESCB's institutional architecture and towards integration into the Eurosystem is feasible.

This chapter has provided insight into the impact of the ESCB on these two different groups of members. With respect to the functional dimension of differentiation, constraints derive from the ESCB's policy-related decisions. These constraints can be assessed to impact differently on 'insiders' and 'outsiders'. With respect to the institutional dimension of differentiation, the ESCB showed traces of separation between 'insiders' and 'outsiders'. At the same time, the system also motivated 'insiders' and 'outsiders' to engage in the system and its decision-making through the General Council. However, 'insiders' additionally engaged in the Governing Council and the Executive Board in order to shape decisions. So, in political practice as well as within the treaty-based foundations, 'insiders' and 'outsiders' form the essential building block of the differentiation of the ESCB's institutional design. The differentiation amongst ESCB members results in several concentric circles: As a consequence of different speeds of rapprochement, 'insiders' form the ESCB 'core Europe group of the able'. 'Outsiders' are arranged around this core Europe group. The overall result is the ESCB as a Europe of concentric circles. Within the core Europe group of the ESCB, a *directoire* of the powerful' can, in analytical conceptual terms, be assumed to form the institutional nucleus of the system.

Elements of institutional differentiation have been found within both the treaties ('legal architecture') and seem to be visible also in its political reality ('living practice'). The treaty-based reform of voting rights and rules in the enlarged Governing Council and a certain *de facto* 'double representation' of some Member States (Germany, France, Italy, and Spain) in the ESCB's governing bodies provide evidence of this process. Provisions of the Lisbon Treaty on the Euro Group, as well as on the two groups of 'countries whose currency is the euro' and those 'with a derogation', additionally strengthen the treaty-based foundations of differentiation. These provisions show that the ESCB is based on a legal foundation that provides for opportunities for the development of a Europe of concentric circles, led by a 'core Europe group of the able' and guided to a certain extent by a *'directoire* of the powerful' (Figure 2.2).

These patterns of differentiation have, however, not induced a strong tendency towards the development of one 'Core Europe group' or one particular differentiation feature for the political system of the EU in general. Quite contrary to such a 'standard differentiation', the number and forms of opt outs from the overall system—that is, the variation of differentiation—have even increased since the creation of EMU. So, the institutional architecture of EMU has not provided for a standard differentiation design for membership across policy areas. The opt outs from the Treaty of Prüm or the Lisbon Treaty indicate at such variations of differentiation not directly following the EMU model.

The most significant impact of EMU differentiation might have been more indirect: it served as an example that, even in highly relevant policy fields, membership did not have to imply equal rights and obligations for all EU Member States. In this way, it might have softened concerns of the 'community orthodoxy' and changed perceptions to view forms of differentiation as acceptable solutions to enhance European integration in areas, in which not all Member States are willing or able to follow. In the wake of the Irish referendum on the Lisbon Treaty, a renaissance of this perception of differentiation concepts as mechanisms to unfetter blockades can be observed (Dahrendorf 2008; Habermas 2008; Hierlemann 2008: 4).

Yet, another expectation related to EMU differentiation did not materialize: In the 1990s, some proponents of the idea of a 'Core Europe' (especially Schäuble and Lamers 1994) regarded EMU not just as a mere example or role model for differentiation. They perceived differentiation within EMU to serve as a strategic 'door opener' to a more federal and integrated Europe of the willing and able Member States. EMU members were expected to move ahead towards closer integration also in other policy fields. They were, thus, assumed to develop into a certain constitutional 'avantgarde' of European integration as a whole. With the enlargement of EMU and in the light of the outcome of the Dutch, French, and Irish referendums, EMU differentiation did, yet, not provide for the basis of a more integrated group of EU members, that go ahead also beyond monetary and economic integration.

Notes

1. The approach of the chapter is based on the research method of the Jean-Monnet Chair for Political Science at the University of Cologne regarding the comparative analysis of the 'legal architecture' (written, treaty-based provisions) and the 'living practice' (its reality in practice) of and within the EU. Additionally, new institutionalism (Bulmer 1994, 1997: 4; Hall and Taylor 1996: 6; Jachtenfuchs and Kohler-Koch 2004: 101; Knodt 2005: 18; March and Olsen 2005: 4 *ff.*; Peters 2000: 4 *ff.*; Stone Sweet and Sandholtz 1998: 16) serves as an explanatory element for the evaluation of the implications of the ESCB for 'insiders' and 'outsiders' both within the 'legal/formal ESCB' (written provisions) and the 'living ESCB' (its reality in practice).
2. Out of the seven to nine annual meetings of the International Affairs Committee two to three are held in EU-27 composition (i.e. one out of three meetings is held in this extended composition). Moreover, there are regular contacts between ECB and NCB (e.g. Bank of England) officials, partially also on a rather informal/personal level. ERM-II links with Denmark for instance are held via the Currency Board meetings.
3. Information provided by ECB officials interviewed for this chapter.
4. Perception of ECB officials interviewed for this chapter.

3

The European Central Bank: The Bank That Rules Europe?

David Howarth

The power of the European Central Bank (ECB) is rooted in its independence established in the Maastricht Treaty of 1992. This power is reinforced through the bank's monetary policy credibility—achieved through meeting its price stability mandate, while resisting political pressures to manipulate monetary policy to other ends. In turn, credibility contributes to the ideational power of the ECB, which is rooted in widespread support for price stability, one of the core objectives of Economic and Monetary Union (EMU). The ECB's relative power, as one of the two leading central banks in the world, is determined by the relative size of the Euro Area economy and the growing importance of the euro as an international reserve currency. It is the leading face of the Euro Area abroad and a new and important presence in several international economic fora. The ECB is effectively the 'captain' of the team of Eurosystem (Euro Area) national central banks (NCBs) as well as the wider European System of Central Banks (ESCB)—which includes all European Union (EU) NCBs. It is responsible for coordinating the policy making of Eurosystem NCBs in a range of areas and NCB discussions on inflation forecasts.

However, there are clear limits to the ECB's power. It controls neither exchange-rate policy nor prudential supervision. Limits have been placed upon its international role. The ECB must work with governments to build support for low inflationary policies and maintain political support for EMU. The ECB is one of the most consistent voices in favour of structural reform in the European Union (EU), yet there is little the bank can do to enforce reform in the short term. Furthermore, the ECB must share many core central banking operations with Eurosystem national central banks (NCBs). This chapter explores the confines of European Central Bank power.

Monetary Policy Power

The basic power of the ECB is to define and implement the monetary policy of the Euro Area. The ECB enjoys unrivalled goal-setting and operational independence in the pursuit of its price stability goals, and its Governing Council members enjoy *ad personam* independence. The Bank is further sheltered from political interference by the need for the unanimous approval of member states to change the Treaty provisions on independence. The Statute of the ECB and the ESCB (principally Article 3) sets out the tasks of Eurosystem NCBs as 'to define and implement the monetary policy of the Community'; 'to conduct foreign exchange operations'; 'to hold and manage the official foreign reserves of the member states'; 'to promote the smooth operation of payment systems'; 'and to contribute to the smooth conduct of policies pursued by the competent authorities relating to the prudential supervision of credit institutions and the stability of the financial system'. The ECB can make regulations (Article 110(1) TEC), principally with regard to the operation of the ESCB and can impose fines or periodic penalty payments for failure to comply with obligations contained in its regulations and decisions (Article 110(3)). This competence applies notably with regard to the reserves that credit institutions should hold with the ECB and the prudential supervision of credit institutions— although the Council of Ministers must first establish the broader framework of rules on these matters.

The ECB's Governing Council (comprising 6 Executive Board members and, in 2009, 16 NCB governors) is the monetary policy committee of the Euro Area. It formulates the monetary policy of the Eurosystem with the aim of maintaining price stability as the Governing Council defines it, including decisions relating to specific monetary objectives, monetary strategy, key interest rates, and the supply of Eurosystem reserves (Article 12.1, ESCB Statute). The Governing Council adopts the internal rules of the ECB and may decide by two-thirds of the votes cast to modify operational methods of monetary control. It exercises advisory functions *vis-à-vis* other European Union bodies. Moreover, it has the power to form opinions on its own initiative on the economic policies adopted by the European Union and member state governments on matters which fall within its jurisdiction, crucially with regard to the pursuit of 'stability-oriented' economic policies.

The six-member Executive Board implements the Eurosystem's monetary policy—giving necessary instructions to the NCBs—in accordance with the guidelines and decisions established by the Governing Council. It decides upon the precise instruments to be used. It also prepares the meetings of the Governing Council. The Executive Board may have certain additional powers delegated to it by the Governing Council (Article 12, ESCB Statute).

Power and Credibility

The power of the ECB relies to a large extent upon the credibility and legitimacy of its monetary policy (see the chapter by Eichbaum in this volume). Despite widespread pessimism about the longevity of EMU and the rapid drop in the value of the euro during the first three years of EMU, the ECB has had considerable success in achieving credibility thanks to its successful pursuit of its price stability mandate. The ECB is frequently seen as the 'the most predictable central bank'—a virtuous reputation in central banking, where controlling expectations about future inflation is seen as crucial in increasing the effectiveness of monetary policy. Its monetary strategy was modelled largely on that used by the respected Bundesbank and was overseen by Otmar Issing, Chief Economist at the ECB from 1998 to 2006 and former director at the Bundesbank. The two-pillar strategy combined an analysis of conventional price and growth indicators with money supply and credit data. Many economists and central banking officials are sceptical with regard to the analytical usefulness of monetary aggregates as a core part of the ECB's monetary strategy (OECD 2007). However, this scepticism has not undermined the credibility of the ECB's policy. The bank has maintained a tight interest-rate policy, successfully targeting inflation that is 'below but close to 2 per cent' over the medium term, even though the actual figure has been frequently just above the target. Yet it appears to have been more flexible with regard to M3 growth, which has regularly far exceeded the bank's official reference value of 4.5 per cent.

During its first decade, the ECB had to deflect regular criticisms of its monetary policy from national politicians and economists. Criticism became particularly vocal with regard to the strong euro from 2003 and its perceived impact upon exports. The ECB was regularly attacked for its pursuit of low inflation, and its tight monetary policy was regularly juxtaposed with the accommodative interest-rate policy and dual mandate of the US Federal Reserve—as in the months following the September 2001 attacks on New York and Washington and following the onset of the credit crunch in the autumn of 2007.

The size of the Euro Area—the second largest economy in the world—and the confidence of financial markets in the credibility of ECB monetary policy have reinforced the euro's position as the world's second international reserve currency. There are debates as to the degree to which the euro can challenge the position of the US dollar as the leading international reserve currency. However, the euro's present position works not only to bolster the position of the ECB as an international actor (in the IMF and other international economic fora) but also to strengthen its position in relation to national governments and EU institutions in European economic governance.

Transparency and Credibility

In several respects, the ECB lacks transparency compared to the US Federal Reserve and the Bank of England. Notably, the ECB has opted not to publish its minutes, principally for fear that NCB governors would come under pressure at home to justify where they had stood in debates. Yet, the ECB has achieved a credibility-enhancing transparency with the markets. The ECB president gives the only press conference following interest-rate setting meetings, thus avoiding the potential for cacophony that could arise if the NCB governors were allowed this responsibility. Moreover, like the Federal Reserve and the Bank of England, the ECB discloses the formal macroeconomic model its uses for policy analysis (Eijffinger and Geraats 2006), which most economists applaud for reducing private-sector uncertainty about the ECB's policy making process and making monetary policy actions more predictable (Geraats 2005, 2006). There remains criticism of ECB transparency. To many economists, its interest-rate setting process and economic analysis remain too opaque (OECD 2007: 7).

Limits to ECB Power Over Monetary Policy

The ECB does not have complete control over all aspects of European monetary policy. The Council of Ministers (the Council of Economics and Finance ministers, Ecofin) is given limited powers over monetary policy and the management of Eurosystem NCBs. These powers are *de facto* exercised by the Euro Group, consisting of the finance ministers of only the member states participating in the Euro Area. Lacking a legal personality, the Euro Group must have Ecofin confirm all its decisions. The Council can adopt complementary legislation concerning the operation of the entire ESCB in a limited number of areas, by qualified majority voting on a recommendation from the ECB after consulting the Commission or by unanimity acting on a proposal from the Commission and after consulting the ECB (Article 42, ESCB Statute). In both situations the European Parliament must be consulted. These areas include, *inter alia* the 'basis for the minimum and maximum reserves to be held by national credit institutions with the ECB, and the maximum permissible ratios between these reserves, as well as the appropriate sanctions in the case of non-compliance' (Article 19.2); the limits and conditions on any increase to the ECB's capital (Article 28.1); and further calls for foreign reserve assets beyond the limit set in the ESCB Statute (Article 30.4). (See Howarth and Loedel (2005) for a more exhaustive list and analysis.)

Ecofin (the Euro Group) is thus empowered to influence future developments of the operation of the ESCB, even though it is unable to modify the objectives or tasks of the ESCB or the provisions regarding its independence. It is responsible for setting the rate at which currencies of the new Euro Area member states are irrevocably fixed in relation to the euro, while the European Council makes the final decision on entry on the basis of a recommendation from the Commission. Notably, Ecofin is responsible for the establishment of exchange-rate agreements with third countries and has final say over most aspects of external monetary policy. However, when performing these tasks, Ecofin must consult the ECB, attempt to reach a consensus, and respect the goal of price stability. The organization of co-ordination in the area of external monetary policy is discussed in greater detail below.

Lack of Control Over Prudential Supervision

During the 1991 Intergovernmental Conference on EMU, it was decided to strongly limit the ECB's potential role in the area of prudential supervision. As noted above, the Maastricht Treaty grants the Eurosystem NCBs the responsibility 'to contribute to the smooth conduct' of prudential supervision and the monitoring of financial stability. The so-called BCCI Directive (96/25/EC of 29 June 1995) lays the foundations for cooperation (exchange of information) but does not contain specific provisions or institutional arrangements to this end. The ECB must be consulted on the adoption of EC and national legislation relating to prudential supervision and financial stability and has the right to perform specific tasks concerning policies relating to this supervision. Moreover, the Maastricht Treaty establishes a simplified procedure (Article 105(6) TEC) that makes it possible, without amending the Treaty, to entrust specific supervisory tasks to the ECB.

The precise role of the ECB in prudential supervision remains the subject of ongoing debate. It is not unusual that the ECB lacks control over banking supervision, in that the central banks in many advanced industrialized countries do not have this power or share it with ministries of finance (more often there are completely separate institutions responsible for supervision). However, the Euro Area is rather unique in that the areas of jurisdiction over monetary policy and over banking supervision—which remains nationally based—do not coincide. ECB Executive Board members thus argue in favour of improved cooperation between Eurosystem central banks (including the ECB) and national banking supervisors on the grounds that central banks are, because of their responsibilities, necessarily concerned with the health of the banking system, and central bank credit control is managed in 'a situation that is generated by problems of interest to the supervisor' (Padoa Schioppa 1999*a*; see also Duisenberg 2002; ECB 2001*a*, 2001*b*; Padoa Schioppa 1999*b*).

The Basle Committee on Banking Supervision assumed the task of promoting cooperation between the ECB, the NCBs, and national supervisory authorities. To give the EU members of this Committee a more specifically Eurosystem profile, their gatherings were officially labelled the Banking Supervision Committee of the ESCB. The ECB has sought to develop this cooperation further: to ensure that the system of national supervisors can operate as effectively as a single authority when required, in particular when dealing with local or national banking problems which may have wider effects.

ECB Executive Board members tend to argue in favour of transferring full supervisory powers to the NCBs rather than centralizing them in the ECB. The emphasis placed on the role of NCBs as opposed to the ECB is due in large part to their role managing the TARGET payment system, which gives the NCBs much greater awareness than the ECB could ever have of the situation of the banks. The precise role of the ECB in the handling of solvency crises remains unsettled, and the lack of crisis management capacity of the Eurosystem has been criticized (see IMF 1998).

The 2002 decision by the German government not to grant the Bundesbank full control over prudential supervision dealt a blow to hopes of an eventual transfer of supervisory powers to NCBs and the ECB (Engelen 2002*a* and *b*). In the new Federal Agency for Financial Market Supervision, the Germans opted instead for the British single regulator model. Shortly, thereafter, the British and Germans further shored up the central role of national prudential supervisors by supporting the conclusions of the Lamfalussy Committee on the regulation of European securities markets (Quaglia 2007*a*). The Brown-Eichel plan (subsequently approved by the Council) proposed the creation of an umbrella EU financial-sector supervisory body which would seek to improve coordination between national regulatory authorities. The creation of such a Lamfalussy-style committee structure for banking and insurance markets was a blow to the existing ESCB Banking Supervision Committee, and ECB President Duisenberg warned that a sideline role of the ECB in bank supervision would risk violating the Maastricht Treaty (Engelen 2002*a*).

The ECB asserted the need for its improved control over banking supervision and unease at the regulatory arrangements in place during the worsening international credit situation of 2007–8. Executive Board members expressed the concern that warnings about threats to the Euro Area's financial systems might not be passed on fast enough at times of crisis because of the fragmented regulatory system in the EU and the insufficient cooperation and exchange of information both between supervisory authorities in different member states and between them and central banks (Stark 2008*c*). Executive Board members (Bini Smaghi 2008) claimed that the effective conduct of the Eurosystem's liquidity-boosting operations from August 2007 relied upon the ECB's access to necessary information concerning the liquidity and solvency problems of the markets and institutions. They argue that banking supervisors needed to strengthen their cooperation to 'exert strong pressure on financial institutions to disclose in a prompt and coherent fashion their balance sheet situations' (ibid.). The ECB also argued that member states—Germany has been frequently cited—must be required to remove all national legislative obstacles preventing supervisors from providing information to the ECB about specific banking institutions.

A Developing but Limited International Role

Since the Delors Committee began meeting in 1988, there has been debate about the role to be played by the ECB in the external representation of the Euro Area in international fora. This issue links into the broader problem of the division of responsibilities among EU institutions over the major elements of economic policy and the respective roles of the Council (Euro Group), the Commission, and the ECB in external representation (Henning and Padoan 2000; McNamara and Meunier 2002). Where the Council represents the Euro Area externally, ECB representatives nonetheless engage in the preparation of Euro Area positions for meetings in international fora within the EU's Economic and Financial Committee, prior to these positions being finalized in the Euro Group.

The ECB made its initial demands for right to external representation on the basis both of Treaty provisions that stipulate that the 'Community' express a single position in external monetary policy, and of ESCB Statute provisions (Article 6) that allow the ECB to decide how Euro Area NCBs shall be represented by the ECB and/or by Euro Area NCBs, on matters falling into its jurisdiction (Padoa Schioppa 1999c). Thus in central banking fora, the participation of the ECB has been straightforward. For example, the ECB president participates in the meetings of the G-10 Governors organized in the context of the BIS and in the committees under the aegis of the governors, notably the Basle Committee on Banking Supervision and the Committee on the Global Finance System. Eurosystem finance ministers also have an interest in ECB participation in intergovernmental fora. For example, the potential success of (eventual) international exchange-rate cooperation [under the aegis of the Group of 8 (G-8)] or concerted intervention in the currency markets relies very much on both *ex ante* and *ex post* internal Euro Area co-ordination that ensures that the ECB will be willing and able to implement the policy bargain.

The ECB's status at the IMF is limited to that of observer. Its representative attends and has the right to speak at meetings on the role of the euro in the international monetary system, multilateral surveillance of the Euro Area and individual countries within the zone, international capital market reports, and world economic and market developments. The ECB has the right to send a representative to IMF Executive Board meetings when agenda items are recognized by both the ECB and the IMF to be of mutual interest for the performance of their respective mandates. The representative can also be invited to other Executive Board meetings, although s/he does not have the *right* to attend. The official Euro Area representative on the IMF Executive Board is the Euro Group chair. The ECB also obtained observer status in the meetings of the G-10 Ministers and Governors, which are organized in connection with the IMF Interim Committee meetings. Although, the ECB's role is limited compared to that of the member state governments, its presence may help to unify the views of the EU participants on particular matters. Moreover, the ECB's observer status does not mean that it assumes a passive role. ECB and Euro Area NCB representatives have taken strong, outspoken positions on major international monetary, financial and other economic issues (see Issing 1998 for one early example).

ECB membership of the OECD, another intergovernmental institution, was also out of the question. However, the organization deals with issues—notably surveillance of the Euro Area—relating to the tasks assigned to the Eurosystem. In February 1999, the OECD Secretary General confirmed that the ECB would be allowed to participate in the work of the relevant committees and working groups as a member of the EC delegation alongside the European Commission. The ECB can make use of its presence in both the IMF and OECD to emphasize the need for ongoing structural reform in the Euro Area (Stark 2008*b*). In the G-8, the ECB president replaces Euro Area NCB governors during the first part of finance minister meetings when monetary matters are discussed. In the G-20, the ECB president attends in addition to the NCB governors from the four member states with the largest economies.

The ECB has called for the reinforcement of the ECB's position in these international fora. Duisenberg (2000*b*) further argued for the gradual but fundamental adaptation of the traditional institutional framework of international relations on the grounds that the existing framework—based on the representation of national governments—'was not tailored to the involvement of monetary unions, nor to the advent of the Eurosystem, and more generally the [Euro Area], as a new actor in international relations'. With regard to Eurosystem representation in international fora where both ministers and bank governors are represented (G-8 Finance, G-20), Duisenberg focused on the capability to speak with one voice (if and when appropriate) and a clearer Euro Area political counterpart for the ECB. Instead of the four Euro Area member state finance ministers (in the G-8 and G-20), he preferred a single Euro Group representative with a higher profile. He wanted to overcome the co-ordination problems among Eurosystem member states on external monetary policy.

Given the diverse circumstances of bilateral economic relations with third countries, the EU finance ministers did not set arrangements for Euro Area representation. The presence of the ECB in these bilateral discussions is now left to the Euro Group chair. The ECB has forged and reinforced bilateral relations with other central banks on issues of mutual concern, including operational facilities, financial stability and the provision of technical assistance. Notably, since November 1999 it has become involved in the EU enlargement process by providing assistance to the central banks of central and eastern European candidate countries to prepare them for participation in the ESCB following accession and their eventual participation in the Eurosystem. In addition to central banks, the ECB has developed contacts with other relevant foreign institutions, such as banking supervisory authorities, local banking associations, stock exchanges, and national public administrations.

Power in Relation to NCBs

The ECB's relatively small Executive Board and its weight on the Governing Council (6 out of 21 places, or less than third) demonstrate an important feature of the Eurosystem. Compared to other federal banking systems, the Eurosystem is relatively decentralized: NCBs have more sway collectively than, say, representatives from the Federal Reserve District Banks. This reflects practical reality: the NCBs are well-established, whereas the ECB is a fledgling, small institution. Eurosystem NCBs perform several operations vital to the operation of the Euro Area: notably, they conduct foreign-exchange operations and ensure the smooth operation of payment systems (including TARGET). The NCBs hold and manage the official foreign reserves of the member states (of which they can provide up to 40 billion euro to the ECB) and hold the capital of the ECB (just under 4 billion euro). However, NCBs must follow the regulations, guidelines, and instructions of the ECB in these and several other areas: buying and selling securities and other claims; borrowing and lending securities; dealing in precious metals; conducting credit operations with banks and other financial institutions based on adequate collateral; acting as fiscal agents for public entities (although they may not grant them credit facilities or buy their debt instruments directly from them). The ECB can also engage in these activities. The precise role of the ECB in relation to the NCBs depends on the kinds of open market operations selected (with regard to aim, regularity and procedures). NCBs are able to perform tasks beyond those specified in the ESCB Statute, except if the Governing Council decides that these activities interfere with the work of the ESCB. The ECB alone attends Euro Group meetings and Ecofin Councils. However, Eurosystem NCBs (and ESCB NCBs) will occasionally attend informal meetings of Ecofin with varying degrees of participation as well as meetings of the EU's Economic and Financial Committee when macroeconomic policy coordination issues discussed directly impinge on them. In 2003, Euro Area NCBs lost their right to sit in Economic and Financial Committee meetings—much to the opposition of several NCBs, including the Bundesbank (Dyson 2008c)—which has reinforced the importance of the ECB in European economic governance.

The degree to which the Eurosystem is centralized will develop over time. The important role of the NCBs in ECB decision-making (in the working groups, committees, and the Governing Council) reflects the ongoing importance of the analytical—including statistical—resources available in the NCBs and in particular the largest. The relative dependence of the ECB on the NCBs has reduced over the past decade, nonetheless the US Federal Reserve remains better endowed analytically than the ECB and less reliant on the state reserve banks. The importance of the NCBs in ECB decision-making encourages a combination of collaborative and competitive work (Goodfriend 1999; Hochreiter 2000; Mayes 1998, 2000). In their attempt to have an impact on

Governing Council decision-making, each NCB governor will use the resources of his own NCB to provide the necessary information and strengthen his position in the ongoing debate with other NCBs and the ECB Executive Board on appropriate policy and the way that the Euro Area economy works. The development of the ECB's autonomous analytical capacity in relation to that of the NCBs will be important in determining the level of centralization in Eurosystem policy making. The ECB has already become the most important centre for monetary policy research in the EU (see below) hiring some of the best monetary economists from NCBs.

Members of the Governing Council are expected to speak with one voice on the basis of the agreed-upon forecasts, although there is no legal requirement to do so. Efforts have been made to ensure a tight coordination of official statements on ECB monetary policy: the President is spokesperson in the official press conference following the bi-weekly meetings, while the other members of the Council have to explain Eurosystem policy in the member states in their own languages. There have been a number of incidents where different NCB governors made ambiguous remarks between Governing Council meetings that led to false predictions of monetary policy decisions (Louis 2002). However, there has yet to be a publicly expressed substantive difference of opinion between members of the Governing Council. Another potential source of divergence in the public expression of policy is the separate national forecasts published by the independent NCBs. Varying NCB forecasts could send different signals to market operators about the development of ECB policy. However, it is the role of ECB working groups and committees to iron out differences and ensure coherence in all the forecasts of the Euro Area prior to their publication.

The relative importance of the NCBs in the Eurosystem also arguably reflects the highly decentralized nature of the EU political system and the problematic legitimacy of the EU in the eyes of many member state citizens. Arguably, European citizens are more likely to accept ECB monetary policy if they know that they are represented, however indirectly and unofficially, by NCB governors, and that policy is designed in the fora of working groups, committees, and the Governing Council, where NCB experts and officials predominate. This concern was of great relevance to discussions in the ECB in 2002–3 on Governing Council reform in the context of Euro Area enlargement (see below).

The ECB Executive Board has been very cautious in its interventions into the operation of NCBs. One of the most controversial developments during the first decade of EMU was the Banca d'Italia Governor Antonio Fazio's handling of the takeover battle for Banca Antonveneta. Despite much criticism, the ECB Executive Board initially took a 'hands-off' approach and warned of a dangerous precedent for ESCB independence if the Italian government used legislation to remove Fazio (*Financial Times* 16 September 2005). The ECB finally adopted a much tougher tone in mid-December 2005, after it was made public that Fazio had received gifts from the former head of a major Italian bank. President Trichet warned that, in accepting gifts, the Italian governor might have breached the ECB's code of conduct (*Financial Times* 17 December 2005). However, the ECB has no investigative powers and was unable to pursue matters further. Ultimately, Fazio's resignation saved the ECB further damage to its credibility and the danger of public battles between Governing Council members.

Independent but in Search of Dialogue

Although the ECB regularly insists upon its independence and directly challenges political leaders who call this into question, it needs to maintain a constructive dialogue with democratically elected officials. The ECB does this in its dealings with the Euro Group of Euro Area finance ministers. The ECB also maintains direct relations with the European Parliament (EP), notably in terms of *ex-post facto* reporting and questioning. The EP must be consulted on appointments to the ECB Executive Board. It receives and debates the ECB's annual report and requests that the president and other Executive Board members appear before the Committee on Economic and Monetary Affairs (TEC Article 113) (see, for example, Duisenberg 2000*a*). Overall, however, the EP has little say over the ECB's management of monetary policy. As Dyson (2000: 69) notes, the model of ECB–EP relations is no match for US Federal Reserve–Congress relations, where a well-staffed and financed Congressional committee maintains constant scrutiny over the central bank. The ECB is not responsible to the EP or other EU institutions; none have the power to dismiss ECB Executive Board members on the grounds of unsatisfactory performance in fulfilment of the Bank's own goals (Taylor 2000).

However, there are signs that the ECB has been responsive to the concerns of the European Parliament and that a certain form of ECB accountability has developed (Jabko 2003; Magnette 2000). While the Treaty and the ESCB Statute establish no specific appearance requirements, the EP succeeded in obtaining Duisenberg's agreement that he would appear before the Committee on Economic and Monetary Affairs four times a year. This accountability has been good for the ECB's legitimacy. The wide-ranging review of the ECB by the Committee on Economic and Monetary Affairs can ensure that the Bank's technical decisions are subject to scrutiny from beyond the ESCB. This review can increase awareness and widen support for the Bank's underlying policies and principles. Accountability to the EP has also arguably induced improvements in ECB transparency, despite the absence of formal disclosure requirements (Jabko 2003). For instance, (nonbinding) EP resolutions on the ECB Annual Report have repeatedly urged the ECB to be become more transparent, and the publication of the ECB's macroeconomic projections appears to have been triggered by the quarterly 'monetary dialogue' between the ECB and the Committee on Economic and Monetary Affairs.

Intervention in Government Policy

The ECB has actively promoted structural reforms with the aim of reducing the public-sector debt burden, in Governing Council member speeches, press conferences, monthly bulletins, and annual reports. It has consistently defended the Stability and Growth Pact, criticized the suspension of the Excessive Deficit Procedure with regard to France and Germany in 2003, and sent strong warnings about the dangers of watering down the Pact in the March 2005 reform (Howarth and Loedel 2004). For the ECB, the Pact is a vital tool to entrench a stability culture in the Euro Area and to avoid conflictual relations with profligate governments. The ECB's pro-reform agenda has been challenged by government and opposition politicians in several member states and labour leaders.

Research and Analytical Capacity

Under the leadership of Otmar Issing, who worked as an academic economist for over 30 years prior to joining the Bundesbank, the ECB developed an impressive research capacity. In addition to its own expanding research staff, the ECB funds a visiting researcher programme to attract some of the best monetary economists in the world. One of the direct effects of the ECB's own research capacity was the development of the New Area-Wide Model—the principal inflation forecasting model—by the staff in DG Research for simulation tasks and scenario analysis. The model is also regularly used to produce research papers that are presented in academic conferences and central bank workshops, thus providing a constant quality check (Trichet 2007b). The ECB has funded policy-relevant research that is not yet available at universities or other research institutes. With the Centre for Financial Studies at the Goethe University of Frankfurt, the ECB runs the Research Network on Capital Markets and Financial Integration in Europe. The ECB has also led and co-ordinated the research efforts of Eurosystem NCBs through four networks on Monetary Transmission, Inflation Persistence, Wage Dynamics, and the Euro Area Business Cycle, the latter also involving the Bank of England and the Centre for Economic Policy Research. In addition to internal and open seminars given by staff and invited speakers, the ECB has become a major venue for conferences on monetary policy and other economic matters of direct relevance to monetary policy. The dissemination of research at the ECB is achieved through the publication of research papers, presentations at international workshops and conferences, and the publication of the ECB's own Working Paper Series. In 2006, 137 working papers were released, with 90 papers authored or co-authored by ECB staff, considerably more than the output of the US Federal Reserve.

There were concerns that, following the departure of Issing and with the decision to divide the management of Directorate Generals economics and research, the latter would lose influence on policy making and resources. However, Lucas Papademos, the Executive Board member in charge of DG research since 2006, sought to allay fears by directing it 'to focus more on policy-related issues' (*Financial Times* 1 June 2006). With a PhD from the Massachusetts Institute of Technology and a stint as an academic at Columbia University, he has a strong background in academic economic research.

Internal Reform

Unlike several NCBs in the Eurosystem, which have had to undergo painful internal cuts and significant reform, the ECB expanded its staff number every year since its creation. It remains a comparatively small and efficient central bank. At the end of 2007, 1,375 members of staff (full-time equivalent) were employed on permanent or fixed term, up from 1,217 staff members at the end of 2003. This number is dwarfed by the number employees working in the largest Eurosystem NCBs. However, the ECB's capacities have been increased considerably, and in some areas (notably, research) its reputation has over-taken that of the other Eurosystem NCBs.

Despite the ECB's reputation for efficiency, bank management had to counter a great deal of publicly expressed discontent from ECB staff who complained that it suffered from poor management, was too bureaucratic, and failed to communicated with its employees (*Financial Times* 5 November 2003). In October 2003, the ECB approved internal reforms aimed at improving working conditions, communication with staff, and management training. A 2003 audit of the bank's information technology services by McKinsey, the consultancy group, found severe management failure in the IT department's project planning, causing heavy budget overruns and major delays (ibid.). Trichet dedicated his first years as president to engineering reform throughout the bank and, in IT, saw off strikes by staff, who were concerned about the potential redundancies resulting from reorganization.

Euro Area Enlargement and Governing Council Reform

The most controversial internal reform undertaken by the ECB was the adoption of a new rotation system for voting in the Governing Council. The complicated nature of the new system has been criticized by many observers, including the well-known monetary economist Daniel Gros (2003). According to the reform agreement, the number of NCB governors exercising a voting right is to be capped at 15, while all governors are to continue to attend and be able to speak at meetings. When the number of NCB governors in the

Governing Council exceeds 15 voting rights is to be exercised on the basis of a rotation system, designed to ensure that the NCB governors with the right to vote are from member states which, taken together, are representative of the Euro Area's economy as a whole. Consequently, the NCB governors are to exercise a voting right with different frequencies depending on an indicator of the relative size of the economies of their member states within the Euro Area. Based on this indicator, NCB governors are be allocated to different groups.

Initially, two rotating groups are established (as took place on 1 January 2009 following the accession of Slovakia to the Euro Area). The governors from the five member states with the largest economies (currently, Germany, France, Italy, Spain, and the Netherlands) form one group, possessing four votes (and thus each have a voting frequency of 80%). The governors from the other member states form the second group, sharing 11 votes. Once the total number of member states in the Euro Area increases beyond 22, three groups are to be established with members of the third group possessing the lowest voting frequency. The members of the Executive Board are to preserve their permanent voting rights.

In 2003, the European Parliament opposed the reform on the grounds of its complicated nature but also because it was felt that population size should have been a factor determining membership of the rotating groups. Many economists and central bankers have also attacked the reform because it does not cut down the number of Governing Council members, which was already considered to be too many to allow for efficient monetary policy making (see, for example, Baldwin et al. 2001; Berger et al. 2004; Buiter 1999; de Haan et al. 2005; Eijffinger 2006). Some argue for a system emulating the Federal Reserve Board, with the ECB Executive Board possessing a larger percentage of the total vote to allow for more efficient policy making (de Haan et al. 2005; Eijffinger 2006; Favero et al. 2000). Others see an entirely centralized system—the creation of a Monetary Policy Board detached from the member state NCBs—as the only effective way to resolve the efficiency problem (Baldwin et al. 2001).

It can be argued (see Dyson 2008; Howarth 2007) that concerns with the efficiency and credibility of monetary policy making were secondary in the design of the rotational groups. More relevant were the corporate interests of the existing 12 NCB governors who agreed the reform—none of whom would be placed initially in the third group. Moreover, legitimacy concerns may have directed the reform. Ensuring representation according to national economic size was potentially important to the legitimacy of ECB policy making, even though this undermined the treaty-established *ad personam* status of the NCB governors. At the same time, the decision to grant all NCB governors the right to attend and speak at Governing Council meetings, and the imposition of rotation—albeit at different frequencies—on all governors (from the Maltese to the German), allowed the ECB to claim that the reform respects the principle of equal treatment.

Conclusion

EMU embodies 'the triumph of technocratic elitism over the idea of political democracy' (Dyson and Featherstone 1999: 801). The ECB can be said to be the principal victor in terms of real power, determining most aspects of monetary policy for the world's second largest economic entity. The burgeoning research and analytical capacity of the ECB has reinforced its power, in relation both to European and national political officials and to the Eurosystem's NCB. Credibility also brings power, and the ECB can be judged to have achieved a considerable amount of credibility thanks to the consistency of its monetary policy and its ability to adopt greater transparency in explaining this policy to both financial markets and democratically elected officials.

The democratic legitimacy of the ECB remains contested by some politicians. However, Governing Council members insist upon its legitimacy. They argue that the ECB's mandate was established by democratically elected governments and is more tightly circumscribed than a dual mandate including growth and employment alongside price stability; that public support for both EMU and the goal of price stability remains high; and that the bank has been accountable to democratically elected officials and the public—without compromising its independence—through the efforts of Executive Board members to explain bank policies regularly to members of the European Parliament, governments and the public in speeches, press conferences, and other public appearances.

The title of this chapter makes direct reference to the title of a much earlier work that focuses upon Bundesbank power (Marsh 1992). On 1 January 1999, the ECB supplanted the Bundesbank as the leading central bank on the European continent. To the extent that we can claim that the ECB 'rules' Europe, it does so differently from the Bundesbank in the era of the European Monetary System. The ECB sets the interest rates for 15 member states and for states in the Exchange-Rate Mechanism (ERM-2), as well as having a strong influence on interest rates for those satellite economies whose currencies shadow the euro (see the chapter by Umbach and Wessels). Yet, NCB governors participate in the setting of these rates—which was certainly not the case prior to 1999, when the Bundesbank was notoriously hostile to interest-rate coordination and set rates to meet its statutory mandate of domestic price stability. Even though the ECB's rates might not be entirely appropriate to the economic conditions of many individual Euro Area member states, they are not the reflection of economic developments in a single member state. The ideational power of the ECB is at least as great as that of the Bundesbank: the former is the guardian of price stability in Eurosystem and one of the world's most visible promoters of the virtues of low inflation. The augmentation of the ECB's research capacity reinforces its ideational power, and it is supported by the Eurosystem NCBs which all share the same mandate. However, the

Bundesbank's influence lay not only in its success in maintaining low inflation but also, to a large extent, on the comparative size and strength of the German economy. The ECB manages the monetary policy of a far larger economic entity—clearly a source of its great clout both at home and abroad—but the Euro Area is, in its great diversity, less economically successful than pre-unification Germany, a fact that inevitably undermines the power of the ECB's anti-inflationary message.

This chapter has shown that the power of the ECB is limited in several important respects. The resistance of member state governments limits the ECB's influence in European economic governance, national macroeconomic policy, and prudential supervision. Despite the ECB's important international profile, EU member states are unlikely to modify its observer status in the IMF and OECD. The resistance of Euro Area NCBs also prevents the extension of ECB activities into several core central banking operations. International developments—and notably the rise of China and India—will limit both the relative economic importance of the Euro Area and, eventually, the importance of the euro as an international reserve currency. Increasingly complicated financial markets—notably the rise of derivatives and hedge funds—have undermined the credibility of ECB monetary policy and will no doubt continue to do so.

Part II

Eurosystem 'Insider' Central Banks

4

National Banks of Belgium and the Netherlands: Happy with the Euro[*]

Ivo Maes and Amy Verdun

Financial integration and monetary union have affected the functions, structures, and powers of European central banks. The scope and content of central bank policies have changed, as has the central focus of the policies. With the creation of the European System of Central Banks (ESCB) and the Eurosystem, European national central banks have become part of a collective system in which monetary policy is set centrally by the Governing Council. The ESCB consists of the European Central Bank and all the EU national central banks (NCBs). The Eurosystem comprises the ECB and the NCBs of EU Member States that have adopted the euro. Given that they are now part of a larger system that sets monetary policy of the euro area, as such, the individual national central banks of the Eurosystem have no sovereignty to set independent national monetary policies as had been the case in the past.

In this chapter, the cases of the National Bank of Belgium (NBB) and De Nederlandsche Bank (DNB) are analysed with a view to what has changed in these central banks of medium-sized European Union member states since the onset of Economic and Monetary Union (EMU). Both central banks played a significant role in the creation of EMU. The National Bank of Belgium played a pace-setting role in the EMU process, whilst De Nederlandsche Bank played the role of gate-keeper (Maes and Verdun 2005). Since the start of EMU, how have these roles of these two central banks changed, both within their domestic context and within the Eurosystem? The core functions of a central bank—monetary policy, issuing banknotes, managing the gold and foreign-exchange

* Ivo Maes wrote the section on the National Bank of Belgium and Amy Verdun the one on de Nederlandsche Bank. The authors would like to thank all those who contributed to this project, especially Kenneth Dyson and Martin Marcussen, the participants at the Cardiff EU-Consent workshop, 2007 UACES (Portsmouth), and British Academy/EU-Consent conference. Amy Verdun thanks some officials and the services of *De Nederlandsche Bank*, especially C.C.A. van den Berg. The usual disclaimer applies.

reserves, and organizing the flow of payments—now take place within a European framework, the Eurosystem, in which the National Bank of Belgium and De Nederlandsche Bank fully participate. Besides their role in the European context both central banks also play an important role in their countries' domestic socio-economic affairs. In this way, they are now 'hybrid' institutions, performing both European and national functions. Both the anticipation of the creation of EMU and actual experience of EMU led to changes in the Belgian and Dutch central banks. Increasingly, there is a growing attention towards financial stability, in line with the globalization and growing complexity of financial markets and institutions. The National Bank of Belgium and De Nederlandsche Bank are evolving towards more knowledge-oriented tasks and are putting more emphasis on cost control and modern management techniques. In sum, these two central banks adjusted their objectives and organization following the creation of EMU. More than before, they focus on policies that support monetary and financial stability.

The National Bank of Belgium

The Pre-Euro National Bank of Belgium

The National Bank of Belgium had a 'monetarist' orientation and played a pace-setting role in the EMU process (Maes and Verdun 2005). It argued for European exchange-rate stability and monetary cooperation as a catalyst for economic convergence. However, it was also convinced of the necessity of parallel progress in the economic and monetary areas.

The National Bank of Belgium was from the outset at the core of the EMU process as Governor Hubert Ansiaux, who was also the chair of the Committee of EC Central Bank Governors, became a member of the Werner Committee in 1970 (Maes 2006). In his memoirs, Pierre Werner (1991) characterized Ansiaux as the *chef de file* of the 'monetarists' in the Committee. Later, at the time of the creation of the European Monetary System (EMS), Governor Cecil de Strycker was the chair of the Committee of EC Central Bank Governors. The National Bank of Belgium was involved in the elaboration of the well-known 'Belgian compromise' (with a role for both the parity grid and the divergence indicator in the exchange-rate mechanism, cf. Ludlow 1982).

The EMU process was relaunched in the second half of the 1980s with the Delors Committee (Verdun 1999b). Governor Jean Godeaux was described by Jacques Delors (2004) as one of the *'grands enthousiastes'* of EMU in the Committee. The Committee of EC Central Bank Governors further prepared the Maastricht Intergovernmental Conference, especially the draft Statutes for the future European Central Bank. The Committee of Alternates, chaired by a Director of the National Bank of Belgium, Jean-Jacques Rey (son of Jean Rey, the second President of the European Commission), played a crucial role. Later, Rey chaired the Monetary Policy Sub-Committee of the European Monetary Institute (EMI), which prepared the Euro Area's single monetary policy.

With its support of European monetary integration the National Bank of Belgium was in line with Belgium's traditional pro-European orientation (Maes 2002). However, there were also differences of opinion at the National Bank of Belgium. Some took a more pragmatic view, regarding Europe as primarily a framework for the stable exchange-rate policy, to ensure discipline in the economy. For others, who were more in favour of a federal Europe, the real goal was a common European monetary policy, both to secure increased influence over the monetary policy stance and as a step towards political union.

The National Bank of Belgium influenced the EMU process primarily via two channels: the Belgian authorities and the central banks of the European Union (Smets, Michielsen, and Maes 2003). At the Belgian level, the National Bank of Belgium helped to formulate Belgium's ideas and positions. Its expertise was a particularly important asset. The National Bank of Belgium also played a role in the world of the European central banks. This was particularly in evidence at times when the Governor was chair of the Committee of EC Central Bank Governors, or when representatives of the National Bank of Belgium chaired a committee or working group (cf. supra).

From a Weak Currency to the Anchoring of the Belgian Franc to the D-Mark

For the National Bank of Belgium, the Snake and the EMS were the beacons of monetary and foreign-exchange policy (Buyst, Maes, and Pluym 2005). It was hoped that a European anchor would have the effect of imposing discipline on domestic economic policy and wage-setting. At first that seemed a vain hope.

Although the early 1970s were a boom period, the seeds of Belgium's economic problems were sown in this period. Not only was inflation gathering speed, nominal wages were also clearly rising faster than prices. The budgetary situation in Belgium was also worsening. In 1981, the public deficit totalled more than 15 per cent of Gross Domestic Product (GDP). This led to discussions between the National Bank of Belgium and the Finance Ministry on ways of financing the deficit. Whilst the National Bank of Belgium was sharply critical of fiscal policy, in practice it often consented to a monetary financing of the deficit. Moreover, the government intervened in interest-rate policy (Buyst, Maes, and Pluym 2005). Thus, in September 1979, the government commissioner exercised his right to suspend an increase in the discount rate, intended by the Council of Regency (the highest decision-making body, composed of the governor, the directors, and 10 regents) of the National Bank of Belgium. One week later, when the situation in the foreign-exchange market had not improved, the minister consented.

In December 1981, a new coalition government of Christian Democrats and Liberals came to power. A key element of its programme was a devaluation combined with accompanying measures. The February 1982 devaluation was clearly designed as a one-off operation. It was accompanied by a series of measures to prevent inflation from getting out of hand. The spectre feared by Belgian policymakers was a 'devaluation–inflation–devaluation' spiral, as previously experienced by other countries.

The Luxembourg government was 'dismayed' at the devaluation announcement by the Belgian government. The Luxembourg authorities asked for the Belgian and Luxembourg gold and currency reserves to be split. New negotiations on the monetary association followed. The Luxembourg authorities dropped their request for a division of the reserves, but the limit on the Luxembourg franc banknote issue was increased.

The devaluation and the recovery policy brought a rapid improvement in the external position of the Belgian economy. The balance of payments current account was restored to equilibrium in 1984. In the periodic EMS realignments during the mid-1980s, the Belgian franc generally held an intermediate position between the strong currencies and the weaker ones. Thanks to the improved performance of the Belgian economy, it gradually became possible to align the Belgian frame more closely to the D-Mark (Godeaux 1989). On 16 June 1990, the Belgian franc was officially pegged to the D-Mark. This new exchange-rate objective also strengthened the National Bank of Belgium's autonomy in relation to the government on interest-rate policy.

Preparing for EMU

The Maastricht Treaty, with its convergence criteria, clearly pointed the way to EMU. The Belgian authorities' strategy was designed to ensure early fulfilment of the criteria concerning price stability, exchange-rate stability, and long-term interest rates. By qualifying sooner on these criteria Belgium hoped to distinguish itself clearly from other countries with a high public debt/GDP ratio (such as Italy). Crucial to this strategy was the exchange-rate policy, anchoring the franc to the D-Mark.

In 1993, the ERM exchange-rate crisis put Belgium's EMU strategy in serious jeopardy. The storm on the foreign-exchange markets reached its peak in October 1993, when the Belgian franc was trading at 6.5 per cent below its central rate against the D-Mark. The National Bank of Belgium defended the exchange rate. It put up the official interest rate from 6.7 per cent in mid-July to 10.5 per cent at the beginning of September. It also intervened in the currency markets on a massive scale. With the approval of the 'overall plan for employment, competitiveness, and social security' in November 1993, the Belgian government took new measures to tighten up fiscal policy and to restrain incomes. In the closing months of 1993, the franc strengthened again.

During the 1990s, the independence of the National Bank of Belgium was not only reinforced through the more ambitious exchange-rate objective. There were also significant reforms, in line with a growing Europeanization of the National Bank of Belgium.

Belgium was in a unique position in the EU, since the National Bank of Belgium had the power to determine the interest rate on short-term treasury paper, albeit after 'consultation' with the Finance Ministry; the responsibilities of the monetary and fiscal authorities were intertwined. In January 1991, the money market and the instruments of monetary policy underwent fundamental reform, thereby ending the intermingling of the National Bank of Belgium's responsibilities with those of the Finance Ministry. The reform made the issue of treasury certificates the exclusive domain of the Treasury. Auction techniques were introduced. Henceforward, the market would determine the interest rate on treasury paper. As in other EU states, the National Bank of Belgium's new range of monetary policy instruments was based on its function as the bank of banks. The National Bank of Belgium influenced market interest rates indirectly, via the volume of its lending to financial institutions and the interest rate charged. The state's credit line was significantly reduced. Furthermore, the state could only take out new loans in foreign currencies if that did not conflict with monetary and exchange-rate policy.

During the 1990s, the statutes of the National Bank of Belgium were further adjusted in line with the provisions of the Maastricht Treaty. The law of 22 March 1993 granted the National Bank of Belgium greater autonomy in the conduct of monetary policy. Limits were imposed on the supervisory powers of the Finance Minister and the government commissioner. In addition, the National Bank of Belgium was absolutely prohibited from lending money to the government. Pursuant to the law of 22 February 1998, the basic law of the National Bank of Belgium was further amended, introducing the principle that the National Bank of Belgium formed an integral part of the ESCB.

In Belgium, preparations for the introduction of the euro were made by the 'General Commission for the euro', which was created in order to prepare the introduction of the euro in Belgium. It had two tasks. It had to encourage the various sectors of the economy to prepare for the advent of the euro, and it had to monitor the cohesion of the measures in order to prevent the adoption of conflicting strategies. The first General Commissioner, who was at the head of the General Commission, was National Bank of Belgium director Guy Quaden. When he was appointed Governor in March 1999, a few weeks after the introduction of the new currency, he was succeeded by National Bank of Belgium director Jan Smets. The National Bank of Belgium also provided the secretariat for the General Commission.

The start of stage three of EMU also brought the abolition of the Belgian–Luxembourg monetary association. From then on, Luxembourg had its own central bank, the Banque Centrale du Luxembourg, which plays a full part in the Eurosystem. The Luxembourg branch of the National Bank of Belgium was taken over by the Luxembourg central bank.

On 1 January 2002, the euro banknotes were introduced in the 12 states of the Euro Area. It was a logistical operation without precedent in monetary and financial history. Since the National Bank of Belgium has its own printing works, it printed banknotes which were placed in circulation on that date. In total 550 million notes were printed. After a brief dual circulation period, the Belgian franc notes ceased to be legal tender on 28 February 2002.

The National Bank of Belgium in the Eurosystem

From 1999 decisions on the single monetary policy were centralized. Most of them are taken by the Governing Council of the European Central Bank. The Governor of the National Bank of Belgium attends the meetings in a personal capacity. In performing his duties, the Governor is strictly independent. Yet Belgium has more influence over monetary policy now than before the introduction of the euro, when the Belgian franc was anchored to the D-Mark, and Belgium had no say in the interest-rate decisions made by the Bundesbank. National autonomy was thus exchanged for a share in supranational decision-making power, a practical illustration of how the effect of European integration can be seen as a means of restoring power of decision, certainly for a small state like Belgium.

One might argue also that with the new policy regime of EMU the power and influence of the National Bank of Belgium in Belgium have been strengthened (e.g. central bank independence, no monetary financing of budget deficits). However, the absence of foreign-exchange crises (certainly an important benefit for the Belgian economy) can sometimes make it more difficult to convince other actors to adjust policies, as the 'drama' and sense of urgency of exchange-rate crises are not there any more. The absence of foreign exchange tensions was even cited as one of the reasons for the long negotiations to form a government in 2007.

This greater role in monetary decision-making, as well as the 'new competition for ideas in the Eurosystem', led to a strengthening of the Research Department of the National Bank of Belgium (a general tendency in the Eurosystem, see the chapter on research by Marcussen in this volume). The Department prepares, twice monthly, a briefing for the Governor, before the meetings of the Governing Council. Moreover, it participates in the Monetary Policy Committee of the Eurosystem, as well as several working groups. The Research Department also prepares the projections for Belgium for the biannual Broad Macroeconomic Projection Exercise of the Eurosystem. Furthermore, this policy work is based on more fundamental economic research. Also, at the level of the Eurosystem, research networks have been set up, for instance, on inflation persistence and wage dynamics, in which the National Bank of Belgium participated actively. In 2000, the National Bank of Belgium started a series of Working Papers and a series of academic conferences. One of the objectives of research at the National Bank of Belgium is also to strengthen links with the Belgian academic community, for instance, through common research projects.

In the implementation of monetary policy the principle of subsidiarity applies. One of the Eurosystem's basic operating principles is a high degree of decentralization. The National Bank of Belgium, like the other national central banks, therefore remains the contact point between Belgian financial institutions or economic agents and the Eurosystem. However, the concept of decentralization has evolved since the Eurosystem was first formed, with some central banks now offering services to the other central banks of the Eurosystem (like TARGET 2). The National Bank of Belgium played a pioneering role here (Quaden 2007). A first example concerns banknotes. The National Bank of Belgium developed an IT tool which manages the flows of banknotes and coins both within the National Bank of Belgium and between the National Bank of Belgium and the financial institutions (or the cash transport firms). This application, called CASH, has yielded significant productivity gains and increased transaction security. The National Bank of Belgium makes this application available for use by the other central banks. In 2006, a partnership was concluded with De Nederlandsche Bank and the Banque centrale du Luxembourg, joined by the Bank of Finland in March 2007.

The second example concerns the implementation of monetary policy. The credit granted to financial institutions has to be backed by appropriate collateral. The National Bank of Belgium developed a new IT system for the efficient management of that collateral. This platform—called ECMS (Euro Collateral Management System)—permits almost totally automated management of this collateral and improves the service provided for financial institutions. A partnership has been concluded here, too, between the National Bank of Belgium and De Nederlandsche Bank.

In Belgium, since the 1930s, the responsibilities of the National Bank of Belgium had been separate from those of the Banking Commission, which is responsible for banking supervision or 'micro-prudential' supervision (Maes and Périlleux 1993). Recently, the National Bank of Belgium acquired a greater role in prudential matters, especially 'macro-prudential' issues, which relate to the stability of the financial system as a whole.

The National Bank of Belgium has traditionally been involved in the stability of the financial system via its responsibility for payment instruments. It is in fact via the payment systems that a crisis in one financial institution threatens to affect other financial institutions, and hence the stability of the financial system and economic activity in general (Lamfalussy 2003; Moran and McCartney in this volume). Also, as the bank of banks, responsible for providing liquidity for the financial system, the National Bank of Belgium performs a macro-prudential function. In the past few decades the National Bank of Belgium has also been involved, via its international role, in developing new prudential rules at international and European levels.

With the law of 17 December 1998, the National Bank of Belgium was given an explicit legal basis for exercising macro-prudential supervision. On 1 January 1999, the National Bank of Belgium took over the functions of the Rediscount and Guarantee Institute, especially the management of the 'Protection Fund for Deposits and Financial Instruments'. The Protection Fund's task is to give financial compensation to depositors and investors who have suffered damages following the bankruptcy of a credit institution or investment undertaking (Vandeputte, Abraham, and Lempereur 1981).

The law of 2 August 2002 fundamentally reorganized prudential supervision in Belgium (Buyst and Maes 2008). As part of that process, the Banking and Finance Commission and the Insurance Supervision Office were merged on 1 January 2004 to form a single supervisory body, the Banking, Finance and Insurance Commission (BFIC). Moreover, stronger links were established between the National Bank of Belgium and the Banking, Finance and Insurance Commission. Thus, three members of the National Bank of Belgium's Board of Directors are members of the Banking, Finance and Insurance Commissions Board of Directors. In addition, a Financial Stability Committee was established in 2003. It comprises the members of the National Bank of Belgium and Banking, Finance and Insurance Commissions boards of directors, and is chaired by the Governor of the National Bank of Belgium. It deals with all matters of common interest, such as the overall stability of the financial system, the coordination of crisis management, and the management of synergies between the two institutions. A Financial Services Authority Supervisory Board was also set up in 2004, combining the Banking, Finance and Insurance Commission supervisory board and the National Bank of Belgium's Council of Regency. However, the Banking, Finance and Insurance Commission retains its powers of micro-prudential supervision and autonomy of decision. The Law of 2 August 2002 also obliged both institutions to cooperate and to pool resources in order to realize synergies.

Several factors contributed to these changes. The liberalization and globalization of the financial markets made the financial system more open and more competitive (Maes 2007). Furthermore, the ever-accelerating pace of financial innovations makes it more difficult to assess and locate the risks. Crucially, during the last decades, there were several mergers of banks and insurance companies in Belgium, leading to the formation of large 'bank assurance' groups. The emergence of very large financial institutions also means that a problem in one large institution could have systemic implications. All these factors are tending to blur the boundaries between macro- and micro-prudential supervision. Moreover, with the introduction of the euro, certain arguments against giving national central banks prudential responsibilities, such as the loss of monetary policy credibility in the case of a bank failure, have lost importance.

The start of the third stage of EMU coincided with an important renewal of the Executive Board of the National Bank of Belgium (in March 1999). Governor Alfons Verplaetse retired and was replaced by director Guy Quaden. In 2000, Governor Quaden launched a strategic management exercise which was triggered by the fundamental changes brought about by the single currency, as well as the spread of new information and communication technologies and the concentration in the commercial financial sector. The exercise led to a strengthening of the National Bank of Belgium's research capacities and communication capabilities, as well as cost control and modern management techniques.

Traditionally, the National Bank of Belgium devoted much attention to macro-economic research. As already mentioned, to participate fully in the Eurosystem, the National Bank of Belgium strengthened its research capacities. Moreover, as a monetary authority it plays a key role in the definition of macro-economic policy in Belgium. Indeed, the National Bank of Belgium's role as an advisor on economic policy has an institutional basis. In the first instance, this role is expressed in the Council of Regency, where the social partners are also represented. The Council of Regency's discussions, which are based on reports prepared by the National Bank of Belgium, help to achieve social consensus in Belgium. With EMU, a crucial issue for the National Bank of Belgium is the coherence between the single monetary policy and economic policy in Belgium.

An important result of the strategic revision was also the strengthening of the communication capabilities of the National Bank of Belgium. In 2000, a Communications Service was created, which reports directly to the Governor. It included also the museum, which was revamped and extended.

It is also noteworthy that during the final three decades of the twentieth century, the National Bank of Belgium was entrusted with various tasks which cannot be classed as strictly central bank functions. Indeed, they fall outside the domain of the ESCB. The reasons are related both to the competences of the National Bank of Belgium and to the weaknesses of other institutions in the Belgian state. Most of these functions concern the collection and circulation of information. The range of functions performed by the National Bank of Belgium is larger and more diverse than that of most other central banks in the Eurosystem. Thus, the National Bank of Belgium is a key player in the provision and analysis of micro-economic information. The law of 24 March 1978 gave the National Bank of Belgium the task of establishing the Central Balance Sheet Office, whose function is to collect and publish the annual accounts of firms. The Central Office for Credits to Enterprises, established in 1967, collects data on lending in the Belgian economy. In the 1990s, the statistical functions expanded as, at the request of the legislature, the National Bank of Belgium took over a substantial part of the activities of the National Statistical Institute, in particular the compilation of the national accounts.

Furthermore, cost control and modern management methods became more important. For instance, the agency network was greatly reduced. Of the 43 provincial branches, 20 were closed between 1974 and 1984. In 1999, a second streamlining operation was launched. Since March 2005, the National Bank of Belgium has only seven establishments outside Brussels. Also, modern management methods were introduced, like master plans and a stronger emphasis on skills management.

There have also been considerable changes in the workforce. The number of employees peaked on 1 January 1987 at a nominal total of nearly 3,300 units. After that the size of the workforce declined sharply. Yet the advent of monetary union did not lead to a significant reduction in traditional activities, whilst new tasks were added. Thanks to productivity increases and restructuring, the workforce contracted. On 1 January 2008 the nominal total had fallen to around 2,250 units, a decrease of nearly one third compared to 1987. This was accomplished without dismissals, but recruitment became very selective. In line with the trend towards more knowledge-based tasks, the proportion of staff in managerial and supervisory positions rose from 11 per cent in 1970 to over 20 per cent in 2008.

De Nederlandsche Bank

De Nederlandsche Bank (DNB) has been the central bank of the Netherlands since 1814, making it one of the older central banks in Europe. Throughout this period its role changed from being commercially involved to serving as a public institution, completely abandoning its commercial activities and acting instead as lender of last resort, and dealing with its three core tasks: managing currency circulation, formulating and implementing monetary policy, and banking supervision (Vanthoor 2005). European integration has always been part and parcel of the modern DNB, and when possible the DNB took action to support the European integration objective.

The DNB in the 1960s–80s

Throughout the late 1960s and 1970s the Dutch monetary authorities favoured close monetary cooperation with other EEC member states. They made alliances with the Germans on policies for further economic and monetary integration. The Dutch were keen to ensure that macro-economic integration was well developed before moving towards deeper monetary integration. The Dutch and German governments both belonged to the 'economists' camp in the well-known debate between 'economists' and 'monetarists' on how best to obtain further monetary integration. Nevertheless, they favoured closer European co-operation in this area. They backed the exchange-rate agreements that were established to promote monetary and trade stability in Europe, such as the Snake and the ERM of the European Monetary System whilst at the same time promoting an EMU based on 'economist' principles (Verdun 1990, 1996, 2000).

In the late 1970s and early to mid-1980s the Dutch economy suffered from low economic growth, rising unemployment, and lack of competitiveness (see also Szász 1988: 208–9). The Dutch monetary authorities reacted to this situation by deciding, among other things, to follow a strong currency policy and closely follow German monetary policies (see Verdun 2002: 241–2, see also Wellink 2008). They aimed at securing fixed exchange rates between the Dutch guilder and the D-Mark. This policy objective was maintained until the launch of the euro in 1999. By 1999 the Dutch exchange rate vis-à-vis the D-Mark had been the most stable of all ERM currencies over a period of two decades.

The Dutch central bank was influential in the relaunch of EMU in the late 1980s and early 1990s particularly during the Intergovernmental Conferences (IGCs) that led to the Treaty on European Union which was signed in Maastricht. The Dutch government, headed by Prime Minister Ruud Lubbers, held the rotating presidency of the EC at a key moment in the history of EMU, when the IGCs preparing the Maastricht Treaty revisions were negotiated in the second half of 1991. The Dutch worked very hard at getting a workable compromise that would satisfy all member states, and the DNB played an important role in this process. The DNB was one of the few central banks that had a record similar to that of the Bundesbank, and was already in these early years all but completely independent.

During the 1980s, the DNB had a record similar to that of the Bundesbank in that it kept inflation rates low, the exchange rate stable, and managed to secure this solid record throughout that decade. As such, the DNB was a strong institution during the negotiations leading up to incorporating EMU in the Treaty on European Union. One of the roles of the DNB was to keep on board the German monetary authorities, who were interested in an EMU that would be built on a price stability objective. The Dutch EU presidency in 1991 needed to find the wording that would be acceptable to even the most sceptical ones, the United Kingdom and Denmark. The end result was the successful incorporation of EMU into the Treaty on European Union with an opt out for the United Kingdom and Denmark. Furthermore EMU would only start with those countries who could meet the convergence criteria.

The DNB: from Maastricht to Frankfurt

Although incorporated in the Treaty, EMU was by no means completely settled in 1991. The interpretation of the convergence criteria remained a hot political topic throughout the 1990s. The Bundesbank and the German Ministry of

Finance were concerned that, once EMU was fully operational, some states might return to their old practices of high public borrowing and high rates of inflation. The Dutch monetary authorities were among those most supportive of these German concerns and thus spoke up about the concerns that the Germans had. As was already touched upon above, the Dutch–German relationship had been carefully crafted throughout the 15 years prior to signing of the Treaty on European Union (Szász 1988, 2001). Also, the German government had to perform a careful balancing act between being pro-active on what it considered important, and not seeming to be too dominant within the broader European context. In particular, the DNB supported the Stability and Growth Pact, which both the DNB and the Bundesbank considered to be a crucial instrument in securing stability in EMU after the adoption of EMU (Heipertz and Verdun 2004, 2005).

The strong record of the Dutch central bank (DNB 1997) and its close relations to the German Bundesbank and the stability culture, put the then President of the Dutch central bank, Willem Duisenberg, in an excellent position to be put forward as the first President of the European Central Bank. Duisenberg personified the new institution in more than one way (De Haas and Van Lotringen 2003). He had been an advocate of European monetary integration since the early days and had ample international experience. Duisenberg had worked with the International Monetary Fund from 1965–9, and then for a year as an advisor to the Director of DNB. Thereafter he was appointed Professor of Macroeconomics at the University of Amsterdam. He left academia to become the Finance Minister in the social–democratic government (1973–7). These were turbulent years for the Netherlands. After his years in the political arena Duisenberg spent a few years in the private sector as vice-president of the Rabobank (a Dutch commercial bank). In 1982 he became the President of De Nederlandsche Bank, a post he kept until he left the position to head the European Monetary Institute in July 1997 and then the European Central Bank from its first day in June 1998.

During his years as President of the Dutch central bank Duisenberg managed to secure a stable exchange rate to the D-Mark and to keep inflation rates low. As part of this strategy he closely followed German monetary policies. But, contrary to many other countries in the 1990s, the Dutch–German exchange rate did not come under pressure at any time, and the Dutch–German exchange rate stayed stable when others were stretched to a ±15 per cent band in 1993. Since the start of the idea of creating EMU, the DNB worked hard to make sure that EMU would be based on the same firm principles the DNB had itself worked long and hard on to achieve.

In 1991 De Nederlandsche Bank's three main tasks were managing currency circulation, formulating and implementing monetary policy, and banking supervision. As DNB looked towards a future role in the Eurosystem where monetary policy would be set centrally, it realized that changes were needed to ensure that it was capable of effectively supporting this ECB monetary policy and of sec-uring the overall financial stability of the Netherlands in this new context.

In preparation for entry into stage three of EMU, the adoption of the euro, and become integrated into the Eurosystem and the ESCB, a few changes were made. First of all, the Dutch parliament passed a change to the Bank Act. The Dutch central bank had effectively operated as an independent central bank, even though, formally, the Minister of Finance had the power to instruct the DNB (in Dutch 'aanwijzingsrecht'). But this power had been rarely used (e.g. in 1945); indeed, according to the new Bank Act of 1948, it was to be used only in *ultimum remedium*—as a last resort, which never happened after 1948 (Vanthoor 2004: 164–7, 201–11). In 1998 the Bank Act was subsequently changed so as to remove this power to comply with the requirement of the ESCB that the national central banks have to be completely independent.

In 2002 another important change was made. Pensions and Insurance Super-visory Authority (Pensioen- en Verzekeringskamer 'PVK'), which traditionally had been a separate institution, was transferred to DNB, which had a major impact on the institutional structure of DNB. A new Act was put in place to replace the older one (which had been in place for 50 years). In 2004 the merger between DNB and the Pensions and Insurance Supervisory Authority was complete.

Other restructuring that took place in light of joining EMU included the closing of seven branches of DNB—a decision taken in 1996 leaving only the main office and four branches open (Apeldoorn, Eindhoven, Hoogeveen, and Wassenaar, DNB 1999: 147). The branches had as one of their tasks to verify the authenticity and the state of banknotes. Following a decision in 2003 to dele-gate some of those tasks to commercial banks, DNB was witnessing a downward trend in the number of banknotes the branches were checking—still as much as 1.8 billion notes in 2004, whereas this number was down to 1.1 million notes in 2007 (DNB 2008a: 95). Given the lower workload, three of the four branches closed on 1 July 2007 and with Apeldoorn (the former seat of the PVK) due to close in 2010, only the headquarters in Amsterdam will remain (DNB 2008a: 120). In the years to come the DNB will still check between 600 and 800 million banknotes per year mainly to intercept counterfeits; the banking sector will examine and re-circulate the rest. Even though there was a reduction in the workload over this period regarding checking for counterfeits, DNB expects a higher workload when second generation banknotes will be introduced. In these early years DNB would still determine itself from which press to order banknotes (5 euro banknotes from France: Oberthur technologies; the 20 euro bills came from the Dutch printer Joh. Enschede, DNB 2008a: 95). DNB states in its 2007 annual report that it is expected that banknotes will be centrally ordered by the ECB in the years to come. Furthermore, a reorganization of the divisions and number of staff in each division was reviewed and changes were made to reflect the new reality of EMU.

Once a member of the Eurosystem, the Dutch central bank became embedded into this new structure and became responsible for some tasks. An example of this joint sharing of tasks is the management of official external reserves. In 1999 part of the reserves of national central banks was transferred to the ECB. In that year the DNB transferred 5 per cent of gold and reserves (2 million euro). These reserves belong to the ECB but are managed by the national central banks, based on instructions and rules set by the ECB (DNB 2000*a*: 179). In addition, the Dutch central bank still holds reserves that have remained its property. Here too, ECB rules and regulations are in place as to how the DNB may manage these reserves: in some cases, it needs to ask prior approval from the ECB for certain investments (DNB 2000*a*: 179). Finally, there are some tasks of the DNB that have not changed because of its becoming a member of the Eurosystem. For instance, in banking supervision, the DNB is responsible to the national Minister of Finance.

The Bank Act of 1998 also changed some aspects of the checks and balances. Similar to what has been envisaged in the Treaty on European Union, the President of De Nederlandsche Bank is responsible for presenting an annual report, which is subsequently discussed in parliament. Furthermore, the Bank Act envisages that either of the two chambers of parliament could request to meet with the DNB President to be given information about DNB policies and decisions. However, the President of DNB remains independent at all times. In the context of monetary policy setting, the DNB President is not obliged to inform the House of Parliament whether he voted and or how he voted in monetary policy decisions taken in Frankfurt [see Bank Act 1998, Article 18 (2) that stipulates that the President may be asked to provide information without, however, compromising the confidentiality of the monetary policy decisions].

When the Bank Act was revised, it was seen as very important to recognize the historic tradition of the DNB's integral role in Dutch society. A Bank Council ('Bankraad') continued to perform this task. The members of the Bank Council are appointed for a period of four years and represent the composition of Dutch society. Its function is to be a sounding board for the DNB's Governing Board. Another aspect of embedding the DNB in society was the regular communication between its President and the Minister of Finance. For many years the two have had weekly luncheons in which financial and economic matters are discussed. Article 18 of the Bank Act envisages that the Bank and the Minister should maintain regular contact. Thus the weekly lunches were kept intact so as to ensure this regular communication (DNB 2000*a*: 180).

Discussions on corporate governance in the Netherlands led to a law named after the chairperson of the committee (Morris Tabaksblat) who oversaw the formulation of a new law. The so-called 'Code Tabaksblat' (Dutch Corporate Governance Code) consisted of 21 principles of sound corporate governance and 113 best practices. After having been discussed by parliament it was formally adopted on 9 December 2003. The code stipulates that, as of 2004, all companies that are listed on the Dutch stock exchange have to provide details on their corporate governance in their annual report. The Dutch central bank, of course, formally fell outside this law as it is not a listed company. Furthermore it felt that its Bank Act of 1998 for the most part already adhered to the principles of good governance and best practices. Nevertheless, DNB decided to change its statutes so as to reflect the Code Tabaksblat. These changes to the statutes included among other things that the Supervisory Board will periodically review its own performance as well as that of the Governing Board; that the Supervisory Board will draw up a profile of its size and composition; and that the profile of the Supervisory Board will in due course be advertised on the website. On 13 March 2007 DNB's statutes were adjusted to reflect the stipulations of the Code Tabaksblat. The annual report of 2003 for the first time included a chapter (albeit an extremely short—two paged—chapter) on 'corporate governance'. Every annual report since has included a substantial chapter on corporate governance, reporting on best practices, cost performance, meeting targets and objectives, etc. Many of the items reported in this 'corporate governance' chapter of the annual reports conform to what is often captured under the header of 'New Public Management' practices. To give an example, the annual report reporting over the year 2007 indicated the cost target for expenses on personnel as having been 167.2 million euro, whereas the actual expenses had been 168.4 million (up from the 162.7 in 2005 and 168.0 in 2004). Elsewhere in the report DNB reported on how in its recent assessment the 2004 merger had met the objective of enhancing efficiency by cost saving of 25 million euro (DNB 2008*a*: 29). One of the objectives had been to keep full-time equivalent (FTE) staff of the new merged DNB on or below the level of the DNB prior to the merger, which has been achieved. Back in 2001 personnel in both organizations were 1,683 FTE in DNB and PVK 177 which changed to DNB 1,672 and PVK 231 in 2003. By the end of 2004 after the two institutions merged the total FTE for the new DNB was 1,774. Since that date there has been a gradual decline in FTE: 1,685 in 2005; 1,630 in 2006; 1,566 in 2007.

In its aim to increase transparency, DNB, besides publishing an annual report, also issues quarterly bulletins and a statistical bulletin, as well as a host of other publications (including a laymen publication 'DNB Magazine'). In 2000, the use of external communications was revised to reach out more to the general public (e.g. increased use of the website first created in 1997—completely revamped in 2004).

The DNB as Part of the Eurosystem: In Search of a New Purpose

With the entry of the DNB into the Eurosystem and the ESCB a number of important changes occurred. As of 1 January 1999 monetary policy was set in Frankfurt (albeit with the DNB President present and voting on monetary policy decisions). The DNB was quick to note that, contrary to what the Dutch media suggested, it did not completely lose or transfer sovereignty. Indeed, as one interview partner put it: 'Before EMU we were just following policies made in Germany; after we joined the ESCB we once again became part of the group of people that were setting monetary policy' (personal interview with DNB official, Amsterdam, August 2006). In fact, the Dutch central bank had been successfully shadowing German monetary policies and thus, effectively, had not used its national sovereignty to set independent monetary policies (see also Wellink 2008). However, the DNB president Nout Wellink takes part in the deliberations and voting of the governing council that sets monetary policy. In this context, the President Wellink has been stressing the importance of price stability and a stability culture in monetary and budgetary policy, very much following in the footsteps of ECB president Duisenberg. President Wellink has continued along the lines set out in the earlier years as to the direction of monetary policy for the Euro Area. Of course, since entering stage three of EMU the Dutch central bank president has one vote on the governing council, whereas in the 1970s, 1980s, and 1990s the Dutch central bank president mostly followed German monetary policies without having a say over it.

The Treaty on European Union stipulates that monetary policy is a common responsibility of the European System of Central Banks. Following the principles of the Treaty, the DNB defined its new function as support for the monetary policy by providing background information and statistics; in other words, an accurate assessment of market sentiments and expectations (Vanthoor 2005: 326). National central banks carry out a number of tasks that are not necessarily part of the EU Treaty. In some states these tasks are the responsibility of an independent regulatory agency that may or may not be the central bank. The Bank Act of 1998 (Articles 3 and 4) captured the tasks of DNB as follows: define and implement monetary policy; conduct foreign-exchange operations and manage official foreign reserves; provide for the circulation of money (banknotes); promote the smooth operation of the payment system; contribute to the supervision of credit institutions and the stability of the financial system; collecting statistical data and producing statistics. Let us bunch a few of these tasks together and discuss them in turn: (1) to ensure financial stability; (2) banking supervision; and (3) economic advisor to the government. Changes have occurred in each of these areas.

The EU treaty stipulates that the ESCB shall facilitate the conduct of policies by the authorities related to the stability of the financial system. These authorities are still predominantly national, but the ESCB can provide information, best practices, and networking.

The DNB has responded to the new monetary environment by focusing more attention on this aspect of its role. For instance, it produces a biannual Overview of Financial Stability (OFS) in the Netherlands (see DNB 2008b). However, many of the changes in this role relate directly to policies set out by the ECB, whereas others are the result of developments in the financial markets. Recent developments in the real economy suggest that there has recently been less supervision by central banks (than before the start of EMU) because in recent years much of the liquidity creation stays outside the control of central banks. The system therefore is more vulnerable than before to stress. To prepare itself for possible future shocks, the DNB and the Belgian Banking Finance and Security Commission and the Belgian central bank signed a memorandum of understanding in 2006 that envisages close coordination in case of a financial crisis. Likewise in February 2007 DNB and the Dutch minister of Finance agreed to consult one another in case of a financial crisis (DNB 2007: 121). For example, during the 2007–8 credit crunch the DNB took rapid action. It sharpened its control on liquidity (DNB 2008a: 61). Even though there was no risk of a similar development in the Netherlands (there is no sub-prime market for mortgages, by law, mortgages may not be more than 30% of the debt of a household, and only 1% of households have a mortgage interest rate set for less than five years, DNB 2008a: 63), the Dutch financial sector still experienced some of the fall out of the sub-prime crises, as some banks and investors had bad debt.

In the Netherlands banking supervision has been the responsibility of the central bank. The creation of the ESCB was no reason to change this role. Although the start of EMU had virtually no impact, a number of changes to banking supervision have been made related to EU directives (Vanthoor 2006: 340). Two directives came into force in July 2002: the Act on the Supervision of the Credit System (which covers the issuing of electronic money since 1 July 2002); and the Money Transactions Offices Act (simultaneously repealing the 1995 Exchange Offices Act) (DNB 2003: 109). In 2002 a crucial change was made. The Pensions and Insurance Supervisory Authority, which traditionally had been a separate institution, was transferred to the DNB, producing a major impact on the institutional structure of DNB. A new Act was put in place to replace the older one (which had been in place for 50 years). The new Act envisages that the Pensions and Insurance Supervisory Authority become part of the DNB and the new merged organization be named DNB. The latter supervises the entire financial sector (including pensions, insurance, collective investment schemes, exchange offices, and the like, Vanthoor 2006: 340–1). In 2004 this merger was completed. The aim of the merger was to reinforce the grip on financial stability, and to enhance the efficiency and effectiveness of supervision.

Since the creation of EMU the Dutch central bank has been more actively promoting its ability to comment on the state of the Dutch economy and on the policies of the government. It is placing more emphasis on research (cf. DNB 2000b: 25, 29). Also, it has been more focal on socio-economic consultation committees and been more outspoken in the media. Furthermore, the traditional weekly 'lunches' of the President of DNB and the Minister of Finance have kept their important place. The President informs the Minister of Finance about strategic direction of the ECB but they also have conversations about the policy mix of budgetary and fiscal policies on the one hand and monetary policy on the other. They also discuss the situation in the financial system (including the payment system). DNB President also has a seat on advice committees such as the Social Economic Council in which employers and trade unions are also represented and that gives advice to the government on socio-economic policy matters. DNB President Nout Wellink also has a seat in the Council on Economic Issues (Raad voor Economische Aangelegenheden, REA). Overall the role of DNB has not so much contracted but rather changed.

In 2007, the so-called 'Holland Financial Centre' (HFC) was created, in which DNB actively participates (DNB 2008*a*: 61). HFC is an organization that seeks to strengthen an international open financial sector in the Netherlands, whilst maintaining international best practices and keeping costs under control (DNB 2008*a*: 62). The DNB also seeks to increase transparency in its operations.

Conclusion

Financial integration, technological change, and monetary union have affected the functions, structures, and powers of European central banks. Both the National Bank of Belgium and De Nederlandsche Bank played significant roles in the creation of EMU. The National Bank of Belgium played mainly a pace-setting role in the EMU process, whilst De Nederlandsche Bank focused on a role as gate-keeper. During the last decades, the Europeanization of the two central banks gathered momentum. With the EMU process accelerating, the independence of both central banks grew, both in a formal way (adaptation of central bank legislation in line with the Maastricht Treaty) and because of the hardening of the exchange-rate objective. With EMU, the core functions of a central bank—monetary policy, issuing banknotes, managing the gold and foreign-exchange reserves, and organizing the flow of payments—take place within a European framework, in which the National Bank of Belgium and the De Nederlandsche Bank fully participate. Thus, the National Bank of Belgium and the De Nederlandsche Bank retain the functions of central banks, although they now share them with the other central banks of the Euro Area.

Thus in their own ways these two central banks played an important role in Europeanizing central banking in Europe and in creating EMU. Over time their differences were reduced and convergence became the name of the game. In so far as National Bank of Belgium and De Nederlandsche Bank power are concerned, the creation of the ESCB and their participation in the Eurosystem, ironically, enabled them to regain some power lost by their own de facto 'tying one's hands' (following German monetary policies through their exchange-rate objective). With the Belgian and Dutch national central bank president now having a voice in the voting, these two actors have, in a certain sense, gained power.

Furthermore, the National Bank of Belgium and De Nederlandsche Bank play an important role in their respective states' socio-economic affairs, in line with their expertise and their special place between the public sector and the financial world, and in providing both a national and European anchorage. So, both central banks have become 'hybrid' institutions, performing both European and national functions. Furthermore, the National Bank of Belgium and De Nederlandsche Bank are evolving towards more knowledge-oriented tasks and are putting more emphasis on cost control and modern management techniques, a general convergence among central banks.

A noteworthy area is financial stability, where both the National Bank of Belgium and De Nederlandsche Bank have been given more responsibilities, something that contrasts with the evolution in certain other states like Germany and the United Kingdom. So, regarding the responsibilities with respect to financial stability, Belgium and the Netherlands show that there is no convergence among the European central banks.

5

Bank of France: The Challenge of Escaping Politicization

David Howarth

Prior to 1994, the Bank of France could be described as the quiet giant of European central banking. Most comparative studies of central bank independence rank the pre-1994 Bank of France as one of the more dependent in its relationship to government. While responsible for the range of operations typical of central banks and exerting potentially considerable influence on policy making, the Bank was very much in the policy making shadow of the Treasury direction of the Ministry of Finance, which held ultimate control over most aspects of monetary policy and considerable influence in prudential supervision (Goodman 1992; Prate 1987). Establishing its subordinate position in republican policy making, the 1936 and 1945 acts that nationalized the Bank placed it under the 'tutelle' of the Prime Minister's office. While in a weak position in relation to the Treasury, the pre-independence Bank and its Governors firmly asserted the importance of defending the value of the national currency during periods of strong inflationary pressure and refused to accede to certain demands that touched upon the limited range of areas under the Bank's control according to legislation (see Prate 1987 for examples). The Treasury had direct say over monetary policy and dominated credit provision until the financial market liberalization that took place from 1985 onwards. The end of the *encadrement du credit* system—by which the state directed credit provision—and liberalization enhanced the relative power of the Bank by increasing the importance of interest-rate policy, over which the Bank had considerable influence by virtue of its unrivalled capacity to monitor French money supply and inflation (Goodman 1992).

Europeanization has had a significant impact on the power of the Bank of France since the 1970s. The operation of the Exchange Rate Mechanism (ERM) of the European Monetary System (EMS) and the strong (stable) franc policy of the second half of the 1980s and the 1990s reinforced the importance of interest-rate policy and currency reserve management, also controlled by the Bank, although the need to follow closely German monetary policy effectively limited Bank of France (and French government) margin of manoeuvre (Howarth 2001). The German insistence on the privileged position of the EU central bank governors in the negotiations on EMU also reinforced the position of the Bank Governor in relation to the Treasury. Governor Jacques de Larosière, former head of the IMF, played a crucial role in the discussions on EMU leading to Maastricht both as a credible interlocutor of the Bundesbank and through his efforts to convince President Mitterrand and others of the need to accept German demands on independence (Howarth 2001).

This chapter will show that Europeanization since 1993—the independence of the Bank of France in 1994 and the transfer of monetary policy powers to the European Central Bank (ECB) in 1999—had a clear and direct impact on the power and roles of the Governor and the members of the *Conseil de la Politique Monétaire* (CPM), but a less obvious impact on the organization and responsibilities of the Bank itself. Independence and the 1999 transfer have also had a direct impact upon the Bank's role in public life. Well over a decade since independence, monetary policy remains more politicized in France than in most Eurosystem member states, thus bucking the trend of apoliticization (Marcussen chapter). In terms of the Bank's core operations, however, political hostility has created only marginal difficulties.

The Difficult Move to Independence

The failure to move towards apoliticized monetary policy in France is due to history and the politically motivated claim that the monetary policy pursued by the independent Bank of France and then ECB has had a negative impact upon the French economy. Following the Second World War, opposition to the delegation of policy-making powers to autonomous agencies was embedded in a new Republican consensus (Fabre Guillemant 1998). Briefly, there are four additional sources of French aversion to central bank independence: the negative perception of the experience of independence prior to the Second World War, when economically powerful private interests were seen as dominating monetary policy; the belief that control over economic and monetary policy should not be separated; the perception—rooted in the history of French political economy—that low inflationary economic policies could be maintained by democratically elected officials guided by enlightened bureaucrats and advisers; and power considerations within the French administration, notably opposition to independence in the Treasury and the elite network of the Financial Inspectorate.

On various occasions prior to independence, the Bank Governor asserted to governments the importance of price stability and the need to maintain the value of the currency (Koch 1983; Mamou 1988; Patat and Lutfalla 1986; Prate 1987; Valance 1996) and occasionally did so in very stern terms. Yet between 1944 and 1994, the Bank Governor rarely intervened publicly in economic and monetary policy and, when he did, could be sorely rebuked and even replaced, as in 1974 (Prate 1987: 210–11). The precise nature of government control and the legal status of the Bank were not defined in the laws on nationalization. Assertions of autonomy depended upon the personalities involved and the degree to which governments diverged from the goal of monetary stability. A January 1973 law clarified Bank powers and granted it greater scope to modify its monetary mechanisms. The 1973 reform set out certain basic principles, allowing the Bank's General Council free rein in their practical application. However, the reform did not eliminate ultimate State control over monetary policy. Various requests from the Bank of France to gain greater autonomy were opposed by governments and the Treasury (Prate 1987). Pre-1994 relations with the Treasury and debates on monetary policy have been frequently described as difficult, with the Treasury maintaining the final say and considerable influence (Koch 1983; Mamou 1988; Prate 1987).

There was strong political opposition to independence right up to the signing of the Maastricht Treaty in 1991. None of the political parties supported the concept of central bank independence (Balleix-Banerjee 1999). Yet, public opinion was generally in favour of the EMU project and the transfer of monetary policy to the European level. The prioritization of European objectives resulted in French government support for EMU and tolerance of central bank independence. In the context of global ideological trends in favour of independence, EMU created an historic opportunity to overcome strong domestic political and institutional resistance. Moreover, the rapid move to independence at the start of Stage II of the EMU project (1 January 1994) was justified as building confidence in the franc in the context of record levels of speculation, not the desirability of independence per se.

The support threshold necessary to pass legislation on independence was raised even further because the French Constitutional Council initially blocked legislation in 1993 on the basis of a constitutional provision that effectively prevented the delegation of policy-making powers to an independent body. The support of three-fifths of the members of both chambers of parliament was also necessary to modify the constitution to achieve independence. Moreover, two core elements of EMU found in the Maastricht Treaty that block governments from soliciting the central bank on monetary policy and establish price stability as the primary objective of monetary policy were removed from the French law on independence.[1] They were successfully challenged by parliamentarians in the Constitutional Court on the grounds that they contradicted the constitutional principle that the government defines the policy of the country. Nonetheless, the real effect of removing these core elements of the EMU bargain from the French law was negligible because they applied by virtue of the provisions found in the Maastricht Treaty. In the Monetary and Financial Code, which replaced the 1993 law at the start of 2001, the wording of the Statute of the ECB and the ESCB was incorporated and the goal of price stability established as primary for the Bank of France. As with the ECB, no requirement of transparency was imposed upon the Bank of France. Article 3 of the 1993 law grants the CPM the power to determine the conditions according to which its minutes could be made public. The non-renewable, nine-year fixed terms of the six external CPM members and the renewable, six-year fixed terms of the Governor and deputy governors (with an age limit of 65) provided a much stronger guarantee of personal independence than was previously the case—when no guaranteed fixed term was provided.[2]

Politicized Monetary Policy in the Post-Independence Era

Despite the broad support for the EMU project in the French political class and consistent public support for EMU, leading French government and opposition politicians have refused to desist from politicizing monetary policy. From early 1994, Government politicians have repeatedly 'scapegoated' the Bank of France and then the ECB for French economic difficulties—worsened by high interest rates and then a strong euro. A surprising number of both government and opposition politicians have been persistent in their challenge to ECB goals and independence, particularly during electoral periods. Several recent examples can be provided. As Finance Minister, Sarkozy, called for the ECB to adopt a Federal Reserve–style target that includes economic growth (*Financial Times*, 11 June 2004), comments that he repeated as presidential candidate[3] and then President. Proposal 89 of Ségolène Royal's 2007 Socialist Party presidential electoral programme called for the inclusion of an employment creation objective in the ECB's statute.[4] In December 2006, when criticizing the ECB's decision to raise its interest rate, Royal insisted that the Bank be 'submitted to political decisions' because it is not its job 'to order [*commander*] the future of our economies'.[5]

Politicized Appointments to the Conseil de la Politique Monétaire

The French law on independence provided less protection against overtly political appointments than the TEU. Members of the Bank's CPM did not have to have any monetary policy experience—the legal requirement was that proposed candidates have experience and recognized competence in monetary, financial, and economic spheres. This opened the way for highly partisan political appointments, with limited or no technical understanding of monetary policy and central banking—unusual in the Euro Area—which was the norm from 1993 to the early 2000s. Moreover, the process of appointment of the CPM members created the possibility of strongly divergent perspectives on monetary policy-making and a less orthodox Bank leadership than that of the pre-independence Bank of France. Initially (from 1994 to 2002), there were six 'external members' and three 'internal members'. Every three years the President and the prime minister selected two external members from a list of six, with two nominees presented by each of the presidents of the National Assembly, the Senate, and the Economic and Social Council. However, given the reach of the President's and prime minister's influence it can be assumed that at least some of the nominees were pre-approved. On one occasion, the President of the Senate complained publicly that his preferred nominee was not appointed. The President alone selects the three 'internal members': the Governor and two deputy governors. Table 5.1 demonstrates that few of the CPM members had any direct experience of monetary policy making, and few had or have any training in the field.

In the first CPM selected in 1993, only one deputy governor had worked previously in the Bank. Four of the first six external members of the CPM could be labelled uncontroversial supporters of the strong franc policy and EMU. However, the two members nominated by the Euro-sceptic president of the National Assembly, Phillipe Séguin, were known opponents of both the strong franc policy and EMU (see Table 5.1). Three of the following four appointees (between 1994 and 1997) held similar opposing positions. In 1997, in a very overt demonstration of his dislike for Bank independence and the strong franc policy, President Chirac appointed Jean-René Bernard and Pierre Guillen to the CPM—both leading conservative opponents of the Maastricht Treaty and the EMS with strong links to senior neo-Gaullist (RPR) politicians. Chirac ignored the preferences of the centrist and pro-EMU president of the Senate, René Monory, who complained to the press. Thus, from 1997 to 2000, five of the six external members, the majority of CPM members, had previously been opposed to EMS membership, the strong franc policy, central bank independence, EMU, and the Maastricht Treaty. *All six had opposed EMU*. Members of this anti-EMS majority called publicly for a rapid drop in French interest rates (*Le Monde*, 29 November 1996; 21 October 1998). In November 1996, two of the externally appointed members, Marchelli and Gérard, publicly expressed their disapproval of the EMU convergence criteria and argued in favour of an additional criterion emphasizing employment levels (*Le Monde*, 22 and 29 November 1996). Given the necessity of respecting the French government's commitments to the inflation and interest-rate convergence criteria of the Maastricht Treaty, the members of the CPM were unable to modify French policy in any significant way. Moreover, the CPM did not modify its monetary policy strategy (established in 1994) of 2 per cent inflation and M3 targeting, which corresponded to Bundesbank practice. Since 1999, the appointments to the CPM have been less controversial and

Table 5.1. Appointments to the Bank of France's Conseil de la politique monétaire (1994–2007) and Comité Monétaire (2007–present)

	Party affiliation	Professional background	Monetary, financial, or economic experience	Relative monetary policy experience (1–5)*	Position on the EMS and EMU
Name and term dates			**Appointments prior to 1999**		
Jean-Claude Trichet (1993–2003)	RPR (loosely)	Treasury	Head of Treasury	3	?
Hervé Hannoun (1993–2006)	PS	Bureaucrat	Ministerial *cabinet*	4	For
Denis Ferman (to 2000)	N/A	Bank of France	Bank of France	5	?
Michel Sapin (1994–5)	PS	Politics	Minister	3	For
Jean Boissonnat (1994–6)	RPR	Journalism	Writings	1	For
Bruno de Maulde (1994–6)	RPR (loosely)	Public administration (financial)	IMF, stock exchange regulator	3	For
Jean-Pierre Gérard (1994–9)	RPR	Business	Head of company	0	Against
Denise Flouzat (1994–9)	RPR	University	Economist (Asia focus)	2	Against
Michel Albert (1994–2002)	RPR	Business/bank/bureaucracy	Bank	1	Against EMU/pro-strong franc policy
Paul Marchelli (1995–2000)	RPR	White collar Unionism	CGC	0	Against
Jean-René Bernard (1997–2005)	RPR	Ministry of Finance/business/banking	Vice-President bank	3	Against
Pierre Guillen (1997–2005)	RPR	Industry	Industry/CNPF	0	Against
Name and date of appointment			**Appointments since 1999**		
Raymond Douyère (2000–9)	PS	Politics	Head of Financial Committee	1	
Michele Saint-Marc (2000–9)	RPR	Academia	Trained monetary economist	4, but theoretical, not practical	
Jean-Pierre Landau (2006–)	UDF	Bureaucracy/cabinet	International (IMF, EBRD)	2	
Christian Noyer (2003–)	RPR/UDF	Treasury	ECB Vice-President	5	
Phillipe Auberger (2007–)	RPR/UMP	Politics	Head of Financial Committee, National Assembly	3	
Monique Millot-Pernin (2007–)	RPR/UMP	Expert-Comptable	Accountancy	0	
Henri de Richemont (2009–)	RPR/UMP	Politics/Lawyer	None	0	
François Caluarin (2009–)	RPR-UMP	Business	Company Head	0	

*This is an approximate, unscientific, figure based on a consideration of the members' professional careers.

more pro-Maastricht. Nonetheless, they remain noteworthy for their highly political character.

Political allegiance also likely determined the appointment of both Trichet and Christian Noyer as governors (in 1993 and October 2003, respectively). Both had previously served in ministerial cabinets in centre–Right governments. Trichet had been the head of Minister of Finance Edouard Balladur's cabinet (1986–8). Balladur was Prime Minister at the time of Trichet's appointment. Noyer was a technical advisor to Balladur as Finance Minister and then head of the cabinet of two centrist (UDF) ministers of finance in the 1990s, Edmond Alphandéry and Jean Arthuis. There was some speculation in the French press (*Le Monde*, 8 October 2003; 23 October 2003) that the two other leading candidates for the post of governor in 2003 (Hervé Hannoun, the first deputy governor and the candidate publicly endorsed by Trichet as his preferred successor, and Jean-Pierre Jouyet, then Treasury director) lost out in large part because of their proximity to the Left.

The two Bank governors of the post-independence era—Trichet and Christian Noyer (since 2003)—were former heads of the French Treasury (respectively, in 1987–93 and 1993–5) with strong links to the Financial Inspectorate—the financial administrative elite—although Noyer himself is not a member. The result is the continuation of a long-standing tradition according to which Bank legitimacy relies upon credible leadership and reputation for managerial and policy making competence that can only be secured through a high-flying career in the French Ministry of Finance. It is unlikely that this situation will change for many years to come. Senior Bank of France officials whose careers have been entirely within the Bank lack this legitimacy, the personal contacts of top-level Ministry of Finance officials and a public profile. However, the strong career links between the governors and the Treasury (Ministry of Finance) should not indicate a lack of autonomous judgement. Direct experience in central banking has not been prized as a criterion of a strong nominee for governor. Moreover, Noyer's appointment to the ECB's Executive Board in 1998 was unusual, although acceptable according to the ECB statute given his experience in the area of monetary policy. He was the only member of the ECB Governing Council (then 18 members) with no prior direct professional or academic experience in central banking.

The Bank as the Public Defender of Sound Money' and Structural Reform

Prior to independence, Bank of France governors were known for their criticism of government policy, especially during the Fourth Republic. However, most refrained from commenting publicly on government policy-making. Following independence, the Bank had to accommodate itself to a more active and public role in promoting a 'stability culture' in France which is one of the clearest expressions of increased bank power since 1994. Governor Trichet made several thinly veiled attacks on the economic and monetary policy statements of presidential candidates in 1994 and 1995 and regularly critiqued government economic policy decisions which appeared to menace the pursuit of 'sound money' policies, the move to EMU, and respect for the Stability and Growth Pact (Aeschimann and Riché 1996; Milesi 1998). Trichet repeatedly criticized the lack of sufficient structural reforms in France. He attacked the new Plural Left's brief freeze on deficit cutting (*Le Monde*, 25 June 1997), the 35-hour week policy (*Le Monde*, 13 December 1997), and in 1999 its handling of the unexpected budget windfall: 'How is it possible to have a windfall when we have debts' (cited in Patat 2003: 110, ft. 1, author's translation). Indeed, in his final public letter to President Chirac as Governor, Trichet urged the President to push for lower public spending and undertake structural reforms *(Financial Times*, 3 August 2003). In June 2004, in response to Sarkozy's attack on the ECB for targeting a very low inflation rate, the Bank of France published a response by Governor Noyer defending the policy in several leading newspapers (*Le Monde*, 13 June 2004). Noyer's concern about rising French government deficit and debt were expressed publicly on several occasions. Most notably, the Bank joined forces with *Insée* (the national institute for statistics and economic studies) and the national court of auditors (the *Cour des comptes*) to produce a succession of reports in June 2004 to express dismay at the state of public finances and to insist on the need for ongoing structural reform. The personal style of the Governor is likely to be of some significance in determining the public profile of the Bank of France. Since his appointment in 2003, Christian Noyer has intervened much less in the national debate on government spending and economic policy than his predecessor.[6]

The Bank attempted to respond to government attacks on its monetary policy by appealing directly to the French public. A 1998 poll by Sofres (27–29 May), undertaken on behalf of the Bank of France and published in the *Le Monde* newspaper, showed that 58 per cent of French people approved of the strong franc (or stable franc) policy, a result that nearly matched the results of a June 1996 poll (56%) which was also published with the 1998 results (*Le Monde*, 2 July 1998). Moreover, four years after independence, 74 per cent of those polled had a positive impression of the Bank (5% 'very much' and 69% 'rather positive'), which is an accomplishment for an institution that was rarely in the public eye prior to 1994. The relatively strong economic growth of 1998 no doubt helped boost these support figures. Only 15 per cent had a negative opinion (12 'rather negative' and only 3 'very negative') with 11 per cent 'without opinion'. On the strong/stable franc policy, only 15 per cent were opposed to the policy and 27 per cent did not have any opinion. French public opinion was thus supportive (or at least tolerant) of the need to maintain low inflation. Trichet, as Governor and then as ECB president, used these polls on several occasions to defend ECB policies within France. The polls also suggest that French public opinion has been at odds with the French political class.

Ongoing Debate on the Bank's Powers

The Bank of France holds all the responsibilities typical of national central banks in addition to several less typical or atypical roles. Since 1999, the Bank ensures the smooth operation of the payments system and the security of financial transactions; monitors the security of the banking system and the stability of the financial markets; conducts bank inspections; runs the committee responsible for granting licenses to new credit institutions and allowing bank mergers; contributes to the drafting of regulations on credit institutions; collects and analyses French monetary, financial, and economic data, including balance of payments data; produces three annual growth and inflation forecasts; manages French exchange reserves, including gold; and provides banking services to individual clients. Independence and EMU have had only marginal impact on these core responsibilities of the Bank. The services of the Bank—notably the Macroeconomic Studies directorate—provide the Governor with quality expert advice on the state of the national and international economy and price developments. Since 1999, they do so to enable him to make competent recommendations on Euro Area monetary policy. The Bank also has a range of atypical roles, two of which it has developed or been assigned since 1999. It provides—uniquely in the Eurosystem—a port of entry to non-EU banks that want to set up euro-accounts; and it provides advice on personal debt management.

Prudential Supervision

The Bank of France has long been the centre of intelligence in the French state on the national banking sector and the financial markets. Prior to 1994, the Treasury's control over prudential supervision—via the Banking Commission chaired by the Governor of the Bank of France but under the '*tutelle*' or control of the Treasury—rested on expertise within the Bank. The latter provided most of the salaried staff to the Banking Commission on temporary secondment (approximately 400 officials at any time) and most of the detailed information about the banking sector by carrying out operational supervision. In 1994, the autonomy of the Banking Commission from the government was established in law, while the Treasury's influence was retained through a single vote on the Banking Commission's governing board of seven members (five of which are nominated by the Minister of Finance). In terms of the day-to-day operation of banking supervision, little changed because of Bank of France independence. However, the elimination of the Treasury's '*tutelle*' ensured the reinforcement of the Governor's leadership position as Commission president with a deciding vote.

This leadership role has been seen in dealing with major problems in the French banking sector, as in the difficulties at *Société Général* of unprecedented losses caused by a single trader. In January 2008, the head of the bank, Daniel

Bouton, met with Christian Noyer who, in effect, chaired a secret crisis committee that also included the head of the Financial Market Authority (Gérard Rameix) to decide how to deal with the massive fraud in the bank and when to make the information public. For a period of five days (19–23 January), in his capacity as President of the Banking Commission and Governor, Noyer discussed the difficulties with Bouton and Rameix without informing the government (let alone other members of the Banking Commission). Despite the Bank's long-standing role in prudential supervision, prior to independence the Governor never played such a central role in the management of a major banking crisis.

Some (*Cour des Comptes* 1996) see the continued influence of the Ministry of Finance, via the selection of five Banking Commission board members and the voting position of the Treasury representative, as unacceptable. Other observers would prefer the elimination of the Commission altogether and the transfer of prudential supervision (indeed, all responsibility for monitoring the financial markets) to the central bank, as in the Netherlands and Belgium. France is one of the few countries in the world with shared control over prudential supervision that involves several public bodies, including the Ministry of Finance. The French Court of Auditors (*Cour des Comptes*) (1996 and 2005) and the National Assembly's and Senate's Finance Committees (Auberger 1996) have called for the full transfer of prudential supervision to the Bank of France as one possible preferred option.

However, transfer to the Bank of France is not the only recommended option. Both the *Cour des Comptes* (1996) and the National Assembly's Finance Committee (Auberger 1996; *Le Monde*, 29 June 1996) called for increased autonomy and capacity for the Banking Commission: the removal of the Treasury representative; the diversification of the recruitment of the Commission's staff (thus decreasing the reliance on the Bank of France); the increased representation in the Commission's decision-making body of members with direct experience in the banking or business sectors (since 1993, only two of the seven members of the Commission necessarily have expertise in the banking and financial sector); the reinforcement of the collegial body in relation to the Commission's Secretariat (dominated by the Bank of France officials) so that the collegial body can gain greater direct control over the process of banking supervision; and the assignment of legal personality to the Commission so that it can pursue banking supervision cases in the courts if necessary.

Thus, the future reform of prudential supervision in France will not necessarily result in a reinforced role for the Bank. An option closer to the British and German models of an autonomous agency might be preferred. Nonetheless, the National Assembly's Finance Committee (1996) also accepted the logic of maintaining a strong link between the central bank and the Banking Commission: 'The role of the Bank in adjusting the liquidity of the entire banking system imposes on the Bank a surveillance role of the liquidity of financial institutions. There is thus a certain logic in assigning Bank of France officials the job of prudential control of banks' (Auberger 1996, author's translation). Banking supervision officials within the Bank (interviews 28 January 2008) insist that the present organization of supervision works well and that full transfer to the Bank is not necessary. Rather, a clarification of certain rules of intervention (as with the difficulties in the *Société Générale*) would be helpful. Another option is the transfer of prudential supervision to the ECB or, at least the transfer of supervision over financial institutions with a strong presence in other EU member state markets. Senior officials in the Bank of France were opposed to this transfer as unnecessary. However, the unofficial position in the bank has shifted and there is growing support for the transfer of some responsibility for prudential supervision to the ECB (interviews 28 January 2008).

Other Roles

Since 1984, the Bank of France Governor has held the presidency of the CECEI (*Comité des établissements de crédit et des entreprises d'investissement*), the body in charge of granting individual licenses and authorizations to credit institutions and investment firms and responsible for approving banking mergers, and 1 of 12 votes on the Committee (another is held by the Treasury Director). Since the CECEI's creation in 1984, the Bank has been one of its principal sources of information and advice, in addition to the Financial Markets Authority (*Autorité des Marchés Financiers*), the French stock market regulator. Moreover, since 1984 the Bank has been in charge of the CECEI's Secretariat. As such it prepares the examination of applications submitted to the Committee. Independence has not had any significant impact on the role of the Bank in this body.

Since 1994, the Bank has also had full responsibility over surveillance of the security of the payment systems, a responsibility possessed prior to 1994 under the '*tutelle*' of the Minister of Finance. From 2001, the Governor gained control over the presidency of the newly established *Observatoire des cartes de paiement*.

The Bank's legitimacy in these areas—banking supervision, financial sector supervision, payments systems, and credit cards—rests upon its unrivalled monetary, financial and economic data, and well-established capacity for analysis. It also exercises a range of functions that in other EU member states are either conducted by the state or left to the private sector. The Bank manages the circulation of fiduciary money, provides a service to analyse local economic development, and is engaged in personal debt management for individuals faced with excessive debt. This unwanted responsibility for personal debt management—'*surendettement*'—was imposed on the Bank in 2006 by the government, which pays the bank for the service. Personal debt management became the central role of 1,300 bank staff members—approximately 10 per cent of the total—and several of the regional branches that were not closed in the 'downsizing' from 2003 to 2006, which also explains why staff and branch cuts during

121

this period were not as large as initially intended. This new social role consists of helping those who are refused bank accounts/credit to sort out their financial affairs. The relatively large number of responsibilities assigned to the Bank of France—and *'surendettement'* in particular—has attracted criticism from the *Cour des Comptes* (2005) which has called for the Bank to be allowed to concentrate on its core tasks.

Down-Sizing at the Bank of France

Prior to 2004, the Bank was not a model of cost-effective public-sector management, which weakened the strength of its calls for structural reform and public-sector staff cuts. The Bank has long suffered from a problem of over-employment and very generous social provisions for its staff including a special pension regime. Prior to independence, the Bank engaged in hesitant cuts, watered down in the face of determined union action and the opposition of local politicians, who baulked at staff cuts in regional branches or their closure. Bitter and lengthy strikes were sparked by reform attempts in 1974 and again in 1987, which led to the resignation of one of the deputy governors. The weakness of New Public Management ideas in the French administration also helps to explain the failure to adopt efficiency enhancing reforms—such as the outsourcing of certain technical functions as in Sweden—which could have also achieved staff cuts. In 2003, the total staff (included seconded staff) reached 15,755. Independence and the transfer of monetary policy in 1999 exposed Bank inefficiency to greater public and government criticism. This criticism intensified when, in 2002 and 2003, the Bank ran deficits. In February 2003, a Bank of France report called for the closure of three-quarters of its regional branches (166 out of 211), over a period of three years, with 3,200 job cuts (out of 9,000 in the branches), amounting to nearly one-third of the Bank's annual budget. A second report called for the elimination of services for individual clients.

Cuts have been significant but were less ambitious than those initially called for by the Bank's own management and other government sources: from 2003 to end-2006, 2,200 jobs were cut leaving 13,500 staff and 120 branches were closed (less than the three-quarters called for) leaving 91 branches. The dilution of cuts allowed the Bank to avert major strikes. Firings were avoided with early retirement packages, which transferred costs onto pension provision. However, the Bank achieved an operational profit in 2006 for the first time in many years. Sixteen of the remaining 91 branches were transformed into 'local economic observatories', debt management centres, or money sorting centres. In December 2005, after 18 months of difficult negotiations, the Bank achieved a major reform to its special pension plan. Further cuts are likely. In its 2005 report, the *Cour des Comptes* recommends the closure of additional branches and insists that the Bank remains over-staffed and suffers from a particularly high unit labour cost in relation to other comparable administrations and from excessively generous social policies. While it is difficult to present the Bank of France as a model of public-sector reform, some observers, notably trade-union officials representing Bank staff, have pointed to the Bank's strong financial position since 2005—due to cuts, the strength of its investments, and the sale of gold—to argue that the internal reform was excessively brutal, stretching the staff available for some Bank services—notably debt management (*Le Monde*, 19 January 2006).

The *Cour des comptes* (2005) and the Finance Committee of the National Assembly also criticized the continued existence of the Conseil de la Politique Monétaire, a body without an obvious role following the transfer of monetary policy to the ECB at the start of 1999 and the independence of the Bank Governor in determining his stance on ECB monetary policy. Responding to these criticisms, in 2002 the government reduced the number of external members to four and then, in 2005, to two. In 2007, the de Villepin Government adopted a law transforming the CPM into the Comité Monétaire (Monetary Committee) consisting of seven members (Governor, two deputies, and four independent 'experts', nominated by the presidents of the National Assembly and Senate). The independent 'experts' are paid only expenses, and their advisory role is emphasized. The 'experts' can also hold other posts (although not in parliament and government), whereas the external members of the CPM could not. The Monetary Committee has continued to attract criticism as an unnecessary body. Officially, it is responsible for examining monetary developments, analysing the implications of Eurosystem monetary policy and adopting necessary measures to transpose ECB decisions into the Bank of France. In 2008, Senator Jean Arthuis, the former financial minister, unsuccessfully sought an amendment to the Economic Modernisation Law, with the explicit aim of eliminating the Monetary Committee. The negligible relevant specialist knowledge of the external members of the Committee remains a problem; only one of the current four external members has any prior professional experience linked to monetary policy. The members are also part of Bank's General Council and thus perform a more general managerial role. The public and media presence of the Monetary Committee members is also very limited—a noteworthy difference from the members of the Bundesbank's Executive Board, not to mention the Bank of England's Monetary Policy Committee.[7]

The Failure to Develop the Bank's Research Capacity

The Bank of France has long possessed a strong capacity for data collection and analysis, which Bank officials argue is unrivalled by other Eurosystem central banks. Through its regional offices, the Bank collects detailed monetary, financial, and economic data and information on French companies that is unavailable to other French and international institutions, and thus has an unrivalled understanding of price developments in France. This data is analysed within the well-staffed and resourced Macroeconomic Studies Directorate of the Bank to produce a detailed monthly update on the state of the French economy. The Bank's capacity to produce growth and inflation forecasts distinguish it from many of its peers, which as in Italy and the UK, rely on Ministry of Finance forecasts. The Macroeconomic Studies Directorate also includes staff who analyse international economic trends. Interlocutors at the Bank claim that the credibility of their Governor's discourse in ECB Governing Council meetings on the impact of international economic developments and the development of prices depends on this analytical capacity and gives the Governor more influence in relation to his peers. There are, however, obvious chinks in the mail of the Bank's analytical armour, as demonstrated by the lead role assumed by the Bundesbank and Banca d'Italia in developing and managing the shared computer platform for TARGET 2—which suggests their superior expertise.

In November 2007, for the first time, the Bank published its own updated growth forecast for the year (2007), which in effect updated and corrected the government's own forecast. Bank staff see this development as a small but significant assertion of the Bank's independence (interviews 28 January 2008; 30 January 2008). In early 2008, the Bank published for the first time its own growth forecast for the year ahead (the Bundesbank began the same practice for Germany in late 2007). Bank of France staff argue that different analyses by the Ministry of Finance and the Bank of France, based on their individual models, result in different forecasts and mutual and productive criticism. The publication of Bank of France figures also serves as a useful counterpoint to politically manipulated government figures. The government, relying on Ministry of Finance analysis of data collected by the national statistical agency, INSEE, publishes the more optimistic upper range economic growth figures, whereas the Bank of France publishes a 'forchette' of upper and lower forecasted rates. Given the Bank's monthly economic studies, it is also in a better position to provide accurate forecast updates than the government.

In juxtaposition to its capacity to conduct statistical and macroeconomic analysis, the Bank is very weak in academic research output, which in turn weakens the intellectual power of the Bank in the 'competition of ideas' in the Eurosystem and its weight in discussions on growth and inflation forecast models. Although a research division was first created in the bank in 1909, there is little tradition of academically oriented research at the Bank. According to one leading historian of the Bank (Olivier Frietag, interview 28 January 2008), the Bank's hierarchy has had little respect for academically oriented research. No top official in the Bank has a background in advanced economic research. Many are graduates of the elite Ecole Polytechnique: they possess a strong analytical capacity that is not, however, academically and theoretically oriented. Bank careers are developed through practical training in a diverse range of the

Bank's activities. With more open recruitment and career progression proced-ures in place, this situation may change with time. There have been no powerful directors of research, who might have been able to attract increased resources. Moreover, the governors, drawn from the Ministry of Finance, possess little academic training and thus limited appreciation of the importance of academic economic research. Governor Noyer, with his experience of top-quality research at the ECB, might be different in this regard, but his appointment did not result in any significant increase in research capacity at the Bank. The small number of Bank staff members with PhDs is in marked contrast to the central banks in many other countries. Several Bank officials also commented on the historic weakness of economic research in France—and notably the weakness of market-oriented research—and the tendency for some of the country's best academic economists to seek training and employment in the United States.

Those working in the Research Directorate of the Bank claim (interviews 28, 30, 31 January 2008) that, following independence, the Bank directors recog-nized that the lack of research output damaged the credibility of the Bank as an independent policy making authority and its influence within the Eurosystem. They deliberately set about to increase the output of research publications that could be accessed outside the Bank. However, the officials interviewed also note that the desire to gain a reputation for the production of academically excellent research has not been supported by a willingness to provide increased financial resources. The financial difficulties of the early 2000s and the power of trade unions that have made the reallocation of resources from the branches to the centre difficult provide additional explanations for this failure. The more academically oriented output of the Bank is limited; the number of peer-reviewed academic journal articles published by Bank staff remains very low in comparison to central banks in the other large EU member states. The reputation of the Bank's research in international banking and academic circles is very weak. It has few research staff: in 2008 only approximately 17 full-time researchers work in the Bank's Research Directorate and publish work in aca-demic journals. The Bank organizes relatively few conferences, although the number has increased since 2000 and four were held in 2007 and 12 in 2008. It is not yet seen as an important centre of debate, discussion on macroeconom-ics and monetary economics. There is some concern for this weakness in French political circles. A French Senate report (May 2001) criticized the con-tribution of the Bank to economic research.

The Bank has undertaken a partial response with a small increase in the number of research staff, although repeated requests from the head of the Research Directorate for more researchers have been rebuffed. Increased efforts have been made to develop links with academic institutions notably through the co-hosting and co-funding of conferences. In early 2008 the Bank was in the process of finalizing a link with an internationally renowned research centre on firms at the University of Toulouse, through which the Bank will finance and be associated with top-level academic research—albeit research that is not connected to monetary policy. In 1995, the Bank of France created a research foundation which provides funding for visiting scholars researching on monetary, financial and banking economics and conferences. The funding, however, has been limited to date. Since 1997, the Foundation has allocated just over one million euros to 48 research projects (to 2008) undertaken by academics from universities based in a number of countries.

All the interlocutors at the Bank accepted that their employer suffers from a weak presence in both national and international discussions and debates on economic developments, despite the occasional interventions of the Governor. Since 1994, the Bank has made some efforts to improve its public profile with new publications, targeted principally at financial journalists and economists working in central banks and the financial sector. The Bank began a working paper series in 1994 (*Notes d' Étude et de Recherche*, NER) published in French and English, with Bank staff writing in a personal capacity but subject to quality validation by other qualified Bank staff. Only one paper was published in 1994 and none in 1995, but the number has increased considerably since then, with 23 published in 2006 and 30 in 2007. By April 2008, 203 working papers had been published. The working papers are written by the full-time researchers but, more often, by officials who engage in applied research for the Bank (forecasting, macroeconomic, balance of payments, and statistical analysis) in the Macroeconomic Studies Directorate. From 2002, annually or biannually, the Bank publishes a *Revue de la Stabilité Financière*, with papers by Bank staff, other French and foreign public- and private-sector officials and leading academic economists, writing on major financial and monetary issues for a non-academic audience, principally finance sector professionals. For example, the April 2007 issue focused on the impact of hedge funds on financial stability and included articles by top central bank officials (from the Federal Reserve Board, ECB Executive Board, and national central banks), leading economists from the London School of Economics and University of Chicago, and major private-sector financial companies.

The present first deputy governor, Jean-Pierre Landau, with experience in the European Bank for Reconstruction and Development (EBRD) and inspired by Bank of England practice, has been a key advocate of improving the communication strategy of the Bank. In 2006, he launched what the Bank labelled its 'publicly oriented' economic debate series: 'Debats Economiques' Occasional Papers series (five to date). In 2007, the Bank also launched 'Documents et débats' (only one to date on whether the euro was inflationist) to address major economic issues in a 'simple but serious manner' but also ensure accessibility to a wider audience (interview 28 January 2008). No other editions are in the pipeline, however, because of Bank sensitivities about covering controversial topics (interviews 30, 31 January 2008). The head of publications at the Bank (interview 30 January 2008) believes that not enough is done to disseminate the impressive data that it collects, for example on national companies. Other efforts have been made to increase the public presence of bank officials in national economic debates. Deputy Governor Landau served on the Attali Commission, examining reforms to stimulate French economic growth. The head of the Macroeconomic Studies Directorate, Gilbert Sette, is a serving member of the Prime Minister's Council for Economic Analysis.

Conclusions: Europeanization, Power, and Convergence

The operations of the Bank of France have been shaped by Europeanization since the 1970s. The strong franc policy of the 1980s and 1990s, the increased importance of interest-rate policy and currency management, owed a great deal to the influence of the German preference for 'sound money' and the low inflation bias of the EMS and the EMU project. Intensified international financial pressures through increased capital flows and the rising exposure of the French economy to non-EU investment further increased the importance of interest rate and currency management. Thus, both Europeanization and international pressures encouraged convergence to the German standard and increased the power of Bank of France in relation to the Treasury prior to independence. The EMU project was the catalyst for independence which in turn enhanced the role and power of the Bank of France governor in a range of bank activities—notably in his chairmanship and voting role on banking supervision and financial sector accreditation and competition—and in national and EU-wide public debate on economic policy and structural reform. Europeanization brought about convergence in the monetary policy strategy of the Bank of France, which—emulating the Bundesbank—in 1994 adopted a two pillar monetary policy targeting inflation and M3 (rather than the M2 targeted previously). EMU has allowed the Bank to engage in some specialized operations. Notably, it provides, uniquely in the Eurosystem, a port of entry to non-EU banks that want to set up euro-accounts. However, apart from the obvious transfer of monetary policy to the ECB, Europeanization since 1994 has had only limited impact on the core operations of the bank.

As the pre-EMU Bank of France lacked the policy making, research, and public role possessed by the Bundesbank and the Banca d'Italia, EMU did not result in the diminished power and status that the German and Italian central banks have suffered in the domestic context because of the transfer of monetary power and research capacity to the ECB. Prior to 1994, the Bank of France sought to influence monetary policy decisions decided upon by the Treasury. However, the power of both French institutions were constrained by the need to follow monetary policy set by the Bundesbank. Attempts by the French government in 1993 to challenge the anchor role of the Deutschmark in the ERM failed (Howarth 2001). Since 1999, the Bank of France Governor is free of

both Treasury control and Bundesbank diktat. France has lost monetary autonomy but the Bank of France has gained an important autonomous voice in
setting Eurosystem monetary policy.

Independence transformed the Bank of France into an autonomous public
actor able to express views on—and often indirect criticism of—government
policy. The Bank has made some—albeit limited—effort to increase its publication output. The Bank's publication of its own growth forecasts—undertaken
by few EU NCBs—can be seen as an expression of its independence. Yet the
Bank's public role has been limited since 1999, which is surprising given its
independence, the diversity of its roles, and its relative size—it employs more
people than any other EU NCB. All officials interviewed at the Bank agree that
the independent Bank of France, as a non-majoritarian institution, should be
cautious in its public role and in its dealings with government and, while
recommending reform, should refrain from direct criticism of government
policy. Since 1999, Europeanization has allowed the Bank to side-step much
of the persistent politicization of monetary policy and central banking in
French politics: French politicians direct most of their antagonism at the
ECB. However, French governments have continued to express frustration
with activities of the Bank of France when they contradict government preferences—as with the handling of the difficulties at the *Société Générale*. Based on
its 1996 and 1998 opinion polls, the Bank appears to have achieved a measure
of public support for its operations, at least in monetary policy. However, these
polls are now dated, and the Bank has not revealed if it has undertaken more
recent soundings of public opinion on its operations since the transfer of
monetary policy in 1999.

There has been a limited degree of convergence with the operations found
in other Eurosystem central banks. With independence and the loss of monetary policy making powers, the Bank of France has faced intensified pressure
to downsize and staff cuts have been significant. However, typical of French
public administration, the Bank of France has long suffered from overstaffing,
inefficiencies, and failed reform efforts due to a strong trade union presence.
When staff cuts came they were diluted and far less severe than those faced by
the Bundesbank. The Bank maintains the largest staff of the EU central banks
and the greatest diversity of roles. The Bank's currently (to 2009) stable
financial situation enables it to resist pressure from the government and the
Cour des Comptes to downsize further in the near future, unless the Bank
manages to shed unwanted tasks, notably '*surendettement*'. On the core operations of the Bank, Europeanization has had a limited effect of convergence.
Unlike the Banca d'Italia which has shed its atypical roles, the Bank of France
continues to perform a range of functions not held by most other EU central
banks and has gained some responsibilities since 1994—for example on '*surendettement*'. There is some pressure from elements within the French administration to reform banking supervision to move to either an autonomous

regulatory body as in the UK and more recently Germany or the full transfer of supervisory powers to the central bank as in Dutch/Belgian model. However, the *sui generis* French system of banking supervision is likely to persist for some time given that it has already survived over a decade and a half of high-profile bank failures and the Treasury is reluctant to surrender its role. The failure of the Bank of France to reinforce its research capacity is particularly surprising given the relevance of research to national central bank influence in the Eurosystem. Some Bank of France officials suggest (interviews 28 January 2008; 30 January 2008) that the impressive data collection and analysis and the relative importance of the French economy in the Euro Area ensures the Bank sufficient influence.

Notes

1. Law no. 93-980, 4 August 1993. LOI no. 93-980 du 4 août 1993 relative au statut de la Banque de France et à l'activité et au contrôle des établissements de crédit.
2. Prior to independence, Governors had no guarantee of longevity and no fixed mandate of sufficient length to protect their independence. Nonetheless, Bank Governors generally occupied their post for long periods: seven years for Jacques de Larosiere (1987–93) and six years for Renaud de la Genière (1978–84). Even so, politics intervened regularly. The Socialists removed De la Genière, and Olivier Wormser had only a short mandate.
3. *'Sarkozy wants "protective EU" to offset globalisation'*, Euroactiv.com, Friday, 23 February 2007, updated Wednesday 28 February 2007, http://www.euractiv.com/en/elections/sarkozy-wants-protective-eu-offset-globalisation/article-161948, accessed on 10 March 2007.
4. The Socialist candidate appears not to have noticed that the ECB already has this as a secondary goal.
5. The precise wording that the Socialist 2007 presidential candidate used was 'soumise à des décisions politiques' *(Le Monde,* 22 December 2006).
6. Bank officials interviewed and journalists have put this down to Noyer's personality, described as lacking the charisma of Trichet, timid, secretive, and averse to risk *(Le Monde*, 23 October 2003). Difficult internal reform at the Bank—of which Noyer had to take charge immediately following his appointment—might have encouraged him to engage in a less public role. Indeed, Trichet, as ECB president, has been more actively engaged in French public debate, appearing several times on high-profile French television and radio talk shows to deflect blame for French economic difficulties from the ECB's monetary policies and the strong euro and to call for further domestic structural reform.
7. In a rare exception to this absence from the media, the four external members of the Monetary Committee published a short newspaper article (written collectively) on possibilities open to France and the Bank of France to respond at the national level to the financial crisis ('Solutions à la crise: commençons en France', *Le Monde*, 21 March 2008). One looks in vain for biographical information on the Bank of France's website for information about these four officials which suggests their negligible role.

6

German Bundesbank: Europeanization and the Paradoxes of Power

Kenneth Dyson

The creation of the Eurosystem in 1998–9 represented a critical juncture in the history of the German Bundesbank, of a kind not experienced by any other national central bank. Under German law it retained some independent international and national responsibilities. The Bundesbank acted as banker for the German government, participated in banking supervision, managed Germany's foreign exchange reserves, decided on gold sales, and represented Germany in the International Monetary Fund. However, with the disappearance of the D-Mark and the loss of its monetary policy-making responsibility to the ECB, the Bundesbank had irrevocably ceded power and status. It lost its international status as the second most important central bank in the world and its premier central banking status in Europe through management of the anchor currency of the Exchange-Rate Mechanism (ERM), the so-called 'D-Mark Zone' (Apel 2003; Heipertz 2001; Loedel 1999a). In a complex reshuffling of power the Bundesbank lost relative power over other actors in European monetary policy making, whilst—paradoxically—the ECB represented a unique extension of its structural power over the terms of debate through institutionalization of the ECB on the basis of Bundesbank ideas and practices. The Bundesbank could claim to be the model on which the ECB had been designed (Dyson and Featherstone 1999; Heisenberg 1999; Kaltenthaler 1998).

Domestically, the Bundesbank could no longer be characterized as the 'fourth branch of government' (Kennedy 1991: 3) or a 'state within the state' (Berger and De Haan 1999). Its symbolic importance as the embodiment of post-war German economic success in delivering a 'hard' currency, around which Germans could retrieve lost pride, and its model character as a European central bank in securing price stability seemed destined to be consigned to historical memory and nostalgia. In becoming an integral part of the

Eurosystem and ceding its core responsibility for monetary policy making to the ECB, the Bundesbank faced difficulties in claiming to be *primus inter pares* amongst NCBs, let alone 'the bank that rules Europe' (Marsh 1992). Its president has only one voice and vote amongst 21 in the Governing Council of the ECB, and its core role in the Eurosystem was defined as 'partnership' (Deutsche Bundesbank 2004).

The Bundesbank's claim to a *Vorreiterrolle* in the Eurosystem had to rest on more than just its unique role in the history of European monetary unification, the relative size of the German economy (accounting for over 40% of the total euro cash in circulation), its weight as the biggest subscriber to the capital of the ECB, and its past superior experience and reputation in managing stability-oriented monetary policies and securing a 'stability culture'. More challengingly, to be a convincing model, the Bundesbank had to invest and renew its remaining functions with high-quality research in order to establish a reputation for top-quality expertise in the new competition of ideas within the Eurosystem (Remsperger 2002, 2004; Weber 2006*a*). It focused on refinements to the ECB monetary policy strategy (notably its 'monetary' pillar, which had been relegated to second pillar status in 2003) and to analysis of risks in financial stability. In addition, the Bundesbank concentrated on excelling in the more 'nuts-and-bolt' areas of modernizing cash management, developing and managing platforms for new pan-European payment and settlement systems (TARGET2 in particular), and banking supervision (notably in negotiating and applying Basle II). This challenge derived not just from a more competitive environment of policy ideas but also from the past reliance of the Bundesbank on its monetary policy performance rather than the quality of its analytical economic modelling, compared for instance to the Banca d'Italia. Its traditional advocacy of a principles-based approach exposed it to critiques of a lack of analytical capacity. In this respect, Axel Weber's appointment as president was important.

The Bundesbank could draw on its strengths in representation of Germany's economic and financial size and its sense of a special vocation to safeguard the Bundesbank legacy of stability to the Euro Area and to promote a long-term culture in financial markets. However, in its new core functional areas, and constraining its development of quality research, it could lay claim to neither the glamour and the gravitational attraction nor the autonomy of action that it had earlier enjoyed in its monetary policy-making function. It faced a new difficult challenge of credibility building across a range of functions to which it had earlier accorded a relatively low strategic profile. In meeting this challenge the Bundesbank's room for manoeuvre was tightly constrained by a more assertive Federal Finance Ministry and by an ambitious ECB Executive Board. Its flank was exposed to German political claims, especially from Social Democratic Federal Finance Ministers, that central bank independence was a less relevant principle outside monetary policy making, for instance, in banking supervision.

This radical change to its functions, and to the structure of opportunities and constraints within which it operated, exposed the Bundesbank to new, continuing public questioning and need to justify its existence. Along with internal reforms and downsizing (between 1991 and 2007 from 16,500 to 11,160 staff and from 202 to 47 branches), it produced profound, disquieting effects on institutional self-confidence and morale and heightened internal conflicts. The Bundesbank experienced a period of defensiveness, introversion, and identity crisis that further threatened its capacity to rebuild credibility and to project a strong shaping presence in the Eurosystem. The ECB could offer higher salaries and more challenging posts to attract the young stars of central banking, on the Bundesbank's doorstep in Frankfurt; whilst the Bundesbank had to make big staffing cuts and in 2006 lost the inducement of special salary bonuses.

The Bundesbank's problems came to a head under the presidency of Ernst Welteke (1999–2004) when internal dissensions over structural reform, and also over use of its gold reserves, along with setbacks to its ambitions to develop its role in banking supervision and financial stability, distracted and weakened the institution within the Eurosystem. The resignation of Welteke proved a cathartic experience, after which Axel Weber sought to develop a sharper profile by consolidating the bank around himself in a more centralizing style than ever before and by pursuing a new image of the central bank as a leader in public-sector modernization. However, the age of powerful Bundesbank presidents like Otmar Emminger (1977–80) and Hans Tietmeyer (1993–8) was ended. Centralizing Bundesbank internal reforms to support the new personal responsibility of the president in ECB monetary policy and to expedite internal managerial reforms failed to halt the decline in Bundesbank profile or to restore team spirit.

The Bundesbank's central problem in redefining a new identity was how to adjust to a major reconfiguration of its power relationships at international, EU, and domestic levels. EMU was just a part of this reconfiguration but one that accelerated adjustment pressures. The following five developments coincided:

- A marked increase in the rate of innovation, in complexity and in opacity in global financial markets. Market developments included the growth in derivative contracts and options, the use of new investment vehicles by banks to offload risk finance, and the emergence of hedge funds and private equity companies as major non-bank players in creating liquidity. These developments confronted the Bundesbank with mounting pressures to be less cautious in its attitudes to financial market liberalization, with new challenges in controlling money supply growth and in monetary analysis, and with new systemic risks to financial stability. This context made the Bundesbank keen to protect the traditional German three-pillar financial system of commercial, cooperative, and public savings banks. It sought to frame financial market liberalization as promoting consolidation *within* each pillar (welcoming the Commerzbank take over of the Dresdner Bank and Deutsche bank of the Postbank); whilst ensuring that retention of the 'narrow' bank concept in the latter two pillars would help retain a strong element of long-term culture in German financial markets that would support a high savings rate.

- The impact of IT and new public management ideas on the provision of central banking services, notably in on-line banking, electronic payment systems, and internal performance-related practices. The Bundesbank was forced to reconsider its essential core functions, which functions could be in whole or part outsourced to the private sector, notably in cash management, and above all staff cuts and less hierarchical working.

- The loss of its role as the 'bank that rules Europe' in monetary policy making (Marsh 1992) to the ECB and the ECB directorate's ambition to centralize functions like banking supervision and payment systems. The Bundesbank had to review its central functions once deprived of the central operational rationale for its intellectual leadership role in European central banking.

- The loss of its international profile in G7, the IMF, and the BIS. The Bundesbank had to strengthen its international bargaining power by working harder to secure EU-wide coordination, for instance, over IMF reform or over Basle negotiations on reform of banking supervision. Its intra-European networking skills and coalition building assumed an even greater importance.

- The release of the German federal government—and the Federal Finance Ministry in particular—from the policy constraint of a strategy of needing to 'bind in' the Bundesbank to its European economic and financial policies, once EMU was achieved. Especially on the political Left, which came to power in 1998, German politicians who had resented Bundesbank domestic power were ready to exploit its loss of domestic political leverage. With the first centre–Left federal coalition government in post-war history, the Bundesbank faced new ideological challenge. In 1998–9 the Bundesbank was confronted with the combative Social Democratic (SPD) party chair Oskar Lafontaine as new Federal Finance Minister and as advocate of neo-Keynesian ideas. Although more supportive, Hans Eichel (1999–2005) and Peer Steinbrück (2005–) placed the Bundesbank under new political pressure with reform of the Stability and Growth Pact, reforms of domestic banking supervision, pressures for gold sales in 2002–3, and even cuts and removal of special salary bonuses. From 1998 the Bundesbank faced the combination of varyingly suspicious SPD finance ministers with the challenges listed above.

In terms of visible power relationships the winners were global financial players, the ECB, and the German Finance Ministry. To add to its domestic difficulties, the 2002 Bundesbank reform weakened the Bundesbank's strong political roots in the German federal structure. Its once powerful domestic political constituency was, in consequence, eroded on two fronts, federal and *Land*. It lost powerful monetary policy instruments and domestic political stature as a core player in the German 'semi-sovereign' state (Katzenstein 1987). In consequence, the post-euro Bundesbank is the story of an institution whose capacity to shape its operating environment—to play domestic 'semi-sovereignty games'—has been eroded. It no longer possesses its former capacity to prevail in domestic conflicts (cf. Berger and De Haan 1999; Duckenfield 1999*b*; Heipertz 2001).

Europeanization and Power

EMU had paradoxical effects on Bundesbank power. On the one hand, EMU collectively empowered central bankers at the EU level to safeguard economic stability on the basis of an Ordo-liberal paradigm of stability-oriented policies inspired by the Bundesbank (and of an institutional design close to that of its more decentralized predecessor, the Bank deutscher Länder, 1948–57). In consequence, the post-euro Bundesbank stressed a fundamental continuity in its special role as the 'guardian' or 'night watchman' of stability: its *Wächterrolle* in the Eurosystem. Central to all its activities remained the mission of 'constructing stability', both in Germany and in the Eurosystem. This mission led it to act as an advance protagonist of the ECB in asserting the institutional and policy attributes of stability against threats: whether from opponents of a predominant role for monetary analysis and money supply growth in ECB monetary policy; from proposals to exclude or marginalize NCBs in banking supervision and financial stability functions; from attacks on ECB independence in successive Treaty and institutional reform proposals; or in principled resistance to reform of the Stability and Growth Pact (Deutsche Bundesbank 2005*a*, *c*). In so doing, it often took up tougher positions than ECB directors. Over the period 1999–2006, Jürgen Stark, its vice-president (earlier chief German negotiator of the Pact and later ECB Chief Economist), encapsulated this role. His departure, like that of Edgar Meister in banking supervision, ended the continuity of personnel at the executive board level with the Tietmeyer Bundesbank.

On the other hand, EMU disempowered the Bundesbank at domestic, EU, and international levels. The effects were most striking in relations with the Federal Finance Ministry (especially over banking supervision reforms in 2002 and 2007 and over reducing salary bonuses in 2006); with certain *Land* governments over the nomination of executive board members (notably in 2006–7 when the Bundesbank had to accept a board member it had opposed); and with the ECB and some other national central banks in the Eurosystem (in the competition for policy ideas). Compared to the US Federal Reserve, the

ECB, and the Bank of England, the Bundesbank lost ground in the IMF and G7 (over financial stability issues) and looked increasingly to achieving common positions in the Euro Group and ECOFIN. Unlike in constructing EMU, the Bundesbank was cast into the position of defending the European monetary constitution, the 'monetary' pillar of the ECB's monetary policy strategy, central banks' role in banking supervision and financial stability, and even retention of extra pay allowances for its staff.

The history of the Bundesbank and the euro reflects the paradox between two types of power: power as the capacity to act in the service of its functions and power as dominance of one actor over others. Paradoxically, in diminishing its power over other central banks, the Bundesbank collectively empowered EU central banks to more effectively promote economic stability within the EU. EMU is the story of the Bundesbank's institutional self-abnegation of power 'over' others for the superior aim of enhanced collective central banking power 'to' deliver a socially valued outcome—economic stability in Europe (on these two forms of power, see Morriss 2006). The legacy of its shaping power over the institutional design of the Eurosystem left intact (even if recurrently challenged) the Bundesbank's power in two of three dimensions—the power to frame how other actors defined their interests in EMU and the power of agenda setting (and keeping issues off the agenda). At the same time the Euro Area reduced the visible face of Bundesbank power in being directly able to change what others did (on the distinction between these three dimensions of power, see Lukes 2005). This self-abnegation testifies to a long-term Europeanization process in the Bundesbank, in which accommodation trumped inertia and resistance to the implications of European market and political integration for monetary policy.

This process of Europeanization and the outcome of accommodation testified to a distinctive conjunction of factors at work both in EMU and in Germany. The Bundesbank was embedded in a broad domestic political consensus about the primacy of European unification in German long-term national interests and about the vital role of monetary union in that process. Debate focused on timing and conditions, not on principle. The Bundesbank was from 1958 onwards a pivotal player in EU central banking, its positions refined and propagated by Emminger. EU central bankers had in turn low collective action problems as a result of both the emerging high professional consensus in monetary economics about price stability by the 1980s, consequent on the collective experience of the Great Inflation of the 1960s and 1970s, and the habits and practices of intensive cooperation in various EU and international fora. Accordingly, EU central bankers readily achieved solidarity around the Bundesbank's detailed prescriptions for European monetary and currency union, presented to and incorporated in the report of the Delors Committee (Dyson and Featherstone 1999). These low collective action costs in EU central banking combined with determined, resolute, and consistent political leadership, not least by the German Federal Chancellor and his astute political skills in 'binding in' the Bundesbank, to facilitate EMU (Dyson 1998).

Both the process and the outcome of EMU illustrated that the power that mattered to the Bundesbank was the professional capacity to shape outcomes—a socially beneficial form of power—rather than the more instrumental power of the Bundesbank over others in gaining their compliance. The Bundesbank focused on whether the Treaty and institutional conditions were right to safeguard the collective professional capacity to deliver price stability. With respect to power relationships, it was concerned to retain influence within the Eurosystem and thereby ensure the Eurosystem's ability to shape the long-term expectations and behaviour of market players, price and wage setters, and governments. The new asymmetrical power of the ECB within European economic governance [what Dyson (2000) calls the 'ECB-centric' Euro Area] compensated in part for the diminished asymmetrical power of the Bundesbank in German economic governance. After 1998–9, on issues like Treaty revision, the application and reform of the Stability and Growth Pact and exchange-rate coordination, the post-euro Bundesbank assigned a special role to itself in speaking out loudly and clearly against any attempts to weaken the collective capacity to deliver price stability. Through Stark, in particular, it specialized in 'voice' on behalf of the policy paradigm that it had collectivized, notably against recurring French suggestions for European 'economic government' (Hirschman 1970).

The Pre-Euro Bundesbank: Europeanization by Stealth

> The Bundesbank is like whipped cream—the more one stirs it, the firmer it gets.
>
> Wim Duisenberg

The Europeanization of the Bundesbank was a long-term, difficult, and at times painful process for a proud, self-confident institution. Its effective outcome in the creation of the Euro Area depended on negotiations that achieved an 'uploading' of Bundesbank ideas and practices of central banking to the EU level. The result was an intellectual and institutional 'fit' of the Eurosystem and the Bundesbank. Underpinning this process was a powerful conjunction of Bundesbank-led argument and persuasion with mostly implicit political threat of domestic German ratification difficulties. The persuasive capacity of the Bundesbank derived from its superior performance in delivering a strong and stable currency and from the association of this performance with the record of sustained growth of the German economy and its resilience in the face of shocks like the oil crises of the 1970s. Its status amongst central banking professionals as *the* EU model was largely unquestioned. Equally, the dependence of the Bundesbank's domestic power on a widely shared 'stability culture' (not on a constitutional anchoring of its independence—which was only secured in statute law) gave it a veto position in EMU negotiations. Hence, in contrast to prevailing norms of German EU behaviour, the Bundesbank—symbolized by Tietmeyer—could play hard in negotiations. The constraint in doing so was loyalty to the political position of the German federal government, whose Chancellor and foreign minister insisted that EMU was pre-eminently a political project.

In consequence, Bundesbank officials could negotiate from strength in EU fora like the EC Monetary Committee and the Committee of Central Bank Governors: notably in defining core ideas of EMU were Emminger as vice-president ((1970–7) and president (1977–9) and Tietmeyer as vice-president (1991–3) and president (1993–9). Emminger was the defining intellectual presence in the background of the Werner Committee deliberations (as was Tietmeyer, alternate member and then in the Federal Economics Ministry), as well as in the European Monetary System negotiations in 1977–9; whilst Tietmeyer played a similar role in the Maastricht negotiations and in the work of the European Monetary Institute in preparing stage three (on details see Dyson 1994; Dyson and Featherstone 1999).

This Bundesbank power over EMU was recognized and embedded in the German federal government's paramount political strategy of 'binding in' the Bundesbank at all points in EMU negotiations (Dyson 1998). The risks inherent in pursuing alternative strategies were highlighted in the gold revaluation crisis of May–June 1997 and the subsequent political victory for the Bundesbank and humiliation for Finance Minister Theo Waigel (Duckenfield 1999a). Not least, the opposition SPD stood ready in the Bundesrat to block any proposal to alter the Bundesbank Act to compel a gold revaluation. The strategy of 'binding in' was designed to accommodate the enormous public support for the competence and effectiveness of the Bundesbank in 'safeguarding the currency'. Historical memory of the painful personal and political consequences of hyper-inflation in the 1920s and 1940s left a deep footprint in German public opinion. In consequence, the guiding strategic principle for the German government was to ensure that the new single currency was 'at least as stable as the D-Mark'. Political credibility in securing this principle depended on Bundesbank support. Hence in intergovernmental negotiations at the European Council and ECOFIN levels the federal government stressed its distinctively narrow 'win set' in domestic outcomes and ceded shaping power over institutional and technical details of EMU to the Bundesbank.

The combination of a political strategy of 'binding in' the Bundesbank throughout EMU negotiations with its institutional reputation as the model EU central bank laid the foundations for a Europeanization process in which accommodation—even to a relatively large Euro Area—triumphed over resistance or inertia. Even so, the process had its moments of risk when the challenges of inertia and resistance threatened to derail EMU. They included the following:

- The continuing insistence of the Bundesbank that its obligations to intervene to support currencies in the ERM were secondary to its domestic statutory mandate under the 1957 Bundesbank Act to 'safeguard the currency'. This position had its origins in the Bundesbank's unhappy memories of the strains created for its mandate by the Bretton Woods system. Release from this system had enabled the Bundesbank to more autonomously and effectively pursue its mandate (Emminger 1986). The famous Emminger letter in 1979 on this point became the reference point for the Bundesbank's resistance to open-ended interventions during a succession of difficult ERM crises, notably in March 1983, January 1987, September 1992, and July 1993 (Dyson 1994 for details). Only a broadening of the bands in 1993—insisted on by the Bundesbank—saved the ERM and kept EMU alive.

- The divided counsels inside the Bundesbank on the role of its president Karl-Otto Pöhl in the Delors Committee in 1988–9. Aware that he was being boxed in, Pöhl had to be persuaded to accept the invitation to join and then to play a constructive role (Dyson and Featherstone 1999 for details).

- The damage limitations on EMU after the German federal government overruled the Bundesbank's recommendations for delay in German–German currency union in 1990 (Marsh 1992: 196–227). This crisis, linked to Pöhl's resignation, cast serious doubt on the Bundesbank's trust in the federal government in EMU negotiations (Duckenfield 1999*b*).

- The hesitations that surfaced in the Bundesbank after 1993 on the adequacy of the excessive deficit procedure in the Maastricht Treaty to provide an effective support for a stability-oriented monetary policy inside stage three. The German agenda-setting on the Stability Pact, with insistence on a tight framework of rules and sanctions, was designed to overcome these hesitations.

- The domestic gold revaluation crisis in 1997 (Duckenfield 1999*a* for details). The Bundesbank mobilized public support behind the principle of central bank independence to resist the proposal of Waigel, Federal Finance Minister, to revalue the gold reserves, in part to offset the fiscal deficit. A panic move to help Germany meet the fiscal convergence criteria threatened to provide an incentive for the Bundesbank to oppose the transition to stage three in 1998–9 and for the opposition SPD to seek political advantage by aligning itself with defence of the Bundesbank.

The enduring loyalty of the Bundesbank to the EMU process, despite these periodic crises, reflected in part acceptance of the primacy of EMU as a political project, in part a shared mind-set that favoured European economic and political unification, and in part its influence in the process and over the content of EMU during all these crises (except German unification).

What factors formed the pre-euro Bundesbank's character? First and foremost, the Bundesbank prided itself on being the most independent of EU central banks (Loedel 1999*b*). This pride had its origins in a distinctive German Ordo-liberalism that favoured a principles-based approach to monetary policy, reliance on monetary rules, scepticism about formal analytical economic modelling, and central bank independence to deliver a long-term predictable framework of price stability free from short-term political pressures (Nicholls 1994; Weber 2006*b*). The historical roots lay in the nightmare memories of hyper-inflation and its corrosive political and economic effects. The earlier, more decentralized Bank deutscher Länder scored two notable victories over Chancellor Konrad Adenauer: when he tried to stop an interest-rate increase: in 1950 during the Korean War crisis; and, most famously, in May 1955 when in his Guerzenich speech Adenauer decried its damage to 'the small fry'. In July 1956 the cabinet rejected Adenauer's proposal to move the planned Bundesbank from Frankfurt to Cologne, close to the political capital Bonn. These practical and symbolic political victories for Wilhelm Vocke, president of the Bank deutscher Länder, and Ludwig Erhard, Federal Economics Minister, were the context for securing its independence in 'safeguarding the currency' in the Bundesbank Act of 1957 (Deutsche Bundesbank 1999; De Haan 2000). Later Chancellors avoided repetition of Guerzenich.

Bundesbank pride was reinforced by the relative success of Germany in avoiding the worse effects of the Great Inflation of the 1970s and in being a pacesetter in devising a monetary rule in 1975 as a domestic discipline once the Bretton Woods system had collapsed (Emminger 1986). In the 1980s the Bundesbank's reputation was further reinforced by mainstream American academic research in monetary economics that established a relationship between central bank independence and price stability and sustained growth without boom and bust. The principle of central bank independence remained the bedrock of its negotiating strategy on EMU and of its post-euro role in consolidating stability.

In the context of an Ordo-liberal orthodoxy that rejected or at least substantially qualified Keynesian demand management, monetary policy possessed an enduring primacy in both macro-economic policy and in the activities of the Bundesbank not seen in any other EU state or central bank (Dyson 1999). The importance of its monetary policy role grew with the Bundesbank's pacesetting role in the ERM, based on the 'anchor' role of the D-Mark, along with its long domestic record of independence. The monetary policy capacity of other EU central banks remained undeveloped because they either lacked this independence in setting interest rates (like the Bank of England) and/or were constrained in monetary policy autonomy by ERM membership, becoming monetary policy 'takers'. This 'benchmarking' role in European monetary policy meant that the Bundesbank director responsible for economic policy enjoyed an unusually powerful internal position, with a large prestigious economic policy division. Examples included Emminger, Helmut Schlesinger, and Otmar Issing. In this way, Bundesbank power was projected onto the European level. Characteristically, the vice-president was responsible either for economic policy (like Emminger and Schlesinger) or for international policy (like Tietmeyer).

In contrast, other central banking functions—notably banking supervision—assumed a secondary importance and prestige. The reigning Bundesbank view was that responsibility for banking supervision might produce conflicts of interest for monetary policy and undermine discharge of responsibility for price stability. Faced with financial difficulties in the banking sector the Bundesbank might be tempted to inject liquidity in circumstances that increased inflationary risks and be drawn into 'moral hazard'. Hence the Bundesbank was content to formally delegate key activities to an independent agency attached to the Federal Finance Ministry, the Berlin-based Federal Banking Supervisory Office (Bundesaufsichtsamt für das Kreditwesen, BaKred). In practice, BaKred worked closely with the Bundesbank.

To the irritation of successive presidents, the Bundesbank combined its European and global commitments and its reputation as a model central bank with a pronounced provincialism. This provincialism reflected the firm political roots of the Bundesbank council and organization in the German federal system, the hostility to creating a single powerful German financial market centre in Frankfurt, and the state central banks' tendency to protect the interests of the public savings banks and hence to be cautious on financial market liberalization. The result was potential tension between the president and the executive board, on the one hand, and the presidents of the state central banks, on the other, about just how best to reconcile domestic responsibilities with European and international obligations. Pöhl, in particular, was a sharp critic of this 'mismatch' between international and European responsibilities and provincialism, arguing that some Bundesbank council members lacked adequate professional expertise in monetary policy.

The potential for this mismatch to spill over into conflict was mitigated by the primacy that Bundesbank thinking gave to building a framework for international and European monetary coordination 'from below' through domestic discipline in delivering economic stability. There was, in short, a firm bias to give primacy to domestic responsibility for 'safeguarding the currency' as the basis for wider exchange-rate stability based on sound domestic fundamentals. Exchange-rate stability was a residual of sound converging domestic policies rather than a prime cause of domestic stability.

This bias to European and international coordination 'from below' reflected another distinctive characteristic of the Bundesbank: the absence of a significant domestic historical context of Keynesian economic thought. The Bundesbank represented the central domestic institutional embodiment of a distinctive German 'Ordo-liberal' tradition of economics. 'Ordo-liberalism' advocated a 'principles-based' approach to economic policy, with regulation to ensure open competitive markets and central bank independence in the service of economic stability as the guiding principles. These principles made the monetarist notion of money supply targeting appealing to the Bundesbank as an apolitical frame of reference unlike the discretionary use of a range of macro-economic indicators, including forecasting, in which it placed little reliance. Hence in the 1970s the Bundesbank was a leader in adapting US monetarist ideas as the key frame of reference for its monetary policy (Johnson 1998). Despite much external criticism, which often ignored its non-mechanistic use of monetarism, it remained the main EU central banking advocate of the primacy of this monetary instrument as the basis for a more secure long-term orientation to securing price stability (Gerberding, Seitz, and Worms 2005).

Following the Maastricht Treaty negotiations the Bundesbank council signalled its critical distance in a statement of January 1992 that underlined the challenges ahead both in achieving sufficient economic convergence and in deepening solidarity through more political union if EMU was to be sustainable. In addition to highlighting 'bottom–up' convergence through sound domestic policies, it argued for a strong political framework to secure competitive markets at the EU level—about whose existence the Bundesbank remained sceptical (Deutsche Bundesbank 1992). This bias to a cautious 'wait-and-see' approach was shifted by the Maastricht Treaty ratification in 1993, by the 1993 ERM crisis centring on the French franc, and by the January 1994 launch of stage two of EMU and the birth of the European Monetary Institute (EMI). They forced internal recognition of the professional as well as political dangers of being reactive to events and of the need for a more comprehensive and pro-active Bundesbank engagement in a project with a clear political timetable and a changed institutional context. This engagement was symbolized by its new high-level European steering committee in October 1994, designed to ensure German influence over the detailed design of stage three.

Between 1994 and 1998 the context changed with the European Monetary Institute as an emerging new intellectual powerhouse in negotiation of the design of stage three. The Bundesbank participated very actively in negotiations on such issues as the role of money in monetary policy strategy, minimum reserve requirements, longer-term refinancing, and seigniorage. It pursued two fundamental principles—central bank independence and continuity with pre-EMU as vital to long-term credibility—and paid close attention to domestic political need to safeguard the specific interests of the German three-pillar financial system (commercial, cooperative, and public savings banks) and in particular retain the critical support of the German savings banks in the transition to stage three of EMU. However, the Bundesbank had to make compromises in what was a consensus-driven process. It was able to secure a role for money, but as one pillar of monetary strategy;

minimum reserve requirements to stabilize money market interest rates, but with banks remunerated at market interest rates; and longer-term refinancing as part of open market operations, but without the subsidy element of discount rates below market rates. These compromises stemmed from a broad emerging consensus, shaped by strong Bank of England positions, that monetary policy instruments should avoid competitive distortions, giving some banks a competitive advantage over others. They also accorded with pragmatism in the Bundesbank's understanding of monetary aggregates and in its recognition of the principle of a 'level playing field' in European competition policy.

In the process of designing stage three, Tietmeyer combined an intellectual ascendancy on detailed technical issues, which derived from a much-longer association with EMU than any of his peers, with highly accomplished negotiating skills and an intense focus on, and commitment to, the negotiations. He was flanked by his Chief Economist, Issing, in preparation of the ECB monetary strategy, and in the EC Monetary Committee by Stark, State Secretary in the Federal Finance Ministry (notably on negotiation of the Stability and Growth Pact). Issing's appointment as the first ECB Chief Economist and Stark's appointment as vice-president of the Bundesbank in 1998 testified to an ongoing axis of Bundesbank centrality in promoting stability in the Eurosystem.

The new internal primacy to Europeanization of the Bundesbank's work post-1993 reflected the determination of the Bundesbank not to lose its grip on the detailed technical issues in transition to stage three and not least to ensure that operational empowerment of the EMI in monetary policy during stage two was kept off the agenda. Equally, the ERM crises of 1992–3 had revealed the risks of political exposure to the Bundesbank and the limits of its statutory mandate. Tietmeyer sought to avoid any association with an image of 'sabotaging' EMU and forcing the federal government to renege on a central EU treaty commitment. His fundamental Europeanism was revealed in his aversion to the high political costs for Germany and for the EU from a failure of EMU that could be credibly attributed to the Bundesbank. As a seasoned German official he recognized that the federal government was ultimately responsible for foreign and EU policies; the Bundesbank was responsible for ensuring that the design of EMU was technically correct.

The Post-Euro Bundesbank

Three Bundesbank Presidents: The Routinization of Charisma

The transformed context of the post-euro Bundesbank was reflected in the differing qualities and experiences of its presidents, who were offered fewer prospects to bask in the public limelight. The context neither favoured nor called for charisma. Tietmeyer's retirement in August 1999 was recognized as the end of an era of 'great' Bundesbank presidents; Ernst Welteke's dramatic resignation in April 2004 represented the worst crisis in its history and was symptomatic of a traumatic period; whilst the appointment of Axel Weber signalled a period of tougher, more centralized but low-profile management of change. Only Tietmeyer merited comparisons with Vocke, Karl Blessing, Emminger, and Pöhl.

Welteke and Weber had to face new, recurring, and uncomfortable questions about whether the Bundesbank was redundant and, if not, whether it was too costly and inefficient and best reduced to being no more than a 'think tank' (*Denkfabrik*) (e.g. Stürmer 2005; Weber 2005*a*). These questions highlighted its problems in encouraging public interest in its remaining operational tasks and thus profiling its identity and securing its influence on domestic economic policies (cf. Fabritius 2004). Welteke talked boldly about creating a 'new' Bundesbank, including a new engagement with promoting Frankfurt as the German and Euro Area financial centre and with using gold sales to increase Bundesbank profits and finance a new role in supporting the Lisbon agenda of education and research. In contrast, aware of the internal Bundesbank dissent provoked by these initiatives and external political constraints, Weber stressed both continuity in its prime concern with strengthening its role in monetary policy and price stability and developing its expertise in financial stability in the context of the new challenges from financial market changes. The credit and insolvency crisis of 2007–8, symbolized by the rescues of the IKB, the Sachsen Landesbank, the Westdeutsche Landesbank (WestLB), and—most systemically serious of all—Hypo Real Estate, increased further the stress on the interdependence of monetary and financial stability.

Initially, the Bundesbank was protected by the 'halo effect' of the Tietmeyer presidency, both his personal legacy in negotiating EMU on German terms and his continuing high international profile in the 1998–9 financial crises, lead role for G7 and IMF in proposing the new Financial Stability Forum, and engagement in IMF reform debates. The active Tietmeyer/Stark role at international and European levels helped to temporarily mask the scale of change. Moreover, the gap between monetary union in 1999 and currency union in 2002 created a hiatus in change. As work on currency conversion was incomplete and absorbed Bundesbank attention, Tietmeyer could limit himself to beginning internal work on structural reform proposals (chaired by Stark). His legacy was approved by the Bundesbank council of *two* reform models (centralized and decentralized) in June 1999. Tietmeyer was also able to counter the critical positions on the EMU institutional and policy arrangements taken by Lafontaine as SPD Federal Finance Minister (October 1998–March 1999). Lafontaine's abrupt resignation, before Tiemeyer's retirement, relieved the short-term pressure on both the Bundesbank and the ECB.

Welteke was left to walk the political minefield of Bundesbank reform. He was initially protected by a two-year timetable as the Bundesbank, especially its large state central banks, were busy ensuring a smooth efficient currency conversion for January 2002. He could also use this European deadline to help force change. However, senior Bundesbank officials and some state central bank presidents were less than enthusiastic about Welteke's appointment, especially his close political association with Eichel, who had been prime minister of Hesse and who had nominated him. Although past president of the Hesse state central bank, Welteke was neither a professional central banker (like Emminger) nor a high-profile international economic figure (like Pöhl, Tietmeyer, and Stark) nor a professional economist (like Schlesinger or later Weber). His combination of a provincial with a political background (as economics and finance minister in Hesse) added to internal Bundesbank fears that he would lack both the international and European experience and weight and the intellectual capacity to profile the Bundesbank effectively in the Eurosystem, especially in the crucial area of monetary policy. Stark emerged as the strong figure on the larger stage of IMF, G7, and Eurosystem and the one whom many felt had been deprived of the post that was rightly his because he did not have the right 'party book' in 1999. In consequence, Welteke felt that he lacked strong internal support.

Welteke's period was characterized by immersion in the domestic politics of Bundesbank structural reform. This issue generated powerful internal conflicts that made agreement on future strategy in the Bundesbank council impossible, which in turn further undermined morale (Engelen 2002a, b). It also provoked criticism that he failed to make time to strengthen the profile of the Bundesbank in the ECB (though structural reform was a condition of, as much as a diversion from, this task). Even when internal reform was agreed, mainly on terms acceptable to Welteke, his attempts to fill out his concept of the 'new' Bundesbank with ideas elicited more suspicion and opposition than support. He proposed a more flexible, profit-oriented management of the large Bundesbank reserves on a more commercial model. In addition, he proposed that gold sales might be used to establish a new fund to invest in the future, specifically in education and research. In these ways, he sought to associate the Bundesbank with 'modernization'. Both proposals met internal Bundesbank resistance on the grounds that the central bank was exposing itself to political interference in reserve management. Colleagues sought to rally around a staunch defence of the principle of central bank independence as essential if Welteke and the Bundesbank were to strengthen their position in the Eurosystem. The Bundesbank position on gold sales hardened in 2003.

The risks of being seen as unreliable on stability within the Eurosystem were a factor in limiting Welteke's desire to carve out a new role for the Bundesbank in actively promoting Frankfurt as an international financial centre and the financial centre of the Euro Area. This was the rationale for the abortive proposals to locate BaFin and the Committee of European Banking Supervisors (CEBS) in Frankfurt and for strengthening ties with Frankfurt University in research on financial markets and monetary policy. Welteke's Hesse background proved a catalyst for political opposition to his centralizing ambitions, especially from Bavaria, and articulated within as well as outside the Bundesbank. His views on the need for a strong German financial centre in Frankfurt, reflected in his preference for a centralized Bundesbank reform model and a shift of financial supervision activities, provoked hostile reactions. Internally, this initiative exposed a dilemma: on the one hand, financial market integration consequent on the euro was sharpening a competition of financial centres, in which the Bundesbank as the German central bank could not be neutral. On the other hand, its image as a reliable guardian of stability in ECB monetary policy depended on not being seen as captive to particular market players. The Bundesbank's stability image in the Eurosystem's monetary policy (continuity) trumped a new image as a promoter of Frankfurt.

Just as the Bundesbank hoped to settle down to a period of stability after currency union and internal reforms, crises multiplied in 2003. The Brown-Eichel proposals for reform of EU financial market regulation and supervision undermined the Bundesbank strategy of using the ECB as an axis for developing its profile in European banking supervision. Eichel put the Bundesbank under pressure to sell gold. Subjected to the excessive deficit procedure, the German government precipitated a crisis of the Stability and Growth Pact. It thereby undermined one of the core German contributions to the design of the EMU. In addition, German negotiators in the European Convention agreed to proposed changes to the European monetary constitution that threatened the Bundesbank position that the Maastricht settlement on EMU must be left intact. Singly and together, these conflicts amounted to a Bundesbank belief that the German government was undermining its capacity to act as guarantor of stability-oriented monetary policies. Relations with the Schröder government deteriorated sharply. Stark advocated most strongly a clear consistent Bundesbank line: no change to the monetary constitution and no reform of the Stability and Growth Pact (just its application) (Deutsche Bundesbank 2005a).

Against this gloomy background, the crisis in March–April 2004 over Welteke's 'hotel-costs' affair (paid for by a leading German bank), and subsequent resignation, and associated allegations of property scandal, tarnished the reputation of the Bundesbank and plunged it into its worst-ever institutional crisis (Einecke 2004). Given its fear that Schröder would use this opportunity to parachute in a Berlin colleague to discipline the Bundesbank, Weber's appointment was a collective relief.

Although without much managerial experience, Weber was a highly respected financial and monetary economist. His priority was not to look for new roles for the Bundesbank but to focus on strengthening its core operational functions, especially in monetary policy, through more high-quality research (Weber 2007). The 'Strategy 2012' and the portfolio allocation in 2006 affirmed this approach. The priorities were symbolized in Weber taking direct responsibility for monetary policy and research (shifting Hermann Remsperger to international affairs) and with Franz-Christoph Zeitler, the vice-president, focusing on banking supervision. Weber intensified cost reductions so that the Bundesbank could argue credibly about structural reforms as itself a pacesetter in the public sector. His insistence on a unified, tightly organized management was made more acceptable in the light of the lessons of the 2004 crisis. However, it provoked much internal unhappiness not just because of job cuts but also because it was unclear how the research-driven approach could be made to work in the context of competition for the bright stars from the better-resourced, neighbouring ECB (including the rumour that Weber might move to the ECB as chief economist). Weber's incentive for consolidating and even reducing involvement in some functions (e.g. privatizing cash management) was to create more space to invest in research capacity.

The departure of Stark in 2006 and retirement of Edgar Meister in 2007 were symbolic of the final disappearance of the shadow of the Tietmeyer era and gave Weber a fresh opportunity to refashion the Bundesbank in his own image. In Weber the post-euro Bundesbank had found a leadership personality and style that suited its more humdrum range of functions.

Living with an Ambitious Federal Finance Ministry and Disgruntled Länder: Internal Reform and Banking Supervision

In seeking to carve out its post-euro identity the Bundesbank faced the challenge that the creation of the Euro Area unleashed new opportunities and incentives for the Federal Finance Ministry to strengthen its roles in macro-economic policy coordination within the federal executive, in fiscal policy co-ordination within the larger federal system, and in financial market supervision. Its only partial success had much to do with the strength of veto players in the German semi-sovereign state with its complex sharing of powers. The most notable development was a major transformation in the relative power of the Bundesbank and the Federal Finance Ministry, exemplified in reforms to German banking and financial market supervision. With EMU in place the Finance Ministry was liberated from the strategic requirement to 'bind in' the Bundesbank to its key policy positions. Faced also by the political difficulties of fiscal consolidation in a federal system it had an incentive to return regularly (in 2003 and in 2006) to the issue of selling Bundesbank gold reserves as a source of revenue. Strikingly, it was not deterred by the memory of the Finance Ministry defeat on the gold revaluation issue in 1997 (Duckenfield 1999*a*).

In addition, the Bundesbank's internal centralizing reform and subsequent job cuts left many *Länder* governments unhappy with the Bundesbank. Although opinion polls suggested that it remained second only to the Federal Constitutional Court in the respect in which it was held by the public, it had fewer political friends. This diminished respect was demonstrated in 2007 when the Bundesrat sought to appoint the head of the State Chancellery of Baden-Wuerttemberg against the opposition of the Bundesbank executive board. The political as well as legal resources of the Bundesbank in playing the German semi-sovereignty game had diminished.

Welteke's close personal and political relations with Eichel were seen as a great bonus for the Bundesbank directorate to gain support for a smaller, more centralized, and streamlined structure, in which the nine *Länder* central banks would lose their independence and the Bundesbank council be abolished. Frictions mounted when presidents of the *Länder* central banks—who were Bundesbank council members—offered public opinions about ECB monetary policy though the president, and not they, was responsible as the ECB Governing Council member. The problem was intensified by the overhang of effects from the Bundesbank's expansion consequent on German unification and the introduction of the D-Mark in the six new federal states.

In 1999–2000 Bundesbank discussions with the Federal Finance Ministry focused in parallel on two issues: the two internal structural reform models (centralized and decentralized) endorsed by the Bundesbank council; and the future of banking supervision. Welteke pressed the case on Eichel, his former political colleague from Hesse, for the centralized reform option—to more effectively support his role in the ECB Governing Council—and for centralizing banking supervision in the Bundesbank—to expand and develop Bundesbank functions and to lay the basis for a more effective role in financial stability as compensation for losing monetary policy. The complex outcomes caused shock waves in the Bundesbank.

In January 2001 Eichel linked the two issues in interrelated legislative proposals. Although in part they offered what the Bundesbank directorate sought, they were also a surprising setback to its ambitions. In his proposed amendment to the Bundesbank Act Eichel accepted the directorate's idea of a small, centralized, and single-tier governing board (to be nominated only by the federal government) and the replacement of the *Länder* central banks by dependent regional offices. This attack on the federal principle underpinning the structure of the Bundesbank triggered the fierce opposition of *Länder* governments, notably Bavaria. The proposal involved abolition of the executive boards of the *Länder* central banks, the removal of a major source of *Land* political patronage, and an end to the remaining tasks of the Bundesbank council. Welteke was happy but faced the bitter opposition of six *Länder* central bank presidents and a deeply divided Bundesbank council.

In a linked reform, Eichel proposed that responsibilities for supervision of banking, insurance, and securities markets—which had been divided amongst three federal regulatory bodies—should be merged in a single new Federal Financial Services Supervisory Authority (*Bundesanstalt für Finanzdienstleistungsaufsicht*, Bafin) under the supervision of the Federal Finance Ministry. Modelled on the British Financial Services Authority, this proposal had the strong backing of the big commercial banks and was justified in terms of an objective sponsored by Welteke—strengthening Germany as a modern financial centre and as a regulatory model in the Euro Area. It was also influenced by the BaKred's proposal for a stronger role in banking supervision in the wake of the Hypo-Bank scandal of the 1990s. However, the objective was pursued in terms that ran counter to Bundesbank interests. Taken by surprise and fearing that the Finance Ministry sought its exclusion from banking supervision, the Bundesbank gained ECB support for its view that central banks must be intimately involved in banking supervision, not just because of their traditional authority and expertise but also so that they could effectively discharge their responsibility for identifying risks to financial stability. Through its regional offices, only the Bundesbank had the appropriate structure for the detailed operational aspects of banking supervision in a highly decentralized and complex banking structure.

Eventually, compromise was reached under which the Bundesbank retained responsibility for the operational aspects of banking supervision. This responsibility mattered because Basel II offered opportunities for staff expansion to take on new tasks in banking supervision. It also ensured that the Bundesbank remained a major player in the ESCB arrangements for EU-wide coordination of banking supervision: Meister of the Bundesbank directorate chaired the ESCB Banking Supervision Committee (BSC). However, the Bundesbank failed to get BaFin transferred to Frankfurt.

From January 2001 to passage of the two bills in March 2002 Welteke faced a serious internal crisis. Eichel's preference for the centralizing reform option brought down the wrath of many colleagues in the Bundesbank council because it strengthened the European role of the Bundesbank to their cost. Simultaneously, Eichel weakened Welteke by his reform proposals for banking supervision on behalf of a modern supervisory system that recognized the closer integration of markets rather than the special character of banking.

Faced with political opposition from state governments in the Bundesrat, the federal government made concessions to secure the passage of the two bills. First, the rights of the Bundesbank to share in banking supervision with BaFin were more clearly recognized, especially in conducting more detailed checks on individual credit institutes, notably the smaller banks, and in maintaining a role in international and European convergence and cooperation. However, decision-making rested with BaFin. Second, the new single-tier executive board of the Bundesbank was to be slightly larger (eight rather than six) and to be nominated half by the federal government and half by the Bundesrat. This return to a plurality of nominating bodies represented a concession to the *Länder* and was justified as better securing the Bundesbank's independence.

Once the single-tier executive board was in place in 2002, internal restructuring around a few dedicated service centres and staff reductions gathered pace. They were reinforced in Weber's 'Strategy 2012', which planned 9,000 staff in 2012: down 40 per cent from 15,600 in 2001 and from 18,000 in 1992, and double the average for the Eurosystem national central banks. Weber also supported the proposal in 2006 to reduce the executive board to six, with federal government and Bundesrat still nominating half each (and the CDU/CSU insisting on the states having the right of proposal for vice-president). These changes fitted his model of a lean, efficient Bundesbank and his strategic view that its tough calls for domestic structural reforms to labour, product, and service markets lacked credibility if it showed lack of will and capacity to reform itself. The Bundesbank had to be a model of structural reform in the public sector.

Banking supervision remained a continuing source of tensions with the federal government. The Bundesbank sought to raise its profile both in Basle II and in the ECB-based Banking Supervision Committee. It actively engaged in the Basle II negotiations on behalf of the distinctive German interests in protecting the credit position of small and medium-sized firms. It also sought to innovate in regulation of liquidity requirements of banks in the context of the new capital standard. In developing a 'principles-oriented' approach, the Bundesbank gave banks the choice between adopting a standard formula and using their own internally developed liquidity risk measurement and management methods (according to certain requirements). The Bundesbank presented this twin-track approach as a model for EU-wide harmonization of banking supervision.

A further setback for the Bundesbank was the failure of its proposals, backed by other NCBs, to strengthen the role of the BSC in promoting banking supervisory convergence and cooperation within the ESCB as well as in stability analyses of the European banking systems. Meister, the Bundesbank director responsible for financial stability and its first chair, identified the BSC as a potential platform for the Bundesbank to raise its profile in EU-wide banking supervision. However, no sooner was BaFin agreed than Eichel, in a joint proposal with Gordon Brown, proposed a comprehensive reform of European financial supervision in April 2002. ECOFIN decided to extend the committee structure established already for securities supervision to banking. The CEBS began work in 2004 to advise the European Commission on preparation of banking directives, to ensure their consistent application, and, increasingly, to encourage convergence in supervisory rules and practices. It fell outside the umbrella of the ESCB, which focused on macro-prudential issues, and symbolically was located in London, not Frankfurt. The Bundesbank unsuccessfully opposed this reform as too insensitive to the national, regional, and local distinctiveness of banking structures. Once again the Bundesbank found itself on the defensive against Federal Finance Ministry proposals.

The Bundesbank had been inhibited by its strategic commitment to retain banking supervision as a national responsibility and prevent its centralization in the ECB, which was sought by members of the ECB Executive Board, including its president. The rationale for this insistence on the principle of subsidiarity was the sheer complexity of different banking structures in Europe, their particular heterogeneity in Germany, and hence the need for locally based expertise. The Bundesbank also doubted that EU states were prepared to cede political authority to the ESCB to deal with financial system issues. At the same time it feared that ECOFIN might seek to establish a pan-European FSA at collective cost to the central banks, ECB, and NCBs. The CEBS was not the worst-case scenario. The Bundesbank not only failed to prevent a sharing of powers with BaFin in CEBS but also failed to prevent CEBS's location in London.

The Bundesbank held up the centralization of banking supervision in the Dutch central bank as the preferred model and rejected the British FSA model as undermining the capacity of the central bank to safeguard financial stability through the early warnings provided by a detailed operational knowledge of the banking system. Although it tried to make the German 'dual' system work, it argued that it was too complex and involved an unclear division of responsibilities and lack of transparency in the process. The Bundesbank argued that BaFin officials tended to duplicate its work and were too removed from the details, whilst tacitly supporting claims by many banks that BaFin lacked the subject-matter competence of Bundesbank officials (a situation that reflected the centralized operation of BaFin and the regional operation of the Bundesbank).

In the coalition agreement of 2005 the Grand Coalition committed to a further reform of banking supervision. The Bundesbank argued for a reform to differentiate more clearly its role from BaFin and to avoid its officials being drawn into the BaFin orbit. For this reason it rejected the proposal that the Bundesbank be given a seat in the management board of the reconstituted BaFin and sought more responsibility in banking supervision.

The Federal Finance Ministry reform proposals in 2007 occasioned major alarm. They prioritized the removal of the supervision of investment funds (many linked to banks) from the Bundesbank to BaFin on the ground that they should not be classified as 'credit institutes'. This reform, which aimed to eliminate dual supervision, reduced the scope of the Bundesbank's involvement. In a critical opinion the ECB argued that the reform undermined the Bundesbank's capacity to safeguard financial stability within the Eurosystem.

More seriously, the Finance Ministry wanted to strengthen its own role by bringing BaFin closer within its own orbit and subjecting both BaFin and the Bundesbank to its own supervisory authority. The Bundesbank argued that this proposal amounted to a major assault on central bank independence and reflected the Finance Ministry's intent to remove the Bundesbank from a significant role in banking supervision. The ministry countered by pointing out that in 2000 the Bundesbank had accepted that banking supervision did not fall within the framework of central bank independence. In turn, the Bundesbank argued that banking supervision was a crucial aspect of the larger function of securing the financial system against risks, that financial stability and monetary policy were complementary functions (a point strengthened by the 2007–8 credit and insolvency crisis), and that correspondingly the Treaty-sanctioned independence of the Eurosystem was at stake. Again, Bavaria assumed the leading political role in challenging this proposal and making it into a major coalition issue.

CDU/CSU opposition (including support for concentrating responsibility in the Bundesbank), combined with the credit crisis in August 2007, and the collapse of the IKB and the Sachsen Landesbank, led Steinbrück to withdraw the proposals (though not reform of supervision of investment funds and not reform of the management structure of BaFin). The Bundesbank gained a reprieve whilst the federal government considered the implications of the 2007 banking crises. Whilst the Finance Minister remained opposed to ideas of strengthening the Bundesbank's role in banking supervision, the elevation of the issue into a 'grand coalition' matter produced a much less radical outcome that sought a clearer division work with BaFin. In the wake of the new banking crises of 2008, especially Hypo Real Estate, the CDU/CSU again returned to the proposal that banking supervision should be centralized in the Bundesbank.

The 2001–2 and 2007—reforms signalled a shift in power between the Federal Finance Ministry and the Bundesbank. The Bundesbank was forced to fight to retain existing functions rather than being allowed to develop them on the lines of the Dutch and Irish central banks. By 2007 Weber was placing less reliance on the Bundesbank gaining new functions than on developing its monetary policy role within the Eurosystem; by 2008 he saw the deepening financial market crisis as a catalyst to strengthen the 'money and credit' pillar as a stabilizing element in a more long-term–focused monetary policy that would focus on dampening the financial cycle (a more symmetrical monetary policy) (Weber 2008b). Focusing on this function enabled it to escape the political constraints of the domestic 'semi-sovereignty game' in favour of the professional games of semi-sovereignty in European central banking.

Strengthening the Bundesbank in Eurosystem 'Semi-Sovereignty' Games: Strategic Consolidation Around Research

The Bundesbank worked its way with difficulty to a consensus around a revamped strategy in 2006, in part because of delayed and painful structural reforms, and in part because of greater Federal Finance Ministry assertiveness.

The new sense of urgency that was imparted by the crisis of 2004 proved useful to Weber. More fundamentally, however, the nature of the strategic consolidation reflected the Bundesbank's weakened position in domestic semi-sovereignty games and its emerging recognition that the primary strategic requirement to overcome this handicap was to strengthen its position in Eurosystem 'semi-sovereignty games'. It had to re-earn credibility and reputation in this new professional context.

The pre-euro Bundesbank's domestic power and professional identity was bound up with its leadership of European monetary policy. The post-euro Bundesbank's domestic power and professional identity was dependent on its perceived competence in the Eurosystem as a key source of innovative ideas and best practices across its range of functions: banking supervision, payment and settlement systems, cash management, and—crucially—ECB monetary policy strategy. In ensuring a clear Bundesbank imprint on the ECB it had advantages other than just an original Bundesbank-shaped design: physical proximity to the ECB; the number of former Bundesbank officials working for the ECB (82 were seconded at senior levels in 2007); and the presence of former Bundesbank directors as successive ECB chief economists (Issing and Stark).

The decentralized structure of the Eurosystem offered an incentive to excel in the competition of ideas. Inspired by New Public Management ideas, internal Bundesbank reforms highlighted strengthening its five roles in applied economic research; in quality of its financial stability analysis and promoting the values of a long-term culture in German financial markets; in developing stress indicators for systemically important banks; in leading operationally and strategically on European cashless payment systems (TARGET2 and TARGET2S); and in pioneering in efficient cash management (through the cash electronic data interchange procedure and multi-denomination banknote processing). The strategic cycle from 2008 to 2012 focused on 'raising the Bundesbank's profile' in these 'core business areas'.

Already, under Welteke in 2000, the Bundesbank set up its Economic Research Centre, along with a scientific advisory council, as the new focus for its research activities. This Centre managed the macro-economic structure model, forged links with applied academic research in universities and outside research institutes on monetary policy and increasingly financial stability issues, and sought to raise the Bundesbank's profile in ESCB policy issues, especially monetary analysis, the dynamics of wage setting, and analysis of household financial situations. Weber (2006) highlighted two papers: on the continuing value of monetary indicators in predicting Euro Area inflation (Hoffmann 2006); and on improving the quality of monetary indicators (Greiber and Lemke 2005). The Bundesbank focused on strengthening its profile in the ECB Governing Council by arming Weber not just to defend the 'monetary' pillar against sceptics but also in refining the contents of this pillar to enhance its use as a long-term framework for identifying inflationary risks from money supply growth.

In reconfiguring its functions under Weber the Bundesbank had to avoid suggestions that its academic president was transforming it into a 'think tank' by emphasizing that its analytical work served its operational roles. This analytical strengthening was justified as necessary to deal with new, inter-related challenges: incorporating a stronger European perspective into its work so as to fulfil its obligations within the new Eurosystem; using IT and New Public Management to modernize its central banking operations; and coping with the rapid changes and closer integration in global financial markets. The Bundesbank was to become a *Vorreiter* in becoming a Europeanized, modernized, and market-focused central bank, notably compared to its French, Italian, and Spanish equivalents.

Research-based strategic consolidation focused on the following:

- Strengthening the monetary policy-making role of its president in the ECB Governing Council, especially following the criticisms of the 'monetary' pillar by those working with neo-Keynesian macro-economic models at the November 2006 Fourth ECB Central Banking Conference. These criticisms were heard even from inside the ECB, as well as from inside the Banque de France and Banca d'Italia. The Bundesbank faced a difficult intellectual challenge as money supply growth repeatedly exceeded its reference values and the 'monetary' pillar was relegated to second place in the 2003 review of monetary policy strategy. The intellectual case for the role of money had to be reformulated.

- Increasing the expertise and quality of Bundesbank representation in international, European, and national committees monitoring the stability of the financial system and investing in the new Bundesbank financial stability reports. Financial stability assumed a new importance both to compensate for loss of monetary policy making and in response to the increased complexity of financial markets and the associated risks to central banking operations.

- Differentiating its role from that of BaFin in banking supervision and internalizing as much operational supervision as possible.

- Reinforcing its reputation as a catalyst in the European integration process by a leading role in developing and managing an efficient euro cashless payment and settlement system and in developing the Single Euro Payments Area (SEPA).

- Opening cash management operations to the private sector and enhancing efficiency of banknote processing (Weber 2006*a*).

With the notable exception of banking supervision (and cash management reforms which produced trade-union opposition) this strategic consolidation avoided domestic semi-sovereignty games. Particularly in relation to cashless payment systems, SEPA, and monetary policy it involved the more comfortable realm of professional European-level semi-sovereignty games, where it adopted the principle: 'as much integration as possible, as much decentralization as necessary' (Weber 2005b). Here the Bundesbank was playing the game of promoting European integration, a game that had broad domestic political support. The situation was more problematic in banking supervision where its corporate interests were thinly veiled behind its professional arguments about the virtues of decentralization.

A notable example of Bundesbank task expansion around European integration was in helping provide the infrastructure that interconnects central banks, the banking industry, stock markets, and financial markets through TARGET2 and the TARGET2 Securities—T2S—proposal. These cashless individual payment and securities settlement systems were provided through a single shared platform for the Eurosystem. With the Banca d'Italia and the Banque de France, the Bundesbank assumed responsibility for developing and operating this platform, including its legal framework and business organization. The Bundesbank was responding to the fact that the largest group of users was German, and German interest required that it be one of the first states to switch to TARGET2. The same three central banks, along with the Banco de Espana, cooperated in the T2S initiative that would use the TARGET2 platform for securities settlement.

Voting Rules, Treaty Change, and Stability and Growth Pact Reform

The triple processes of Euro Area enlargement, of drafting the Constitutional/ later Reform Treaty, and of Stability and Growth Pact reform created strong incentives for Bundesbank engagement in safeguarding European stability culture. In the case of the two latter, the Bundesbank's principled opposition opened up tensions with some members of the ECB executive board. Common to its positions was the stress on retaining the 'monetary constitution' of Maastricht. Retaining the Stability and Growth Pact mattered not just as a discipline on other EU governments but also as an external means of compensating for the loss of the Bundesbank's domestic capacity to discipline the German federal government for lax fiscal behaviour through monetary policy.

EU enlargement was linked to evidence that the Bundesbank model remained an important influence on the establishment and reform of national central banks in east central Europe, like the Czech Republic and Poland (Rentzow 2002). The Bundesbank was also a major source of technical advice and training to accession state central banks on such matters as payment systems, banking supervision, and financial market stability. This role was formalized in its restructured Centre for Technical Central Bank Cooperation (Deutsche Bundesbank 2005d). However, enlargement was also a source of new challenges. On behalf of the Bundesbank, Stark strongly opposed proposals for a diminished role for national central banks in the powerful Economic and Financial Committee, which prepares for meetings of, and advises, ECOFIN. In 2003 it was agreed that, in the interests of a more efficient committee in the wake of EU enlargement, NCBs would only attend when issues involved their tasks and expertise. Stark saw this change as weakening the capacity of the Bundesbank to address German fiscal policy problems at the EU level. Stark also stressed the strictest application of the 'nominal' convergence criteria to the new member states, with added attention to 'real' convergence in GDP per capita.

Similarly, EU enlargement provoked an anticipatory reform of the governing council of the ECB in 2003 (for details Dyson 2008c). The outcome—a rotation system—was supported by the Bundesbank. It retained the principle of 'one man/one vote' that the Bundesbank had proposed in the Maastricht Treaty negotiations whilst differentiating by size in voting rules. The negotiations kept off the agenda the issue of a smaller ECB monetary policy committee that the Bundesbank feared would centralize too much power in the ECB directorate. The Bundesbank would be in the large state grouping of five, with four out of five voting in rotation (a voting frequency of 80%) once there were 18 NCBs in the governing council.

However, it was reform around a lowest common denominator that satisfied no particular interest inside the ECB (Dyson 2008c). Members of the German Bundesbank, and leading German politicians, were critical of an outcome that did not involve a permanent right to vote of its president, as for the New York Fed in the US system and that would see the share of the large NCB group in the total vote fall. Domestic critics viewed the outcome as a further threat to the primacy of 'stability-oriented' policies at a time when this primacy was being tested by the troubles of the Stability and Growth Pact.

In pursuit of what it defined as its special historical role in the Eurosystem as the guardian of stability culture, and again led by Stark, the Bundesbank played an active role in ensuring that the European Convention (2002–3) and the subsequent IGC did not challenge and undermine the Maastricht Treaty principles on which the ESCB had been designed. The Bundesbank viewed the Convention's final Draft Treaty of July 2003 as highly problematic (Deutsche Bundesbank 2003). The commitment in the EU objectives to 'non-inflationary growth' was replaced by 'balanced growth'; only the ESCB was obliged to maintain price stability. Guarantees of independence for the NCBs within the ESCB were weakened. In addition, the ECB lost its special status as a *sui generis* institution and was to become an EU body. These proposals were seen as reducing the centrality of price stability, creating opportunities to weaken central bank independence, and facilitating moves to *ex ante* coordination of monetary with other EU policies. On this last point, the Bundesbank took a stronger stance than the majority in the ECB Governing Council.

In contrast to the original draft, the final document signed in October 2004 lay down not only 'balanced growth' but also 'price stability' as EU objectives. The Bundesbank was notably active on this issue.

German breaches of the Stability and Growth Pact from 2001, the crisis of November 2003 over the German federal government's mobilization of support in ECOFIN to avert the next stage in the excessive deficit procedure, and subsequent discussion about reform of the Pact highlighted the diminished power of the Bundesbank. It illustrated a more assertive Federal Finance Ministry, no longer needing to 'bind in' the Bundesbank to its positions. Led by Stark, who had been chief negotiator of the original Pact with Tietmeyer, the Bundesbank adopted a position of fundamental opposition to reform (Schäfer and Hagelueken 2005). It identified the problem as a failure to apply its provisions. The Schröder government sought flexibility in both its terms and its application so that the Pact would function not just to flank the ECB monetary policy but also to give governments greater scope for using public spending and tax policies to facilitate painful domestic structural reforms. Unlike the Federal Finance Ministry, the Bundesbank was very dissatisfied with the final outcome in the 2005 reform (Bundesministerium der Finanzen 2005; cf. Deutsche Bundesbank 2005c).

Conclusion

Monetary union transformed the Bundesbank into the most Europeanized institution in Germany; whilst, to a greater extent than the Bank of France and Bank of Italy, internal reforms helped it to carve out a new role as a model for domestic public-sector modernization. These two transformations were crucial to the credibility of its domestic advocacy roles. It promoted the Europeanization of other German institutions: in particular, those responsible for fiscal policies (including constitutional reforms to the federal system to enable an effective national stability pact), for collective bargaining (more flexibility to compete on unit labour costs), and more generally for economic policy advice (so that the Euro Area became the frame of reference) (e.g. Deutsche Bundesbank 2005b). In addition, it became the champion of domestic public-sector modernization. However, the Bundesbank's own Europeanization and modernization remained difficult 'works in progress'. Its internal transitional problems weakened its capacity to be an influential player in the Eurosystem.

The loss of the Bundesbank's authority over monetary policy and migration of associated expertise to the ECB was the central factor in its diminished power. This decline was apparent in its power over other domestic actors, notably the Federal Finance Ministry, and over other NCBs. To characterize its position in the Eurosystem, Zeitler (2007: 3), vice-president (2006–), resorted to a sporting metaphor: 'Earlier we were the only player on a small pitch. Today we are part of a team and the pitch has grown in size.' Extending this metaphor, the Bundesbank felt that it lacked adequate off-pitch support, above all from the federal government in fiscal policy and in banking supervision. The Bundesbank was weakened in domestic semi-sovereignty games, and this domestic weakening undermined its capacity within the Eurosystem.

Nevertheless, power moves in complex, shifting ways. In certain respects the Bundesbank retained and even increased its power. Whilst it suffered declining relative power over others, it focused on a *Wächterrolle* over its unique historical, intellectual, and legal legacy to the Eurosystem. This 'guardianship' role reflected the Bundesbank's ongoing indirect structural power—now collectivized—to effect policy outcomes through the Treaty mandate of the ECB. The key tests of whether this structural power would endure were represented in the ECB monetary policy strategy (especially the role and significance of its 'monetary' pillar) and in Treaty changes to the 'monetary' constitution (Deutsche Bundesbank 2003). The revised monetary policy strategy and the Constitutional/Reform Treaty changes suggested that this power remained intact—though the 'monetary' pillar was now secondary to the 'economic' pillar. Monetary policy decisions were also consistent with a Bundesbank trajectory for the Euro Area (Smant 2002). In addition, the gold sales issue reflected its continuing ability to defend its independence in managing the foreign exchange reserves. Although no longer able to benefit from the 'binding in' strategy of the federal government, it could count on partisan veto players threatening Bundesrat veto of government proposals. No less significantly, the Bundesbank retained the support of German public opinion as the most reliable, expert, and independent economic policy institution: and, consequent on its centralizing restructuring in 2002, it was released from the former constraints of the federal system on its internal reforms.

This enduring structural power and release from domestic constraints could not hide the reality that the post-euro Bundesbank was a more humdrum central bank and, in a dissimilar way to other Eurosystem 'insiders', had been substantially disempowered. It was confined to developing its role in technical areas like implementing ECB monetary policy, euro payment, and settlement systems, modernizing cash management, and operational aspects of banking supervision. Any more heroic pretensions to intellectual leadership were constrained by the Bundesbank's less glamorous formal powers. It had limited success in developing its macro-economic research capacity to strengthen its intellectual power in the Eurosystem or its influence in domestic economic debate; in helping promote Frankfurt and Germany as a financial centre (London remained pre-eminent); in becoming the lead domestic actor in banking supervision (the Federal Finance Ministry favoured BaFin); or in shaping the development of financial market supervision at the EU level or debate about IMF reform and global financial stability. In macro-economic research it was overshadowed by the economic research capacity of the ECB (though the appointment of Axel Weber as president in 2004 strengthened its reputation). The federal government further undermined its gravitational pull by cutting back special Bundesbank salary bonuses. Compared to the Federal Finance Ministry, it had few levers of power to assist Frankfurt as a financial centre. Eichel seized the initiative to sweep key decision-making in banking supervision into a new integrated financial services authority on the British model; whilst Steinbrück sought to further limit the Bundesbank's role. The potential for leadership in European banking supervision through the ESCB was frustrated by Eichel's sponsorship of the new CEBS. Although its international role in the IMF remained, it was more dependent for influence on coordinating policies in the Euro Group and ECOFIN. Against this background, central banking talent tended to drift away to the ECB.

Not least, the prestige of the Bundesbank as a privileged economic policy adviser to the federal government had fallen. No longer was it necessary to bind in the Bundesbank to economic policy proposals. Possibly the clearest testament was the powerlessness of the Bundesbank's opposition to the Schröder government's support for a more flexible Stability and Growth Pact. Symptomatic of its strategic interest in strengthening its visibility in German economic policy debate, above all vis-à-vis the Finance Ministry, was the publication of the Bundesbank's own projections of German economic development from late 2007. This move aimed to capitalize on greater public trust in the Bundesbank to avoid politically motivated economic projections and to project its role in the Eurosystem to domestic audiences.

7

Bank of Greece: Latecomer, Uphill Adjustment

George Pagoulatos[1]

Why should the Bank of Greece warrant particular attention? In the early 1990s, Greece posted the worst record among all EU member states in terms of deficits and inflation. The story of Greece's EMU accession is the uphill adjustment course of the most laggard of EU-15 economies, steered successfully by the country's central bank, the Bank of Greece. Thus, Greece was a latecomer in the Euro Area. It was the only state that wanted but could not enter in 1999 and remained in the antechamber for two more years before finally managing to accede alone in 2001, into stage three of EMU. This late accession was not a function of weak will but of acutely problematic initial macroeconomic conditions, testifying to the intensity of the adjustment enterprise and the scale of the final achievement. The Bank of Greece steered this arduous monetary adjustment course, led by Governor Lucas Papademos, who subsequently became vice-president of the European Central Bank. The wide initial gap between capabilities and expectations, and the central bank's leading role in bridging the gap, makes Greece a particularly revealing case study. The Bank of Greece offers a hard case of successful application of the orthodox EMU adjustment strategy, led by a rigorous and consistent disinflationary monetary policy.

The Bank of Greece (BoG) historically underwent three main evolutionary stages, following closely the European trend. Initially, a strong central bank was founded in 1928, in order to establish the monetary guarantees that would safeguard the interests of international creditors. The BoG was one of the central banks established by the League of Nations Financial Committee, endowed with the exclusive right to issue currency, a strong orthodox monetary and exchange-rate policy orientation, and important statutory guarantees of legal independence (Mazower 1991: 103 *ff.*; Pepelasis-Minoglou 1998).[2] Subsequently, in the early post-war period, the Bank was subjected to extensive financial intervention, seeking to combine monetary stability under the Bretton Woods system with the provision of targeted credit to sectors and activities deemed to be conducive to economic development. As had occurred in other countries such as France or Spain, in 1946 the Bank of Greece was subsumed under a governmental Currency Committee, which undertook all responsibility for exchange-rate, monetary, and credit policies. The Currency Committee was abolished in 1982, but the post-war interventionist apparatus persisted for a few more years, until a piecemeal process of deregulation began in 1987. Subsequently into the 1990s the Bank was gradually freed from government intervention and vested with full institutional autonomy in the process of preparing to join the EMU institutions.

While the chapter will focus on this latter third period of central bank convergence under the EMU programme, it is worth noticing the crucial impact of the European political economy context on every major stage of the BoG's historical development. But before examining the external 'push' factors of central bank change, we shall take a closer look at the domestic context within which the BoG operated.

Although the definitive driving force in transforming the central bank's role into one of full institutional independence came from the external EMU framework, its impact was mediated by the domestic structural, institutional, and politico-economic context.

Two main arguments will be advanced:

(a) Domestic economic governance failures and the institutional features of the domestic capitalist and politico-administrative system over the years generated significant demand for a more influential role of the central bank (Quaglia 2005a).

(b) The BoG's widely perceived success (defying negative expectations) in navigating the Greek currency into the Euro Area endowed it with formidable political capital, which, however, in the new post-accession EMU framework, was not to remain entirely intact.

The Politico-Administrative System, National Capitalism, and Patterns of Economic Governance

By the time of initiation of EMU and the Maastricht Treaty of 1993, the long-standing and structural features of Greece's political economy corresponded to what has been broadly, albeit impressionistically, identified as a Southern European model. Several—though certainly not all—of the main patterns of the Greek system may be generalizable across Southern Europe: a post-war tradition of far-reaching financial intervention, with a traditionally credit-based, under-developed financial system (Zysman 1983), weak, mostly state-controlled and domestic-oriented banks, and a use of state-administered credit for a combination of developmental and political purposes. In addition, these countries exhibited a lack of proper social concertation in a version of *parentela* pluralism, distinguished by party/government control over the unions, the latter dominated by wider public-sector representatives (Pagoulatos 2003*a*: 160 *ff.*). The private business sector had been traditionally dualistic and protected, losing significant ground in terms of productivity growth and international competitiveness during the high-inflation, post-1973 period until the early 1990s.

The extensive though ineffective state control over the economy and society has been rooted in structural features of the politico-administrative system, the Greek state being characterized as a 'colossus with feet of clay' (Sotiropoulos 1996). Public administration has been the principal target of party political patronage, intensified in the framework of an adversarial parliamentary system. Two parties (centre–right New Democracy and socialist PASOK) have alternated in government since the 1974 transition to democracy. For the first two post-authoritarian decades, party competition was characterized by intense politico-ideological polarization in a centrifugal two-party system, where differences between the two parties were deliberately magnified, especially on the part of PASOK. It was only after 1993–4, with the socialists' return to power, that the two parties converged over a commonly shared objective of acceding to EMU. Since then the two-party system has acquired strong centripetal tendencies. Each party, while in power, attempted to colonize the bureaucracy with clientelistic appointments, not just in the higher echelons but throughout the public sector. It was only as late as 1994 that a general examination process of entry to the public administration was instituted, and even after that occasionally circumvented. As a result of such patterns, the Greek state overall fell short of an elite civil service that could vest public policy with higher consistency and continuity, filtering out excess politicization.

Policy discontinuity had been a steady feature of economic policymaking until the early 1990s, marking not only government alternation in power but often policies under the same government. Dismal economic performance had been another feature, especially between the late 1970s and early 1990s, reaching its worst in 1989–90, when a prolonged electoral climate, three consecutive national elections within less than a year, and successive coalition governments had raised the public deficit and inflation to record levels in 1990 (Figures 7.1 and 7.2). Under government control, the BoG in the post-authoritarian period was forced to accommodate expansionary or at best 'stop-go' macroeconomic policies. The political identification of price stability with the mostly Right-wing or authoritarian post-war governments blunted socio-political reflexes against inflation. By the second half of the 1970s, a considerable section of the Greek public and body politic even positively identified a more lax and inflation-accommodating macroeconomic stance with progressive politics.

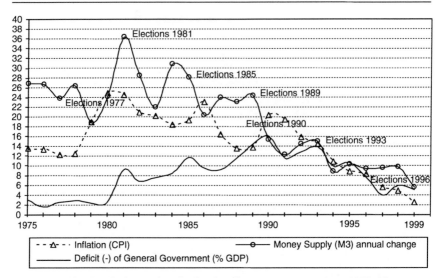

Figure 7.1. The Greek electoral cycle: fiscal and monetary expansion, 1975–99

Sources: Pagoulatos (2003*a*); Ministry of National Economy (1998, 2001); Bank of Greece (1993–2001).

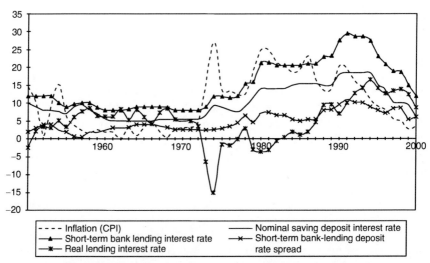

Figure 7.2. Greek inflation, interest rates, and short-term bank-lending deposit rate spread, 1950–2000

Sources: Pagoulatos (2003*a*); Bank of Greece (1992, 2000); Ministry of National Economy (2001).

After 1974, monetary authorities relied extensively on crawling peg or currency devaluation as means of recovering the losses of competitiveness under conditions of high inflation. After exceeding 25 per cent in 1973, double digit inflation persisted for three decades, peaking in 1980–1, 1985, and 1989–90, all key moments of the electoral cycle (Figure 7.1). Indeed, electoral cycles in the exercise of monetary and fiscal policy were evident throughout the period in question, exacerbating inflation and deficits in the aftermath of national elections. Given its obvious lack of independence, the BoG was not to be blamed for the monetary policy failure. It stood however to receive much of the credit for the successful EMU adjustment that was about to follow in the 1990s.

Overpoliticization, bureaucratic inefficiency, prolonged economic policy failure, and declining trust in the two main parties' capacity to spearhead Greece out of its economic crisis by the early 1990s had created favourable conditions for a more active and autonomous policy role of the BoG in bringing about macroeconomic stabilization. The conditions of intense and prolonged macroeconomic instability, and the fear that Greece was bound to miss the EMU train and become marginalized in the EU, led business and socio-economic groups from the beginning of the 1990s and throughout the decade to demand greater effectiveness in curbing the high levels of inflation. This also generated positive political capital for the BoG. Non-governmental actors, especially business, aspired to enter the framework of stability and predictability associated with a strong European currency. The transition cost of getting there (high lending rates) was not an adequately discouraging factor: business owners also held financial assets such as government bonds and repos, whose value increased during transition. Except for the communist and post-communist Left, trade unions (mostly leaning towards the socialist PASOK) also partook in the bi-partisan consensus over EMU accession (Pagoulatos 2003a: 129–30).

Thus in the early 1990s, two important, causally related processes were simultaneously witnessed: first, a long tradition of economic policy failure rooted in persisting patterns and domestic structural features; and, second, the emergence of a clear, tangible, and widely shared programmatic objective (EMU accession), whose desirability was proportionate to the gravity of Greece's perceived economic failure and fear of EU marginalization. The disjunction between policy desideratum and reality generated demand for a leading BoG role in pursuing nominal macroeconomic adjustment, even more so given the primacy of monetary stabilization in the entire EMU convergence programme.

Along with the demand conditions, the supply factors were there. The main supply factor was, of course, the EMU programme of central bank independence. A second supply factor operated at the domestic level and had to do with the government itself. The BoG institutional weakness of the 1970s and 1980s fostered the conditions for its drastic strengthening in the 1990s as precondition for the successful exercise of monetary policy. It derives from the orthodox literature that governments may well have a positive interest in allowing their central bank a significant degree of autonomy, institutional independence being considered a factor enhancing central bank credibility and effectiveness in combating inflation (Cukierman 1992; Giavazzi and Pagano 1988; Gilardi 2002). This is even more the case with governments plagued by inadequate resources, poor policy effectiveness, and questionable credibility. Of particular concern to state actors is the issue of creditworthiness: harsh market penalties (in the form of higher premiums) await borrower governments lax in combating inflation. For these reasons, the dominant orthodoxy held, it is desirable for democratic governments to have one macro-economic policy instrument which can respond exclusively to the technical requirements of the economy, and to achieve that it is in their interest to extend a significant degree of central bank autonomy (Woolley 1985: 334).

By the early 1990s prolonged macroeconomic instability was turning into serious political liability. The socio-economic demand for currency stability in the face of persisting high inflation ended up empowering the central bank, leading government to entrust it with more decisive control over monetary instruments in pursuit of disinflation. Thus, domestic economic policy failure, rooted in enduring patterns and structural factors, created favourable conditions for a bolder, active BoG involvement in the EMU adjustment process. The growing distance between the emboldening pace of European economic integration and Greece's lagging policy performance in meeting its challenges during the 1980s and early 1990s generated a vacuum of economic policy leadership. Bolstered by the rapidly rising importance of central banking after Maastricht, and the favourable economic, politico-institutional, and ideational conditions in the EU, the Bank of Greece rushed to fill the void.

From Interventionism, Through Liberalization, to Independence to the Eurosystem

The Bank of Greece: Resource Superiority and Policy Continuity

Since its establishment the BoG was endowed with ample finance and a consistently high quality of human resources. The governor's seat has been normally held by high-level technocrats, who overall exhibited significant job tenure and continuity (Table 7.1). A combination of undisputed technocratic competence, a consistent appearance of political neutrality, flexibility in dealing with government, and a long-standing career with the BoG have historically proven strong assets for survival from government changes.

The sheer number and quality of the BoG staff always placed it in a position of unrivalled superiority compared to any other government agency or bank

Table 7.1. Bank of Greece governors, 1946–2008

Appointment year	Governor	Previous office held
1946	Georgios Mantzavinos	BoG Deputy Governor
1955	Xenophon Zolotas	BoG Co-Governor
1967	Dimitrios Galanis	BoG Deputy Governor
1973	Constantinos Papayiannis	One-time Finance Minister
1974	Xenophon Zolotas	BoG Governor
1981	Gerasimos Arsenis	UNCTAD official
1984	Dimitris Halikias	BoG Deputy Governor
1992	Efthymios Christodoulou	Alternate Economy Minister
1993	Ioannis Boutos	Ex-Coordination Minister, MP
1994	Lucas Papademos	BoG Deputy Governor
2002	Nicolaos Garganas	BoG Deputy Governor
2008	Georgios Provopoulos	Former Commercial Bank CEO

institution. Career tenure and favourable employment circumstances of the higher-ranking personnel, their similarity of academic backgrounds, closeness of technocratic views and professional attitudes, considerable exposure to European policy milieus (especially since Greece's 1981 entry to the EC), and considerable stability in service have all been factors enhancing the Bank's effectiveness in formulating policy. Such conditions have been rather atypical in the Greek civil service, where remunerations have been lower, working conditions poorer, recruitment mostly non-meritocratic, and promotions more subject to party political criteria (Spanou 1998).

Consistency and continuity characterized the Bank's policy orientation over the years, not unrelated to the exposure of BoG staff to similar epistemic influences. Evident in the similarity of content and style of the governors' annual reports, continuity owed much to the fact that the Bank was traditionally able to develop its own internal hierarchy. Successive BoG administrations relied strongly on the same infrastructure of economic advisors, department directors, and deputy directors for the formulation of policy. As a result, when the surrounding conditions became conducive for a major monetary policy shift, the BoG commanded all the necessary resources for shaping policy, knew what its policy objectives were, was willing to pursue them, and was able to do so effectively by keeping its policy realm relatively under control.

Liberalization as Precondition for Monetary Policy Effectiveness

The introduction referred to a third stage of BoG evolution defining its course towards institutional independence and EMU accession. Three sub-stages can be distinguished: first, transition to institutional independence via credit deregulation (1987–94); second, steering EMU convergence (1994–9—1999 being the year of the EU Council decision on Greece's EMU entry—coinciding with stage two); and, third, 2000–present, with official participation in preparing stage three of EMU, the launch of the euro, and life in the Eurosystem.

The BoG course to institutional independence, monetary stability, and EMU accession began with pursuing a vital precondition of monetary policy effectiveness: domestic credit liberalization. Direct state-administered interest rates (over 90 different categories existed in the early 1980s) prevented the central bank from applying its monetary policy. Usually fixed at low levels in order to benefit favoured recipients including predominantly the government, nominal interest rates rose much more slowly than inflation, and remained negative in real terms through most of the 1973–87 period (Figure 7.2). Monetary stabilization required the central bank to be able to raise real interest rates to European levels and above, and that was predicated on interest rate liberalization (Figure 7.3).

Two facets of the financial regime got in the way of central bank policy effectiveness: credit intervention and its lack of institutional autonomy. The BoG's political dependency, government control over the majority of the banking system, and the obligatory bank investment requirement in government securities, all amounted to a soft budget constraint that enabled the heavy politicization of economic intervention in the late 1970s and especially through the 1980s.

Credit intervention had rendered monetary policy highly inflexible by multiplying the political cost of either monetary stabilization or the return to a less discretionary regime. Thus, following PASOK's 1985 re-election, after which an alarming balance of payments shortfall, a galloping public deficit, and inflation in the 20 per cent area was revealed, the BoG prioritized credit deregulation as a vital precondition for obtaining monetary policy

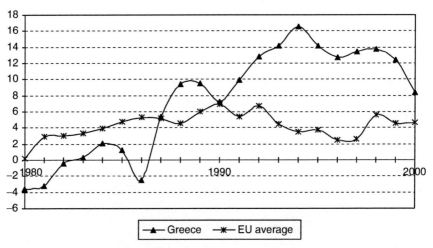

Figure 7.3. Real short-term interest rates: Greece and EU, 1980–2000
Sources: Pagoulatos (2003a); IMF (2000); Ministry of National Economy (1998, 2001).

effectiveness. The European single market programme (dictating the abolition of a range of subsidies granted through the credit system) and a post-election EC balance of payments support loan (incorporating measures of credit deregulation among its terms) offered the crucial opportunity (in the form of an external constraint) for the BoG to initiate a gradual programme of financial liberalization. This was concluded in the first half of the 1990s, amounting to what the *Financial Times* characterized as a 'silent revolution'.

As part of the European single market programme, the prospect of capital liberalization in the EU (which for the countries of the periphery, including Greece, had to be completed by 1994) necessitated far-reaching domestic financial reform. For the right sequencing to be followed, domestic credit—including interest rate—liberalization had to precede external capital liberalization. Several important, mostly preparatory, measures were taken during 1985–7, but the seminal act of liberalizing the lending rate was implemented in June 1987 (Figure 7.2). Rising real interest rates testified to the restrictive direction of monetary policy, which led macroeconomic adjustment. Although the 1985 stabilization programme was abandoned in 1987, it was the first systematic move towards the orthodox economic adjustment orientation that would prevail throughout the 1990s. The gradual deregulation process was slowed down for electoral purposes in 1988–90 but acquired new momentum with the 1990 rise of the centre–Right New Democracy government. A key element of this piecemeal 'revolution' was the momentous monetary policy shift from direct to indirect monetary control.

The BoG discourse of the 1980s–90s illustrates the argument underpinning the policy shift. It recognized that the emergence of persistent fiscal deficits and inflation after the 1970s had dramatically altered the conditions for the effective exercise of monetary policy. Direct credit controls, the post-war state's leading stabilization instrument, were becoming increasingly incapable of stabilizing the economy: as public deficits were pushing money supply growth upwards, it was hard to control credit supply without changing the interest rate levels. However, as administered interest rates were subject to political bargaining, they prevented the central bank from applying its own interest rate policy. Special obligatory investment ratios and the borrowers' recourse to the informal credit markets precluded the central bank's exercise of effective monetary control (BoG 1987: 37). Government securities forced upon the banking system at a government-determined interest rate forestalled the central bank's exercise of open market policy. Without open market operations (buying and selling government securities), the central bank was unable to control effectively the interest rate. Only a developed money market, according to the underlying central bank view, would allow effective control of monetary aggregates by enabling the central bank's regular unobstructed response to short-term liquidity changes (BoG 1987: 42). Domestic financial liberalization was thus deemed necessary to allow the central bank to employ its indirect monetary policy instruments more effectively towards disinflation, and respond more flexibly to the restrictive conditions of international markets.

External Pressures and Transmission Belts

The two major reform projects of the BoG in the 1980s and 1990s (financial liberalization and monetary reform culminating in Euro Area accession) were both externally induced and domestically demanded, brought about as a result of converging pressures and the pull factors already mentioned.

Gradually, from the second half of the 1980s, the international and European disinflationary regime was internalized into domestic economic policy-making and institutional design. Various transmission belts cooperated in bringing about adjustment to the disinflationary international regime and the neo-liberal–leaning economic paradigm of the 1980s, helping transform external pressures into domestic policy output.

In one of the various proposed typologies, Europeanization mechanisms have been classified using a two-dimensional framework and distinguishing between material versus cognitive, and direct versus indirect (Dyson 2002*b*: 13 *ff.*). Material mechanisms involved processes of hard or softer regulation and harmonization, for example, the Exchange-Rate Mechanism of the EMS (direct) and market interdependence or the threat of capital flight (indirect); cognitive mechanisms referred to the vertical diffusion of ideas of the sound finance paradigm (Dyson 2000, 2002) (direct) and the horizontal emulation of 'best practices' in central banking through processes of elite networking (indirect). These processes operate as transmission belts in passing international policy pressures and blueprints into the national policymaking system. Sector-level developments underlay the broader epistemic shifts towards greater profession-alization and 'scientization' in the banking and financial communities, as argued by Marcussen in this volume. Adjustment was a Europe-wide phenom-enon, though implemented with different timing, sequencing, and scope. Cross-national variation resulted from dissimilarity of institutional endow-ments, domestic economic conditions, and socio-political context.

Over the 1980s and into the 1990s, South European financial intervention (in Greece as well as Italy, Spain, and Portugal) was dismantled by liberaliza-tion (Pagoulatos 2003*b*). The European single financial market programme, complemented by EMU, represented an affirmation of the rising importance and power of the internationalized financial sector and central banks (Dyson, Featherstone, and Michalopoulos 1995). Moreover, the new strict 'sound finance' orientation satisfied the typically inflation-averse European bankers.

This paradigm shift incorporated the additional dimension of elite network-ing and peer pressure within the European expert community of central bankers. Long before the negotiation of the Maastricht Treaty, the central banks of EC member states had developed numerous informal cooperation practices and networks, cultivating their mutual relations (Andrews 2003). These practices evolved rapidly in the 1990s. From the second half of the 1970s, in view of Greece's prospective entry into the EC in 1980, expert contacts and exchange between BoG officials and technocrats and their European counterparts became more systematic. The interaction of EC with Greek government and central bank officials was intensified after the 1985 EC balance of payments support loan and the European single market programme. The domestic expert banking community became increasingly subject not only to the fashionable monetarist ideas of the time but also to the personal influence of their peers. By the mid-1970s the idea that 'money matters', the case for banking competition and the perception that credit regulation was responsible for serious 'rigidities', 'distortions', and 'misallocation of resources' (terms that were to prevail in the Greek banking discourse of the 1980s) had already captured the minds of European central bankers and were being elevated to virtual monetary orthodoxy.[3]

International monetary instability, combined with growing levels of capital mobility, eventually necessitated a more or less universal shift of Western countries to disinflation over the 1980s. The Greek domestic response to the international momentum of financial liberalization and disinflation was delayed, initiated only well into the second half of the 1980s, mediated as it was by domestic socio-political factors. Thus the initial response was inertia, if not retrenchment. But at that initial stage external pressure was still mostly ideational or structural and indirect (related to the changing international economy) and had not yet been vested with the force of hard conditionality. Such became the case after the European single market programme, the balance of payments support loans of 1985 and 1991, and finally the EMU programme.

The Decade of Adjustment (1990–2000)

The April 1990 election brought to power a neo-liberal–leaning, centre–Right New Democracy government, whose official ideological and political proclamations contained unambiguous commitment to liberalization and macroeconomic adjustment. So the EC, whose pressure by that time had intensified, found a cooperative partner. By 1990 the bulk of credit deregulation was completed, though specific loan categories were still being subsidized. For three consecutive years before 1990 monetary targets had been overshot, with liquidity expanding due both to the abolition of credit controls and to the swelling government deficit. In 1990 the BoG's restrictive monetary policy was closely adhered to—facilitated by the 1990 Stock Exchange boom, which alleviated demand previously exerted on the credit system.

The non-accommodative monetary policy inaugurated in 1990 ('hard drachma' and high real interest rates) continued with new vigour under the

PASOK governments of Andreas Papandreou in 1993 and Costas Simitis in 1996. Garganas and Tavlas (2001: 45 *ff.*) single out 1994 as the actual transition year to the 'hard drachma' policy regime, with 1991–4 being the transition phase to an increasingly effective monetary policy. Throughout the 1990s, the EMU roadmap sustained an overall ambitious reform momentum, anchored on a sequence of tangible, measurable, and increasingly feasible steps, at the end of which lay the prize of euro accession. Euro Area accession was contingent on the participation of national currencies in the Exchange-Rate Mechanism (ERM). The combination of liberalized capital movements and stable exchange rates necessitated the full alignment of national monetary policies behind the ERM, even for those EC/EU member states that had not yet entered the ERM. By 1998, when Greece joined the ERM, there was a growing sense of attainability of the EMU nominal convergence targets. Greece was officially admitted to the Euro Area in June 2000 and joined on 1 January 2001.

The importance of the external constraint factor cannot be exaggerated (cf. Dyson, Featherstone, and Michalopoulos 1995; Featherstone 2003). The successful drachma devaluation in March 1998 and ERM entry, in an environment of free capital movements (fully liberalized after spring 1994) and high interest rate differentials, led to massive inflows of mainly short-term capital. Apart from causing a liquidity surplus in the interbank market, which necessitated sterilization operations by the BoG, these inflows posed constant threat of a reverse outflow at the first signals of a government retreat from its announced policy targets. The imminence and salience of this external constraint exercised a most potent suasion for economic adjustment. The BoG viewed the ERM as a stabilizing framework on inflationary expectations, wage bargaining, and pricing behaviour and as a reinforcing factor for policy credibility, allowing consistent stability-oriented monetary, fiscal, incomes, and structural policies (Voridis, Angelopoulou, and Skotida 2003: 34).

The Monetary Policy Shift and the Political Ascendance of the BoG

Over the 1990s, financial liberalization and monetary adjustment led to macroeconomic convergence in three closely related ways. First, as mentioned, financial liberalization was the *sine qua non* precondition for allowing monetary policy to become assertive and carry the brunt of stabilization. Liberalization allowed the introduction of new instruments of monetary management. It enabled the BoG to rely flexibly on open market operations, seeking to influence short-term interest rates in the interbank market as its main intermediate goal. Second, financial liberalization generated flexible conduits of intermediation: mostly short-term government securities markets and the associated distribution channels such as mutual funds. After the government had shifted away from deficit monetization, they allowed for public deficits to be absorbed by private investors. Third, the greater role of private investors in public deficit financing subjected government to stricter discipline in its monetary and fiscal policies (OECD 1995: 58–60).

In its annual reports of the early 1990s, the BoG mentioned the balance of payments, GDP growth, and banking liberalization as additional secondary objectives to the reduction of inflation. Following other central banks, however, it was already succumbing to the appeal of monetary targeting. After capital movements were fully liberalized in 1994, the BoG adopted an exchange-rate intermediate target (publicly announced on an annual basis), alongside its monetary target. Progressively the monetary target was de-emphasized, and the BoG after 1997–8 endorsed a version of inflation targeting, setting the ultimate inflation objective for two years ahead (Bank of Greece, various years; Voridis, Angelopoulou, and Skotida 2003).

Until 1994, the BoG was clearly not independent (Pagoulatos 2003a).[4] After 1994, when the Maastricht-imposed abolition of the monetary financing of government deficits entered into force, the BoG satisfied all the formal criteria of economic independence. Finally, in the context of full statutory harmonization with the Eurosystem, law 2548 of December 1997 ('Provisions relating to the Bank of Greece') granted the BoG complete institutional independence and stipulated that 'the primary objective of the Bank of Greece shall be to ensure price stability. Without prejudice to this primary objective, the Bank shall support the general economic policy of the government.' The law established BoG independence from any government instructions or advice, exclusive authority in the exercise of monetary policy, a six-year renewable term for the governor and deputy governors, and a Monetary Policy Council (comprising the governor, the two deputy governors, and three additional members). The Monetary Policy Council, which began to operate in 1998, was assigned responsibility for decisions pertaining to monetary policy definition and implementation and to the conduct of exchange-rate policy, the operation of payment systems, and the issue of banknotes.

The primacy of the euro accession objective, in an adverse environment of large deficits and a tradition of lax monetary and fiscal policies, endowed the central bank with extraordinary political authority. The BoG has been widely credited for Greece's accession to the Euro Area. Crucial after 1994 was the presence at the helm of Professor Lucas Papademos, a widely respected monetary economist and pragmatic proponent of the orthodox mix of drastic disinflation and fiscal overhaul, combined with growth-enhancing structural liberalization.

Thus the cross-party political adoption of euro entry as a 'national objective', combined with the acute macroeconomic conditions, led to a momentous increase of central bank power. In sum, the gains of central bank authority in the domestic socio-political system were a combined result of its endowment with formal institutional independence after 1994 and the successful implementation of the Euro Area accession mission.

Financial System Transformed

Although monetary austerity implied burdensome restrictions on their liquidity, Greek commercial banks were able to benefit in the high interest-rate period that followed liberalization by retaining wide interest-rate spreads, indicative of the sector's persisting oligopolistic structure. The 'hard drachma' policy that followed banking liberalization until ERM entry was a boon for the (sheltered) financial sector, allowing banks to reap sizeable profits from a growing volume of financial transactions in a steadily appreciating (in real terms) national currency. Higher interest rates served not just the 'public' objective of disinflation but also eventually the commercial banks' preference for market-determined interest rates. The large volume of bad loans accumulated by the state-controlled section of the Greek banking system necessitated a central bank strategy of enhancing bank profitability, in view of the Second Banking directive and the subsequent capital adequacy standards of the Basle framework (Pagoulatos 1999).

In the aftermath of liberalization, and despite competition by non-bank financial institutions, Greek commercial banks overhauled their portfolios, solidified their capital bases, and reaped remarkable profits by colonizing the new financial markets and institutions. Liberalization (especially after 1994 when capital movements were freed) advanced banking interests by lifting imposed obligations and restrictions, and releasing opportunities for profit. Government recourse to public debt markets enhanced the banks' bargaining power, given their role as principal buyers of government paper. They were able to place their assets in risk-free government securities, and negotiate not only market rates but also other significant concessions, such as underwriting privatization schemes and financing large-scale infrastructure projects.

Euro Area membership entailed far-reaching transformations. Among others, the transition from a high-inflation to a low-inflation economic environment generated certain long-term financial markets (such as fixed-interest mortgages or long-term debt instruments) that were non-existent or dormant during the inflationary period. As EMU convergence was realized in Greece, the yield curve for government securities was extended to 20 years, a marked improvement over the conditions until just 1998, when only short-term maturities were issued. EMU consolidated the disintermediation shift of the 1980s and 1990s: that is, the shift from bank lending to transactions in securities. In Europe as well as in Greece, the movement from bank-based towards increasingly securitized finance was followed by growing 'equitization' from the late 1990s.

Equity capitalization in Greece rose from 2 per cent of GDP in 1985 to 15 per cent in 1994 up to 169 per cent in 1999, then receding to 98 per cent in 2000 following the decline of stock prices (Capital Market Committee 2001: 40). As in continental Europe, financial liberalization in Greece has notably increased the role of the capital market but has not as yet reversed the financial system's bank-based character. Liberalized banking competition is thus the main aftermath of financial deregulation, involving important efficiency as well as systemic safety implications. These shape the novel environment in which the BoG's supervisory responsibility is exercised. Liberalization increased bank competition in interest rates, though with a significant time lag. Falling lending rates and more aggressive banking competition animated demand for credit, which had been suppressed by the high interest rates over much of the 1990s. Consumer credit grew at an average annual rate of about 40 per cent over the period 1994–2000, but the ratio of consumer credit to GDP in 2000 was only 4.5 per cent in Greece compared to 10 per cent in the Euro Area members. Similarly, the corresponding ratio for mortgage lending in 2000 stood at about 8 per cent compared to the EU average of 40 per cent. By 2006 the figures were converging to Euro Area standards.

On the assets side, banks developed trading activities and securitization operations (including fees opportunities for advising and underwriting), while the fall of traditional deposits from the 2000s was countered by the rise of money market mutual funds and other liabilities (Belaisch et al. 2001). Income from the management of investment and pension funds controlled by the larger banking groups has been assuming important proportions in Greece and throughout the Euro Area. In 2000, the majority of mutual funds operating in the Greek market were banking group subsidiaries. Moreover, the copious windfall income achieved from securities trading, especially during the Greek stock market boom of 1998–9, allowed banks previously burdened with bad debts to clean up their portfolios and list very high profits.

Under the Eurosystem: A Redefined Role

Surrendering monetary policy to the ECB allowed the BoG to focus on its other areas of institutional responsibility. The new role entailed increased emphasis on two main areas: banking supervision (an area of weakness in the past), and research and information. The BoG developed communication policies of public dissemination and systematic promotion of special studies and research initiatives. It also undertook a new set of responsibilities for the more efficient functioning of the Eurosystem, involving mainly the modernization of material and technological infrastructures, the establishment of collaboration networks, and their staffing with personnel of high quality and expertise.

The BoG has always relied on an elite research department, but Euro Area accession placed renewed emphasis on the recruitment of high-level technocratic personnel of postgraduate and PhD level. As Dyson and Marcussen underline in this volume, the Eurosystem brought a major adaptation of the central bank's mission towards stronger research and data analysis. The staff training programmes reveal the novel areas of BoG interest as part of the Eurosystem: the operation and security of information systems; the global understanding and evaluation of Greek and international capital and money markets; the operation and efficient use of new financial instruments in risk management; foreign exchange management; e-banking risks; new international accounting standards; and effective banking supervision.

Facing these new circumstances, the BoG restructured its Economic Research Department to respond to its obligations under the Eurosystem to improve the analysis of current economic developments and participate in drafting economic projections. In 2000 a separate Statistics Department was created, under which came several services formerly belonging to the Economic Research Department. Thus the BoG acquired two distinct Departments specializing in research. Both have been staffed with expert scientific personnel, producing a significant number of BoG publications. Over the last few years, the Governor's Annual Report has been visibly upgraded, in both volume and quality, and two publications have been added (Monetary Policy Annual Report and Monetary Policy Interim Report), all officially submitted to the Greek Parliament. As part of central bank accountability, the BoG Statute (Article 5B) provides that the Governor, when asked, shall appear before the competent parliamentary committee to report on BoG-related matters. The BoG has expanded its statistical and economic bulletin series,[5] and in 2003 a new series of BoG Working Papers was launched (around 20 academic and policy-oriented papers in English are published annually).

The Information Systems Department was restructured. The BoG launched the Electronic Secondary Securities Market and created a Help Desk Unit, an Information Systems' Security Unit, and an Alternative Information Technology Centre. The Information and Communications Office, assigned with mastering the Bank's website, was upgraded in 2002 into the Communication, Press and Management Section within the Administration Department. This latter change was justified as part of the ECB strategic plan of improving national central bank communication policies, in a twin effort to facilitate the understanding of monetary policy and Eurosystem functioning and to promote the ECB principles of openness, transparency, and accountability.

With the surrender of national monetary policy to the ECB, the responsibilities of the BoG Monetary Policy Council were reduced to a mere analysis of monetary and economic policy developments and of the domestic impact of monetary policy. The BoG contribution in the monetary policy domain is thus confined to implementing ECB guidelines and supervising the payments system. Here too organizational restructuring followed institutional and policy change. Initially, in 2000, the Monetary Policy and Banking Department acquired an office assigned with the oversight of payment systems, aiming to safeguard the latter's integrity and credibility. In 2003, the Monetary Policy and Banking Department was abolished, and its operations were subsumed under the newly established Financial Operations Department and Department for the Supervision of Credit and Financial Institutions (see Figure 7.4).

The BoG structure was affected by the transfer of exchange-rate policy to the ECB. Its operations and activities were partly re-oriented from international markets and transactions to the Eurosystem, aiming to strengthen the cooperation networks of Euro Area central banks at the expense of a more independent international orientation. In 2000, a Risk Management, Performance Measurement and Foreign Exchange Liquidity Section, and an International Markets Research and Analysis Section were created under the Foreign Exchange Department. In 2003, the International Transactions Department was abolished, and the Foreign Exchange Department was restructured into Financial Operations Department. This new department was upgraded, undertaking the exchange-rate policy-related responsibilities of the recently abolished Monetary Policy and Banking Department, and assuming a broader role within the Eurosystem. The office for the Oversight of Payment Systems was upgraded into a fully fledged Payment Systems Department, while a novel Strategic Planning and Organization Department was created.

Banking liberalization shifted the central bank's approach in banking supervision from emphasizing compliance with administrative regulations to focusing on the risks involved in the functioning of the banking system. Mirroring the evolution of regulatory standards under the Basle capital adequacy framework, the central bank's supervisory agenda addresses not only solvency, liquidity, and concentration of risks but also matters of effective corporate governance of credit institutions in terms of good administrative and accounting organization and internal control structures.

The scope of the BoG supervisory responsibility grew following the expansion of non-bank financial market institutions subject to its supervisory jurisdiction. In addition to commercial banks, its responsibility includes special credit institutions (e.g. the Loans and Consignment Fund and the Postal Savings Bank), cooperative banks, leasing, factoring, and financing companies and exchange bureaux. The Capital Market Committee supplements the BoG in supervising the financial sector.

Geographical expansion through cross-border banking mergers and acquisitions further enhanced the importance of the supervisory function. Indicatively, the size of the banking system in 2000 involved a total of little less than 500 branches of Greek banks and their subsidiaries. By that time Greek banks had just started to expand dynamically into South-eastern Europe. By 2007, total branches of Greek banks in the Balkans had risen to 2,100, an indication of the breadth and complexity of the supervisory task. As Moran and Macartney observe in this volume, the central bank thus acts as a significant

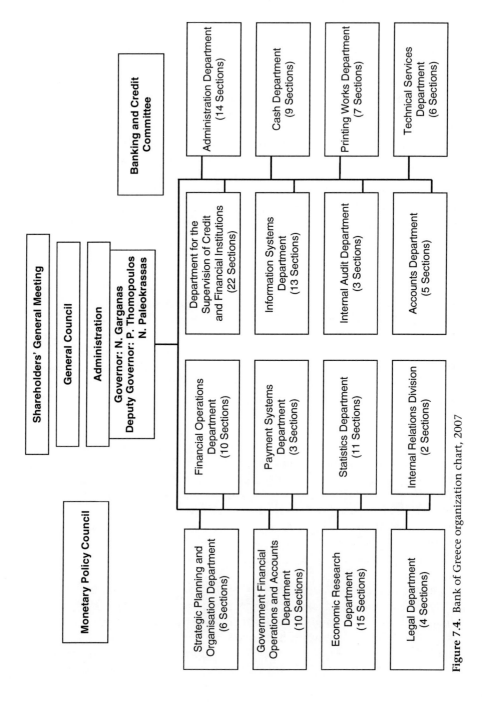

Figure 7.4. Bank of Greece organization chart, 2007

agent of cross-border institutional and policy transfer—in the South-eastern European region.

Conclusion: A Changing Political Role and the 'Paradox of Depoliticization'

The turn of the century finds the BoG part of a different balance between state and financial system, in a novel political economy. The banking system is no longer government-controlled and forced to subsidize developmental or redistributive priorities, but free to operate along profit-maximizing lines. The central bank is vested with full political independence, is institutionally prohibited from participating in the primary market for public debt, and is officially endowed (as part of the Eurosystem) with a statutory commitment to price stability. The government has no channel of access to preferential credit by taxing the banking system, but is forced to finance its deficit by resorting to the internationalized money markets. On the ascending side in terms of importance and bargaining power are financial markets, banks, financial investors, institutional stockholders, and bondholders. Disinflation becomes a principal normative determinant, given that both government and the private-enterprise sector as deficit units rely exclusively on liberalized financial markets able to demand constantly higher returns, and given the supreme bargaining power of the (typically inflation-averse) creditors within the system.

Since the second half of the 1980s and especially over the 1990s, the BoG steered the structural transformation of the Greek financial system and the momentous change of monetary policy that landed an erstwhile problematic economy at the monetary core of the EU. The prize of the BoG's leading role in the economy's nominal adjustment process was its own institutional independence, if only short-lived, as its 'sovereign' policymaking authority was surrendered to the Euro Area. The BoG was transformed to national-level executive branch of an independent European supranational institution. For an economy with a long track record of monetary instability, such surrender of monetary independence meant that much more was to be gained than lost. However, significant structural, organizational, and functional transformations of the BoG have been associated with this development.

The BoG continues to operate as a custodian of the national economy, authoritative source of independent technocratic assessment of economic conditions, and *par excellence* 'objective' economic advisor to the government. In the initial climate of euphoria that followed successful accession to the Euro Area, the BoG enjoyed public visibility, cross-party respectability, and considerable popularity. The latter was soon to recede as life under the euro gave rise to a new generation of problems. Its institutional role as part of the Eurosystem renders the BoG a representative of the orthodox central banking doctrine that (given the commitment of ECB monetary policy to price stability and of national fiscal policy to flanking budgetary discipline and fiscal sustainability) economic growth can only result from structural reforms, that is, most prominently market liberalization, labour-market flexibility, and far-reaching pension reform. The BoG has been the most persistent advocate of wage moderation and structural reforms in these politically controversial policy areas, consequently becoming the target of widespread political attacks, to an extent unseen in the past. Susceptibility to such political hostility is further aggravated by the central bank being perceived as a banking system ally and apologist of its galloping profitability. Being the flipside of the rapidly increasing indebtedness of Greek households, bank profits and what is perceived as the BoG's 'neo-liberal agenda' are becoming a focal point of political opposition from the Left and the populist Right.

We are thus faced with what we might call 'a paradox of central bank depoliticization'. Before acquiring independence the central bank was subject to the government's politicized macroeconomic governance. While being used as an instrument in the service of the government's objectives, the central bank was nonetheless rarely accused of pursuing a politico-ideological agenda, not least because the government absorbed the political heat of such opposition. As an independent institution, however, and especially as executive arm of the ECB, the national central bank becomes the domestic focal point of opposition against what a significant part of the political spectrum regards as 'monetarist' and 'neo-liberal' economic policy. In other words, the national central bank's depoliticization, by way of independence from national governmental political objectives, has subjected it to far greater political controversy than it had ever elicited during its long period of supposed 'politicization'. The answer to this apparent paradox is, of course, that, for all its technocratic robustness, central banking orthodoxy is not distributionally neutral: it affects socio-economic interests in different ways, it involves gains and losses.

Notes

1. The chapter has benefited from the research assistance of Christos Triantopoulos.
2. The 1928 Charter provided for a five-year term of BoG governors and for an independent arbitration commission to resolve disputes in case of disagreement between BoG and government, and seriously restricted the BoG's direct or indirect financing of government or public enterprises.
3. The book of Halikias (1978) (BoG governor for 1984–92) is representative of the monetarist-leaning central bank orthodoxy.
4. Until 1994 the BoG satisfied only 3 of the 10 generally accepted formal criteria of political independence. Among the formal criteria of economic independence, until

end 1993 only the discount rate criterion was satisfied (but then, the discount rate was of minimal importance anyway in a regime of administered interest rates). In terms of formal political independence, Grilli, Masciandaro, and Tabellini (1991) ranked the BoG over the central banks of Britain, Portugal, Japan, Belgium, and New Zealand and at the same level as those of France and Spain. However, in overall pre-1994 formal independence, the BoG was outranked by all, except Portugal and New Zealand.

5. Economic Bulletin (since 1992), Monthly Statistical Bulletin (since 1999), Monthly Statistical Bulletin of Economic Conjuncture (since 1997), and Monthly Bulletin of Regional Economic Conjuncture Macedonia-Thrace (since 1999).

8

The Banca d'Italia: Between Europeanization and Globalization

Lucia Quaglia

The Banca d'Italia is one of the largest central banks in the European Union (EU). It is a relatively powerful player in the Eurosystem, which it joined when the third stage of Economic and Monetary Union (EMU) began in 1999. In an interview released in the run up to the third stage, its Governor, Antonio Fazio, expressed his concerns about Italy's membership of the single currency, arguing that it would be a 'purgatory' (*Financial Times*, 10 November 1998).

This chapter addresses the question of what have been the main changes experienced by the Banca d'Italia as a result of Europeanization and globalization over the last 20 years, but with the focus on the most recent period, from its entry into the Euro Area. To what extent has the Italian central bank been able to resist or mediate external pressure for change, namely, Europeanization and globalization, and how has it adapted to them? Has this led to convergence of institutional structures, policy templates, and roles performed by the Banca d'Italia? How has its power in national, EU, and international monetary and financial matters changed after the establishment of European monetary union?

The chapter is organized according to a temporal sequence, taking a diachronic perspective in order to explain continuity and change over time. As Europeanization is a long-term incremental process, its direct and indirect effects should be traced and assessed over time. The chapter first examines the independence, internal governance, legitimacy, policies, and atypical roles performed by the Banca d'Italia prior to the establishment of European monetary union. The second part examines these issues with reference to the period after the creation of monetary union. These sections, which help to trace institutional and policy convergence over time, also discuss the institutional context and power relations in which the central bank is embedded. Finally, the chapter explores the role of the Banca d'Italia in the Eurosystem, including the interactions with the European Central Bank (ECB), and its interactions in the international system, first and foremost in central banking networks dealing with banking supervision. Its international role is necessarily less important than its position in the Eurosystem, given that the Banca d'Italia, unlike the German Bundesbank, was not one of the top three world-wide players. The concluding section elaborates further the themes of Europeanization, convergence, and power.

The Banca d'Italia has undergone significant changes in the last 20 years, and the pace of change has quickened in the last decade or so, first and foremost as a result of preparation for Euro Area entry and then membership. However, certain policies, such as banking supervision, have been only marginally affected by Europeanization, limiting the process of convergence. Globalization has also promoted convergence, especially through the structural power exerted by financial markets and the 'power of ideas' (paraphrasing Hall 1989), that is the spread of a specific policy paradigm centred on central bank independence and price stability. In certain instances, the Banca d'Italia has been able to resist or at least to delay externally triggered convergence. Indeed, the Italian central bank seems to have experienced some difficulties in re-designing its role in the Eurosystem and adapting to membership, difficulties that re-shaped its power relations at the national and EU levels. It has been a difficult, delayed process of Europeanization for the Italian central bank, a process that is far from complete, but which was given extra momentum by the appointment of a new Governor in 2005.

The Banca d'Italia Prior to European Monetary Union

The Banca d'Italia has often been described as the least independent among the group of independent central banks or, to put it another way, as the more independent within the category of the dependent central banks (*Financial Times*, 22 November 1989). Indeed, until the changes introduced in the early 1990s in preparation for monetary union and discussed in the following section, in economists' rankings the Banca d'Italia used to be awarded fairly high scores as far as political independence (especially, personnel independence) was concerned, but scored rather low on economic independence (Alesina and Summers 1993; Cukierman 1992; Grilli, Masciandaro, and Tabellini 1991).

The Bank's personnel independence was safeguarded by the legal provisions and established practices for the appointment of the Executive Board (*Direttorio*), the length of its members' tenure in office, and difficulties of dismissal, as well as by the distribution of power within the Bank. The procedures for the appointment process and the practices that developed over time, as well as the position of the Governor, as discussed below, very much limited the power of the political authorities in selecting the top management of the Bank, strengthening its independence.

Before the 2005 reform, legislation limited the direct influence of the political authorities in the appointment process of the Governor and the other members of the Executive Board. The Executive Board consists of the Governor, the Director-General, and three Deputy Directors-General. In 2006 the number of deputy directors-general was raised from two to three, so as to have an odd number of members. Prior to 2005, the nomination of all four members of the Executive Board, including the Governor, was proposed by the Board of Directors (*Consiglio Superiore*). It had to be approved by a decree of the president of the Republic, acting on the proposal of the prime minister together with the Treasury minister, after discussion in the Council of Ministers. Furthermore, the practice of internal appointments to senior and top positions in the Bank generally prevailed. Hence the Governor was generally chosen from among deputy governors, and deputy governors were normally chosen from among senior officials at the Bank.

Moreover, before 2005, all four members of the Executive Board were appointed *sine die*, that is, their mandate was open-ended and there was no age limit. In practice, since the Second World War the longest period for governors to have remained in office was for a decade or more, like other members of the Executive Board. The same body that proposed the appointment of the members of the Executive Board, the Board of Directors, could repeal their appointment through a joint decision-making procedure, involving the government and the President of the Republic (Finocchiaro and Contessa 2002). However, the members of the Board of Directors are elected by the holders of the Bank's capital quotas by a secret vote in a process apparently immune from interference from the government of the day, generally following the proposals put forward by the Bank itself (interviews, Rome, March 2002).

The appointment of the members of the Executive Board for life, together with the distribution of power within the Bank, as determined by its governance structure, contributed to make the Governor a powerful figure. Until 2005, the Banca d'Italia was one of the most centralized and hierarchical central banks in Europe. The distribution of power within the Bank was very much skewed in favour of the Governor. He had wide powers and discretion, in that all responsibilities in monetary, exchange-rate, and supervisory policies were concentrated in his hands.

In contrast to this relatively high personnel independence, the economic independence (in economists' studies also referred to as 'instrument' independence, see Cukierman 1992; Grilli, Masciandaro, and Tabellini 1991) of the Bank was low and was completed only in 1993, when the overdraft account of the Treasury at the central bank was closed down, in order to prepare for the final stage of monetary union. Nonetheless, the financial and organizational independence in terms of economic resources available to the central bank was and is remarkable. For example, Bank officials are among the best-paid civil servants in Italy, and the Governor is one of the best-paid governors in the world. This is important because it has allowed the central bank to attract and retain high calibre, well-trained officials, who, in turn, have provided the Bank with advanced economic knowledge. In the macroeconomic field, this is a clear instance of 'when knowledge is power' (Haas 1990).

The other side of central bank independence and power is its accountability and legitimacy. Until the 2000s, the legitimacy of the Banca d'Italia had hardly ever been questioned in Italy, for a variety of reasons. Before the statutory changes introduced in order to comply with the Maastricht Treaty in the early 1990s, the Banca d'Italia was not legally independent of the government. Hence the issue of accountability was not very significant. Moreover, the Banca d'Italia could rely on widespread domestic public acceptance of its activities and the policies that it delivered. Public opinion surveys reveal that the Banca d'Italia was the most trusted institution in Italy. Indeed, the intangible assets of the Bank, such as expertise in monetary and financial matters and a distinctive operational culture, were important in fostering public support, as were some of the atypical roles performed by the central bank over time, as elaborated below.

Let us now look briefly at the power of the Banca d'Italia in the main policies in which it was involved before the establishment of the Eurosystem: monetary policy, exchange-rate policy, and financial stability.

Monetary Policy

Before the changes implemented in the early 1990s in preparation for monetary union, power in the conduct of monetary policy in Italy was formally shared between the Treasury and the central bank. It should be noted that, before the amendments introduced in order to comply with the Maastricht Treaty, the Italian central bank was not assigned the statutory objective of maintaining price stability. On the one hand, in practice, the Bank had a preponderant power in the conduct of monetary policy, because it had the technical expertise, macroeconomic credibility, and knowledge of the market that until the early 1990s the Treasury (or any other governmental body) lacked (Quaglia 2005a). On the other hand, the Bank's power in monetary policy was *de facto* limited by the conduct of fiscal policy, which, unlike monetary policy, was in the hands of the political authorities, negatively affecting the economic independence of the Bank.

Together with the institutional arrangements for central bank independence, monetary policy is the domain in which the impact of economic ideas, in the form of 'policy paradigms' (cf. Hall 1993) has been greatest in promoting convergence in Europe and worldwide (Dyson 1994; Marcussen 2000; McNamara 1998). In the 1980s, the monetary policy paradigm at the Bank changed substantially, switching from a Keynesian approach to a stability-oriented one, whereby the main objective of monetary policy became the fight against inflation. The spread of stability-oriented economic ideas led to a gradual (and at times difficult) convergence of monetary policy towards the German model, outlined by Dyson (this volume). Such convergence can also be seen as a 'downloading' effect of Europeanization, prior to the establishment of European monetary union and triggered by Italy's membership of the European Monetary System (EMS).

Exchange-Rate Policy

Italy joined the technical part of the EMS, the Exchange-Rate Mechanism (ERM), in 1979. Afterwards, exchange-rate policy became a key component of the monetary policy strategy followed by the Banca d'Italia, whereby the quantity of money (M2) was the intermediate target and the exchange rate was a 'quasi final objective' (Sarcinelli 1995). Hence, the ERM was used by the Italian central bank as a mechanism to foster macroeconomic convergence, first and foremost convergence of monetary policy and inflation performance (Ciampi 1990). Exchange-rate policy was crucial in this strategy, deploying 'Europe' (to be precise ERM membership) as an external constraint, which augmented the decision-making power of the Bank domestically, shielding the conduct of monetary policy from political interference.

Before European monetary union, decision-making power in exchange-rate policy was shared between the Banca d'Italia and the Treasury. The Bank was responsible for the day-to-day management of the exchange rate, while the government decided on the exchange-rate regime, and the Treasury, together with the Bank, was involved in parity realignment in the ERM. *De facto*, the domestic power of the Bank in exchange-rate policy went well beyond what was prescribed by legal provisions, for the same reasons as in monetary policy: advanced macroeconomic knowledge, market expertise, and limited Treasury's technical capabilities.

However, the external power of the Bank in exchange-rate policy was curtailed by the dominant role of the Bundesbank, which was the 'leader' of the ERM (on the functioning of the ERM, see Giavazzi and Giovannini 1989; Giavazzi, Micossi, and Miller 1988). In other words, the other central banks in the system had largely to adapt to the Bundesbank's monetary policy, which indirectly influenced the conduct of the monetary and exchange-rate policies in other European states.

Participation in the EMS, which was an exchange-rate regime based on an adjustable peg, produced a major shift in Italian exchange-rate policy and monetary strategy. In short, Europeanization effects were at work well before the establishment of monetary union. From the first half of the 1980s onwards realignments of the lira never fully compensated for the inflation differentials between Italy and the low-inflation states within the ERM (Ciampi 1990). Furthermore, from 1987 to 1992, no realignments took place, leading to an appreciation of the lira in real terms (Gaiotti and Rossi 2003,). It was the so-called 'strong' exchange-rate policy (or 'hard currency' option) coupled to a relatively tight monetary policy.

The withdrawal of the lira from the ERM in September 1992 reversed the exchange-rate policy followed by the Italian authorities during the 1980s. The subsequent floating lira became an important element of the Italian strategy, fostering an export-led boom, which in turn sustained Italian economic growth in a phase of fiscal retrenchment and slow growth in the EU. The lira re-entered the ERM in November 1996, which was essential to fulfil the nom-inal convergence criteria in order to join monetary union in the first wave in January 1999.

Those critical of Euro Area membership argue that the loss of competitive-ness that affected Italian goods and services and the deficit in the balance of payments since the late 1990s suggest that, as far as variables in the real economy are concerned, Italy was not ready for European monetary union. Not enough 'real' convergence had taken place in preparation for the final stage of EMU. Governor Antonio Fazio and some of his close advisers were leading proponents of this 'Eurosceptic' interpretation of Italy's membership in European monetary union (Quaglia 2004). In an interview released shortly before the beginning of the final stage Fazio argued that Italy was not ready for European monetary union because in particular structural reforms had not been carried out (*Financial Times*, 10 November 1998). A senior official at the Bank interviewed in 2001 likened Italy's performance in the Euro Area to a medium-weight boxer fighting a match against a heavy-weight opponent without proper training (interview, Rome, June 2001).

Financial Stability

The Banca d'Italia is responsible for the systemic stability of the financial sector, including all financial intermediaries; the prudential supervision of banks and securities market intermediaries; the oversight of relevant markets for monetary policy; and the oversight of the payments system. Financial supervisory tasks have not substantially changed with European monetary union. The main change took place in 2005, as discussed below, in that until that date the Bank had been responsible for safeguarding competition in the banking sector. Overall, as compared to other European central banks prior to monetary union, the Banca d'Italia had extensive and largely discretionary power concerning banking policy and prudential supervision. Indeed, it was the only central bank in Europe in charge of competition policy in the banking sector. This almost unchecked power became evident in 2005, as elaborated below.

Other Roles

Besides the three core central banking policies (monetary policy, exchange-rate policy, and financial stability and supervision), the Banca d'Italia has performed a variety of services for the government. However, they have been reduced over time, as a certain degree of convergence of the 'other functions' performed by central banks has taken place in the Eurosystem. The Bank used to act as banker to the government, a function that came to an end in 1993 and was ruled out by the EMU provisions in the Maastricht Treaty. Nowadays the government has a non-interest–bearing deposit at the Bank, and the overdraft facility has been closed. The Bank used to manage the public debt, in conjunction with the Treasury, but in the 1990s this task became the competence of the Treasury alone. The Bank manages the payments system, a task that is shared with other central banks in the Eurosystem (see below). All banks based in Italy are obliged to keep a non-interest–bearing deposit at the Bank, which acts as lender of last resort. In addition, the Banca d'Italia has often acted as an adviser to the government on a variety of matters.

Over time the Banca d'Italia has performed other functions that can be regarded as 'country-specific', that is to say, result from the configuration of the Italian socio-economic and political system. It was a 'strong' central bank in a 'weak' state (cf. the Banque de France). This meant that the Banca d'Italia acted outside the traditional boundaries of a central bank, performing certain functions that should arguably have been carried out by other parts of the Italian state apparatus or civil society. This situation strengthened the power of the central bank, but also made its functions more complex. Once in European monetary union some of these functions came to an end, so that the Italian central bank has converged towards practices of other central banks. At the same time, as we see below, some new self-assigned roles have been taken on board by the central bank.

A Strong Central Bank in a Weak State

For most of the post-war period, the Banca d'Italia acted as an 'economic counter power to the government'. For all the reasons mentioned above, notably central bank personnel, financial, and organizational independence; its access to advanced macroeconomic expertise, and knowledge of the financial markets, the Bank was a strong institution in a weak state. The state was composed of fragmented political institutions, and the executive had limited political capacity, which was further weakened by frequently changing coalition governments. There was an inclination on the part of government, and politicians more generally, to let the Bank make difficult decisions, supposedly on technical rather than political grounds (Quaglia 2005*a*). This was part of a larger picture, where the tacit acknowledgement of the absence of strong political institutions fostered policymaking by technocrats, several of whom moved to important political positions in the 1990s.

Until the early 1990s, the Banca d'Italia had a near monopoly of expertise in Italy, a trend that continued in the 2000s, even though the Treasury augmented its technical capabilities from the 1990s onwards. The Bank has been at the forefront of the development of Italy's 'economic culture'. Its Research Department has been the research centre *par excellence* in the economic field in Italy. The Bank has awarded scholarships for post-graduate education abroad. Many of these award holders later joined the Bank. The cutting-edge economic expertise enjoyed and deliberately developed by the Banca d'Italia was a clear case of 'when knowledge is power' (Haas 1990) for several reasons. First, at the domestic level, the wider implications of certain 'technical' decisions taken by the central bank were not always understood, *a priori*, by the government and the political class, which did not have direct access to technical knowledge (Quaglia 2005*b*). Second, the Italian central bank's strategy to strengthen its informal power in international and EU policy fora was to deploy the 'force of argument' (or of 'numbers') as a way to tip the balance in the policy discussions in certain directions and to persuade other macroeconomic authorities. As argued below, the quality of economic knowledge and the calibre of experts to which central banks have access has become an important source of informal power in the Eurosystem.

The Banca d'Italia has also been a breeding ground for talented civil servants and the financial elite. It has 'exported' credibility, expertise, and personnel for the conduct of Italian economic policy to other parts of the Italian state apparatus, the private sector, and international organizations. Interestingly, the Bank has been the 'exporting' institution, whereas central banks in other countries more usually 'import' senior officials from outside (cf. the Bundesbank and the Banque de France). This was also an indicator of the power (power of appointment, technocratic power) enjoyed by the Bank.

The Banca d'Italia has represented a 'credible interface' for Italy with the outside world—the 'power of credibility'. Since the post-war period it has interacted with foreign institutions (i.e. other monetary authorities and international organizations) and, more generally, has kept contacts with the outside world. After the upgrading of technical capabilities and human resources at the Ministry of the Treasury, which led to the 'empowerment' of the Treasury (later reformed into the Ministry for the Economy), the function of external economic representation and credible interface between the domestic arena and the international environment has largely been taken over by this Ministry.

Adapting to the Euro Area: The Crisis of 2005

A set of institutional reforms that formally increased central bank independence took place shortly after the Treaty on European Union (TEU) was signed in Maastricht. These reforms fostered institutional convergence towards the German model of central bank independence (see Dyson, this volume) among all the members of the Eurosystem. In 1992, the Banca d'Italia was granted exclusive power to set interest rates without approval from the Treasury. In 1993, the Treasury's overdraft facility at the Banca d'Italia was transformed into an interest-bearing deposit that must always be in credit. Legally, such changes were needed to comply with the EMU provisions contained in the TEU. They also completed the economic independence of the Italian central bank.

In approaching the final stage of EMU, the Banca d'Italia had to undergo further formal institutional changes in order to comply with the EMU institutional and policy templates. These stipulated that the members of the Board of Directors were to be appointed for five years, rather than three, as had previously been the case; the Treasury minister's power to suspend or abrogate the deliberations of the Board of Directors falling within the competence of the European System of Central Banks (ESCB) was abolished; and the Treasury minister's approval of deliberations concerning the investment of reserves was abrogated (Law decree N 43, March 1998, issued to permit the integration of the Banca d'Italia into the ESCB).

Another set of reforms to internal governance, policy competences, and personal independence took place in 2005, in the wake of a scandal that involved Fazio. The Law on Savings had been in the making since 2002 and was eventually adopted in December 2005. It introduced a fixed-term mandate for the Governor and the Executive Board and modified the procedures for appointing and dismissing them. The reform increased the power of the government in the appointment procedures, in that the members of the Executive Board (including the Governor) are appointed by a presidential decree, acting on the proposal of the prime minister, followed by a deliberation of the Council of Ministers, having consulted the Board of Directors. In other words, after the 2005 reform the Board of Directors is only consulted—its opinion is not legally binding. Since 2005 each member of the Executive Board has a six-year mandate, which can be renewed only once and can be repealed by the government after consultation with the Board of Directors—here again the opinion of this body is no longer binding.

Moreover, the ownership structure of the central bank was changed, so that only the state and public bodies are allowed to hold shares of the bank's capital. Before 2005, and as a consequence of the process of privatization of the banking sector that unfolded in Italy in the 1990s, private banks had held a large part of the central bank's shares.

The decision-making process within the Banca d'Italia was made more pluralistic in 2005, so that decisions with external implications for the Bank are no longer to be taken by the Governor alone, as it had been the case in the past, but are instead taken by the five members of the Executive Board, through a formal voting procedure. In other words, power is no longer concentrated in the hands of the Governor. This procedure of collective decision-making by the Board does not apply to decisions concerning the activities of the ESCB/Eurosystem, where the Governor votes in her or his personal capacity.

Notably, during the drafting of the Law on Savings, which amended central banking legislation, the Italian government requested the ECB's legal opinion three times (May 2004, October 2005, and December 2005, see CON/2004/16; CON/2005/34; CON/2005/58.). In its opinion issued in October 2005, the ECB suggested the introduction of the principle of collegiality for the Executive Board's decision-making on measures related to non-ESCB tasks and the introduction of a fixed-term mandate, renewable once, for all members of the Executive Board. This suggestion was eventually incorporated into the relevant legislation in December 2005. The ECB also repeatedly highlighted the need for ensuring that the planned transfer of the Banca d'Italia's share capital to the state was compatible with the provisions of the TEU concerning the avoidance of monetary financing and the need for sound fiscal policy (Quaglia 2008*a*).

The adaptation of the governance structure and the internal organization of the central bank to membership of the Eurosystem has so far been very limited. Within the Economic Research Department, four of the five existing sectors have been given competences for the analysis of Euro Area data. Also, additional structures, such as the Monetary Policy Coordination Committee and the Euro Policy Liaison Office, have been created, with co-ordination tasks on issues relating to the Euro Area and the Eurosystem monetary policy. Another new internal structure is a division to co-ordinate the whole set of activities related to the ECB Governing Council, which puts together the dossier for the Governor and for an accompanying person, generally from the Economic Research Department, for the meeting of the Governing Council in Frankfurt. The Bank has approximately 8,000 employees. There have been no substantial cuts in staff numbers in preparation for or after Euro Area membership. However, this status quo has begun to change after the appointment of the new Governor, Mario Draghi, in 2006, and there are plans in place for a reduction in personnel as well as an internal reorganization of the Bank, as elaborated further below.

When the legal independence of the Banca d'Italia was increased in the run-up to the final stage of EMU, there was hardly any domestic debate on the need to step up the procedures for accountability. Moreover, unlike central bank independence, central bank accountability was not subject to a process of convergence, and there were no 'European templates' to be adopted at the domestic level. The Bundesbank itself could hardly provide a model, given that its procedures for accountability were not particularly robust. The procedures for central bank accountability were beefed up in Italy by the reform in 2005, following the Fazio affair, which brought to the fore the high degree of discretion and low level of accountability of the top officials at the Bank, first and foremost the Governor, who had the ultimate decision-making power at the Bank.

As a result of the changes introduced in 2005 in order to step up the transparency and accountability of the central bank, written justifications for decisions taken, especially in the supervisory field, have to be provided by the Bank, and the minutes of the meetings of the Executive Board have to be kept. The report on supervisory activities is due twice a year, not once a year.

Since 1999, the monetary policy in the Euro Area is conducted by the ECB and the Eurosystem, which very much adopted a German model for the conduct of monetary policy and central bank independence (Dyson 2000). The Banca d'Italia participates in policy formulation and implementation as a member of the Eurosystem. Similarly, exchange-rate policy is conducted at the Euro Area level. For these two policies convergence has been complete. On the one hand, the Banca d'Italia has lost the power to conduct these policies at the national level. On the other hand, this power is now shared with the ECB and other participating central banks at the Euro Area level.

In contrast, financial stability and financial supervision remain largely national competence, even though the mechanisms for institutional cooperation in the EU and the Euro Area have been stepped up. Unlike in monetary policy and exchange-rate policy, 'positive integration'—characterized by specific EU models or provisions to be adopted by the member states—has been minimal in the EU as far as financial supervision is concerned. Even within the Eurosystem, different institutional frameworks and policy paradigms persist. This is not only because financial systems vary remarkably across Europe, but also because, unlike the stability-oriented paradigm in monetary policy, based on central bank independence, there is not a benchmark institutional model or widely accepted technical framework in financial supervision (Busch 2004). It should also be noted that the Banca d'Italia during the Fazio governorship opposed any expansion of the ECB's competence in the supervisory field (*Sole 24 Ore*, 16 February 2002), and by closing ranks with some other national central banks, it was successful in doing so.

At least until the 2000s, the Banca d'Italia had traditionally been regarded as an effective supervisor, which also made the Bank intellectually powerful in European and international supervisory networks and fora. Except for the bankruptcy of Banco Ambrosiano in 1981, there were no major financial scandals in Italy in the 1980s and 1990s. Hence Italian policymakers had no need to consider alternative supervisory models. However, the early 2000s proved to be a more turbulent period, with the insolvency of the Argentinean bonds, the financial collapse of Cirio in 2002, and Parmalat's insolvency in 2003. Although these episodes could hardly be attributed to systematic supervisory failures, they triggered a heated debate about the configuration and allocation of supervisory responsibilities in Italy and weakened public confidence in the existing supervisory framework.

In 2005, two episodes threatened the credibility and reputation of the central bank, weakening its ability to resist changes, which were incorporated at the 11th hour in the Law on Savings. The cases made the headlines across Europe because they involved foreign banks and related to two proposed takeovers of Italian banks in 2004–5: one of Banca Nationale del Lavoro by a Spanish group, Banca Bilbao Vizcaya Argentaria; and the other of Banca Antoniana Popolare Veneta (Antonveneta) by ABN Amro. In both cases Governor Fazio intervened to block the foreign takeover bid, while endorsing counterbids launched by two Italian banks, Banca Popolare di Lodi and Unipol, respectively.

Both foreign banks involved in the attempted takeovers complained to the European Commission, which had given its authorization on the grounds that the bids did not jeopardize competition in the banking sector. An antitrust enquiry launched by European competition Commissioner, Neelie Kroes, was dropped on the grounds of lack of conclusive evidence. The European internal market Commissioner, Charlie McCreevy, also expressed his concern in a letter to Governor Fazio in 2005 (*Financial Times*, 18 February 2005).

Pressure from other EU member states, EU bodies, and financial markets, hence a mixture of Europeanization and globalization effects, coupled with sharp domestic criticisms, led to the resignation of Fazio in the autumn 2005, followed by a change of competition policy in the banking sector in Italy (see Quaglia 2008*b*). The reform, which was inserted in the Law on Savings, basically left untouched the extensive supervisory powers of the central bank. However, banking competition policy was transferred to the Competition Authority, which had been established by law in 1990 and is separated from the central bank. Whereas the Banca d'Italia would conduct its evaluation of mergers and acquisitions by taking into account 'sound and prudent management issues', the Competition Authority would base its assessment on the impact of mergers and acquisitions on competition (my translation, Law 262, December 2005).

Moreover, the crisis prompted the EU to legislate on this matter. After the controversial foreign takeovers in Italy and a similar case in Poland, Commissioner McCreevy proposed to amend the existing EU banking directive with a view to limit the discretion of the competent national authorities in authorizing (or denying) foreign takeovers and more generally entry of foreign banks into national markets. The amendment was approved and constitutes an interesting instance of how events at the national level affect EU developments.

The Banca d'Italia has always paid a considerable amount of attention to the configuration and development of the financial system in Italy, especially in the banking sector. It performed an 'educational function and protective role' vis-à-vis the Italian banks. This self-appointed role became more prominent after the establishment of European monetary union, partly because the Bank had lost some core functions and partly because foreign banks, largely as a consequence of EMU and more generally financial globalization, tried to penetrate the Italian market in the 2000s. The Banca d'Italia reacted by endeavouring to protect the *italianita' delle banche* (basically, Italian ownership of the banks operating in Italy). As part of the Bank's 'grand design' for reshaping the banking system in Italy, Governor Fazio consistently opposed foreign shareholdings and never authorized a foreign takeover, in an attempt to prevent, or at least to slow down, foreign penetration of the Italian market (*Financial Times*, 11 February 2005; 17 February 2005; 31 March 2005). The Bank's official explanation was that this strategy was designed to give the domestic banking system time to adjust and to become competitive internationally. Critics (e.g. the *Financial Times* was particularly vocal on this) argue that it was economic protectionism, coupled with *dirigiste* attitudes.

Mario Draghi, former vice-president and managing director of Goldman Sachs (an international investment bank), based in London, and former Director General of the Italian Treasury in the 1990s, took over from Governor Fazio in 2006. From the outset, Draghi gave clear signals of change, albeit emphasizing the continuity of the prestigious tradition of the Bank of Italy. Following the new rules agreed in 2005, three new members of the Executive Board were appointed: they all had considerable international experience and were either internal to the Bank, or had spent a considerable part of their career there. Besides changes at the level of the senior management, the approach adopted by the new governor and the Executive Board can be summarized as more openness, accountability, and efficiency. The priority was to regain 'credibility'.

The first objective was to open up and modernize the Italian financial sector, in marked contrast to the approach taken by Fazio. Draghi was keen to encourage mergers in the banking sector, making clear that, if banks' executives failed to take the initiative, he would not oppose foreign takeovers. The second objective was to rationalize the Bank's structure and its resources by initiating the process of closing down the existing delegations in EU capitals, but strengthening the Bank's delegations in the United States and Japan. Third, Draghi expressed positive attitudes to membership of the Eurosystem, seeking to specialize the Bank of Italy on specific activities. Finally, in the new management style, there has also been deliberate emphasis on accountability and transparency. For example, given the fact that Draghi was a former executive at Goldman Sachs, when taking office he announced that he would abstain from any decisions involving his former employer for one year.

Despite the appointment of Draghi in 2005 and the changes that have gradually taken place since then, unlike the Swedish central bank (see Marcussen, this volume), the Banca d'Italia, like the Banque de France (see Howarth, this volume) has not embraced a new public management approach, which emphasizes performance indicators, monitoring, outsourcing, and so on. It might therefore be seen as closer to the Banque de France as a laggard in this respect. There are two explanations for this: no major impulse has come from the top management of the bank for the adoption of new public management practices, and several changes introduced so far had to be negotiated with public-sector trade unions, which are not very receptive to new public management doctrines.

The Role of the Banca d'Italia in the Eurosystem and in International Central Banking Networks

The Banca d'Italia is the third largest central bank in the Eurosystem and has been eager to remain an influential actor there. Among the national central bank governors, Fazio was one of the most determined to safeguard the competences of national central banks within the Eurosystem—or, to put it another way, to limit the competences and power of the ECB and its Executive Board in Frankfurt.

The contributions of the Banca d'Italia to the design and setting up of the ESCB, Eurosystem, and ECB are not comparable to those of the Bundesbank, which largely provided the institutional and policy templates for the ECB (Dyson 2000). However, three types of inputs can be identified. First, the Banca d'Italia seconded a considerable number of officials to the ECB headquarters in Frankfurt when the ECB was established. This was important in the early years of the ECB, when it was in the process of hiring its own staff. Some of the Italian officials seconded to Frankfurt subsequently returned to the Banca d'Italia, and the ECB has established procedures to hire its own staff, also at senior level, even though the number of senior officials initially employed by national central banks remains high.

Second, the Banca d'Italia played an important role in the establishment of the Trans-European Automated Real-time Gross Settlement Express Transfer System, or TARGET, which was completed in 1999. TARGET was created by interconnecting 12 national euro real-time gross settlement systems and the ECB payment mechanism and is used for the settlement of central bank operations, large-value euro interbank transfers, and other euro payments in real time. In October 2002, the Governing Council of the ECB decided to establish TARGET 2 in preparation for the enlargement of the Eurosystem, based on a single shared platform for the central banks that decided to join it and were willing to give up their own national real-time gross settlements platform. The central banks of Italy, France, and Germany, building on their expertise in payment systems, offered to provide the technical platform in 2002, and the ECB Council accepted in 2004. TARGET 2 is operational and the Banca d'Italia is also involved in the setting up of TARGET 2 Securities, a system for the clearing and settlement of securities in the Euro Area.

Third, the Banca d'Italia is an important source of technical knowledge in the Eurosystem. The number of research staff at the Banca d'Italia is the highest among European central banks, *ex equo* with the Bank of England (St-Amant et al. 2005). Moreover, this is not a relatively recent trend, even though the Bank considerably expanded its research staff in the period 1996–2003 as part of a deliberate strategy to strengthen the Bank's influence within the Eurosystem and in ECB decision-making (cf. a similar strategy followed by the Bundesbank). A study of the quantity, quality, and relevance of research in 36 central banks in developed countries since 1990 indicates that the number of journal articles published by members of the Banca d'Italia is one of the highest, with an upward trend post-1999 (St-Amant et al. 2005). Moreover, the Banca d'Italia, the Bank of England, and the ECB are the sole non-American representatives among the top 10 central banks in quality-adjusted output (i.e. publications in top-quality academic journals) (Quaglia 2008*a*).

Adaptation to membership of the ESCB has been relatively difficult for the Banca d'Italia, especially among the top-level management, notably in the case of Governor Fazio and some of his closer advisers. The Governor and other senior officials were rather sceptical of Italian membership of the single currency, even though no formal statement was ever made in this respect (Quaglia 2004). More generally, senior officials were intent on safeguarding the role of the Banca d'Italia within the Eurosystem. Some high-calibre officials (often the most outward-oriented) have left the Bank to take up senior positions in international organizations, at the ECB, at the Treasury, and in private banks. In terms of personnel employed and internal organizational structures, no major restructuring has taken place since joining monetary union, although this began to change after the appointment of Draghi as Governor in 2006.

Outside the Eurosystem, the Banca d'Italia is part of international networks dealing with banking supervision, first and foremost the activities of the Basel Committee on Banking Supervision (BCBS). Within this committee, which brings together banking supervisors from 13 states, the Banca d'Italia tends to be an intellectually powerful member, although its structural position in the network is not comparable to those of the Federal Reserve or the Bundesbank. The influence of the Banca d'Italia in the BCBS has been strengthened by the fact that, unlike the Bundesbank and the Bank of England, the Banca d'Italia, with its extensive supervisory powers, is the sole representative for Italy. Moreover, the Banca d'Italia has a considerable amount of expertise in this field and has generally been regarded as an effective supervisor, given the absence of significant banking crises in Italy in the last two decades.

The role of the Banca d'Italia in the BCBS, for example, during the negotiations of the Basel II agreement, has not substantially changed as a result of European monetary union, especially as the ECB and the European Commission participate in the meetings in Basel as observers, without decision-making power, which rests with the national central banks and the national supervisory authorities sitting on the BCBS. This status quo might, however, change if the composition of the BCBS is amended or if the ECB is given new competences in the supervisory field.

In the negotiations of both the Basel I and the Basel II Accords, the Banca d'Italia endeavoured to make sure that issues that were important for the competitiveness of the Italian banking system were taken into account. On certain issues, the Banca d'Italia forged an effective alliance with the Bundesbank, given their similarity of interests (interviews, Rome, July 2006; Frankfurt, January 2006), such as preventing negative effects of the Basel II agreement on small and medium-sized enterprises (Wood 2005), which are widespread in both Italy and Germany. During the negotiations, German and Italian policymakers co-operated on this matter—for example, by conducting joint studies—and achieved positive results, with the final draft of Basel II regarded as providing favourable treatment for small and medium-sized enterprises. Another important goal of the Italian, British, and German authorities was to make the new accord less pro-cyclical, in which they were successful, as becomes obvious when the first draft of the accord is compared with the draft eventually agreed in 2004.

Conclusion: Europeanization, Power, and Convergence

This chapter examined the evolution of the Banca d'Italia between Europeanization and globalization. These two processes promoted institutional and policy convergence, and redefined the power of the Italian central bank, domestically, internationally, and in the EU. The chapter argued that convergence of institutional and policy templates has mainly been imposed by external factors, such as European monetary union and Eurosystem membership, EU legislation, other (non-legally binding) international agreements, pressure exerted by the financial markets, and international circulation of ideas in the form of policy paradigms.

Some of these factors were at work well before the establishment of European monetary union, reminding us that Europeanization and globalization are long-term phenomena and can be better understood by taking a diachronic perspective. These external factors triggered changes that affected both the institutional framework of central banking in Italy and the main policies conducted by the central bank, though to a different extent. Some policies, first and foremost monetary and exchange-rate policies, have converged completely in the Euro Area, whereas others, above all financial supervision, have not converged significantly, and divergence persisted across the EU/Euro Area. Overall, the atypical roles performed by the Banca d'Italia converged, leading, not without some hitches, to a 'normalization' of central banking in Italy. Persistent divergence in certain domains, such as financial supervision, is explained by the specific tangible and intangible assets of the central bank, the distinctive configuration of the Italian system of governance, and the lack of specific policy templates at the EU level.

Membership of the Eurosystem reconfigured the power of the Banca d'Italia. On the one hand, it has diminished the power of the central bank domestically, given the fact that monetary and exchange-rate policies are decided at the Euro Area level. On the other hand, even before European monetary union, the room for manoeuvre left to national central banks operating in the ERM was relatively limited, as they largely had to follow the policy set by the Bundesbank. At least in monetary union they have a voice (and, to date, a vote) in the decision-making process.

After the establishment of European monetary union, there has been a genuine difficulty in defining a new role for the Banca d'Italia, partly because several special functions performed by it have been transferred to other parts of the state apparatus, and partly because it has lost many of its traditional functions to the ECB. The adaptation of the Banca d'Italia to monetary union in the early years of the project was rendered more difficult and/or slowed down by the rather Eurosceptic attitudes of Governor Fazio and other senior officials, for the decision-making power was concentrated in his hands. It was a delayed (and at times difficult) process of Europeanization.

In the Eurosystem, the Italian central bank has taken a leading role in the development of the payments system and the clearing and settlement of securities, provided (or seconded) personnel to the ECB, especially at senior level, and stepped up its technical capabilities in economic knowledge, which can be an intangible source of power in the Eurosystem—a strategy that was fully embraced by Draghi when he took over from Fazio in early 2006. Unlike his predecessor, Draghi displayed a different, more positive approach to monetary union and a more constructive engagement of the Bank with the Eurosystem. Building on the legislation passed in late 2005, he also set in motion overdue reforms to the Bank and its policies at the domestic level.

Acknowledgements

I wish to thank the editors, Charles Goodhart, John Woolley, and the participants in the workshops in Cardiff and at the British Academy for their comments on an early draft of this chapter.

Part III

'Temporary' Outsiders: Pace Setters and Laggards

9

Estonia, Hungary, and Slovenia: Banking on Identity

Béla Greskovits

A powerful new institution, the independent central bank, emerged rapidly from the transformation of inherited financial systems in postcommunist Central and Eastern Europe (CEE). Its power entailed the ability to define macro-economic stability as a policy priority, institutionalize it against rival preferences, and shape economic performance in line with its own agenda. However, rather than converging on a single uniform model, the new central banks adopted varied institutional features. They also diverged in terms of their performance and central bankers' identities.

In section two, this chapter examines variation of central bank power across the cases of Estonia, Hungary, and Slovenia on four dimensions. First, new monetary authorities differ in the extent to which they have retained the traditional functions of a central bank. Second, there are differences in central banks' 'interaction across different political-economic arenas' (Iversen and Pontusson 2000: 2), especially with fiscal authorities, industrial relations regimes, and commercial banks. Third, diversity in institutional interactions reflects variation in the degree to which the monetary authority is divorced from the political system. Finally, these configurations shape central bank capacity to affect economic performance.

Central bank power also exhibits variation over time. Importantly, the relative speed at which central bank independence (CBI) had been instituted, and macroeconomic stability restored, contrasts with the difficulties of compliance with the Maastricht convergence criteria for euro entry.

The chapter asks three questions. What were the sources of central banks' power after communism? In what way have these sources of power influenced their refashioning as varied configurations of institutions, performances, and identities? Have the origins of their power and the institutional features adopted in the course of preparing for EU membership had a bearing on the political economy dynamics of preparing for euro entry?

Answers are sought through a comparative analysis of political opportunity structures defined by three main trials of transformation: Europeanization, economic challenges, and nation building. Section three argues that adoption of central bank independence, the main task of preparing the monetary regime for EU accession, could advance fast *because—and to the extent—of its compatibility* with domestic agendas of nation building and monetary stabilization.

Section four tests this proposition in the context of the new political opportunity structures after EU accession, shaped by growth-driven inflation, hitherto pent-up demands for welfare, and public concerns about losing national currencies. It argues that Europeanization after EU accession is delayed because preparation for euro entry is *less compatible* with national agendas than central bank independence had been. The conflict manifests itself in different forms in new and old nation states. The Estonian central bank lacks not only the means of inflation control in a fast-growing economy but also the political support for shifting to less minimalist monetary coordination. Equally controversial is the prospect of abandoning the Estonian currency as it is considered as a loss of national identity. Losing national currency and policy autonomy are less feared in Hungary. However, there, demands for welfare and security come into conflict with public-sector retrenchment and reform required for euro entry compliance. From east central Europe Slovenia fulfilled the conditions of euro entry first. This unique success is traced to the embeddedness of monetary coordination in neocorporatist institutions, which helped to accommodate and distribute adjustment costs in a balanced and politically acceptable manner, both before and after EU accession.

Alarmed by the danger of repetition of negative experiences of some insiders, rather than encouraging new entrants, the European Central Bank (ECB) has scrutinized and questioned their capacity to secure *sustainable* macroeconomic stability. As a result, some new EU members may join the camp of semi-permanent outsiders, not least because of their central banks' clustered, partial, and increasingly contested route to the euro. The chapter concludes with some lessons for the study of central bank convergence, power, and Europeanization.

Ascendance of Central Bank Independence after Communism

By EU accession in 2004, Estonia, Hungary, and Slovenia advanced far in institutionalizing central bank independence (Feldmann 2006; Greskovits 2006; Silva-Jáuregui 2004). Central bank governors were appointed to their legally well-protected and generously remunerated positions for six years, exceeding the length of terms granted to elected governments. Governors gained significant, albeit varied influence over appointments of their deputies and monetary council members. Professional credentials became a condition for appointments to executive positions. Internationally well-connected, sizeable research departments enabled the monetary authorities to become sources of trusted macroeconomic data, analyses, and forecasts. Increasingly, EU-compliant acts limited and ultimately abolished central banks' role in financing fiscal deficits.

Adopting the legal standards and norms of European central banking coincided with success in macroeconomic stabilization. Over the 1990s all three central banks accomplished challenging tasks. In Estonia and Slovenia these included disentangling the national monetary authority from quasi-federal structures, ending galloping inflation and introducing new convertible national currencies, the Estonian kroon and Slovene tolar, which replaced the multiple-currency regimes of the Soviet rouble, Yugoslav dinar, and German D-Mark. Management of inherited foreign debt was an important issue in Hungary. Similar as they are on the above dimensions, these central banks differ in a number of crucial aspects.

Configurations of Institutions and Performances

The three central banks differ in how far they accommodated the traditional functions of a central bank. The currency board mechanism adopted by the Bank of Estonia prevented the central bank from influencing money supply through interest-rate policies and acting as lender of last resort. Money supply has been determined by foreign currency reserves, and the central bank refused to bail out troubled commercial banks and industrial firms. In contrast, both the Bank of Slovenia and the National Bank of Hungary have retained the right to control interest rates and function as lenders of last resort. The economic consequences included varied tolerance for non-performing loans and varied access to new credits. While Estonian firms were not allowed to accumulate 'bad debts' and faced a credit-crunch in the first half of the 1990s, Hungarian and Slovene firms enjoyed longer 'grace periods' in case of non-payment and had easier access to new credits (Table 9.1).

The varieties of capitalism literature help to capture other differences. Authors in this tradition propose that 'Political economies are complex systems of interlocking institutions that mutually reinforce and condition the effects of each other' (Iversen and Pontusson 2000: 19). Arguably, interaction with three key institutions—fiscal authorities, business and labour organizations, and commercial banks—matters most for central bank independence and its economic impact.

Independent central banks have acted in tandem with ministries of finance to (re)produce macroeconomic stability through coordinated, prudent monetary and fiscal policies in Estonia and Slovenia. In contrast, recurrent conflicts between the monetary and fiscal authorities have tended to undermine efficient macroeconomic coordination in Hungary. It was only in exceptional

Table 9.1. Non-performing loans, and domestic credit to private sector and households in Estonia, Hungary, and Slovenia, 1993–2006

	1993	2000	2006
Non-performing loans (% of total loans)			
Estonia	3.5 (1994)	1.3	0.2
Slovenia	13.8 (1994)	9.3	5.6
Hungary	29.6	3.1	3.0
Domestic credit to private sector (% of GDP)			
Estonia	11.1	23.3	78.4
Slovenia	22.1	37.8	67.1
Hungary	20.7	30.1	54.6
Domestic credit to households [of which mortgage lending] (% of GDP)			
Estonia	n.a.	7.1 [4.7]	38.7 [32.1]
Slovenia	n.a.	11.3 [1.7]	17.0 [4.5]
Hungary	n.a.	3.3 [1.1]	18.5 [13.9]

Sources: EBRD Transition Report (2001, 2006, 2007, London).

moments, such as the stabilization package of 1995, that Hungarian fiscal and monetary policies could be coordinated.

As to central bankers' interaction with social partners, business associations, and trade unions, varieties of capitalism scholars identified patterned variation within the club of OECD economies. They argue that 'the effects of monetary policies cannot be understood without paying attention to the conditioning influences of wage bargaining structures and processes' (Iversen and Pontusson 2000: 12). If wage bargaining is centralized and coordinated, social partners concerned about the economy-wide levels of inflation and unemployment are likelier to respond to central bank signals with wage restraint. Such response pre-empts the need for overly restrictive monetary policies. In turn, highly decentralized, fragmented industrial relations regimes make such accommodation unlikely (Franzese and Hall 2000: 178–9). Adapted to east central European cases, the varieties of capitalism approach help to identify important differences. Central bank policies in Slovenia, just like in many West European states, have been backed by centralized and coordinated neocorporatist institutions of social partnership. In contrast, central banks in Estonia and Hungary (and all other east central European states) have operated against the background of highly fragmented, decentralized industrial relations regimes, and monetary policy has remained exogenous to atomized wage bargaining. Generally, the interplay between central banks and the regimes of industrial relations has developed in rather *'un-European'* directions in the region (Table 9.2).

Both the Bank of Estonia and the National Bank of Hungary interact with commercial banking sectors, which, to much larger extent than Slovene banks, have undergone almost complete privatization to transnational investors. Again, the almost complete transnationalization of commercial banking exhibits striking *divergence* from what Europeanization of this sector would mean.

Table 9.2. Employer organization, union density, and pattern of wage bargaining in Estonia, Hungary, and Slovenia, 2002–3

	Private employer organization (%) 2002	Union density (%) 2002	Wage bargaining index of centralization of 2003	Wage bargaining index of coordination 2003
Estonia	31–40	11–20	0.25	0.17
Slovenia	91–100	41–50	0.43	0.63
Hungary	n.a.	11–20	0.26	0.28
EU-15 average	n.a.	n.a.	0.45	0.47

Source: Visser (2005). Index of centralization: maximum 0.71 (Austria), minimum 0.13 (U.K.). Index of coordination: maximum 0.64 (Finland), minimum 0.11 (Lithuania).

Foreign dominance in the banking sector of most EU old member states has been the exception rather than the rule. It is only in Luxembourg and Greece where foreign banks' power compares with the situation in east central Europe (Claessens, Demirgüc-Kunt, and Huizinga 1998; Table 9.3).

However, the un-European ownership pattern proved helpful in the course of 'extreme "top-down" Europeanization that has required a rapid alignment of financial sector regulation with EU regulations as part of the accession process' (Mohácsi Nagy 2006: 259). Foreign banks have deepened domestic financial markets and rapidly 'imported' high standards of management and governance in Estonia and Hungary, while the coordination of Slovene banking sector has remained somewhat rudimentary and less transparent. At the same time, in the former two countries foreign subsidiaries' ability to borrow from their parent institutions has impaired the effectivity of changing reserve requirements as a monetary policy instrument.

Table 9.3. Transnationalization of commercial banking in Estonia, Hungary, and Slovenia, 1988–2006

	1988–95 average	2001	2006
Estonia			
Number of foreign banks in total (%)	43	57	86
Foreign bank assets in total (%)	35	98	99
Slovenia			
Number of foreign banks in total (%)	12	21	40
Foreign bank assets in total (%)	n.a.	15	30
Hungary			
Number of foreign banks in total (%)	61	76	70
Foreign bank assets in total (%)	61	67	83
EU-15 average			
Number of foreign banks in total (%)	30	n.a.	n.a.
Foreign bank assets in total (%)	20	n.a.	n.a.

Sources: Claessens, Demirgüc-Kunt, and Huizinga (1998): table 1; EBRD Transition Report (2007).

The above institutional configurations reflect variation in the degree to which the monetary authority is sheltered from governmental and partisan efforts to exploit or impair central bank independence. Indeed, the paths leading to central bank independence have differed in terms of radicalism and political contestation. In Estonia the divorce of the monetary authority from the political system is more complete than in Slovenia, let alone Hungary. The Bank of Estonia's hegemony in macroeconomic coordination has not been challenged since the adoption of the currency board in 1992. Central bank independence and its political implications have been somewhat more controversial in Slovenia. However, after an eruption in the first years of independence, the debates later largely subsided. Hungary's advance towards central bank independence has been gradual, partial, and provoked recurrent party-political struggles.

Overall economic performance seems to reflect the above institutional patterns. Measured by combined rates of inflation and unemployment, the Slovene configuration of central bank independence, institutionalized social partnership, and cooperative fiscal institutions performed best. In comparison, the Estonian and Hungarian patterns, which combine fragmented industrial relations with uncontested versus challenged central bank independence and cooperative versus conflicting fiscal institutions, respectively, appear as inferior (Table 9.4).

Compatibility Between International and Domestic Agendas

Interpreters of the rapid ascendance of central bank independence tend to split into two groups. International Political Economy approaches question that central bank independence in east central Europe followed a domestic economic rationale, and stress the role of the region's quest for international creditworthiness, reinforced by advocacy of the central bankers' transnational community (Johnson 2006; Maxfield 1997). Accordingly, the process of refashioning the inherited authorities as independent central banks 'by and for international actors ... occurred without the need to build extensive domestic support for the new institutions' (Johnson 2006: 91). However, the assumption of a missing domestic economic rationale and political support for postcommunist central bank independence sits uneasily with facts.

Table 9.4. Economic performance of Estonia, Hungary, and Slovenia, 2004–6

	Estonia	Slovenia	Hungary
Inflation rate (2004–6 average)	3.8	2.9	4.8
Unemployment rate (2004–6 average)	8.0	6.4	7.0
Inflation and unemployment (2004–6 average)	11.8	9.3	11.8

Source: EBRD Transition Report (2007).

The salience of a domestic rationale, namely, taming high inflation and ending chaotic multiple-currency regimes and economic recession in these small states, is highlighted by authors in Comparative Political Economy (Ennuuste et al. 2004; Feldmann 2006). Central banks could hardly have accomplished these tasks without strong domestic support. Indeed, in the Baltic states a 'largely home-grown stability culture that has been well-established since the early transition' brought about widespread support for the extreme version of central bank independence manifested in the currency board arrangements (Feldmann 2006: 128). This view is supported by facts on the amazing *political careers* of Siim Kallas, Einars Repse, and Ivan Tosovsky, Estonian, Latvian, and Czech central bank governors who founded and/or led political parties, and became ministers of finance or even prime ministers of their states.

Although not denying the salience of international factors, *national politics must be brought back in* especially as the rapid shift to central bank independence implied social welfare losses. Polányi's ideas on the original role of central banking under the gold standard system clarify the crucial link between central bank independence and national politics. '[T]he great institutional significance of central banking lay in the fact that monetary policy was thereby drawn in the sphere of politics' (Polányi 1957 [1944]: 197–8). In Polányi's term, independent central banks served as *buffers* in relation to the international gold standard system, since '[c]ompletely monetized communities could not have stood the ruinous effects of abrupt changes in the price level necessitated by the maintenance of stable exchange rates unless the shock was cushioned by the means of an independent central banking policy' (ibid. 194).

The social risks associated with abandoning central banks' buffer role imply that the *de-politicization* of monetary policy after the collapse of communism could not be anything but an inherently *political* process. International actors could press for and contribute to its emergence, but were unlikely to set in motion and consolidate it on their own. Features of domestic polities must have had a bearing on how fast, and through what trials, errors, and compromises, central bank independence could advance. What then were the characteristics of central bank independence and power after communism?

This chapter proposes that central bank independence, the single most important focus of monetary regimes' Europeanization before EU accession, could advance relatively fast in east central Europe because of its *compatibility* with the domestic agenda of ending crisis, monetary stabilization, and nation building, which empowered central bankers no less or even more than their international connectedness. (For a similar argument on the popularity of the gold standard in the age of nation building, see Helleiner 1999.)

However, 'objective' economic challenges and constraints capture only part of the story. Notwithstanding their actual seriousness, recession, inflation, and monetary chaos must first be *perceived as critical*, with identified causes and remedies, before they can prompt publicly supported extraordinary measures. Revisiting his path-breaking study of successful small states in postwar Europe, Katzenstein (2003: 11) asserted that '[A]n analysis that focused only on the objective data of economic openness missed the crux of the matter. Small size was a code for something more important ... it was concealing an underlying and politically consequential causal connection. What really mattered politically was the perception of vulnerability, economic and otherwise.' What were the politically consequential perceived vulnerabilities of postcommunist small states?

Central Bankers as Nation Builders, Social Partners, and Partisans

The majority of east central European countries had to build new nation states. All of them faced recession, inflation, and chaos, and wanted to 'return to Europe'. This section traces their initial decisions empowering or limiting the power of central bankers to past legacies and their perception as either assets or threats from the viewpoints of national independence, economic success, and the perspective of Europeanization.

Estonia

Since inherited institutions and skills of monetary coordination were absent in Estonia, central bankers' power could not originate from public trust in their professional competence. Given that the rapid shift to a national currency with fixed exchange rate and a currency board mechanism, backed by a constitutionally enshrined balanced budget provision, led to massive social dislocation, the sources of political support for such radical measures are far from trivial. Their support could not purely stem from international backing, as crucial decisions had been taken in 1992 *before* massive external pressure or assistance could materialize. Indeed, former Estonian prime minister Mart Laar (2002: 114) recalled that '[i]n the Spring of 1992 the International Monetary Fund (IMF) initially urged Estonia to postpone monetary reform until its technical capabilities were more advanced.' The engagement of *émigrée* policy advisors is noted in the literature. However, the fact that Estonia's exclusive monetary reform committee included Jeffrey Sachs's doctoral student Ardo Hansson (hardly a senior representative of global academic or financial circles at the time,) seems less a proof of powerful external influences than of a pre-existing domestic consensus favouring radical solutions.

Since the technicalities and risks of monetary policy had been hardly intelligible for politicians, let alone ordinary citizens, the origins of such consensus are puzzling. 'The fact that politicians that outwardly supported the currency board were at the same time sure that after monetary reform the central bank would continue to deliver "cheap credits" to inefficient factories and collective farms indicates that many politicians probably never understood exactly what they supported' (Laar 2002: 121–2). How then could a socially particularly costly variant of a 'stability culture' (Dyson 2002*a*) sink roots in Baltic soil? The answer points to its *close fit* with 'sentiments of wider resonance', especially the '*collective commitment to nationhood . . . and independence*' (Landes 1991: 49, emphasis added).

According to Anderson (1991: 7, emphasis added), '*regardless of the actual inequality and exploitation that may prevail in each*, the nation is always conceived as a deep horizontal comradeship'. Regained freedom to 'imagine' and craft a national community has enjoyed immense popularity in the Baltics over the whole period of transformation (Lagerspetz and Vogt 2004). Stability culture and trust in its guardians, the currency board, a balanced budget, and central bankers, could become a cornerstone of national identity, especially as measures to foster national independence and transformation have been introduced as part and parcel of the same policy package.

The link among identity politics, the monetary regime, and tolerance for social hardship has been reinforced by the issue of a new currency, a core means and symbol of sovereign statehood (Laar 2002: 125). The enthusiasm with which the stable kroon was received elevated the symbolic status of the monetary authority, and enhanced the popularity of *central bankers as nation builders*. Institutional insulation of monetary policy resonated well with the public sentiment that the cause of national independence ought to be removed from the everyday struggles of democratic politics. It was on these grounds that the Bank of Estonia governor in 1991–5, Siim Kallas, could build political capital around his role as 'father of the national currency'. Still in office, in 1994 he founded the Reform Party that came in second in the 1995 parliamentary elections and remained politically influential afterwards (Smith 2002). Kallas became minister of finance (1999–2002), prime minister (2002–3), and Estonia's EU Commissioner (2004).

'De-politicization' of monetary coordination has not been buttressed by democratic means alone. In the early 1990s Estonia introduced restrictive citizenship laws that deprived many ethnic Russian 'losers of the transformation' of the right to oppose radical transformation by democratic vote (Smith 2002). These measures muffled conflicts and relieved central banks and other sites of public policy from losers' pressures.

Identity politics cemented the hegemony of stability-oriented institutions in yet other ways. Estonian policy makers refused to help troubled industrial firms and banks by subsidies and grace periods for restructuring bad debts (Table 9.1). Lack of protectionism, however, could be more easily justified on grounds of perceived vulnerability of the national economy to post-colonial influences. In Laar's words, after 1940 a 'large Soviet military garrison and the continued influx of Russian speaking colonists who acted like a "civilian garrison" re-placed the lost population. In order to effect colonialization, rapid industrial-ization was launched by Moscow' (Laar 2002: 37). By implication, after independence, since most managers and workers were ethnic Russians, radical *de-industrialization* could be perceived as a means of *de-colonialization*. The imminent atrophy of business and labour organizations has not been viewed as too painful a loss, even if it led to highly fragmented industrial relations that impaired the prospects for socially embedded coordination, and reinforced exogenous monetary policy as the 'only game in town'.

Furthermore, faced with the banking crises of the early 1990s and the tasks of bank privatization, the Bank of Estonia acted as a *substitute police force*.

The government soon found out that it was not possible to compete against the influx of Russian organized crime into Estonia with a police force which was still in the process of being built up. And so the government had no alternative other than to try to weaken organized crime by introducing a series of economic measures designed to cut its sources of income and prevent its entry into the banking sector.

(Laar 2002: 191–3)

In consequence, the Bank of Estonia urged the demise and bankruptcy of banks with suspicious portfolios by the abrupt withdrawal of public assets and setting strict prudency standards. It also encouraged acquisitions by Western banks, which rapidly emerged as 'absolute market leaders' (ibid.).

Slovenia

Since Slovenia faced a triple transformation to nation state, democracy, and capitalism (Offe 1991), some factors that empowered Estonian central bankers have been at work in Slovenia too. The new currency fostered identity through its national imagery, replaced the cacophony of a multiple-currency regime with 'unity in "economic language" ', and consolidated the 'trustworthiness of the institution that issued it or guaranteed its value' (Helleiner 2003: 101, 112–13). However, the Bank of Slovenia has never acquired the unchallenged hegemony of its counterpart in Estonia.

Unlike policy makers in Estonia, Slovene monetary strategists opted for a separation between policies to achieve independence and to foster transform-ation. 'In the belief that the new country could start as a genuine market economy' banks and industrial firms were granted grace periods, subsidies, and loans to adjust and restructure (ibid.). Over the 1990s, administrative barriers hindered foreign takeover, especially in the banking sector. Consistent with the above, macroeconomic independence had been sought by a 'prag-matic economic policy and a floating exchange rate system for the new cur-rency … It was hoped that such a policy would result in smaller output losses and lower unemployment by allowing some inflation' (Mencinger 2004: 78).

This approach continued in the face of external advice. Although the *same* team of foreign advisors, led by Sachs, proposed similar remedies to the economy's woes in Slovenia as in Estonia, namely, fixed exchange rates, radical stabilization, liberalization, and privatization, their suggestions were 'stubbornly rejected' in Slovenia (Mencinger 2004: 76).

Due to gradualism in commercial bank transnationalization, reserve requirements remained effective tools at the Bank of Slovenia's disposal until (and even beyond) the early 2000s when recurrent EU pressures ultimately forced Slovenia to grant private and foreign capital freer access to its banks (Lindstrom and Piroska 2007: table 1.3). Ironically, then, resistance to some of the top–down pressures of accession Europeanization in the banking sector helped the Bank of Slovenia to succeed in the main task of membership Europeanization: full compliance with the Maastricht convergence criteria.

To a large extent, the divergence of Estonian and Slovene paths can be traced to differences in legacies and their perceptions. First, in contrast to Estonia, Slovenia did not have to build institutions of macroeconomic coordination from scratch. Second, Slovene gradualists generally 'considered the legacy of the past an exploitable advantage' (Mencinger 2004: 76). Domestic policy makers' credibility was enhanced by their competence acquired in the last decades of Yugoslav communism when 'many economists studied abroad, acquiring a solid understanding of Western economics, and were therefore not easily awed by foreign advisers' (ibid.)

An important Yugoslav legacy was the long experience with workers' self-management that added a level of participatory decision making unknown in other east central European states. Independent Slovenia embraced this legacy and developed it into a system of negotiated industrial relations. Especially after the initial recession removed from power the Right-wing coalition that won the first parliamentary elections, 'political exchange between centre-Left governments and organized economic interests became a permanent feature and the key mode of interest concertation, giving social legitimacy to market reforms' (Stanojevic 2003: 290). Centralized institutions of industrial relations strengthened cooperative social partners and mitigated the costs, and facilitated the political acceptance, of stability-oriented monetary policies. In essence, encompassing social partnership has become the expression of a *Europeanized and inclusive* variant of nationalism that did not perceive Slovenia as permanently threatened by enemies from within and without.

For all these reasons, central bank independence and power emerged in the context of a *power-sharing arrangement* with other important economic interests and institutions. Above all, Slovene central bankers' power originated from their negotiated relationship with social partners. On the one hand, central bank independence has become part and parcel of an inclusive and balanced national agenda that successfully resisted external pressures for radicalism. On the other hand, as Slovene nationalism unambiguously favoured a 'return to

Europe', bottom–up Europeanization proved to be much less divisive than in other east central European states.

Hungary

The Hungarian route to central bank independence is distinguished from the Estonian path by its gradualism, and from the gradualist Slovene path by fierce partisan struggles around central bank independence. Since the Hungarian nation state and national currency survived communism, central bankers could not pose in the role of nation builders. Nor could they gain power as the monetary guardians of encompassing social partnership, as Hungary lacked such institution. Essentially, Hungarian central bankers' *power depended on partisan struggles mitigated by top–down pressures for Europeanization.*

Similarly to Slovenia, Hungary inherited foundations of macroeconomic coordination. Importantly, a two-tier system that separated the central bank from commercial banks had been put in place as early as the second half of the 1980s. Indeed, from the early 1980s, market-oriented economic reforms and the management of accumulated huge foreign debt had facilitated the integration of Hungarian financial technocracy into international networks. Fellowships, conferences, debt negotiations, lobbying for new external resources, education, and training grants were as important in fostering such linkages as Hungary's early IMF and World Bank membership. New skills were developed during this integration process, such as familiarity with the logic of stabilization programmes, statistical and analytical capacities, and negotiating with foreign creditors and investors, skills that were even more badly needed after 1989.

One consequence was that Hungary's shift to the monetary coordination of a market economy could be relatively organic, gradualist, and 'home-grown', similar to that of Slovenia. While the role of foreign assistance was more accentuated before than after the collapse of communism, the task of maintaining international creditworthiness has remained an important driving force of the National Bank of Hungary's Europeanization. Given the imperative of foreign debt management, the reluctance with which central bank independence was adopted seems surprising.

The apparently weak support for a stability culture can be traced to the fact that Hungarian elites and publics have not perceived the overarching social purpose of transformation in terms of national identity or social partnership. For historical reasons, the popular legitimating principle of Hungarian capitalist democracy has been *public social provision* that typically contradicted macroeconomic stability (Bohle and Greskovits 2007; Kornai 1996). As in the other two cases, initial choices take us far in understanding the difference.

Hungarian reformers were well aware of the social hardship coming with economic collapse and market reforms, but could not fall back upon identity politics, gain support on nationalist grounds, and muffle protest by disenfranchising large parts of the affected population, as Estonia did. At the same time, they shied away from offering institutionalized voice to trade unions and the losers of reforms, the way Slovenia did. Rather, fearful of losers' protest, Hungarian reformers decided to offer compensation in the form of relatively generous, targeted social protection packages in order to overcome opposition to reforms (Vanhuysse 2006).

Prime minister Ferenc Gyurcsány's words before the spring 2006 elections capture the structural roots of implied imbalance. 'A labour-friendly but anticapitalist policy is an oxymoron ... Labour-friendly policies can only succeed if they also foster entrepreneurship. If we overshoot in supporting workers, we are left without jobs. If we overdo supporting entrepreneurs, we are left without social peace. During the transition Hungary has been stumbling from one extreme to the other' (Interview, Népszabadság, 24 February 2006).

Hungary's 'stumbling' has been closely linked to the issue of social protection and its conflicts with macroeconomic stability, which has been mostly unsuccessfully guarded by the National Bank of Hungary. The routine of buying acquiescence through welfare spending and industry subsidies at the expense of sound finances had lasting consequences for party competition. Rival mass parties usually stressed the intrinsic relationships between economic and welfare protectionism, promised both kinds, and, once in power, tried pragmatically to implement some mix at the expense of fiscal overspending and/or lax monetary policies. This complex and contradictory agenda left its mark on bureaucratic politics.

While top–down pressures for Europeanized macroeconomic coordination empowered the National Bank of Hungary and supported fiscal reforms, advances on both accounts were subordinated to *partisan considerations*, reflecting short-term electoral risks and opportunities. First, political struggles over the control of the ministry of finance and the central bank recurred over the 1990s and early 2000s. Delegation of power for fiscal centralization, rationalization, and adjustment depended crucially on the extent to which prime ministers governed cohesive legislative majorities and perceived finance ministers as brothers-in-arms rather than rivals in politics. Institutional reforms could advance in the former but were watered down or stalled in the latter cases (Greskovits 2001; Haggard, Kaufman, and Shugart 2001).

Second, Hungary's muddling towards central bank independence reflected efforts of partisan control, which impaired the coordination of fiscal and monetary policies even after EU accession. Ironically, steps towards central bank independence made the monetary authority an even more attractive target for partisan capture both from the ranks of incumbent parties and the opposition. Appointments of new National Bank of Hungary governors and efforts to strengthen central bank independence occurred in a revealing sequence. 'Unreliable' governors were not allowed to enjoy the longer terms in office, legally better-protected jobs, and enhanced policymaking authority guaranteed by the more and more Europeanized central bank laws. Rather, advances to stronger central bank independence typically favoured and empowered their 'party-loyalist' successors.

Hence, the replacement of president György Surányi by Péter Ákos Bod of the MDF (Hungarian Democratic Forum) in 1991 coincided with the passing of the first National Bank of Hungary Act, which limited (though without entirely abolishing) the central bank's role in financing fiscal deficits. Surányi could not stay because he signed the Democratic Charter, a left–liberal protest leaflet against the rise of extreme–Right forces under the centre–Right government. Similarly, Gyula Horn's Left-led coalition started its term in 1994 by replacing Bod with Surányi, whose authority was not questioned as long as the Horn government was in power. Although Surányi served his term, by its end in 2001 he was vehemently attacked, on grounds of alleged serious mismanagement of the National Bank of Hungary's office in Austria, by prime minister Orbán's minister of finance, Zsigmond Járai. While Surányi helped to prepare the new act of June 2001 that further strengthened central bank independence, and declared direct financing of the public deficit by the National Bank of Hungary no longer possible, the new EU-compliant law empowered his successor Járai. Járai became in turn the prime example of a central banker blamed with the abuse of his sheltered position for partisan political advantage. Ironically, then, while over the past one-and-a-half decades Hungary succeeded in creating the legal institution of central bank independence, it had to wait until 2007 to have a central bank president whose personal independence and non-partisanship appeared credible to, and could be accepted by, the whole political community. Prior to 2007 National Bank of Hungary presidents were typically viewed as *advocates of partisan agendas*.

Passing and Failing the Euro Entry Test

How have the increasing pressures for *sustainable* compliance with the Maastricht convergence criteria affected the fortunes of central banking around, and especially after, EU accession? This section argues that central banks' origins in terms of power and the institutional features adopted in the course of preparing for EU accession have had an impact on the dynamics of Europeanization after membership.

In the early 2000s, all three central banks optimistically prepared for joining ERM II in 2004 and changeover to the euro in 2007. However, only Slovenia could introduce the euro as planned. The Bank of Slovenia mastered this task by utilizing the same neocorporatist institutions that had shaped and helped its Europeanization during the accession period. Uniquely in the region, in April 2003 Slovene social partners signed an encompassing pact on future wages and income policy 'with important provisions on issues such as employment, training, social dialogue, equal opportunities and taxation ... Undoubtedly, this social agreement, with its ambitious objectives and comprehensive agenda, matches the "social pacts" reached in "old" Member States with the aim of coordinating the whole adjustment process in the course of joining the euro-zone' (EIROnline 2004: 19).

In contrast, in 2007 the Estonian government admitted that it would not be able to keep inflation within the Maastricht limit. Indeed, in 2007 the Baltic states ended up as EU leaders in inflation rates, and the financial community became increasingly concerned about the possibility of their 'crash-landing'. Estonia thus remained in ERM II and by early 2008 lacked a target date for euro entry.

It is tempting to explain this fiasco by the discouraging demonstration effect of the ECB's refusal to endorse Lithuania's Euro Area membership in 2006. However, the ECB's uncertainty and negative signals have not *caused but rather responded to* the Baltic states' apparent inability to counter accelerating inflation and mounting current account deficits, which were fuelled by rising energy and food prices, and especially firms' and households' hitherto pent-up domestic demand (EBRD Transition Report 2007, London). Central bankers have been clear about the reasons. Bank of Latvia's governor Ilmars Rimsevics expressed scepticism about the possibility of curbing domestic demand by fiscal restriction since both Latvia and Estonia already run sizable budget surpluses. Both Rimsevics and Bank of Estonia governor Marten Ross complained about lack of control over the expansionary credit policy of their states' Scandinavian and German banks associated with a housing and real estate boom (Farkas 2008: 68; Table 9.1). The ECB, then, seems to have serious reasons for scrutinizing new members' capacity for sustained macroeconomic stability.

After repeated postponements, by 2007 Hungary even lacked a new target date for entering ERM II. This is less surprising as the partisan and bureaucratic struggles for control over fiscal and monetary coordination, which character-ized the transition period, further intensified after Hungary's EU entry. The strategies and arguments used by rival advocacy coalitions (Sabatier 1991) have been thoroughly shaped both by 'top–down' and 'bottom–up' processes of Europeanization. Mainly 'top–down' compliance requirements affected the competition for power over monetary policy, since they empowered the presi-dent of the National Bank of Hungary and allowed him to use the increasingly critical Convergence Reports of the ECB and the European Commission to buttress his own position. In contrast, struggles over fiscal and exchange-rate policies have been stronger affected by a divisive process of 'bottom–up' Euro-peanization, in which domestic actors instrumentalized a variety of European models, such as the European mixed economy or the European Social Model, to strengthen their positions in electoral and party competition (Greskovits 2006).

Despite repeated calls for emulating West European practices (Bruszt, Oblath, and Tóth 2003), Hungarian macroeconomic stability could not be backed by an encompassing social pact. Government disinterest, business strength, and labour weakness obstructed the institutionalization of a social partnership. Sharing of adjustment burdens has thus been left entirely to the process of democratic competition, with troubling consequences for economic performance and ultimately political balance.

In autumn 2006, a huge fiscal deficit and public debt forced Hungary to implement a radical programme of macroeconomic stabilization and public-sector reform and retrenchment. The appointment of independent András Simor as National Bank of Hungary president in 2007 paved the way for ending the trench warfare between the central bank and the Ministry of Finance. However, since the attempted termination of the social contract provoked fierce political and social resistance and undermined political stability, the belated cease-fire among Hungary's top policy makers may fall short of restoring macroeconomic balance.

The difficulties encountered by most east central European states on the road to euro entry can be ultimately traced to the crucial *differences between the political opportunity structures* shaping Europeanization before and after accession. First, the 'heroic' times when central bankers successfully fought high inflation and chaotic multiple-currency regimes by introducing new national currencies are over. However, while ordinary citizens had strong reasons to support the cause of taming galloping inflation, it is far less trivial for them why compliance with the Maastricht criteria ought to be viewed as a basic public good. Instead of further nominal convergence, it is now *real convergence* of output, employment, and living standards that East Europeans demand.

Second, the prospect of *'de-nationalization of money'* (Helleiner 1999) implied by euro entry fuelled fears of losing national identity—just as earlier in older EU member states. However, '[n]ational currencies do not have the same meaning for national identity in all countries' (Verdun 1999a: 208). In east central Europe, it is in the new states where the link between money and nation appears to be strongest. Accordingly, the conflict between preparations for euro adoption and national agendas manifested itself in *different forms* in the new Estonian and the old Hungarian state (Table 9.5).

The Eurobarometer data reveal interesting cross-country variation of citizens' hopes and fears about the euro. To the extent that low inflation remains important for them, a large majority of Estonians and a sizable minority of Hungarians expect euro entry to *undermine* price stability, at least in the short run. Furthermore, a large majority of Estonians and more than half of Hungarians are sceptical about the euro's impact on real convergence: rates of growth and employment. Hungarians' relative optimism is less puzzling when their despair and dissatisfaction with the ongoing radical welfare-state retrenchment and confusion about its rationale is factored in.

While identity gains and losses seem to matter little for 'materialist' Hungarians, Estonians appear as more 'idealist' in expressing their hopes and

Table 9.5. Hopes and fears about the euro in Estonia, Hungary, and Slovenia (% of answers)

Dominantly expected euro zone entry date	Estonia (09/07)	Slovenia (09/06)	Hungary (09/07)
	2012 (*2008* in 2006)	2007	2013 (*2012* in 2006)
Happy about the euro	30	72	48
Material gains and losses			
Ensure price stability	40	24	58
Increase prices when introduced	89	63	72
Improve growth, employment	30	31	49
Identity gains and losses			
Feel more European	40	68	30
Lose national identity	51	35	30
Lose control over economic policy	37	30	28
Trust in European Institutions versus National Central Bank for information about the changeover to the euro (%)	75	89	91

Sources: Introduction of the Euro in the New Member States. Flash Eurobarometer November 2006, 2007. The Gallup Organization—European Commission. Country Scorecards.

fears about the euro mainly in terms of identity. In concrete terms, more than half of Estonians are concerned about loss of national identity (and a third about loss of control over economic policy) associated with the changeover to euro. Only a minority of Estonians expects to feel more European after the adoption of Europe's single currency. In the light of recent incapacity to sustain macroeconomic stability, the fact that Estonians trust their central bank significantly more than EU institutions as a source of reliable information on the euro is no less ironic than Hungarians' trust in EMU as an engine of fast growth and employment. Nonetheless, such puzzles of trust and mistrust seem to support those who believe in the *power of ideas and even of misperceptions.*

For the above reasons, the EMU project appears to be less compatible with national agendas than central bank independence had been, and this conflict impairs its public acceptance and political support. Bearing this in mind, it is less than surprising that the euro has lost popularity all over the region. In September 2007 only less than half of Hungarians and hardly a third of Estonians were happy with the prospect of having euro as their official currency (Table 9.5). Indeed, in 2008 inflation accelerated and social protest intensified even in Slovenia. A general strike in March 2008 signalled a possible end to wage moderation and the strength of demands for convergence in real wages.

Conclusions

What do these cases reveal about central bank convergence, power, and Europeanization? They show that the convergence of postcommunist central banks

on the norms and standards of central bank independence paralleled and interacted with processes of *divergence*. Varied configurations of central bank responsibilities and policy instruments have emerged, along with distinctive patterns
of dominance, involving collaboration or rivalry with fiscal authorities, industrial relations regimes, commercial banks, and political parties.

It follows that, although independence became a common key aspect of
central bankers' identity and institutional power, their profile also responded
to particular political opportunity structures, placing them in the varied roles of
nation builders, *social partners*, and *partisan agents*. Accordingly, central bank
power has been as much shaped by perceived national vulnerability and
other sentiments of wider resonance, such as trust in social partnership or
demands for social welfare, as by their demonstrated technocratic competence
and international connectedness.

The chapter offers some lessons for students of Europeanization. One finding is
about its dynamics over time. Central banks' *origins of power and institutional
features adopted in the course of Europeanization before EU accession have had an
impact on the dynamics of Europeanization afterwards*. In the case of Slovenia, the
former process reinforced the latter. Institutionalization of social partnership
during the transition period helped the Slovene central bank to complete Europeanization by rapid euro entry. In the Estonian case, the opposite influence is
evident. Success in nation building and Europeanization leading to accession
empowered the central bank as Estonia's most reputed economic institution.
However, public trust backfired after EU accession, since the central bank delayed
necessary institutional adjustment, even if on the route to euro entry the currency
board appears to be dysfunctional as the guardian of stability.

Finally, the chapter's findings confirm earlier research on the interplay of
Europeanization processes *across varied policy issue areas* (Bohle and Greskovits
2006). Europeanization of economic policies is not a 'seamless web'. Rather,
advance in one issue area might undermine or delay advance in another, and
thus simultaneous compliance 'with everything' might prove to be either
impossible or undesirable.

10

Czech Republic and Poland: The Limits of Europeanization

Rachel Epstein and Juliet Johnson

The Czech Republic and Poland underwent rapid economic transformation in the first decade of post-communism, which included embracing international standards of central bank independence and the depoliticization of monetary policy. However, they have shown much less appetite for adopting the euro since acceding to the European Union in 2004. 'Europeanization' in terms of meeting, or even striving to meet, the criteria for euro entry has been incomplete. We argue that two broad conditions explain *both* the relative susceptibility of Czech and Polish central bankers and politicians to international financial institutions' advice on central bank independence and price stability *and* these states' more recent resistance to rapid adoption of the euro: the uncertainty of domestic actors and the credibility of international institutions' policy prescriptions.[1] Given the presence or absence of domestic uncertainty and credibility, external actors have either more or less authority to define the contours of domestic policy debates and privilege particular institutional arrangements. The Czech Republic and Poland faced similar measures on actor uncertainty and the perceived credibility of international institutions' policies over time and thus rapidly institutionalized central bank independence while procrastinating on euro entry.

Actor uncertainty, a domestic variable, manifested itself in Poland and the Czech Republic in the search for policy and technical guidance early in the transition. The first post-communist Czech and Polish leaders were uncertain in the sense that they had never before managed a transition from state socialism to capitalism or governed a market economy. They therefore looked to international institutions for guidance as to what constituted best practice. New parliamentarians and the public had little sense of how institutional relations in the financial sector like central bank independence would affect distributional outcomes. In addition, there was considerable technical uncertainty. Even once politicians had decided to emulate Western models, turning socialist-era mono-banks into two-tiered systems anchored by effective central banks required extensive legal and economic expertise that mono-bank bureaucrats lacked. As international institutions imparted this technical advice, they also had the opportunity to prioritize central bank independence and price stability above competing policy aims.

While domestic uncertainty explains Czech and Polish openness to central bank independence and price stability in the first decade of transition, the *lack* of uncertainty among domestic actors more than a decade later helps explain their scepticism towards euro entry. By the early 2000s, Central and East European (CEE) politicians and central bankers were very familiar—in part from more than a decade of direct experience—with the costs and benefits of a range of monetary and exchange-rate policies. Moreover, although Czech and Polish central bankers were keener to adopt the euro sooner than many of their political counterparts, even central bankers questioned the wisdom of the Maastricht convergence criteria (Dyson 2007; Johnson 2006).

The perceived credibility of international institutions' prescriptions, an international variable, has also varied over time in the Czech Republic and Poland in ways that help explain the institutionalization of central bank independence and the rejection of rapid euro entry. We assess the 'credibility' of international institutions' policies in two ways: the extent to which different international institutions endorsed similar policy prescriptions, and the consistency between what international institutions prescribed for target states and what the Western states themselves actually did. Post-communist transition began at precisely the moment when a Western consensus around central bank independence and low inflation was crystallizing (Maxfield 1997). The consistency between international institutions' simultaneous urgings that the Czech Republic and Poland adopt central bank independence and what the majority of Western states were doing—which was themselves to move monetary policy out of the political fray—left little argumentative space for east central European states to deny the credibility of central bank independence (Epstein 2006). The EU's decision to make the institutionalization of central bank independence a firm requirement for EU accession further emphasized its importance to the international community.

But while the credibility of international institutions on central bank independence was high in the 1990s, the same cannot be said for the euro. First, Sweden, Denmark, and the United Kingdom had all opted out of joining the euro, albeit on varying legal grounds.[2] Second, the Maastricht convergence criteria for euro entry and the Stability and Growth Pact have both been undermined by the failure of some members to meet the criteria or to stay within the confines of the Pact. Ongoing criticism of the ECB from France and Italy has also called into question the desirability of a single monetary policy for Europe. Third, while many international institutions presented a united front in pushing post-communist states to adopt central bank independence and price stability, no such consensus or shared stakes existed on when and how the east central European states should adopt the euro.

Moreover, mixed messages from the ECB itself undermined the credibility of the euro in east central Europe. Although these states promised to enter the Euro Area as a part of EU membership, the ECB has used the toughest interpretation of the convergence criteria to evaluate their adoption bids— much tougher than was used in Western Europe (Johnson 2008). When compared with Greece's compliance with the convergence criteria, for example, Lithuania's 2006 exclusion from the Euro Area based on a slightly higher than prescribed inflation rate appeared somewhat arbitrary. Tensions between the ECB and CEE states have continued, with Slovenian inflation in the post-Euro adoption period calling into question the ability of post-communist states to sustain the necessary macroeconomic criteria. Such doubts did not ultimately prevent the European Commission's positive recommendation in May 2008 that Slovakia was qualified to join the euro zone on 1 January 2009. There had been ongoing disagreement between European officials and Slovak leaders over the sources of inflation and need for greater fiscal consolidation and structural reform. Finally, as of the time of writing, the Czech Republic was considering a delay in euro adoption of another decade or more, underlining how politically problematic the euro zone had become in CEE.

Greskovits (in this volume) offers a competing explanation based on variation in domestic conditions, arguing that the institutionalization of central bank independence and the adoption of the euro have been more or less compatible across cases with nation-building goals and national identities. But we believe that our explanation, which draws on both domestic and international forces, better explains pro-central bank independence and Euro-sceptic outcomes in east central Europe. Partisan disagreement over central bank independence and the euro, as evidenced in Poland, Hungary, and the Czech Republic, can neither confirm nor disconfirm an identity-based explanation. Moreover, domestic uncertainty and international credibility are quite good at explaining change over time. Looking beyond the Polish and Czech cases in this chapter, both Romania and Ukraine had much lower levels of domestic actor uncertainty at the outset of transition and consequently showed much less willingness to embrace central bank independence early on. Although Romanian identity did not change during the 1990s, the measure on actor uncertainty did—with the victory of the Democratic Convention of Romania over the communist successors in 1996. With uncertain actors in office and central bank independence enjoying broad international credibility, Romania began to institutionalize central bank independence much more strongly in the late 1990s than previously (Epstein 2008).

Central Bank Internationalization: Independence and Price Stability

By the time the Berlin Wall fell in 1989, a hard-won consensus had developed among international financial institutions, governments, and central banks in the advanced industrial democracies on the importance of central bank independence and price stability. As a result, during the early years of transition, international institutions presented a unified policy front to post-communist governments. A wide range of external actors such as the IMF, the World Bank, USAID, the Bank for International Settlements (BIS), and central banks such as the Bundesbank and the Bank of England came together to encourage post-communist states to create independent central banks. They not only promulgated the twin mantras of central bank independence and price stability, but also provided the technical assistance and training necessary to put these ideals into practice. This assistance included everything from IMF missions and resident experts to sophisticated training programmes designed for post-communist central bankers. For example, approximately 4,500 central bankers from the 10 post-communist states that would later join the EU took part in training courses at the Bank of England's Centre for Central Banking Studies (CCBS), the Joint Vienna Institute (JVI), and the IMF Institute between 1991 and 2000 (Figure 10.1). The Polish and Czech central banks were among the leading recipients of this training. By the end of 1993, over 300 of their central bankers had already taken a CCBS, JVI, or IMF course.

The EU itself did not become significantly involved with central bank transformation until later, when EU enlargement came onto the agenda and the European Central Bank (ECB) began operations. The ECB then worked to harmonize the relevant accession-state legislation with the EU *acquis communautaire* (which requires a high level of central bank independence), to improve central bank operations, to upgrade payment and settlement systems to EU standards, and to ensure consistency of statistics and IT infrastructure and applications with current EU members. EU accession conditionality reinforced domestic commitment to these efforts, but the possibility of future EU membership did not represent the initial or primary impetus for change. The transformation of post-communist central banks into independent guardians of price stability thus represented not so much Europeanization as internationalization, with central banks adapting to an established international model. As we discuss below, in Poland and the Czech Republic the concerted, credible efforts of international institutions to promote central bank independence practically guaranteed success in the face of domestic uncertainty over appropriate post-1989 policy choices.

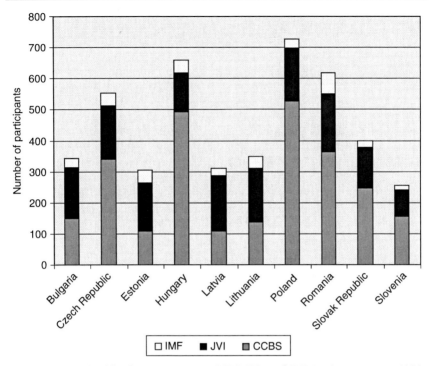

Figure 10.1. Central bank participants in CCBS, JVI, and IMF institute courses, 1991–2000

Source: Data provided to the authors by the CCBS, JVI, and IMF.

Poland

By the close of 1997, the National Bank of Poland (NBP) was among the most independent central banks in the world (Cukierman, Miller, and Neyapti 2002). Two sets of legislation, in 1990 and 1997, as well as the adoption of a new constitution in 1997 that supported central bank independence and price stability resulted from domestic political conflicts in which Polish supporters of central bank independence prevailed. The internationalization of Polish monetary and bank regulatory policy was in turn linked to international institutions' consistent involvement in Polish economic reform. Indeed, a transnational coalition overpowered a serious challenge to central bank independence in the mid-1990s, which led to further institutionalization of international norms towards the end of the decade.

Polish actor uncertainty was strongest in the first four years of the transition when post-communist states experimented with approaches to macroeconomic stabilization and the introduction of markets. There is evidence of Polish uncertainty regarding how to structure the central bank and of the

225

influence that such uncertainty afforded international institutions. Already in 1989, Poland passed the 'Banking Act' and the 'Act on the National Bank of Poland'—two pieces of legislation converting the socialist-era mono-bank into a two-tiered banking system modelled on Western, capitalist principles. In that instance, the US Agency for International Development (USAID) provided detailed advice on the legislation (Stirewalt and Horner 2000). The World Bank's 1991 Financial Institutions Development Loan (FIDL) also shaped the central bank's role in the economy in so far as it required the curtailment of subsidized and directed credit (World Bank 1997*b*). The Enterprise and Financial Sector Adjustment Loan (EFSAL) of 1993 was similarly designed to define and limit the central bank's funding authority by shielding the central bank from pressure to bail out banks or enterprises undergoing restructuring (World Bank 1997*a*). This last loan also guaranteed IMF and World Bank officials' access to the NBP's supervisory activities in order to help 'contain systemic risk in the banking sector and to support the NBP's larger objective of price stability' (Borish and Company Inc. with Triumph Technologies Inc. 1998).

The Polish case shows not only a willingness to call on international institutions to deal with policy uncertainty but also a tendency to rely on external expertise to train central bankers. One long-serving head of bank supervision in Poland recalled that there were initially sharp disagreements between NBP bureaucrats and international institutions on everything from the need for bank supervision to government deposit insurance (interview with Śleszyńska-Charewicz). In addition, before her tenure as the central bank's chairwoman and her intense exposure to the international financial institutions' counsel, Hanna Gronkiewicz-Waltz supported executive authority over the central bank. That international institutions prevailed in all of these debates demonstrates the significant power of external actors in defining best practice—in part because of domestic actor uncertainty, but also because the international financial institutions had strong credibility—not least because of the evolution of standard practice in the West.

The international institutions also forged strong personal and intellectual ties in Poland in the early years, both with the central bankers and with members of various post-Solidarity governments. This transnational coalition of central bank independence and price stability supporters proved crucial to stronger institutionalization of these principles in law and in the 1997 Polish constitution. For, beginning in the mid-1990s, after the Democratic Left Alliance (the SLD, the communist successors) prevailed in the 1993 parliamentary elections and formed a governing coalition with the Polish Peasant Party (PSL), central bank independence came under attack.

Finance Minister Grzegorz Kołodko first called into question the NPB's policies and governing structure. Although Kołodko defended central bank independence in principle, he took exception to the practice of central bank independence in Poland. Arguing in the press that the central bank president's responsibilities were 'not confined to those of God and History' but were also to 'society and the national economy', he took aim at what he called 'excessively restrictive monetary policy'.[3] He also lamented the fact that power within the NBP was, in his view, dangerously centralized with respect to monetary policy and bank regulation. Finally, Kołodko complained that the Ministry was never consulted on major central bank policy shifts (interview with Kołodko). As a potential remedy to these perceived problems, the SLD–PSL coalition tabled legislation to increase political control over the central bank (particularly through appointments), remove its regulatory authority, and loosen limits on central bank lending to the government.[4]

The government's legislation drew an immediate and negative reaction among Poland's external advisors. At this point international actors had no more central bank independence-related conditionality agreements pending, while EU membership was not explicitly tied to the nuances of central bank governance at that time. Lacking any 'hard' tools of enforcement, IMF, World Bank, and USAID representatives turned first to their Polish allies, including those who had been heavily influenced by international financial institutions' training. A transnational coalition comprising international financial institutions' officials, Gronkiewicz-Waltz, Śleszyñska-Charewicz, and politicians from the Freedom Union party (chaired by Leszek Balcerowicz) worked together to perfect arguments in defence of central bank independence to present to the public and the Sejm. In addition, the international financial institutions contributed to alternative legislation to insure that legal changes would reflect international trends towards greater central bank independence. The Freedom Union ultimately put forward that legislation. Finally, in public settings, the international financial institutions and the EU lobbied heavily against the SLD–PSL legislation, which undermined its legitimacy in Poland.

After more than a year of political conflict, the Freedom Union's central bank independence-preserving legislation prevailed, while the SLD–PSL proposals were 'quietly shelved'.[5] This was a surprising outcome, not least because the SLD–PSL coalition had an overwhelming majority in the Sejm. But it is explicable because of the overwhelming rejection of the SLD–PSL legislation by the international financial institutions and the EU. Given their unified pro-central bank independence position and the increasing consistency in Western practice, Poland's external advisors had enormous credibility. Although Poland's EU membership or access to financial assistance was not at stake, the potential reputational costs of violating international norms were sufficiently threatening to cause Poland's communist successors to relent. In 1997, the Sejm approved a new constitution in which central bank independence was further institutionalized, including clarifying the president's role in selecting the NBP chair and banning government borrowing from the central bank.[6] Thus central bank independence was institutionally stronger in the wake of the conflict (Cukierman, Miller, and Neyapti 2002: 242).

Czech Republic

As in Poland, Czech policy makers turned to international models and assistance to transform their central banking institutions. The November 1989 Velvet Revolution initiated a sharp break with the previous regime, bringing to power individuals with a strong commitment to political democracy and economic liberalization. Like the NBP, the Czech National Bank (CNB) quickly became one of the world's most independent central banks (Neyapti 2001). The CNB took advantage of foreign expertise and encouragement to transform itself into a formidable, capable institution. As a result, again like the NBP, the CNB later defeated a serious challenge to its independence. By the time the Czech Republic entered the EU, the CNB had already become a respected member of the international central banking community.

The transition empowered a small circle of neo-liberal Czech economists such as Václav Klaus, then a leading figure in the Civic Forum, and Josef Tošovský, named governor of the Czechoslovak State Bank (CSSB) in January 1990. These individuals had internalized the international central banking consensus through their studies and experiences abroad in the 1980s, and looked to international institutions to legitimize and assist efforts to transform the CSSB along these lines. Beyond this small circle, however, few domestic actors held strong opinions about central bank independence, and its ramifications were not widely understood. Therefore, its international legitimacy and clear break from the communist past made implementing the initial changes relatively uncontroversial.

An interim central banking law came into force on 1 January 1990, but did not include central bank independence. Uncertain policy makers quickly brought international expertise to bear upon the process of revision. The IMF and the World Bank advised the government on drafting a new Law on the CSSB during 1990–1, one modelled heavily on the Bundesbank. This law, which passed nearly unanimously on 20 December 1991, and took effect on 1 February 1992, established central bank independence and made currency stability the CNB's primary aim (Mataj and Vojtíšek 1992). As a leading Czech economist noted, 'passage of the Act in this form confirms how rapidly a political consensus has been achieved regarding the positive significance of central bank independence on currency stability in this country' (Pospíšil 1996). After the Velvet Divorce separating the Czech and Slovak Republics, the new Czech constitution and Act on the CNB (both of which came into force on 1 January 1993) further institutionalized the CNB's economic role and independence, and transferred the rights and duties of the CSSB to the CNB.[7] The CNB also kept most high-level personnel from the CSSB, making the transition from CSSB to CNB nearly seamless in the Czech Republic.

The CSSB under Tošovský's leadership also took advantage of international technical assistance and training. As Vladimir Valach, CSSB first deputy chairman, observed, 'On 1st January 1990, development became much faster. The whole top management of the new federal Central Bank changed. . . . I got the chance to be at the centre of an unrepeatable process of bank reform, of the ferment of seeking new routes, approaches and mechanisms' (Valach 2004). The CSSB sought these new approaches in the West. One Czech central banker stated strongly that 'We didn't hesitate. We knew we had to join the West. . . . In the CNB, these changes are Tošovský's work. He constituted the bank as a typical Western European bank. He took the structure, methods, and technical ways of the West and put them in the CNB' (personal interview, 2000). With a lack of experience and training, the central bankers relied heavily on the assistance efforts of international institutions and central banks (Czech National Bank 2003; Tůma 2004). By the mid-1990s, the CNB had firmly adopted the norms and practices of the international central banking community. As in Poland, the CNB's international support would prove vital in defending central bank independence against a domestic political attack.

The CNB's formerly secure status became politicized after an exchange-rate crisis in May 1997 forced the CNB to abandon its exchange-rate peg and significantly raise interest rates. The ensuing economic turmoil contributed to the resignation of Prime Minister Václav Klaus (by then head of the Civic Democratic Party, ODS) and his temporary replacement by CNB governor Tošovský in December 1997. Tošovský led a caretaker government until Miloš Zeman's newly elected Social-Democratic (CSSD) minority government took power in July 1998. Circumstances surrounding the 1997 events turned both Klaus and Zeman against the CNB. Klaus blamed the CNB's tight monetary policy for the 1997 crisis and his own political troubles, while Zeman blamed the same restrictive CNB policies for the Czech Republic's slow post-crisis recovery (Bönker 2006; Klaus 2000).

Ironically, Zeman and Klaus used the need to harmonize the Act on the CNB with the EU *acquis* in 2000 to rein in the independence of the central bank. In preparing the Act's amendment, Klaus's ODS introduced new limitations on the CNB, including a requirement to set the inflation target in consultation with the government, to get parliamentary approval of the CNB budget, and to get governmental approval of the president's choice for the CNB governor and board. Zeman's government accepted Klaus's proposals in June 2000. The IMF, ECB, and European Commission all spoke out against the draft amendment, as did the CNB and President Václav Havel. Nevertheless, the CSSD and ODS-dominated parliament not only passed the amendment, but overrode Havel's veto. The revised Act on the CNB took effect in January 2001. It briefly seemed as if central bank independence had suffered a devastating blow in the Czech Republic.

The influence of international institutions ultimately foiled Klaus and Zeman's efforts, however, as the CNB's protected constitutional status and EU accession pressures undid the amendment's damage to central bank independence. The first strand unravelled as Zeman unwittingly pushed his luck with the CNB. In November 2000, Tošovský resigned from the CNB to head the Financial Stability Institute at the Bank for International Settlements, and President Havel appointed Zdenek Tůma as his replacement. The Zeman government appealed the appointment to the Constitutional Court, arguing that the appointment should have required governmental approval. In response, the Constitutional Court not only rejected the government's petition, but declared that the portion of the amendment on appointments violated the CNB's independence and was thus unconstitutional. The 1993 Constitution's protections for central bank independence, inspired by international experience and advice, had successfully shielded the CNB from this challenge seven years later. Then, under pressure from the EU—which argued that the other ODS-sponsored parts of the 2000 amendment contradicted the *acquis*—a new amendment fully restoring the CNB's previous status came into effect in May 2002. In the end, the Act on the CNB protected the CNB's independence, changed its primary objective to price stability, and prohibited it from providing short-term credit to the government. As a result, like in Poland, Czech central bank independence emerged from this challenge strengthened both in law and in practice.

The Limits of Europeanization: Partial and Delayed Compliance

The prevailing international norms of central bank independence and price stability became institutionalized in Poland and the Czech Republic because of the consistency of international institutions' advice and actions, and the post-1989 uncertainty of domestic actors. With the euro, however, the situation was reversed. By the time the east central European states joined the EU, domestic policy makers had developed their own expertise in macroeconomic affairs and had no need or desire to rely on outside advisors. In addition, while politicians generally agreed on the desirability of EU accession (for which central bank independence was a prerequisite), no such political consensus existed on euro entry. Once EU accession had been successfully accomplished, east central European politicians also grew more assertive and confident in their dealings with EU institutions. More importantly, international actors not only gave inconsistent policy advice regarding the euro; the actions of Euro Area authorities undermined the attractiveness of the Euro Area. As a result, they lacked credibility with Polish and Czech policy makers on whether, when, and how to adopt the euro.

Not only had there been open dissent among West European countries about the Euro, ECB policy, and the Stability and Growth Pact, as well as notable opt-outs by influential states (the UK, Denmark, and *de facto* Sweden). Also, international actors sent mixed messages to east central Europe on euro entry timing. On the one hand, the IMF, OECD, World Bank, and international investors pushed the east central European states to develop euro entry strategies, with firm time commitments, even before these states had become EU members (Bönker 2006). On the other hand, the ECB strongly discouraged the new member states from pursuing rapid euro entry. ECB president Jean-Claude Trichet even argued, somewhat pedantically, that east central European states were akin to young but underdeveloped athletes seeking to join a 'champion league' before they were fit.[8] Given existing troubles in the Euro Area, and the increased risks of financial instability that expansion would present, the ECB was wary of bringing in new members who may not be completely prepared. Western central bankers and economists have sent similarly mixed messages. Some advocated rapid adoption or even unilateral euroization (Breuss, Fink, and Haiss 2004; Buiter 2004; Eichengreen 2003; Schoors 2002), while others urged great caution and lengthy postponements (Begg 2006; Dumke and Sherman 2000; Égert, Gruber, and Reininger 2003; Krenzler and Senior Nello 1999). On institutionalizing central bank independence, there were never such disagreements among external advisors to east central Europe.

International actors faced perhaps the greatest credibility challenge regarding the mandated *process* of euro adoption: fulfilling the Maastricht convergence criteria. Although EU accession states committed to joining the Euro Area at some future date, there is no fixed timetable or deadline for doing so. The European Commission and the ECB insisted that the east central European new member states meet the Maastricht criteria to the letter before Euro Area accession. However, other external actors widely criticized the criteria as being too restrictive, especially the requirement that the fast-growing prospective Euro Area members both maintain very low inflation rates and remain in the ERM II pegged exchange-rate regime for at least two years. The ECB has explained this requirement as the best method available for ascertaining the appropriate convergence rate between national currencies and the euro to prevent destabilization upon entry to the euro zone or after. But despite this rationale, an IMF report otherwise praising the ECB argued that 'the Maastricht criteria—specifically the inflation criterion together with the exchange rate stability criterion—could be overly binding for the CECs' (Schadler et al. 2005).

Moreover, unlike with central bank independence, in the case of euro entry the central bank internationalization and Europeanization processes conflict. Best practice in international central banking calls for inflation-targeting monetary policy regimes. Both Poland and the Czech Republic became inflation targeters in 1998, well before their 2004 EU entry. Indeed, the ECB itself is an informal inflation targeter. Entering ERM II would force east central European central bankers to revert to a less flexible peg.

In short, international institutions have little credibility with Polish and Czech policy makers on the euro entry issue because of their inconsistent advice and actions regarding the desirability, timing, and mechanisms of adoption. This lack of credibility left the door open for domestic debates about the euro in Poland and the Czech Republic, battles which confident east central European policy makers, central bankers, academics, and populaces were by that time relatively well-equipped to wage.

Poland

Whereas international institutions exercised substantial authority over central bank structures and the terms of debate concerning central bank independence and price stability from 1989 until 1997, external actors, and particularly the EU and ECB, largely failed to facilitate Poland's rapid convergence with Euro Area membership criteria. Although monetary indicators have been moving in the right direction, fiscal measures have not. Because of the absence of domestic actor uncertainty and lack of euro credibility by the late 1990s and early 2000s, the contours of conflict on this issue evolved, not between political parties, but instead between the central bank and politicians—from across the political spectrum. Central bank–government conflict has essentially resulted in a stalemate with no immediate prospects for euro entry. This development occurred because Poland's central bankers, who generally favour euro entry, are no longer empowered by international institutions' credibility, changing the domestic balance of power. In the battle with successive governments, central bankers have become relatively weaker on the question of European monetary integration.

Since 1997 when the NBP's independence was strengthened, the central bank has been in a strong position to pursue EMU convergence on the monetary side, even as it has had virtually no power to persuade politicians to meet the fiscal requirements. NBP governors Gronkiewicz-Waltz until 2000 and Leszek Balcerowicz (2000–7) have been inflation hawks (along with their Monetary Policy Councils, a result of the 1997 legislation). Between 1997 and 2004, the central bank at times used restrictive monetary policy to try to negotiate out of successive Polish governments commitments to fiscal austerity (Zubek 2006). One such episode became so heated that the centre–left SLD–UP–PSL governing coalition threatened in 2001 and 2002 to limit the bank's independence, a proposal that ultimately went nowhere (Epstein 2002). Motivated in large measure by the perceived benefits of macroeconomic stability and the structural reforms that EMU convergence would require, the Polish central bank has been a strong supporter of early euro entry. Indeed in 2002, Balcerowicz had plans for Poland to join ERM II by 2004 in hopes of adopting the euro by 2007. That timetable, as well as subsequent central bank aspirations, fell by the wayside.

While the central bank has been eager, politicians have been unwilling to undertake the structural reforms that would cut annual government outlays, even though the 1997 constitution limits government debt to the 60 per cent of GDP prescribed by the Maastricht convergence criteria. For Poland, the state's enormous distributional obligations make such structural reforms particularly problematic politically (Rhodes and Keune 2006). Exacerbating pressure on the government to engage in social spending has been very high unemployment, which neared 20 per cent in 2004. Moreover, although Poland's finance ministers have sometimes formulated fiscal 'stabilization' packages in order to align with the Maastricht criteria, when it came to implementation, governments consistently violated their terms (see Zubek 2006 for details). And, as noted above, because the European Commission and the ECB were not pushing for rapid nominal convergence (and in some cases actively discouraged rapid convergence for Poland), Polish cabinets have perceived themselves free to delay euro entry.

Since Poland's EU accession in 2004 and the victory of the centre–right Law and Justice Party (PiS) in the 2005 elections, this general pattern of political conflict has been recurring. PiS and its coalition partners, more than their predecessors, articulated a nationalist and Euro-sceptical political platform. This scepticism included public government doubts about whether euro entry would benefit the Polish economy. It also led to the halting of further privatization, and thus to potential privatization revenue. But, although in many respects the rhetoric out of Warsaw became more hostile to euro entry during PiS's tenure (with the government refusing to discuss full monetary convergence until 2009), macroeconomic measures did not deteriorate.

With respect to monetary policy, for example, Poland stayed on track. In 2004, the first Monetary Policy Council adopted a target inflation rate of 2.5 per cent. The second Monetary Policy Council (which took office in 2004 and remains until 2010) retained this policy and, because it was largely successful, reduced a key interest rate to its lowest level ever: 4 per cent in 2006. Citing inflationary pressure thereafter, rates climbed back up to 4.5 per cent in 2007, but this was similar to the ECB's own rate-setting. Poland also managed to contain overall levels of debt below the constitutional and Maastricht limit. Only on deficit spending has Poland remained consistently out of compliance.[9]

Whether the AWS-led government in the late 1990s, SLD-led in the early 2000s, or PiS-led in 2005–7, the lack of Europeanization is clear in that in every case politicians prioritized short-term political exigencies over the possible long-term benefits of rapid euro entry. Whether the Civic Platform, which prevailed in the October 2007 elections, will prove more Euro-friendly depends on two factors. First is whether European institutions become more consistent in their support of Polish entry. Second is whether these same European institutions can convince Polish central bankers that ERM II is the correct mechanism through which to demonstrate 'euro readiness'—a mechanism about which there is substantial doubt (Buiter 2004). In September 2007 NBP governor Sławomir Skrzypek expressed his scepticism by stating that he would again ask the EU to reduce the mandatory two-year term in ERM II, citing the precedents of Ireland and Spain.[10]

Czech Republic

The Czech experience with the euro shares much in common with that of Poland. International actors lacked credibility on this issue in the Czech Republic, and so could do little to effectively support the Czech National Bank in its push for early euro entry. As in Poland, the CNB retained its reputation as an inflation hawk, but Czech politicians could not maintain conservative fiscal policies. The CNB also faced an additional obstacle in the person of Vaclav Klaus, a long-time Euro-sceptic and CNB foe, who used his influence to undermine the CNB's early euro entry efforts. As a result, not only did the CNB lose a key battle over early euro entry in 2004–5, but the CNB itself became divided over how quickly to introduce the euro.

The independent CNB under both Tošovský and Tůma avidly pursued monetary convergence with Europe. Since moving to its inflation targeting regime in 1998, it has kept a tight hold on monetary policy, to the chagrin of many Czech politicians, academics, and businesspeople. Geršl (2006) found in a survey of articles in the leading Czech financial newspaper from 1997 to 2005 that every government comment expressing dissatisfaction with the CNB signalled the CNB to ease monetary policy. The signals from other interest groups did the same: the financial sector (70%), employers (100%), unions (100%), and 'others' (96.5%). The CNB resisted this pressure, and by 2002 Czech inflation met the Maastricht convergence target.

In contrast, the Czech Republic began running significant fiscal deficits after the 1997 crisis, reaching a high of 11.3 per cent in 2003—the largest deficit among the prospective EU new member states. The CNB felt powerless to restrain politicians on its own, so it promoted early euro entry to impose fiscal discipline on the government (Johnson 2006). However, the CNB found itself in a relatively weak position to fight for the euro, because of both the lack of outside support from the ECB and its own sharp criticism of the Maastricht criteria, especially ERM II.[11] In short, the CNB berated the government for not meeting one set of the Maastricht convergence criteria, while itself challenging the legitimacy of another. This position did not raise the credibility of either the CNB or the euro entry process.

Without useful levers of international influence, the CNB faced difficulty in rallying domestic support for its euro entry campaign from either of the largest Czech political parties. The leftist CSSD generally approved of Europe but preferred higher social spending than meeting the Maastricht fiscal criteria would allow. On the other hand, while Klaus's centre–right ODS party supported fiscal rectitude, it also had a deep Euro-sceptic streak. Klaus in particular often berated European 'socialism' and questioned the efficacy and desirability of the Euro Area. To make matters worse for the CNB, Klaus succeeded Vaclav Havel as Czech president in February 2003, ironically giving him the sole appointment power over the CNB governor and board members that he had fought to take away from the presidency just a few years earlier. Finally, the divided electorate repeatedly forced Czech parliamentarians to form tenuous governing coalitions or to rule as minority governments, with little mandate for or ability to implement fundamental policy reforms. As a result, the appropriate timing of euro entry became an issue of heated political debate, with conflict coming to a head over the Czech euro entry strategy.

In its draft strategy of December 2002, the CNB ambitiously suggested 2007 as the Czech Republic's target entry date.[12] Although new CSSD Prime Minister Vladimír Špidla was willing to use the Maastricht criteria as an excuse for stepping up fiscal reforms, many in his own party failed to support him. The government also feared making a euro entry strategy public until after the June 2003 Czech EU referendum, given the relatively Euro-sceptic Czech public (Bönker 2006). As a result, months of discussion followed, during which the CNB criticized the Špidla government for badly missing its fiscal deficit targets and not taking the Maastricht criteria seriously. President Klaus hit back by criticizing the CNB's inflation targeting as 'fiction' and stating that it would be 'unwise' to adopt the euro.[13]

In September 2003, the CNB and the government finally agreed on a revised strategy, one which represented a significant compromise for the CNB.[14] It stated that joining the Euro Area in 2007 would not be possible because 'the current outlook ... does not indicate that the public budget deficit criterion will be fulfilled by [June 2006]', and it revised the expected entry date to 2009–10 at the earliest. Even this agreement proved unsustainable, however, and tensions grew as the government continued to spend in excess of the promised targets. Persistent high deficits exacerbated by another spate of pre-election spending in mid-2006 finally forced a complete revision of the strategy in August 2007. Despite the protests of CNB governor Tůma and Finance Minister Miroslav Kalousek, the revised strategy did not set a new target date for euro entry. ODS Prime Minister Miroslav Topolanek said that he refused to set a date because his tenuous government –with 100 ODS deputies plus their smaller coalition partners facing off against 100 CSSD opposition deputies—could not ensure long-term compliance with its plans for fiscal reform.[15]

Not only did the CNB lose the political battle over early euro entry, but its pro-euro stance has been undermined from within. When the terms of three CNB board members expired in February 2005, President Klaus replaced them with close allies and fellow Euro-sceptics. Klaus did so again in November 2006, when he replaced two more outgoing board members with like-minded economists. Afterwards, only Governor Tůma and Vice-Governor Niedemeyer remained from the seven-member board that had approved the CNB's initial ambitious euro strategy in 2002. Once on the board, the Klaus appointees publicly spoke with great wariness about the euro. For example, Mojmir Hampl urged caution and argued that successful euro entry did not represent a meaningful measure of a country's economic health.[16] Faced with challenges from without and within, Tůma simply stated that the timing of Czech Euro-Area entry is now 'a political decision'.[17]

Convergence and Central Bank Power

The Czech and Polish central banks have, in a surprisingly short period of time, converged with European central banks in terms of internationally accepted norms and practices. Both eagerly defend central bank independence and their inflation-targeting regimes. Both have developed sophisticated economic modelling and research capabilities. Both have ensured that their states' central banking legislation, payment systems, statistical departments, and so forth substantially comply with international best practice and EU/ESCB requirements. The international consensus on the value of these developments and international assistance to achieve them made it possible to transform these central banks. Importantly, this transformation took place primarily immediately after the transition when domestic actor uncertainty was at its height.

In addition, because central bank independence was firmly institutionalized in this early era, and reinforced by international practice and pressures, it became difficult for domestic political leaders to overturn it later. The combination of the institutionalization of central bank independence, the development of extensive economic expertise within the central banks, and the active support of an influential transnational community of central bankers sharing the same beliefs and responsibilities, have dramatically increased the domestic power of east central European central banks. In a short period of time, they moved from simple communist-era accounting bureaucracies to prestigious and influential domestic economic policy makers.

But ironically, internationalization also gave east central European central bankers the tools with which to challenge certain aspects of Europeanization. Polish and Czech central bankers critique European practices with great authority. They are not willing to accept ECB arguments in favour of the inflation criterion or ERM II membership at face value, and they forcefully upbraid the EU for not enforcing the fiscal rules of the Stability and Growth Pact. Moreover, they are wary of giving up their flexible inflation-targeting regimes without the promise of rapid euro entry in return. In short, they behave just as national central bankers in Western Europe or in North America would. In this sense, the NBP and CNB have experienced significant convergence with Europe.

Yet, although Czech and Polish central banks have gained enormous stature at the international level, their power has not increased commensurately at either the European or domestic levels. The east central European central bankers have been unable to alter the terms of debate on euro entry and will clearly remain (and be treated as) junior partners at the ECB and in the ESCB. As a result, Czech and Polish central bankers have defended early euro entry, but without international support and, increasingly, without as much enthusiasm. Although the CNB and NBP promote the positive aspects of euro entry in order to press fiscal restraint on their governments, the central bankers themselves appreciate very well the arguments both for *and* against entering the euro in the near term. They resent the ECB and EU for their inflexibility and inconsistency on the Maastricht convergence criteria, and have become more reluctant to spend their limited political capital on shooting at a moving goalpost.

This situation in turn ultimately threatens the power of European central banking. The EU and ECB are divided between the 'in' Euro-Area states and the 'out' states. For European central bankers to speak with a common and powerful voice in the face of increasing challenges to central bank authority from politicians and markets, and for east central European central banks to retain their hard-won domestic influence and credibility, the EU cannot afford to long exclude the largest of its new member states from the 'euro club'.

Notes

1. For further elaboration on these variables across a range of issues, see Epstein (2008).
2. The UK and Denmark have legal 'opt-outs' negotiated into the Maastricht Treaty. Sweden is under obligation to join, and plans to hold a referendum on the issue in 2012.
3. G. Kołodko, 'Central Bank Responsibilities: Not Only to God and History', *Polish News Bulletin*, 6 September 1994. Also see 'Between Inflation and Recession: A Dispute over Interest Rates', *Polish Press Agency*, 30 September 1994.
4. See the 'Central Bank Facing Changes', *Polish News Bulletin*, 20 September 1995; and K. Kowalczyk, 'The NBP's Fortress', *Polish News Bulletin*, 5 October 1995.
5. K. Bobinski, 'Survey—Poland: The Central Bank', *Financial Times*, 26 March 1997: 4.
6. See the Constitution of the Republic of Poland, Article 227 and Article 220–2.
7. 1993 Constitution of the Czech Republic, Chapter 6, Article 68.
8. J.-C. Trichet, 'Looking at EU and Euro Area Enlargement from a Central Banker's Angle: The Views of the ECB', speech at the Diplomatic Institute, Sofia, 27 February 2006.
9. This data come from *Economist Intelligence Unit: Poland*, 10 July 2007.
10. 'NBP Head Skrzypek Expects Euro Adoption Not Before 2012, Wants Fast ERM II Path', *Poland Today*, 25 September 2007.
11. See Z. Tuma, 'Europe's Club of Nations Needs a Rule Change', *Financial Times*, 4 January 2007.
12. Czech National Bank, 'The Czech Republic and the Euro—Draft Accession Strategy', 23 December 2002, www.cnb.cz.

13. 'Klaus Says Deflation in Czech Rep Not Good, Blames CNB', *CTK Business News*, 22 April 2003.

14. The Czech Government and the Czech National Bank, 'The Czech Republic's Euro-area Accession Strategy', September 2003, www.cnb.cz.

15. 'Czech Euro Strategy Says Public Finances Still Hamper Adoption', *CTK Business News*, 27 August 2007.

16. 'Czech Central Banker Urges Patience in Shift to Euro Zone', *Dow Jones International News*, 19 October 2007.

17. 'Czech Central Banker: Euro-Zone Entry Is Political Decision-Report', *Dow Jones International News*, 5 November 2007.

Part IV

'Semi-Permanent' Outsiders

11

Bank of England: Learning to Live with the Euro

Charles Goodhart[1]

1997 was a climacteric year for the Bank of England, and for political developments in the UK. In early May, the Labour Party won a resounding General Election victory. Thirteen years of Conservative government came to a crashing end, marked in the years since 1992 by internal infighting between euro-sceptics and euro-philes.

Within a week the incoming Chancellor of the Exchequer, Gordon Brown, had awarded the Bank of England operational independence,[2] and within two weeks had stripped it of its role in both banking supervision and debt management.[3]

Prior to the departure of the UK from the Exchange Rate Mechanism in September 1992, the Bank had been one of the more subservient central banks, in the sense that the key (interest rate) decisions for determining macro-monetary policy were taken by the Chancellor, often after consultation with the Prime Minister. The Bank could, and did, advise on these, in private and behind the scenes, and was often influential; but the politicians and, especially, the Treasury kept pressure on the Bank *not* to reveal publicly when the Bank's advice differed from the action taken. The Bank was discouraged from publishing its own forecast, (for fear of commentators focussing on discrepancies between the two, Bank and HMT, forecasts), and its Quarterly Bulletin Assessments were submitted to, read, and sometimes censored by HMT.

Changes in Core Purposes: The Bank and Euro Entry

In the 1980s and 1990s, the Bank had three core purposes (CP). As articulated in the Annual Report of 1997, they were the following:

1. **Maintaining the integrity and value of the currency**. Above all, this involves securing price stability as a precondition for achieving the wider

economic goals of sustainable growth and employment. The Bank does this by influencing decisions on interest rates, on the basis of economic and financial analysis of development both at home and abroad; by participating in international discussions to promote the health of the world economy; by implementing agreed policy through its market operations and its deal-ings with the financial system; and by maintaining confidence in the note issue.

2. **Maintaining the stability of the financial system, both domestic and international**. The Bank seeks to achieve this through supervising individual institutions and markets; through monitoring the links between financial mar-kets; through analysing the health of the domestic and international economy; through co-operation with other financial supervisors, both nationally and internationally; and through promoting sound and efficient payment and settlement arrangements. In exceptional circumstances, the Bank may also provide or organise last resort financial support where this is needed to avoid systemic damage.

3. **Seeking to ensure the effectiveness of the UK's financial services**. The UK needs a financial system that offers opportunities for firms of all sizes to have access to capital on terms that give adequate protection to investors, and which enhances the international competitive position of the City of London and other UK financial centres. The Bank aims to achieve these goals through its expertise in the market place; by acting as a catalyst to collective action where market forces alone are deficient; by supporting the development of a financial infrastructure that furthers these goals; by advising HM Government; and by encouraging British interests through its contacts with financial authorities overseas.

So long as the Bank remained subservient, its ability to influence, and its contribution to, CP1 (i.e. to maintain price stability) remained limited. Not surprisingly therefore, it invested more of its energies into CP2 (maintaining financial stability), and CP3 (enhancing the efficiency and role of the UK's financial system in general, and of the City of London in particular). With the abolition of exchange control, the ending of the building societies' cartel, and of restrictive practices in the London Stock Exchange (Big Bang) the 1980s was the heyday of CP3. The government was strongly supportive, but the Bank played a major effective role (David Walker being one of the key protagonists in the Bank). During the 1970s and 1980s, banking supervision (CP2) became the fastest growing part of the Bank, though a series of crises—fringe bank crisis, 1973–4; Johnson-Matthey Bank failure, 1984; Barings, 1995; and BCCI, 1991—seriously tarnished its reputation in the eyes of many external commentators.

After the UK had been forced out of the ERM, the then Chancellor, Norman Lamont, adopted the strategy of inflation targetry in October 1992. This new strategy was announced and implemented with remarkable speed after the ERM exit. But, after the relative failures of the government's earlier monetary targeting strategy (the Medium-Term Financial Strategy, MTFS, 1979–85) and of its external peg strategy (1988–92), the government itself had little credibility left. As an expert, non-political institution the Bank did have credibility. So Lamont turned to the Bank to provide independent support, by now *requiring* it to publish its Inflation Report (without any prior censorship). A few years later, Ken Clarke as Chancellor reinforced this by having the Governor's advice published verbatim in the 'Ken and Eddie show' (Eddie George being the then Governor). All this is detailed at much greater length in Goodhart (2008).

But these changes to the role and status of the Bank were comparatively small, in contrast to the devolution of operational independence to the Monetary Policy Committee of the Bank of England in May 1997. Suddenly this elevated the role of CP1, and the decision on interest rates, to primacy in the Bank. Meanwhile, the removal of banking supervision to the Financial Services Authority simultaneously led to a downgrading in the importance of CP2.[4]

At a stroke, the role of the Bank had been shifted from one in which they were akin to central banks on the Continent (such as the Banca d'Italia and Banco de España), with little role in macro-monetary policy because of the ERM, but a large role in banking supervision, to bring it to a position like the Bundesbank, with monetary policy autonomy and a much lower profile on financial stability issues.

Amongst continental central banks the Bundesbank was the 'big loser' in the shift to the European System of Central Banks (ESCB). But, if the Bundesbank had opposed the creation of the ESCB, it is doubtful whether the German people, or their legislature (Bundesrat and Bundestag), would have approved it. Largely in order to gain the (reluctant) assent of the Bundesbank to the launch of the ESCB (and the euro), the Bundesbank was, in effect, enabled to shape the ESCB and ECB in its own image (or so it is widely believed in the UK). This involved features such as almost total independence from government, (indeed much more so than the Bundesbank had), considerable goal independence to decide its own definition of price stability, a prominent 'monetary' pillar, and a collegiate, consensual approach to decision-making.

All this was quite at odds with the British approach, which followed on from the initial New Zealand model in many respects. This latter model allowed the Bank of England operational independence, but no goal independence, emphasizing the focus on an inflation target, set by the Chancellor. Decision-making was to be individualistic, and, so the British contend, much more transparent than that of the Governing Council of the European Central Bank. These differences of viewpoint are highlighted in the entertaining papers by Buiter (1999) and Issing (1999). The then Chancellor, Gordon Brown, is believed to be (justly) proud of the constitutional structure that he set out for the Bank and for the conduct of monetary policy, as codified by the Bank of England Act 1998. He, and many others in the UK, believes this structure to be superior to the German model adopted for the ECB. That may be one of the reasons for Brown's supposed coolness towards joining the Euro Area.

Be that as it may, by his regime change in May 1997 Brown revised the role of the Bank from one in which its position and status would not be greatly altered by entry into the Euro Area to one in which it too would be a 'big loser'. Everyone knew this, at least at the back of their minds. Nevertheless the Bank prided itself, and rightly so, on the professionalism, expertise, and independence of its staff. Whatever the implications for the Bank itself, the case—the benefits and disadvantages—of UK entry into the euro were carefully and fairly laid out by its economic research staff, notably its Chief Economists, John Flemming followed by Mervyn King. I was not myself working in the Bank in those years, but my (reasonably well-informed) understanding was that there was much the same balance of euro-philes and euro-sceptics in the Bank, both after 1997 as well as before, as in the intelligentsia as a whole.

There were two major reasons why the Bank would have found it extremely difficult to have expressed an overt view/position on the merits of euro entry, prior to the government itself coming to a decision on the economic merits of the case. First, it was a major, strategic political decision. As public-sector officials, the Bank had to be prepared wholeheartedly to implement whatever people and government decided to do. Taking a clear, overt position could leave the Bank in a very exposed position if the decision went the other way. Second, there was an obvious potential conflict of interest, especially after May 1997. The Bank's own role would now have been dramatically affected by entry. Under these circumstances any public position-taking, especially if advocating staying outside, could have been attacked as self-seeking.[5]

So, from a fairly early stage, certainly by 1997, the Bank's strategy was decided. The Bank would *not* give any view on the overall question, whether or not UK entry into the Euro Area would be desirable. Thus, in his speech to the British/Swiss Chamber of Commerce on 12 September 2000, the Governor Eddie George said the following:

But let me make clear, from the outset, that monetary union is fundamentally a political rather than an economic issue. It necessarily involves the deliberate pooling of national sovereignty over important aspects of public policy, in the interest not just of collective economic advantage, but of a perceived wider political harmony within Europe.

As a central banker, I have nothing to say about the politics of monetary union—that's for elected politicians and clearly political opinion is divided—not just in the UK—about how far and certainly how fast to go in the sensitive matter of pooling national sovereignty. But monetary union is also an economic issue and that is my concern.[6]

He went on to outline the economic pros and cons,[7] but neither he, nor any of the other spokespersons for the Bank in these years, like Howard Davies and

David Clementi, successive Deputy Governors; Ian Plenderleith and John Townend, respectively, then Executive and Deputy Directors; ever tried to reach a conclusion about the balance of advantages and disadvantages. The two-handed economist, 'on the one hand and on the other', appeared up-front in this context. Some close observers of Governor George felt that he may have placed slightly more emphasis on the disadvantages, especially 'one size fits all' than on the countervailing advantages, but that would have been a subjective, personal judgement, in the ear of the beholder. And views about the balance of the pros and cons varied from person to person, as in the wider community.

I DREAMED I WAS TOLD TO SELECT AN
INTEREST RATE TO SUIT GERMANY
EIRE AND THE T.U.C.

There were many, especially in Anglo-Saxon countries, who drew the (incorrect) inference from the difficulties of the Exchange Rate Mechanism in 1992–3, and the UK's exit from it, that the Eurosystem would never start, and, if it should start, would rapidly beak down. In an associated vein, many wonder whether the views of the Bank (and Treasury) were tilted against euro entry by that experience. In my view both suppositions were mostly, perhaps entirely, mistaken. Bank (and Treasury) officials were good enough economists to know that a single currency is a much more robust regime than a pegged exchange rate. The former cannot be subject to speculative attack. Once adopted, it can only break apart, if some internal segment makes a (political) decision to do so.

The problem with a single currency is, instead, that it may condemn some parts of the zone to long-lasting inflationary, or deflationary, pressures in the face of asymmetric shocks. That is why issues of whether the UK economy had converged to its Continental neighbours, and of the flexibility of adjustment mechanisms, figured so large in the commentaries and discussions, both in the Bank and in the Treasury.

Through all this, the Bank's strategic position remained constant; that the issue of entry was primarily a political matter, on which it would be inappropriate for the Bank to comment. There were, of course, economic advantages and disadvantages. The Bank would enumerate and report these, but would consciously abstain from reaching any conclusion about the overall balance of pros and cons. In this respect, the Bank's position was, rather nicely, the mirror-image reverse of that taken up by the government, and in particular by the Chancellor. For the Labour government, the political and constitutional issues pointed, fairly clearly, to a case *for* UK entry into the Euro Area. Instead, the issue for them was primarily economic.

The Five Economic Tests for Euro Entry

As Ian Plenderleith stated in a speech to the conference organized by the International Centre for Monetary and Banking Studies on 'the International Monetary System after the Decision on EMU' in Geneva on Friday, 7 November 1997:

The Government's conclusions, as the Chancellor of the Exchequer set them out in his statement to Parliament on 27 October, began by addressing three issues of principle. It concluded first that, in principle, a successful single currency within a single European market would be of benefit to Europe and to Britain. Second, to share a common monetary policy with other Member States represents a major pooling of economic sovereignty; but, while this constitutional issue is a factor in the decision, it is not in the Government's judgment an overriding one. Rather it signifies that in order for EMU to be right for Britain the economic benefit should be clear and unambiguous. If, in the end, a single currency is successful, and the economic case is clear and unambiguous, then the Government believes Britain should be part of it. There is a third issue of principle, namely popular consent, which the Government has reiterated will be tested through a referendum.

The UK Treasury has published its assessment of five economic tests that define whether a clear and unambiguous case can be made for the UK to join EMU. These are: whether there can be sustainable convergence between Britain and the economies of a single currency; whether there is sufficient flexibility to cope with economic change; the effect on investment; the impact on the UK's financial services industry; and whether it is good for employment.

Applying these five economic tests leads the Government to the following clear conclusions. British membership of a single currency in 1999 could not meet the tests, so that joining at the start of EMU is not in the country's economic interests. The Government will therefore be notifying our European partners, in accordance with the Maastricht Treaty, that we will not seek membership of the single currency on 1 January 1999. The Chancellor emphasised that there is no need—legally, formally or politically—to renounce our option to join for the period between 1 January 1999 and the end of the current Parliament; nor would it be sensible to do so. But he concluded that, barring some fundamental and unforeseen change in economic circumstances, making a decision during this Parliament to join is not realistic. It is therefore sensible for business and the country to plan on the basis that, in this Parliament, the Government does not propose to enter a single currency.

HAS HE PASSED HER FIVE KEY ECONOMIC TESTS ?

The basic economic rationale for not joining the euro, as set out then in 1997, was that sustainable and durable convergence with the rest of the prospective Euro Area had not yet been achieved. In particular, short-term interest rates on the Continent were around 3–4 per cent, compared with over 7 per cent in Britain. HMT's accompanying paper, setting out the five tests that Britain would have to pass before joining the Euro Area, noted that Britain had more non-EU trade, more home loans at variable interest rates than its partners, and that it was the only oil exporter in the EC. Those factors made it hard for the UK's economic cycle to match those on the Continent, and for its interest rates to be the same. Moreover, sterling had appreciated strongly at this time, and was expected by many to fall back shortly, so there was a disinclination to lock in a high real exchange rate. So, there was quite general approbation of the decision to defer the decision, though *The Economist* (1 November: 31) grumbled that not enough was being done to *promote* convergence. Nevertheless, many euro-philes were encouraged by the generally pro-European tone of the 27 October statement, while the euro-sceptics were cheered by the actual decision to stay out, if only for the time being.

Anyhow, these same five economic tests gained a totemic importance for the Chancellor, and, without his imprimatur, it was generally accepted that the promised referendum on entry would have no chance of success. His October statement ruled out British entry for the life of that Parliament, but no longer. So when Labour was re-elected in 2001, shortly thereafter a major exercise for the Treasury became to subject these same five tests to much more detailed scrutiny. This was a major analytical study, in which a large number of outside academic economists (including me) participated. Note, however, that the Bank did not participate in this exercise,[8] and was neither used, nor sought to be involved, as an official adviser.

At the same time as the 'five test' exercise was being conducted, preparations had to be run in tandem to consider the practical implications, if the decision went in favour of UK entry. Having been marginally involved myself in the former exercise as an outsider, my own impression was that the write-up of those tests which might *not* prove favourable was left very much in an 'either/ or', 'on the other hand/on the other', mode until the last moment. Officials did *not* know, nor could they presume to guess, the outcome in advance. So, practical preparations for possible entry continued to be made until June 2003.

PLEASE DECIDE WHETHER YOU WANT
TO SPEND A PENNY OR A EURO

These practical preparations for possible UK entry under the government's policy of 'prepare and decide' were also led by HM Treasury. The Bank was involved in the key committees chaired by HMT, and was delegated the responsibility by HMT for co-ordinating preparations in sterling wholesale markets. This was done through the City Euro Group (CEG), which the Bank proposed, established, and chaired, and which represented all the City's main constituencies. CEG met regularly between 1999 and 2005, and still meets once a year (to discuss developments in the Euro Area, such as infrastructure projects, rather than euro preparations). As a result of cooperation with the City through CEG, the Bank was able to publish a change-over plan in sterling wholesale markets in *Practical Issues*, and keep it up-to-date on the Bank website. This is discussed in much more detail in the next section. The Bank also contributed to the UK National Changeover Plan and the regular reports to Parliament coordinated by HMT.[9]

The conclusion of the five test study—*UK Membership of the Single Currency: An Assessment of the Five Economic Tests*, June 2003—effectively repeated the negative conclusion about sustainable convergence (and flexibility) that had been made in October 1997. Thus the concluding, and crucial, paragraph 6.6, p. 228, reads as follows:

Overall the Treasury assessment is that since 1997 the UK has made real progress towards meeting the five economic tests. But, on balance, though the potential benefits of increased investment, trade, a boost to financial services, growth and jobs are clear, we cannot at this point in time conclude that there is sustainable and durable convergence or sufficient flexibility to cope with any potential difficulties within the euro area. So, despite the risks and costs from delaying the benefits of joining, a clear and unambiguous case for UK membership of EMU has not at the present time been made and a decision to join now would not be in the national economic interest.

In the immediately following years the Euro Area grew more slowly than the UK. Also, London reinforced its position as the leading capital market centre for the Euro Area, despite being an 'out'. Moreover, the sterling exchange rate against the euro became rather stable (till 2007–8), even while the paths of interest rates in London and Frankfurt continued to diverge. For all these, and other, reasons advocacy in the UK for entry into the Euro Area waned, indeed largely disappeared. The lobby group in favour of entry, Britain in Europe, wound itself up.

Through all this discussion, the Bank had consciously kept to the side lines on the wider issue of whether the UK should enter, or not. There was, however, a more operational, educational, and technical field, related to the establishment of the Euro Area into which the Bank flung itself with enthusiasm and conviction.

The Bank and the City of London: The Co-Ordination Unit for Europe

London is the largest *international* financial centre in the world; New York and Tokyo are perhaps bigger overall, but the predominant part of their business is domestic, rather than international. London had become, by the 1990s, the site of much of the financial intermediation involving its European partners. So, whether in, or out, of the euro, much of the business undertaken in legacy currencies in London would have to switch onto a euro basis when the Euro Area commenced on 1 January 1999.

That this change-over to the euro would be important for the City, and essential to get right, was not fully recognized by commercial institutions in the early years. As early as 1995 from senior conversations across the City, Bank officials all too frequently heard that, even if the euro started, about which there was considerable scepticism in the City, the UK would not be a member 'and so we don't need to do anything'. The Bank, notably the Governor Eddie George, and John Townend, George's Alternate at the European Monetary Institute, were convinced that this view was wrong. The Alternate's Committee was charged with responsibility for all the technical preparations for the euro. Because of this work which was just beginning, Townend was well placed to understand precisely how the euro was going to be introduced, both at the retail and at wholesale levels, as decisions were taken—strictly by the EMI Council but the Alternate's Committee was very influential. So George asked Townend to write a paper for circulation to senior executives across the City, to explain why practical preparations in the London wholesale markets were as critical as on the Continent, whether or not the UK was to become an initial member of the euro. Hence the first *Practical Issues* was published in May 1996. It was only a dozen pages long but went to 200 or so senior people across the City and was influential in helping to serve as a wake-up call. From that point on, the euro responsibility came gradually to dominate Townend's Bank role.

As another indication of the delayed recognition in the City, and the appreciation of the euro's importance in the Bank, Howard Davies, then Deputy Governor, stated in his speech to the Futures and Options Association International Derivatives Week Conference on 4 June 1997, that

The assessment was that relatively few market participants in London had made serious preparations for EMU, and seemed unsure of how to proceed. Only 6 per cent of brokers and own account traders had made contingency plans for the introduction of EMU. But this survey was undertaken in April of last year, and I am confident that the responses would be different today.

Certainly a lot of work has been done in the London market, co-ordinated and steered by a team in the Bank, to ensure that London is as well prepared as other European centres for EMU. And our assessment now, which I believe is shared by the EMI and the Commission, is that London is as well prepared as most if not all European centres.

I can assure you that the Bank of England itself will be ready for EMU on 1 January 1999, whether or not the UK is a member. We will be able to offer euro accounts and euro settlement facilities. We have taken the lead in work on market conventions across

251

Europe. EMU is likely to bring harmonisation of conventions such as day count and frequency of coupon payments among Europe's bond markets, and the London market is ready to do that.

Prior to 27 October 1997, when the decision to enter the Euro Area was deferred into the next Parliament, the Bank had to work under the assumption that entry was a real possibility, despite the agreement by both main political parties to submit any proposal to join to a referendum, and the continuing apparent majorities in the opinion polls against joining. Opinions can change. A note outlining the main features of the Bank's work, pre-October 1997, is contained in the Bank's Annual Report and Accounts for 1996.[10]

The 27 October statement did not, in the event, slow down work on preparation for the euro, especially in wholesale markets in London. In any case, there remained a need to prepare in advance, should Britain eventually decide to join. 'Prepare and decide' was the then common watchword.

Thus John Townend in his Bank of Wales lecture, 29 October 1997, on 'The U. K. and the Euro', stated that

The other condition for London to thrive as a financial centre after EMU begins is that it must be well prepared for the introduction of the euro. The Bank of England is playing a substantive role in the preparations in two complementary ways. First, through our participation in the work of the EMI, we aim to make sure that the design of EMU is capable of being delivered in a technical sense. I referred to this earlier.

Our other role is to co-ordinate the preparations for the introduction of the euro across the financial sector, to the extent that co-ordination is required. The Bank's role in helping the financial community to prepare for the euro was recognised and reconfirmed by the Chancellor this summer when he launched his complementary initiative to begin preparing the business community for the euro. In addition to making our own internal preparations at the Bank, we play a co-ordinating role in the financial community in three main ways:

- First, our job is to ensure that the necessary infrastructure is developed in the UK to allow anyone who wishes to do so to use the euro in wholesale payments and across the financial markets from the first day of EMU.

- Second, we aim to promote discussion between the EMI, national central banks and market participants across Europe about practical issues on which the market is seeking a degree of co-ordination.

- And, third, we provide information: for example, through our quarterly series of editions on *Practical Issues Arising from the Introduction of the Euro*, which is distributed to around 32,000 recipients across the City and beyond, including many (I hope) to Wales and 4,000 directly abroad. And following the successful symposium we held early this year, we are planning to hold a further symposium, next January at the Bank, on London as the international financial centre for the euro.[11]

" I'M LOOKING FORWARD TO HEARING "
JOHN TOWNEND'S INSIGHTS ON THE EURO

This work needed to involve at differing times many of those working in various operational parts of the Bank, (though the Monetary Analysis wing serving the MPC was less affected). In order to pull this work together, and to take the lead in the Bank's educational, and Core Purpose 3 (City efficiency), role the Governor introduced a new and separate group in the Bank, initially called the Euro Preparation Division, but renamed the Co-ordination Unit for Europe some time after the 27 October 1997 Statement. The work of this unit was directed by John Townend, from its start until his retirement in June 2002 (to climb mountains in the Himalayas). Townend became a Director of the Bank, with special responsibilities for Europe at the start of 1999, promotion that derived in part from the considerable success of the wholesale market change-over to the euro on 1 January 1999. He had previously been a Deputy Director of Market Operations, under Ian Plenderleith, in that part of the Monetary Stability wing that had taken over the functions of what had once been the Chief Cashier's Department, undertaking the market oper-ations and home finance issues of the Bank. But Townend had already be-come 'Mr. Europe' in the Bank. Before taking on this role, while still heading

Market Operations, he had also been the Governor's Alternate on the EMI Council, which means that he did the main donkeywork, together with Stephen Colllins, the second Alternate. Prior to the 1998 establishment of the ECSB, the EMI was the main centre for the technical preparations for EMU.[12]

The role of the Co-ordination Unit, as set out in the Annual Report of 1999, was to be

responsible for co-ordinating the Bank's work on Europe, which is carried out by each of the Bank's main operational areas. It takes a lead on the issues that affect the Bank as a whole but which do not fall within the ambit of any of the operational areas. It is also responsible for co-ordinating the Bank's involvement with the European Central Bank, other EU central banks and the EU Economic and Financial Committee. It maintains contact with, and provides technical information to, financial institutions operating in euro markets and with responsibility for euro infrastructure.

The Coordination Unit was a relatively small part of the Bank, involving not much more than about 1 per cent of the total staff, and of its direct costs, see Table 11.1 and Figure 11.1, taken, respectively, from the Bank's Annual Reports in 2000 and 2001.

Despite being small, the senior staff[13] in the Unit were of very high quality, including top-class officials such as Bill Allen, who became Director for Europe after John Townend's retirement in June 2002, Stephen Collins, Jon Carr, and Paul Richards, a financial expert in the City who was seconded to the Bank in February 1997 and joined full time in 2002.

In the first year of the existence of the Euro Preparation Division, 1996–7, its main function was to prepare for possible UK entry. But after the 27 October 1997 Statement its most immediate task was primarily an educational and co-ordinating exercise to prepare the City of London, and indeed the Bank itself, for the change-over to the euro on 1 January 1999, though of course it also continued preparations for euro entry until after 2003.

Table 11.1. Bank of England expenditure budget

	1999/00 Budget	1999/00 Out-turn	2000/01 Budget
Business units			
Monetary Analysis and Statistics	16.5	16.9	18.9
Financial Market Operations	43.6	41.3	45.7
Financial Stability	8.1	8.4	8.9
Co-ordination Unit for Europe	1.3	1.3	1.4
Centre for Central Banking Studies	1.5	1.3	1.5
Printing Works	39.5	37.7	34.5
Registrar's Department	4.0	3.8	3.6
	114.5	110.7	114.5

Numbers of Staff by Area 2000 and 2001 (Chart 1)

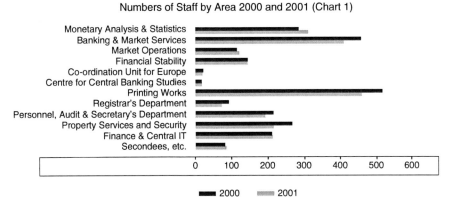

Figure 11.1. Bank of England: numbers of staff by area, 2000 and 2001

As already noted, the City of London was the largest financial centre affected by the change-over in wholesale financial markets from legacy currencies to the euro at its launch at the beginning of 1999. The Bank was integrally involved in co-ordinating the preparations in the City for the launch of the euro. Although individual firms were responsible for their own preparations, the Bank sought to achieve a consensus where a common approach was required, and to communicate the results across the market as a whole (e.g. through the early editions of *Practical Issues Arising from the Introduction of the Euro* in 1997 and 1998). The Bank was also concerned to ensure that large firms and the financial infrastructure in the City were prepared for the 'conversion weekend' at the beginning of 1999. In the run-up to the conversion weekend, during the weekend itself, and in its immediate aftermath, the Bank kept in regular contact with all the key firms in the City to check that they were ready, and in case there were any problems. In the event, the change-over went without any significant hitches, as the City was well prepared. The change-over to the euro in wholesale markets was one of the largest operations ever undertaken in the City. The Bank's involvement was consistent with its 'CP3' role at the time.

The details are set out in the early editions of *Practical Issues*. These were widely used, not only in the City, but also across the Euro Area. Indeed the circulation list of *Practical Issues* was literally global, issuing some 32,000 copies, by far the largest circulation of any Bank publication. The other central banks in Europe helped and co-operated in the publication of *Practical Issues*, but none of them published anything comparable in quality or circulation. Many experts (including European Commissioner Mario Monti) regarded *Practical Issues* as equivalent to 'the Bible' for the wholesale euro launch in 1999, which was remarkable given the likelihood, later confirmed, that the UK would be an 'out' central bank.

IT WAS !

The Bank also monitored the retail banking change-over in the Euro Area between 1999 and 2001 and the issue of euro notes and coin and withdrawal of legacy national notes and coin at the beginning of 2002. This was consistent with the UK's policy of 'prepare and decide'; and it was felt that there was a one-off opportunity to learn from the experience of the Euro Area, particularly in the large countries, before memories faded. The Bank was in a unique position to learn these lessons because of its own responsibilities and its good relations with the national central banks (NCBs) in the Euro Area. The details are set out in later editions of *Practical Issues* (1999 to 2002), to which a number of NCBs contributed.[14] The issue in May 2002 provides a very comprehensive account of the completion of the retail banking change-over and of the issue of euro-currency, together with drawing some lessons for subsequent entrants, whether the UK or not.

In this largely educational role, much of the work of the group involved the dissemination of advice about the practical issues arising from the euro, in the pamphlets that they published, mostly via the web on the Internet, semi-annually. Prior to 1 January 1999, this publication was entitled *Practical Issues Arising from the Introduction of the Euro*, but once the euro was introduced in January 1999, the title had to be shortened to *Practical Issues Arising from the Euro*; it was more familiarly known throughout as *Practical Issues*. There were some 18 issues circulated by November 2002.

Much of the work involved was somewhat technical, concerned with the details of the new systems and market processes involved. For markets to work, it is, however, essential to get such details exactly right. However, I doubt whether the readers of this book want to be taken through them in any detail, and those that do can directly consult the Bank of England's website.[15]

For the reasons already stated, the Bank and the City of London played a key role in the conversion of wholesale markets to the euro in January 1999. The subsequent adoption of euro-currency, notes, and coin, in January 2002, a technical triumph, had much less impact on the 'out' countries.

". . . SO THEY CHANGED INTO EUROS AND LIVED HAPPILY EVER AFTER "

Once it became clear in June 2003 that the UK would remain 'out' for the foreseeable future, (which in economics is a rather short horizon of about 2/3 years!), interest in the subject waned, and *Practical Issues* ceased. During the years of 'prepare and decide' much had been done to assess the implications of the UK's potential entry for retail markets and the currency change-over. This was pulled together in a stand-alone document, dated September 2005, entitled *Publications on Europe: City Guide to a UK Euro Changeover.*[16]

The conversion weekend in January 1999 represented the high point of the work of the Euro Co-ordination Group. Although no one knew, with any assuredness, what the outcome of the 'five tests' exercise would be until the last moment, the different and rather better trajectory of the UK economy than of its Continental partners, the belief of the Chancellor that the institutional structures for monetary and fiscal policies that he had created in the UK were superior to those in the Euro Area, and the continuing (opinion poll) majority against entry made entry increasingly unlikely. After June 2003 it rapidly disappeared as a current issue. Yet, under slightly different circumstances that need not have been so, and, should circumstances change (as they will), the issue of UK entry might revive. Who knows? If so, the preparatory work done in the Bank on the retail side and for the currency change-over would come in very useful.

Whither Now?

Despite the UK being an 'out' country, relationships between the Bank and both the NCBs and the ECB of the Eurosystem have remained mostly good. The Bank still plays a (minor) role in the ESCB through its membership of the General Council of the ESCB, though, of course, the key macro-monetary decisions are taken by the Governing Council, from which the 'outs' are excluded. The members of the Governing Council of the ECB would welcome the 'outs' to join them, and hope that it will happen soon.

One must assume that it is somewhat galling for the Euro Area members to have the main capital market of the Euro Area sited in London, in an 'out' country. There are, I believe, suspicions that a few of the rare areas of discord have related to a disinclination in the Euro-Area members to give London an easy ride. An example was the initial discussions of how the 'out' countries might link into the Euro-Area TARGET payments system, though this latter is a tortuous and technical matter with which I am not personally familiar.

With domestic price stability being the main monetary objective, both in the Euro Area and in the UK, and with floating exchange rates, the key requirement both for the Eurosystem and the Bank of England has been to keep their 'own houses in order', and both have achieved that. Within the wider international political scene, the ECB and its President wield even more weight and influence than the Bundesbank and its President used to do; but, equally, the governors of the NCBs have a diminished role. If the UK were to join the Euro Area, the Bank would become a small fish in a much bigger pool.

Meanwhile, the importance of London as *the* main international financial market, notably for euro business, and the relative success of the UK's macro-monetary policies, gives the Bank and its Governor a platform and a weight in international monetary discussions considerably above its comparative standing in terms of national GDP.

But the Bank's primary focus is not so much on international issues, but to achieve its inflation target, as set for it by the Chancellor. To do this the MPC varies interest rates. It can do so because the exchange rate is allowed to float, although in practice remaining rather stable against the euro in recent years. In the interest rate setting exercise, the Euro Area is just part of the 'Rest of the World' (ROW), important because it is the UK's largest trading partner but perhaps less so than the United States, whose fluctuations tend to drive the world economy. In this exercise the Bank has been both independent and extremely successful, when measured by the record of inflation (and output) outcomes.

In comparison in recent years, the other historical functions of the Bank have been removed (debt management, bank supervision) or have played a lesser role than in former years. Until the credit crisis of 2007–8, there had been no systemic financial crisis in recent years, and so not much public role for the financial stability wing of the Bank. Quite what a central bank charged with responsibility for contributing to the maintenance of financial stability, but with no supervisory functions, should do—outside of crisis periods—remains unclear.[17] Unlike the MPC, there are virtually no instruments for a companion Financial Stability Committee (or Board) to wield, and precious little economic analysis, theory or useful forecasts to inform such a committee on how to vary such instruments (if any) that they may have. That leaves them with the *Financial Stability Review* report, describing current developments and recording current, subjective concerns, with little, or no, ability to forecast and not much quantitative measurement.

Even more important in this context, Core Purpose 3, relating to the enhancement of the efficiency of the UK financial system, has been quietly dropped in recent years. No doubt the private sector should (normally) take the lead in such structural innovations, though the ECB appears not to think so in its (controversial) TARGET2S proposal for handling Euro Area capital markets' securities settlements centrally. Its mission statement includes the objective of promoting financial integration.

The Co-ordination Unit for Europe was essentially a CP3 exercise. Its dissolution, and the recent structural changes in the Bank, effectively represents a bet that the UK will remain outside the Euro Area for future planning purposes. So far that bet looks rather good.

If that bet went wrong, however, there would be serious internal, practical, staffing problems for the Bank.[18] Its primary focus, for the MPC to set interest rates on UK grounds, would disappear in an instant, to be replaced by the need

259

to advise the Governor on conditions in the Euro Area more widely at the monthly ECB meeting, one vote amongst many, perhaps 1 in 25. The idea that the Bank could fashion for itself a special position in the ESCB, rather as the Federal Reserve Bank of New York has in the Federal Reserve System is, in my view, highly unlikely. Why should the ESCB transfer any special operational role from Frankfurt to a 'Johnny-come-lately' in London; anyhow such operations now mostly get done in cyberspace.

With their macro-monetary policy roles much diminished, national central banks within the Eurosystem and the ESCB have, naturally enough, been hanging on, like grim death (an apposite analogy?), to such supervisory and CP3 (financial efficiency) roles as they found themselves left with. But, as already noted, the Bank has either been stripped of, or has abandoned, most of these in its focus on CP1.

If the UK should join the euro, it could be argued that the optimal size of the Bank of England would be two persons,[19] the Governor and her/his secretary. The building on Threadneedle Street could easily be put to other uses.

Notes

1. My thanks are due to Bill Allen, Jon Carr, Stephen Collins, Nigel Jenkinson, Paul Richards, and John Townend for advice, assistance, comments, and suggestions. All interpretations and errors, however, remain my own. I also want to thank Mrs. Margot Hone for permission to reproduce her husband's, Basil Hone's, excellent cartoons, which had previously appeared in the Bank of England's publication, *Practical Issues*, under the pseudonym, Ben Shailo. Finally, I want to thank Marina Emond for excellent secretarial assistance.
2. From then onwards the Monetary Policy Committee of the Bank of England, chaired by the Governor, and consisting of four other internal Bank officials and four external members, (appointed by the Chancellor), were delegated the power to set the short-term policy interest rate, without direction or interference from politicians. The MPC was not, however, given goal independence. The MPC's goal, of achieving an inflation target, was set for it by the Chancellor.
3. Neither of these structural changes had any connection, as far as I am aware, with wider European developments.
4. Indeed it remains to this day unclear exactly what is the prudential role and functions of a central bank retaining responsibility for overall financial stability but without *any* supervisory operations, though it certainly has some, notably oversight of the payments systems.
5. If the Government had decided that the economic case had been met, the Bank would most likely have been pressed to state whether it agreed with that, or not. It is, of course, an untestable counterfactual, but I, and most others, believe that the Bank would have assessed the balance of economic advantage then dispassionately and analytically without giving any weight to the implications for its own future status and position.

6. George used almost identical words in his speech on 11/04/2000.

7. There became something of a well-rehearsed litany on this topic. Amongst the pros mentioned were the following:

   Nominal exchange-rate certainty (Townend, 29/09/87; Davies, 04/06/97; George, 23/09/97; George, 26/03/98; George, 12/02/2000; George, 11/03/2000; Townend, 16/03/2001; George, 31/05/2001).

   Broader, more liquid financial markets (George, 11/03/2000; George, 12/09/2000; Townend, 16/03/2001; George, 31/05/2001).

   Lower transactions costs (George, 23/09/97; Townend, 29/09/97; Townend, 16/03/2001; George, 31/05/2001).

   More price transparency, competition, and hence dynamism (George, 23/09/97; Townend, 29/09/97; George, 26/03/98; Townend, 16/03/2001; George, 31/05/2001).

   Amongst the cons were the following:
   Asymmetric conditions, 'one size fits all' (George, 23/09/97; Townend, 29/09/97; George, 26/03/98; George, 11/04/2000; George, 12/09/2000; George, 24/10/2000; Townend, 16/03/2001).

   Limited adjustment mechanisms (George, 23/09/97; Townend, 29/09/97; George, 26/03/98; George, 11/04/2000; George, 12/09/2000; George, 24/10/2000).

   Some points to notice are
   That the Governor especially placed so much emphasis on nominal exchange-rate certainty. There was much less emphasis on greater transparency and competition leading to any dynamic productivity enhancement.

   One of the additional arguments sometimes made *for* euro entry was that that could be necessary to safeguard and advance the cause of further European (political) union. Since this latter was primarily a political question, it was not discussed by the Bank.

8. There is one minor qualification to this. Dr. Peter Westaway had by this time left the National Institute of Economic and Social Research for the Bank. He was seconded by the Bank to HMT for this exercise; this was not because of any expertise gained at the Bank, but because of his prior modelling work at NIESR, which models played a role in this overall exercise (see, for example, Annex A of the Assessment of the Five Tests); where Westaway is mentioned (e.g. HMT 2003: 229, 232), reference is made to his NIESR former work, not to his current Bank position.

9. My thanks for the information in this last paragraph, as also for much more of this Chapter, are due to Paul Richards.

10. If a reader should like a copy of this, it is available as Annex A of the original draft. The annexes were omitted from the book Chapter to save space.

11. Also see Annex B, available on request from the author.

12. 'The Bank continues to play a full role in all of the technical preparations for EMU at the European Monetary Institute (EMI) in Frankfurt and in the European Union (EU) Monetary Committee. Much of the preparatory work undertaken at the EMI was brought together in a document specifying the operational framework for the single monetary policy in Stage 3, published in January 1997. The Bank welcomed the publication of this document and its substance. There are only a small number of areas where it has not proved possible to reach a unanimous view among central

banks: one of these relates to the need for reserve requirements on the banking system and another to the terms of access of non-euro area Member States to intraday liquidity within TARGET (the proposed interlinking of Real-Time Gross Settlement payments systems). Other topics on which national central banks have been heavily engaged with the EMI include the drafting of the legal Regulations on the euro, the design of the revised Exchange Rate Mechanism (membership of which will be voluntary), the specification of euro banknotes and the specification of the statistical requirements for EMU.' *Annual Report* (1997)

13. The junior staff were no doubt top-class too, but I never got to know them.
14. Once again, I am entirely indebted to Paul Richards for the information in these last couple of paragraphs.
15. In order to give readers a slight flavour of what went on, the Contents Pages of the December 1998 issue provide an idea of the scope of the change-over, Annex C, and the opening five pages of the June 1999 issue, Annex D, give a good, general account of what occurred and the Bank's role in it. These, again, are available from the author on request.
16. The first three contents pages also available as Annex E, on request from the author.
17. That should not be taken to imply that I think that it has *no* useful role. It can try to analyse the nature of systemic risks and threats to the overall financial system and to promote solutions to collective action problems and other sources of market failure that strengthen financial resilience and are justified on cost–benefit grounds. A few examples would be analysis of networks, especially of the payments systems, of the resilience of market and funding liquidity, and—on the risk reduction side—approaches to strengthen the wholesale payment systems and to improve the access to funding and the use of standing facilities in stressed conditions.
18. Although less so than for several national central banks within the Euro Area, which entered the Eurosystem with a far more bloated staff size than the Bank of England has achieved.
19. This is, of course, hyperbole. London would become, even more than it already is, the financial centre of the Euro Area. The Bank of England would have access to market intelligence, e.g., about financial stability issues that the ECB should want to know. But the Bank would need to become *much* smaller with a focus totally different from its present one.

12

Denmark and Sweden: Networking by Euro-Outsiders

Martin Marcussen

Both Denmark and Sweden have a paradoxical relationship to the European Union. Their populations clearly favour international cooperation in general and membership of the EU in particular. They are also among the most informed about matters related to European integration overall. Still, although public support for the euro seems to have increased over the last 15 years, the two countries' populations belong to the most EMU-sceptical in the EU. Only about half of their populations thinks it would be a good idea to replace their national currencies with the euro, the Danes being slightly more positive than the Swedes (Figure 12.1).

In addition, while we are dealing with states in which the issue of introducing the euro has been put to public referendums on various occasions, we see almost no day-to-day public debate about the euro, or about the EU as such. The national debates oscillate between almost complete silence about everyday activities in the EU, on one hand, and very intensive campaigns preceding EU referendums, on the other. In Denmark, the euro was rejected in a referendum in 1992; in 1993, a so-called opt-out from the stage three of EMU was adopted; and in 2000 the euro was rejected once again in a referendum. In Sweden, the euro was rejected once in the 2003 referendum (Table 12.1). With turnouts well beyond 80 per cent, the majority against the euro in both countries was around 53–56 per cent. In Sweden, the political elite has sworn not to put the euro on the agenda before 2010, and among the four Danish EU opt-outs (defence cooperation, police cooperation, European citizenship, and the euro), the euro opt-out is generally considered to be the most difficult hurdle to overcome in a future referendum. Yet, in Sweden as well as in Denmark, the political elite remains generally in favour of entering the Euro Area.

However, public debate is only one face of the EU in these countries. The other face is the professional and pro-active diplomatic European activities that take place continuously—but which are typically hidden from the attention of

Denmark and Sweden: Networking by Euro-Outsiders

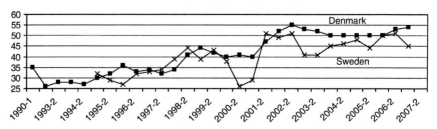

Figure 12.1. Public support for the euro in Sweden and Denmark
Sources: Standard EuroBarometer, EB43-EB67.

the broader public. Underneath the surface, Danish and Swedish civil servants are negotiating their ways through and beyond the EU labyrinth, creating cross-national networks of contacts and adapting their institutions to the reality of European integration (Jacobsson, Lægreid, and Pedersen 2004; Lindahl and Naurin 2005; Vifell 2006).

In line with the rest of the book, this chapter focuses exclusively on this second and hidden face of European integration processes: the everyday life of central bankers who continuously are forced to negotiate their ways in European decision-making. Central bankers in Denmark and Sweden are in a very particular situation because their domain—monetary and financial policies—is exempted from European integration while, at the same time, highly interwoven into the European macro-economic organizational field. This situation distinguishes these two small central banks that traditionally have been decision-takers from a third euro-outsider, the Bank of England, which has a completely different historical legacy and tradition of working on the global level as a decision-maker and with a different position in Europe interlinked with the City of London (see Goodhart's chapter in this volume). In this light, the Swedish and Danish central bankers, more urgently than is the case with the Bank of England, need to compensate for being Euro-outsiders (Marcussen 2007a). The paradox is that Danish and Swedish central bankers, despite their

Table 12.1. Referenda in Denmark and Sweden on EMU

	Yes	No	Turnout	Result
Denmark				
2 June 1992: Referendum about the Maastricht Treaty with a protocol in which the Danish government promises to organize another referendum before adoption of the Euro	49.3	50.7	83.1	Rejected
18 May 1993: Referendum about the Maastricht Treaty with a declaration stating that the Danish government has obtained an opt-out from the third stage of EMU	56.7	43.3	86.5	Accepted
28 September 2000: Referendum about abolishing the opt-out and introducing the Euro	46.9	53.1	87.5	Rejected
Sweden				
14 September 2003: Referendum about introducing the Euro	42	55.9	82.6	Rejected

semi-permanent position as euro-outsiders, have to formulate and implement their monetary and financial policies as integrated parties on the European macro-economic organizational field. How do they do that? Thus, the central question concerns *the ways in which the Danish and Swedish central banks cope with being euro-outsiders.*

Over the years, a very dense institutional framework has been established between the euro-insiders, with an obvious acceleration since the mid-1990s (see Umbach and Wessels, and Howarth in this volume). Seen from the point of view of the euro-outsiders, such a dense institutionalized network of euro-insiders is characterized by the strong, regular, and formalized ties between network members, recurrent, long-term patterns of face-to-face relationships, and a large degree of proximity, homogeneity, and reciprocity. Over time, the Euro-insiders begin to constitute a distinct policy community, and the institutional framework of the Euro Area provides a sense of belonging to its members, giving meaning to both collective and individual actions and driving its members by smoothing out and facilitating interaction (Puetter 2006). Dense relations and heavy embeddedness are furthermore likely to increase trust and cohesion among in-group members. They reduce transaction costs and minimize the need for control and monitoring, while improving the quality of delivery and performance. They also facilitate collaboration, cooperation, and exchange, not least easing and speeding up circulation of information and diffusion of best-practices within the group. In other words, the network literature provides a set of reasons for why euro-outsiders would strive to become euro-insiders, or at least relate actively to the euro-insiders.

However, there are caveats to the general argument about the attractiveness of being a fully integrated member of the euro-network. First, it comes out clearly from studying the relationship of the Bank of England to the Euro Area (see Goodhart in this volume) that the attraction of the Euro Area network varies considerably from one function to another. The resource dependencies between the actors differ in financial market integration, financial stability and supervision, and the planning and execution of monetary policy. In Britain and in Sweden, ECB monetary policy seems to have no attraction at all. In contrast, Swedish central bankers seem to pay much attention to European efforts at creating some sort of a 'European Organization for Financial Supervision' (Ingves 2007), whereas in Britain central bankers are highly alert to European financial regulation. Second, the attractiveness of the euro-network may depend on the extent to which socialization and mutual learning in the Euro Area foster some sort of 'group-think' among the euro-insiders that prevents innovation. A main text-book argument for entering the Euro Area has been that being an insider promotes discipline around a set of commonly agreed rules of appropriateness, such as those enshrined in the Stability and Growth Pact. However, if it is generally perceived among the euro-outsiders that those inside the Euro Area have become less, not more, inclined to undertake necessary reforms, then the attractiveness of the Euro Area network may decrease (see Epstein and Johnson in this volume).

In a historical perspective, both the Danish and Swedish central banks have been involved in formal and informal international cooperation for the purpose of maintaining a stable exchange rate (Table 12.2). Over the last 150 years, stable exchange rates and participation in some kind of cooperative framework have been the rule rather than the exception. Seen in that perspective, the current position of the Danish and Swedish central banks as euro-outsiders is abnormal, all the more so for Sweden than for Denmark, which in 1999 chose to link its currency to the euro within the framework of the Exchange Rate Mechanism II (ERM II).

The question about how Danish and Swedish central bankers cope with being euro-outsiders highlights the role of *organizational reform* and how they implement *networking strategies* to compensate for their exclusion from the euro-club. The chapter adopts both an 'outside-in' perspective (on the impact of European monetary integration on Danish and Swedish central bank institutions) and an 'inside-out' perspective (on the network strategies pursued by these two euro-outsiders in the European macro-economic organizational field). The conclusion is that, on both these levels of analysis, Europeanization has taken place, but that Europeanization takes different forms in Sweden and in Denmark. Whereas the Danish central bank copes with Euro-outsiderness by modernizing its organizational culture while essentially maintaining its structural features intact, the Swedish central bank has been in a constant reform process over the last 10–15 years, profoundly altering its structures, relations, and functions in line with a global trend of public-sector modernization. Whereas the Danish central bank is opening up and increasingly engaging actively in all sorts of central bank networks in Europe and elsewhere, it suffices for the Swedish central bank to exploit the large networks it has built up over the last 75 years. Thus, it is hard to observe any kind of convergence between the two banks. However, in their different ways, both

Table 12.2. The Danish and Swedish central banks in successive cooperative currency arrangements

Cooperative currency arrangements	Sweden	Denmark
ERMII		01.01.1999–present
ERM	17.05.1991–19.11.1992	01.01.1979–01.01.1999
Snake Cooperation	03.1972–29.08.1977	19.02.1972–01.01.1979
Smithsonian Agreement	19.12.1971–19.03.1973	19.12.1971–19.03.1973
Bretton Woods	31.08.1951–23.08.1971	12.12.1946–23.08.1971
Interwar Gold Standard	01.04.1924–27.09.1931	01.01.1927–29.09.1931
Classical Gold Standard in the form of a Scandinavian Currency Union from 01.01.1877	27.05.1873–02.08.1914	01.01.1875–06.08.1914

Sources: Jonung (2000); Mikkelsen (1993); Olsen and Hoffmeyer (1968); Svendsen and Hansen (1968).

central banks remain powerful, legitimate, and independent political authorities in their respective domestic contexts. They play considerable roles in defining the direction and content of macro-economic policy-making. So far, therefore, the Danish and Swedish central banks have not lost out as a result of their euro-exclusion. This stands in sharp contrast to some of the euro-insider central banks, of which the Bundesbank is the obvious example (see Dyson in this volume).

The Danish Central Bank

For a long period before, during, and after the Second World War, the former Social Democratic Minister of Finance, Carl Valdemar Bramsnæs, was Danish central bank governor (1936–49). Written correspondence, board minutes, and personal diaries retrieved from the archives of the Danish central bank show clearly that Denmark had no permanent and strong network of international contacts to exploit during these years. In addition, the Danish central bank had no significant international capacity. There was not much travelling, and the Danish central bank governor did not seem to be informed about, interested in, or participating in international policy formulation or exchanges. One of the few links to the outside world was to neighbouring Sweden, where the Riksbank had become a member of the Board of Directors of the Bank for International Settlements (BIS). Not being at ease with other foreign languages, the link to the Riksbank and its governor, Ivar Rooth, allowed communication on the basis of the mother tongue and between two relatively similar political and administrative cultures. Thus, occasionally and almost randomly, the Danish central bank received scattered information about central bank business in Europe and policy issues in general. For instance, during the Second World War, Denmark was isolated from, and mostly unaware about, negotiations taking place in Bretton Woods. The Danish diplomat, Henrik Kauffmann, who during the years of German occupation of Denmark walked the corridors of Washington, did not formally represent the Danish government and was only present during the Bretton Woods negotiations in his personal capacity (Lidegaard 2005). In short, before the Second World War, the Danish economic governance structures including the central bank and the Ministry of Finance seemed to be sheltered from international developments and influence (Østergaard 1998).

During the 1950s and 1960s, Svend Nielsen (governor 1950–64) focused his attention on the US and British central banks. The perception inside the Danish central bank was that the locus of decision-making power was placed in organizations such as the International Monetary Fund (IMF) and that particularly the British and American central banks constituted gateways to information. With the establishment of the Marshall Plan and the Organization for

European Economic Cooperation (OEEC), a pattern of international contacts was established constituting a very sparse portfolio of network ties. The network strategy seemed to be that since Denmark was not, and had no aspiration of becoming, centrally located in the international network of central bankers, the Danish central bank should concentrate on cultivating contacts with actors who were located in these central positions. After the Second World War, the BIS fought hard to re-establish its credibility and legitimacy which had been badly damaged during the war as a result of allegations about buying and selling looted gold from Germany (Toniolo 2005). As a result, the BIS was not perceived to be the most central organization on which to focus attention. Thus, during Nielsen's period as governor, the BIS did not figure in his mindset, and the Scandinavian connection became overshadowed by the Anglo-Saxon connections.

From the mid-1960s, the number of European forums in which central bankers could gather on a regular basis increased drastically (Marcussen 2006c). Denmark became a member of the European Monetary System (EMS), and Erik Hoffmeyer (governor 1965–94), consequently, participated actively in the Basel-based Committee of EC Central Bank Governors. However, there were no illusions that the important decisions were made in the European institutions (Marcussen 2008). The idea that the Committee of Central Bank Governors should develop a club mentality and consequently become a motor for European monetary integration was mostly 'wishful thinking', according to Hoffmeyer (Hoffmeyer 2000: 14). As a result, over three decades, attention was directed at the local hegemon of the Exchange Rate Mechanism, the German Bundesbank. Here power was located in European monetary cooperation. In continuation of the strategies traditionally pursued by Danish central bank governors, sparse resources were concentrated on the regular cultivation of good and stable links with the most powerful actors in the most relevant monetary regimes (on the Bundesbank, see Dyson in this volume).

The result of the second referendum on the Maastricht Treaty in May 1993, when Denmark got a formal opt-out from the third stage of EMU, challenged the traditional network strategy which focused mainly on cultivating contact to the regional hegemon. The possibilities were slim that Denmark would be able to enter the euro on 1 January 1999. Moreover, since August 1993 the fluctuation bands of the ERM were widened to $\pm$ 15per cent, as a result of which the Danish central bank stood *de facto* alone in the defence of the stable currency policy. On 13 August 1993, Governor Hoffmeyer issued a press release stating that he intended to stick to a much narrower fluctuation band, in practice $\pm$ 2,25per cent. With Denmark in ERM II, the ECB promised that, if a situation arose that threatened to push the Danish currency out of these much narrower bands, it would intervene immediately and in an unlimited fashion, provided that such an intervention would not make it more difficult for the ECB to realize its objective of keeping inflation low in the Euro Area as a whole. This 'guarantee'—or 'security net', as it is sometimes called in Denmark—has been evoked once, in the autumn of 2008.

From 1993, the Danish central bank started to develop a diversification strategy, which implied a multiplication of unilateral ties to central bank actors inside and outside Europe. Increasingly employees were seconded to international economic organizations and other national central banks as part of their individual career planning. Inside the Eurosystem, the Danish central bank and other euro-outsiders worked diplomatically in many contexts to obtain observation status in the forums from which they were excluded. In general, a new internationally oriented communication strategy was implemented, and participation in the many different central bank forums world-wide was prioritized. This line has been broadly continued. The intensification of contacts to the outside world can be illustrated by registering the extent to which Danish central bank personnel participate in meetings in the ESCB committees (Figure 12.2).

Figure 12.2 shows that the Danish central bank participates in the various committees and sub-committees to various degrees. Generally, over the last four years, the level of attention paid to ESCB committees and the intensity with which Danish central bank officials participate in their meetings have increased. In particular, the Market Operations Committee, which assists the Eurosystem in carrying out monetary policy operations and foreign exchange transactions, and in managing the ECB's foreign reserves and the operation of ERM II, plays a more central role for Danish central bankers.

The ESCB Banking Supervision Committee has always been relatively open for Euro-outsiders. As noted by Moran and McCartney in this volume, banking supervision is not a prime competence of the ECB. Supervisory issues are dealt with by national supervisory authorities and in other European and international forums. In contrast to the Banking Supervision Committee, the Monetary Policy Committee goes to the heart of key ECB competences. It advises on the formulation of monetary and exchange rate policies in general and is responsible for the projections of macro-economic developments in the Euro Area. Interestingly, also in this area the Danish central bank is increasingly involved in ESCB work. Among other important committees, the participation of the Danish central bank in the International Relations Committee and the Payment and Settlement Systems Committee has been intensified. The International Relations Committee assists ECB work in forums such as the IMF, OECD, and BIS, and the Payment and Settlement Systems Committee advises on the operation and maintenance of TARGET, general payment systems policy, and oversight issues, and issues in the field of securities clearing and settlement.

Unlike the Riksbank, the Danish central bank has no official opinion about being a euro-outsider, though Bodil Nyboe-Andersen (governor 1995–2005) and Niels Bernstein (governor 2006–) helped to consolidate a life outside the

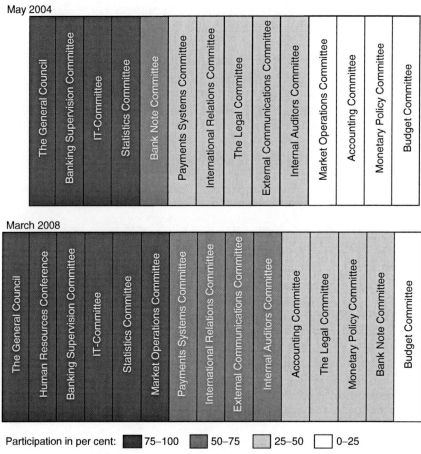

Figure 12.2. The Danish central bank's participation in ESCB committee work, 2004 and 2008

Source: Danmarks Nationalbank, May 2004 and March 2008.

Euro Area in their own ways—simply by not explicitly engaging in public debate about the issue, by minding their own business. With the help of consenting politicians, monetary policy and all related issues have been entirely depoliticized in Denmark, as a result of which the option of letting the Danish currency float like the Swedish currency is never mentioned as a realistic alternative to the fixed exchange rate policy.

The Danish central bank has not engaged in radical organizational reforms since the Second World War. In fact, the central bank law has remained basically the same since 1936. However, consecutive governments implemented a profound change in the macro-economic policy paradigm from 1982 onwards

(Table 12.6). Fixed exchange rates, low inflation, and stable budgets became the solid pillars of Danish macro-economic policy (Marcussen 2002). In addition to structural reforms in the labour market, a permissive consensus seemed to have developed around traditional central bank 'sound policy' values. Inside the Danish central bank, formal changes have been minimal. In 1998, a so-called 'information office' and a website were installed, underlining a felt need to respond regularly and systematically to inquiries. In the following years, a number of regular publications were streamlined, in terms of both form and content, thereby appealing to a larger readership.

The number of employees has, overall, remained relatively constant. However, the composition of employees has changed. Slowly but steadily, an increasing number of university-educated economists define the central bank, replacing employees from other lower-educated branches. The bank has quite a low turn-over rate and the average years of service seem to be very high (13–15 years on average; 21–2 years at top level). The number of employees with more than 25 years of service amounts to 20 per cent. A survey conducted among the employees concluded that employment satisfaction is high. In addition, the Danish central bank has for many years figured among the 15 most popular workplaces in Denmark for newly graduated economists (www. universumeurope.com). From 2000, a personnel directive was adopted emphasizing the importance of employee satisfaction and human resource development. Increasingly, emphasis is placed on education and skill-upgrading of employees. Over the last decade, the budget consecrated to education and training has increased manifold. Interestingly, the Danish central bank actively encourages its younger economists to take a stage in one of the many international financial institutions. On average 15–20 persons are permanently on leave from the bank, spending time in an international organization.

From 2000, like many other public organizations, the bank explicitly stated its basic values. One central element is to safeguard traditions while attempting to engage in renewal. Another central value is to provide services to the public. Transparency becomes central in that regard (see Jabko in this volume). The level of transparency institutionalized in the Danish central bank does not, however, measure up with other euro-outsiders such as the Swedish Riksbank and the Bank of England, nor does it compare with the ECB (Figure 12.3). The Danish governor does not have an obligation to explain his policies in parliament, and no minutes are released from decision-making forums. Inside the Danish central bank, this relatively low level of transparency is explained by the fact that the Bank on a day-to-day basis is demonstrating to the world that it is pursuing a stable currency objective within the framework of the ERM II. Since the markets can observe directly whether the Bank is succeeding or not, it is argued that there is not much more to tell the financial markets. This argument stands in contrast to central banks, such as the ECB, the Bank of England, and the Swedish Riksbank, which manage floating currencies

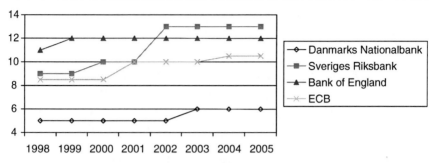

Figure 12.3. Central bank transparency, 1998–2005*

* The transparency index is constituted by the following five elements: political transparency (openness with regard to policy objectives), economic transparency (openness concerning information used for monetary policy), procedural transparency (openness about the ways in which policy decisions are being made), policy transparency (prompt disclosure and explanation of decision made), operational transparency (openness in relation to the implementation of the policy actions). Minimum score is '0', maximum score is '15'.

Source: Dincer and Eichengreen (2007: 41).

and which implicitly or explicitly target inflation. To a much greater extent these central banks need to inform the public about what they are doing to meet this target, simply because it is much more difficult to evaluate how successful they are.

In terms of organizational structure, the number of departments has remained relatively constant over the years at 16–17. Very few people have been dismissed over the last decade as a result of streamlining the organization and outsourcing of functions. As regards the internal allocation of resources, no resources have been invested in a distinct research department. This too stands in sharp contrast with the Riksbank as well as with many other central banks around the world, where research seems to constitute a major source of authority and legitimacy (see Marcussen in this volume). A certain tendency towards decentralization has taken place in recent years. Decisions about promotion, for instance, are now being made in the various departments rather than in the executive board.

The Danish central bank explains the 'non-reforms' by the fact that it undertook the major part of its reforms earlier than the world trend (Pedersen 2006: 10). For instance, the last regional branch was closed in 1989. In addition, the costs of running the bank are, in international comparison, quite low. This is taken to be an indication of the continuous streamlining which is taking place in a gradual manner, rather than through large-scale reforms and outsourcing. In addition, the Danish central bank is cheaper in operational costs because it is normally regarded to be more labour-demanding to run a system of inflation targeting such as the Swedish Riksbank than to tie one's currency to the euro. Finally, although the salaries of the employees in the Danish central bank are

Table 12.3. Staff costs in the Danish and Swedish central banks

2004	(1) Annual salary in industry in Dkr.	(2) Staff costs per employee per year in Dkr.	(2)/(1)	Relative price level	Staff costs per employee per year in Dkr., PPP corrected	Index of PPP-corrected staff costs
Danmarks Nationalbank	309.000	529.000	1.7	100	529.000	100
Swedish Riksbank	277.000	536.000	1.9	89	602.000	114

Source: Pedersen (2006: 12).

higher than in manufacturing, they are among the lowest in European central banking (Table 12.3).

Reforms or not, the Danish central bank governor has for years topped the rankings of the most trusted and most powerful decision-makers among Danish elites (Berlingske Nyhedsmagasin, various years). The Danish central bank governor does not have to face continuous contestation like, for instance, the president of the ECB. He or she rarely has to stand up and defend his actions in order to remain a recognized and legitimate public authority in the Danish society. In contrast to Sweden, the Danish governor receives a relatively modest salary (Table 12.4) while tending to remain much longer in office (Table 12.5).

Table 12.4. Danish and Swedish central bank governors' salaries, 2003 (US$)

Lars Heikensten	Sveriges Riksbank	$241.000*
Bodil Nyboe-Andersen	Danmarks Nationalbank	$253.000

*Membership of the Board of the Bank for International Settlements adds another $90.000 to the salary.
Source: www.centralbanknews.com, 18 August 2003; annual reports.

Table 12.5. Average tenure in the Danish and Swedish central banks

Denmark (employment to the age of 70)	Sweden (5 year terms)
Bramsnæs (1936–49)	Rooth (1929–48)
Nielsen (1950–64)	Böök (1948–51)
Hoffmeyer (1965–94)	Lemne (1951–5)
Nyboe-Andersen (1995–2005)	Åsbrink (1955–73)
Bernstein (2006–)	Wickman (1973–6)
	Nordlander (1976–9)
	Wohlin (1979–82)
	Dennis (1982–93)
	Bäckström (1994–2002)
	Heikensten (2002–2005)
	Ingves (2006–)
Average tenure: 17.25 years	Average tenure: 7.6 years

The Swedish Central Bank

For the Swedish Riksbank, the 1930s constituted a formative decade that had lasting impact on its international strategy. In those years, political, entrepreneurial, and academic elites were driving forces in the construction of broad, diversified, world-wide networks of contact. Ivar Rooth (governor 1929–48) drove the creation and helped cultivate a large portfolio of formal and informal contacts. At an early stage, he was the only Scandinavian central banker who engaged himself actively in the formative period of the BIS. Rooth's personal archive at the Riksbank shows the ways in which he emphasized international contacts. During his very first months as governor he travelled among the major European capitals with a view to personally securing good relationships with the most important players in the field. Detailed travelling notes demonstrate how he deliberately assembled a portfolio of preferred contacts that could be activated in the future if need be. In the following two decades, while working hard to maintain established links, a large amount of new persons and institutions were added to his personal network.

The direct and indirect results of this work were many. At the most basic level, Rooth simply obtained information about opportunities and threats on the international financial scene. During the first years, for instance, he obtained a privileged position in observing the financial unrest emanating from the United States; he gained inside information about the plans for the new BIS (referred to as the 'International Bank' in those early days); and he even entered an operational partnership with the Bank of England about an informal mutual early warning system in the event of interest rate modifications. Indirectly, Rooth inspired confidence in his partners abroad. This comes out clearly when members of the BIS Board were to be selected from among the shareholders of the organization. Many central bankers stood up to defend his candidacy in the closed process. In addition, during the Second World War, by representing neutral Sweden, Rooth was able to function as an effective and trusted channel of communication between central bankers from Allied as well as from aggressor countries. Over the years, the web of central bankers around Rooth grew larger and became increasingly intimate and personal in character. During the Second World War, he often ran a personal risk in travelling through war-torn Europe to maintain and expand essential contacts.

Per Jacobsson, another Swedish economist, occupied for many years the influential role of Head of the Monetary and Economics Department at the BIS. Rooth paved the way for his international career, which started at the BIS. Whereas Rooth was respected and liked for his integrity and social intelligence, Jacobsson was highly valued for his academic skills. As the main author of almost two decades of annual reports for the BIS, Jacobsson travelled the world as a very knowledgeable and effective consultant (Jacobsson 1979). Thus, he was actively involved in Jean Monnet's modernization plan in

France; in Ireland's struggle to establish a set of credible financial institutions, including a central bank; and in Bretton Woods where a new international financial order had to be spelled out in operational detail. If Rooth was the diplomat, Jacobsson seemed to be the fixer. After the Second World War, Sweden became a member of the IMF quite late, but once a member, Rooth stood out as a natural candidate for the important and influential post as its managing director. Just as Rooth was able to run the IMF during a couple of years in which the organization established itself as a legitimate world player, so Jacobsson replaced him as managing director (1956–63) when the organization was in need of innovation.

Rooth and Jacobsson were not the only high-flying Swedes on the global financial scene during these years before, during, and after the Second World War. In other international organizations, Swedes took central positions. Dag Hammarskjöld who was secretary-general of the UN (1953–61) is an obvious example. More importantly, the networks established by Swedish central bankers during the 1930s until the1950s have remained in place. With a central location in the BIS, Sweden took part in the Group of Ten, for instance. With G10 membership, access to the OECD Working Party 3 (WP3) and the Interim Committee of the IMF (later referred to as the International Monetary and Financial Committee, IMFC) was assured, and so on. The work of Rooth and Jacobsson helped to lay the path that could be followed by their successors.

During the 1970s and 1980s, with the building up of European monetary cooperation, another layer of contacts was added on top of an already very dense constellation of Riksbank contacts. When Bengt Dennis (governor 1982–93) was forced to withdraw the Swedish krone from the ERM in November 1992 (Dennis 1998), there were no direct consequences for the Riksbank's network strategy. The network could hardly be any wider or more diversified.

Unsurprisingly, therefore, the modern Riksbank is closely knit together with other central banks from all around the world, the European scene being one among others. At one level, there are the annual meetings of the G10, BIS, and IMF, involving the participation of the central bank governors, sometimes joined by their economic and finance ministers. At a second level, the governors and their deputies participate in the more numerous meetings related to board work in the BIS and the IMF, the General Council of the ECB, the informal ECOFIN meetings in Brussels, and the International Monetary and Financial Committee of the IMF, as well as the Nordic central bank meetings. At a third level, a very large number of committees in various areas require the attention of a large range of central bank personnel. These forums include Working Party 3 and the Economic Policy Committee of the OECD, the Economic and Financial Committee of the EU, a series of committees within the framework of the ESCB, and the Basel Committee in the BIS. A simple count of the international forums in which the Riksbank is represented on a regular basis concludes that on an annual basis the Riksbank's personnel prepares for

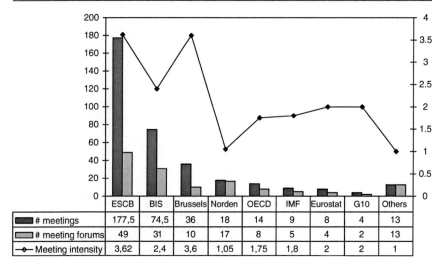

	ESCB	BIS	Brussels	Norden	OECD	IMF	Eurostat	G10	Others
▬ # meetings	177,5	74,5	36	18	14	9	8	4	13
▬ # meeting forums	49	31	10	17	8	5	4	2	13
◆ Meeting intensity	3,62	2,4	3,6	1,05	1,75	1,8	2	2	1

Figure 12.4. Busy Danish and Swedish euro-outsiders

Source: Own data.

meetings in no less than 139 forums, amounting to 354 meetings (Figure 12.4). These data are only rough indicators of international networking for they ignore the informal dimensions of trans-national central bank cooperation. But it clearly underlines the fact that euro-outsiders, like Sweden, need not be excluded from international cooperation.

Whereas the Danish central bank has not engaged in radical institutional reforms since the Second World War, the Swedish central bank has gone through comprehensive modernization programmes since the end of the 1980s (Table 12.6). Already in 1988, the Swedish central bank stood out as a first mover among central banks in the world. A reform of the Riksbank act granted the governor more *legal autonomy*, thereby leading a world-wide trend of central bank reform in that direction. Having left the ERM in November 1992, the Riksbank in 1993 explicitly declared an *inflation target* (IT) regime. Given that the first to declare an explicit inflation target were the Reserve Banks of New Zealand in July 1989 and of Australia in April 1993 (see Eichbaum in this volume), the Bank of Canada in February 1991, and the Bank of England in October 1992 (see Goodhart in this volume) the Riksbank was again among the first movers in what a decade later became a distinct global fashion. At about the same time, but initially without success, initiatives were taken to grant the Riksbank even more legal autonomy. A new central bank law was not adopted, however, till 1998 and entered formally into force in 1999.

Also, in the area of central bank *transparency* the Riksbank took the lead (Figure 12.3). Inflation reports are regularly published; press releases explain monetary policy decisions; the minutes of the meetings of the Directorate are

Table 12.6. Two worlds apart: institutional reforms in the Swedish and the Danish central banks

	Denmark
1982	The government declares its support for a fixed exchange rate regime.
	A so-called 'sound policy'/'stability-oriented' macro-economic policy strategy is being pursued, implying sound money (low inflation) and sound finances (balanced budgets)

	Sweden
1982	The government announces a 16 per cent devaluation within the framework of the ERM
1988	A new Riksbank Act:
	The chairman of the Governing Board is no longer appointed by the government, but by the other seven members of the Board.
	The Governor's term in office is made longer (five years) than that of the rest of the Board and the parliament (three years, at the time).
	There is no indication of the objective for monetary policy-making.
1991	The government declares that low inflation is an overriding goal for stabilization policy.
1992	*November:* After repeated speculative attacks against the Swedish currency the Riksbank abandons the pegged exchange rate policy.
1993	*January:* The Riksbank declares an explicit inflation target.
	February: A parliamentary committee presents a proposal for a new Riksbank Act, including a price stability objective for monetary policy and increased central bank independence. The proposal does not achieve enough political support and is not formally presented to the parliament.
	October: The first internal Inflation Report is published.
1995	*January:* Sweden becomes a member of the European Union.
	November: The first Inflation Report signed by the Governor is published.
1997	The Riksbank starts to publish its inflation forecasts and Financial Stability Reports.
1997	A new proposal for a price stability objective and increased central bank independence is presented, this time based on broad political consensus.
1999	An amended Riksbank Act comes into effect.

Source: Heikensten and Vredin (2002: 9); Hoffmeyer (1993).

made public two weeks after the meeting; and the governor meets with the Parliamentary Financial Committee twice a year. Interestingly, today's central banking in Sweden very much resembles the experience of the 1930s (Berg and Jonung 1998). In 1931–7, Sweden declared an explicit inflation target with a view to anchoring expectations. In addition, the Riksbank produced regular reports spelling out the details of monetary policy, and Ivar Rooth met regularly with the Parliamentary Banking Committee to explain and defend his decisions. Finally, the media gave wide coverage to monetary policy-making, thereby emphasizing yet another aspect of central bank transparency.

Today, Riksbank personnel talk about 'a clash of reform cultures' between the prominent idea in Sweden that a central bank that demands reforms elsewhere in the economy ought to be a first mover and show the way for the others and the continental perspective, according to which central bankers are classical institutions with long established traditions that ought to be maintained and protected from outside involvement (though see Dyson in this volume on Axel Weber and the Bundesbank). For this reason alone, very few Riksbank managers feel attracted by the European way of running central banking and often indicate that it would be easier to sell European monetary cooperation to the Swedish population if the continental model would actively engage with modern management philosophies, thereby constituting a lodestar.

Within the Swedish central bank, these structural and policy reforms implied considerable organizational and procedural changes. Over the decade from 1997 the organization and culture of the Riksbank have been completely overhauled. Competences were gradually transferred from the top level management to the individual departments. The number of departments has been reduced from 16 to 11 in 2000 and then again from 11 to 7 in 2004. The regional offices were closed down, and a considerable number of employees in these offices as well as in the Riksbank building have been dismissed. For instance, in 2003 the Board of the Riksbank decided that the number of employees (FTEs) would be reduced by 10 per cent over a three-year period (Figure 12.5). Regular attitude surveys among bank staff have been carried out since 1997. Not surprisingly, a recent survey concludes that the employees in the units that have been cut down 'tend to have more negative impressions' of the Riksbank and its governor (Sveriges Riksbank 2007: 52). Towards the end of the 1990s, the Riksbank used to be one of the most attractive workplaces in Sweden for newly graduated economists. This is no longer so. The Riksbank has dropped out of Universum Communication's ranking of the top-15 most popular workplaces for economists in Sweden (www.universumeurope.com).

All managers of the Swedish central bank have been going through intensive management training with particular focus on communication and output performance. The official corporate culture statement in 2002 is based on openness, competence, cooperation, overall view (whole of government), initiative, and

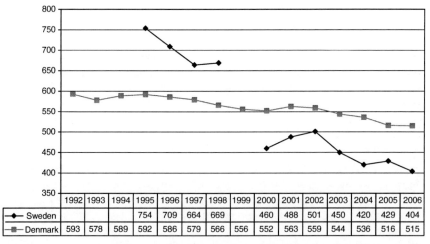

	1992	1993	1994	1995	1996	1997	1998	1999	2000	2001	2002	2003	2004	2005	2006
Sweden				754	709	664	669		460	488	501	450	420	429	404
Denmark	593	578	589	592	586	579	566	556	552	563	559	544	536	516	515

Figure 12.5. Development in staff numbers (FTEs) of the Danish and Swedish central banks

Source: Annual Reports from the Swedish and Danish central banks.

respect. The Executive Board adopted a so-called strategic plan in 2005, with strategic targets emphasizing quality, efficiency, and confidence, and in 2006 this plan was turned into a 'new vision' for the Riksbank. By constantly comparing itself to other central banks as well as other public authorities and private corporations, and by constructing an organization prepared for change, the 'new vision' is supposed to be transformed into reality. Over the years, the central bank has, by example and choice, taken a lead in the discussion among central banks about central bank efficiency. The point of departure is that central banks are not, like private corporations, exposed to market competition as a result of which other efficiency-enhancing mechanisms have to be installed. Completely in line with values associated with the New Public Management doctrine, the recommendation is to reduce the number of tasks entrusted to central bankers. These tasks should focus on the efficiency of the payment system and maintaining price stability, on spelling out precisely when an outcome has been achieved (by introducing inflation targeting, for instance), and on improving the transparency of the organization thereby allowing for internal and external evaluations of the bank (Blix, Daltug, and Heikensten 2003). In short, the Riksbank seems to have closely followed mainstream advice about central bank modernization (Marcussen 2009; Mendzela 2002, 2003, 2006).

Managing a Role as Euro-Outsiders

In the absence of Euro Area membership, which compensation strategies have been adopted in these two Scandinavian central banks? Clearly, tremendous internal and constitutional reforms have been undertaken in Sweden. The ongoing reform programmes implemented since 1997 have fundamentally altered the central bank on almost all dimensions. Such policy and constitutional reforms have been largely absent in the Danish case. If anything, mainly informal changes have taken place. Gradually, the composition of employees has been altered. Today, the Danish central bank is a 'knowledge organization' like any other central bank. A quite substantial amount of the budget is being spent on education and human resource development. In addition, increased emphasis has been placed on establishing a more differentiated relationship to other international actors in central banking. For instance, young employees are being encouraged to take up positions in international financial organizations, and travel activity has increased. In short, there is a strategy to cultivate international contacts and consolidate lines of information.

In contrast to the Swedish central bank, the Danish central bank does not automatically obtain information through central positions in the IMFC, the BIS Board, the G10, and other major international decision-making centres. As a result of its already very wide networks, the Riksbank does not seem to need further expansion and diversification with regard to external networking. In

Table 12.7. Danish and Swedish strategies of coping with being euro-outsiders

	Sweden	Denmark
Networking	*Little* change as a result of Euro-outsiderness	*Large* change as a result of Euro-outsiderness
	Sweden already did diversify its international relations before EMU	From having few links, DK started deliberately to cultivate diversification after EMU
Organizational reform	*Large* formal changes—modernization programmes: managementization, transparency, and accountability	*Little* formal change—but some change in organizational culture (informal change)

contrast to the Danish central bank, it has traditionally been very well integrated into international financial circles (Table 12.7). In short, being in the same position as euro-outsiders does not imply convergence in the ways in which structural reforms are undertaken and international networking is being diversified. Formulated differently, the fact that the two banks do not take part in substantial elements of European monetary integration does not mean that Europeanization has not taken place. Both central banks have changed, but in quite different ways and in conjunction with broader global reform trends.

Over a 70-year period, the Danish central bank altered its networking strategy to a much larger extent than the Swedish Riksbank. The Riksbank seems to have consistently followed an internationally oriented diversification strategy, establishing strong as well as weak ties with a large number of relevant actors, inside and outside Europe. The Danish central bank was gradually internationalized after the Second World War, but for many years it strategically linked itself to what it perceived to be the most powerful actor on the scene of global finance (first Sweden, then Britain and the United States, and finally Germany). With its non-membership of the Euro Area, it opened up, and diversified its links to other actors, thereby trying to compensate for its lack of information. In recent years, despite being a euro-outsider, the Danish central bank also put much more emphasis on committee work in the ESCB context. In principle, Denmark has only access to committee work in the so-called extended composition. On occasions, however, Denmark has received specific invitations to participate in committee work in standard composition. Clearly, when it comes to voting in these committees, Denmark does not participate. In addition, the analytical capacity of the Danish central bank has been boosted by, for instance, increasing the ratio of employees with a formal education in economics. Over recent years, more PhDs are being employed by the Danish central bank.

Traditionally, the Riksbank has been accustomed to being present in international economic organizations. Denmark was always a decision-taker, not Sweden. The Riksbanks has always been part of the powerful G10—a forum of decision-makers. The only problem faced by the Danish central bank is that it is no longer sufficient to be linked to a local hegemon with a view to obtaining information. In the Euro Area, monetary decision-making is collective, and not formally based on the discretion of a local hegemon. Euro-insiders get information easily, whereas, depending on the issue-area, euro-outsiders have increasing difficulty in obtaining basic information. Therefore, a new network strategy has been implemented by the Danish central bank—not to get more and better information than in the 1980s but to avoid being totally excluded from information flows.

The creation of the Euro Area and the consolidation of a position as semi-permanent euro-outsiders through various referendums underpinned reforms that were already on their way in these two central banks. In Sweden, so-called modernization reforms mirror global management fads implying operational autonomy, modern management methods, technocratization, transparency, and accountability. In Denmark, the reforms have manifested themselves not in new regulation or procedures but in a new culture and redefined relations with the public. It is a paradox, however, that the central bank that has altered its network strategy to the greatest extent is the one that has undertaken the least amount of institutional reforms to support its new network strategy.

Thus, even though the Danish and Swedish central banks as euro-outsiders have found ways to compensate for their exclusion from the Euro Area, the ways in which compensation takes place vary considerably. It seems that path-dependency offers some explanation for the different strategies over the decades running from the Second World War, but so does more recent economic history. Thus, in the early 1990s, Sweden was exposed to one of its most severe economic shocks. This shock opened a window of opportunity, allowing for considerable reforms that turned Sweden into a first-mover in management reform in general and central banking in particular. Neither before nor since has it been possible to undertake such wide-ranging reforms without encountering resistance from at least some members of the Swedish Parliament. This stands in sharp contrast to the Danish administrative apparatus, including the central bank, which has not been challenged in the same way. In Denmark, there has not been an obvious opportunity for a reform-coalition to drive through change that went beyond a consensus about sound macro-economic policy-making. The passive linking of the national currency to the euro in the ERM II has not served as a reform catalyst either. As illustrated above, the ERM II is a continuation of a very long Danish tradition of being involved in a stable currency regime. In both countries, therefore, exclusion from the Euro Area served from the mid-1990s to help consolidate a path that had already been laid out and that explains why Europeanization materializes so differently in these two central banks.

The status of euro-outsiders seems to correlate quite significantly with two other trends. One concerns the widespread belief among the euro-outsiders in the value of pursuing a stability-oriented macro-economic policy. Another trend seems to be that Euro Area exclusion at least has not hindered, maybe even encouraged, processes of micro- as well as macro-innovation in central banking. Thus, in both Sweden and Denmark central bank stability-oriented values constitute the locus around which all national debates oscillate. Independent from the choice of currency regime, in both Sweden and Denmark it is uncontested that wage-negotiations, public spending-programmes, and private investments should support, not threaten, the underlying stability of the economy. Low inflation, public budgets in surplus, and a sustainable balance of payments seem to constitute deep core values among the major political parties and other opinion makers. The euro-outsider status has not diminished this particular stability-oriented consensus. If anything, it seems to have helped to further consolidate a basic belief in the value of stability and the role of central banks in fostering stability. In this context, it comes as no surprise that the authority and legitimacy of central banks in the respective states is considerable. Central banks in Denmark and Sweden are safely located in powerful positions right at the centre of macro-economic decision-making. On this score, the Swedish and Danish central banks seem to differ from continental European central banks in the sense that these former maintained and even consolidated their traditional powerful positions in national policy processes, whereas the latter transferred much of their authority to the ECB together with the competence of making monetary policy. Even the Danish central bank, which in reality does not exercise any sovereignty in the area of monetary policy-making, is perceived as a natural authority on the Danish political scene.

Both Sweden and Denmark rank high in international bench-marks that value competitiveness, flexibility, and innovation. Their status as euro-outsiders had as a consequence that economic stakeholders in these two small and open countries were exposed to risk in a different way from many euro-insiders. Indeed, euro-insider status has often functioned as a safe heaven for large as well as small EU member-states, and as an external anchor that can provide stability and eliminate some key risks. Whether the status as a euro-insider also eliminates some of the incentives to undertake structural reforms is debatable (Duval and Elmeskov 2005). It is clear, however, that the status as a euro-outsider in no way hindered profound structural reforms to labour and product markets and that these reforms seem to have placed these euro-outsiders among the most innovative economies in the world. In addition, it is clear that central banking in Sweden and Denmark has encouraged, and to some extent created, the right conditions for structural reforms. Continuously, central bankers have pointed to the necessity of streamlining economic institutions, have urged politicians, businesses, and trade unions to work together on these reforms, and have provided economic analysis and data to scientifically underpin economic reforms.

If this kind of continuous reform can be referred to as a form of macro-innovation relating to the function of the overall economic system, then it may also be relevant to associate being a euro-outsider with micro-innovation, which concerns the ways in which the direct economic stakeholders have compensated for their exclusion from the Euro Area. Micro-innovation can take many different forms (Marcussen 2007*a*). As we have seen in this chapter, the Danish and Swedish central banks have engaged in processes of micro-innovation—such as organizational change and network diversification—in order to be better able to navigate in an external environment loaded with risk. In Sweden the central bank has been a forerunner in organizational reform. In conclusion, on all dimensions central banking in Sweden and Denmark is as powerful as ever. Central bank power manifests itself in different ways in the two states, but, in contrast to some national central banks in the Euro Area, theses euro-outsiders seem to be exploiting their position to the widest possible extent.

Part V

Lessons from Non-European Central Banks

13

The Political Economy of Central Banking in Australia and New Zealand

Chris Eichbaum

This chapter examines the political and economic context of central banking in Australia and New Zealand and seeks to illuminate the causes and consequences of markedly different trajectories of institutional reshaping in the two nations. The focus is largely on institutional reshaping over the past 25 years and on patterns of similarity and difference over that period. Both Australia and New Zealand are classified as Westminster political systems. However, the former has a federal constitution and a bi-cameral legislature (with the governing party only infrequently commanding a majority in both houses). The latter is a unitary state, with a single legislature. Until the 1980s the political economy of both states reflected what Castles (1984, 1988) termed the 'politics of domestic defence', dominated by recourse to barrier protection through tariffs and import licensing, and quasi-corporatist, centralized systems of wage fixing (the 'wage earners welfare state'). The 'unmaking of the politics of domestic defence' served to liberate the central banks of both states as finance markets were liberalized and currencies floated (with attendant challenges in terms of the stability of the financial system), border protection removed, and wage-fixing systems decentralized (largely by agreement in Australia, and by legislative fiat in New Zealand during the early 1990s). Central banks in both states directed policy (or have been tasked with directing policy) to the maintenance of price stability, and have, by evolving practice or legislative fiat, become operationally independent. Fiscal policy has increasingly become subject to sanction or accommodation by independent monetary policy authorities. In short, central banks have become extremely influential policy actors in their own right.

In 1989 the Reserve Bank of New Zealand Act gave New Zealand's central bank operational independence to pursue a single economic objective—achieving and maintaining price stability. The 1989 Act repealed legislation passed in 1964 which had enjoined the Bank to direct policy to multiple objectives—the maintenance and promotion of economic and social welfare, and promoting the highest level production and trade and full employment. Under the 1964 legislation the Bank was required to give effect to the monetary policy of the government of the day; under the 1989 Act monetary policy is directed to meeting the terms of a Policy Targets Agreement agreed between the relevant Minister (typically the Minister of Finance) and the Bank Governor. These terms are also incorporated into the Governor's contract of employment. The 1989 Act vests full authority for the determination of monetary policy in the Governor—not in the Board of the Bank or a monetary policy committee. Under the 1964 legislation the Secretary of the New Zealand Treasury was a member of the Board of the Bank; that is no longer the case under the 1989 Act. The role of the Board is to monitor the Bank and the Governor on behalf of the Minister. In the event of a vacancy in the position of Governor the Board is tasked with recommending an appointment to the Minister. Since 1989 a number of central banks have been granted operational independence, but with a measure of goal dependence—typically the goal has been that of price stability.

While, from the vantage point of both New Zealand and Australian policymakers it is now acceptable to posit a degree of convergence as regards the practice of central banking, it has not always been so. Indeed, in the 1990s for New Zealand policymakers (and for those enamoured of the New Zealand model) it was almost *de rigueur* to point out the institutional inadequacies of the Australian arrangements. And in a formal sense at least, those arrangements (or institutional 'pillars') have not changed: the Reserve Bank of Australia is still enjoined to direct policy towards multiple objectives, it still maintains a relationship of 'consultative independence' with the government of the day, the Secretary to the Treasury still has a seat as of right on the Board of the Reserve Bank, and it is the Bank Board (which combines 'professional' or full-time members with individuals drawn from a range of industry sectors) that is formally tasked with the development of monetary policy. Policy is informed, to a degree, by an inflation target—a target developed largely by the Bank itself, a target of an annual rate of inflation of between 2 and 3 per cent over the cycle. This target was imported into a statement on the conduct of policy agreed between former RBA Governor Ian Macfarlane and Treasurer Peter Costello shortly before Macfarlane assumed office in 1996. So far as the formal statutory arrangements are concerned, the Australian statute remained largely intact since the tempestuous times of 1945, as have—notwithstanding remarkable changes in context—the formal institutional arrangements within which policy has been determined and implemented. But while the trajectory of institutional reform in Australia has been evolutionary and incremental, and, in the post-War period transacted largely in the extra-legislative sphere, the same could not be said of New Zealand.

This chapter examines the scope, content, processes, and outcomes associated with central bank reforms in Australia and New Zealand. Both have seen significant reforms to the institutional arrangements governing relationships between political (and administrative) executives and central banks. In both cases there has been a move to greater operational independence. In the Australian context operational independence has not been accompanied by goal independence to the same degree. In both cases the focus on price stability has been codified in an agreement between central bank and government (with a more explicitly contractual basis in the New Zealand context). In New Zealand, reflecting in no small part the *Zeitgeist*, changes were explicitly informed by an *ex ante* theoretical case, and were made manifest in a 'first-principles' and comprehensive approach to legislative change. In Australia the statutory anchor for the institutional arrangements—the Reserve Bank of Australia Act 1959 with its dualist charter—remained substantially intact.

The Dimensions of Difference

There are obvious limits in focusing on differences in the formal (as distinct from conventional or behavioural) markers of central bank independence. In the final analysis it is behaviour that counts. But one key issue raised by a focus on the two Australasian central banks is how to account for and explain institutional difference—why it is that certain institutions have been shaped or reshaped in certain ways—and the logic of institutional reshaping. The extent and specific manifestations of this difference vary over time. The political-economy code that shapes or reshapes the institutions of central banking is suggested by elements of the statutes governing the two Australasian 'banks of reserve'.

While until 1989 both institutions were formally given status and function by statutes that did not, in substantive terms, differ significantly in institutional form, this changed with the passage of the Reserve Bank of New Zealand Act in 1989. The differences between this Act, and the corresponding Australian statute, the Reserve Bank Act 1959 are captured in elements of the formal institutional arrangements which govern the development and implementation of monetary policy. The charters of the two central banks prescribe the objective(s) to which policy shall be directed and the governance and accountability arrangements in pursuit of the objective(s), and, at the level of policy goals, defines the relationship between the bank and the government of the day.

The functions of the RBA are detailed in section 10 of the Reserve Bank Act, the wording of which clearly indicates the status of the Board of the Bank in terms of its statutory authority in both policymaking and governance:

(1) Subject to this Part, the Board has power to determine the policy of the Bank in relation to any matter and to take such action as is necessary to ensure that effect is given by the Bank to the policy so determined.

(2) It is the duty of the Board, within the limits of its powers, to ensure that the monetary and banking policy of the Bank is directed to the greatest advantage of the people of Australia and that the powers of the Bank under this Act, the Banking Act 1959 and the regulations under that Act are exercised in such a manner as, in the opinion of the Board, will best contribute to:

(a) the stability of the currency of Australia;
(b) the maintenance of full employment in Australia; and
(c) the economic prosperity and welfare of the people of Australia. (Section 10, Reserve Bank Act 1959)

By contrast, the charter prescribed in the Reserve Bank of New Zealand Act 1989 directs the Bank to a single *economic* objective:

The primary function of the Bank is to formulate and implement monetary policy directed to the economic objective of achieving and maintaining stability in the general level of prices. (Section 8, Reserve Bank of New Zealand Act 1989)[1]

The Australian statute provides that the Board of the Bank has the power to determine the policy of the Bank. It is sufficient to note at this point that it is the Board, and not the Governor alone, in which the power of policymaking resides, and that, typically, in making appointment to the Reserve Bank Board successive Australian governments have sought to bring a range of interests to the task of policymaking, including, at various times and in varying combinations, manufacturing, rural, mining, and employee interests, and academic economists.

In contrast, the New Zealand policymaking arrangements are premised on a set of contractual arrangements between the government of the day, through the Minister of Finance or Treasurer, and the Governor of the Bank, and subject to the Bank's primary objective. While the primary objective of monetary policy is prescribed in the statute, the specific target to which monetary policy is directed is codified in a policy targets agreement between the Minister and the Governor. The Governor is tasked with ensuring, 'that the actions of the Bank in implementing monetary policy are consistent with the policy targets fixed under section 9 of [the] Act' (Section 11, Reserve Bank of New Zealand Act 1989). The Governor is appointed by the Minister on the recommendation of the Bank's Board of Directors, (Section 40, Reserve Bank of New Zealand Act 1989), and is duty bound, 'to ensure that the Bank carries out the functions imposed on it by [the] Act' (Section 41, Reserve Bank of New Zealand Act 1989). While the Bank has a Board of Directors, the role of the Board is largely directed to ensuring that the Governor of the Bank fulfils the terms of the contracted Policy Targets Agreement.

The statute prescribes the grounds on which a Governor may be removed from office, either on the initiative of the Minister or on the recommendation of the Board, grounds which include a failure to achieve contracted policy targets, and actions inconsistent with the Bank's primary function (Sections 49 and 53, Reserve Bank of New Zealand Act 1989).

The accountability requirements for both central banks are detailed in statute, and, in the case of the RBA evolved in ways consistent with the statute, and have in recent years been codified in an agreement between the Governor and the Treasurer. Both Banks publish reports or statements on the conduct of monetary policy, and both appear before committees of the respective parliaments. And both statutes specify the rights of bank and government in policy determination and in the event of the government of the day requiring the bank to significantly modify the course of a preferred policy path.

In the case of the New Zealand statute the Reserve Bank Governor and the government of the day codify agreed policy targets in a Policy Targets Agreement (which must be consistent with the Bank's principal target). However, the government possesses a residual power to direct the Bank to formulate and implement policy for any economic objective, other than the economic objective specified in section 8 of the Act (the principal, objective), for a period (Section 12, Reserve Bank of New Zealand Act 1989). This provision has, to date, not been activated by any government.[2] In the New Zealand context, however, the possibility of the government seeking recourse to this facility was raised by the Minister of Finance in 2007. The Australian statute also provides for an override or disputes procedure. Section 11 of the Reserve Bank Act requires the Board of the Bank to inform the government of Bank policy from time to time, and prescribes a process to be followed in the event of a difference of opinion between the Government and the Bank Board. This process allows the government of the day, through the Treasurer, to determine the policy to be adopted by the Bank, but requires that the Parliament (and through the Parliament, the public at large) be provided with all relevant information relating to the difference of opinion and the rationale for any government override.

Both central banks have responsibility for financial system stability, and increasingly are cooperating on a trans-Tasman basis on issues of prudential regulation and financial stability (the more so given the recent period of international financial instability). The RBNZ is tasked in statute with using its powers to promote the soundness and efficiency of the financial system, and to avoid the significant damage to the financial system that could be caused by the failure of a registered bank. The approach taken by the bank involves three pillars—self-regulation, market discipline, and regulatory and supervisory arrangements (Bollard 2005), and these are directed at prevention of financial crises (e.g. through the prudential supervision of banks and a registration system for banks directed to ensuring appropriate governance arrangements and capability, and adequate capitalisation). They are also aimed at correction and crisis management (ranging from speeches by the Bank's Governor drawing attention to any risks, through to the Bank acting as a lender of last resort, exercising powers by which it may give directions to a registered bank, or direct foreign-exchange intervention) (Orr 2006). In November 2004 the RBNZ commenced publishing a six-monthly Financial Stability Report.

Financial system stability is also a responsibility of the RBA. Significant changes were introduced to Australia's financial regulatory arrangements in 1998. These included the establishment of a new regulator, the Australian Prudential Regulation Authority (APRA) and the creation of a Payments System Board within the RBA. APRA is the prudential regulator of the Australian financial services industry. It oversees banks, credit unions, building societies, general insurance and reinsurance companies, life insurance, friendly societies, and most members of the superannuation industry. For its part the RBA publishes a half-yearly Financial Stability Review which incorporates the Bank's assessment of the soundness of the financial system and potential risks. The Bank also has responsibility for the Payments System Board, which has authority for payments system safety and stability and recourse to regulatory powers and instruments.

In the domestic context the RBA is a member of the Council of Financial Regulators, which is chaired by the Bank's Governor, and which brings together the RBA, APRA, the Treasury, and the Australian Securities and Investments Commission (ASIC). The Council is tasked with contributing to the efficiency and effectiveness of regulation and the stability of the financial system. The RBA is also one of the 26 national authority members of the Financial Stability Forum, established in April 1999 to promote international financial stability.[3]

Contrasting Narratives of Antipodean Central Banking

The contrasting trajectories of institutional reform in Australia and New Zealand provide a useful complement to the meso-historical perspective on central banks and central banking (see Marcussen, this volume). From the preceding discussion it is clear that, in terms of the formal statutory provisions, Australian and New Zealand central banks (but perhaps not central banking practice) can be viewed as representative of different *stages* of central banking (ibid.). This conclusion is suggested by the dates at which central banking statutes came into being: the Reserve Bank of New Zealand Act in 1989, and the Reserve Bank of Australia Act in 1959 (incorporating the charter provided for in the Commonwealth Bank Act of 1945).

With its focus on price stability, and the formal context for relations between bank and government influenced by agency theory, the Reserve Bank of New Zealand Act 1989 is very much a reflection of the intellectual climate of the times. But as we have already noted, Australian central banking continues to operate according to an institutional scheme reflecting the third stage in the development of central banking. In some respects the current statutory arrangements—and the Bank's dualist charter and the structure of its board are most often cited here—evoke aspects of an earlier Keynesian settlement. Equally, however, those arrangements are quite consistent with what Blinder (1998) characterized as 'modern central banking'.

The somewhat 'dated' Australian arrangements could perhaps be excused if they simply reflected an institutional 'overhang' from an earlier time, and if central bank policy and practice (as articulated by Australia's central bankers) was not couched in terms of the formal statutory arrangements. However, successive governors of the Bank appeared to be quite comfortable operating with a charter that directs the Bank to multiple objectives, and defended the Bank's governance arrangements against the accusation that they compromise the independence of the institution.[4] The chapter considers below the extent to which antipodean central banking might be exhibiting the characteristics of a fifth age of central banking.

In order to fully illuminate and account for the patterns of similarity and difference between central banks and central banking in Australia and New Zealand—and to complement the standard historical taxonomy of ages of central banking—two particular drivers need to be factored into the discussion. They are institutional credibility and institutional legitimacy. The argument (which is more fully developed in Eichbaum 1999) is that a stable institutional settlement (in essence, a political settlement) requires high endowments of both credibility and legitimacy. Institutional (and policy) credibility is required to counter the problem of dynamic inconsistency (Kydland and Prescott 1977). Politically porous institutional arrangements, it is argued, lack credibility. Opportunistic and discretionary monetary policymaking, conducted with a short-term bias, will cause price setters to factor a risk premium into forward contracts. Institutional legitimacy has two dimensions. The central bank and the conduct of monetary policy more generally will be perceived as legitimate where monetary policy balances the need for stable prices with the needs of non-financial actors with real economy interests (addressing both stabilization and growth imperatives); and, second, to the extent that they satisfy tests of democratic governance and accountability (mitigating the perception or actuality of a democratic deficit). Conceived in this way, the 'equilibrium' condition for a stable institutional settlement is one in which endowments of both credibility and legitimacy are optimized.

The Reserve Bank of New Zealand Act 1989 represented a regime shift of paradigmatic proportions. But it was a shift that was, at its core, designed to address a significant credibility deficit. The RBNZ, which had *de facto* since late 1984 enjoyed the kind of 'independence' codified in the 1989 Act, was a significant actor in its own institutional reshaping. It drove the process of policy formation, and, significantly, mobilized sufficient support within the government to ensure that its own preferences as regards the detail of institutional form prevailed over those advocated by the New Zealand Treasury.

The fact that an incumbent government might wish to limit its own capacity for discretionary policymaking is, given the behavioural assumptions that inform the rational choice case for central bank independence, conceptually somewhat problematic. Some accounts (e.g. Goodman 1992) seek to remedy this by postulating that an incumbent government will act where it faces the prospect of imminent defeat and wishes to limit the capacity for discretionary action on the part of its successor. There is much in the New Zealand case to support this line of argument. By 1988–9 the fourth Labour Government was facing the probability of defeat in the 1990 election, and the public justification for the Act, captured in the political discourse of the time, was one predicated on the policy failings of earlier governments and the prospect for those failings informing the conduct of policy under future governments. Faced with the opportunity to codify its *de facto* independence in a more durable form, the government created the conditions for a significant reconfiguration of the domestic political economy, and for a more independent political role for the central bank. In so doing, it nurtured a critical mass of support for the kinds of legislative changes that it initiated in 1988.

Moreover, by zero-basing the process of institutional design, the architects of the Act—within the government and within the Bank—were able to draw on the prevailing institutional prescription, one that privileged operationally independent central banks, tasked exclusively with the achievement and maintenance of price stability. For the architects the principal objective was the restoration of credibility to the conduct of monetary policy. There was not total disregard of institutional legitimacy. Those most closely involved in the design of the Act were concerned to arrive at an institutional settlement that respected the rights of the legislature in a Westminster-style democracy. But, to the extent that legitimacy was a consideration, it was captured and disposed of in the contractual nature of the accountability regime, and not viewed as a consideration in designing either objectives or wider governance arrangements. The fact that the government retained the right in statute to provide the governor with policy targets, and, in limited circumstances, to override the principal objective, was viewed as sufficient.

The dominant economic interests demanded credibility in the conduct and substance of policy, and the Bank, concerned to administer a further circuit breaker to inflationary expectations, was also driven by this imperative. In the context of an environment in which the institutions of the New Zealand state were being progressively reshaped according to the tenets of agency theory, the vehicle of a contract between the government, as principal, and the central bank governor, as agent, was readily at hand. The *de facto* changes in the post-1984 period shifted the Bank's position, and the subsequent codification of these changes in the 1989 Act was informed by the quest for credibility. The Bank's stock of credibility had appreciated.

If the New Zealand changes represented a paradigm shift, institutional reshaping in Australia has been of a more incremental kind, based on the legislative changes of the early post-War period. Whereas New Zealand entered the 1980s with institutional arrangements carrying a significant credibility deficit, the institution of Australian central banking had been subject to a searching evaluation through the 1981 Campbell Committee Inquiry into the financial system. Its report recommended the liberalization of the finance sector (and presaged the floating of the Australian dollar), and, with reference to the RBA, endorsed the institutional status quo (Bell 2006: 21–5). However, the 1980s, and the early 1990s in particular, were to see a political contest over the Australian central bank predicated on the allegation of an acute credibility deficit as the basis for radical institutional change—along the lines of the New Zealand model. The case for reform rested on the low score of the RBA on the standard formal indices of central bank independence. The intellectual climate of the times (no better demonstrated than in the 'New Zealand model') privileged an institutional model in which central banks focused exclusively on price stability, and in which operational independence from government—and indeed the implementation of monetary policy clearly at variance with the political interests of incumbent governments—was held to be virtuous. In a climate in which the quest for low inflation was the only game in town, a central bank tasked to deliver multiple objectives 'invited' a credibility deficit. The RBA was governed by a Board, in which membership of financial actors was specifically precluded (and which included a 'representative of the Treasury'), and was enjoined to develop and implement policy in consultation with the government. This credibility deficit was pronounced amongst those actors who held the assumption of a direct correspondence between statute and behaviour (which standard textbook accounts implied).

The perception that the Australian institutional arrangements were politically porous was further encouraged by the imprudent remarks of politicians, who claimed to be able to influence the conduct of monetary policy. These politicians were, in the words of the Reserve Bank Governor of the time, 'chastised' for these observations, and may well have regretted them. However, while within the domestic environment financial actors may have been inclined to dismiss such observations as evidence of political hubris, in overseas markets such comments merely served to reinforce the appearance of a systemic weakness in institutional design. There was little, if any, evidence of direct political involvement in the conduct of monetary policy decision-making; if anything, the evidence was that 'political considerations' influenced the Board of the Bank to time policy changes specifically to avoid the appearance of political influence. However, the prevailing view—particularly in offshore markets—was one of a politically porous set of institutional arrangements, and of an increasingly acute credibility deficit.

Two competing political prescriptions were on offer in Australia in the early 1990s. One prescription sought to replicate the New Zealand model; the other, to effect an increase in institutional and policy credibility without any consequential diminution in the legitimacy of the institution (and without the requirement to revisit the statutory framework). The second prevailed. Having moved to a position where both endowments of legitimacy and credibility have been optimized, the reshaping of the Australian central bank resulted in a position of relative equilibrium, reflected in a bi-partisan policy settlement.

Two aspects of the on-going institutional reshaping of Australia's central banking arrangements have been particularly significant. The first was the development by Bank and government of an inflation target: of an annual rate of inflation of between and 2 and 3 per cent over the course of the business cycle. The development of an inflation target was seen as mitigating the deleterious consequences of the credibility deficit, while at the same time being consistent with the maintenance of the dualist approach suggested by the Reserve Bank charter. The second was the agreed statement on the conduct of monetary policy embodied in an exchange of letters between the Bank Governor and the Treasurer in August 1996, subsequently reaffirmed in July 2003 and September 2006.

The agreed statement was reviewed following the change of government in Australia in November 2007. One of the first items of business for the incoming government was to recommit to an agreed Statement on the Conduct of Monetary Policy. On 6 December 2007, the new Prime Minister Rudd and Treasurer Swan released a revised Statement, outlining the 'mutual understanding on the conduct of monetary policy between the new Government, represented by the Treasurer, and the Governor as Chairman of the RBA Board'. The Statement contains a number of new elements. The positions of Governor and Deputy Governor of the Bank are to be raised to the same level of statutory independence as the Commissioner of Taxation and the Australian Statistician. This means that appointments will be made by the government, but that any termination will require parliamentary approval (now a higher threshold than applies in the New Zealand legislation, where the formal power to terminate the Governor's employment—albeit subject to a number of tests—resides with the government). In respect of future Board appointments, the Secretary to the Treasury, and the Governor of the Reserve Bank will maintain a register of 'eminent candidates' from which the Treasurer will make appointments to the Board. These developments were heralded as bringing in a 'new era of independence for the RBA'. The Prime Minister and the Treasurer viewed the revised Statement on the Conduct of Monetary Policy as 'an important step towards ensuring the appointment processes, debates and decision making of the RBA are as independent and transparent as possible'.

On 5 December 2007, the RBA announced some modifications to its arrangements for communicating policy decisions. The Board of the Bank now releases a short statement each month explaining its monetary policy decision; the Board's decision is announced on the same day that the monthly meeting of the Board is held; and the Board now releases the minutes of its monetary policy meeting each month. The minutes record the factual material available to the Board, the Board's policy assessment and decisions; comments are not attributed to individual board members (Reserve Bank of Australia 2007).

Equally, New Zealand's arrangements have also been the subject of incremental changes over time. As in Australia, these changes have, in the main, been prosecuted within the context of existing legislative arrangements. However, if the narrative of institutional reform in Australia is suggestive of a need to appreciate the stock of institutional and policy credibility, the contrasting New Zealand narrative is one more suggestive of the need to achieve a better alignment between the Bank's price stability objective and other aspects of macroeconomic management. Since the 1989 legislation governments of various political complexions have at times struggled with (and been tempted to revisit) the Bank's resolute (some would say 'single-minded' pursuit of price stability). The Policy Targets Agreement between Bank and the government carried the burden of codifying the precise nature of the Bank's policy responsibilities, in the context of the government's wider policy objectives.

The first Policy Targets Agreement directed the Bank to formulate and implement monetary policy with the intention of achieving price stability in the year ending in December 1992. An annual inflation rate in the range of 0 to 2 per cent was to be taken to represent the achievement of price stability. Although the target date was later extended to 1993, the Bank met its objective ahead of time. The current Policy Targets Agreement is somewhat less 'hard-edged' and more flexible, requiring the Bank to keep future CPI inflation outcomes between 1 and 3 per cent *on average over the medium term*. Moreover, paragraph 1 (b) of the current PTA reads as follows:

The Government's economic objective is to promote a growing, open, and competitive economy as the best means of delivering permanently higher incomes and living standards for New Zealanders. Price stability plays an important part in supporting this objective.

While the overall scheme of the Reserve Bank Act remains, in terms of the sentiment (certainly politically, and possibly within the Bank) that is expressed in the Policy Targets Agreement, there is a tacit acceptance of the need for a measure of policy dualism and—notwithstanding statutory references to economic policy objectives in isolation—of the interdependence of economic and social policy.

The New Zealand arrangements have also been the subject of a technical review, conducted in 2000 by Professor Lars Svensson. On balance the Svensson report was supportive of the monetary policy regime and the Bank's conduct of monetary policy.[5] Svensson (2001) did, however, recommend a number of changes, including to the inflation target and to the Bank's governance arrangements. They included that

- The Bank's inflation target be restated as a point target of 1.5 per cent
- A formal monetary policy committee, comprising the Governor and four other Reserve Bank staff, be formed (with the change to be made at the beginning of the next term of the Governor)
- Changes to the accountability arrangements and Bank governance, specifically that the Board of the Bank consist only of non-executive directors, with the Chair of the Board selected by these non-executive directors (under the 1989 Act the Governor and Deputy Governors were members of the Board and the Governor the Chair of the Board)[6]

Svensson's recommendations regarding changes to accountability arrangements and specifically to the composition of the Board of the Bank were largely accepted. However, the government chose not to act on his recommendation to establish a monetary policy committee or to amend the Policy Targets Agreement to provide for an explicit mid-range point target.

While the New Zealand arrangements are unlikely to be revisited in the short term, recent developments suggest that there is every prospect of a further refining of those arrangements. Both Australian and New Zealand central banks, in common with those in a number of other jurisdictions, have been faced with the challenge of asset-price (house price in particular) inflation (Bell 2006: 181–97 on the Australian case). New Zealand policymakers have, since late 2005, been exploring whether supplementary policy instruments might be deployed to complement monetary policy in the task of managing inflation pressures (RBNZ/The Treasury 2006). And in both jurisdictions there are clearly on-going challenges associated with the alignment of monetary and fiscal policy.[7]

For over two decades the RBA has intervened, as appropriate and necessary, in the foreign-exchange markets. The policy rationale for recourse to foreign-exchange intervention dates from the Campbell Committee inquiry into the financial system, which indicated that, in the absence of a clean float, some intervention may be required from time to time. On 11 June 2007 the RBNZ confirmed that, for the first time, it had intervened in the foreign-exchange market.

In July 2007, with the US/NZ dollar cross rate reaching 'exceptional' levels, the level of political discomfort with the conduct of monetary policy surfaced again. The Leader of one of the parties supporting the coalition government raised concerns about the Reserve Bank Governor's implementation of the Policy Targets Agreement. Reflecting perhaps the pressure emanating from this source, on 18 July 2007 the Minister of Finance was asked in the Parliament whether he had given any consideration to using the powers of the Reserve Bank Act to direct the Bank to formulate and implement monetary policy for different economic objectives. He replied as follows:

Under section 12 of the Reserve Bank of New Zealand Act there is the power to suspend the policy targets agreement and to incorporate objectives other than the primary object-ive outlined within the Act. I have given no specific consideration to that matter, but the section is clearly there for a purpose and as Minister of Finance I would never rule out its potential use.

In a speech in August 2007 Finance Minister Cullen signalled his concern with aspects of New Zealand's monetary policy framework, noting that

The accepted consensus has been that our monetary policy framework doesn't have an impact on long run growth. In other words, monetary policy helps keep the economy stable by moderating economic cycles, without impacting on the sustainable rate of growth of the economy.

My overriding concern is that this view no longer holds. . . .

So I think we need to look seriously at the monetary policy framework and whether it can be made more effective at curing the inflation disease without killing the patient in the process. (Cullen 2007)

Conclusion: Implications of Antipodean Convergence and Difference

The Australasian experience provides an interesting case study in the logics, consequences, and durability of institutional reshaping. In 1989, New Zealand implemented an institutional reform that was based largely on the rational expectations model, and that was codified in statute on the basis of bi-partisan political support. By contrast, institutional reshaping in Australia was—over the period of the late 1980s and early to mid-1990s, but less so more recently—much more the subject of partisan contestation. In both states there is now a large measure of multi-party support for the present institutional arrangements: a condition of institutional equilibrium and a settlement of kinds. But in New Zealand the settlement is a somewhat uneasy one.

As the preceding discussion suggests, the broader institutional frameworks for the conduct of monetary policy in Australia and New Zealand—by which is meant the statutory and the less formal or more conventional elements of the institutional mix—have seen a measure of both convergence and continuing difference. The differences, such as they are, are more marked in the formal or statutory realm and much less so in the actual conduct of monetary policy and in relationships between central banks and governments. Australia still 'offends' against an earlier orthodoxy by retaining a statute that codifies policy dualism, by a mode of policymaking by a mixed board of professionals and 'lay' representatives, and by continuing to have the Secretary of the Treasury on that Board. The defining features of New Zealand's formal arrangements have already been well rehearsed. They are a single focus on price stability, policymaking vested in the Governor and in a contractual relationship between Governor and government that provides operational autonomy for the former on the basis of goal dependence stipulated by the latter, and a Board that is tasked principally with oversight of the performance of Governor—as agent—on behalf of the Minister—as political principal. Both formal regimes provide for a policy override, but—to date at least—there has been no recourse to this facility.

Looking closer at the second tier of the formal arrangements—the exchange of letters in the Australian case, and the Policy Targets Agreement in New Zealand—one detects a high degree of similarity. Australia's exchange of letters in 1996 incorporated an inflation target, developed by the Bank itself as a means of providing a more explicit (and credible) anchor for monetary policy. This target remained unchanged for 11 years. It is a soft-edged and medium-term target that enjoins the Bank, and the government, to direct policy to the objective of keeping underlying inflation between 2 and 3 per cent, on average, over the cycle. It bears a striking similarity to the target first incorporated into the New Zealand Policy Targets Agreement in September 2002, some 8 years after the Macfarlane/Costello exchange of letters, and 13 years after the passage of the Reserve Bank of New Zealand Act 1989. The 2002 PTA is, as we noted, significant also because it locates monetary policy within a wider set of policy objectives. Although perhaps not policy dualism in the same way that it is expressed in the charter of the RBA, it is as close as one might come to an explicit commitment to policy dualism without revisiting the overall scheme of the Act.

Both Banks produce regular reports on monetary policy: Monetary Policy Statements in the case of the RBNZ, and Statements on Monetary Policy released four times a year by the RBA. Both Banks appear regularly before committees of their respective national legislatures: the RBNZ before the Finance and Expenditure Committee of the New Zealand Parliament, and the RBA before the House of Representatives Standing Committee on Economics, Finance and Public Administration.

While the election of a centre-right government in 2008 has seen a slight shift away from the policy dualism that formerly linked economic and social policy, there is still less distance now between the approaches of New Zealand and Australia approaches.

As Bell (2006: 198) observed:

The RBA has changed in many important ways, but the Bank's statutory provisions have not. This suggests that informal institutions and arrangements matter a great deal. The Bank operates in an invisible force field of institutional incentives and disincentives. It needs credibility in the markets and elsewhere to operate effectively, and the search for credibility has preoccupied it. But as its clout and independence have risen has its need to achieve wider community and democratic legitimacy. This credibility—legitimacy frame, and the search for balance between the two, is a good way to describe the key institutional dynamics that enmesh and shape the RBA.

Central banking is, in substance and in form, a particular and different variant of democratic decision-making (see Marcussen in this volume). In the case of both the antipodean central banks there has been a progressive move towards depoliticization. Indeed the quest for institutional and policy credibility is in large part about inoculating central banks and the conduct of monetary policy from the democratic distemper that is evidenced in short-term and electorally opportunistic decision-making. It is not, however, clear that the Australasian central banks have embraced, or been embraced by the imperatives of apoliticization (Marcussen, this volume). Policymaking within the RBA is characterized by a Board bringing both 'expert' and 'lay' perspectives to the process. It is clearly decision-making by committee, but is hardly a new trend (and, as we noted, offends against the orthodox prescription by providing representation for the Treasury on the Bank Board). New Zealand in fact moved from decision-making by committee to one-person decision-making by the Governor alone in 1989. While this could be seen as at variance with the putative 'fifth age' of central banking, the change reflected the tenets of agency theory and the hard-edged contractualism of the New Zealand variant of the New Public Management (Boston et al. 1996). It was also consistent with the orthodox institutional prescription (Rogoff 1985).

Both central banks embraced the need for a much greater measure of transparency in the conduct of monetary policy, and a recent decision by the Board of the RBA will now see minutes of Board meetings released. The RBNZ publishes three-year forward projections of monetary conditions, but this is not a practice favoured by the RBA. Accountability arrangements for both Banks include regular briefings to, and questioning by, committees of their respective parliaments. Both central banks have adopted inflation targeting of the flexible kind. New Zealand arrived relatively recently, and through an iterative process of the review and renegotiation of Policy Target Agreements, at a target almost identical to that developed by the RBA in the early 1990s. As one of the architects of the Australian inflation target argued, this target, along with the other pillars of the Australian settlement, has been less an aspect of science, and more a feature of the 'art of monetary policy' (Fraser 1994).

What then of the scope, content, processes, and outcomes associated with central bank reforms in New Zealand and Australia and the lessons that might be taken from the experience of the antipodean central banks? Clearly context—and, more to the point, differences in constitutional, political, and economic contexts between Australasian and European central banks—is vitally important. The two Australasian central banks are national institutions, notwithstanding the interdependencies associated with the international qualities of financial markets and, increasingly the governance of those markets. The ECB is, in charter and function, a supranational institution and one that operates under a very different governance structure. However, ideas travel, and benchmarking and policy transfer are integral to central banking, whether in Europe or in Australasia. Unsurprisingly therefore, the Australasian experience speaks to the challenges of European central banking.

The first, somewhat self-evident point to note is that central banks are creatures of politics: if only because, whatever their quasi-constitutional status in the administrative topography, they are established, tasked, and held accountable by way of statutes (or treaties).

The second is that endowments of credibility are clearly important in enabling central banks to achieve and maintain price stability. However, though necessary, credibility may be by no means sufficient as a basis for establishing an enduring institutional settlement. Institutional arrangements and the conduct of policy also needs to meet the test of legitimacy. This test is in part about the specific nature of inflation targets and the conduct of monetary policy, and in particular about ensuring that price stability does not come at the cost of undue variability in output. It is, in other words, about being conscious of trade-offs. In this sense, one can argue that monetary policy will meet the tests of credibility and legitimacy if the cure ensures the continuing rude good health of the patient. But legitimacy is also about other aspects of the institutional mix, including the governance arrangements for central banks and the wider context within which central banks, governments, economic actors, and civil society more generally engage.

In part the legitimacy issues relate to the formal tasking or charters of central banks, The primary objective of the European Central Bank is to maintain price stability, operationalized as inflation rates of 'below but close to 2 percent' over the medium term. But the ECB charter also directs the Bank, 'without prejudice to the objective of price stability' to, 'support the general economic policies in the Community with a view to contributing to the achievement of the objectives of the Community', and these include a high level of employment and sustainable and non-inflationary growth.

So what is the nature of the ECB's charter or mandate—a sole focus on price stability or a measure of policy dualism? Responding to a question at the ECB's monthly press conference in February 2008, its president Jean-Claude Trichet reflected on the uncertainties facing central bankers (including financial market turbulence and wage pressures) and remarked that, in the face of such uncertainty,

[W]hat is certain is that we have an anchor. *We have only one needle in our compass*, as I have always said, which is that we have to deliver price stability in the medium term. (Trichet 2008, emphasis added)[8]

One of the central arguments of this chapter—and to a large extent substantiated by the Australian and New Zealand experiences—is that a 'one-needle' approach to the conduct of monetary policy may not always be appropriate. This is not to deny the fundamental contribution that low and stable inflation makes to economic—and social—policy outcomes, or the significant credibility gains that come from anchoring monetary policy in a flexible medium-term target. But, though necessary, credibility is not sufficient. What then of legitimacy?

In a normative sense, the ECB acknowledges that legitimacy is a necessary characteristic of central banking institutional arrangements. Juergen Stark (2008*a*), a member of the Executive Board of the ECB, argued that 'the far-reaching independence granted to the ECB does not mean that it lacks democratic legitimacy', suggesting that the principles of democratic legitimacy needs to be located in the context of constitutional principles or conventions relating to the separation of powers, the rule of law, and the provisions of the EC Treaty. His analysis is strikingly evocative of that advanced in support of the decision to place the RBNZ on an independent footing, where independence was equated with a single goal of price stability and the operational independence to pursue that goal. Stark (ibid.) argues that democratic legitimacy is the product of robust accountability arrangements; but that such arrangements are much more efficacious if there is only the one objective:

Problems of accountability could only arise if the ECB—having only one instrument at its disposal—had the mandate to pursue several objectives. Then, it would have to explain potential conflicts between the objectives, and, if necessary, to justify its own prioritisation of objectives in a democratic manner.

But legitimacy is perhaps best conceptualized as having two dimensions:

First, public policy decisions are legitimate if they are, directly or indirectly, the will of the people.... This is often referred to as 'input legitimacy' or 'legitimacy by procedure'. Second, decisions can be considered legitimate if they meet the justified expectations and needs of the people ... a notion which is also referred to as 'output legitimacy' or 'legitimacy by result'. (ECB 2002)

The experience of the Australian and New Zealand central banks suggests that the imperatives of legitimacy cannot simply be satisfied by procedural or accountability mechanisms that address the kinds of potential democratic deficits attendant upon central bank independence. Legitimacy is as much about what central banks do as how they do it.

303

The narrative of central banking in the antipodes is a tale of two banks taking markedly different pathways but arriving, broadly, at a common destination. It is a narrative that illuminates a number of the challenges of institutional design and of the conduct of monetary policy. This chapter has emphasized the distinction to be drawn between institutional *and* policy credibility and legitimacy, has contrasted two different trajectories of institutional reshaping—one radical and the other much more incremental—and has noted the importance of moving beyond literal interpretations of formal structures to examine actual behaviour. Given that scholars and practitioners of central banking share an international currency of ideas, the antipodean experience speaks to some of the challenges—present and emergent—of central banking in Europe.

Indeed, the narrative of central banking in the antipodes may ultimately be a story of a single central bank and of a common Australasian currency (Holmes 2002; Hunt 2005). If this outcome occurs, there will be important lessons to be drawn from the scope, content, processes, and outcomes associated with central banking in the EU.

Notes

1. Moreover a number of other elements of the institutional framework are clearly subject to this single charter objective. Section 9 of the New Zealand statute requires the Minister to negotiate policy targets with the Governor, 'for the carrying out by the Bank of its primary function. . . . ' (Section 9 (1), Reserve Bank of New Zealand Act 1989); and the override facility, which we examine in more detail below, requires that a manifestly public and transparent process be followed in seeking to provide, for a finite period, that policy be directed to, 'any economic objective, other than the economic objective specified in section 8. . . . ' (Section 12 (1) Reserve Bank of New Zealand Act 1989).

2. It is noteworthy in this respect that in form and function section 12 of the New Zealand Act owed a great deal to the Australian legislation. The Australian arrangements were viewed as being consistent with the hierarchical nature of political and administrative relationships in Westminster-styled systems (thereby addressing, to some extent at least, the challenge of a democratic deficit—in the final analysis the views of the government of the day can prevail), providing for operational independence for the central bank, and requiring transparency in the event of the use of the override. So far as this third element of institutional form is concerned, while the institutional regime in which the override or disputes provisions are situated differ, the guiding principle informing each—transparency of process—is common to both, and there are common procedural elements.

3. In recent years initiatives have also been taken to strengthen the harmonization and coordination of banking supervision in an Australasian context. In 2005, a Trans-Tasman Council on Banking Supervision was established, with terms of reference

which cover supervisory co-operation, preparedness for responding to crises that involve banks that are common to both countries, and whether legislative changes may be required to ensure Australian Prudential Regulation Authority (APRA) and the RBNZ support each other in their regulatory responsibilities, at least regulatory cost (Orr 2006).

4. See Fraser (1996) for an interesting discussion of the institutional pillars underpinning Australian central banking.

5. As Singleton et al. note, Svensson was, 'known to be generally sympathetic to the New Zealand regime and to Brash's performance as Governor' (2006: 201).

6. Arthur Grimes, now Chair of the Reserve Bank of New Zealand Board, commented at the time that, [i]f the same review were applied to the current Australian arrangements, one would expect approval of the monetary policy implementation regime based on a short-term interest rate. The soft-edged nature of the inflation target would be regarded as reasonable, although possibly a little vaguely expressed and the central target of 2.5 per cent may be regarded as somewhat higher than necessary. Further, an improvement in transparency could be sought through the provision of more detailed forecasts for macroeconomic and financial variables. The most notable recommendations are likely to pertain to governance and accountability structures. In particular, the decision-making structure involving a board of largely non-expert outsiders would be regarded as close to the worst available arrangement. In addition, as with the New Zealand recommendations, a non-executive Chair for the Board would be recommended, with the Board having a monitoring, rather than decision-making role. (2001: 319).

7. In the New Zealand context decisions relating to the tightening of monetary policy in March and April 2007 were justified in part by the stimulatory impact of fiscal policy. The Reserve Bank of New Zealand's March 2007 Monetary Policy Statement noted that Government spending had been rising in recent years, that increases in spending in recent years may have stimulated activity, and that fiscal policy was expected to remain stimulatory over the next two fiscal years.

8. This comment was interpreted by one observer as marking a significant degree of difference between European and US central banking (Dougherty 2008).

14

The US Federal Reserve and the Politics of Monetary and Financial Regulatory Policies

John T. Woolley[1]

As a model independent central bank in the world's economic superpower, the US Federal Reserve System (the Fed) has never been far in the background for planners of European monetary union and the European Central Bank (ECB). Since 1980, the Fed has seemed to consolidate a dominant position in US macroeconomic affairs. A consensus emerged that inflation, widely seen as the pre-eminent macroeconomic challenge, could be solved only through steady, but technically supple, politically independent monetary policy (Woolley 1998). While the Fed experienced occasional political challenges to its regulatory powers and public disclosure, these challenges did not extend to monetary policy.

However, if the Fed's power over its policy domain seemed secure, its power to shape economic outcomes has diminished since 1980. Financial innovation, which the Fed encouraged through regulatory policy, spread through growing global capital markets to make the Fed's macroeconomic job more complicated and less certain. The Fed has struggled to keep its balance in responding to asset bubbles and international financial crises. Despite the post-1980s' increased stability in inflation, unemployment, and growth, the year 2007 marked the onset of financial instabilities that clearly surprised Fed officials in their depth and disruptive potential.

This chapter examines major developments at the Fed in recent decades bracketed by the crises of late 1979 and late 2007. It focuses primarily on the conduct of monetary policy in that period of moderation—the strategies used and the outcomes achieved. However, in the wake of the turmoil in financial markets arising from innovations in mortgage finance, it also discusses the Fed's role in regulation of financial institutions. In late 2007, serious challenges emerged for the Fed, arising directly from the failure of financial markets and regulators to identify and contain financial risks. The Fed, together with the US Treasury and other agencies, responded aggressively and creatively to those events, fundamentally, perhaps temporarily, reshaping the US financial industry. Deep criticism seemed certain to yield major reforms of financial regulation. It seems unlikely that these reforms will call into question the Fed's fundamental autonomy and authority, but the circumstances pose political risks for the Fed unlike any since the 1970s.

The chapter focuses on influences on the central bank that have figured prominently in scholarly writing: the *structure of political institutions* and the place of the central bank among these institutions; the varying *distribution of interests and preferences* across these institutions; the development of *policy ideas* about the conduct of monetary policy; and the *changing problems* arising from the developing economic system. Because these influences often interact, they are to some degree interwoven in the analysis.

The central argument is that, in terms of the usual indicators of central bank independence, very little has changed about the Fed. In terms of pressure from other institutions and interests, the Fed's environment became more benign. The preferences that were arrayed within and outside the Fed in the 1980s created space in which the Fed was able to establish not just its own credible commitment to low inflation but also the political sustainability of this commitment. With respect to issues of disclosure and transparency, the Fed has been remarkably sensitive to its environment. The linked notions of transparency and inflation targeting have been welcomed at the Fed, but not officially embraced precisely because of the legal environment that commits the Fed to consider both output growth and inflation. The consolidation of European monetary union and rise of the ECB have clearly affected the Fed, but in relatively modest ways. By the end of 2007, however, the Fed was shocked by unanticipated financial crisis.

The dominant policy problem for central banks during this period was how to manage inflation—the risks of financial collapse seemed remote. In a useful and comprehensive essay, Blinder (2004) wrote that worldwide in the past 20 years there have been three developments in central bank behaviour so important as to justify calling them 'revolutionary': (1) increasing policy transparency; (2) increasing reliance on collective rather than individual decision-making; and (3) increasing reliance on financial market indicators to guide policy. Blinder's second point does not, of course, apply to the Fed, where collective decision-making has long been the rule. In other essays, Goodfriend (2003, 2005) argued that the most important developments in US monetary policy were in the realm of policy-makers' understanding of the constraints imposed by the working of the economy. The basic lesson of the early 1980s was that, in an economy of agents with forward-looking price expectations, the only stable inflation rate was a low rate, and that could only be achieved as a result of a credible long-term commitment. The most important development, Goodfriend argues, was the rise of inflation targeting, albeit implicit rather than explicit, as the core of the Fed's monetary policy strategy.

This chapter draws on data derived from the transcripts of 197 regular meetings of the Fed's key policy-making committee, the Federal Open Market Committee (FOMC), between 1978 and 2001. More details and technical information about these analyses can be found in Woolley (2007). Briefly, counts of keywords and phrases used in the FOMC meetings are used to create indexes that reveal trends in its focus of attention. The analysis uses the ratio of the number of transcript lines containing index keywords to the total number of lines in the file. Because some of the results discussed below indicate a pronounced trend over time, it is relevant to note that there is very little trend over time in the length of FOMC meetings as expressed in lines of text.

Recent Economic Trends and Monetary Policy Stance

A landmark shift in US monetary policy occurred in 1979, under the leadership of Paul Volcker. In dramatic fashion, the Fed announced that, in order to better contain inflation, it was shifting focus from controlling interest rates to controlling monetary aggregates. The year 1984 roughly marks the consolidation of this vigorous anti-inflation policy. Since the mid-1980s, on a wide variety of indicators, economic policy and economic outcomes in the United States have become more stable and have remained positive.

Figures 14.1–14.4 recapitulate some of the most important facts about the US economic context and the stance of monetary policy before and after 1983. The data in these figures begin in 1964 and extend through the most recent data available in early 2008. In the latter half of the time-period, all four graphs reveal a dramatic reduction in volatility, accompanied by average economic performance that is as good or better than before. The statistics showing the improved performance are summarized in Table 14.1.

Real GDP Growth. Figure 14.1 shows that, since 1984, there has been less volatility in real GDP growth rates, and recessions have been less frequent and less severe, although average growth has not changed.

Inflation. Figure 14.2 plots the so-called 'headline' inflation and 'core' inflation (net of inflation in food and energy) for the United States as measured by the Consumer Price Index.[2] It also displays the Euro Area inflation index (Harmonized Index of Consumer Prices) for 1990–2008. As with GDP, since the early 1980s there has been greater price stability. Core inflation has fluctuated around 2 per cent per year in recent years. Since 2000, Euro Area inflation has been less volatile than US 'headline' inflation.

Unemployment. Figure 14.3 plots the US unemployment rate. The unemployment rate also declined since the early 1980s and became more stable.

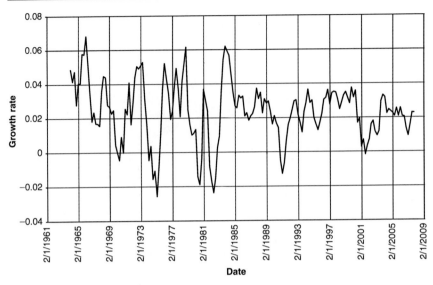

Figure 14.1. US real GDP growth over quater year prior, 1964–2007

Source: U.S. Department of Commerce, Bureau of Economic Analysis.

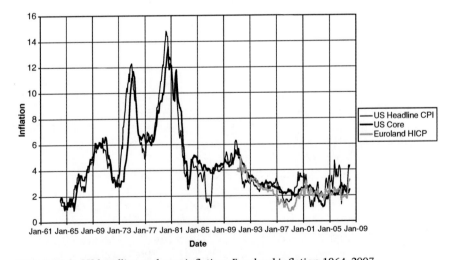

Figure 14.2. US headline and core inflation; Euroland inflation 1964–2007

Sources: CPI: US Department of Labor, Bureau of Labor Statistics. All Urban Consumers NSA, Chg over 12 months; CUUR0000SA0. HICP: European Central Bank, Overall Index, Annaual Rate of Change, ICP.M.U2.N.000000.4.ANR.

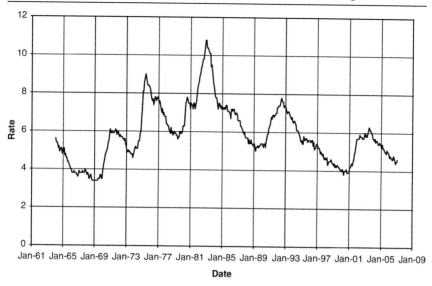

Figure 14.3. US unemployment rate, 1964–2006

Source: US Department of Labour, Bureau of Labour Statistics, Civilian Unemployment Rate Seasonally Adjusted.

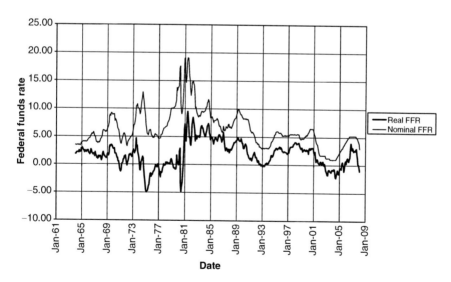

Figure 14.4. Nominal and real rederal funds rate January 1964–February 2008

Sources: Nominal Rates: US Board of Governors of the Federal Reserve System. Real Rates: Nominal rate minus the contemporaneous CPI, calculated by author.

Table 14.1. Greater US economic stability after 1983

	1964–83		1984–2003		Change	
	Mean	Standard deviation	Mean	Standard deviation	Mean	Standard deviation
Real GDP growth rate	0.024	0.023	0.024	0.013	0.000	−0.010
Headline inflation (CPI)	6.130	3.450	3.120	1.130	−3.010	−2.320
Unemployment	6.030	1.890	5.840	1.070	−0.190	−0.820
Nominal federal funds rate	7.640	3.710	5.670	2.350	−1.970	−1.360

Data Sources: GDP, US Department of Commerce, Bureau of Economic Analysis; CPI and Unemployment, US. Bureau of Labor, Department of Labor Statistics; Federal funds rate, US Board of Governors of the Federal Reserve System.

Federal Funds Rate. The Federal funds rate, or overnight interbank rate, has been the main monetary policy instrument in the United States. Figure 14.4 plots the monthly average nominal and real Federal funds rate (FFR) from 1964 to 2008. In general, the nominal rate has been more volatile than the real rate. Following a very volatile period in real and nominal rates in the period 1974–82, the FFR has become more stable. Since 1983, the real FFR has usually been between 2 and 5 per cent. However, the real FFR rate was *negative*, a very stimulative policy stance, in 1992–3 and again in 2003–4 (contrast especially the period from 1974 to 1980).

Altogether, these data show an economy that seemed to be functioning exceptionally well on the aggregate. Missing from these pictures, and from monetary policy discussions, was a sense that the financial economy was moving toward a period of crisis.

Federal Reserve Institutions and Policy Responsibilities

The Fed has three main components: the Board of Governors, the District Banks, and the Federal Open Market Committee (FOMC). Collectively, the System's legal authority stems from the Federal Reserve Act.[3] In 1978 the Act was amended in two critical ways. First, it required semi-annual Congressional testimony on the conduct of monetary policy, later regarded as a core element in Fed transparency. Second, it codified explicitly the Fed's obligation to pursue the goals of long-run growth and price stability.[4] This two-goal legislative mandate has been one important factor in the Fed's reluctance to embrace explicit inflation targeting, and is an important source of many contrasts between the Fed and the ECB.

Uniting all the components of the Fed is a large and exceptionally talented staff including scores of PhD economists. The intellectual power of the staff means that the Fed is at the forefront worldwide of discussion and analysis in relevant epistemic communities. However, interestingly, the Fed has frequently not been among the world's leading central banks when it comes to institutional innovation and policy leadership. The Fed has resisted almost every panacea or fad that has swept markets or academia, including Keynesianism, monetarism, commodity price targeting, the separation of monetary policy from financial institutions regulation, and inflation targeting. This resistance reflects an institutional culture of reluctance to interfere with markets and an inbred scepticism toward fads. It also reflects important preferences in the Fed's political environment, especially Congressional insistence on balancing the pursuit of growth and the fight against inflation.

The Board of Governors is a seven-member board, also called the Federal Reserve Board (FRB), located in Washington D.C. The members are appointed to 14-year terms (or portions of unexpired terms) by the US President, with the consent of the Senate. The Chair is appointed by the President, with the consent of the Senate, from among the members of the Board, to serve a four-year renewable term.[5] The Board is responsible for setting reserve requirements for member banks. It also sets the discount rate, that is, the rate at which the Fed lends directly to eligible financial institutions. The discount rate is changed upon the request of the Boards of Directors of Federal Reserve district banks. Policy innovations adopted in December 2007 to address the financial crisis (see more below) had the interesting characteristic of clearly placing the initiative for new policy directions in the FRB, not the FOMC.

The FRB also sets and implements regulation of a variety of financial institutions under authority granted by law. While demanding and time-consuming, Board members have considered these tasks to be far less engaging than monetary policy (cf. Meyer 2004: xvi). Regulations are referred to alphabetically— Regulation A through Regulation GG. Regulation A, for example, deals with borrowing at the discount window (i.e. 'extending credit to depository institutions and others').[6] Regulation C governs Home Mortgage Disclosure for some lenders. Regulation K covers the operation of foreign banks in the United States.

The Board's economic staff provide highly influential technical assistance to the Board and the Federal Open Market Committee. They prepare the crucially important monetary policy forecast. The Board's three main economic research divisions have some 450 staff, of whom about half are PhD economists.[7] Fed staff report to the chair (Meyer 2004: 26–7). By far the heaviest weight of staff resources resides with the Board rather than the district banks.

The 12 *Federal Reserve District Banks* are headed by Presidents, appointed by local boards of directors subject to approval by the Board of Governors of the Federal Reserve System. Five of the 12 Presidents participate each year as voting members of the FOMC. Among them is always the president of the Federal Reserve Bank of New York, who by convention is also always selected as Vice-Chairman of the FOMC. Voting seats rotate among the other Presidents, but all of them attend FOMC meetings and participate fully in deliberations. In some circumstances, not involving formal votes on policy, but in questions of procedure and public openness, the views of all Presidents are considered in seeking a consensus. The opportunity to participate in monetary policy deliberations is a major motivation for becoming a district bank president.

While initially the district banks were dominant in the Fed, by 1935 a series of reforms had shifted authority to the FRB. Over time, the district banks have come to be engaged primarily in commercial bank supervision and in the provision of financial infrastructure services—especially cheque clearing and currency distribution. In the total 2007 budget of the Fed, the district banks accounted for about 90 per cent of total expenditures. Of the total district bank budget expenditures, only about 12 per cent is classified as being involved in 'monetary and economic policy' (BGFRS 2007b: tables 1.2; E.3). Of the 19,828 employees at district banks in 2006, only 928 (or 5 per cent) were involved in monetary and economic policy. However, the district bank economic staff provide an alternative view of the economy to that taken by the Board staff, and this diversity of views is generally agreed to be a source of institutional strength. Historically, some of the district banks have been particularly hospitable to insurgent groups of economists, such as the monetarists. White's (2005) estimates suggest that about 270 economists are employed by the district banks. A disproportionate share is located at the Federal Reserve Bank of New York, with some 15–20 at each of the other banks (Goodfriend 2000: 14). Over 70 per cent of the articles on monetary policy published by US-based economists in US-edited journals appear in Fed-published journals or are co-authored by Fed economists (White 2005).

The district banks have no budgetary autonomy vis-à-vis the FRB. However, fee-based services delivered by the district banks generate revenues for the banks as a group that offset nearly half their budget expenditures. The balance of System revenues is generated from earnings on the assets that are held in the Open Market portfolio. These earnings *far* exceed the total expenses of the Federal Reserve System, and the balance is returned to the US Treasury. This financial autonomy is one key element in making the Fed independent of Congress.

The Federal Open Market Committee (FOMC) is the locus of decision-making in open market policy—setting the level of the Federal funds rate and, increasingly, interpreting that action for the benefit of outside observers. The FOMC meets regularly—now eight times per year—in Washington D.C. in the offices of the FRB. While there are only 12 voting members, there are many others in attendance, including non-voting Presidents, Board staff, and district bank staff. By convention, the Chair of the FRB is selected to be Chair of the FOMC. All observers concur that the Fed Chair is far and away the most influential member, as he controls the agenda and the staff (Woolley 1984). Her or his personal style looms large for most participants. Alan Greenspan, for example, was famous for opening the policy discussions in the FOMC by offering his analysis and stating a policy preference. On occasion, Greenspan would use that opportunity to explicitly ask for Committee support for his preferred policy.

Greenspan routinely led a lengthy discussion of monetary policy issues with the Board on Mondays prior to FOMC meetings. Meyer (2004: 51) suggests this contributed to the near absence of FOMC dissents by Board governors.

Financial Institutions Regulation and the Fed

Turmoil in financial markets starting in late 2007 highlighted the complex responsibilities of central banks for addressing financial instability and monetary policy. As lender of last resort, all central banks must balance the risks of bailing out irresponsibly risky private behaviour (moral hazard) and stabilizing the overall economic system. At the same time, events have raised the question of whether a well-informed lender of last resort has a duty to warn forcefully in advance against unsustainable or irresponsible behaviour—even if actual supervisory responsibility lies elsewhere. In retrospect, the optimism within the Fed about the benefits of financial innovation, emphatically shared by Greenspan, seems to have been far too great.[8]

Prior to 1980, the regulation of US financial institutions was sharply divided in terms both of geography and of function. For much of the twentieth century, there was a sharp distinction between commercial banks and other financial institutions. Additionally, banks were geographically restricted to conducting business in a single state. Regulation responded slowly to financial innovations in the 1970s. However, by 1994, legislation essentially allowed full interstate banking, and the Gramm-Leach-Bliley Act of 1999 eliminated the separation of banking from other areas of finance (GAO 2007).

US financial regulatory structure continues to be highly fragmented despite various efforts to create bridging institutions designed 'to foster communication, cooperation and coordination' such as the Federal Financial Institutions Examination Council (FFIEC 2006).[9] The Fed has regulatory responsibility for bank holding companies and for state-chartered banks that are 'member banks' of the Fed. State-chartered member banks hold only 10 per cent of the assets of US depository institutions (FFIEC 2006: 23).

However, the Fed's authority over bank holding companies makes it the lead for 'consolidated supervision' of their activities. As of the end of 2006, US bank holding companies controlled over 6,000 insured commercial banks, with about 96 per cent of all insured commercial bank assets in the United States (BGFRS 2007a: 66). Additionally, the Fed has regulatory authority over the US operations of foreign banking companies (BGFRS 2007a: 63 *ff*). Thus, in banking, the Fed's regulatory reach is extensive. Along with other regulators,[10] the Federal Reserve Board implements the internationally harmonized banking capital standards, Basel I and II[11] through regulations H and Y.

The Fed's continued involvement in banking supervision runs contrary to one idea popular among central bank reformers: separating financial institutions regulation and supervision almost completely from monetary policy. The views expressed in 1998 by Board member Lawrence Meyer continue to reflect views in the Fed: 'I cannot grasp how we could possibly understand what is happening in banking markets, what innovations are occurring and their implications, and the nature and quality of the risk exposures and controls so critical for crisis management and policy formulation without the hands-on practical exposure that comes from supervision' (Meyer 1998). This may explain the Fed's determined fighting to retain a regulatory role following the financial institutions reforms of 1999 (Greenspan 2007: 198–9). Additionally, Fed officials are aware of the potential political benefits of a close relationship with the banking industry, should challenges arise in Congress.

At the outset of the crisis in late 2007, the Fed did not regulate investment banks, brokers, and dealers in securities, futures traders, insurance companies, thrift institutions, or the government-sponsored secondary-mortgage lenders known as Freddie Mac and Fannie Mae.[12] Thus, its authority did not reach to the derivative contracts and other financial instruments that linked US sub-prime mortgage lending to a worldwide crisis. Most subprime[13] mortgage lending in the United States was by firms not supervised by *any* bank or thrift regulators (Gramlich 2007: 21). In 2005, only 20 per cent of subprime loans were made by banks or thrifts subject to careful regulatory scrutiny, while around 30 per cent more had some, but weaker, forms of supervision. Securitized subprime loans created yet another set of financial instruments substantially exempt from public-sector regulation. The securities were assigned risk ratings by private bond rating agencies, which badly misjudged their risk (Ip and Hilsenrath 2007; Lucchetti 2008).

Any concerns within the Fed about these new market instruments were largely hidden from public view prior to the market meltdown of late 2007. Excessive optimism must have played a part, for the Fed staff have been known for its belief in the generally beneficial effects of financial innovation (Greenspan 2007: 373–6). While Governor Gramlich spoke publicly on the issue of predatory mortgage lending as early as 2000, he did not address the risks involved in securitization. In Congressional testimony in April 2005, Greenspan warned against 'systemic risk' flowing from the implicit government guarantees extended to Fannie Mae and Freddie Mac.[14] As late as *June* 2007, Chairman Bernanke expressed considerable optimism:

> ... fundamental factors—including solid growth in incomes and relatively low mortgage rates—should ultimately support the demand for housing, and at this point, the troubles in the subprime sector seem unlikely to seriously spill over to the broader economy or the financial system. (Bernanke 2007*b*)

By the end of *August* 2007, however, the existence of a widespread crisis was clear, and Bernanke's tone became more cautious. He essentially said that 'nobody saw it coming'.

Although this episode appears to have been triggered largely by heightened concerns about subprime mortgages, global financial losses have far exceeded even the most pessimistic projections of credit losses on those loans.... [T]he difficulty of evaluating the risks of structured products that can be opaque or have complex payoffs has become more evident. (Bernanke 2007c)

Given that central banks' reputation for competence is a significant element in establishing their overall reputation as credible managers, there is great potential for damage to the Fed arising out of this profound crisis.

The Fed's Reaction to the Financial Crisis

Beginning in August 2007, the Fed adopted a sequence of novel and aggressive intervention strategies intended to address the collapse of markets for certain kinds of financial instruments.[15] When the crisis intensified in September 2008, these novel strategies were expanded further. The Fed's new measures had been studied years earlier by the staff as hypothetical responses to two potential threats: deflation and resulting zero nominal interest rates, or the sharp reduction in outstanding government debt possible with sustained budget surpluses.[16] These new strategies radically changed the Fed's balance sheet, which more than doubled in size and profoundly increased in risk.[17]

The Fed began in August 2007 by liberalizing the terms of access to the discount window. In December, the Fed defined new intervention 'facilities' that presented a way to address liquidity problems without generally lowering interest rates. The Term Auction Facility[18] (TAF, launched in December 2007) provided funds through the discount window; the Term Securities Lending Facility (TSLF, created in March 2008) lends treasury securities to primary dealers[19] in exchange for less liquid securities at rates determined through auctions. The Primary Dealer Credit Facility (PDCF, created in March 2008) lends through the discount window to Primary Dealers. At the same time, the Fed announced an aggressive programme of 'repurchase agreements' through the open market desk.[20]

By October 2008, near-collapse in credit markets brought another round of innovations. Some actions, by the Fed alone, were authorized under the 'unusual and exigent circumstances' clause of Federal Reserve Act Section 13(3) which had never been invoked.[21] These included the Asset Backed Commercial Paper Money Market Mutual Fund Liquidity Facility (AMLF, September 2008), Commercial Paper Funding Facility (CPFF, October 2008), and the Money Market Investor Funding Facility (MMIFF, October 2008). The Fed began purchasing obligations of Fannie Mae and Freddie Mac. The remaining investment banks, Goldman Sachs and Morgan Stanley, were declared to be 'bank holding companies', bringing them under the direct regulatory supervision of the Fed. The Fed began paying interest on required reserves for the first time.

Perhaps most stunning, the Fed and Treasury cooperated in promoting what was widely called 'the bailout bill' to create a $700 billion fund to be used to buy government equity positions in financial institutions (and indeed, any firm).[22] This abrupt reversal of prior free-market rhetoric seemed to have the perverse effect of telling investors that conditions were far worse than they had previously thought. Stock markets swooned worldwide and US consumer confidence hit a record low. Credit markets did show signs of recovery, as spreads between government and interbank borrowing rates began to narrow.

At the technical level, the Fed's new strategies were similar to intervention techniques widely used in Europe. Through loans, swaps, and outright purchases, these programmes replaced billions of dollars of illiquid financial assets with high-quality treasury securities, all in an effort to keep financial markets functioning.[23]

Repeatedly during the crisis, actions were undertaken in close coordination with the G-10 central banks. On numerous occasions central banks simultaneously undertook parallel interventions to address liquidity issues.[24] Extraordinary swap lines were created with the ECB, BOE, and SNB; and later expanded and extended.[25] There were additional coordinated interventions conducted by G-10 central banks.[26]

Critics were justified in calling the undertaking a bailout of financial markets, but it was incorrect to suggest there were no costs for the financial institutions and thus that moral hazard was unquestionably being encouraged.[27] Politically, however, the perception was widespread in the United States that the central bank was bailing out Wall Street, while ordinary citizens were losing their homes. The future strengthening of financial regulation in the United States looks quite certain.

Transparency

Public disclosure and communication have come to be seen as powerful monetary policy instruments, distinct from decisions about the interest rate. Beginning in the mid-1960s, the Fed has taken many steps to release more complete records more quickly. Today, the Fed is one of the most open central banks in the world, especially with respect to the historical record of the FOMC.

Until May 1999, all these moves, including the decision to release verbatim transcripts of FOMC meetings, were taken defensively in response to pressure coming from Congress or the courts. The Fed acted reluctantly to forestall demands for even greater openness, seeking to preserve the integrity of the FOMC deliberative process. To deal with the Freedom of Information Act, the Fed began in 1967 to release the 'Record of Policy Actions' only about 90 days after the each FOMC meeting rather than annually. In response to adverse Court decisions relating to the Freedom of Information Act and the pending passage of the Government in the Sunshine Act, the FOMC in 1976 expanded the Record of Policy Actions and discontinued keeping a semi-verbatim record that had previously been released with a five-year lag.

In 1992, the House Banking Committee began to request information from the FOMC about meeting records. The inquiry was preparatory to introduction of legislation to require the creation and preservation of audio–visual and textual records of FOMC meetings. Tense exchanges continued for months as House Committee Chair Henry Gonzalez pressed for the creation and immediate release of FOMC transcripts. Greenspan revealed in October 1993, to the surprise of just about everyone, the existence of unedited FOMC transcripts dating back to 1976.

In these circumstances, the Clinton Administration Justice Department issued new guidance to agencies about implementation of the Freedom of Information Act. The Administration indicated it would only defend agencies in court if the information requested would threaten their core functions. In light of prior court decisions, it seemed unlikely that the Fed could prevail in asserting that claim with respect to the vast bulk of FOMC transcript records.[28]

In 1994, the FOMC decided to release the existing transcripts with a five-year lag, and to release expanded records of committee action—henceforth called 'The Minutes'. Also in 1994 the committee began what later became a regular practice—announcing publicly when policy had been changed.[29] In 1995, having concluded that politically there was no viable alternative, the FOMC agreed to continue creating verbatim meeting transcripts and to release them with a five-year lag. The Committee also agreed to continue the 'prompt announcement' of policy changes—which was judged to have been a success. In these actions as well, the threat of Congressional legislation loomed in the background.[30]

Starting in May 1999, the Committee released statements after every meeting, even if there were no change in policy. These statements included what was referred to as 'the tilt', which seemed to indicate the likely next move of policy. Markets were uncertain how to interpret this new information, and subsequent discussion revealed that FOMC members themselves disagreed about the message they were trying to convey. In January 2000 the Committee decided to try to clarify its intent by referring to the 'balance of risks'—to indicate what kinds of adverse developments in the economy seemed most likely. In March 2002 the Committee began releasing information about member votes as part of the immediate post-meeting press release (rather than only later with the more complete policy record). Beginning with 2005 the committee accelerated the release of the policy record ('The Minutes') and began to report forecasts for two years ahead rather than just one. As of late 2007, the FOMC announced a plan to release forecasts more often, to extend their forecasting horizon to three years, and to include inflation projections (Bernanke 2007*d*). These changes from 1998 forward have primarily reflected the desire of FOMC members to increase the efficiency of policy—an idea that gained momentum due to turnover in the FOMC membership.

The Fed's Institutional Power and Independence

Central bank independence is commonly cited to 'prove' the policy importance of institutional structure. In recent years, measures of central bank independence have been incorporated in vast numbers of cross-national and time-series studies (Bernhard 1998; Cukierman 1992; Franzese 2002). Studies have frequently found that increasing central bank independence is associated with reduced inflation.

By all measures, the Fed is a very independent central bank, but since 1978 these indexes show no variation in the Fed's formal institutional status. Blinder (2004) observed that since 1989 more than two dozen countries have increased the degree of central bank independence, while none have moved in the other direction. In contemporary advanced industrial countries it is taken for granted that central banks are independent, so that institutional status no longer can account for variation among central banks in their policy behaviour. Thus, in a cross-national study, Cecchetti, Flores-Lagunes, and Krause (2005) conclude that decreased GDP volatility is not robustly correlated with central bank independence. In short, institutional change at the Fed *cannot* help us understand the changes in US monetary policy since 1979.[31]

Relations with Other Political Institutions and the Media

Two factors shape the Fed's relationships with other political institutions and with the media. First, when conservative (i.e. Republican) politicians control any one of the House, Senate or Presidency, they are in a position to veto any legislative initiatives hostile to the Fed (Krehbiel 1998; Morris 2000). Second, when the economy is doing well, the Fed's political environment has been benign, no matter what the distribution of partisan preferences.

Since the Carter administration (1977–80), Democrats have had unified control of Congress and the Presidency for only two years, 1993–4. That is, Republicans controlled at least one veto point at all other times. Although the Reagan Presidency (1981–8) saw ample tension between the administration and the Fed (Greider 1987; Woodward 2001), the relatively supportive political context provided the political cover that the Fed needed in order to establish the notion that a credible low-inflation policy could yield acceptable rates of employment and economic growth.

Congress

One relevant indicator of Congressional interest is the proportion of all hearings in both House and Senate dealing with monetary policy, inflation, prices, interest rates, and price controls.[32] Consistent with the notion that a good economy yields benign monetary politics, hearings peaked in the tumultuous years of 1979–81, followed by a period of relative stability. There was no upsurge in Congressional hearings in the Democratic-dominated 1993–4 period, even though interest rates increased substantially.

The FOMC transcript data provide a fine-grained look at the Fed's reaction to its environment. One naïve expectation would be that, as an independent central bank, the FOMC would conduct its policy essentially without reference to Congress or the President. That would, of course, be quite incorrect.

The transcript data confirm that extensive Congressional hearings arouse substantial attention inside the Fed. In 1992–3 the demands of a single committee chair with respect to information, discussed above, provoked lengthy FOMC discussion. In 1995–6, after Democrats lost control of Congress, Republican Senator Connie Mack introduced legislation to repeal the Humphrey-Hawkins Act and to assign the Fed a single goal of price stability.[33]

While FOMC members favoured Senator Mack's bills, they debated whether their benefits were worth the risk that the ultimate legislative product might be worse than the status quo. The legislation was never even referred out of committee, illustrating nicely the difference between the power to initiate and the power to veto. But it did provoke an interesting discussion inside the FOMC about the virtues of inflation targeting and about the appropriateness of explicitly emphasizing a single target despite a legislative mandate to pursue multiple objectives (more below).

Another glimpse of Fed/Congress relations can be gained from the Congressional testimony by Fed officials between 1996 and 2007.[34] Of the 239 instances of testimony during that period, *none* involved legislation to reform the Fed's budget, transparency, appointments procedures, monetary targets, etc. Including routine and recurring policy testimony, only about 20 per cent of all Fed testimony dealt with monetary policy. The rest addressed financial regulation, fiscal policy, and international financial developments—apparently with more prescience than was evident at the Fed.

The Administration

Classic studies of the politics of macroeconomic policy in the United States have been based around two assumptions. First, Presidents dominate macroeconomic policy. Second, Democrats seek to reduce unemployment, while Republicans try to reduce inflation (Bartels and Brady 2003; Hibbs 1977). There are many accounts from studies of US monetary policy of Presidents and their advisors trying to influence monetary policy, usually in an expansionary direction, and commonly as a presidential election approaches (Woodward 2001).

The FOMC transcripts show that the Administration and fiscal policy get regular attention from the FOMC, more so than Congress, with more frequent, sharper upswings (Woolley 2007). This record belies any notion that the Fed's inflation responsibilities, independence, and power enable it to be indifferent to fiscal policy. Increases in FOMC attention to the Administration are linked to major new budget and taxing initiatives generated from the White House. For example, in 2001, FOMC members devoted a lot of time to discussing Bush administration fiscal policy and its likely effects on the economy.

The Media

Increased media attention to policy problems and institutions often presages policy innovation (Baumgartner and Jones 1993). The pattern of attention to the Fed and monetary policy by major US newspapers since 1978 has essentially followed the path of inflation—trending steadily downward. A combined count of articles reporting on monetary policy by three leading newspapers, *Wall Street Journal*, *Washington Post*, and *New York Times*, from 1977 to 2006 reveals a steady decline during the period (Woolley 2007). From a journalistic perspective, monetary policy became less interesting and less newsworthy.

In summary, in recent years the political environment of the Federal Reserve has been very benign. It is a near-certainty that this flows from macroeconomic performance that has been good *and* steady. With the financial crisis and economic slowdown of early 2008, joined with the context of a Presidential election year, Congressional and media attention has increased dramatically as one would expect.

Policy Problems and How They were Understood

The heart of discourse inside the FOMC has to do with the conduct of monetary policy in response to inflation and economic output. This is where the policy action really is, and it is where we would expect to see considerable change during this period, given accounts by informed 'insider' observers like Blinder and Goodfriend. The results from the FOMC transcripts confirm that important changes occurred. Over time, there was less focus on the details of the implementation of policy—interest rates, money supply targeting, etc.—and more on understanding and steering the primary targets—inflation and growth of output.

Inflation and Inflation Targeting

Many observers have suggested that the Fed is institutionally obsessed with inflation. Recall that one often-repeated characterization of Fed behaviour is that since 1994 it has engaged in 'implicit' inflation targeting.

My examination of the FOMC transcripts clearly confirms the FOMC's increasingly intense focus on inflation. Since 1978, as inflation rates have

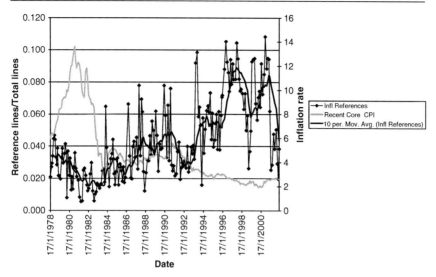

Figure 14.5. References to inflation, FOMC meetings
Source: Author's calculations, see Woolley (2007).

declined and stabilized, the proportion of meeting time devoted to inflation has at least doubled (see Figure 14.5). In the initial period from mid-1978 through mid-1983, attention to inflation declined roughly as the observed core rate of inflation declined. However, the increasing core rate from 1984 to 1990, while modest by standards of prior history, was accompanied by large increases in FOMC concern. In this period, the FOMC was determined to demonstrate the credibility of its own commitment to stable, low inflation. From then on, the Fed's rhetorical responses to inflation became, by historical standards, hypersensitive. This may be expected in an institution intent on building a credible commitment to maintaining low rates of inflation.

As early as 1978, the FOMC discussed a proposal from district bank presidents to set long-term targets for the monetary aggregates as a way of trying to influence long-run expectations about inflation, especially on the part of people engaged in contract negotiations throughout the economy (FOMCT, 18 April 1978). Objections were based on the fear that their instruments were insufficient to assure that they could hit the target—and the result for Fed credibility would be worse.

Nearly a decade later, another district bank president argued explicitly for inflation targets (FOMCT, 15 December 1986). He argued that, given the problems with relying on the monetary aggregates as guides to policy, announcing long-run targets for inflation would be an effective way of communicating more clearly with the public. However, despite some expressions of interest, the topic was dropped with little extended discussion.

A few members continued to raise the issue from time to time. Partly in response, in February 1995, at a time when related legislation had been introduced in Congress, Chairman Greenspan organized an FOMC discussion on the topic, with 'pro' and 'con' statements from members in order to be able to define a Fed position on anticipated Congressional legislation on inflation targets. The debate in the FOMC was framed as one between considering a single goal as opposed to multiple goals. Again, the argument was made that setting such a target would not be credible and, thus, would undermine Fed reputation. Doubts were expressed that the Bundesbank had, *in practice*, either a single overarching price stability objective or that its alleged credibility actually bought it much of a reduced cost of fighting inflation. Greenspan concluded the discussion by observing:

We now understand why this Committee has had difficulty confronting this issue. It is because we are as split down the middle as we could possibly get.... My own impression is that even if we now locked into law a fixed inflation rate—say, 2 per cent or 1 per cent— and the Congress voted for it with a large majority, in the first recession everyone would be arguing to go in a different direction.... You may recall that a couple of years ago, we all basically said we were going to have to move early on the up side or we would not achieve anything resembling price stability. Now, I submit to you that is exactly what we did.... But that objective is not being implemented in a straight line because we have recognized, and I think correctly, that the Congress would not give us a mandate to do that.... We [sh]ould always be moving in the direction of price stability, recognizing that we would not do so in a straight line because I do not think we have the philosophical, cultural, or political support in this society for that.   (FOMCT, 1 February 1995: 58)

The committee returned to the issue again in late 1999 and in 2000. In June 2000, Greenspan again ended the discussion by arguing that the claims for the benefits of inflation targeting were empirically dubious and the practice politically risky. 'It is too soon', he stated, 'to make a judgment as to whether official inflation targeting actually works' (FOMCT, 27 June 2000: 84). Moreover, Greenspan observed that attempting to get agreement within the FOMC to pursue a specific price level, without regard to the cost of getting there, would be too divisive.

With the appointment of Ben Bernanke as Chair in February 2006, the Fed, for the first time, was headed by someone whose reputation was almost exclusively as an academic.[35] All Fed Chairs starting with William McChesney Martin (1951–70; Burns 1970–8; Miller 1978–9; Volcker 1979–87; Greenspan 1987–2006) had been distinguished by their pragmatic, eclectic approach to the conduct of policy. They emphatically were not partisans for any panaceas popular in academia. Bernanke, by contrast, was known as an advocate of inflation targeting long before entering public life (e.g. Bernanke and Mishkin 1997). In September 2006, Bernanke was joined on the Board by Frederic Mishkin, a long-time academic collaborator and inflation targeting advocate.[36] It seems likely that there was an understanding involved in Bush's appointing in quick succession long-time Fed staff 'baron' and Greenspan advisor

Donald Kohn as Fed Vice-Chair in May 2006, followed a few weeks later by the appointment of Mishkin as governor.[37] Kohn was known to financial markets and was understood to be a critic of inflation targeting. In May 2006, Bernanke appointed Kohn to head a committee to study how the Fed communicates with financial markets. Its work eventually generated a consensus in favour of announcing longer-term forecasts, similar to practice at the ECB and the Bank of England.[38]

Output and Employment

The flip side of the stereotype of the Fed as obsessed with inflation is that it is relatively indifferent to output and the real economy. Some would assert that the world of money is a world of nominal events, and there is no enduring way to stimulate the real economy through the use of monetary policy. Thus central bank discussions of output are pointless. Based on the FOMC transcripts, this kind of stereotype is not only badly wrong, but it became increasingly wrong as the post-Volcker era evolved. Substantial and increasing FOMC discussion focused on questions of output and growth (see Figure 14.6). Discussion of output appears to get only about half the volume of attention given to inflation. Nevertheless, as FOMC discourse has become increasingly focused on inflation, the proportionate emphasis on output has been maintained.

Europe and Globalization

Neither Blinder (2004) nor Goodfriend (2005) discusses globalization and increasing financial integration as issues for monetary policy. Several high officials at the Fed have recently written or spoken about the implications of globalization for monetary policy, including Chair Bernanke (2007a), Board Vice-Chair Kohn (2005), and Board member Mishkin (2007b). All agree that globalization is not, thus far, a big deal for US monetary policy. Globalization of financial markets 'has not materially reduced the ability of the Federal Reserve to influence financial conditions in the United States' (Bernanke 2007a: 4). However, it has made financial conditions more complex. Additionally, the impact of globalization on the US inflation rate is mixed, and 'there seems to be little basis for concluding that globalization overall has significantly reduced inflation in the United States' (Kohn 2005: 6). Moreover in recent years, inflows of capital from abroad have probably helped reduce the interest rate for long-term debt—complicating the ability of policy-makers to draw information about inflation expectations from the yield curve.

In the FOMC transcripts, international matters are a focus of attention second only to inflation. Drivers include large shifts in the exchange rate and, especially prominent at the end of the data series, international financial crises. The transcripts are also interesting with respect to American perceptions of an

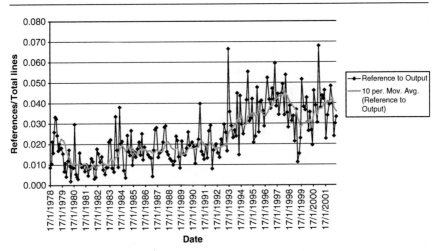

Figure 14.6. References to output and [un]employment, FOMC meetings

Source: Author's calculations, see Woolley (2007).

emerging Europe, both in the details of specific comments and in the broad trends in discourse in the FOMC.

The FOMC received staff briefings from time to time that mentioned the Maastricht process and progress toward European monetary union, but Maastricht was hardly a big issue in its discussions. The first references one can find from FOMC members (as opposed to staff) reveal a plainly sceptical tone—dubious about the politics of monetary union; dubious about the political will required to meet the criteria specified for monetary union; and uncertain about where the project was really going. In 1994 members discussed the implications of the creation of the European Monetary Institute for the Bank for International Settlements. Would the BIS 'be effectively neutered'?[39] Would the problem of meeting the Maastricht convergence criteria provoke an economic slowdown in Europe?[40] In 1995, the FOMC heard that moves toward European monetary union were a source of uncertainty, and would lead to increased market volatility.[41]

In 1996, the FOMC was briefed that France and Germany will likely lead 'a small band' into full economic and monetary union.[42] Again in 1996, doubts were expressed that the future ECB and the euro could match the standard of value achieved by the D-Mark. Therefore there was a need for the FOMC to think clearly about 'what kinds of arrangements we will want to have with that central bank.'[43] Also in 1996, participants asked whether the French were fiddling the Maastricht criteria and whether this will get the blessing of the European Commission.[44]

Doubts begin to recede in 1997, when the FOMC was advised that European monetary union was likely to begin on schedule with 11 participants, but the fiscal criteria in the Maastricht Treaty would be 'missed or fudged' by most.[45] In mid-1998, they were told 'jitters' about the introduction of the euro were 'out of the way', and there was a risk that the US dollar would decline against European currencies.[46] In September 1998, the FOMC was briefed on technical issues concerning the exchange of D-Mark-denominated assets for euro-denominated assets. In December 1998, it was noted that the Fed and the ECB are likely to maintain official interest rates for the early months of 1999, which should provide 'a very good background for a successful introduction of the euro'.[47] It was noted in February 1999: 'The weekend conversion to the euro went quite smoothly. . . .'[48] In August 1999, the FOMC were reminded, unfavourably, of the strong market response to statements made by ECB president Duisenberg.[49]

The discussions inside the FOMC about Europe, as revealed by systematic keyword searches, have two important characteristics: First, in the period 1978–82, over half the references to institutions or actions located in the European continent (including the UK) referred to a specific country, central bank, or currency. As is illustrated in Figure 14.7, from August 1998 forward, in a striking change, 80 per cent of those references were exclusively to 'European' institutions.[50] Europe became a reality for the FOMC.

Second, the frequency of FOMC references to institutions or events located in the European continent increased continuously from 1992 to the end of 2001. In short, not only did FOMC participants substitute 'euro-talk' for discussions

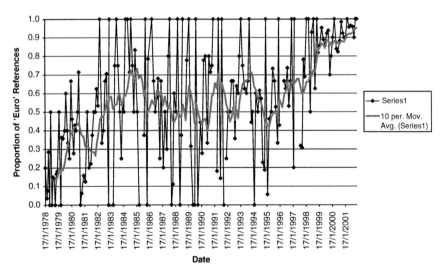

Figure 14.7. 'Euro' references (EMS, EMU, ECB, Euro) as share of FOMC references to European countries and institutions (e.g. Bundersbank, Bank of France, Germany, France)

Source: Author's calculations, see Woolley (2007).

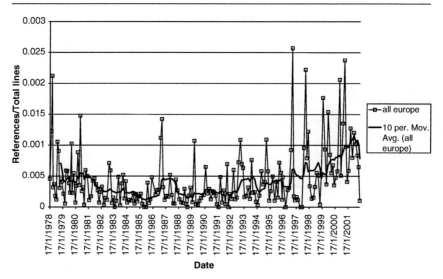

Figure 14.8. All references to european currencies, central banks, or countries, FOMC meetings 1978–2001

Source: Author's calculations, see Woolley (2007).

of individual European countries, but also the prominence of Europe in FOMC discourse shot upward (Figure 14.8).

Conclusions

US economic performance in the period from 1979 to 2007 was quite good— economic growth remained strong and was less volatile; inflation dropped and became more steady; unemployment fell and also became more steady. In part, the 'good news' for policy-makers reflected little more than good luck. In part, it reflected conscious choices and adjustments that policy-makers made. Both the luck and the choices were conditioned by political alignments that facilitated good (or poor) choices. Mainstream analysts, however, failed to anticipate the growing risks that convulsed the economy in 2008.

The Fed's control over the key monetary policy instrument, the Federal funds rate, was never seriously criticized, much less contested. In short, the Fed's power over its monetary policy instruments has hardly been greater. While economic performance, as measured by outcomes, was quite good, a close observer will see that the Fed has been surprised repeatedly by developments in capital markets and foreign-exchange markets. Despite a determination to be ahead of the game in fighting inflation, policy-makers have nonetheless been reactive, and that is certainly true with respect to their Congressional audience.

There were dramatic changes in the way policy was discussed and conceptualized inside the FOMC. Monetarism and monetary targeting bloomed and faded. Discussion of indicators of real output increased dramatically. Attention to inflation soared, despite objective evidence that inflation was well under control. Europe became a reality for the FOMC and of increasing importance.

While Europeanization mattered at the Fed, the Fed did not look to Europe or the ECB for inspiration or guidance at a technical level. Nonetheless, many within the Fed have followed with great interest the ECB's engagement with inflation targeting and the different approaches to transparency at the ECB, Bank of England, and elsewhere. These projects are viewed with great sympathy at the Fed, but, as reflected by the statement of Alan Greenspan quoted above, the Fed has been sceptical about inflation targeting on empirical grounds and cautious given the US legal context. The clear misgivings about US policy from the European side have had to do with the fear that the Fed is mistakenly unleashing a round of inflation.

The crisis of 2007–8 showed that the world's leading central banks shared quite similar understandings of their context, and similar optimism about the pricing of risk in financial markets. Central banks responded in coordination using very similar techniques. It is hard to imagine more compelling evidence of 'convergence' than what is offered in these events. This convergence is driven by the profound globalization of finance, which spread primarily US-originated securitized mortgages to financial institutions worldwide. The Fed is at the heart of this process, but it is not clear as of today, that the Fed weighs very heavily the impacts its policies create outside the United States.

The crisis also illustrated clearly that Fed's unilateral power of action in cleaning up after financial crises is not in question—although in sorting through the wreckage after the still-unfolding crisis is over, conditions may change. The challenge for coming years will be for private markets, central banks, and financial regulators across the world to devise means to expose and control financial risks. The magnitude of the crisis, despite the Fed's rescue efforts, assures that the United States will see a searching examination of financial regulation.

Notes

1. I appreciate the helpful comments on previous drafts from the editors, Michael Moran, Randall Henning, Benjamin Cohen, and Robert Franzese. The work benefited from the research assistance of Andrea Haupt and David Weaver.
2. In recent years the Federal Reserve has regarded the deflator of Personal Consumption Expenditures (PCE) as a more accurate measure of inflation. The CPI and PCE are highly correlated.
3. US Code Title 12, Chapter 3.

4. The Full Employment and Balanced Growth Act of 1978, also known as the Humphrey Hawkins Act, revised the Employment Act of 1946. The 1946 Act had stated that the government's goals, and only by implication the Fed's, were 'to promote maximum employment, production and purchasing power'.

5. For many years, the term of the chairman happened to be renewable during a presidential election year. However, starting with Bernanke, the terms are aligned to the middle of the Presidential term.

6. The regulations are codified in the *Code of Federal Regulations* (CFR) title 12, Banks and Banking and include parts 201 through 233. The CFR is officially updated yearly, and is now available online: http://www.access.gpo.gov/nara/cfr/cfr-table-search.html#page1.

7. Division of Research and Statistics, the Division of Monetary Affairs, and the Division of International Finance. Other divisions also employ PhD economists. http://www.federalreserve.gov/research/default.htm.

8. In October 2008, Greenspan admitted in Congressional testimony that he had mistakenly presumed that the self-interest of banks and other financial institutions would be sufficient to protect shareholders. See Kara Scannell and Sudeep Reddy, 'Greenspan Admits Errors to Hostile House Panel', *Wall Street Journal*, 24 October 2008. [http://online.wsj.com/article/SB122476545437862295.html.]

9. The FFIEC, created in 1978 by the Financial Institutions Regulatory and Interest Rate Control Act, is intended to create common standards for financial institutions examinations among the Federal Reserve System, the Federal Deposit Insurance Corporation, the National Credit Union Administration, the Office of the Comptroller of the Currency, and the Office of Thrift Supervision.

10. Office of the Comptroller of the Currency, the Federal Deposit Insurance Corporation, and the Office of Thrift Supervision.

11. The Basel Committee on Banking Supervision (previously the Standing Committee on Banking Regulation and Supervisory Practices) was launched in 1975 by G-10 central banks at the Bank for International Settlements (BIS) in Basel. Now, the Committee includes representatives from Belgium, Canada, France, Germany, Italy, Japan, Luxembourg, the Netherlands, Spain, Sweden, Switzerland, the United Kingdom, and the United States. Countries are represented by their central bank and/or also by other authorit(ies) with formal responsibility for the prudential supervision of banking. The United States and UK have been driving forces in the Basel process (Calomiris and Litan 2000); http://www.bis.org/bcbs/index.htm.

12. Freddie Mac: Created in 1970 as Federal Home Loan Mortgage Corporation; Fannie Mae: Created in 1938 as Federal National Mortgage Association; 1989 legislation severed Fannie Mae's supervision by the Federal Home Loan Bank Board.

13. 'Subprime' is not precisely defined. Generally, subprime mortgages have adjustable rates following a fixed low rate for the first two years. The adjustable period is typically 28 years—the so-called 2/28 mortgage. The down payment may be zero. Borrower income may not be documented fully or at all. By contrast 'prime' mortgages involve a substantial down payment of 10 to 20 per cent of the home price, no low introductory rate, and careful documentation of borrower income.

14. *'Regulatory reform of the government-sponsored enterprises'* Before the Committee on Banking, Housing, and Urban Affairs, US Senate 6 April 2005, http://www. federalreserve.gov/boarddocs/testimony/2005/20050406/default.htm.
15. In Fed-speak, 'pressures emerged abruptly' in August, reflected in 'the elevated level of unsecured term interbank rates'. The spread between the US Overnight Index Swap rate and the Libor rates increased dramatically in mid-August. See Federal Reserve Bank of New York (2008).
16. See especially Ahearne et al. (2002) and Federal Reserve System (2002), Small and Clouse (2004) for historical studies. Gaithner (2008) usefully summarizes the new actions. Also see Federal Reserve Bank of New York (2008), and 'Forms of Federal Reserve Lending to Financial Institutions', http://www.newyorkfed.org/markets/ Forms_of_Fed_Lending.pdf.
17. These data are reported weekly in what is called the H.4.1 release: http://www. federalreserve.gov/releases/h41/. From October 2007 to October 2008, various forms of direct lending to financial institutions and others increased by over $500 billion. A programme of securities lending to dealers grew by over $250 billion. 'Other' lending, which by May 2008 was about $30 billion, most maturing within 15 days, by October became over $400 billion, with nearly a quarter maturing in over 90 days.
18. The TAF opened with auctions of $20 billion for 28 days, and was increased in October 2008 to auctions of $150 billion for 85 days. The minimum bid rate was set to equal the expected future FFR, thus initially it was at least 25 basis points lower than conventional discount window lending.
19. Primary Dealers are investment banks, not the commercial banks regulated by the Federal Reserve.
20. 'Operating Policy Statement', Federal Reserve Bank of New York, 7 March 2008, http://www.newyorkfed.org/markets/operating_policy_030708.html.
21. According to section 13(3), dating from 1932, the Fed is authorized to make loans to 'any individual, partnership, or corporation' in 'unusual and exigent circumstances', if 'adequate credit accommodations' cannot be secured from other banking institutions.
22. The Emergency Economic Stabilization Act of 2008 (HR 1424); PL 110-343. Passed on 3 October 2008. Preliminary outlines of the plan were made public only around September 19.
23. By April 2008, the Fed had replaced nearly half of the risk-free Treasury securities in its portfolio (i.e. over $300 billion of securities) with risk-bearing securities; an unsustainable trend. Source: Author's calculation from the Federal Reserve's H.4.1 Statistical Release.
24. These 'repo' transactions provide temporary liquidity. The announcement of the Bank of Canada is here: http://www.bank-banque-canada.ca/en/notices_fmd/2008/ not110308.html.
25. From March 2008: http://www.federalreserve.gov/newsevents/press/monetary/ 2008-0311a. htm; from October 2008: http://www.federalreserve.gov/newsevents/ press/monetary/20081013a.htm.
26. For example: http://www.bankofengland.co.uk/publications/news/2008/017.htm; http: // www.federalreserve.gov/newsevents/press/monetary/20080926a.htm.

27. From their peak values in 2007, NYSE financial stocks had fallen some 45% by November 2008. Lehman Brothers stock went from $65 + to $0 in seven months. Bear-Stearns stockholders lost something like 90% of the value of their investments in a matter of days. Banks took losses estimated at over $200 billion (Bloomberg 29 March 2008). Collateral for loans and advances through the Fed's discount window for non-government securities without current market prices have been valued at 70 to 85 of par, which is a substantial allowance for risk by the Fed. See http://www.frbdiscountwindow.org/discountmargins.cfm?hdrID=21&dtlID=83.

28. Especially the rulings in Merrill v. FOMC 585 F 2d 778 (1977) The 'domestic policy directive', the instructions to the Open Market Desk were distinguished from the transcripts and accorded greater confidentiality by the Supreme Court. FOMC v. Merrill 443 US 340. Department of Justice statement may be found here: http://www.usdoj.gov/oip/foia_updates/Vol_XV_2/page3.htm.

29. The 1994 move to a tighter policy stance came after a long period of stable policy and was the first tightening action in nearly five years.

30. Greenspan, FOMCT, 31 January 1995, p. 21: 'It is my impression that House Banking Committee Chairman Leach has been holding off on any legislative initiatives in this area on the grounds that we are going to do it ourselves ... if we don't set our own policy, there will be real interest in that committee in trying to do something.'

31. We might not expect to find policy-makers in truly independent institutions regularly pondering their independent status. In 1981, arguing for immediate public release of the policy directive, Governor Henry Wallich suggested that his colleagues should 'look at what other central banks do'. The Bundesbank, he observed, calls a press conference every time they take action and explain what they are doing. 'How could that be?' responded another Governor. Wallich answered, 'Well, I guess they are an independent central bank' FOMCT, 2 February 1981.

32. These data are at: http://www.policyagendas.org/datatools/toolbox/analysis.asp.

33. Mack's legislation was known as the 'Economic Growth and Price Stability Act'. In 104 it was S1266/HR2445; in 105 it was S611/HR 1396; in 106 it was S1492.

34. This testimony is archived on the FRB website.

35. Bernanke joined the Board as a Governor in 2002, then resigned in 2005 to become Chairman of the Council of Economic Advisors. Arthur Burns had much more public involvement.

36. Mishkin was research director at the Federal Reserve Bank NY from 1994 to 1997.

37. Mishkin and Kohn were both under consideration as possible appointees as Vice-Chairman (Ip 2006).

38. Bernanke's appointment followed a precedent of assigning similar tasks to the FRB Vice-Chairmen including Roger Ferguson, Alan Blinder, and David Mullins.

39. Greenspan, FOMCT, 20 July 1994 conference call.

40. Governor Lindsey, FOMCT, 6 July 1995.

41. Staff advisor Truman, 26 September 1995.

42. Staff advisor Truman, 21 May 1996.

43. President Jordan, 2 July 1996.

44. Colloquy between Governor Lindsey and Staff advisors Truman and Fisher, 24 September 1996. Truman opined, 'The question, Governor Lindsey, is whether we are talking about high politics or grass root politics and that is another source of

uncertainty. The high politics may bring it about. The question is whether the grass
root politics will follow the high politics.'
45. Staff advisor Truman, 2 July 1997.
46. Staff advisor Hooper, 30 June 1998.
47. FOMC Vice-Chair McDonough, 22 December 1998.
48. Staff advisor Fisher, 2 February 1999.
49. Staff advisor Fisher.
50. That is, EMU, EMS, ECB, or any word or phrase with 'euro' in it.

Part VI

Convergence and Divergence

15

Financial Supervision: Internationalization, Europeanization, and Power

*Michael Moran and Huw Macartney**

Three Faces of Convergence/Divergence

Understanding central banking in the European Union since the introduction of the euro turns critically on one question that is central to this volume: how far has the experience of monetary union been accompanied by convergence? It also raises a further vital political question: what is all this doing to the way power is wielded in central banking? Our opening question immediately brings us to others: how far convergence, if it is occurring, is traceable to the introduction of monetary union; how far, if it is occurring, it is characteristic of those systems that have joined the Euro Area; and, alternatively, how far does it embrace those occupying varying positions outside the Euro Area. As Marcussen's discussion of Sweden and Denmark in this volume shows, formal Euro Area membership need not be the key consideration—a good deal of convergence can take place independent of these formalities. His chapter also alerts us to an important point that shapes much of what follows here: 'convergence' or 'divergence' has many faces, and, in attempting to estimate change, we need at least some notion of how to explore these different faces. That is particularly so in the case of financial market regulation and supervision because, as we shall see, there are complex connections between wider market conditions, the organization of regulatory institutions, and the understandings that underpin both perceptions of the significance of market change and the purpose and workings of regulatory institutions.

* We are grateful for many helpful comments offered in the British Academy Workshop of November 2007, at which drafts of chapters were presented; to the editors for their acute comments, and their patience; and above all to Lucia Quaglia for numerous perceptive comments and characteristically generous sharing of information.

These last remarks provide the shape of what follows, for they allow us to make a distinction between three different faces of change that deeply affect supervisory worlds: the structural, the institutional, and the epistemic. The *structural* face of convergence/divergence refers to changes in the scale, organization, and trading patterns of financial markets and in the key actors in those markets. The extent to which, for instance, convergence is, or is not, taking place through the cross-national integration of markets is obviously a crucial underlying force—though not necessarily a determining force—in the extent to which regulatory and supervisory institutions are being reshaped. The *institutional* face of convergence/divergence refers to the extent to which institutions responsible for regulation and supervision are coming to resemble each other in their structures and responsibilities and, at the most developed, the extent to which European Union–level institutions are appearing. Finally, the *epistemic* face refers to the extent to which the creation of an epistemic community of banking regulators has been hastened in the age of the euro; the extent to which, if it has been hastened, that process can be traced to the experience of European monetary integration; and the extent to which an epistemic community characterizes the borders of either the EU as a whole or the Euro Area?

These distinctions are important for one obvious analytic reason: that we should not expect the three faces of convergence/divergence to change in unison, or even to vary in the same direction. But they are also important for substantive (historical) reasons. Structural convergence, and the supervisory issues that it raises, is hardly the creation of the age of the Euro Area. Likewise, the organization of supervision neither dates from the establishment of the Euro Area, nor is it confined to the Euro Area or the EU. On the contrary, for a long time the key arena of supervision has lain, and continues to lie, in the Basel Committee on Banking Supervision of the Bank for International Settlements. That is a natural and unavoidable outcome of structural convergence in global banking markets (Basel Committee on Banking Supervision 2003, 2007). Perhaps most important of all, the epistemic community of central bank regulators and supervisors has a long history—and, as Marcussen's work (2007b, and in this volume) shows, may indeed be subject to a process of convergence that is more or less independent of anything that is happening either in the EU or in the Euro Area.

Of these three faces of convergence/divergence, the epistemic face is the most important, for it affects the exercise of 'soft' power (Nye 2004). Power in cross-national banking supervision is 'soft' because governance operates via dispersed networks, not hierarchically authoritative institutions; because compliance is the product of negotiation; and because the 'soft technology' of bank regulation depends on the development of shared understandings about the purposes, the techniques, and the substantive rules of banking supervision. All these reasons help explain why it makes sense to speak of an epistemic community in cross-national banking supervision and regulation.

Reflecting on the language root of the complex concept of 'epistemic' community clarifies what this means. An epistemic community is a *knowledge* community: that is, it is unified by a common acceptance of what constitutes appropriate knowledge about its regulatory and supervisory world and, by extension, by agreement about an appropriate language in which to discuss this world. The growth of epistemic convergence therefore does not necessarily imply the growth of a substantive consensus about what the substance of banking supervision arrangements should amount to. On the contrary, our case confirms Marcussen's picture (2007*b* and this volume) of the growth of an intellectual world where central banking discussions are conducted in the language of science: arguments are validated by appeals to evidence which can be scrutinized for confirmation or disproof. This growth moves policy debate from reliance on practical experience to reliance on evidentially backed claims. In so doing it also replaces tacit knowledge accrued from practical experience, only available to insiders, with knowledge available in public domains. In 'modernizing' central banking it creates a special new politics of transparency and accountability (Blinder 2004; Jabko in this volume). It is consequently as likely to *decrease* as to increase substantive agreement about how to conduct banking supervision, for it has the hallmark of scientific exchange: it can be contested by anyone equipped with technical skill, rhetorical capacity, and access to (increasingly easily accessible) data. In this world power is 'soft', therefore, because 'evidence, argument and persuasion' are central to the exercise of influence over policy outcomes (Majone 1989).

The chapter contends that an analysis of central banking—within wider processes of financial internationalization—reveals the degree of soft power accorded to central bankers. Whilst we highlight the remaining specificities of national politics and the slow pace of institutional convergence, the extent of epistemic convergence within the central banking community reveals the importance of banking elites and common (scientized) language to our understanding of the dynamics of convergence.

We examine these three faces of convergence/divergence—structural, institutional, and epistemic—in turn. We then use them in a case study of the first great regulatory crisis of the system, that following the US 'sub-prime' crisis of 2007. The chapter begins, however, with a brief organizational summary of regulatory arrangements in the age of the euro.

Organizing Bank Regulation and Supervision in the Age of the Euro

The formal arrangements governing the supervision of EU financial systems have been neatly summarized as follows: 'The banking model adopted by the EU is the universal banking model, which permits banks to undertake investment banking activities, while leaving it to national banking regulators to control financial conglomerates, the ownership structure of banks, and their relationship with industry' (Dermine 2006: 59). The legal framework for this arrangement is contained in key clauses of the Maastricht Treaty of 1993, which simultaneously allocates supervision to the national sphere but leaves open a residual responsibility for financial stability to the European Central Bank. According to Article 105(2),

The basic task to be carried out by the ECSB (European System of Central Banks) shall be:

- To define and implement monetary policy of the Community
- To conduct foreign-exchange operations consistent with the provisions of Article 109
- To hold and manage the official foreign reserves of the Member States
- *To promote the smooth operations of the payment systems* (emphasis added).

Article 105:5 fleshes out this last provision:

The ECSB shall contribute to the smooth conduct of policies pursued by the competent authorities relating to the prudential supervision of credit institutions and the stability of the financial system.

But Article 105:6 sets boundaries to the exercise of any powers by the ECSB that might intrude into the competence of national supervisory authorities:

The Council may, acting unanimously on a proposal from the Commission and after consulting the ECB and after receiving the assent of the European Parliament, confer upon the ECB specific tasks concerning policies relating to the prudential supervision of credit institutions and other financial institutions with the exception of insurance undertakings.

In Dermine's (2006: 61) words again 'The Treaty is explicit on the principle of decentralization and allocation of regulatory powers and supervisory powers to national central banks. It is only in very special circumstances, and with unanimity in the European Council, that the ECB will be allowed to regulate or supervise financial institutions.'

This formal picture of decentralization needs to be qualified in three ways. First, the pattern of financial supervision at national level is a complex patchwork, often plagued by coordination problems—evident in the crisis of 2007, examined below. It is a curious mix of different historical institutional legacies (central bankers); of different private and public partnerships (depositor protection schemes); and the diffusion of independent regulatory agencies, such as the UK Financial Services Authority (FSA), dating from 1997, and the German Bundesanstalt für Finanzdienstleistungsaufsicht (BaFin), dating from 2002 (for overview, Kahn and Santos 2004). What is more, the patchwork is becoming more complex with the accession of new EU member states carrying a wide range of institutional histories and supervisory traditions (Johnson 2006;

McDermott 2007). This institutional mess obviously creates opportunities for the ECB to intervene.

Second, even under the formal statement of institutional arrangements, the ECB is endowed with an advisory role in the regulatory process, and we shall see that there are good grounds for believing that this role is important in the process of epistemic convergence. Third, even under the established nationally based supervisory arrangements, the supervision of cross-border banking has developed important coordinating institutions. Two particularly significant examples are described in detail by Quaglia (2007*a,b*). The first is the European Banking Committee, a Commission-chaired, 'level-2' Committee under the Lamfalussy procedure, established in 2005, underpinned by a number of working parties, and concerned principally with aspects of the transposition of the Basel 2 agreement (see below) on capital adequacy standards. The second is the Committee of European Banking Supervisors, established in 2004, which is composed of representatives of national banking supervisory authorities. Quaglia's summary catches exactly the significance of this two-part committee structure: it is instrumental in the creation and strengthening of the epistemic community of bank regulators. Hence 'it advises the Commission ... as regards the preparation of draft-implementing measures in the field of banking activities.... It contributes to the consistent implementation of EU directives by issuing "standards" and "guidelines" and to the convergence of member states' supervisory practices.... Finally, it promotes supervisory co-operation, including through the exchange of information' (Quaglia 2007*b*: 12).

It will be plain even from this brief account that the organization of regulation and supervision is more complex than can be comprehended from the formal arrangements alone; we need to explore the different faces of the system, the task of the next section.

Structural, Institutional, and Epistemic Convergence

The growing extent of structural convergence in financial markets is virtually a truism—one of the key features of the modern financial services revolution. In contrast, the degree of integration of both institutions and market practices between the national banking systems of the EU has lagged behind integration in many other important markets (see Véron 2007). In the last 15 years, however, 'Europeanization' has accelerated significantly, creating a broader structural convergence that lies behind 'headline' cases like the acquisition of Abbey in the UK by Gruppo Santander. The most up-to-date summary comes from ECOFIN in 2007:

Integration in EU banking markets is foremost taking place at wholesale level and through the cross-border consolidation activity of a limited number of larger banking groups. Out of approximately 8700 licensed banks in the EU, 46 large banking groups with cross-border activities (both wholesale and retail) have emerged. They represent 58 per cent of total EU banking assets and more than one quarter of their assets (over 14 per cent of total) are in other Member States. 21 of these groups have significant operations outside their home country.... In the Member States which acceded in 2004, on average 70 per cent of banking assets are foreign-owned and the market share of foreign banks often exceeds 50 per cent.

(Economic and Financial Committee 2007*b*: para. 22)

It is precisely this history of growing structural convergence which has given rise to an extended debate about the extent of, and desirability of, institutional convergence. The formal institutional structure of the regulatory and supervisory system has been striking for its lack of institutional convergence. It is a hybrid (Kahn and Santos 2004) which formally assigns the ECSB only a subsidiary and advisory role in the prudential management of the system. As we have seen, it is charged with a responsibility to promote the smooth operation of payment systems; its Banking Supervisory Committee is the most important forum where the national banking supervisors meet to consider issues of coordinated management; and, as we saw above, it has established a presumptive right to an advisory role in supervision discussions. Meanwhile, the organization of banking supervision remains heavily biased to national institutions, and, as we noted above, there is considerable diversity in the way that individual EU states organize their supervision arrangements.

It is striking how far this contrasts with both the expectations of the Lamfalussy 'Wise Men' (2001) and academic prediction (Lee 2005). Whilst stipulating that increased cooperation between national regulators was the most obvious immediate solution to banking supervision, the Wise Men (2001: 95, emphasis added) contended that future developments might engender 'a Treaty change, including the development of a *single* EU regulatory authority'. Lee (2005) argued that, precisely as a result of national diversity, regulation would become increasingly centralized. But there have proved to be two obstacles to institutional convergence, both of which are important for our argument. First, banking regulation remains a highly sensitive national policy area: we shall see that in the 2007 crisis domestic political calculations overrode everything. Second, a substantive consensus on how to supervise banks remains elusive. Epistemic convergence does not imply increased substantive agreement on regulatory options.

These assertions have been further compounded by former ECB director Padoa-Schioppa's recently rejected proposals for a European financial authority. Following a review of the Lamfalussy Process he suggested that, whilst current arrangements were a dramatic improvement on its predecessor, 'current arrangements for co-ordinating national supervisory activities are overly complex and burdensome' (Padoa-Schioppa 2007). His solution: an 'integrated supervision of EU-wide groups, resting on a complete pooling of information and the enhancement of the powers of the colleges of supervisors' (ibid.). Significantly though, and as our argument suggests, his proposals were rejected within ECOFIN where national interests continue to override collective Eurozone concerns (Economic and Financial Committee 2007*a*).

That said, there is not only considerable diversity in the way the component parts of the EU and the Euro Area manage supervision, but also in the way they approach the task of managing the stability of the banking system in crisis conditions—in other words, of organizing the 'lender-of-last-resort' role, traditionally the way central banks have both tried to create trust in the stability of banking institutions and, when that trust breaks down, stood behind individual institutions. There is no Euro-Area-wide capacity to provide a 'lender-of-last-resort', because whilst 'the ECB can manage overall liquidity through monetary operations ... the arrangements put in place in the Eurosystem, namely the pre-specification of what the ECB can accept as collateral, make it impossible for the ECB to meet the liquidity needs of an illiquid financial institution that runs out of assets qualifying as a collateral according to the established list' (Kahn and Santos 2006: 352).

Within states there is also some diversity in how this role is managed. In most cases, responsibility is assigned to member-state central banks, but even here there is national diversity. Germany, for instance, has a specialized liquidity consortium, the Liquiditäts-Konsortialbank GmbH, 'a private company jointly owned by the central bank and the private banks' (Kahn and Santos 2006: 52). It is precisely this diversity which led to calls in 2007 for the creation of a more uniform, centralized system of inspection and regulation (Véron 2007). We will return to this issue in considering the crisis of autumn 2007.

This simple sketch of modes of convergence suggests that there is a considerable disjunction between the first two faces, the structural and the institutional. Whilst, by the wider standards of the European economy, the banking industry has been a laggard in structural convergence, in recent years the degree of convergence has increased considerably. By contrast, there is considerable 'stickiness' in the development of the institutional system, with regulatory and supervisory responsibility and authority continuing to reside at the national level. It is precisely this apparent disjunction—and, of course, attempts at empire building—which has led to calls for the enhancement of capacity at the EU level (Véron 2007). Both the institutional 'stickiness' and the empire building are precisely what we would expect from standard neo-institutional rational choice theory.

Easily the most striking feature of European banking regulation is the increasing degree of epistemic convergence. There are four indicators. First, European central banking exemplifies the signs of epistemic transformation highlighted by Marcussen in this volume: the shift from an image of banking regulation as primarily a 'practical' activity, involving the mobilization of the tacit knowledge of those with business experience to the rise of those who claim a professionalized, systematic knowledge of bank regulation. The most developed version is the emergence of the profession of bank regulator, either in specialized divisions within central banks or in 'non-majoritarian' regulatory organizations like the United Kingdom FSA. Whilst there exists no single policy paradigm, there is a high degree of homogeneity within the 'community' of banking regulators. It is composed predominantly of trained research economists and specialists with PhDs in financial economics. For example, the Committee of European Banking Supervisors (CEBS) comprises 46 active members from respective national regulatory agencies. Of this number, three are professors at the universities of Amsterdam, Portugal, and Vienna (Arnold Schilder, Pedro Duarte Neves, and Andreas Ittner), whilst a further three are university lecturers (Rumen Simeonov, Jukka Vesala, and Mihaly Erdos). At least eight of the members hold PhDs, whilst a further three have postgraduate qualifications in economics. Of the remaining members, the majority are trained research economists. This is clearly a 'scientific' community.

Second, the creation of the ECB has itself been a major contribution to this epistemic convergence, for it functions as a highly technocratic institution: a big employer of the professionally qualified; a big supplier of standardized data conforming to agreed technical forms; and a major disseminator—through its working paper publications, its monthly review, and its twice-yearly Financial Stability Review—of bodies of data. Just how far the discussion of regulatory issues is now encapsulated in a highly technical language that the professionals use to communicate is illustrated by a passage in the June 2007 issue of the ECB Financial Stability Review. A boxed study offers an elaborately modelled account of banking and insurance risks, which covers three pages. It introduces the features in the following way:

From a financial stability perspective, it is useful to decompose the risks faced by the financial sector into systematic, sector-specific and idiosyncratic components. The aim of this Box is to apply a latent factor model framework to achieve such a decomposition for both the banking and insurance sectors. Principal component analysis is a dimension reduction technique that makes it possible to approximate large multivariate datasets with a limited number of factors which account for the largest share of the changes in the original data. The variance of the data can be explained by a model of unobserved factors that are common to all or most of the variables, and an idiosyncratic component which corresponds to variable-specific factors. In this way, each variable can be represented as a linear combination of common factors plus idiosyncratic ones. (ECB 2007: 115)

This scientific turn is not confined to the ECB. In states within the Euro Area the very creation of the ECB has led to significant changes in goal definition for those domestic institutions that carried out the central banking functions now performed at supranational level. The consequence has been a major adaptation in mission—a turning to data analysis and research. As Marcussen notes (this volume, Chapter 17), with the advent of the euro national central banks in the Eurosystem have turned increasingly to research, investing in specialized personnel, in part to compensate for the disappearance of some historically important functions.

Third, this new spirit of scientific rationality is being used to forge an epistemic community of supervisors and regulators via the institutional developments described earlier: the creation of networks of advisory committees that engage with the most technical details of regulation. The advisory committees help create the institutional networks that are the necessary underpinning of the epistemic community, along with the specialized language that gives the community its epistemic character. In this process they reflect the wider epistemic transformation of central banking since, as we saw, they are in part concerned with transmitting concepts from the wider international epistemic community of central bankers, in the form of the transformation of the Basel (II) framework rules. The words of the European Commission exactly catch the rise of a world where participants speak a common technical language, and work to solve regulatory problems in that language:

Increasingly, standards and best practices are set and defined at global level, for example on accounting, auditing and banking capital requirements. Considering the size of the EU market, and Europe's experience in pragmatically uniting the legitimate call for harmonised rules and the diverging needs of different markets/cultures/players, the EU must have a leading role in standard setting at global level.

(Commission of the European Communities 2005: 15)

Fourth, the politics of enlargement for the new EU accession states—notably those in the former command economies—have seen a considerable expansion of the range of this epistemic world, principally through the activities of the ECB as an evangelist of responsible banking regulation. The ECB has built and consolidated its sources of prudential capacity and expertise. In the process it has been able to act as a significant agent of institutional and policy transfer of central banking supervisory expertise. The ECB has also been able to offer institutional support to embattled central bankers in the accession states. This support has been necessary because the success of the attempt to extend the epistemic central banking community has in some individual national cases confronted the raw politics of economic and political change in states still attempting to make a painful transition to democratic capitalism (e.g. Johnson 2006).

This sketch of convergence and divergence in the age of the euro suggests three obvious conclusions. First, and most important, our opening suggestion is plainly vindicated: it is not possible to speak of convergence as if it were a unified phenomenon. Structural convergence has been moderately encouraged by the new monetary regime, and more importantly by the long-term consequences of the Maastricht Treaty. Second, in comparison with structural convergence in other sectors, that in banking remains modest. Institutional convergence—in the sense of the creation of authoritative institutions charged with responsibility for supervision—has been much more limited. Indeed, the tendency in some cases to create specialized independent regulatory agencies in response to regulatory crises has, if anything, increased the diversity of the institutional patchwork that is concerned with bank regulation across the EU. Third, the most significant form of convergence is epistemic in character, and it has both social and intellectual aspects. Socially, it consists of the creation, and strengthening, of networks joining regulators across national domains; intellectually, it amounts to the creation of a shared language that expresses regulatory issues in a technically complex discourse.

We have argued that, whilst the phenomenon of epistemic convergence is part of a wider global phenomenon, it has been given a considerable impetus since the creation of the Euro Area. One conclusion that might be inferred from this argument is that the functional effectiveness of banking regulation is assured because of the capacity of epistemic convergence to compensate for any lack of institutional coordination. But, as the brief account of the 2007–8 banking crisis shows, this cannot be safely assumed.

The Crisis of 2007–8: Convergence or Divergence?

Regulatory systems rarely change radically without being subjected to some intense external stress. 'Crisis' in regulatory change has a double significance: it marks, usually, a moment of dramatic failure in regulatory arrangements; and it marks what 'crisis' exactly means—a turning point, when all kinds of established ways of doing things are suddenly abandoned. It has that double significance because it constitutes a moment of great danger, where averting the danger often means abandoning existing institutional practices and modes of thought. In other words, crisis is a moment for policy creativity, involving sharp increases in levels of institutional and epistemic convergence. What is most striking about the crisis of 2007 is the absence of these features. It did indeed produce radically new ways of thinking about the problem of bank regulation, especially in the national system that was most publicly and intensely affected by the crisis; but the extent of institutional and epistemic learning at the systemic level of either the EU or the Euro Area has been slight. To this judgement must be attached an obvious caveat: at the time of writing the story of the crisis is still unfolding, and what is more is being written from the outside. We cannot yet know how far the continuing unravelling of the crisis, or reflections on the crisis by policy actors, will impel change.

The character of the crisis has been concisely summarized by the Vice-President of the ECB as follows:

The month of August (2007) was characterised by a substantial increase in financial market volatility and a reappraisal of risk. The financial market turbulence was triggered by a series of events which intensified tensions in the US subprime mortgage market. This resulted in an adjustment of investors' attitudes towards risk—a diminished appetite for risky assets—and led to an increase in uncertainty about financial market conditions and prospects. Market volatility rose sharply in almost all asset classes. Stock markets tumbled, as investors sold equities and moved funds into safe-haven investments, like government bonds. Several investment funds holding asset-backed securities—with subprime mortgage elements—suspended withdrawals. At roughly the same time, a number of European banks made public their direct and indirect exposures to the US subprime mortgage market. These exposures were sometimes sizeable but were not sufficiently significant to materially impact the soundness of core financial institutions. In addition, several banks, especially in Europe, were subject to rumours about severe losses stemming from exposures to mortgage-backed securities. (Papademos 2007)

Banking crises usually spring from wider problems in the macro-economy, and this crisis fits that pattern. Its origins lie in the financial history of the United States in the new millennium: an age of cheap money, intense competition between financial institutions, and a continuing history of financial innovation; in other words, an extension of the now quite familiar history of the financial services revolution. That competition opened up new markets, in particular the notorious market in 'sub-prime' mortgage-backed loans, when poor credit risks were encouraged to take out property-backed mortgages—often on the basis of fraudulent declarations of ability to repay loans. The extent of bad debt problems in that market became clear in spring 2007. The mechanism by which these problems were more widely, indeed internationally, transmitted shows one aspect of convergence that we identified earlier: structural convergence. The growth of internationally integrated markets in securitized debt led to the packaging of these sub-prime loans at attractive rates. It was the packaging, and therefore the aggregation of these dubious loans into securitized bundles, that left many financial institutions with commercial paper that was of dubious worth—or in some cases actually worthless. That in turn led to a climate revealed in any anatomy of financial crises: a crisis of trust between actors in markets, an unwillingness to do business in this atmosphere, and a consequential inability of some institutions to finance their loan books. As always in financial crises, there were two elements which interacted in complex ways: a 'real' crisis as some institutions discovered that large parts of their loan book were worthless, or of considerably less worth than imagined, since the value of the paper which had been securitized had been greatly overvalued; and a crisis of trust encompassing a much wider range of institutions as, in conditions of non-transparency, institutions

347

declined to deal with, especially to loan to, each other, in the absence of good information about the scale of systemic problems.

The mechanism by which this was transmitted to Europe was the global organization of this market in securitized paper. August saw bailouts for two German banks, arranged in an *ad hoc* fashion by the Bundesbank, and disclosure of serious losses at a range of other institutions in France and the Netherlands. In the same month the ECB, in its role as system manager, made the largest injection of funds into the market since the '9/11' crisis of 2001. In September the crisis prompted the first public bank run in the United Kingdom since the nineteenth century when customers queued outside the branches of Northern Rock, a former building society converted into a bank with a large mortgage property-backed loan book financed by borrowing on the inter-bank market. The crisis of 9 August caused a sharp change in behaviour in the inter-bank loan market; Northern Rock found it increasingly difficult to fund its borrowing, and was obliged to reveal that it had turned to the Bank of England for assistance. This announcement prompted a collapse of confidence in the bank on the part of large numbers of individual investors, who queued to withdraw their money. Repeated assurances from the elite of the domestic regulatory community (the governor of the Bank of England, the Chancellor of the Exchequer, and the head of the Financial Services Authority) failed to convince depositors. Only the announcement on day five of the crisis that the Exchequer—that is, the full resources of the state—stood behind Northern Rock, and would guarantee all £28 billion of its deposits and, by implication, the deposits of all other banks in the UK, saw an end to the public panic, though not to Northern Rock's problems, as a further loosening of the terms of assistance in October showed (Bowers and Inman 2007). The exact connection between the contagion of panic and real problems with the worth of Northern Rock's loan book has still to be established at the time of writing.

The crisis shows that *structural convergence* is now particularly important, though it is not clear that we can identify an independent Euro Area effect. The signs of this convergence are plain both in the development of integrated markets dealing in the tainted paper, and in the rapid spread of the contagion of panic across markets in different national jurisdictions.

In contrast, the crisis shows the persistence of institutional divergence. This was naturally the case in the instance of the UK, which has remained outside the Euro Area, and where the management of the crisis was largely determined by domestic political pressures. In the case of the Euro Area, the diversity of institutional responses is also striking. The epicentre of the crisis, the two German banks that went under, was largely managed domestically, by *ad hoc* coalitions organized principally by the Bundesbank.

The organization of the British crisis is particularly striking, for here we are talking about the dominant banking centre in the EU. As we have noted, the UK was not the only national system to experience crisis, but what makes the case special are two considerations: the UK—or rather the City of London—is the linchpin of the European banking system; and the crisis of Northern Rock was peculiar in its public character, its scale, and its prolonged form. It involved a complex system of bureaucratic politics between four institutional actors: the Bank of England, as central bank responsible for the orderly conduct of the markets; the Financial Services Authority, the responsible regulatory body; the Treasury, which in the end was the only effective ultimate guarantor because the resources of the state stood behind it; and other key actors in the core executive, notably the Prime Minister, anxious that the crisis not fatally damage public confidence in the capacity of the Labour Party to manage financial markets. In part this bureaucratic politics involved the familiar search for some means of effective coordination under the pressure of a crisis which demanded rapid response, and the equally familiar 'blame game' which is played in all regulatory disasters.

But above all what is striking about the UK crisis is the way its attempted resolution was prescribed by the high politics of the core executive. The Treasury's guarantee to cover all the deposits was prompted by the fear that otherwise New Labour would experience its own 'Black Wednesday', the currency crisis that destroyed public confidence in the financial capacity of the Conservative Party for more than a decade. What is more, the institutional and epistemic faces of the UK system after the crisis were largely conditioned by the domestic UK context. The intellectual content of the debate about the regulation of systemic stability has been dominated by the interests of small and medium-sized depositors: in the crisis-driven guarantee by the Chancellor, as he desperately sought to avoid meltdown at the height of Northern Rock panic, that all deposits would be safeguarded by the state; in the subsequent *ad hoc* extension of the generosity of the deposit protection scheme; and in the announcement that this is indeed only *ad hoc,* contingent on a review of the scale of the whole scheme. The Chancellor has now foreshadowed the legislation that will be introduced to reform the system in the spring of 2008. It is still not clear who the big winner will be. The Chancellor's initial thoughts advantaged the Financial Services Authority, which would be given more statutory control over the banking system (Parker and Strauss 2008). But the most recent intervention in the debate about blame—the report of the House of Commons Treasury Select Committee on the affair—is scathing in its judgement of FSA regulatory incompetence (Treasury Committee 2008).

This interpretation is confirmed by the tentative scheme announced in January 2008 to rescue Northern Rock through a convoluted public–private partnership—a package designed to avoid tainting the Labour government with the stain of nationalization of a major financial institution. Likewise the institutional face of the crisis has been dominated by the 'blame game': the attempt to blame the present administration for the allegedly uncoordinated character of the present system; the attempt to avert blame, notably by the key actor in the core executive, the Prime Minister, who is the official author of that system; and the attempt by the different institutional actors (the central bank, the Financial Services Authority, the Treasury) to shift blame between each other.

If structural convergence, and institutional divergence, was the mark of the crisis, the epistemic face of the crisis is remarkable for its lack of change. Crises in any regulatory system are important because they typically force actors to think in entirely new ways, not just about the management of the particular crisis, but about the management of the whole system. There is very little evidence of this here. The 'don't panic' response of the ECB president, Jean-Claude Trichet, in mid-August 2007—'I call on all parties concerned to continue to keep their composure'—catches this resistance to anything epistemically radical. Likewise the response of European Commissioner Charles McCreevy after the mid-September meeting held when the Northern Rock crisis was still at its most intense: 'We are making progress, but I would not want to put it any stronger than that. . . . We are moving to the next stage. You can only move as fast as you are allowed' (Barber 2007). It is true that as the systemic crisis intensified in the spring of 2008 central banks were propelled to a more activist stance in trying to stabilize the system; but this activism was belated, ad hoc and uncoordinated.

Why is a system which is experiencing significant structural convergence, and which in the crisis of 2007 suffered so dramatically the consequences of that structural convergence, showing such an inability to converge institutionally and epistemically? The modern age of banking instability began in the early 1970s, and what has been most marked is precisely the capacity of policy actors to learn from the successive crises—to remake institutions radically, and to refashion their epistemic worlds. Why is the Eurosystem finding this so difficult?

Three possibilities suggest themselves. The first may be expressed in the question: crisis, what crisis? The little local difficulties of summer and autumn 2007 were, after all, managed Trichet-fashion—by a little flexibility. It is, however, hard to maintain this equable response in the face of problems that continue to unfold, the collapse of banks, and the first public run on a bank in the EU's leading banking member for over a century. A second possibility in effect derives from neo-institutional theory: that the EU's institutions are so laden with veto points that, in McCreevy's words, 'you can only move as fast as you are allowed'. But this is hard to reconcile with the evidence presented earlier of the dense organized epistemic community, itself linked to wider global communities of banking regulators, used to confronting problems of regulation in a well-developed technical language. The 'scientization' of central banking identified by Marcussen (this volume) has provided regulators with a set of well-developed intellectual tools. A third possibility is that, writing still as the crisis unfolds, we are too early to pick up the transformations that may be taking place. It is, indeed, a feature of the transforming power of crisis that even participants may not be aware just how much they are changing under the pressure of critical events. And, as we have noted, the crisis has already forced a growth in central bank activism in crisis management.

Soft Power, Banking Regulation, and the Eurosystem

The exercise of power in banking regulation and supervision is necessarily 'soft': it depends crucially on the appropriation of effective symbols, specialized discourses, and communicative competence. That is what makes the evolution of epistemic communities so critical. But there is a paradox in the recent regulatory history of central banking, and it is a paradox which immensely complicates the regulatory life of the Eurosystem.

The story of epistemic convergence is not just, or even mainly, a European story. The centre of the epistemic community of banking regulators lies in the Basel Committee. European regulators, though important, are only one subset of the Basel participants. The age of the financial services revolution has also been the age of the emergence of a highly distinctive epistemic world. Blinder's (2004) central banking revolution encapsulates this epistemic transformation. The modernization of central banking has seen the growth of a more transparent, accessible world, where issues of regulation are expressed in a technical language widely accessible, both to insiders and to outsiders. Banking regulation has become more 'scientific'.

But since the age of the financial services revolution has also been an age of crisis, collapse, and scandal, we must conclude that regulators have become less successful at their core task—to ensure financial stability. Over nearly two decades the transformation of central banking has been accompanied by success in the search for macro-economic stability, and failure in the search for prudential stability. Central bankers have become better at helping to manage whole economies, but worse at managing the prudential stability of banking institutions. They have become better at talking about the techniques of prudential supervision and stabilization, and worse at practising those techniques. They live in a world of carefully constructed regulatory models—and in the world of panic, chaos, and bafflement revealed in the great crisis of 2007–8.

The Regulatory State is Dead! Long Live the Regulatory State!

Panic, chaos, and bafflement intensified throughout 2008 and culminated in a global crisis of bank supervision in September–October of that year. The collapse of Lehman Brothers, the American investment bank, on 15 September 2008, led to the final eruption of that crisis. It also produced an astonishing increase in epistemic convergence in the world of bank regulation. The crisis showed that the distinction alluded to in the preceding paragraph—between macro-economic stability and prudential stability—is illusory. The two are bound together. The failure of prudential regulation is a disaster for macro-economic stability. The new 'long boom' in the global economy has abruptly ended, on foot of which we will experience global recession. This catastrophe explains the epistemic convergence. It also explains the form taken by convergence.

Financial supervision in the first years of the Euro was an attempt to practice the principles of the regulatory state sketched nearly two decades ago by Majone: a Madisonian, technocratic ruling order which excluded democratic politicians in favour of non-majoritarian regulatory institutions. In the crisis of 2007–8 that regulatory state was weighed in the balance and found wanting. Confronted by crisis the bankers and the technocratic regulators froze, petrified like rabbits before a stoat. Now, the great agents of transformation are not the central bankers and financial regulators who until recently reigned supreme. The agents of transformation are democratic governments driven by fear of the electoral consequences of macro-economic collapse. The crisis produced rapid learning and innovation—a common social function of any crisis. But it was politicians who learnt most rapidly, not central bankers still trapped in the mind world of the long boom. The epistemic convergence that occurred killed the old regulatory state—and is creating a new one. Across the capitalist world it turned banks into public utilities. Every big capitalist economy has taken significant public ownership stakes in the banking industry. The leader in innovation was the United Kingdom. That is not surprising, for the UK economy teetered most precariously on the extraordinary financial pyramid revealed by the crash of September–October 2008. But the UK was soon followed by other major EU economies, by frenzied coordination among the G7, and then—astonishingly—by the Bush Administration in Washington.

The terms of regulatory discourse were also transformed. It became impossible credibly to use the language of light touch flexible regulation. The crisis is the precursor of a new wave of controls: more adversarial, more juridified, and more exposed to the pressures of democratic politics. This is the new regulatory state now being born. The regulation of financial markets—and probably of capitalist economies generally—has been irreversibly transformed into an object of democratic political struggle. The age of the long boom was also the age of the scientization of financial supervision—a scientization anatomized in Marcussen's contribution to this volume, and in some of the account of EU supervision offered earlier in this chapter. It may be that powerful interests in the markets will still be able to capture the regulatory process; but to do so they will now have to struggle against democratically elected politicians and the social forces that press on those politicians. Control of trading practices and of reward systems is no longer in the hands of the markets. As the global crisis deepens it may even be that the crown jewels of the old regulatory state—central bank independence in setting short-term interest rates—will be lost to the politicians. This is why the crisis signals more than the end of the long boom; it also signals the death of one state order, and the birth of a successor. The Madisonian regulatory state is dead; a more democratic form is coming into being. Death and rebirth will be accompanied by chaos and suffering.

16

Monetary Policy Strategies

Iain Begg[1]

Contemporary macroeconomic policy places a premium on achieving stability and largely eschews active demand management. In the pursuit of macroeconomic objectives, monetary policy has become relatively more dominant over the last two decades and central bankers have evolved from being shadowy figures who cultivated their own mystique, such as Montagu Norman at the Bank of England, in the inter-war years to become—in many eyes—the leading actors in economic policy-making. Some, such as Alan Greenspan, are revered, while others (such as European Central Bank President Jean-Claude Trichet) attract critics as well as fans, but notwithstanding Bank of England Governor Mervyn King's stated ambition to make monetary policy boring, none is ignored.

In parallel, there have been far-reaching changes in the strategies adopted by the monetary authorities and there is an apparent convergence in approaches, to the extent that what distinguishes different monetary policy strategies today can appear minor compared with strategies that were in place 20 or 30 years ago. This chapter argues that the evident convergence has been driven by a combination of theoretical developments in monetary economics and the progressive intensification of research input into decision-making, together with a recognition of the pitfalls of monetary and fiscal laxity. Yet, as Rose (2007) points out, in the history of monetary policy, changes of strategy have been frequent and even the variant on Bretton Woods with capital controls and fixed but adjustable exchange rates only lasted 13 years from 1959–71. It is, therefore, interesting to speculate on whether the convergence visible today is likely to endure. Monetary policy strategies clearly continues to evolve, albeit with pressures for change coming more from within the central banking community and the academic specialists in the area (see, also, the chapter in this volume by Marcussen) than from Europeanization as it is usually understood. The credit market turmoil that started in August 2007 may, however, be a source of new pressures for change insofar as it has raised questions about whether central bankers have focused too much on price stability, to the neglect of the underlying stability of the financial system.

The chapter sets out what appear to be the main features of the state-of-the art, delves into why they have arisen, and explores emerging directions for monetary policy and unresolved debates. It shows that today's strategies reflect evolving ideas about what monetary policy can, cannot, and should do, and that in the EU, at least, there has been an intriguing iteration between institutional and constitutional changes and the development of strategies. There may not be a single model of best practice, but it is clear that there are systematic preferences.

Aims of Monetary Policy

Monetary policy has evolved considerably over the last quarter of a century. In many parts of the world it has become the primary instrument of macroeconomic policy, with fiscal policy relegated to a supporting role. Price stability has been elevated to be the principal policy objective, while granting of independence from political control and various other institutional changes in central banking, such as resort to monetary policy committees (MPC) and new approaches to transparency, have come to characterize the broad approaches deployed (Blinder 2004; Blinder and Wyplosz 2004; Mishkin 2007a; Siklos 2002). In this process, power has shifted from politicians to central bankers and an intriguing element has been that this transfer has happened with only limited public debate and, despite occasional rumblings, has not elicited much opposition.

New ideas about the purpose and scope of monetary policy have been highly influential, leading in some cases to significant legal and institutional transformations, such as those that altered the role of the Bank of England during the 1990s (see Goodhart's chapter in this volume). In others (notably the US Fed), the effects of new ideas have been more subtle, with substantial changes of style or emphasis which draw on new thinking about how to conduct monetary policy, even though the institutional framework has been stable (see Woolley, this volume). Amidst these changes, it is evident that the manner in which the European Central Bank (ECB) has been constructed partly reflects the Bundesbank tradition, but is partly also attributable to the evolving norms and practices of the central banking community of the advanced nations (see, also, Howarth's chapter in this volume).

Bernanke (2004b) suggests that two over-arching frameworks for monetary policy can be distinguished. Although he draws parallels with the distinction between 'instrument rules' and 'targeting rules' common in much of the literature, he contends that these labels are somewhat misleading and opts instead for the terms *simple feedback policies* and *forecast-based policies* as more accurate descriptions of what lies behind the respective frameworks. The former are exemplified by well-known options such as the Taylor rule and are suited to contexts in which information on how the economy is evolving is incomplete or hard to obtain and validate. Because a simple feedback relies on a limited range of variables, it can also help to shape expectations, since economic agents and the monetary authority are privy to similar and readily understood information. Using forecasts rather than rules to anticipate how the economy will evolve, including in response to policy changes, necessarily requires more information as well as judgement on how to interpret risks and uncertainties. As Bernanke stresses, it also offers better means for making use of judgements, but has the drawback that the strategy of the central bank is then more difficult for other actors to interpret. The approach therefore needs to be complemented by more extensive communication aimed at explaining the strategy. Despite its layers of complexity, Bernanke argues that the forecast-based approach is winning over a growing number of central banks and that this trend seems to have been associated with better results.

The monetary policy-maker has to be alert to underlying variables such as the capacity of the economy and how it varies over time, the structural characteristics that may influence when inflation is prone to accelerate and the rate of interest likely to be consistent with stability (Tucker 2006). He observes that judgements on such variables are very hard to make, partly because they cannot be directly observed and partly because, as the economy itself changes, the relationships between key variables will also change. In addition, monetary policy has to reflect the conduct of fiscal policy which is not just a flanking policy, but can (as happened in Germany in the early 1990s) be a source of inflationary pressures. The character of structural policies—certainly those affecting wage trends, but increasingly also those that have bearing on product markets—will, too, shape what monetary policy has to do (for a survey, see Leiner-Killinger et al. 2007). Tucker also stresses that well-anchored nominal variables (such as prices) make the task of stabilizing the real economy easier and he makes the link to central bank credibility by pointing out that if a cut in interest rates is made, private agents will accept that what monetary policy is trying to do is to prevent demand falling below capacity, rather than engineering a short-term boost to demand that will result in higher inflation in the future. However, he rejects the idea that monetary policy can fine-tune the economy, preferring to describe what a central bank can do as 'rough-tuning'.

Monetary policy also has to be good at anticipating change, and cannot afford to be largely reactive. Bernanke (2004b: 1) alludes to 'several reasons for concluding that good policies must be primarily forecast-based'. These reasons include the need for pre-emptive policy-making, the importance of taking account of the changing structure of the economy, and the value of what he terms a risk-management approach to policy. The second of Bernanke's reasons is one of the most tricky because of the uncertainty about how the economy will evolve (see, also, Tucker 2006). While some trends lend themselves relatively straightforwardly to prediction, certain structural changes are, by their nature, much harder to factor into decision-making or to identify as they happen. In the UK, for example, the wave of immigration following the 2004 enlargement of the EU was bound to have effects on labour market pressures, but these could not be fully predicted. Breakthroughs that result in new sources of supply or new ways of producing may result in step-changes, and it is too easily forgotten that economics is a behavioural rather than a hard science: consumption or savings patterns will not always respond identically to particular signals. Bernanke cites the productivity surge in the late 1990s as such a change.

From Monetary to Inflation Targeting

From the mid-1970s, monetary targeting was in vogue, a shift that can be attributed partly to the growing influence of ideas rooted in monetarism, and partly to the search for answers to the empirical phenomenon of the world-wide surge in inflation from the late 1960s onwards. Monetarist analyses stressed that expansionary monetary policy does not produce enduring effects on the real economy, that inflation is costly, and that there are considerable benefits from having the sort of strong nominal anchor offered by stabilizing the growth of the money supply (Mishkin 2007a). The approach started to lose support because of the breakdown of the underlying empirical relationship between the quantity of money and inflation (i.e. variations in the velocity of circulation) and the effects of what came to be known as Goodhart's Law, the finding that 'any observed statistical regularity will collapse once pressure is placed upon it for control purposes' (Goodhart 2006).

Mishkin also notes that some central banks may have pursued monetary targeting less vigorously than they should have done if the approach were to work as advertised. At the same time, the Swiss and German monetary authorities, despite frequently failing to hit their monetary targets, were successful in keeping inflation low, an achievement that Mishkin ascribes to their activism in communicating their aims and strategy to the public. Their success also established the credentials of independent central banks, paving the way for the gradual conversion of others as part of the broader paradigm change. In both cases, too, the message conveyed was that even if there were slippage in the short-term, it was long-run price stability that mattered. Mishkin contrasts this consistency of communication with what he describes as the game playing of the central banks of the UK, Canada, and the United States which he believes hindered their communication process. For example, he notes the targeting of multiple aggregates and a willingness to redefine targets if they were not met, thereby undermining their credibility.

Over the last 20 years, dissatisfaction with monetary targeting caused by the lack of stability of the relationship between monetary growth and prices (Mishkin 2007a) has been superseded by forms of inflation targeting as the preferred approach. In essence, inflation targeting shifts the focus from the intermediate target of monetary growth to the outcome variable—price stability. Its emergence as a nominal anchor for policy reflects the conjunction of new thinking about how to deal with the time inconsistency problem[2] and to manage expectations better. Mishkin (2007a) makes the point that central bankers can, in practice, cope straightforwardly with time inconsistency problems by refusing to let the short-term dominate, but if politicians—who typically have shorter time horizons—are able to instruct the central bank, time inconsistency will remain. This is one of the reasons why independence of central banks has become part of the contemporary monetary policy package.

What Should be Understood by Price Stability?

At one level, the core aim of monetary policy is obvious and there is little dispute about the goal espoused by all monetary authorities of preserving the value of money by assuring price stability. Price stability is valued as a public good because the alternative—inflation—is acknowledged to cause welfare losses. However, price stability is only one component of macroeconomic stability and it is clear that society only values the former as part of a broader set of objectives. Buiter (2006) points to a dichotomy between those central banks which have price stability as their primary mandate and a smaller, but weighty minority (it includes the US Fed, and the central banks of Australia and Norway) for which it is not. Among the latter group, real economy aims are as prominent as nominal stability.

The advantages of price stability are sufficiently compelling for it to be a key goal of policy and most monetary policy strategies take for granted that this is so. Uncertainty about price movements undermines the unit of account function of money, weakening the signalling role of prices, and leads to behaviour by economic agents that is potentially disruptive. Hence, anchoring price expectations is a core aim of monetary policy. However, as Bordes and Clerc (2007) note, there can be departures from short-term trends that cannot easily be pulled back without triggering sharp fluctuations in economic activity and it is in this regard that certainty calls for monetary policy strategy also to have the long-term price level in its sights. A price-level target might be an answer, but has its own problems, not least the potential for increasing output volatility. Instead, policy strategy has to map out a trajectory towards the long-term trend, possibly with reference to intermediate variables such as monetary aggregates.

While the definition of price stability might be intuitively obvious, Bordes and Clerc (2007: 268) show that it has distinctive short-term and long-term properties. In the short-term, price stability means anchoring price expectations, whereas in the latter sense, it means 'the absence of long-term price-level uncertainty'. They argue that most research focuses on the short-term anchoring role of monetary policy, but that the ECB monetary policy strategy can only properly be understood by considering both objectives. In essence, the distinction between the short- and the long-term hinges on the notion of the neutrality of money vis-à-vis economic activity over the long-term, whereas in the short-term fluctuations in money can affect economic activity.

The Inexorable Rise of Inflation Targeting

Rose (2007) documents the steady rise of inflation targeting as the preferred monetary policy strategy. The start of inflation targeting can be traced to the decision by the Reserve Bank of New Zealand to adopt it as its monetary strategy in 1988, even before the 1989 Act that enshrined the new approach was passed. Its spread since has been quite remarkable and the inflation targeting approach, in various guises, rapidly became the dominant monetary policy strategy. Its advantages, apart from providing a way round the instability of the velocity of circulation, include the fact that more information will then be brought into policy decisions, that the target can be more easily explained to the public, and that a highly visible target (rather than one subject to vagaries of interpretation) makes holding the central bank to account more practicable.

He also points out that no country has yet abandoned inflation targeting (although Finland and Spain replaced their own inflation targeting regimes when they acceded to the euro area).

Svensson (2007: 187) notes that there is a growing consensus about the merits, not to mention achievements, of inflation targeting as a monetary policy strategy, yet he observes that despite the impression that 'monetary policy bliss, or something very close to it, may have been reached', there is still room for improvement. He identifies three features of 'good' inflation targeting, while pointing to ways in which these facets of the strategy could be improved:

- An explicit numerical target for inflation, coupled with the aim of avoiding volatility in either inflation or output. He observes that many central banks acknowledge that they implement what he calls 'flexible' inflation targeting—that is paying attention to stabilization of the real economy—but suggests that the aims for the real economy and information about trade-offs and weightings given to different objectives are neither explicit nor consistent.

- Targeting forecasts of inflation rather than the inflation rate itself. However, he is critical of monetary authorities that do not build-in to their forecasts changes in the instrument rate itself, noting that for private sector agents what shapes their behaviour is expectations of future rate movements. Indeed, the information conveyed by the current policy rate is only useful to the extent that it conveys information about future rate developments.

- A high degree of transparency that simultaneously enhances central bank accountability and contributes to the effective implementation of policy. Svensson maintains that if inflation forecasts or output forecasts do not include the projected effects of policy rate changes that would be consistent with the optimal instrument rate path, they risk misleading private agents. He therefore argues for publication of the optimal projection, including information on the optimal policy rate path.

According to Rose (2007), what is striking about inflation targeting regimes is that they are the reverse of all three main elements of Bretton Woods: capital movements are free, exchange rates are free to float, and it is the price level which is targeted. He also notes that countries have not adopted inflation targeting because of adherence to a rule-based international system, but have taken this direction independently, resulting in a system that has grown in what he describes as a 'Darwinian' way. Consequently, Rose (2007: 671) comments, 'the key players are central banks; these are now more independent, accountable and transparent than under Bretton Woods'. He notes, further, that where Bretton Woods was increasingly criticized by prominent academic economist, inflation targeting seems to find favour.

Best Practice?

There are, not surprisingly, differing views on the best approach to monetary policy. Svensson (2006: 2) makes the simple point that

the implementation of best-practice monetary policy takes into account that monetary policy is actually the management of private-sector expectations...[and that]...what matters for private-sector decisions are the private sector's expectations about future interest rates. Therefore, the implementation of best-practice monetary policy consists of announcing and motivating the bank's forecasts of inflation, the output gap, and, importantly, the instrument rate. This is the most effective way of managing private-sector expectations.

Svensson consequently argues that the central bank should have its own view of the optimal interest rate path, based on its analysis of economic developments. Whether or how much to divulge about the trend is a matter of judgement. Indeed, judgement is widely regarded as the key component of monetary policy strategy—after all why would we need central bankers if the models they use were sufficient for the right decisions to be made?

Observing that the transformation of the monetary environment over the last two to three decades has been extraordinary, Mishkin (2007a) highlights six key ideas that have come to be widely accepted by monetary authorities and against which there is little dissent, although he also notes that his list shows how far monetary policy has moved since the 1960s—a decade in which the outcomes of monetary policy were poor. They are as follows:

1. There is no long-run trade-off between output and inflation, with the implication that monetary policy cannot provide a lasting stimulus to output, even if it can do so in the short-run. Put another way, this first tenet is a re-assertion of the statement that inflation is always a monetary phenomenon.

2. Expectations, especially of financial markets, are critical in shaping the outcomes of monetary policy decisions, and therefore have to be actively managed.

3. Inflation, especially beyond low single digit rates, has high costs that diminish welfare.

4. There is always a risk that monetary policy will be vulnerable to what Mishkin refers to as the time inconsistency problem—the temptation by the monetary authority to choose a looser monetary policy in the short-run, even though it has long-run costs.

5. Independent central banks are able to conduct monetary policy more effectively than those subject to political control, a corollary of which is that monetary policy should be de-politicized.

6. A strong nominal anchor is needed to ensure that monetary policy achieves its desired outcomes.

To the extent that there is an approach that does amount to a 'state-of-the-art', it arguably comprises the following:

- Inflation targeting—perhaps more accurately rendered as inflation-*forecast* targeting—in which the aim is to achieve medium-term price stability.

- Putting a premium on pre-emptive action to ensure that inflation is unable to take hold, an approach which necessarily means that policy has to be alert not just to current developments, but also to forecasts of likely changes.

- Using the short-term interest rate (repo) as the main policy instrument, but complementing it by using various forms of communication to signal to economic actors (especially financial markets) what the orientation of monetary policy is to be and to hint at the direction of change (tightening or loosening).

- Awareness of the risks associated with prospective economic developments.
- A preference for small changes in policy rates and only rare use of surprises, partly to reinforce a sense of both commitment and credibility, with the latter a very fragile commodity—as Tucker (2006: 220) notes, 'credibility needs to be earned and re-earned, over and over again'.

Formally, neither the ECB nor the Fed explicitly targets inflation, and it could be argued that with the world's two largest central banks eschewing this approach, inflation targeting cannot easily be described as a state-of-the-art. However, the ECB comes very close[3] to inflation targeting in the way it defines its reference value, while the Fed, despite its dual mandate, appears to have a de facto inflation target that is not that different from those of the ECB or the Bank of England. Moreover, the fact that the two most prominent central banks do not conform fully could simply mean that they are 'behind the curve'.

Institutional Structures

Different facets of the institutional structure within which central banks operate can affect the approach to monetary policy. They include whether or not the government retains powers to set operational targets, the power over appointments, including whether central bank board members can be fired, and the arrangements for holding the central bank to account. At an operational level, the composition of the monetary policy committee that makes policy decisions and the manner in which it functions varies among leading central banks.

All these factors, and more, can have some impact on monetary policy strategy. The Bank of England, for example, has an MPC with nine members, five of whom are internal and four external. While Eddie George was Governor, he always voted last on interest rate decisions, and always sided with the majority (and hence, on close decisions, acted as the swing voter). His successor has sided a couple of times with the minority, a tactic than can itself be a signal about future intentions if markets assign greater weight to the Governor's view. Alan Greenspan, by contrast, signalled his view in advance, arguably defying the rest of the open-market committee to contradict him. The Governor of the Reserve Bank of New Zealand is the sole decision-maker, but is advised by a committee, with the result that the decisions are, in fact, more collegial than the formal arrangements imply, according to Svensson[4] (2007).

Point Target or Range?

There are aspects of the detail of implementation of monetary policy that distinguish different approaches, but they are hardly strategic and hence need not be analysed in this chapter. But some aspects of decisions frameworks do have strategic ramifications, a good illustration being the form that the inflation target takes. In some cases, the objective is set in terms of a range, which can give the central bank some leeway, though at the expense of increasing uncertainty. Others specify a point target, making it more evident to private agents when conditions presage a change of interest rates, thereby enhancing predictability. Some, such as the Fed (not an inflation targeter), do not disclose a value for inflation, leaving it to be inferred by market actors.

Two central banks that employ very similar approaches are the Swedish Riksbank and the Bank of England. Both have symmetrical inflation targets with a 1 percentage point tolerance band. The Riksbank's framework also provides for inflation being returned to the target rate within two years of any deviation from it. Yet, it does allow for the possibility that where a deviation from target is larger, it may make sense to allow a longer period. So far, this prospect has been only theoretical. The Riksbank makes clear that, although it has an explicit target for CPI inflation, it recognizes that there are other relevant definitions of inflation. It therefore monitors a second consumer price index (UND1X) which strips out from the CPI the effects of indirect taxes, subsidies, and mortgage payments, and states that it pays attention to asset price inflation. However, the Riksbank also states that it distinguishes between inflation measures that bear on the inflation forecast and the targeted variable itself. Thus it may comment on trends in other series, but does so as part of its decision on how to meet the CPI target.

The empirical evidence is also revealing in other respects. On the surface, the ECB should not adopt a Taylor rule, since it has hierarchical objectives in which price stability has pride of place. Yet, among others, Surico (2003) suggests that it has come very close to following such a rule, erring if anything on being soft on the inflation component of the rule. Similarly, Hayo and Hofmann (2006) suggest that the ECB has given much more weight to the output gap than the Bundesbank ever did. The fact that central banks have only imperfect knowledge is, however, highlighted by Issing (2005*b*) who observes that not being sure about the true output-level gap or the likely impact of major institutional developments creates uncertainty and calls for the exercise of judgement. This renders difficult the use of simple rules—such as the Taylor rule—that assume the output gap can be monitored straightforwardly.

Central Bank Communication

As explained in greater detail in the chapter in this volume by Jabko, transparency has become a vital part of the monetary policy toolkit, and is also now seen as part of the state-of-the-art. But what is meant by transparency and the manner in which it is used as a technique to achieve monetary policy aims— as opposed to other motivations such as underpinning accountability—needs to be examined in detail (Begg 2007). Eusepi and Preston (2007) look at what forms of communication are needed to ensure that monetary policy strategy is understood by economic agents, and show analytically that more extensive transparency will be more effective than partial communication in avoiding a de-stabilizing path for expectations. Thus, it is better for the central bank to announce not just the inflation target, but also how it will be reached. Publication of extensive information, including inflation forecasts, is seen by the Riksbank as part of its monetary policy strategy and it is clear (see Tucker 2006 for a recent exposition) that the Bank of England has a similar viewpoint. Geraats (2007) shows that how central banks choose to communicate can affect the role of transparency in a monetary policy strategy. She argues that a central bank should be precise in communicating its inflation target, but may achieve better results by fostering a perception of ambiguity in what will induce it to act.

Here the debate on price-level versus inflation targeting is salient. Because price-level targeting means clawing back any deviation from the target by aiming for a lower or higher inflation rate in the short-term, it would make communication of the target more complicated (Tucker 2006). In a simple example, if the economy were subject to a shock that meant that inflation had been above a price-level target consistent with an annual rate of inflation of 2 per cent for five years by half a percentage point, the path to bring it back on course would (in round numbers) imply an inflation rate of 1.5 per cent for the following five years. Alternatively, it could be two years at 1 per cent to restore credibility followed by a gradual return to the long-term target rate of 2 per cent. Explaining a range of values for current inflation to the public would be significantly more difficult than a consistent 2 per cent inflation target.

Similarities and (Limited) Differences

While there are manifestly differences in approach to monetary policy strategy among leading central banks, partly because of their traditions and mandates, what is more striking are the similarities. Independence is critical, in that monetary policy strategists plainly take a long view and feel no need to court popularity. Resort to formal rules varies. The Fed is usually described as having a dual mandate[5] which consists of having regard to both price stability and the level of employment (or unemployment)—in other words, it simultaneously targets the nominal and the real economy. Yet, there have been repeated calls for the Fed to adopt an explicit inflation target, and there was considerable speculation at the end of the Greenspan era about whether Bernanke, who had seemed in some of his academic writings to be well-disposed to an explicit inflation target, would seek to implement such a strategy. The dilemma is that it is not easy to alter a long-established mandate, especially as it will generally require legislation, and often easier to have a hidden rule, an example of limits to the power of central bankers.

The ECB's definition of price stability as a reference value of 2 per cent for HICP inflation for the euro area as a whole is consistent with the practice of the member central banks in the years leading up to the start of the single currency, and it has made clear that the target range is above 0 per cent inflation, then (after an evaluation of its strategy in 2003) further clarified the aim as being close to 2 per cent. Strictly, though, the ECB does not have an inflation target and the ECB approach explicitly acknowledges that price stability is a medium-term goal, thereby allowing for some short-term deviation from the reference value. Some critics have argued that the ECB reference value is too restrictive (see, for example, Svensson 2002) and that it would be better if the ECB adopted a more symmetrical target, as in Sweden or the UK.

The ECB's two-pillar strategy (Issing et al. 2001) gave considerable notional weight to the growth of the monetary stock, with a reference value of 4.5 per cent for annual monetary growth (M3) ostensibly setting a rule for intervention. The ECB's strategy, described as hybrid by Bordes and Clerc (2006), is more difficult to explain than pure inflation targeting or monetary growth targeting. Issing (2006: 6) defends the approach in the following terms: 'the two pillars serve the purpose of organising the incoming data in a structured way basically under the aspect of the relevant time horizon. The cross-checking is a means of reconciling the shorter-term analysis with the longer-term perspective leading to a consistent, "unified" overall assessment'.

Even a cursory look at the data suggests that the monetary pillar reference value is a rule honoured above all in the breach. However, as explained in Fischer et al. (2006), the Quarterly Monetary Assessment (QMA) undertaken by the ECB staff, but not made public, is more comprehensive than just looking at the monetary aggregate, since its purpose is to understand how monetary conditions bear on price stability. They conclude that the use of the monetary pillar has allowed more rounded analysis—sometimes referred to as a cross-check—of inflation dynamics than reliance solely on the economic analysis pillar and, thus, made for better decisions. Yet, their evidence also suggests that, although both pillar have tended to point in the same direction most of the time, the economic pillar has been the more influential overall in interest rate decisions when, in their words, the monetary pillar gives a blurred signal.

The ECB approach prompts the broader question of whether money matters in monetary policy-making. In 2003, the ECB appeared to diminish the role of the monetary pillar, re-branding it as 'monetary analysis' and reversing the order of the two pillars. For the ECB, the monetary pillar provides a cross-check on price movements in the longer-run, whereas the economic analysis is considered to be more revealing about the short-run. In fact, most central banks take some account of monetary growth according to the OECD (2007: annex to chapter 2, paragraph 2) which comments that 'only the US Fed does not put any noticeable weight on money supply'. However, the degree to which other central banks take account of money is limited (Woodford 2007).

By contrast, critics of the ECB suggest that it places too much weight on monetary aggregates, but the issue is not easy to verify because the ECB has never signalled an explicit weight and, in all probability, would expect to vary the weight over time in any case.

Thus, one dimension that distinguishes different strategies is the precise manner in which money is taken into account. The euro area is adjudged to have a relatively stable demand for money, which means that it is a relatively more reliable indicator for policy purposes. The euro area (according to the OECD 2007) has also had less financial innovation than other currency areas so that there is less distortion of the relationship between money supply and inflation, although the OECD reports that the stability of the relationship may be diminishing, as shown by a less stable velocity of circulation. The housing market is considered to be a particularly important factor and the OECD cites evidence that most of the overshoot of M1 in the euro area is attributable to mortgage lending.

Consensus or Debate

One of the more striking inferences to draw from a review of monetary policy strategies is how little room there appears to be for debate about the social welfare aims central banks, with all their power, are trying to achieve, and this lack of debate pervades approaches to monetary policy. It would scarcely be an exaggeration to say that most of the discourse is around how to conduct policy, not why or for whom it is being conducted. Buiter (2006) argues that to target inflation, even in the flexible inflation targeting manner, is a policy approach bereft of any microeconomic foundations about what improves welfare and, with customary robustness, he casts doubt on the consensus that says inflation targeting and independent central banks are optimal. Similarly, Bean (2007) points to the problem within flexible inflation targeting that the choice of what weight to give to a real economy variable is ultimately a normative one, and he notes that some micro-foundations of the approach ignore legitimate distributive issues of an uneven incidence of unemployment. The fallout from the 2007–8 credit market turmoil is likely to be another source of disquiet.

A pointed question posed by Buiter (2006: 24) is whether the strength of the independence granted to some central banks is such that they are devoid of incentives. As he puts it:

while many central bankers may be motivated in their approach to the job by a sense of public service, by duty and by unflinching commitment to the central bank's mandate, one would like to see these higher motives reinforced by such primitive but frequently more reliable motives as the desire for power, prestige, wealth, comfort and leisure. This problem is especially acute when the monetary policy decision is a group decision; it gets more severe the larger the monetary policy making committee.

For Buiter the problem cannot readily be solved because independence and accountability are, in many ways, incompatible. However, he argues forcefully for limiting the tasks assigned to the central bank to monetary policy, excluding tasks such as supervision of financial intermediaries and control of payments systems, and he also advises central bankers to avoid commenting on fiscal or structural policies that are not part of their direct remit.

Beyond Price Stability

One contentious area is whether monetary policy strategy should have much regard to variables other than price stability. As Bean (2007) points out, governments might be interested in distributive questions or in regulatory ones such as how to curb carbon emissions, but they tend to be tangential to what monetary policy can plausibly do. Nevertheless, it is pertinent to ask whether monetary policy strategy should, on occasion, give greater weight to aims other than price stability, even when the latter is formally identified as their primary objective. Many central banks, for example, have financial stability as part of their mandate, notwithstanding Buiter's concerns that they should stick to monetary policy and only monetary policy. As an illustration, financial stability is part of the Swedish Riksbank's remit, but it does not regard movements in the repo rate as an instrument for promoting financial stability, and a statement of objectives on its web-site is at pains to emphasize this distinction. Even so, the Riksbank gives itself some flexibility, noting that large corrections may have effects that are better avoided, the implication of which is that interest changes may be phased in if, for example, there is undue turbulence in asset prices.

In fact, asset prices could be seen as either a complementary or a distinct target, and the relationship between monetary aggregates and asset prices is another of the more contentious areas, with some central banks more willing than others to countenance policy action to counter an asset bubble. Bean (2007) suggests that the argument runs as follows: when an asset boom turns to bust, borrowers' net worth deteriorates and lenders will react by imposing a credit crunch with rapid effects on the real economy. A low inflation environment may, moreover, accentuate the impact. However, Bean argues that interest rate increases cannot regulate a surge in asset prices, will exacerbate the problems of borrowers, and thus will have a negative impact on activity, all for uncertain policy gains. The problem may, according to Kohn (2006), be that it is often difficult to distinguish between 'normal' movements in asset prices that pose no threat to the stability of output and prices, and fundamental misalignments in asset prices that become a threat to economic (and/or financial) stability as they unwind. One strategic answer is for the monetary authority simply to respond to the consequences of the asset movement on the variables that it usually monitors, while a second approach is to bend policy so as to go beyond such reactions. Another would be to pay more attention to money.

As the 2007–8 credit market problems have shown, central banks also need to be vigilant about financial stability (see also the chapter by Moran and Macartney in this volume). These recent events have highlighted the role of central banks in providing liquidity to the markets at times when banks and other financial intermediaries face problems, and may call for a fresh look at how the 'lender-of-last-resort' function is exercised. Central banks have tended towards ambiguity in how they approach liquidity problems, preferring not to intervene in ways that inhibit the functioning of financial markets. But to achieve stable monetary conditions, such intervention may on occasion be necessary as the differences that became apparent in 2007–8 in how the ECB and the Bank of England confronted this challenge made plain.

Validation by Performance?

Monetary policy strategies seem to attract only limited debate outside specialist circles, and even then the differences of opinion are typically more about the timing of decisions or the quality of analysis than the underlying strategies. It may therefore be reasonable for a performance yardstick to be used to assess them, rather than more politicized judgements. Indeed, it is in some ways a surprise that inflation targeting has not been more problematic, given the expectation that while it offered a compelling solution for achieving price stability, it was likely to be at the expense of greater output volatility. In fact, most inflation targeters can take comfort from the out-turns. Bean (2007: 15), commenting on the period since the UK adopted inflation targeting (becoming known as the 'Great Stability'), observes that 'the *really* remarkable thing is how stable output growth has been' [emphasis in original]. He accepts that an absence of shocks and other structural factors that can be characterized as 'good luck' have played a part, but having reviewed a variety of such other explanations, implicitly favours the view that good policy has played a considerable part.

This would come as no surprise to Mishkin (2007a) who notes that while inflation targeting pushes central banks to avoid a focus on short-term real economy variables, thereby dealing with time inconsistency, it is not incompatible with output stabilization over the longer term. He notes, too, that countries that have adopted full inflation targeting monetary policy strategies have fared well economically, with no apparent cost in terms of output volatility. However, Mishkin qualifies his praise by noting that prominent countries that have not adopted inflation targeting have also performed well, notably the United States,[6] and he offers the explanation that these countries have been able to find alternative strong nominal anchors. Nevertheless, the emerging evidence that Mishkin reviews suggests that inflation targeting may be better at curbing expectations of inflation and at diminishing inflation persistence.

In a careful analysis, Rose (2007) finds that despite a floating exchange rate being a feature of inflation targeting regimes, exchange rate volatility is marginally lower, on average, than for other monetary regimes. This is not as paradoxical as it seems in that the inflation targets are typically very similar (2% CPI, for example, is typical). Rose (2007) also finds that inflation targeting countries do not seem to be at risk from capital 'stops' which arise when short-term capital flows suddenly desert a country, even though inflation targeting implies no controls on capital. The obvious explanation is that capital is attracted to the stability that the monetary regime provides.

There has been some criticism, especially since the launch of the euro, that price increases have been higher (or perceived to be so) than revealed by the core inflation index used by the ECB (and the Bank of England). Yet in this regard, it is important to recognize that highly visible price increases (the baguette or the café au lait) are offset by falls in the prices of less frequently purchased items; in other words, the move to the euro has resulted in some relative price adjustments. While it is probably true that some sellers exploited the opportunity of the conversion to the euro, it is important to recognize that the transition is a one-off change.

Concluding Remarks

In shaping contemporary approaches to monetary policy strategy—while recognizing that non-trivial differences remain—some explanations resonate more widely than others. Considerable influence can be ascribed to changes in understanding of what monetary policy can and should do. Many of the 'big ideas' have come from outside Europe or from non-euro area countries and have been pioneered elsewhere: for instance, the time inconsistency concept or the adoption of inflation targeting in New Zealand. An intriguing feature of much of the literature on monetary policy strategy is that so many of the leading protagonists seem to straddle the academic and policy worlds. In terms of the overall themes of this volume, this establishment of an international central banking 'intelligentsia' suggests that the sound money paradigm has led European approaches, rather than there being a distinctive European approach, and the apparent convergence on so many agreed aspects of monetary policy strategies is striking.

Particularly notable is the strength of the consensus around the view that inflation targeting (preferably of the flexible variety), buttressed by independence, is the preferred monetary policy strategy, notwithstanding the ECB and the Fed—custodians of the two largest monetary areas—not being strict inflation targeters. Dissent from this consensus is rare. Willem Buiter (2006: 39) is a prominent exception, arguing that

flexible inflation targeting . . . is incompatible with the mandate of every central bank that has price stability as its primary objective. It risks imparting an upward bias to inflation. It sets monetary policy design and implementation back to before 1989—the year New Zealand first adopted inflation targeting. The solution is to drop flexible inflation targeting and replace is with *lexicographic* or *hierarchical* inflation targeting.

By this, Buiter means giving price stability pride of place and, by implication, playing down the weights given to stabilization of the real economy so long as price stability has not been assured.

However, it deserves to be stressed that central banking is about more than price stability and, as regards financial stability, recent events have exposed greater divergences (and, arguably, failures) in approach. It may be, therefore, that the pursuit of price stability has over-shadowed other dimensions of stability, notably financial stability, though as Pisani-Ferry et al. (2008) point out the resilience to shocks of the macroeconomic system as a whole is another vital facet of stability. Here, European countries may have more in common with each other than with other parts of the world, especially in the relationship between fiscal policy and monetary policy, though with continuing ambivalence about how structural policies enter the equation.

It can be argued, further, that today's consensus on monetary policy strategy reflects the rather benign conditions that have prevailed in recent years. Increased global competition has held down consumer prices and although there have been periodic swings in oil prices, they have, on the whole, not led to attempts by wage negotiators to push up nominal wage rates in a compensating manner, as occurred in the 1970s and 1980s. Immigration to OECD countries with relatively tight labour markets has probably also played a part, while persistent unemployment in others has meant that labour markets have had some slack.

Nevertheless, there are several areas where reform or refinement of monetary policy strategies can be contemplated. Some are largely technocratic issues, such as the degree to which the central bank should seek to present an interest rate path in both its forecasts and its pronouncements. In 2005, for example, the Riksbank shifted its forecasting strategy to factor-in changes in interest rates anticipated by the markets, rather than forecasting on the assumption of an unchanged repo rate and has since (2007) further refined its approach, whereas the Bank of England appears to be more hesitant. Other disputed areas are more political, for example Mishkin (2007a) argues that there four aspects of monetary policy strategy on which there is debate about the way forward:

- What definition of an inflation target to favour given the distinction between the price level and the current inflation rate.

- The optimal degree of transparency. At issue here is whether more is always better, or whether there should be limits to transparency, either to avoid confusing the public or because central bank mystique can still be a valuable attribute (Geraats 2007).

- How to deal with asset price movement and whether asset prices should be explicitly targeted, irrespective of any pass through into inflation, or simply monitored as a potential influence on prices.
- Whether the exchange rate should be treated as a separate aim of policy, an issue that manifestly came to the fore in the 2007 French election.

There is also some evidence of a renewed interest in how much attention to pay to money in monetary policy (see, for example, Issing 2006). A further area for development in monetary policy strategy is in how to exercise judgement in what Svensson (2007: 190) describes as 'a disciplined and systematic way rather than in a completely discretionary and ad hoc way'. Models and analytic work can provide a strong basis, but can never (Issing 2005*b*) be sufficient, and behavioural changes are, by definition, difficult to anticipate. If, in addition, political economy influences are allowed for, there is good reason for caution in any presumption that monetary policy strategy has reached its own 'end of history'.

Notes

1. The research on which this chapter draws is part of the Integrated Project 'New Modes of Governance' (www.eu-newgov.org), financially supported by the European Union under the 6th Framework programme (Contract No. CIT1-CT-2004-506392). I am grateful to Charles Goodhart and the editors of this volume for helpful comments on a previous draft.
2. The notion that the monetary authority may be tempted to court popularity by opting for looser monetary policy in the short-term, despite being aware of the adverse longer-term consequences of igniting inflation.
3. Nevertheless, Pisani-Ferry et al. (2008) argue that it would benefit from fully adopting an inflation targeting approach.
4. Who, it should be noted, has advised the Reserve Bank that it should have a broader decision-making committee.
5. In fact the statutory instruction to the Fed identifies moderate long-term interest rates as a further objective, along with a general duty to promote financial stability and a sound banking system.
6. More controversially, he also cites Germany, a country which has undoubtedly achieved enduring price stability, but given the record of that country's real economy since the early 1990s, the verdict on other aspects of economic performance may be less flattering.

17

Scientization of Central Banking: The Politics of A-Politicization

Martin Marcussen

Central banks across the world are embedded in a variety of national contexts and histories. They are exposed to a multitude of challenges that require learning and adaptation in very specific situations. Globalization, regional integration processes, financial crises, wars, and terrorist attacks impact differently on central banks. In most cases, the central banks feel that flexibility and change are imperative because of these challenges. Seen in that light, we would not expect central banks across the globe to display isomorphic characteristics. Although central bankers model each other's practices, structures, and ideologies, they do not copy these features one-to-one. Instead, they translate and convert institutional fashions from other contexts into a format that resonates with the existing domestic structures, relations, and ideas. Emulation does not necessarily imply institutional convergence. Indeed, in preparation for major institutional reform, a comparative study commissioned by the Reserve Bank of New Zealand concluded that in the 1980s 'there was little commonality among central banks in their precise functions, objectives, or even the question of who should set the objectives. The evidence was that few central banks at the time had well-defined, stable, objective functions' (Singleton et al. 2006: 140). Central bankers are therefore commonly regarded as an 'oddly assorted bunch'. Many national idiosyncrasies persist that may no longer have a place, though ' ... these may have deeper roots than many people assume' (Deane and Pringle 1994: 338).

Despite the danger of oversimplification, the chapter neglects many of the differences that exist between central banks. It adopts a meso-historical perspective on central banks and central banking in order to identify the conjunctures through which central banking has developed over the last couple of centuries. In short, at this level of abstraction, the chapter considers central banking and central banks to be distinct analytical categories, thereby neglecting micro-developments. The conception of time with which the chapter works is possibly best described in Fernand Braudel's notion of *moyenne durée* (Hufton 1986: 210–11). In contrast to the *longue durée*, in which the basic parameters of human existence are stable, the *moyenne durée* allows for a level of analysis which draws our attention to the conjunctural cycles, in this chapter referred to as 'ages', through which central banking and central banks are developing as a group. In contrast to the *courte durée*, which is connected to detailed historical studies of individual and possibly—in a longer historical perspective—abnormal phenomena, the *moyenne durée* tends to neglect idiosyncrasies in central banking, while aspiring to develop theories about meso-historical dynamics. Thus, the dynamic meso-historical perspective implies that we are interested in learning from past cycles with a view to formulating so-called 'plausibility probes' about possible future developments (Eckstein 1975: 108). In other words, the intention is to develop and forward an argument that intuitively sounds plausible and puzzling.

Thus, the purpose of this exercise is to substantiate *a claim about where central banks are at present and where they are heading.* In short, the chapter claims that central banking may be heading towards a *new age, characterized by scientization and including horizontal bureaucratic extension, external communication, collective decision making, and outcome management.* Max Weber's concept of rationalization describes this development in terms of a striking *intellectualization* of the world; an *objectification* of things and actions via formal analysis and mathematical abstraction; a *technical mastery* via specialized practices and discourse; and *reification* of policies, power relations, and institutions. The last part of the chapter discusses the possible implications that scientization might hold for central bank governance, knowledge production, and accountability.

Global Trends in Central Banking

It is common practice among central bank historians to distinguish four stages in the development of central banking (Fischer 1994: 262–329). In the first stage, governments created special banks to raise loans for themselves, typically to cover war expenditures. These central banks also assumed responsibility for issuing and regulating notes. In the second stage, central bankers were defined as the sort of entities we now recognize as central banks proper. Central banks started to become banks to other banks, thus accepting responsibility for the stability of the financial system. They were occasionally the lenders of last resort and were responsible for the management of the external value of the national currency. In the third stage, many central banks were nationalized. They were entirely subordinated to their government and merely implemented the general macro-economic policy. Monetary policy had multiple goals such as full employment, economic growth, price stability, and a stable exchange rate. Finally, in the fourth stage, central banks were granted formal autonomy to pursue a single objective, most typically price stability (see Begg in this volume). They maintained their currency function and responsibility for the overall stability of the financial system (although their supervisory functions vary from country to country).

The shift from the first to the second stage can be explained by the gradual development of private banking and the consequent risk of bank failure. The government's bank simply had to take on additional functions to assist in situations of financial default, sometimes as lender of last resort (see Moran and Macartney in this volume). The shifts from the second to the third stage and from the third to the fourth stage can be accounted for by successive crises in the form of the inter-war economic depression, the two world wars, and the great inflation of the 1970s. With that background in mind, this chapter asks the question whether globalization implies that yet another stage in the development of worldwide central banking is taking shape. In other words, is there indicative evidence to support a plausible claim that central banking is moving into a fifth age (Table 17.1)?

The question is whether key trends are so significant and general in scope that they contribute to laying the foundations for a new stage in the development of central banking. Attention will be directed towards a major trend, scientization, and the way in which scientization is being bolstered by horizontal bureaucratic extension, collective decision making, external communication, and outcome management.

Scientization

While the 1990s were characterized by a worldwide surge in organizational reform enhancing the instrument autonomy of central banks, that is, freedom from being supervised by political authorities in the process of implementing monetary and financial policies, the 2000s appear to be characterized by scientization. In the previous decade, monetary and, to the extent that banking supervision was in the hands of central bankers, financial policy making were *de*politicized. These two policy areas were shielded from what were seen to be short-term political considerations. The arena for ideological debate and political deliberation shifted away from the world of central banking towards other areas of political life. Central banking was institutionally and legally exempted from ordinary democratic decision making.

In the 2000s, however, central banking is becoming increasingly *a*politicized. Max Weber referred to this process as 'rationalization': 'the process by which explicit, abstract, intellectually, calculable rules and procedures are increasingly substituted for sentiments, tradition, and rules of thumb' (Wrong 1970: 26). When ideology is being displaced by science, central bankers gain legitimacy and authority by basing their views on, and applying,

Table 17.1. Central banking throughout the ages

	First age 1600s–1800s	Second age 1873–1914	Third age 1930s–1970s	Fourth age 1980s–1990s	Fifth age? 2000s
Regime	Mercantilism/colbertist Nationalism	Gold standard/Laissez faire internationalism	Bretton Woods/Keynesian nationalism	Washington consensus/ Monetarist internationalism	Post-Washington consensus/ transnationalism
Arena shifting	Few state-owned central banks	De facto autonomous central banking	Integrated central banking	Formally autonomous central banking	Scientization
Bureaucratic scope	Small—disparate	Establishment of basic structures	Building up	Building down	Building out (alliances)
Decision making	Subdued the will of the principal	Discretionary	Public service machine bureaucracy. Process administration	Let managers manage. Business and output management	Committees and outcome management
Communication	Non-existent	Non-existent	Legalistic—formalistic	Techno-speak	Transparency
Targets	Servicing the state and its war-economy	Currency stability	Multiple goals—internal and external	Monetary targeting	Inflation targeting

the language of science. Human affairs are being reduced to 'calculable, cold, hard, "matter-of-factness" ' lying outside—indeed transcending—the sphere of political action (Gregory 2007). Scientization implies that power is being concentrated in the hands of those who master the discourse of science, scientific 'techno-speak'. Central banking is becoming a matter for intellectuals, thus implying that it is an elite phenomenon with which elected politicians would not even consider dealing (Woods 2002: 25–45, 34–7). It is being dehumanized, eliminating personal ideological and emotional features that escape calculation. In line with Weber's portrayal of the ideal typical civil servant, central bankers are being presented, and sometimes present themselves, as passionless machines and specialists without spirit (Marcussen 2006a).

Scientization, which apoliticizes the art of central banking, is fundamentally different from autonomization, which depoliticizes central banking. Autonomous central banking does not imply that media and politicians and other opinion makers do not care about or pay attention to the métier of central bankers; scientization does. Autonomous central banking does not imply that central bankers are automatically considered to be right when they make decisions; scientization does. And autonomization does not imply that central bankers are being uncritically listened to as the Delphi oracle, even when speaking out on matters that lie far beyond the narrow field of monetary and financial policy; scientization does. For instance, Alan Greenspan's inclination to speak out on issues that are formally beyond the authority of the Federal Reserve was legendary, and he possibly inspired central bankers elsewhere to do the same (Meyer 2004: 215).

The claim is not that central banking is 'scientistic'. Genuine science is open-ended, keeping alive a continuing conversation between theory and practice, not attempting to close debates and not presenting general, everlasting truths about human affairs. Central banking, on the other hand, appears to be 'scientific', representing a closed scientism which is 'self-confirming, essentially an ideology or dogma presented in the guise of science' (Gregory 2007). Importantly, the argument here is *not* that scientization and the ways in which it unfolds are universal phenomena. The meso-perspective adopted in this chapter is more interested in attempting to identify trends that, at some point in the future, may end up being more general phenomena in the world of central banking.

The American Federal Reserve Banks account for more than half of all published central bank research output (St-Amant et al. 2005: v), but the European Central Bank (ECB) also qualifies as a research powerhouse. In terms of full-time researchers, for instance, the ECB has a larger research directorate than the Department of Economics at the London School of Economics and Political Science (Marcussen 2006a: 93). Over its 10 years of existence, however, it has yet to achieve the level of authority enjoyed by the Bundesbank, the bank on which it was modelled (Jabko 2003). Since the ECB can still not speak without any visible opposition, the rationalization of the bank remains incomplete.

Scientization expresses itself in relation to many dimensions of central banking. Central bankers start to make epistemic alliances with other members of the scientific community ('building out'); coincidence, prejudices, and discretion are being filtered out of decision making in an 'instrument rational' manner (collective decision making); procedures are being instituted to minimize haphazard and random reactions to central bank decision making, so-called 'irrational exuberance' (transparency and communication); and measurable performance is based on few and exact standards (inflation targeting). In the following, these components of scientization will be discussed individually.

Building Out

The first central banks were established more than three hundred years ago, but the real upsurge in central bank institutions proper took place in the inter-war years. Since then, the world has witnessed a steady increase in the number of central bank institutions. Indeed, '[if] the fundamental, evolutionary criterion of success is that an organization should reproduce and multiply over the world, and successfully mutate to meet the emerging challenges of time, then central banks have been conspicuously successful' (Goodhart, Capie, and Schnadt 1994: 91). Today, almost all sovereign states have established a central bank. It has become a sign of statehood on the same level as a national anthem, flag, and army (ibid. 26).

With the politicization of central banking in the immediate post–Second World War period, most central banks were charged with additional functions and grew considerably in size. Together with the rest of the national public administration, the number of personnel, departments, sections, and administrative levels continued to grow. Central banks developed their administrative structure. Integrated central banking could be characterized as a paternalistic, formalistic, and hierarchical machine bureaucracy in which employees held steady career prospects and where form and process mattered more than substance.

The global wave of New Public Management changed all that. Central bank organizations everywhere underwent considerable trimming—'building down' (Morgan Stanley 2004: xi). To reduce the number of employees became an objective in itself and a single measure of success of central bank reform. Modernization became synonymous with downsizing. The administrative and management culture also shifted. Whereas central banks were regarded as distinct bodies of public administration in the immediate post–Second World War period, during the 1980s and 1990s they came to be considered businesses in their own right, or a subspecies of the category of state-owned enterprises. Managers were asked to manage their business, and each individual was evaluated on his or her ability to perform, that is, to deliver a certain kind of output in time according to contractual obligations (BearingPoint 2005).

As a result of scientization and rationalization in the 2000s, this may be changing. As epistemic communities, many central banks work in entirely different ways. They are opening up their distinct knowledge networks to like-minded allies and closing off their relations to the uninitiated (Marcussen 2006b). Organizational boundaries are blurring, as are territorial and cultural boundaries. Central banks are no longer building up or down; they are simply 'building out'. They form collegial alliances in the national as well as global organizational fields. Hierarchies are being broken down, and co-equal central bankers work closely together from project to project. Interesting and influential allies are being sought, preferably among those actors on the global institutional field of monetary policy making who share central bank notions of rationality. Veritable transnational, epistemic clan structures or communities may be emerging in the world of central banking. Such a development does not require fewer personnel (building down): it requires a different sort of personnel, possessing doctorates in economics and engaging directly and actively with the scientific community (Apel, Heikensten, and Jansson 2008). We may gradually see research departments established in central banks. Such research departments could expand and assume prestigious roles inside central banks. This could involve central bankers creating scientific working paper series and financing their own scientific journals, as well as management being recruited from universities (Marcussen 2006a). Within the central bank, scientific credentials could thus become effective career-enhancing factors.

Committee Decision Making

The history of central banking has typically been written with a particular focus on strong, decisive men, who created, consolidated, and defended the integrity and autonomy of their institution. One scholar concluded that '[t]hroughout the Fed's history, its power over the economy has depended more on the political leadership of its chairman than on any other factor' (Kettl 1986: 193). Bank of England Governor Montagu Norman and a great number of Fed Chairmen were presented as superhuman beings who constitute strong elements in the institutional legacies of these two central banks as well as role models for central bankers around the world. Throughout most of his governorship, Fed Chairman Greenspan simply personified the central bank institution: not by law, but in practice (Meyer 2004: 50–1, 74–5, 216, see also Woolley in this volume). Thus, an ordinary member of the Federal Open

Market Committee (FOMC), the main decision-making forum of the Federal Reserve System, holds that '[f]rankly, to this day I do not know if I ever actually influenced a FOMC decision in my five and a half years' (Meyer 2004: 166). In other countries, the personal role and responsibility of the central bank governor is spelled out in contractual form. The Reserve Bank of New Zealand offers a case in point: Alan Bollard and, before him, Don Brash were personally responsible since 1989 for achieving the inflation targets established together with the Treasury. Because of this personal responsibility, it is also ultimately the Reserve Bank governor, and him alone, who makes decisions about interest-rate changes. If unable to fulfil these stated objectives, the central bank governor can be fired by parliament (see Eichbaum in this volume).

The focus on one-person performance may now be changing. Rationalization and scientization require that decisions cannot be left to charismatic individuals. Instrumental rationality (*Zweckrationalität*) stands in contrast to value-rational (*wertrational*), affectual, and traditional forms of social action. It is therefore simply natural that collective decision making is gaining ground in the world of central banking. In countries as different as the UK, Japan, Sweden, Norway, Switzerland, Brazil, and many others, a monetary policy committee has been established. The same goes for the committee-based ECB, which thus far has replaced 16 central banks that were formerly run by individual governors (see Umbach and Wessels, as well as Howarth, in this volume). There has yet to be a central bank with collective decision making that has replaced this form of internal consensus building with a one-man show.

The increased depoliticization of central banking in recent years largely explains why such a major change in the decision-making mode has taken place. When central banking was fully integrated into the state apparatus during most of the Bretton Woods period, there was not much point in establishing decision making in committees. Governmental orders were not meant to be discussed, even less criticized. The governor was responsible for carrying out the decisions of others rather than making informed decisions of his own. With central bank autonomy flourishing in the 1990s, central banks were made accountable for efficient and effective decision making. In recent years, many central banks have shifted to collective deliberation to enhance the knowledge repertoire behind decisions and, not least, to spread accountability between more persons.

Arguments about the decision-making efficiency, in contrast to arguments about representative democracy, are being applied in favour of collective decision making in central banks. Indeed, some experimental research demonstrates that committees actually make better and more informed decisions than individuals (Lombardelli, Proudman, and Talbot 2005). Majority voting cancels out the worst performers in the committee, and more knowledge is being shared. When Lars Svensson was asked to evaluate single-governor

380

decision making in the Reserve Bank of New Zealand, he thought change ought to be made. He '... considered it risky for one individual to have so much power over monetary policy', and recommended that a monetary policy committee was established (Singleton et al. 2006: 201).

Transparency and Communication

Many myths about central banking date back to the Classical Gold Standard, when central bankers constructed the art of central banking in esoteric and almost religious fashion, keeping the functioning of the central bank temple as the best kept secret of all (Greider 1987: 54). The legacy is that, as a rule, central bankers do not interpret their role as consisting of communicating with the public on a regular basis or explaining their policies. No wonder that 'central banks traditionally [have been] surrounded by a peculiar and protective political mystique' (Goodfriend 1986: 64). Speaking about central bankers, Milton Friedman once observed that they had two principal objectives: 'avoiding accountability on the one hand and achieving public prestige on the other' (Fischer 1990: 1181).

All this may be about to change in many places. Today, there is a 'general consensus among central bankers that transparency is not only an obligation for a public entity, but also a real benefit to the institution and its policies' (Issing 2005a: 66). Within central banking, arguments related to efficiency drive the case for central bank transparency and external communication, rather than arguments about democratic legitimacy and accountability (Begg 2007, see also Jabko in this volume). Although central bankers recognize that their institution cannot exist in a vacuum cut off from public scrutiny, they primarily spend their time on making the scientific case for how transparency can enhance the effectiveness of their monetary policies. In other words, central banks translate the globally accepted norm of 'good governance' in their own way, which condemns secret and closed bodies of public administration to fit their own world. By way of targeted one-way communication, central bankers do not communicate with a view to learning from or adapting whatever argument may be raised against central bank policies. On the contrary, such market insensitivity or 'leaning against the wind' is helping central bankers to consolidate their reputation of integrity and autonomy in the financial markets. When central bankers talk, they do so with the financial markets, not with the general public. The argument is simple: central banks depend on financial and monetary markets to be effective and 'rational'. If markets are irrational, it will become difficult for the central bank to lay down a monetary policy strategy that helps it to reach its stated goals. One way in which the central bank improves the rationality and effectiveness of the financial markets is that it reveals not only its policy decisions but also the arguments and data leading to its decisions. The clearer the central bank is about what it is doing and why, the easier it becomes for the financial markets to form an opinion of how the short term develops. If the financial markets are clear about the short term, then, it is argued, the central bank can more easily achieve its objective in the medium to long term.

Central banks with a long history of policy effectiveness and credibility do not necessarily need to talk as much as central banks with a low level of perceived credibility. That is 'why "nouveau riche" institutions with poor credibility "talk," and why institutions that have a great "wealth" of credibility can afford to whisper' (Eijffinger et al. 2000: 119). This may explain why a hitherto unheard of degree of transparency has been adopted in Norway. The Norwegian Governor, Svein Gjedrem, decided that his quarterly inflation reports ought to contain projections of interest-rate levels three years into the future (*Financial Times*, 26 May 2006). Other central banks plan to follow the trend in the name of transparency, but critics argue 'that there is no point in announcing intentions for the future if that future is clouded in mystery' (Grauwe 2006).

Increased and improved communication with the external world is closely connected to the habit of making decisions collectively rather than on an individual basis. Committee decision making simply helps open the doors to the inner circles for professional central bank watchers in the financial media, stock exchanges, and private banks. Transparency is also closely connected to the next global trend in central banking: inflation targeting. Former Swedish central bank governor Lars Heikensten (2005: 6) argued that inflation targeting is now being conducted 'almost by necessity with a high degree of openness and clarity'.

Inflation Targeting

Inflation targeting—the notion that the bank, typically together with the national treasury, determines an acceptable range within which price inflation is allowed to settle—is now recognized as a worldwide central banking trend (Mahadeva and Sterne 2000). During the Classical Gold Standard, central bankers were most interested in external stability in the value of the currency. By contrast, central bankers in the post–Second World War period were asked to pursue several objectives simultaneously, such as growth, employment, and financial as well as price stability. During the late 1970s and the 1980s, many central banks started establishing monetary targets, which is an arrangement under which the central bank aims for a certain money supply growth rate (see Begg in this volume). In the United States, the idea of monetary targets entered political discourse in 1974, but it took until 1979 before Fed Chairman Paul Volcker implemented it. It lasted only a couple of years as a watered-down kind of 'pragmatic monetarism' (Kettl 1986: 144, 173). In practice, monetary policy was based on an eclectic application of economic theory. It proved to be incredibly difficult to determine the exact money supply and its impact on price levels.

A new era of targeting started when New Zealand, as a first mover, formally announced an inflation target in 1990. The New Zealanders and outsiders, having been accustomed to double-digit inflation levels for more than two decades, thought the first targets agreed in March 1990, 0–2 per cent, seemed radical. However, the objective was already reached after two years (see Eichbaum in this volume). A very large number of the world's central banks have since adopted explicit or implicit inflation targets (Mahadeva and Sterne 2000: 38). Both as a professor of economics, an ordinary member of the FOMC, and now as Chairman of the Fed, Ben Bernanke has been an ardent supporter of inflation targeting (*Time Magazine*, 23 July 2006: 'Gentle Ben. Inside the Head of the Fed'). The IMF is now also taking an active part in diffusing the idea worldwide. It has therefore entered high on the agenda, not only among the largest and richest countries in the world, but also—and maybe particularly— among the poorest and most peripheral countries in the world, such as Albania, Botswana, Romania, Uganda, and many others.

Former central bankers are sceptical. Paul Volcker, for instance, held that inflation targeting 'is a little bit too tight for me. The inflation rate is bound to go up and down a little bit and it should go up and down a little bit' (*Bloomberg.com*, 14 July 2006). Harvard professor Benjamin Friedman is also extremely reluctant to embrace inflation targeting: 'By forcing the entire conversation to take place in terms of only one aspect of economic activity that the central bank and the government care about . . . inflation targeting tends to hide what the true objectives of the monetary policy are and therefore undermines transparency' (*CentralBankNet.com*, 11 February 2005). The debate is classical in central bank circles; it is one of discretionary policy making versus rule-based policy making (Fischer 1990). Although inflation targeting can be understood as 'constrained discretion' (King 2004: 5), most analysts actually consider the explicit focus on one single performance criterion defined within a narrow band of fluctuation as an excessive breach of the extended discretion for which central bankers have fought over decades and actually obtained. When Congress established the Fed in 1913, the job was thought to be relatively automatic. This rule-based automaticity was supported by monetarist theory from the 1930s and onwards. From the 1960s, however, consecutive Fed Chairmen made it a central feature of central banking to adopt a discretionary, holistic, eclectic, and pragmatic approach to monetary policy making, that is, not narrowly focusing on one single objective maintained within a narrow band (Kettl 1986: 194). Targeting was not only considered to be an excessively constraining activity that could seriously undermine the utility of monetary policy. It was also perceived to be a threat to central bank independence, and, as we have seen, a setback for accountable policy making in central bank circles. Furthermore, most recently, some of the first-movers in inflation targeting, for instance Sweden, have in practice interpreted the targets in quite flexible ways. This has prompted some commentators to ask whether this is the beginning of the end for inflation targeting (Wolfgang Munchau, *Financial Times*, 5 June 2006).

However, inflation targeting can be seen as just another key element of rationalization and scientization. By explicitly and strictly determining the criteria for success and failure, monetary policy making is dehumanized in many ways. The scope for discretion and intuition—holistic and pragmatic central banking—is being narrowed down considerably, thereby confirming the stereotype of central bankers as passionless machines. The art of central banking is becoming objectified, thereby concealing the social character of monetary policy. The interests of real human beings and the political and power-related structures underlying central banking are being obscured by scientific and almost 'divine' rules. An abstract and complex affair is simplified and objectified: made a thing rather than a malleable social relation (reification). Thus, reification may conceal what is actually arbitrary and socially changeable by representing it as immutably given (Berger and Luckmann 1966: 106). As such, reification, through scientization and rationalization, could be considered an excellent form of social control, since those who have a stake in central banking, ordinary citizens as well as elected politicians, may be expected to exercise self-control and self-censorship rather than engage in direct debate or other efforts at politicizing central bankers.

Scientization and rationalization may challenge our existing understanding of accountability, legitimacy, and power relations between civil servants and politicians. This is the subject for the next section, which argues that the scientization process may have consequences for our conceptualization of governance, for how and what kind of knowledge is produced, and for political accountability (Table 17.2).

Table 17.2. The impact of scientization on governance, knowledge, and accountability

Governance Transnationalization	
Governance Communities	→ Knowledge Communities
Political Governance	→ Knowledge Governance
Knowledge Production	
Scientific Pluralism	→ Scientific Overlay
Civil Servant—Politician Relationship	
Depoliticization	→ Apoliticization
External Accountability	→ Internal Accountability

New Rules of the Game in Central Bank Governance

Scientization implies that governance—the regulation of social behaviour—is being transnationalized: that *a movement from territorial 'governor communities' to non-territorial 'knowledge communities'* is taking place (Table 17.2). Central bankers have usually been involved in international cooperation. During the era of the Classical Gold Standard, international cooperation between central bankers was characterized by *ad hoc* and informal contacts. Since the Second World War, international cooperation has become formalized in a large number of international organizations. It has also become globalized, in view of the fact that an increasing number of countries are becoming involved with one another in increasingly complex ways (Marcussen 2006c).

So far, the many forums in which central bankers meet have been defined by their national members and the territory that they represent. It has been possible to speak of communities of national central bank governors. International central bank forums have had a distinct territorial dimension, larger or smaller, depending on the number and type of members. International organizations such as these are fundamentally based on a territorial principle of organization and governance. This may now be about to change. If scientization is truly taking hold of central banking, and central bankers are merging to form a transnational knowledge community, territorial borders will cease to play a role and non-territorial principles of organization and governance will increasingly define the field. Conflict structures and patterns of governance within a knowledge community do not respect territorial borders; they become supra-territorial phenomena (Scholte 2005). Cleavage structures are defined according to the rules of the scientific game: intra-paradigmatic quarrels about theory, methods, data, etc. (Fourcade 2006). Knowledge communities are being constructed, partly replacing and partly supplementing or overlapping with governor communities.

Governor communities consist of central bank governors who represent clearly demarcated territories. Knowledge communities, by contrast, include all scientists within a field—whether central bank personnel or not. A knowledge community may be broader or narrower in scope than a governor community, and knowledge communities are more dynamic and porous than governor communities. Membership of a knowledge community cannot be inherited in the same way as membership of a governor community. For instance, the president of the Bundesbank will always be part of the G10, but he will only be a member of the knowledge community as long as he continues to contribute to the generation of scientific knowledge.

Transnational knowledge communities will be inclined to exercise 'soft' governance to a much greater extent than international governor communities. Central bankers in knowledge communities are more in the business of producing rules of appropriateness, standards, and guidelines, that is, *normative governance*; knowledge and data, that is, *cognitive governance*; as well as meaning, common histories, myths about the past, and visions about the future, that is, *imaginary governance* (Marcussen 2006*b*). It is therefore possible that *a movement from political governance to knowledge governance* is taking place as a result of scientization. Political governance can, for the sake of argument, be simplistically defined as using regulation to solve a concrete societal problem (Chandler 1958: 260). The practical aspects of problem solving—'the art of central banking'—rather than theorizing for the sake of theory—'the science of central banking'—have traditionally been central to the business of central banking. Theoreticians have not been held in high esteem in central bank circles, and it has been argued that the art of central banking is driven by intuition and life experience. John Maynard Keynes, for instance, was viewed among central bankers as a distant theoretician, and Strong and Montagu Norman feared that people like him would overshadow the 'practical bankers' (Jacobsson 1979: 45). However, this may cease to be the case. In contrast to political governance, knowledge governance can be defined as the production and dissemination of norms, knowledge, and identity. Central to knowledge governance is the idea that knowledge production is an objective in itself, that is, more knowledge is better than less knowledge.

Related to the development of knowledge governance is the question of what knowledge is and which aspects of knowledge ought to be expanded through intensified and systematic research. It is possible that scientization within central banking implies *a movement from scientific pluralism to a strategic overlay of particular research disciplines and approaches*. Since many central banks provide for their own income and to a large degree have a free hand when spending that money, and as central bankers tend to spend considerable amounts of money on a few areas of research activity, one would expect to see a more noticeable expansion of research activity in some areas of research than others. Through the massive injection of central bank money into research activities in delimited fields of research, many more actors will suddenly become players in the field of generating knowledge within a particular subset of macro-economic research. This is already a noticeable phenomenon in the North American scientific community. Here, central bank research appears to 'crowd-out' research on alternative monetary regimes (White 2005: 326). In other words, the scientization of central banking may cause a bias in research focus, since very few other sources of research funding, private or public, will be able to match the cash flow emanating from central bank circles. It is difficult to predict whether this potential research bias will have enduring consequences for the development of the economic sciences in particular and the social sciences in general. However, it is to be expected that the scientific disciplines of most relevance to central bankers will tend to play a dominant role in the overall field of macro-economic research (Apel et al. 2008). In consequence, the central banks have a sort of oligopoly on monetary opinion (White 2005: 327).

By the same token, just as specific scientific disciplines can become over-emphasized by an extraordinary injection of funding, so also can specific scientific approaches. The new impetus to macro-economic research may have an impact on the scientific discourse in general and, consequently, also on which approaches are considered to be marginal or peripheral and which are considered to be central or important. Indeed, it has been documented that central banks tend to subsidize research that takes the institutional status quo for granted (White 2005: 344). Since the new actors in the knowledge game are relatively well financed, and since it may reasonably be expected that they will have quite a narrow agenda, central bankers may be able to discipline the kind of discussions held in certain domains of economic research. Within the field of research on monetary policy, some voices in the ongoing academic debate may be strengthened, while others become weaker. If central banking ideas about obtaining stability via sound money, finances, and institutions have achieved the status of hegemony, this status can be expected to be further consolidated by additional funding in its favour.

Within central bank circles, this power to actually influence the entire research climate and the conditions of research is fully recognized and even valued. A Swedish central bank governor held that '[s]everal of my academic contacts have stressed how valuable the contact with the central bank world is for their research' (Heikensten 2005). For instance, the most recent evaluation report written by ECB researchers argued that the benefits to be attained by a central bank from engaging actively in academic research include the fact that the central bank 'can stimulate and encourage external research on issues of interest to the central bank through publications, conferences, and consulting relationships' (Goodfriend, König, and Repullo 2004: 5). The 'research power-house', the ECB itself, has ostensibly grasped the overall idea behind the concept of research management, since it 'uses its research capacity to encour-age, coordinate, and lead research efforts of the national central banks of the Eurosystem' (ibid. 22). And this is apparently not in vain. The evaluation concludes that '[g]iven its place at the centre of a continental system of central banks, it is not surprising that the ECB has already had a major effect on academic discourse throughout Europe' (ibid. 24).

The scientization of central banking may also have an impact on the power relationship between civil servants and politicians, typically in favour of the unelected civil servant, that is, the central banker. As mentioned, one result of scientization may be *a movement from depolitization to apolitization of the civil servant–politician relationship*. First, scientization consolidates the autonomous status of civil servants by objectifying monetary policy making. It becomes 'unthinkable' to start a political argument with a civil servant who possesses recognized scientific authority. Rather, to boost their own credibility, politi-cians might instead tend to socialize with and even publicly flatter the civil servant in question (Marcussen 2006a). The subtle longstanding relationship between the Governor of the US Federal Reserve and the American Congress can serve as an illustrative, albeit not necessarily entirely representative, example. Twice a year, in February and July, the Fed's Federal Open Market Committee reports to Congress on the conduct of economic and monetary policies—the so-called Monetary Policy Reports (see Woolley in this volume). The release of the report is followed up by the Fed Chairman testifying in Congress before the Banking Committees of both the Senate and the House. As an example, a transcript of the so-called Humphrey-Hawkins hearings in the Senate's Banking, Housing, and Urban Affairs Committee reads as follows:

I have had the privilege over an extended period of time as a Member, as Chairman, as Ranking Member, to work with Alan Greenspan in his capacity as Chairman of the Board of Governors, and it is something that I will always be proud of. I will always be proud to be able to say that I worked with the greatest central banker of the era.... I think one of the great services you provided to this country has been the wisdom of your views and the credibility that they contain when you have been willing to speak out.... In reviewing the great bankers in world history, I think Alan Greenspan qualifies as the greatest central banker in the history of the world. (Senator Phil GRAMM, Republican from Texas, banking.senate.gov/_files/107835.pdf, pp. 1–2)

As always, I welcome [Alan Greenspan] and thank him for the service he gives our Nation. (Senator Jon S. CORZINE, Democrat from New Jersey, banking.senate.gov/_files/107835.pdf, p. 5)

Second, scientization may imply that civil servants with recognized scientific authority are encouraged to engage in policy issues and domains that are not part of their primary area of responsibility. The functions and responsibilities of the civil servant grow exponentially with the degree of scientization. This may take two forms. One is the case where the central banker takes the initiative to engage in questions related to education policy, public administrative reform, and even cultural matters. Thus, researchers employed in the ECB do not hesitate to express criticism of the efficiency of the public sector in various European countries (e.g. Afonso et al. 2003). In an American context, Chairman Greenspan earned a notorious reputation for speaking out on issues lying far beyond the authority of the Federal Reserve, including politically contentious issues. Another form is the case where politicians and media alike consult central bankers on their own about questions that are only marginally related to central banking. This may take place in various hearings or in other public spheres.

Third, scientization has an impact on the mode and type of communication taking place in the political sphere. Apolitization through scientization means that the entire language of the field is changing. In contrast to political and administrative statements, a major characteristic of scientific statements 'is that they are privileged in the sense that, if derived in accordance with scientific procedures, they are considered to give greater assurance of truth. It is more useful if conclusions on, say, what works and what does not work in government are scientific because scientific propositions are understood to be more reliable' (Farmer 1995: 71). In other words, scientized civil servants become immune to political argumentation, because only the language of science is a valid means of communication.

All of these considerations suggest that the locus of accountability in central banking may be about to shift. We may see *a movement from external to internal accountability*. Central bankers were formerly accountable to the financial markets (during the 1990s) and politicians (during Bretton Woods). Now, central bankers may be increasingly accountable, first and foremost, to their scientific colleagues within the knowledge community. In knowledge communities, central bankers can only enhance their legitimacy and authority by complying with a number of scientific standards and by subjecting themselves to continuous peer review processes. Whereas central bankers were formerly obliged to communicate broadly with politicians, citizens, and the financial markets, their communication may be narrowing down to communicating with their peers. In doing so, they in some cases apply an arcane scientific terminology that excludes a large number of people, including many economists. Thus, the current fashion in central bank circles for engaging in a debate about how central banks should talk or whether it is a good or a bad thing that central bankers talk should not be interpreted as a general attempt to open the business of central banking to the broader public or to elected politicians.

The Fifth Age: From 'Art' to 'Science'

Do scientization and rationalization constitute a qualitatively and quantitatively new era for central banking? Is central banking developing from being an 'art' to becoming a 'science'? As emphasized throughout this chapter, Max Weber pointed to rationalization as a mega-trend in modern society as embodied in the reality of public administration. Later, Gouldner (1979) argued that public administration is on its way to becoming fundamentally scientized. Thus, scientization as a phenomenon is, strictly speaking, hardly a new, revolutionary phenomenon. It may not even adequately describe the world of central banking in all detail. However, there may be three solid reasons for why it is worthwhile to pay attention to elements of scientization in central banking. A first reason concerns the role of the state in the globalized world. As the reality of globalization is taking shape, the state is embarking on new roles and functions; new actors continue to pop up in global governance; and a multitude of authoritative governance instruments are being applied. In this situation, the possible scientization of central banking might serve as an early indicator of what is possibly becoming a more general phenomenon in global governance, that is, that the production of knowledge, norms, and identity—rather than the production of traditional, enforceable regulation—is what matters. Scientization can simply be seen as a new mode of governance in transnational regulation, according to which rational, technical, and objectified knowledge becomes central for the authoritative allocation of goods in society.

Second, it is worth paying attention to the nascent scientization of central banking, because it problematizes the relationship between science producers and science consumers. The literature on epistemic communities tends to view these two spheres as separate. According to that argument, scientific knowledge is injected into the policy process from outside in situations of uncertainty with a view to helping policy makers construct meaning. The case of central bank scientization illustrates that those producing science are not easily distinguished form those consuming science. Science and politics are not easily disassociated. Central banks do not necessarily produce relevant, open, debatable, and testable science. But they obtain a certain level of authority by presenting themselves as true scientists. Likewise, elected politicians appear to have tacitly agreed to leave large trunks of macro-economic policy making to the discretion of unelected bureaucrats. This delegation of power can be justified in the name of science, and it conveniently shifts responsibility for a problematic political arena away from the sphere of interest of elected politicians. The matter is objectified and, therefore, no longer an art subject to the discretion of individuals; rather, it is a science subject to generalizable social rules.

Finally, and connected to this latter point, a critical study of the case of central bank scientization helps us unravel the objectification of power structures. By doing so, we may better understand why national, regional, and global governance structures suffer from democratic deficits. If monetary policy is somehow transcending politics, lifted out of the political game all together, how can support and demand then be channelled into the formulation, adoption, and implementation of monetary policy? Traditional political systems analysis simply assumed that policy issues are salient and that concerned individuals and groups would attempt to channel their demands and support into the political system. Scientization and rationalization suggest that it may not be the case that interested parties engage in politics at all, particularly if the contentious issues and procedures are being brought beyond politization into the world of pseudo science, hidden in techno-speech, and reserved for the few initiated. Scientization points to the need for uncovering these processes with a view to repoliticizing monetary policies.

18

Transparency and Accountability

Nicolas Jabko

In the contemporary discourse of financial and monetary officials across the world, 'transparency and accountability' are usually lumped together as paired requirements. The spread of this global ethos is puzzling if we consider that central bankers not long ago derived pride and authority from their power to make important decisions outside the public eye. In 1986, Marvin Goodfriend, a vice-president of the Federal Reserve Bank of Richmond, acknowledged—and questioned—central bankers' adherence to a 'mystique' of secrecy surrounding monetary policy (Goodfriend 1986). By contrast, transparency and accountability now seem to be the object of a global consensus about modernity in central banking. Reflecting on his experience as vice-chair of the US Federal Reserve, Alan Blinder comments at great length upon the shift toward more transparency as one of three key elements of a 'quiet revolution' in central banking (Blinder 2004: 2–3, 5–33). The question therefore is how can we account for this apparently complete turnaround in less than two decades?

This chapter envisions the emergence of transparency and accountability as the normative embodiment of a historically contingent balance of power between central bankers and other actors. It argues that conventional accounts in terms of economic benefits and of democratic concerns are insufficient. Beyond the apparent convergence on a new global consensus, the equilibrium point of the balance of power between central bankers and other actors varies considerably across political systems. Even though everyone agrees on the need for 'transparency and accountability', there remain many different ways for central banks to live up to this global ethos. After developing a critique of conventional explanations, the chapter demonstrates the argument in the cases of the world's two most important central banks today—the Federal Reserve and the European Central Bank.

Transparency and Accountability in Historical–Political Perspective

At the most commonsense level, a central bank that lives up to the norm of transparency is one that makes its decisions in the public eye and renounces the 'mystique' of secrecy. This is the case if central bankers communicate abundant and timely information about their decisions and about the process that leads them to make these decisions. A commonsense definition of accountability is arguably somewhat more demanding. A central bank can be called accountable if it can be held to account for its decisions—both in the sense of explaining its decisions and in the sense of taking responsibility for its decisions. This, in turn, requires a constituency or even perhaps a political body to which the central bank must be brought to account.

Although these two basic definitions are widely open to discussion, a variety of techniques that purport to enhance central bank transparency and accountability have spread across the world since the 1980s. The most commonly cited transparency enhancements are the dissemination of inputs to the monetary policy process (including inflation and other economic forecasts and models that central bankers use as information for making policy); the publication of data about the process and output of monetary policy (minutes of monetary policy meetings, voting records, press conferences, and other central bank statements about policy trends). The most commonly cited accountability enhancements—in addition to the above—are the holding of regular parliamentary hearings of central bankers, the holding of increasingly open appointment (or re-appointment) procedures for central bankers, and more generally the existence of a regular debate and interaction between central bankers and various outside constituencies.

The value that is generally ascribed to transparency and accountability in central banking rests on two conventional rationales—one economic and one political. The economic rationale puts great emphasis on the need for transparency in order to achieve economic policy goals. According to this reasoning, both real changes in the economy and the evolution of economists' thinking call for enhanced central bank transparency.[1] As financial markets became more global and instantaneously responsive, monetary policy has become the central avenue not only for ensuring price stability, but also for macroeconomic demand management. Interest rates are now the main instrument for economic stabilization. In this new context, the expectations of market actors and the credibility of monetary policy become increasingly important. Central bankers need the cooperation of market actors in order to set medium- and long-term interest rates. This in turn would explain the new emphasis on transparency and the increasing importance of 'how central bankers talk' (Blinder et al. 2002). Transparency is part and parcel of the public relations strategies that central bankers develop in order to communicate their intentions to market actors.

The political rationale for the new consensus seems to stem from the global trend of increasingly independent central banks.[2] Accountability, in particular, is a normative requirement in a democratic context. As one central banker put it, 'independence and accountability are two sides of the same coin' (Issing 1999: 505)—or, this is the way things *should* be from a normative democratic perspective. The delegation of important policymaking powers to unelected central bankers raises serious concerns about the compatibility between central bank independence and democratic ideals. Some scholars have echoed these concerns and have questioned whether independent central bankers can truly be held accountable for their decisions [Berman and McNamara 1999; Cerny 1999; Pauly 1997; for a rather harsh view from a (British) central bank insider, see Buiter 1999]. The resonance of such arguments in a democratic context helps explain, in turn, the insistence of politicians on the norm of accountability and the willingness of central bankers and financial officials to adopt it—at least in rhetoric.

Does this conjunction of powerful economic and political rationales mean that there is now a strong consensus on the need for transparency and accountability in modern central banking? The problem with this view is that there are good political reasons to question the strength of the consensus.

How Central Banks Relate to Their Political Systems

Even though everyone pays lip service to transparency and accountability, different actors push for different versions of the new mantra. In order to see this, it is important to understand that the concept of central bank transparency has several meanings and therefore can easily become an object of contestation among the actors (Begg 2007). Central bankers may generally welcome increased opportunities for communicating their views to outsiders, but they are likely to resist when politicians desire to scrutinize (and potentially criticize) their decisions. In the case of accountability, the problem is even worse because accountability is perhaps the single most important argument that critics have levelled against what they see as the excessive independence of central bankers (see for example Berman and McNamara 1999). Practical disagreements are compounded by the notorious difficulty of envisioning meaningful accountability from a theoretical perspective—*a fortiori* in the absence of meaningful electoral sanctions.[3] Therefore, scholars' sharp disagreements on the awarding of accountability credentials to central bankers are perhaps not surprising.[4] Although everybody agrees that central bankers should not be left 'unaccountable', there is no normatively neutral definition of accountability.

Once we envision 'transparency and accountability' no longer as a monolithic ideal but as a field of contest, it makes little sense to continue the largely elusive search for a universally applicable definition or checklist of transparency and accountability mechanisms. Across the world, apparently similar measures (e.g. the definition of a policy targets, or the practice of parliamentary hearings) are being introduced for markedly different reasons, following different modalities, and with different effects. This in turn helps understand the sharp disagreements on the definition and measuring of central bank transparency and accountability. Rather than assuming a homogenous economic and democratic push for transparency and accountability, the crucial task then is to assess different distributions of resource endowments among actors, and their effects on various patterns of central bank transparency and accountability.

Just as in other movements of modernization in history, the possibility of retaining one's differences contributes to explain the attraction and diffusion of the global model. Each local elite can embrace economic modernity without however renouncing its distinctive political system and culture. Transparency and accountability become part and parcel of a broader set of trends—financial deregulation, central bank independence, the increasing importance of ratings, and new public management techniques of all kinds—that appear to diffuse on a worldwide scale under the broad label of 'neoliberal reforms'. While some of these shifts have massive consequences for the evolution of the world economy, considerable variation remains possible within a broader-than-expected spectrum of possible outcomes. Actors thus do not simply follow the example set by the United States or the IMF—let alone New Zealand or Sweden. More often than not, they appropriate terms that have gained global currency for their own idiosyncratic purposes.

Three Sources of Variation in Transparency and Accountability

Three institutional factors stand out as critical sources of variation in central bank practices between the United States and the EU. These factors usually encapsulate not only well-entrenched formal characteristics of the political–administrative system but also culturally accepted, informal ways of doing things that actors rarely question in normal circumstances.[5]

The first, and perhaps most obvious, factor is the solidity of the central bank's claim to independence. If the central bank's claim to independence is (virtually) uncontested, central bankers will be better able to resist what they feel are overly intrusive forms of transparency and accountability. That is the case, for example, in the United States, where the Fed's record of independent and largely successful monetary policy—with the exception of the 1970s—protects it against fundamental outside challenges. The European Central Bank is a situation similar to the Fed, albeit for different reasons. Its independence is entrenched because of the aura of its German predecessor and model, and also and above all because of the sheer difficulty of challenging its treaty-defined statute. The more their claim to independence is institutionally entrenched, the better central bankers will be able to resist forms of transparency and accountability that might encroach on their independence.

A second factor in explaining variation in transparency and accountability practices is the power of the legislature to oversee the central bank. Interestingly, the principle of legislative oversight is no longer really contested anywhere. Even when central bankers are independent from the executive branch of government, it is now generally accepted practice that they must publicly report on what they do to the legislative branch. But there remains considerable variation in oversight power. The US Congress's claim to oversee the Fed is virtually uncontested due to its power and prestige within the American system of government. As for the European Parliament, it started from a particularly weak position within the EU and had to work hard to assert a relatively modest claim to oversee the ECB.

The third factor that fosters variation is the capacity of the executive branch to assert policy leadership in relation to the central bank. Monetary policy operates in a broader context of economic policies that remain, for the most part, executive prerogatives. In the United States, the executive claim to economic policy leadership stems from the President's democratic mandate to implement the policies for which he has been elected, notwithstanding the important powers of the US Congress in fiscal matters. Executive power at the EU level is neither unified, nor a straightforward expression of democratic will. The Euro Group—which brings together the finance ministers of the countries that have adopted the euro—would be the most likely candidate for policy leadership on fiscal matters. Yet, it is far from a cohesive body of government and is therefore largely unable, at this point, to exert genuine policy leadership.

Although each of the above three factors provides only a partial picture of the institutional context within which the central bank operates, they interact to produce rather different equilibrium points for transparency and accountability practices in the United States and in the EU. The nature of central bank transparency and accountability practices ultimately depends less on the presence or absence of specific transparency and accountability provisions than on local institutional dynamics.

The United States: A Strong Bank in the Midst of Divided Powers

As the Fed acquired growing clout in the determination of US economic policies since the 1970s, it has also become more forthcoming about its decision-making process. Against a backdrop of relative stability in the Fed's legal and political environment, Woolley's chapter in this volume highlights 'considerable change with respects to issues of disclosure and transparency'.[6] Perhaps the most obvious and internationally replicated change was the introduction in 1975 of regular and increasingly publicized hearings of Fed officials in Congress. But there were many other changes as well: the publication of forecasts starting in 1979; the introduction of the Beige Book about regional economic conditions in 1983; the publication of minutes of Federal Open Market Committee (FOMC) meetings after 1994; and, most recently, Ben Bernanke's pledge to publish 'enhanced projections' by FOMC members about key economic aggregates (Bernanke 2007*d*). At the same time, the United States is relatively late in adopting certain measures that have become accepted practice in many other states and that can be described as transparency-enhancing, like inflation targeting. The question is what factors provoked these various moves and what is pushing the United States to adopt its own, relatively singular version of transparency and accountability. When we examine this question, the evolving political environment of the Fed looms large in comparison to strictly economic or democratic concerns.

The Fed's Rise to Prominence and the Mounting Pressures for Transparency and Accountability

The 1970s were years of turmoil for the Federal Reserve as well as for successive administrations. As the US economy ran into double-digit inflation figures, politicians in Congress increasingly questioned the executive branch's economic policies, including the Fed's. Of course, the Federal Reserve exists by virtue of an act of Congress, the Federal Reserve Act of 1913. As former Fed chairman Paul Volcker famously put it, 'Congress has made us, Congress can unmake us.' The Senate also has the power to confirm or invalidate the president's appointments of the Fed's governors and chair. Yet, during the first few decades of the Fed's history, Congress deferred to the administration in matters of economic policies and the Fed had trouble asserting its independence.[7] Until the 1970s the Fed's accountability was mostly vis-à-vis the administration and the Department of Treasury—and thus outside the reach of Congress.

In fact, the first steps toward the present framework of Fed's transparency and accountability stemmed from Congressional efforts to clip the wings of the executive in matters of monetary policy. After a long period of 'imperial' presidency, the 1970s saw a reassertion of Congressional oversight over the Federal Reserve as well as other executive agencies. Only in the mid-1970s did Congress start a practice of regular hearings of Federal Reserve Board officials, in addition to the normal appointment hearings at the Senate. The Federal Reserve Reform Act (1977) and the Full Employment and Balanced Growth (Humphrey-Hawkins) Act (1978) reasserted Congress's oversight role and redefined the Fed's mandate. Inflation projections, for example, stemmed from the Fed's obligation to publish its 'prospects for the future'. Court cases also played a role in prompting the Fed to become more open, especially the Merrill versus Federal Open Market Committee ruling by the US Supreme Court (following a lawsuit under the Freedom of Information Act), which limited the Fed's latitude in withdrawing information from the public eye (Goodfriend 1986). By the time Paul Volcker was appointed Fed chairman in 1979, then, the Fed was already subject to unprecedented amounts of public criticisms.

Under Paul Volcker (1979–87), the Fed grew its own wings, which created a new kind of transparency and accountability problem. Volcker asserted the Fed's claim to independence more forcefully than ever before. Breaking with the relatively accommodating monetary policy of the 1970s, he inaugurated a policy of high interest rates designed to kill inflation. As Volcker established the Fed as a Washington power broker, however, he also faced a barrage of critics. The Fed's harsh medicine of high interest rates was blamed for the recession of the first Reagan Presidency, and pamphlets against the Fed and its lack of accountability proliferated. *Secrets of the Temple*, a best-selling book by journalist William Greider (1987), expressed the American Left's widespread suspicion that the 'independent' Fed actually catered for the special interests of Wall Street rather than for those of the general population. Despite all the criticisms, Paul Volcker's Fed was above all widely credited with its successful victory over the inflationary pressures of the 1970s. Yet, the Federal Reserve's aloof and secretive culture was its Achilles' heel. More important change was brewing on both sides of the aisle in Congress and within the Federal Reserve Board itself.

After Alan Greenspan took over as chair, the Fed adopted a less confrontational approach but, if anything, gained voice and influence in the US economic policymaking process—which seemed to magnify the transparency and accountability problem. Greenspan's advocacy of fiscal prudence was clearly a central consideration in the Clinton administration's decision to adopt a programme of deficit reduction in the 1990s. Some members of the Clinton administration resented this rapid rise to power of a Republican appointee.[8] As the US economy boomed in the late 1990s, Greenspan became the character depicted in a biography by Bob Woodward (1997) as the 'Maestro'. He was universally hailed as the chief architect of an economic policy that ensured both low inflation and remarkably robust growth, along with dwindling federal deficits.

It is easy to overstate the Fed's claim to exert policy leadership, however. In law but also in practice, the Fed is not only 'subject to the oversight of the US Congress' but also 'must work within the overall objectives of economic and financial policies established by the government' (Board of Governors of the Federal Reserve 2005: 3). Of course, the administration's prevalence over the Fed declined after the 1970s and the Fed was never as deferential to the administration as under Roosevelt. Yet the President retained the power of appointment, which implies a form of central bank accountability *to the President*—especially given the fact that the Fed chair can be *re*appointed. Even under Clinton, Greenspan's seemingly huge influence over government policies was probably the product of a good cooperation between the Fed and the administration, rather than of an undue power grab by the Fed. Above all,

Greenspan was able to develop a good working relationship with Clinton and his long-time Treasury Secretary Robert Rubin. Clinton chose to reappoint Greenspan—and he would presumably have acted differently if Greenspan had not been a good 'team player' (Woodward 1997: 159–60). The administration's claim to policy leadership was reasserted with a vengeance by the post–2000 Bush administration, when Greenspan endorsed the president's tax cuts despite mounting fiscal deficits.

Once again, therefore, the key factor that pushed the Fed to change its approach to transparency and accountability was really the renewed pressure coming from a powerful Congress—a structural characteristic of the US political system. In the early 1990s, Congress was demanding more transparency and accountability as a prerequisite to approval of the administration's funding of international organizations. In that context, the Fed and some other federal agencies fell under the same Congressional axe. The single most important consequence was the 1994 decision to publish minutes of the FOMC meetings. The consequences of this decision are actually ambiguous. According to Meade and Stasavage (2008), it may have rigidified the style of FOMC debates, as participants apparently began to voice their opinions less freely. Critics would add that the publication of minutes is a rather limited form of accountability, especially since the minutes are edited and were revealed only many weeks after the decision. (The delay was shortened to three weeks in 2005.) All this may be true, but it was nonetheless a departure from existing practice.

Increasingly, and perhaps surprisingly, voices from within the Federal Reserve System were heard supporting the push for greater transparency and accountability. The central bankers were above all concerned not so much about their own accountability, but about the benefits of explaining monetary policy decisions to the markets.[9] But they also knew there was an outside demand for more transparency and accountability. Most vocal among them in the 1990s was vice-chair Alan Blinder, a Clinton appointee to the Federal Reserve Board.[10] Blinder's reasoning was political as well as economic, since he believed that both the Fed's democratic credentials and its credibility would be best served by enhanced transparency and accountability. Originally a product of distinctively American political pressure coming from the US Congress, the Fed's conversion to transparency and accountability was now complete—or was it?

The Debate Over Inflation Targeting and the Problem of the Dual Mandate

Let us examine the substance of the Fed's transparency and accountability. One glaring aspect that seems to be missing in the case of the US Federal Reserve is a clear policy target. There is an interesting political story behind this absence—one that highlights potential contradictions in the new ethos of transparency and accountability. And the resistance to this particular step once again comes from the particular political environment in which the Fed finds itself, namely, as an independent central bank subject to strict legislative oversight from the US Congress.

The first episode of this story about inflation targeting started as a technical debate in central banking and economist circles. After the heyday of monetarism in the early 1980s, central bankers were looking for a policy target that would be both an appropriate intermediate goal for monetary policy and a way to anchor market expectations. Inflation targeting emerged as a potential solution to this problem in New Zealand and Europe. The Bank of New Zealand pioneered the use of numerical inflation targets for monetary policy in the late 1980s. The Maastricht Treaty's definition of price stability as the 'primary' goal of monetary policy in 1992 was a step in the same direction. One of the benefits of this approach was to enhance the transparency of the decision-making process. If there were a clear target that everybody could see, central bank transparency and accountability would be presumably enhanced.

Yet in the United States these international developments toward greater transparency were controversial because of the so-called 'dual mandate' of the Fed since the 1978 Humphrey-Hawkins Act. The Fed's task is not only to fight inflation but also to pursue 'full employment and balanced growth' at the same time. On the one hand, the Fed's defence of its growth-enhancement mandate is often largely a matter of rhetoric. There were times when the Fed acted as a very hawkish inflation fighter—especially under Paul Volcker in the 1980s. The Fed could argue that it was impossible to make progress on all fronts at the same time, and thus arguably obfuscate its mandate (e.g. Wyplosz 2001: 5). On the other hand, the dual mandate also means that the governors are legally bound to worry about growth as much as about inflation. In the Fed's recent history, 'doves' who argued that growth should not be sacrificed to the fight against inflation have been able to invoke the dual mandate in support of the argument.[11] From this perspective, the dual mandate may be argued to ensure that central bankers are held accountable for the goals set for them by Congress.

The US debate on inflation targeting quickly became partisan. On the Republican side of the aisle, Congressmen Coney Mack and Jim Saxton argued that the Fed should have a single hierarchical mandate of price stability, meaning zero inflation. They favoured not only inflation targeting but a change in the mandate of the Fed. Others, especially among Democrats, argued that the mandate should not be changed and the Fed should stay away from inflation targeting. They feared that an inflation target would assign more weight to the price stability mandate of the Fed and would authorize the Fed to disregard its employment mandate. After some hesitations, Greenspan sided with the second camp in the name of flexibility, and the Mack-Saxton proposal went nowhere in the 1990s.

The next episode of this inflation-targeting saga started when Ben Bernanke was appointed chair of the Fed in 2006 and is still being played out. Bernanke came in with a reputation as an advocate of inflation targeting and started defending a move of the Fed in that direction, in the name not only of policy effectiveness but also of transparency and accountability. The lines of debate among economists had changed, since inflation targeting is no longer a rallying cry for inflation 'hawks'. Many supporters of the dual mandate in US central banking circles now support 'flexible' inflation targeting via a small but definitely positive inflation target, especially Alan Blinder and Janet Yellen (see Meyer 2004: 40–3). But the topic remains politically sensitive. In Congressional hearings, Bernanke pledged that any adoption of an inflation target would be progressive and would not require a change in the mandate. The Fed's new communication strategy, unveiled by Bernanke (2007d), introduces an extended inflation forecast (with a time horizon of three years instead of two) and additional information about the FOMC members' views about the economy. Yet Bernanke stopped short of introducing a formal inflation target: 'My colleagues and I strongly support the dual mandate and the equal weighting of objectives that it implies.'

This inflation-targeting debate illustrates the importance of Congress in steering the Fed toward a particular model of transparency and accountability. For Congress, accountability is not just a concern in and of itself. It is also a way to assert legislative oversight, to acquire a role in the policy debate, and to defend its turf against the administration and the Fed. To this day, the Fed's mandate remains the dual, non-hierarchical mandate set by Congress in the 1970s, and hard inflation targets are eschewed. No matter how successful its policies and how powerful its voice in US economic policies, the Fed could not afford to ignore the argument against inflation targeting—since it came from Congress. Thus, abstract considerations of efficiency or democracy were clearly secondary to the institutional framework of central banking in the United States. The same was true in Europe, but there the institutional dynamics were remarkably different.

The European Union: A Strong Bank in a (Still) Weak Polity

Central bank transparency and accountability were not paramount concerns in the late 1980s and early 1990s, when European political leaders designed the European Central Bank (ECB) as an independent central bank to manage the new European currency. According to an extensive investigation of this process, Europe's economic and monetary union embodied 'the triumph of technocratic elitism over the idea of political democracy' (Dyson and Featherstone 1999: 801). Yet after the ECB started to operate in 1998, its officials quickly pledged to make the ECB 'the most transparent and accountable central bank in the world' (Issing 1999: 105; see also Padoa-Schioppa 2000: 28). The ECB has therefore developed its own model of transparency and accountability. This model is characterized by extensive but often unilateral communication. The ECB was the first major central bank to systematically hold press conferences after the meetings of its Governing Council. Compared with the Federal Reserve, the ECB has a relatively clear inflation objective, and Executive Board members also appear before the European Parliament. Yet, the ECB does not publish a Beige Book, nor the minutes or the voting patterns of its Governing Council meetings. Let us now turn to the factors that shaped the development of this model.

The ECB's Problem of 'Institutional Loneliness'

On the face of it, the ECB did not really need to go in the direction of transparency and accountability. The primary purpose of the Treaty of Maastricht was to create a single European currency under the supervision of an independent central bank, not to enhance democracy. Central bank independence was granted quasi-constitutional value, whereas the Maastricht Treaty's formal transparency and accountability provisions were scarce. Treaties are the functional equivalent of constitutional documents for the EU, and it requires a unanimous agreement between the member states to change them. Because the ECB is a Treaty creature, it is particularly entrenched. And yet the ECB is part of an EU political system that still lacks the historically produced power and legitimacy of its constituent member states. This situation is, in a sense, the exact opposite of the situation in the United States, where the Federal Reserve is a venerable century-old institution, yet has no constitutional status whatsoever.

As a consequence, EU central bankers could not completely ignore widespread concerns about the EU's 'democratic deficit'. After the harsh criticisms against the Maastricht process, the young ECB needed to restore its democratic image. As soon as it was established, the ECB started a practice of numerous press conferences and outreach, by which it attempted to communicate its policies to the markets, to the general European public, and to other political bodies. Not only the ECB's monetary policy decisions but also many key announcements of monetary policy strategy are announced by way of press conferences and speeches. In addition to this all-out communication strategy, the ECB also endeavoured to break out of what one ECB Board member called its 'institutional loneliness' (Padoa-Schioppa 2000: 37). Despite its initial reluctance to engage in 'politics', the ECB increasingly looked for partners to break its isolation and to enter into a normal dialogue with other bodies.

This eagerness of Europe's central bankers to restore their democratic image was met favourably by some other actors. In particular, the European Parliament saw it as an opportunity to develop for itself something akin to the oversight function of the US Congress over the Federal Reserve, which members of Parliament cited as a constant reference in parliamentary discourse about the (desirable) 'democratic accountability' of the ECB. At the end of

2000, the ECB acknowledged that the European Parliament is the only body 'directly elected by the European citizens and, consequently, plays a crucial role—the ECB must be accountable to the Parliament for the conduct of monetary policy. (. . . .) In this sense, the relations between the ECB and the European Parliament must be considered as more than a simple statutory requirement' (European Central Bank 2000: 54). Early on, therefore, the ECB started a practice of sending Executive Board members to explain monetary policy before the European Parliament (see Jabko 2003).

The sheer force of democratic ideals is insufficient, however, to explain the growing importance of transparency and accountability in the official rhetoric of both the Parliament and the ECB. Since the Maastricht Treaty did not explicitly provide for it, an accountability relationship developed progressively as a practical result of interactions between key actors. By the ECB's own admission, the hearings 'contribute to safeguard the independent status of the ECB. Consequently, it is certainly in the ECB's enlightened interest to carry on with such relations' (European Central Bank 2000: 54). Thus, the evolution of the ECB's official position is, for the most part, the result of a calculation. The expected gains in terms of consolidated independence are perceived as far higher than the expected costs of acknowledging the European Parliament's role as a privileged interlocutor.

In the absence of strong parliamentary powers at the EU level, the 'dialogue' is in fact not very constraining. A new routine of quarterly hearings of the president of the ECB before the European Parliament's Economic and Monetary Affairs Committee has been established. The main actors looked at foreign models as sources of ideas, especially the US model. Yet despite the recurrent reference to the Fed's accountability to the US Congress, the staging of ECB hearings is revealingly different from the hearings of the chair of the US Federal Reserve by Congressional committees. Whereas the chair of the Federal Reserve stands in the witness box and must answer questions asked by a small number of Congressmen who sit above him like judges, the president of the ECB addresses a floor of European Parliament members from a platform where he is seated next to the chair of the Economic and Monetary Affairs Committee. Moreover, the ECB president's hearings only last two hours, and members of Parliament are only allowed to ask the President two questions, which he can therefore dodge quite easily. Here again, the difference with the US situation is striking, since the chair of the Federal Reserve is subjected to a barrage of questions from Congressmen.

In sum, the ECB and the European Parliament came to an agreement on the rules of the accountability game because both bodies had a clear interest in playing that game. Accountability became a terrain of political contest between two bodies that defended what they had identified as their primary interests. The ECB wanted more democratic legitimacy, which it could acquire through good relations with the European Parliament. Conversely, the European

Parliament desired a greater say on the conduct of economic policy within the EU, which it could gain from its relations with the ECB. Thus, in many respects, the 'dialogue' between central bankers and members of the European Parliament developed into a form of exchange.

The real question is whether the game of central bank accountability between the ECB and the European Parliament really serves democracy, or merely the interests of the various actors who play that game. It is important to realize that both hypotheses could well be valid at the same time. The evolving debate on central bank accountability represents an interesting attempt to 'muddle through' a new democratic practice, yet it is also, and perhaps inevitably, a power play between the main actors—just as in the United States. Despite the continuous upgrade of its powers since the 1980s, the European Parliament does not in any sense match the power and prestige of the US Congress. The European Parliament gained its oversight role over the ECB only by courtesy of the member states, and, furthermore, this oversight is limited to mere 'reporting requirements'. This affects the Parliament's power to hold the ECB accountable. The practice of parliamentary hearings has different parameters and results, despite the superficial similarity between the EU and the United States.

Just as important, there is almost no form of accountability to the executive in Europe—largely because there is no unified executive able to claim policy leadership. Thus far, the Euro Group—that is, the caucus of Euro Area finance ministers within the EU Council—has not asserted very strongly its preferences vis-à-vis the ECB. This is due to the difficulties of coordinating member governments' economic policies, as well as to the extent of ECB independence in the Treaty. Only with the nomination of Jean-Claude Juncker as the chair of the Euro Group did this situation begin to change. But the chair has no hierarchical powers over his colleagues, so his room for manoeuvre is limited. By contrast, member states are still vested with so much power and legitimacy that central bankers are very cautious when it comes to accountability toward the member governments. This also explains the relative opaqueness of the ECB when it comes to minutes and voting patterns. In the absence of a truly unified EU-level economic stance, the governors of national central banks refuse to be exposed to the heat of national debates on their positions within the Governing Council.

Limits and Dilemmas of Transparency and Accountability

A good example of the limits and dilemmas of transparency and accountability in the EU is the definition of the ECB's mandate. The Maastricht Treaty defines 'price stability' as the primary objective of the ECB, with other objectives like growth and employment only permissible 'without prejudice' to price stability. The effects on accountability depend on the analyst's definition of accountability. On the one hand, it could be argued that in practice there is almost no difference of behaviour between the single-mandate ECB and the dual-mandate

Federal Reserve. Those who hold this view favour the ECB's mandate from a transparency and accountability perspective, which has the advantage of being clearly hierarchical. From this perspective, the mandate is transparent, and the ECB is 'accountable for the fulfillment of its mandate' (Issing 1999).

On the other hand, it is also possible, and indeed more conventional, to argue in favour of more open-ended goals for policymakers as a way to *reinforce* their accountability. In political theory, the standard conception of accountability assumes that there is room left for policymakers to exercise discretion, and that the evaluation of policies takes place *ex post*. The existence of meaningful accountability is then *opposed* to the definition of a strict mandate (Pitkin 1967). In this conception, therefore, too much transparency can actually come at the cost of accountability.

Second, the self-definition of their role by central bankers is different in the ECB and in the United States. While the Fed is an independent central bank, it has had to live with a particularly broad mandate that includes growth and employment as well as low inflation. In the Euro Area, the situation is very different because the ECB's mandate is narrower—with price stability defined as a 'primary objective'. But arguably even more important is the fact that Eurosystem central bankers have come to see a narrow technical definition of their task as a guarantee of their hard-won independence. Unlike their American counterparts, they are in an EU sphere where nobody has sufficient legitimacy to make clear—let alone partisan—policy choices. The consequence is that central bankers attempt to escape political debate and to deny the existence of difficult trade-offs altogether.

Does an inflation rate 'below 2 per cent', namely, the ECB's unilaterally chosen 'reference value', strictly correspond to the Treaty's objective of 'price stability'? This is debatable—to say the least. In 2003, the ECB chose to specify its objective and announced a target of 'below but close to 2 per cent'. The first remarkable fact is that, unlike the US situation (or the Japanese situation), there was no unified political body able to really discuss—let alone to disagree—with the ECB on this matter. Despite a formal recognition of the Euro Group and the introduction of a stable chairmanship during the EU Constitutional Convention of 2002–3, the forums toward which the ECB is supposed to be transparent and accountable remain ill designed. If this situation ever changes, it will not be simply because of a universal realization that change is desirable from the viewpoint of transparency and accountability—some very serious political obstacles stand in the way.

In addition, it is possible to question, from a substantive perspective, the ECB's adherence to a rather rigid conception of central bank independence and its refusal to engage in a debate about its policy target. While understandable in its own terms, given the ECB's political environment, the absence of substantive debate is not necessarily the way of ensuring satisfactory standards of transparency and accountability.[12] After all, the fact that price stability and central bank independence are given such high priority in the Maastricht Treaty must itself be understood as the output of a political process, not simply as a legal translation of economic rationality. In the French referendum of May 2005 on the EU Constitutional Treaty, one of the recurrent arguments of opponents was the 'democratic deficit' of the EU and specifically the 'lack of accountability' of the ECB. But then, again, there is a gap between a diagnosis of the situation and a political cure.

Concluding Remarks

Everybody today talks about enhancing central bank transparency and accountability, but the fact is that institutional designs to ensure these goals remain quite different. It is not clear that they will deeply converge in the future, since varieties of transparency and accountability have deep roots, and no system can claim to be completely coherent and ideal. To be sure, the frameworks that govern central banking will probably continue to evolve with a view to achieve more effectiveness and more democracy. But, as we saw, efficiency-enhancing transparency and democracy-enhancing account-ability sometimes generate different prescriptions for change. Thus, mutual emulation will likely continue, but there is no inherent reason to believe that it will necessarily lead to homogeneity.

In addition, new problems emerge, sometimes very powerfully, and they do not always call for the same remedies. For example, the financial crisis of 2007–8, with its near-collapses of several banks on both sides of the Atlantic, highlighted the need for good prudential supervision as well as good monetary policy. In keeping to the scholarly literature on central bank transparency and accountability, this chapter has given no attention to financial supervision. Yet if we briefly consider this question, it is obvious that the requirement for good prudential supervision may well involve *less* transparency on the part of central bankers. This is because transparent decision-making in this area may create moral hazard. If banks and other financial firms know exactly at what point and how quickly central bankers will come to their rescue, they might be tempted to push the envelope and take on excessive risks. Thus, the on-going redeployment of central bankers' energy toward the task of prudential super-vision may also lead to a more sceptical assessment of the requirement for transparency—at least in this area of central bank operations.

More generally, as John Freeman (2002: 904) puts it, 'consensus with respect to the goals of monetary institution is a *false perception*.' This raises the possi-bility that the widespread support for central bank independence, transpar-ency, accountability, and other holy cows among political economists, actually indicate a 'crisis of imagination in institutional design' (ibid. 906). Trends that look overwhelming for the progress of modernity may actually be much less seamless than they appear at first sight. As long as there is room for incoherence within and deviation from the consensual norms, the façade can nonetheless cover the reality without generating too much cognitive dissonance. Only when we stop believing in the reality of the façade will we need to move to another (consensus) view.

Notes

1. The importance of monetary policy credibility is one way to address the time consistency problem pointed out by Kydland and Prescott (1977). On the importance of transparency to help central banks achieve their policy objectives and buttress their credibility, see Geraats (2002), Stasavage (2003).
2. McNamara (2002) lists 38 countries that have made their central banks independent in the course of the 1990s. Pollilo and Guillen (2005) calculate that more than 80 countries have adopted legal provisions that increase the independence of their central banks; Marcussen (2005) finds roughly similar numbers.
3. Political theorists have typically conceptualized accountability in the context of electoral representation and often concluded that it was difficult to achieve in practice. The addition of power delegation from elected officials to independent central bankers arguably makes accountability even harder to operationalize. See Pitkin (1967), Mansbridge (2003).
4. See for example the heated Buiter–Issing and Elgie–De Haan–Amtbrink debates on the issue of whether or not central banks in Europe had become more accountable in the 1990s: (Buiter 1999; De Haan and Amtenbrink 2000; De Haan and Eijffinger 2000; Elgie 1998, 2001; Issing 1999).
5. These factors can thus be called institutions in an anthropological sense, like 'planets fixed in the sky' (Douglas 1986: 46–7).
6. This change contrasts with Woolley's (1984: 26) earlier assessment that monetary policy was 'made in great secrecy'.
7. For a narration of William Cheshire Martin's role in securing the Fed's independence not from but 'within the government', see Bremner (2005).
8. Labor Secretary Robert Reich (1997) was one of the most outspoken critics of Greenspan's influence on the administration's policies.
9. According to Woodward (1997: 114, 226–7), Greenspan favoured transparency also because he thought it magnified his own power. For an early expression of this concern for the benefits of transparency, see Goodfriend (1986).
10. Blinder (2004: 5–33) offers his own account of his advocacy of transparency within the Board of Governors.
11. Meyer (2004) cites a 1996 meeting at which Janet Yellen, a member of the FOMC, boldly challenged Alan Greenspan on this issue.
12. See Stasavage (2003) for an argument that reconciles monetary policy credibility with a degree of democratic accountability, but on the condition that central bank independence ceases to be an absolute principle.

References

Adolph, C. (2003). 'Paper Autonomy, Private Ambition: Theory and Evidence Linking Central Bankers' Careers and Economic Performance'. Paper presented at the annual meeting of the American Political Science Association, Philadelphia, 28–31 August.
—— (2005). 'Three Simple Tests of Career Influences on Monetary Policy'. Paper presented at the annual meeting of the American Political Science Association, Washington, DC, 1–3 September.
Aeschimann, E. and Riché, P. (1996). *La guerre de sept ans: histoire secrète du franc fort, 1989–1996*. Paris: Calmann-Lévy.
Afonso, A., Schuknecht, L., and Tanzi, V. (2003). 'Public Sector Efficiency: An International Comparison', *ECB Working Paper, no.* 242, July.
Ahearne, A., Gagnon, J., Haltmaier, J., and Camin, S. with Erceg, C., Faust, J., Guerreri, L., Hemphill, C., Kole, L., Roush, J., Rogers, J., Sheets, N., and Wright, J. (2002). 'Preventing Deflation: Lessons from Japan's Experience in the 1990s'. *International Finance Discussion Papers #729*, Board of Governors of the Federal Reserve System.
Alesina, A. and Summers, L. (1993). 'Central Bank Independence and Macroeconomic Performances', *Journal of Money, Credit and Banking*, 25, 2: 151–63.
Anderson, B. (1991). *Imagined Communities. Reflections on the Origins and Spread of Nationalism*. London and New York: Verso.
Andrews, D. M. (2003). 'The Committee of Central Bank Governors as a Source of Rules', *Journal of European Public Policy*, 10, 6: 956–73.
Apel, E. (2003). *Central Banking Systems Compared: The ECB, The Pre-Euro Bundesbank and the Federal Reserve System*. London: Routledge.
Apel, M., Heikensten, L., and Jansson, P. (2008). 'Monetary Policy and Academics: A Study of Swedish Inflation Targeting', in A. B. Shani, S. A. Mohrman, W. A. Pasmore, B. Stymne, and N. B. Adler (eds.), *Handbook of Collaborative Management Research*. London: Sage Publishers, 375–402.
Armstrong, J. (1973). *The European Administrative Elite*. Princeton, NJ: Princeton University Press.
Auberger, P. (1996). Rapport d'information de l'Assemblée Nationale, no. 2940.
Baldwin, R., Berglof, E. Giavazzi, F., and Widgren, M. (2001). 'Preparing the ECB for Enlargement' Centre for Economic Policy Research Discussion Paper, no. 6.
Balleix-Banerjee, C. (1999). *La France et la Banque Centrale Européenne*. Paris: PUF.
Bank Act (1998). 'Wet van 26 maart 1998, houdende nieuwe bepalingen inzake De Nederlandsche Bank NV in verband met het Verdrag tot oprichting van de Europese Gemeenschap', *Staatsblad 2004*, 556 (version as of 30 October 2004).
Bank for International Settlements (2008). *Global Monetary and Financial Disorder*, www.bis.org/events/conf080626
Bank of England (1996–2001). *Annual Report*. London: Bank of England.
—— (1999–2002). *Practical Issues Arising from the Euro*. London: Bank of England.

References

Bank of England (1996–1998). *Practical Issues Arising from the Introduction of the Euro*. London: Bank of England.

—— (2005). *Publications on Europe: City Guide to a UK Euro Changeover*. September, www. bankofengland.co.uk/publications/other/europe/cityguide/index.htm

Bank of Greece (various). *Report of the Governor for the Year*. Athens: Bank of Greece.

Barber, T. (2007). 'EU Adopts Flexible Stance on Bank Crises'. Financial Times, 16 September.

Bartels, L. and Brady, H. (2003). 'Economic Behavior in Political Context', *American Economic Review*, Papers and Proceedings, 93 (May): 156–61.

Basel Committee on Banking Supervision (2003). *High-level Principles for the Cross-branch Implementation of the New Accord*. Basel: Bank for International Settlements.

—— (2007). *Principles for Home-Host Supervisory, Cooperation and Allocation Mechanisms in the Context of Advanced Measurement Approaches (AMA)*. Basel: Bank for International Settlements.

Baumgartner, F. and Jones, B. (1993). *Agendas and Instability in American Politics*. Chicago: University of Chicago Press.

Bean, C. (2007). 'The Meaning of "Internal Balance" Thirty Years On'. Speech at the James Meade Centenary Conference, London, July 13.

BearingPoint (2005). *Central Bank Modernisation. How to Plan and Implement Reforms*. London: Central Banking Publications.

Begg, I. (2006). 'Real Convergence and EMU Enlargement: The Time Dimension of Fit with the Euro Area', in K. Dyson (ed.), *Enlarging the Euro Area: External Empowerment and Domestic Transformation in East Central Europe*. Oxford, Oxford University Press, pp. 71–89.

—— (2007). 'Contested Meaning of Transparency in Central Banking', *Comparative European Politics*, 5, 1: 36–52.

Belaisch, A., Kodres, L., Levy, J., and Ubide, A. (2001). 'Euro-Area Banking at the Crossroads', *IMF Working Paper*, 01/28, March.

Bell, S. (2006). *Australia's Money Mandarins: The Reserve Bank and the Politics of Money*. Cambridge: Cambridge University Press.

Berg, C. and Jonung, L. (1998). 'Pioneering Price Level Targeting: The Swedish Experience 1931–1937', *Working Paper* 290, Stockholm: Stockholm School of Economics.

Berger, H. (2006). 'Unfinished Business? The ECB Reform Ahead of Euro Area Enlargement', *CESifo Forum*, 4: 35–41.

—— and De Haan, J. (1999). 'A State within the State? An Event Study on the Bundesbank (1948–1973)', *Scottish Journal of Political Economy*, 46, 1: 17–39.

—— de Haan, J., and Inklaar, R. (2004). 'Restructuring the ECB', in H. Berger and T. Moutos (eds.), *Managing European Union Enlargement*. Cambridge, Mass.: MIT Press, pp. 29–66.

Berger, P. and T. Luckmann (1966). *The Social Construction of Reality*. London: Penguin Books.

Berman, S. and McNamara, K. (1999). 'Bank on Democracy: Why Central Banks Need Public Oversight', *Foreign Affairs*, 78, 2: 2–8.

Bernanke, B. (2004a), 'Central Bank Talk and Monetary Policy'. Remarks at the Japan Society Corporate Luncheon, New York, 7 October.

—— (2004b). 'The Logic of Monetary Policy'. Speech to the National Economists' Club, Washington, DC, December 2.

—— (2007a). 'Globalization and Monetary Policy', speech at the Fourth Economic Summit, Stanford Institute for Economic Policy Research, Stanford, California, March 2.

—— (2007b). 'The Housing Market and Subprime Lending'. Speech to the 2007 International Monetary Conference, Cape Town, South Africa, June 5.

—— (2007c). 'Housing, Housing Finance and Monetary Policy'. Speech at the Federal Reserve Bank of Kansas City's Economic Symposium, Jackson Hole, August 31.

—— (2007d). 'Federal Reserve Communication'. Speech to the Cato Institute 25th Annual Monetary Policy Conference, Washington, DC, November 14.

—— and Mishkin, F. (1997). 'Inflation Targeting: A New Framework for Monetary Policy? *Journal of Economic Perspectives*, 11, 2: 97–116.

—— Thomas, L., Mishkin, F., and Posen, A. (1999). *Inflation Targeting*. Princeton, NJ: Princeton University Press.

Bernhard, W. (1998). 'A Political Explanation of Variations in Central Bank Independence', *American Political Science Review*, 92, 2: 311–27.

BGFRS (Board of Governors of the Federal Reserve System) (2007a). *Annual Report 2006*. Washington, DC: Federal Reserve System.

—— (2007b). *Annual Report: Budget Review*. Washington, DC: Federal Reserve System.

Bini Smaghi, L. (2008). 'Financial Stability and Monetary Policy: Challenges in the Current Turmoil'. Speech at CEPS joint event with Harvard Law School on the EU-US financial system, New York, 4 April.

Blinder, A., Goodhart, C., Hildebrand, P., Lipton, D., and Wyplosz, C. (eds.) (2002). *How Do Central Banks Talk?* London: Centre for Economic Policy Research.

—— (2004). *The Quiet Revolution: Central Banking Goes Modern*. New Haven: Yale University Press.

—— (1998). *Central Banking in Theory and Practice*. Cambridge, Massachusetts: The MIT Press.

—— and Wyplosz, C. (2004). 'Central Bank Talk: Committee Structure and Communication Policy', prepared for the session on 'Central Bank Communication' at the ASSA meetings, Philadelphia, January 9, 2005.

Blix, M., Daltug, S., and Heikensten, L. (2003). 'On Central Bank Efficiency', *Economic Review of the Riksbank*, 3: 81–93.

Board of Governors of the Federal Reserve (2005). *The Federal Reserve System: Purposes and Functions*. Washington, DC: Federal Reserve System.

Bohle, D. and Greskovits, B. (2006). 'Europeanization and the Variety of Competition States in Central-Eastern Europe', in A. Ágh and A. Ferencz (eds.), *Deepening and Widening in an Enlarged Europe: The Impact of Eastern Enlargement*. Budapest: 'Together for Europe' Research Centre of the Hungarian Academy of Sciences, pp. 245–86.

—— —— (2007). 'Neoliberalism, Embedded Neoliberalism and Neocorporatism: Towards Transnational Capitalism in Central-Eastern Europe', *West European Politics*, 30, 3: 443–66.

Bollard, A. (2005). 'Bank Regulation and Supervision in New Zealand: Recent and Ongoing Developments', address to the Australasian Institute of Banking and Finance, 23 March, Wellington: Reserve Bank of New Zealand.

Bönker, F. (2006). 'From Pacesetter to Laggard: The Political Economy of Negotiating Fit in the Czech Republic', in K. Dyson (ed.), *Enlarging the Euro Area: External Empowerment and Domestic Transformation in East Central Europe*. Oxford, Oxford University Press, pp. 160–77.

Bordes, C. and Clerc, L. (2007). 'Price stability and the ECB's Monetary Policy Strategy', *Journal of Economic Surveys*, 21, 2, 268–325.

References

Bordo, M. (2007). 'The Crisis of 2007: The Same Old Story, Only the Players Have Changed', paper presented at the Federal Reserve Bank of Chicago and International Monetary Fund conference 'Globalization and Systemic Risk', Chicago.

Borish, M. and Company Inc. with Triumph Technologies Inc. (1998). 'An Assessment and Rating of the Polish Banking System'. Washington, DC: USAID.

Boston, J., Martin, J., Pallot, J., and Walsh, P. (1996). *Public Management: The New Zealand Model*. Auckland: Oxford University Press.

Bowers, S. and Inman, P. (2007). 'Bank of England Throws Northern Rock Another Lifeline by Loosening Loan Terms'. *The Guardian*, 10 October.

Bremner, R. (2005). *Chairman of the Fed*. New Haven: Yale University Press.

Breuss, F., Fink, G., and Haiss, P. (2004). 'How Well Prepared Are the New Member States for the European Monetary Union?' *Journal of Policy Modeling*, 26, 7: 769–91.

Broz, J. (1997). *The International Origins of the Federal Reserve System*. Ithaca: Cornell University Press.

Bruszt, L., Oblath, G., and Tóth, A. (2003). 'Összehangolt cselekvés' (Coordinated action), *Népszabadság Online*, September 27.

Buiter, W. (1999). 'Alice in Euroland', *Journal of Common Market Studies*, 37, 2: 181–209.

—— (2004). 'To Purgatory and Beyond: When and How Should the Accession Countries from Central and Eastern Europe Become Full Members of EMU?' *CEPR Discussion Paper* No. 4342.

—— (2006). 'Rethinking Inflation Targeting and Central Bank Independence', inaugural Lecture, LSE, October 26.

Bulmer, S. (1994). 'The Governance of the European Union: A New Institutionalist Approach', *Journal of Public Policy*, 13, 4, 351–80.

—— (1997). 'New Institutionalism, the Single Market and EU Governance', *ARENA Working Papers WP 97/25*, Olso.

Bundesministerium der Finanzen (2005). 'Erfolgreiche Debatte um Reform des Stabilitaetspakt', *Pressemitteilung 36*, Berlin, 21 March.

Busch, A. (2004). 'National Filters: Europeanization, Institutions, and Discourse in the Case of Banking Regulation', *West European Politics*, 27, 2: 310–33.

Buyst, E. and Maes, I. (2008). 'The Regulation and Supervision of the Belgian Financial System (1830–2005)', Working Paper, no. 77, June, Bank of Greece.

—— Maes, I., and Pluym, W. (2005). *The Bank, the Franc and the Euro. A History of the National Bank of Belgium*. Tielt: Lannoo.

Calomiris, C. and Litan, R. (2000). 'Financial Regulation in a Global Marketplace'. *Brookings-Wharton Papers on Financial Services*, 283–339.

Capital Market Committee (2001). *Annual Report 2000*. Athens: CMC.

Castles, F. (1984). *The Working Class and Welfare: Reflections on the Political Development of the Welfare State in Australia and New Zealand, 1890–1980*. Wellington: Allen and Unwin/Port Nicholson Press.

—— (1988). *Australian Public Policy and Economic Vulnerability*. Sydney: Allen and Unwin.

Cecchetti, S., Flores-Lagunes, A., and Krause, S. (2005). 'Assessing the Sources of Changes in the Volatility of Real Growth'. Paper at the conference on 'The Changing Nature of the Business Cycle', Reserve Bank of Australia.

Cerny, P. (1999). 'Globalization and the Erosion of Democracy', *European Journal of Political Research*, 36, 1, 1–26.

Chandler, L. (1958). *Benjamin Strong – Central Banker*. Washington, DC: The Brookings Institution.

Chappell, H., McGregor, R., and Vermilyea, T. (2005). *Committee Decisions on Monetary Policy: Evidence from Historical Records of the Federal Open Market Committee*. Cambridge, MA: MIT Press.

Chirac, J. (2000). Unser Europa, Rede vor dem deutschen Bundestag in Berlin am 27.6.2000, http://www.bundestag.de/geschichte/gastredner/chirac/chirac1.html

Ciampi, C. (1990). 'L' Autonomia della Banca d'Italia nella Conduzione della Politica Monetaria', *Bancaria*, 1, 1: 65–70.

Ciocca, P. (2000). *La Nuova Finanza in Italia*. Torino: Bollati Boringhieri.

Claessens, S., Demirgüc-Kunt, A., and Huizinga, H. (1998). *How Does Foreign Entry Affect the Domestic Banking Market?* Washington, DC: The World Bank.

Cohen, B. (1998). *The Geography of Money*. Ithaca: Cornell University Press.

Collins, H. (2007). *Rethinking Expertise*. Chicago: University of Chicago Press.

Commissariat Général du Plan (ed.) (2004). *Perspectives de la coopération renforcée dans l'Union européenne*. Paris: Commissiariat Général du Plan.

Commission of the European Communities (2005). *White Paper: Financial Services Policy 2005–2010*, SEC(2005) 1574. Brussels: Commission of the European Communities.

Council of the European Union (2000). *Council Decision 2000/604/EC of 29th September 2000 on the Composition and the Statutes of the Economic Policy Committee*, Brussels: Council of the European Union.

—— (2006). *Council Recommendation to the United Kingdom with a View to Bringing an End to the Situation of an Excessive Government Deficit – Application of Article 104(7) of the Treaty*, 5367/06, ECOFIN 12, UEM 17, Brussels: Council of the European Union.

Cours des comptes (1996). *La Banque de France*, January.

—— (2005). *La Banque de France*, March.

Cukierman, A. (1992). *Central Bank Strategy, Credibility, and Independence: Theory and Evidence*. Cambridge, MA: MIT Press.

—— Miller, G., and Neyapti, B. (2002). 'Central Bank Reform, Liberalization and Inflation in Transition Economies – An International Perspective', *Journal of Monetary Economics*, 49, 2: 237–64.

Cullen, M. (2007). 'The Role of Tax in Transforming the Economy', Speech notes for address to Ernst & Young Tax Partners/Managers Breakfast. Clearwater Resort, Christchurch, 16 July.

Czech National Bank (2003). *Czech National Bank, 1993–2003*. Prague: Czech National Bank.

Dahrendorf, Ralf (2008). 'Europa – oder die irische Frage. Plädoyer für die Rückkehr zu den Quellen und für einen Neubeginn', *Neue Züricher Zeitung*, 2nd July 2008.

Davies, H. (1997). Speech at the Futures and Options Association International Derivatives Week Conference, 4 June.

De Haan, J. (2000). *History of the Bundesbank: Lessons for the European Central Bank*. London: Routledge.

—— and Amtenbrink, F. (2000). 'Democratic Accountability and Central Bank Independence: A Response to Elgie', *West European Politics* 23, 3, 179–90.

—— and Eijffinger, S. (2000). 'The Democratic Accountability of the European Central Bank: A Comment on Two Fairy Tales', *Journal of Common Market Studies*, 38, 3: 393–407.

References

De Haan, J., Eijffinger, S., and Waller, S. (2005). *The European Central Bank: Credibility, Transparency, and Centralization*. Boston: MIT Press.

De Haas, B. and van Lotringen, C. (2003). *Wim Duisenberg: Van Friese Volksjongen to Mr. Euro*. Amsterdam: Business Contact.

De Nederlandsche Bank (1997). *Monetaire Stabiliteit en Bestendigheid. Smalle Marges Optimaal Benut 1981–1996*. Amsterdam: De Nederlandsche Bank.

—— (1999). *Annual Report 1998*. Amsterdam: Kluwer.

—— (2000*a*). *Jaarverlag De Nederlandsche Bank 1999*. Amsterdam: De Nederlandsche Bank.

—— (2000*b*). *Quarterly Bulletin*. March. Amsterdam: De Nederlandsche Bank.

—— (2002). 'Smooth Euro Changeover, Higher Prices? Results of a Survey among Dutch Retailers', DNB Research Memorandum No. 682.E.

—— (2003). *Jaarverslag De Nederlandsche Bank 2002*. Amsterdam: De Nederlandsche Bank.

—— (2007). *Annual Report 2006*. Amsterdam: De Nederlandsche Bank.

—— (2008*a*). *Jaarverslag De Nederlandsche Bank 2007*. Amsterdam: De Nederlandsche Bank.

—— (2008*b*). *Overview of Financial Stability in the Netherlands*. Amsterdam: De Nederlandsche Bank.

Deane, M. and Pringle, R. (1994). *The Central Banks*. London: Harmish Hamilton.

Delors, J. (2004). *Mémoires*. Paris: Plon.

Dennis, B. (1998). *500%*. Stockholm: Bokförlaget DN.

Dermine, J. (2006). 'European Banking Integration: Don't Put the Cart Before the Horse', *Financial Markets, Institutions and Instruments*, 15, 2: 57–106.

Deutsche Bundesbank (1992). 'Die Beschluesse von Maastricht zur Europaeischen Wirtschafts- und Waehrungsunion in Europe', *Monatsbericht*, 2: 45–54.

—— (2003). 'The Monetary Constitution under the Constitution for Europe', *Monthly Report*, November: 65.

—— (2004). 'Die Deutsche Bundesbank als integraler Bestandteil des Eurosystems', *Die Europaeische Wirtschafts- und Waehrungsunion*, Frankfurt, February: 57–8.

—— (2005*a*). 'The Changes to the Stability and Growth Pact', *Monthly Report*, April: 15–21.

—— (2005*b*). 'Deficit-limiting Budget Rules and a National Stability Pact in Germany', *Monthly Report*, April: 23–37.

—— (2005*c*). 'Stabilitaets- und Wachstumspakt entscheidend geschwaecht', *Pressenotiz, Stellungnahme der Deutschen Bundesbank*, Frankfurt, 21 March.

—— (2005*d*). 'Establishment of a Centre for Technical Central Bank Cooperation', *Press Release*, Frankfurt, 20 July.

—— (ed.) (1999). *Fifty Years of the Deutsche Mark. Central Bank and the Currency in Germany since 1948*. Oxford: Oxford University Press.

DIE ZEIT (2007). 'Jetzt wird's ungemütlich. Der Euro steigt und steigt. Eine ungewöhnliche Reisegruppe soll für Abhilfe sorgen', 18 October: 28.

Dincer, N. and Eichengreen, B. (2007). 'Central Bank Transparency: Where, Why, and With What Effects'? *NBER Working Paper Series*, no 13003, Cambridge: National Bureau of Economic Research.

Dougherty, C. (2008). 'In Europe, Central Banking Is Different', *The New York Times*, 6 March.

Douglas, M. (1986). *How Institutions Think*. Syracuse: Syracuse University Press.

Downs, A. (1957). *An Economic Theory of Democracy*. New York: Harper and Row.

Draghi, M. (2008). 'How to Restore Financial Stability: Bundesbanl Lecture 2008', Aus-zuege aus Presseartikeln, Deutsche Bundesbank, 17 September: 7–11.

Duckenfield, M. (1999*a*). 'The *Goldkrieg*: Revaluing the Bundesbank's Reserves and the Politics of EMU', *German Politics*, 8, 1: 106–30.

—— (1999*b*). 'Bundesbank-Government Relations in Germany in the 1990s: From GEMU to EMU', *West European Politics*, 22, 3: 87–108.

Duisenberg, W. (2000*a*). 'Hearing before the Committee on Economic and Monetary Affairs, European Parliament', March 20.

—— (2000*b*). 'The Role of the ECB at the International Level'. Speech at the Annual meeting of the Institute of the International Finance, Inc. (IIF), Prague, 23 September.

—— (2002). 'The Role of the Eurosystem in Prudential Supervision', speech at the con-ference organized by the De Nederlandsche Bank on the occasion of the 50th anniver-sary of Dutch bank supervisory legislation, Amsterdam, 24 April.

Dumke, R. and Sherman, H. (2000). 'Exchange Rate Options for EU Applicant Countries in Central and Eastern Europe', in B. Granville (ed.), *Essays on the World Economy and its Financial System*. London: The Royal Institute of International Affairs, pp. 153–95.

Duval, R. and Elmeskov, J. (2005). 'The Effects of EMU on Structural Reforms in Labour and Product Markets', *OECD Economics Department Working Papers*, no. 438, Paris: OECD.

Dyson, K. (1980). *The State Tradition in Western Europe*. Oxford: Martin Robertson.

—— (1994). *Elusive Union*. London: Longman.

—— (1998). 'Chancellor Kohl as Strategic Leader: The Case of Economic and Monetary Union', in C. Clemens and W. Paterson (eds.), *The Kohl Chancellorship*. London: Frank Cass, pp. 37–63.

—— (1999). 'German Economic Policy after 50 Years', in P. Merkl (ed.), *The Federal Republic of Germany at Fifty. The End of a Century of Turmoil*. New York: New York University Press, pp. 219–30.

—— (2000). *The Politics of the Euro-Zone. Stability or Breakdown?* Oxford: Oxford University Press.

—— (ed.) (2002*a*). *European States and the Euro: Europeanization, Variation and Convergence*. Oxford: Oxford University Press.

—— (2002*b*). 'Introduction: EMU as Integration, Europeanization, and Convergence', in K. Dyson (ed.), *European States and the Euro. Europeanization, Variation, and Convergence*. Oxford: Oxford University Press, 1–27.

—— (2006). *Enlarging the Euro Area: External Empowerment and Domestic Transformation in East Central Europe*. Oxford: Oxford University Press.

—— (2007). 'Euro Area Entry in East-Central Europe: Paradoxical Europeanization and Clustered Convergence', *West European Politics*, 30, 3: 417–42.

—— (2008*a*). 'The Treaty of Rome at Fifty: The 'Hard and Stony' Road to Economic and Monetary Union', in D. Phinnemore and A. Warleigh-Lack (eds.), *Reflections on European Integration*. London: Palgrave, pp. 143–173.

—— (ed.) (2008*b*). *The Euro at 10*. Oxford: Oxford University Press.

—— (2008*c*). 'The European Central Bank: Enlargement as Institutional Affirmation and Dif-ferentiation', in E. Best, T. Christiansen, and P. Settembri (eds.), *The Governance of the Wider Europe: EU Enlargement and Institutional Change*. Cheltenham, UK: Edward Elgar, pp. 120–40.

—— and Featherstone, F. (1999). *The Road to Maastricht: Negotiating Economic and Monetary Union*. Oxford: Oxford University Press.

References

Dyson, K. and Goetz, K. (eds.) (2003). *Germany, Europe and the Politics of Constraint*. Oxford: Oxford University Press.

—— and Quaglia, L. (2009). *European Economic Governance and Policies: Commentary on Key Documents*. 2 vols. Oxford: Oxford University Press.

—— Featherstone, K., and Michalopoulos, G. (1995). 'Strapped to the Mast: EC Central Bankers between Global Financial Markets and Regional Integration', *Journal of European Public Policy*, 2, 3: 465–87.

Eckstein, H. (1975). 'Case Study and Theory in Political Science', in F. Greenstein and N. Polsby (eds.), *Handbook of Political Science. vol. 7, Strategies of Inquiry*, Addison-Wesley Publishing Company, pp. 79–137.

Economic and Financial Committee (2007a). *Developing EU Financial Stability Arrangements: Final Report*. 5 September, ECFIN/CEFCPE(2007)REP/53990, Brussels: EFC.

—— (2007b). Press Release (15698/07), 4 December.

Égert, B., Gruber, T., and Reininger, T. (2003). 'Challenges for EU Acceding Countries' Exchange Rate Strategies after EU Accession and Asymmetric Application of the Exchange Rate Criteria', *Focus on Transition*, 2: 152–72.

Eichbaum, C. (1999). *Reshaping the Reserve: A Political Economy of Central Banking in Australasia*. PhD dissertation, Massey University, New Zealand.

Eichengreen, B. (1985). 'Editor's Introduction', in B. Eichengreen (ed.), *The Gold Standard in Theory and History*. London: Methuen, pp. 1–35.

—— (2003). 'The Accession Economies' Rocky Road to the Euro', *East-West Conference 2003*. Vienna: National Bank of Austria.

Eijffinger, S. (2006). 'Change at the ECB Executive Board', *Intereconomics*, 41, 2: 93–9.

—— and Geraats, S. (2006). 'How Transparent Are Central Banks?', *European Journal of Political Economy*, 22, 1: 1–21.

—— Hoeberichts, M., and Schaling, E. (2000). 'Why Money Talks and Wealth Whispers: Monetary Uncertainty and Mystique', *Journal of Money, Credit, and Banking*, 32, 2: 218–35.

Eijffinger, S. C. W. (2006). 'Change at the ECB Executive Board', *Intereconomics*, March/April: 93–9.

Einecke, H. (2004). 'Bundesbank in der Krise', *Sueddeutsche Zeitung*, 10 April.

EIROnline (2004). 'National-level Tripartism and EMU in the New EU Member States and Candidate Countries'. www.eiro.eurofound.eu.int/2004/03/study/tn0403102s.html accessed on 7/23/2004.

Elgie, R. (1998). 'Democratic Accountability and Central Bank Independence', *West European Politics*, 21, 3: 53–77.

—— (2001). 'Democratic Accountability and Central Bank Independence: A Reply to Various Critics', *West European Politics*, 24, 1: 217–21.

Emminger, O. (1986). *D-Mark, Dollar, Waehrungskrisen. Erinnerungen eines ehemaligen Bundesbankpraesidenten*. Stuttgart: Deutsche Verlags-Anstalt.

Engelen, K. (2002a). 'Central Bank Losers: The Inside Story of How the ECB and the Bundesbank Are Being Pushed Aside as Financial Regulators', *The International Economy*, Summer.

—— (2002b). 'Buba's Internal Politics', *The International Political Economy*, 16, 3: 22.

Ennuuste, U., Kukk, K., Pyss, T., and Viies, M. (2004). *A Political Economy Analysis of Estonian 1987–2006 Capitalist Market Reform Process*. Estonian Institute of Economics at Tallinn University of Technology. Unpublished Manuscript.

Epstein, G. (2005). 'Central Banks as Agents of Economic Development', *Working Paper* #104. University of Massachusetts Amherst: PERI.

Epstein, R. (2002). 'International Institutions and the Depoliticization of Economic Policy in Post-communist Poland: Central Banking and Agriculture Compared', *EUI Working Paper*, RSC No. 2002/69, Florence: The Robert Schuman Centre.

—— (2006). 'Cultivating Consensus and Creating Conflict – International Institutions and the (De)politicization of Economic Policy in Post-communist Europe', *Comparative Political Studies*, 39, 8: 1019–42.

—— (2008). *In Pursuit of Liberalism: International Institutions in Post-communist Europe.* Baltimore: Johns Hopkins University Press.

European Central Bank (2000). *ECB Monthly Bulletin* (October). Frankfurt: ECB.

—— (2001*a*). 'The Role of Central Banks in Prudential Supervision', Frankfurt: ECB, www. ecb.int/pub/pdf/other/prudentialsupcbrole_en.pdf

—— (2001*b*). 'Opinion of the ECB at the Request of the German Ministry of Finance on a Draft Law Establishing an Integrated Financial Services Supervision', CONV/2001/35, 8 November. Frankfurt: ECB.

—— (2002). 'The Accountability of the ECB', *Monthly Bulletin*, November, Frankfurt: ECB.

—— (2005*a*). 'Opinion of the European Central Bank of 23 December 2005 at the request of the Italian Ministry of Economy and Finance on the draft law on the protection of savings', CON/2005/58.

—— (2005*b*). 'Opinion of the European Central Bank of 6 October 2005 at the request of the Italian Ministry of Economy and Finance on the draft law on the protection of savings', CON/2005/34.

—— (2007). *Financial Stability Review, June.* Frankfurt: European Central Bank.

—— (2008). 'Price Stability and Growth', *Monthly Bulletin*, May: 75–87.

European Commission (2007). *DG Economic and Financial Affairs: Future Enlargements of the Euro Area – State of Preparations*, June, ec.europa.eu/economy_finance/euro/transition/preparations.pdf, Brussels.

—— (2008). *EMU@10: Successes and Challenges after 10 Years of Economic and Monetary Union.* COM (2008) 238, 7 May, Brussels: European Commission.

Eusepi, S. and Preston, B. (2007). 'Central Bank Communication and Expectations Stabilization', *NBER Working Paper*, no. 13259, Cambridge, MA.

Fabre Guillemant, R. (1998). *Les réformes administrative en France et en Grande Bretagne.* Paris: l'Harmattan.

Fabritius, H.-G. (2004). 'Die Deutsche Bundesbank im Wandel', *Auszuege aus Presseartikeln*, Deutsche Bundesbank, 5 May.

Farkas, Z. (2008). 'Hiánymátrix' (A Matrix of Shortages), *Heti Világgazdaság*, January 26: 67–70.

Farmer, D. (1995). *The Language of Public Administration: Bureaucracy, Modernity and Post-modernity.* Tuscaloosa, Ala.: University of Alabama Press.

Favero, C., Freixias, X., Persson, T., and Wyplosz, C (2000). *One Money, Many Countries: Monitoring the European Central Bank 2*, London: CEPR.

Featherstone, K. (2003). 'Greece and EMU: Between External Empowerment and Domestic Vulnerability', *Journal of Common Market Studies*, 41, 5: 923–40.

—— and Radaelli, C. (eds.) (2003). *The Politics of Europeanization.* Oxford: Oxford University Press.

References

Federal Reserve Bank of New York (2008). 'Domestic Open Market Operations During 2007'. A Report for the Federal Open Market Committee by the Markets Group, February.

Federal Reserve System Study Group on Alternative Instruments for System Operations (2002). 'Alternative Instruments for Open Market and Discount Window Operations'. Washington, DC: Federal Reserve System.

Federal Trust (2005). *Flexibility and the Future of the European Union*. London: Federal Trust.

—— (2005). *Flexibility and the Future of the European Union*. London.

Feldmann, M. (2006). 'The Baltic States: Pacesetting on EMU Accession and the Consolidation of Domestic Stability Culture', in K. Dyson (ed.), *Enlarging the Euro Area: External Empowerment and Domestic Transformation in East Central Europe*. Oxford: Oxford University Press, pp. 178–96.

FFIEC (Federal Financial Institutions Examination Council) (2006). *Annual Report 2006*. Washington, DC.

Finocchiaro, A. and Contessa, A. (2002). *La Banca d'Italia e i Problemi della Moneta e del Credito*. Roma: Bancaria.

Fischer, B., Lenza, M., Pill, H., and Reichlin, L. (2006). 'Money and Monetary Policy: The ECB Experience 1999–2006', paper presented at the ECB Central Banking Conference, Frankfurt, November 6.

Fischer, J. (2000). *Vom Staatenbund zur Föderation – Gedanken über die Finalität der Europäischen Integration*, speech given on 12 May at the Humboldt-University Berlin, in M. Hartmut (ed.), *Die neue Europadebatte. Leitbilder für das Europa der Zukunft*. Bonn: Europa Union Verlag, pp. 41–54.

Fischer, S. (1990). 'Rules Versus Discretion in Monetary Policy', in B. M. Friedman and F. H. Hahn (eds.), *Handbook of Monetary Economics*. vol. 2. Amsterdam: North Holland, pp. 1169–78.

—— (1994). 'Modern Central Banking', in F. Capie, C. Goodhart, S. Fischer, and N. Schnadt (eds.), *The Future of Central Banking. The Tercentenary Symposium of the Bank of England*. Cambridge: Cambridge University Press, pp. 262–308.

—— (2001). 'Exchange Rate Regimes: Is the Bipolar View Correct?', *Journal of Economic Perspectives*, 15, 2: 3–24.

Fourcade, M. (2006). 'The Construction of a Global Profession: The Transnationalization of Economics', *American Journal of Sociology*, 112, 1: 145–94.

Franzese, R. (2002). *Macroeconomic Policies of Developed Democracies*. New York: Cambridge University Press.

Franzese, R. J. and Hall, P. A. (2000). 'Institutional Dimensions of Coordinating Wage Bargaining and Monetary Policy', in T. Iversen, J. Pontusson, and D. Soskice (eds.), *Unions, Employers, and Central Banks. Macroeconomic Coordination and Institutional Change in Social Market Economies*. Cambridge: Cambridge University Press, pp. 173–204.

Fraser, B. (1994). 'The Art of Monetary Policy', *Reserve Bank of Australia Bulletin*, Sydney: Reserve Bank of Australia, October.

—— (1996). 'Reserve Bank Independence', *Reserve Bank of Australia Bulletin*, Sydney: Reserve Bank of Australia.

Freeman, J. (2002). 'The Political Economy of Monetary Institutions', *International Organization*, 56, 4: 889–910.

Fry, M., Julius, D., Mahadeva, L., Roger, S., and Sterne, G. (2000). 'Key Issues in the Choice of Monetary Policy Framework', in L. Mahadeva and G. Sterne (eds.), *Monetary Policy Frameworks in a Global Context*. London: Routledge, pp. 1–216.

Gaiotti, E. and Rossi, S. (2003). 'La politica monetaria italiana nella srolta degli anni '80', in S. Colaziri, P. Craveri, S. Pons, G. Quagliariello (a cura di) *Gli anni '80 come storia*, Rubettino.

Gaithner, T. (2008). 'Statement Regarding Actions by the Federal Reserve Bank of New York in Response to Liquidity Pressures in Financial Markets', before U.S. Senate Committee on Banking Housing and Urban Affairs, April 3.

GAO (Government Accountability Office) (2007). *Financial Regulation: Industry Trends Continue to Challenge Federal Regulatory Structure*. GAO-08–32, October.

Garganas, N. and Tavlas, G. (2001). 'Monetary Regimes and Inflation Performance: The Case of Greece', in R. C. Bryant, N. C. Garganas, and G. S. Tavlas (eds.), *Greece's Economic Performance and Prospects*. Athens: Bank of Greece-The Brookings Institution, pp. 43–95.

George, E. (2000). 'Britain and Europe', speech to British Swiss Chamber of Commerce Lunch, 12 September.

Geraats, P. (2002). 'Central Bank Transparency', *Economic Journal,* 112, 483: 532–65.

—— (2005). 'Transparency and Monetary Policy: Theory and Practice', on-line paper, December; http://www.econ.cam.ac.uk/faculty/geraats/tpmptp.pdf, accessed 24 March 2008.

—— (2006). 'Transparency of Monetary Policy: Theory and Practice', *CESifo Economic Studies*, 52, 1: 111–52.

—— (2007). 'The Mystique of Central Bank Speak', *International Journal of Central Banking*, 3, 1: 37–80.

Gerschenkron, A. (1965). *Economic Backwardness in Historical Perspective*. New York: Praeger.

Geršl, A. (2006). 'Political Pressure on Central Banks: The Case of the Czech National Bank', *Finance a úvěr- Czech Journal of Economics and Finance*, 56, 1–2: 18–39.

Giavazzi, F. and Giovannini, A. (1989). *Limiting Exchange Rate Flexibility: The European Monetary System*. Massachusetts: MIT Press.

—— and Pagano, M. (1988). 'The Advantage of Tying One's Hands. EMS Discipline and Central Bank Credibility', *European Economic Review*, 32, 5: 1055–82.

—— Micossi, S., and Miller, M. (eds.) (1988). *The European Monetary System*. Cambridge: Cambridge University Press.

Giblin, L. (1951). *The Growth of a Central Bank: The Development of the Commonwealth Bank of Australia*. Melbourne: Melbourne University Press.

Giering, C. (2007). 'Flexibilisierung', in W. Weidenfeld and W. Wessels (eds.), *Europa von A bis Z. Taschenbuch der europäischen Integration*, 10. Auflage. Baden-Baden: Nomos, pp. 257–60.

Gilardi, F. (2002). 'Policy Credibility and Delegation to Independent Regulatory Agencies: A Comparative Empirical Analysis', *Journal of European Public Policy*, 9, 6: 873–93.

Godeaux, J. (1989). 'The Working of the EMS: A Personal Assessment', in *Committee for the Study of Economic and Monetary Union*, Luxembourg: Office for Official Publications of the European Communities.

Goodfriend, M. (1986). 'Monetary Mystique: Secrecy and Central Banking', *Journal of Monetary Economics*, 17, 1: 63–92.

—— (1999). 'The Role of A Regional Bank in a System of Central Banks', *Federal Reserve Bank of Richmond Working Paper*, 99–4.

References

Goodfriend, M. (2000). 'The Role of a Regional Bank in a System of Central Banks'. Federal Reserve Bank of Richmond, *Economic Quarterly* 86 (Winter), 7–25.

—— (2003). 'Inflation Targeting in the United States?' in B. Bernanke and M. Woodford (eds.), *The Inflation-Targeting Debate*. Chicago: University of Chicago Press, pp. 311–37.

—— (2005). 'The Monetary Policy Debate Since October 1979: Lessons for Theory and Practice'. *Federal Reserve Bank of St. Louis Review*, 87 (March/April, part 2), 243–62.

—— König, R., and Repullo, R. (2004). 'External Evaluation of the Economic Research Activities of the European Central Bank', Frankfurt: ECB.

Goodhart, C. (2009). 'The Political Economy of Inflation Targets: New Zealand and the U.K.', in R. Leeson (ed.), *David Laidler's Contribution to Macroeconomics*. Basingstoke: Palgrave Macmillan, p. 243.

—— (2005). 'Dear Jean-Claude', *Central Banking*, 16, 1: 32–6.

—— and Persaud, A. (2008). 'A Party Pooper's Guide to Financial Stability', *Financial Times*, 5 June, 15.

—— Capie, F., and Schnadt, N. (1994). 'The Development of Central Banking', in F. Capie, C. Goodhart, S. Fischer, and N. Schnadt (eds.), *The Future of Central Banking. The Tercentenary Symposium of the Bank of England*. Cambridge: Cambridge University Press, pp. 1–231.

—— (2006). 'The ECB and the Conduct of Monetary Policy: Goodhart's Law and Lessons from the Euro Area', *Journal of Common Market Studies*, 44, 4: 757–78.

Goodman, J. (1992). *Monetary Sovereignty: the Politics of Central Banking in Western Europe*. Ithaca, N.Y.: Cornell University Press.

Gouldner, A. W. (1979). *The Future of Intellectuals and the Rise of the New Class*. London: The MacMillan Press Ltd.

Gramlich, E. (2004). 'Subprime Mortgage Lending: Benefits, Costs, and Challenges'. Remarks at the Financial Services Roundtable Annual Housing Policy Meeting, Chicago, Illinois May 21.

—— (2007). *Subprime Mortgages: America's Latest Boom and Bust*. Washington, DC: Urban Institute Press.

Grauwe, P. de (2006). 'A Central Banking Model for Neither Gods Nor Monkeys', *Financial Times*, 26 July.

Green Cowles, M., Caporasa, J., and Risse, T. (eds.) (2001). *Transforming Europe: Europeanization and Domestic Change*. Ithaca: Cornell University Press.

Greenspan, A. (2007). *The Age of Turbulence: Adventures in a New World*. New York: Penguin.

Gregory, R. (2007). 'New Public Management and the Ghost of Max Weber: Exorcised or Still Haunting?', in T. Christensen and P. Lægreid (eds.), *Transcending New Public Management*. Aldershot: Ashgate, pp. 221–44.

Greiber, C. and Lemke, W. (2005). 'Money Demand and Macro-Economic Uncertainty' *Deutsche Bundesbank Discussion Paper Series 1*, No. 26.

Greider, W. (1987) *Secrets of the Temple: How the Federal Reserve Runs the Country*. New York: Simon and Schuster.

Greskovits, B. (2001). 'Brothers-in-Arms or Rivals in Politics? Top Politicians and Top Policy Makers in the Hungarian Transformation', in J. Kornai, S. Haggard, and R. Kaufman (eds.), *Reforming the State. Fiscal and Welfare Reform in Post-Socialist Countries*. Cambridge: Cambridge University Press, pp. 111–41.

—— (2006). 'The First Shall Be the Last? Hungary's Road to EMU', in K. Dyson (ed.), *Enlarging the Euro Area: External Empowerment and Domestic Transformation in East Central Europe*. Oxford: Oxford University Press, pp. 127–44.

Grilli, V., Masciandaro, D., and Tabellini, G. (1991). 'Political and Monetary Institutions and Public Financial Policies in the Industrial Countries', *Economic Policy*, 6, 13: 342–92.

Grimes, A. (2001). 'Review of New Zealand Monetary Policy', *Agenda*, 8, 4: 303–20.

Gros, D. (2003). 'Reforming the Composition of the ECB Governing Council in View of Enlargement. How Not to Do It!', Briefing Paper for the Monetary Committee of the European Parliament. Brussels: Centre for European Policy Studies, February.

H.M. Treasury (2003). *UK Membership of the Single Currency: An Assessment of the Five Economic Tests*. London: Cm 5776, June.

Haas, E. (1990). *When Knowledge is Power*. Berkeley: University of California Press.

Haas, P. (1992). 'Introduction: Epistemic Communities and International Policy Coordination', *International Organisation*, 46, 1: 1–36.

Habermas, Jürgen (2008). 'Ein Lob den Iren', *Süddeutsche Zeitung*, 17th June 2008, http://www.sueddeutsche.de/ausland/artikel/310/180753/

Haggard, S., Kaufman, R. R., and Shugart, M. (2001). 'Politics, Institutions, and Macroeconomic Adjustment: Hungarian Fiscal Policy Making in Comparative Perspective', in J. Kornai, S. Haggard, and R. R. Kaufman (eds.), *Reforming the State: Fiscal and Welfare Reforms in Post-Socialist Countries*. Cambridge and N.Y.: Cambridge University Press, pp. 75–110.

Halikias, D. J. (1978). *Money and Credit in a Developing Economy: The Greek Case*. New York: New York University Press.

Hall, P. (1993). 'Policy Paradigms, Social Learning and the State', *Comparative Politics*, 25, 3: 275–96.

—— (ed.) (1989). *The Political Power of Economic Ideas: Keynesianism Across Nations*. Princeton, NJ: Princeton University Press.

—— and Taylor, R. (1996). *Political Science and the Three New Institutionalisms*, Max-Planck-Institute for the Study of Societies, MPIfG Discussion Paper 96/6, Cologne.

Hallerberg, M. (2002). 'Veto Players and the Choice of Monetary Institutions', *International Organization*, 56, 4: 775–802.

Hawke, G. (1977). *Between Governments and Banks: A History of the Reserve Bank of New Zealand*. Wellington: Government Print.

Hawtrey, R. (1932). *The Art of Central Banking*. London: Longman.

Hay, C. (2000). 'Globalization, Regionalization and the Persistence of National Variation: The Contingent Convergence of Contemporary Capitalism', *Review of International Studies*, 26, 4: 509–31.

Hayo, B. and Hofmann, B. (2006). 'Comparing Monetary Policy Reaction Functions: ECB versus Bundesbank', *Empirical Economics*, 31, 3, 645–62.

Heikensten, L. (2005). 'Monetary Policy and the Academics', inaugural lecture at Umeå University, October 28. Umeå, Sweden.

—— and Vredin, A. (2002). 'The Art of Targeting Inflation', *Penning- och valutapolitik*, Stockholm: Rikskbanken, 5–34.

Heipertz, M. (2001). 'How Strong was the Bundesbank: A Case Study in the Making of German and European Monetary Union', *Working Document No. 172*. Brussels: Centre for European Policy Studies.

—— and Verdun, A. (2004). 'The Dog that Would Never Bite? On the Origins of the Stability and Growth Pact', *Journal of European Public Policy*, 11, 5: 773–88.

—— —— (2005). 'The Stability and Growth Pact – Theorizing a Case in European Integration', *Journal of Common Market Studies*, 43, 5: 985–1008.

References

Heisenberg, D. (1999). *The Mark of the Bundesbank*. Boulder, CO: Lynne Rienner Press.

Helleiner, E. (1999). 'Denationalising Money? Economic Liberalism and the 'National Question', in Currency Affairs', in E. Gilbert and E. Helleiner (eds.), *Nation-States and Money. The Past, Present and Future of National Currencies*. London and New York: Routledge, pp. 139–58.

—— (2003). *The Making of National Money. Territorial Currencies in Historical Perspective*. Ithaca: Cornell University Press.

Henning, C. R. and Padoan, P. C. (2000). *Transatlantic Perspectives on the Euro*. Washington, DC: Brookings/Pittsburg: ECSA.

Hibbs, D. (1977). 'Political Parties and Macroeconomic Policy', *American Political Science Review*, 71, 4: 1467–87.

Hierlemann, D. (2008). 'Irish Vote, Europe's Future: Four options after the "No" ', *Spotlight Europe*, special edition 2008/06.

Hill, C. (2006). 'The Directoire and the Problem of a Coherent EU Foreign Policy', *CFSP Forum*, 4, 6: 1–4.

Hirschman, A. (1970). *Exit, Voice, Loyalty*. Cambridge, MA: Harvard University Press.

Hix, S., Hoyland, B., and Vivyan, N. (2007). 'From Doves to Hawks: A Spatial Analysis of Voting in the Monetary Policy Committee of the Bank of England, 1997–2007. London School of Economics: Unpublished.

Hochreiter, E. (2000). 'The Current Role of National Central Banks in the Eurosystem', *Atlantic Economic Journal*, 28, 3: 300–8.

Hoffmann, B. (2006). 'Do Monetary Indicators Still Predict Euro Area Inflation?', *Deutsche Bundesbank Discussion Paper Series 2*.

Hoffmeyer, E. (1993). *Pengepolitiske problemstillinger 1965–1990*. Copenhagen: Danish Central Bank.

—— (2000). 'Decision-making for European Economic and Monetary Union', *Occasional Paper*, 62, Washington, DC: Group of Thirty.

Holmes, F. (2002). 'An Anzac Union?' *IPS Policy Paper*, Institute of Policy Studies, Victoria University of Wellington.

Howarth, D. (2001). *The French Road to European Monetary Union*. Basingstoke: Palgrave.

—— (2007). 'Running an Enlarged Euro-Zone – Reforming the European Central Bank: Efficiency, Legitimacy and National Economic Interest', *Review of International Political Economy*, 14, 5: 820–41.

—— and Loedel, P. (2004). 'The ECB and the Stability Pact: Policeman and Judge?', *Journal of European Public Policy*, 11, 5: 832–53.

—— —— (2005). *The ECB: the New European Leviathan*. Basingstoke: Palgrave, revised second edition.

Hufton, O. (1986). 'Fernand Braudel', *Past and Present*, 112: 208–13.

Hunt, C. (2005). 'A Fresh Look at the Merits of a Currency Union', *Reserve Bank Bulletin*, 68, 4: 16–30.

IMF (1998). 'International Capital Markets', September, Washington, DC: IMF.

Ingves, S. (2007). 'Regulatory Challenges of Cross-border Banking: Possible Ways Forward', speech at Reserve Bank of Australia, Sydney, July 23.

Ip, G. (2006). 'Columbia Economist Is Considered for Fed Board', *Wall Street Journal*, April 10.

—— and Hilsenrath, J. (2007). 'How Credit Got So Easy and Why its Tightening', *Wall Street Journal*, August 7.

Issing, O. (1998). 'Crisis Prevention: IMF Surveillance, Need for New Teeth?', Statement at the IMF conference on the role of the IMF in the world economy, held in Frankfurt am Main on July 2.

—— (1999). 'The Eurosystem: Transparent and Accountable or "Willem in Euroland" ', *Journal of Common Market Studies*. 37, 3: 503–19.

—— (2008). *Der Euro*. Geburt – Erfolg – Zukunft, München: Verlag Franz Vahlen.

—— (2005*a*). 'Communication, Transparency, Accountability: Monetary Policy in the Twenty-First Century', *Federal Reserve Bank of St. Louis Review*, March/April, part 1, 65–84.

—— (2005*b*). *Imperfect Knowledge and Monetary Policy*. Cambridge: Cambridge University Press.

—— (2006). 'The ECB's Monetary Policy Strategy: Why Did We Choose a Two-pillar Approach?' Paper presented at the 4th ECB Central Banking Conference, Frankfurt, November 10.

—— (2008). *The Birth of the Euro*. Cambridge: Cambridge University Press.

—— Gaspar, V., Angeloni, I., and Tristani, O. (2001). *Monetary Policy in the Euro Area*. Cambridge: Cambridge University Press.

Iversen, T. and Pontusson, J. (2000). 'Comparative Political Economy: A Northern European Perspective', in T. Iversen, J. Pontusson, and D. Soskice (eds.), *Unions, Employers, and Central Banks*. Cambridge: Cambridge University Press, pp. 1–37.

Jabko, N. (2003). 'Democracy in the Age of the Euro', *Journal of European Public Policy*, 10, 5: 710–39.

Jachtenfuchs, M. and Kohler-Koch, B. (2004). 'Governance and Institutional Development', in T. Diez and A. Wiener (eds.), *European Integration Theory*. Oxford: Oxford University Press, pp. 97–115.

Jacobsson, B., Lægreid, P., and Pedersen, O. K. (2004). *Europeanization and Transnational States. Comparing Nordic Central Governments*. London: Routledge.

Jacobsson, E. E. (1979). *A Life for Sound Money. Per Jacobsson – His Biography*. Oxford: Clarendon Press.

Janning, J. (1997). 'Dynamik in der Zwangsjacke – Flexibilität in der Europäischen Union nach Amsterdam', *integration*, 20, 4, 285–91.

Johnson, J. (2006). 'Post-communist Central Banks: A Democratic Deficit?', *Journal of Democracy*, 17, 1: 90–103.

—— (2006). 'Two-track Diffusion and Central Bank Embeddedness: The Politics of Euro Adoption in Hungary and the Czech Republic', *Review of International Political Economy*, 13, 3: 361–86.

—— (2008). 'The Remains of Conditionality: The Faltering Enlargement of the Euro Zone', *Journal of European Public Policy*, 15, 6: 826–42.

Johnson, P. (1998). *The Government of Money – Monetarism in Germany and the United States*. Ithaca, NY: Cornell University Press.

Jones, E. (1998). 'The Netherlands: Top of the Class', in E. Jones, J. Frieden, and F. Torres (eds.), *Joining Europe's Monetary Club. The Challenges for Smaller Member States*. New York: St Martin's Press, pp. 149–70.

Jonung, L. (2000). 'Från guldmyntfot till inflationsmål—svensk stabiliseringspolitik under det 20:e seklet', *Ekonomisk Debatt*, 28, 1: 17–32.

Junge, K. (2006). 'Differentiated European Integration', in M. Cini (ed.), *European Union Politics*. Oxford: Oxford University Press, pp. 391–404.

References

Juppé, A. (2000). 'Pioniergruppe als Übergang. Ein Gespräch mit Alain Juppé über das Europa von Morgen', *Frankfurter Allgemeine Zeitung*, 8 July, 7.

Kahn, C. and Santos, J. (2004). 'Allocating Lending of Last Resort and Supervision in the Euro Area', in A. Volbert, J. Mélitz, and G. von Furstenberg (eds.), *Monetary Unions and Hard Pegs – Effects on Trade, Financial Development, and Stability*. Oxford: Oxford University Press, pp. 347–60.

Kaltenthaler, K. (1998). *Germany and the Politics of Europe's Money*. Durham, NC: Duke University Press.

Katzenstein, P. (1987). *Policy and Politics in West Germany*. Philadelphia: Temple University Press.

—— (2003). '*Small States* and Small States Revisited', *New Political Economy*, 8, 1: 9–30.

Kayser, M (2005). 'Who Surfs, Who Manipulates? The Determinants of Opportunistic Election Timing and Electorally Motivated Economic Intervention'. *American Political Science Review*, 99, 1: 17–27.

Keefer, P. and Stasavage, D. (2003). 'The Limits of Delegation: Veto Players, Central Bank Independence, and the Credibility of Monetary Policy', *American Political Science Review*, 97, 3: 407–23.

Kenen, P. B. (1995). *Economic and Monetary Union in Europe*. Cambridge: Cambridge University Press.

Kennedy, H. (1991). *The Bundesbank: Germany's Central Bank in the International Monetary System*. London: Pinter Publishers, Chatham House Papers.

Kettl, D. (1986). *Leadership at the FED*. New Haven: Yale University Press.

Kindleberger, C. and Aliber, R. (2005). *Manias, Panics and Crashes: A History of Financial Crises*. Basingstoke: Palgrave Macmillan.

King, M. (2004). 'The Institutions of Monetary Policy', *American Economic Review Papers and Proceedings*, 94, 2: 1–13.

Klaus, V. (2000). 'Three Years after the Exchange Rate Crisis: Recapitulation of the Events and Their Consequences', *Politiká Ekonomie*, 48, 5: 595–604.

Knodt, M. (2005). *Regieren im erweiterten europäischen Mehrebenensystem. International Einbettung der EU in die WTO*. Baden-Baden: Nomos.

Koch, H. (1983). *Histoire de la Banque de France et de la monnaie sous la IVe république*. Paris: Dunod.

Kohn, D. (2005). 'Globalization, Inflation and Monetary Policy', remarks at the James R. Wilson Lecture Series, The College of Wooster, Wooster, Ohio, October 11.

—— (2006). 'Monetary Policy and Asset Prices', paper given at the ECB conference on 'Monetary Policy: A Journey from Theory to Practice', Frankfurt, March 16.

Kornai, J. (1996). *Paying the Bill for Goulash-Communism. Hungarian Development and Macro Stabilization in a Political-Economy Perspective*. Discussion Paper 23. Budapest: Collegium Budapest/Institute for Advanced Study.

Krehbiel, K. (1998). *Pivotal Politics: A Theory of US Lawmaking*. Chicago: University of Chicago Press.

Krenzler, H. and Senior Nello, S. (1999). 'Implications of the Euro for Enlargement: Report of the Working Group on the Eastern Enlargement of the European Union', *RSC Policy Paper*, 99, 3, Florence: Robert Schuman Centre.

Kydland, F. and Prescott, E. (1977). 'Rules Rather Than Discretion: The Inconsistency of Optimal Plans', *Journal of Political Economy*, 85, 3: 473–91.

Kynaston, D. (2002). *The City of London: Club No More, 1945–2000, Vol. 4 (History of the City)*. London: Pimlico.

Laar, M. (2002). *Little Country that Could*. Centre for Research into Post-Communist Economies. London: St. Edmundsbury Press.

Lagerspetz, M. and Vogt, H. (2004). 'Estonia', in S. Berglund, J. Ekman, and F. H. Aarebrot (eds.), *The Handbook of Political Change in Eastern Europe*. Cheltenham, U.K.: Edward Elgar, pp. 57–94.

Lamfalussy, A. (2003). 'Central Banks and Financial Stability', 2nd Pierre Werner Lecture, Luxembourg: Banque Centrale du Luxembourg.

—— (2001). *Committee of Wise Men on the Regulation of European Securities Markets (Lamfalussy), Final Report (February 15th)*. Brussels: Commission of the European Communities.

Landes, D. (1991). 'Does It Pay to Be Late?', in J. Batou (ed.), *Between Development and Underdevelopment*. Geneve: Publications du Centre D'Histoire Économique Internationale de L'Université de Geneve, pp. 43–66.

Le Horen, E. (2007). 'The New Governance in Monetary Policy: A Critical Appraisal of the FED and the ECB', in P. Arestis, E. Hein, and E. Le Heron (eds.), *Aspects of Modern Monetary and Macroeconomic Policies*. Houndmills/Basingstoke: Palgrave, pp. 146–71.

Lee, R. (2005). *Politics and the Creation of a European SEC: the Optimal UK Strategy – Constructive Inconsistency*. Washington, DC: AEI Brookings Joint Centre.

Leiner-Killinger, N., Lopez Perez, V., Stieger, R., and Vitale, G. (2007). 'Structural Reforms in EMU and the Role of Monetary Policy', *ECB Occasional Paper*, No. 66, Frankfurt: European Central Bank.

Lidegaard, B. (2005). *I Kongens navn. Henrik Kauffmann i dansk diplomati 1919–58*. København: Samlerens Forlag.

Lindahl, R. and Naurin, D. (2005). 'Sweden: The Twin Faces of a Euro-Outsider', *Journal of European Integration*, 27, 1: 89–110.

Lindstrom, N. and Piroska, D. (2007). 'The Politics of Privatization and Europeanization in Europe's Periphery: Slovenian Banks and Breweries for Sale?' *Competition and Change*, 11, 2: 117–35.

Loedel, P. (1999a). *Deutsche Mark Politics: Germany in the European Monetary System*. Boulder, CO: Lynne Rienner Press.

—— (1999b). 'The Lasting Legacy of the Bundesbank: Fifty Years of Deutschmark Politics', in P. Merkl (ed.), *The Federal Republic of Germany at Fifty: The End of a Century of Turmoil*. New York: New York University Press: pp. 231–42.

Lohmann, S. (1998). 'Federalism and Central Bank Independence: The Politics of German Monetary Policy, 1957–92', *World Politics*, 50, 3: 401–46.

Lombardelli, C., Proudman, J., and Talbot, J. (2005). 'Committees versus Individuals: An Experimental Analysis of Monetary Policy Decision Making', *International Journal of Central Banking*, 1, 2: 181–205.

Louis, J.-V. (2002). *Euro in the National Context*. London: BIICL.

Lucchetti, A. (2008). 'As Housing Boomed, Moody's Opened Up', *Wall Street Journal*, April 11.

Ludlow, P. (1982). *The Making of the European Monetary System*. London: Butterworth.

Lukes, S. (2005). *Power: A Radical View*. 2nd edition. Basingstoke: Palgrave Macmillan.

Maes, I. (2002). *Economic Thought and the Making of European Monetary Union*. Cheltenham, UK: Edward Elgar.

423

References

Maes, I. (2006). 'The Ascent of the European Commission as an Actor in the Monetary Integration Process in the 1960s', *Scottish Journal of Political Economy*, 53, 2: 222–41.

—— (2007). *Half a Century of European Financial Integration. From the Rome Treaty to the 21st Century*. Brussels: Mercatorfonds.

—— and Périlleux, V. (1993). 'De Prudentiële Controle van de Kredietinstellingen', *Economisch en Sociaal Tijdschrift*, 47,4: 611–34.

—— and Verdun, A. (2005). 'Small States and the Creation of EMU: Belgium and the Netherlands, Pacesetters and Gatekeepers', *Journal of Common Market Studies*, 43, 2: 327–48.

Magnette, P. (2000). 'Towards "Accountable Independence"? Parliamentary Controls of the European Central Bank and the Rise of a New Democratic Model', *European Law Journal*, 6, 4: 326–40.

Mahadeva, L. and Sterne, G. (2000). *Monetary Policy Frameworks in a Global Context*. London: Routledge.

Majone, G. (1989). *Evidence, Argument and Persuasion in the Policy Process*. New Haven, Conn.: Yale University Press.

Mamou, Y. (1988). *Le Tresor: Une machine de pouvoir, la Direction du Trésor*. Paris: Editions la Decouverte.

Mansbridge, J. (2003). 'Rethinking Representation', *American Political Science Review*, 97, 3: 515–28.

March, J. and Olsen, J. (2005). 'Elaborating the "New Institutionalisms" ', *ARENA Working Papers* 05/11, Oslo: ARENA.

Marcussen, M. (2000). *Ideas and Elites*. Aalborg: Aalborg University.

—— (2002). 'EMU: A Danish Delight and Dilemma', in K. Dyson (ed.), *European States and the Euro – Europeanization, Variation, and Convergence*. Oxford: Oxford University Press, pp. 120–44.

—— (2005a). 'Central Banks on the Move', *Journal of European Public Policy*, 12, 5: 903–23.

—— (2005b). 'Denmark and European Monetary Integration: Out but far from Over', *Journal of European Integration*, 27, 1: 43–63.

—— (2006a). 'Institutional Transformation? The Scientization of Central Banking as Case', in T. Christensen and P. Lægreid (eds.), *Autonomy and Regulation: Coping with Agencies in the Modern State*. Cheltenham, UK: Edward Elgar Publishing, pp. 81–109.

—— (2006b). 'The Basel Committee as a Transnational Governance Network', in M. Marcussen and J. Torfing (eds.), *Democratic Network Governance in Europe*. Hampshire: Palgrave-Macmillan, pp. 214–31.

—— (2006c). 'The Transnational Governance Network of Central Bankers', in M.-L. Djelic and K. Sahlin-Andersson (eds.), *Transnational Governance. Institutional Dynamics of Regulation*. Cambridge: Cambridge University Press, pp. 180–204.

—— (2007a). 'Handling Euro-Outsiderness', *Working Paper* 2007:6, Roskilde University: Center for the Study of Democratic Network Governance.

—— (2007b). 'Central Banking Reform Across the World: Only by Night Are All Cats Grey', in T. Christensen and P. Lægreid (eds.), *Transcending New Public Management: the Transformation of Public Sector Reforms*. Aldershot: Ashgate, pp. 135–53.

—— (2008). 'The Danish Central Bank – The Reluctant European', *CEP Working Paper Series*, 2008/1, Copenhagen University: Department of Political Science.

—— (2009). 'Leading Central Banking in Europe', in J. A. Raffel, P. Leisink, and A. E. Middlebrooks (eds.), *Public Sector Leadership: International Challenges and Perspectives*. Cheltenham: Edward Elgar Publishing, pp. 73–90.

Marsh, D. (1992). *The Bundesbank: The Bank That Rules Europe*. London: Heinemann.

Mataj, J. and Vojtíšek, P. (1992). 'Právní a ekonomické aspekty nového zákona o SBČS (Legal and Economic Aspects of the New Law on the SBCS)', *Finance a úvěr- Czech Journal of Economics and Finance*, 42, 3, 109–15.

Maxfield, S. (1997). *Gatekeepers of Growth: The International Political Economy of Central Banking in Developing Countries*. Princeton, NJ: Princeton University Press.

Mayes, D. G. (1998). 'Evolving Voluntary Rules for the Operation of the European Central Bank', *Current Politics and Economics of Europe*, 8, 4: 357–86.

—— (2000). 'Independence and Co-ordination – The Eurosystem', paper presented at the UACES 30th Anniversary Conference and 5th UACES Research Conference, Central European University, Budapest, 6–8 April.

—— and Virén, M. (2007). 'The SGP and the ECB: an exercise in asymmetry', *Journal of Financial Transformation*, 19: 159–75.

Mazower, M. (1991). *Greece and the Inter-War Economic Crisis*. Oxford: Oxford University Press.

McDermott, G. (2007). 'Politics, Power, and Institution Building: Bank Crises and Supervision in East Central Europe', *Review of International Political Economy*, 14, 2: 220–50.

McNamara, K. (1998). *The Currency of Ideas: Monetary Politics in the European Union*. Ithaca: Cornell University Press.

—— (2002*a*). 'Rational Fictions: Central Bank Independence and the Social Logic of Delegation', *West European Politics* 25, 1: 47–76.

—— (2002*b*). 'State Building, Territorialization, and the Creation of American Currency', in D. Andrews, C. Randall Henning, and L. Pauly (eds.), *Governing the Word's Money*. Ithaca: Cornell University Press, pp. 128–47.

—— (2006). 'Managing the Euro. The European Central Bank', in J. Peterson and M. Shackleton (eds.), *The Institutions of the European Union*. Oxford: Oxford University Press, pp. 169–89.

—— and Meunier, S. (2002). 'Between National Sovereignty and International Power: What External Voice for the Euro?', *International Affairs* 78, 4: 849–68.

Meade, E. and Stasavage, D. (2008). 'Publicity of Debate and the Incentive to Dissent', *Economic Journal*, 118, 525: 695–717.

Mencinger, J. (2004). 'Transition to a National and a Market Economy: A Gradualist Approach', in M. Mrak, M. Rojec, and C. Silva-Jáuregui (eds.), *Slovenia: From Yugoslavia to the European Union*. Washington, DC: The World Bank, pp. 67–82.

Mendzela, J. (2002). 'Leadership and Management in Central Banking', *Central Banking*, 13, 2: 40–6.

—— (2003). 'Leadership and Management of Central Banks', *Central Banking*, 13, 3: 59–66.

—— (2006). 'How to Manage the 21st-Century Central Bank?', *Central Banking*, 16, 4: 31–9.

Meyer, L. (1998). 'Issues and Trends in Bank Regulatory Policy and Financial Modernization Legislation'. Remarks at the Bank Administration Institute, Finance and Accounting Management Conference, Washington, DC, June 9.

—— (2004). *A Term at the Fed – An Insider's View*. New York: Harper Business.

Mikkelsen, R. (1993). *Dansk pengehistorie 1960–1990*. Copenhagen: Danmarks National Bank.

Milesi, G. (1998). *Le Roman de l'Euro*. Paris: Hachette.

Mishkin, F. (2002). 'Inflation Targeting', in B. Snowdon and H. R. Vane (eds.), *An Encyclopedia of Macroeconomics*. Cheltenham: Edward Elgar, pp. 361–65.

References

Mishkin, F. (2004). 'Can Inflation Targeting Work in Emerging Market Countries?' *NBER Working Paper*, no. 10646, Cambridge, MA.

—— (2007a). *Monetary Policy Strategy*. Cambridge, Mass: MIT Press.

—— (2007b). 'Globalization, Macroeconomic Performance, and Monetary Policy'. Speech at the 'Domestic Prices in an Integrated World Economy' Conference, Board of Governors of the Federal Reserve System, Washington, DC, September 27.

—— and Schmidt-Hebbel, K. (2001). 'One Decade of Inflation Targeting in the World'. *NBER Working Paper*, no. 8397, Cambridge, MA.

Mohácsi Nagy, P. (2006). 'Financial Market Governance: Evolution and Convergence', in K. Dyson (ed.), *Enlarging the Euro Area: External Empowerment and Domestic Transformation in East Central Europe*. Oxford: Oxford University Press, pp. 237–60.

Moran, M. (1984). *The Politics of Banking*. London: Macmillan.

Morgan Stanley (2004). *Central Bank Directory 2004*. London: Central Banking Publications Ltd.

Morris, I. (2000). *Congress, the President and the Federal Reserve: The Politics of American Monetary Policy-Making*. Ann Arbor, MI.: University of Michigan Press.

Morriss, P. (2002). *Power: A Philosophical Analysis*. Manchester: Manchester University Press.

—— (2006). 'Steven Lukes on the Concept of Power', *Political Studies Review*, 4, 2: 124–35.

Munchau, W. (2006). *Financial Times*, 5 June.

Neyapti, B. (2001). 'Central Bank Independence and Economic Performance in Eastern Europe', *Economic Systems*, 25, 4: 381–99.

Nicholls, A. (1994). *Freedom with Responsibility. The Social Market Economy in Germany, 1918–1963*. Oxford: Clarendon Press.

Nye, J. (2004). *Soft Power: Means of Success in World Politics*. New York: Public Affairs Press.

OECD (1995). *Economic Surveys: Greece 1995*. Paris: OECD.

—— (2007). 'Economic Survey of the Euro Area, 2007', *Policy Brief*, January. Paris: OECD.

Offe, C. (1991). 'Capitalism by Democratic Design? Democratic Theory Facing the Triple Transition in East Central Europe', *Social Research*, 58, 4: 865–92.

Olsen, E. and Hoffmeyer, E. (1968). *Dansk pengehistorie 1914–1960*. Copenhagen: Danmarks Nationalbank.

Orr, A. (2006). 'Towards a Framework for Promoting Financial Stability in New Zealand', *Speech to the Institution of Professional Engineers New Zealand*, 22 March. Wellington: Reserve Bank of New Zealand.

Østergaard, H. (1998). *At tjene og forme den nye tid. Finansministeriet 1948–1998*. Copenhagen: Ministry of Finance.

Padoa Schioppa, T. (1999a). 'EMU and Banking Supervision', lecture at the London School of Economics, Financial Markets Group, 24 February.

—— (1999b). 'EMU and Banking Supervision'. *International Finance*, 2, 2: 295–308.

—— (1999c). 'The External Representation of the Euro Area', introductory statement at the Sub-Committee on Monetary Affairs, European Parliament, Brussels, 17 March.

—— (2000). 'An Institutional Glossary of the Eurosystem', *ZEI Policy Paper*, B 16.

—— (2005). 'Es ist eine gute Sache, die Bankenaufsicht den Zentralbanken zu ueberantworten', interview in *Frankfurter Allgemeine Zeitung*, 25 May.

—— (2007). 'Europe Needs a Single Financial Rulebook', *Financial Times*, 10th December.

Pagoulatos, G. (1999). 'European Banking: Five Modes of Governance', *West European Politics*, 22, 1: 68–94.

—— (2003*a*). *Greece's New Political Economy: State, Finance and Growth from Postwar to EMU*. London and New York: Palgrave Macmillan.

—— (2003*b*). 'Financial Interventionism and Liberalization in Southern Europe: State, Bankers, and the Politics of Disinflation', *Journal of Public Policy*, 23, 2: 171–99.

Papademos, L. (2005). *'Banking Supervision and Financial Stability in Europe'*. Speech by the Lucas Papademos, Vice-President of the ECB, delivered at the Conference: 'Supervision of International Banks: Is a Bank Crisis still Possible in Europe?' organized by the European Banking Federation, Brussels, 28 October 2005, http://www.ecb.eu/press/key/date/2005/html/sp051028_2.en.html

—— (2007). 'The Financial Market Turmoil, the European Economy, and the Role of the European Central Bank', speech by the Vice President of the ECB at an event organized by The European Institute, New York, 27 September.

Parker, G. and Strauss, D. (2008). 'Interview Transcript: Alistair Darling, January 3', www.ft.com/cms/s/0/ec63ba08-ba27–11dc-abcb-0000779fd2ac.html

—— Larsen, P., Giles, C., and Saigol, L. (2007). 'Darling Caught off Guard by First Big Test', *Financial Times*, 18 September.

Passacantando, F. (1996). 'Building an Institutional Framework for Monetary Stability: The Case of Italy (1979–92)', *BNL Quarterly Review*, 196: 3–37.

Patat, J.-P. (2003). *L'ere des banques centrals*. Paris: Harmattan.

—— and Lutfalla, M. (1986). *Histoire monetaire de la France au XXe siècle*. Paris: Economica.

Pauly, L. (1997). *Who Elected the Bankers? Surveillance and Control in the World Economy*. Ithaca: Cornell University Press.

Pedersen, E. (2006). 'Danmarks Nationalbank's Operating Costs and Number of Employees in International Comparison', *Working Papers* no. 35. Copenhagen: Danmarks Nationalbank.

Pepelasis, M. I. (1998). 'Transplanting Institutions: The Case of the Greek Central Bank', *Greek Economic Review*, 19, 1: 33–64.

Peters, B. (2000). 'Institutional Theory: Problems and Prospects', *Political Science Series 69*, Institute for Advanced Studies, Vienna.

Pisani-Ferry, J., Aghion, P., Belka, M., von Hagen, J., Heikensten, L., Sapir, A., and Ahearne, A. (2008). *Coming of Age: Report on the Euro Area*. Blueprint No. 4, Brussels: Bruegel.

Pitkin, H. (1967). *The Concept of Representation*, Berkeley: University of California Press.

Plenderleith, I. (1997). 'London as a Financial Centre after EMU', speech at a conference organized by the International Center for Monetary and Banking Studies on 'The International Monetary System after the Decision on EMU', Geneva, 7 November.

Polányi, K. (1957). *The Great Transformation: The Political and Economic Origins of Our Time*. Boston: Beacon Press.

Polillo, S. and Guillén, M. (2005). 'Globalization Pressures and the State: The Worldwide Spread of Central Bank Independence', *American Journal of Sociology*, 110, 6: 1764–802.

Pollitt, C. and Bouckaert, G. (2000). *Public Management Reform. A Comparative Analysis*. Oxford: Clarendon Press.

Posen, A. (1995). 'Declarations Are Not Enough: Financial Sector Sources of Central Bank Independence', *NBER Macroeconomics Annual*. Cambridge, MA: MIT Press.

Pospíšil, J. (1996). 'Inflation and Central bank Independence – Do We and Can We Have Experience in the Czech Republic?' in *A Collection of Lectures from the Conference in Honour of the 70th Anniversary of Central Banking in the Czech Republic*. Prague: Czech National Bank.

References

Prate, A. (1987). *La France et sa monnaie: Essai sur les rélations entre la Banque de France et les gouvernements*. Paris: Julliard.

Puetter, U. (2006). *The Eurogroup. How a Secretive Circle of Finance Ministers Shape European Economic Governance*. Manchester: Manchester University Press.

Quaden, G. (2007). *Foreword. Annual Report 2006 – Part II: Activities, Governance and Annual Accounts*. Brussels: National Bank of Belgium.

Quaglia, L. (2004). 'Italy's Policy towards European Monetary Integration: Bringing Ideas Back In?', *Journal of European Public Policy*, 11, 6: 1096–111.

—— (2005*a*). 'An Integrative Approach to the Politics of Central Bank Independence: Lessons from Britain, Germany and Italy', *West European Politics*, 28, 3: 549–68.

—— (2005*b*). 'Civil Servants, Economic Policies and Economic Ideas: Lessons from Italy', *Governance*, 18, 4: 545–66.

—— (2007*a*). 'The Politics of Financial Services Regulation and Supervision Reform in the European Union', *European Journal of Political Research*, 46, 2: 269–90.

—— (2007*b*). 'Committee Governance in the Financial Sector in the European Union'. Brighton: University of Sussex European Institute, Working Paper No. 96.

—— (2008*a*). *Central Banking Governance in the European Union: A Comparative Analysis*. London: Routledge.

—— (2008*b*). 'The Reform of the Supervisory Authorities: the Case of the Bank of Italy', in M. Donovan and P. Onofri (eds.), *Italian Politics*. Oxford: Berghahn Books, pp. 141–156.

Reich, R. (1997). *Locked in the Cabinet*. New York: Knopf.

Reinhart, C. and Rogoff, K. (2008). 'This Time is Different: A Panoramic View of Eight Centuries of Financial Crises', *Working Paper*, 13882, March.

Remsperger, H. (2002). 'The Role of the Deutsche Bundesbank in the European System of Central Banks', *Journal of Asian Economics*, 13, 2: 137–56.

—— (2004). 'Research Matters', *Auszuege aus Presseartikeln*, 51, 1: 7–8. Frankfurt am Main: Deutsche Bundesbank.

Rentzow, S. (2002). 'The Power of Ideas: How Bundesbank Ideas Have Influenced the Reconstruction of the National Bank of Poland', *German Politics*, 11, 1: 173–90.

Reserve Bank of Australia (2007). *Reserve Bank Board—New Arragements for Communication*, Media Release No: 2007-252, 5 December 2007, Sydney: Reserve Bank of Australia.

Reserve Bank of New Zealand (2007). *Opinion Article by Reserve Bank Deputy Governor Grant Spencer*. Wellington: Reserve Bank of New Zealand, 27 June.

Rhodes, M. and Keune, M. (2006). 'EMU and Welfare State Adjustment in Central and Eastern Europe', in K. Dyson (ed.), *Enlarging the Euro Area: External Empowerment and Domestic Transformation in East Central Europe*. Oxford, Oxford University Press, pp. 279–300.

Roberts, R. and Kynaston, D. (eds.) (1995). *The Bank of England: Money, Power and Influence, 1694–1994*. Oxford: Oxford University Press.

Rogoff, K. (1985). 'The Optimal Degree of Commitment to an Intermediate Monetary Target', *Quarterly Journal of Economics*, 110, 4: 1169–90.

Rood, J. Q. Th. (1990). 'The Position of the Netherlands: A Lesson in Monetary Union', in H. Sherman, R. Brown. P. Jacquet, and D. Julins (eds.), *Monetary Implications of the 1992 Process*. London: Pinter/Royal Institute of International Affairs, pp. 124–47.

Rose, A. (2007). 'A Stable International Monetary System Emerges: Inflation Targeting is Bretton Woods, Reversed', *Journal of International Money and Finance*, 26, 5: 663–81.

Rossi, S. (1998). *La Politica Economica Italiana 1968–98*. Roma: Laterza.

Sabatier, P. (1991). 'Toward Better Theories of the Policy Process', *Political Science and Politics*, 24, 2: 147.56.

Sarcinelli, M. (1995). 'Italian Monetary Policy in the '80s and '90s: the Revision of the Modus Operandi', *BNL Quarterly Review*, 195: 397–423.

Schadler, S., Drummond, P. F. N., Kuijs, L., Murgasova, Z., and Elkan van, R. (2005). 'Adopting the Euro in Central Europe: Challenges of the Next Step in European Integration' *Occasional Paper*, No. 234, Washington, DC: International Monetary Fund.

Schäfer, U. and Hagelueken, A. (2005). 'Stabilitaetspakt: Bundesbank legt sich mit dem Kanzler an', *Sueddeutsche Zeitung*, 18 January.

Schäuble, W. and Lamers, C. (1994). *CDU/CSU-Fraktion des Deutschen Bundestages, Überlegungen zur europäischen Politik*, Bonn, 1. September.

Schedvin, B. (1992). *In Reserve: Central Banking in Australia. 1945–1975*, Sydney: Macmillan.

Scholte, J. (2005). *Globalization. A Critical Introduction*. 2nd edition, London: Palgrave-Macmillan.

Schoors, K. (2002). 'Should the Central and Eastern European Accession Countries Adopt the EURO Before or After Accession?' *Economics of Planning*, 35, 1: 47–77.

Schüler, M. (2003). 'Incentive Problems in Banking Supervision – The European Case', *ZEW Discussion paper 03–62*, Mannheim.

Siklos, P. (2002). *The Changing Face of Central Banking. Evolutionary Trends since World War II*. Cambridge: Cambridge University Press.

Silberman, B. (1993). *Cages of Reason: The Rise of the Rational State in France, Japan, the United States, and Britain*, Chicago: University of Chicago Press.

Silva-Jáuregui, C. (2004). 'Macroeconomic Stabilization and Sustainable Growth', in M. Mrak, M. Rojec, and C. Silva-Jáuregui (eds.), *Slovenia: From Yugoslavia to the European Union*. Washington, DC: The World Bank, pp. 115–31.

Singleton, J. with Grimes, A., Hawke, G., and Holmes, F. (2006). *Innovation and Independence: The Reserve Bank of New Zealand 1973–2002*. Auckland: Auckland University Press.

Small, D. and Clouse, J. (2004). 'The Scope of Monetary Policy Actions Authorized under the Federal Reserve Act', July 19. www.federalreserve.gov/Pubs/Feds/2004/200440/200440pap.pdf

Smant, D. (2002). 'Has the European Central Bank Followed a Bundesbank Policy? Evidence from the Early Years', *Kredit und Kapital*, 35, 3: 327–43.

Smets, J., Michielsen, J., and Maes, I. (2003). 'Belgium and the Creation of the Euro', in M. Dumoulin, G. Duchêne, and A. Van Laer (eds.), *La Belgique, les Petits États et la Construction Européenne*. Brussels: P.I.E.-Lang, pp. 295–318.

Smith, D. J. (2002). 'Estonia. Independence and European Integration', in D. Smith, A. Pabriks, A. Purs, and T. Lane (eds.), *The Baltic States: Estonia, Latvia and Lithuania*. London and New York: Routledge, pp. vii-196.

Smits, R. (1997). *The European Central Bank. Institutional Aspects*. The Hague: Kluwer Law International.

Sotiropoulos, D. (1996). *Populism and Bureaucracy. The Case of Greece under PASOK, 1981–89*. Notre Dame: Notre Dame University Press.

Spanou, C. (1998). 'Les sirènes de la politisation. Fonction publique et politique en Grèce', *Revue Française d'Administration Publique*, 86: 243–54.

References

Stadler, R. (1996). *Der rechtliche Handlungsspielraum de Europäischen Systems der Zentralbanken*. Baden-Baden: Nomos.

Stanojevic, M. (2003). 'Worker's Power in Transition Economies: The Cases of Serbia and Slovenia', *European Journal of Industrial Relations*, 9, 3: 283–301.

Stark, J. (2008*a*). 'Monetary Policy and the Euro'. Speech at the Conference on 'Advantages and Benefits of the Euro – Time for Assessment', European Economic and Social Committee, Brussels, 15 April.

—— (2008*b*). 'Bullet Points for Intervention Delivered at the OECD-IMF Conference on Structural Reforms', Paris, 17 March.

Stark, J. (2008*c*). 'The Agenda for the Competitiveness of Europe's Economy and Financial System', speech delivered at Ambrosetti Finance Workshop, Cernobbio, 5 April.

Stasavage, D. (2003). 'Transparency, Democratic Accountability and the Economic Consequences of Monetary Institutions', *American Journal of Political Science*, 47, 3: 389–402.

St-Amant, P., Tkacz, G., Guérard-Langlois, A., and Morel, L. (2005). 'Quantity, Quality, and Relevance: Central Bank Research, 1990–2003', *Working Paper*, 2005–37. Ottawa: Bank of Canada.

Stiglitz, J. (1997). 'Central Banking in a Democratic Society', *Tinbergen Lecture*, Amsterdam, 10 October. Washington, DC: The World Bank Group.

Stirewalt, B. D. and Horner, J. E. (2000). *Poland-National Bank of Poland: Final Report*. Washington, DC: USAID.

Stone Sweet, A. and Sandholtz, W. (1998). 'Integration, Supranational Governance, and the Institutionalization of the European Polity', in A. Stone Sweet and W. Sandholtz (eds.), *European Integration and Supranational Governance*. Oxford: Oxford University Press, pp. 1–26.

Stürmer, M. (2005). 'Buba ohne Land', *Die Welt*, 31 March.

Surico, P. (2003). 'Asymmetric Reaction Functions for the Euro Area', *Oxford Review of Economic Policy*, 19, 1: 44–57.

Svendsen, K. and Hansen, S. (1968). *Dansk pengehistorie 1700–1914*. København: Danmarks Nationalbank.

Svensson, L. (2001). *Independent Review of the Operation of Monetary Policy in New Zealand: Report to the Minister of Finance*. Wellington: The Treasury.

—— (2002). 'A reform of the Eurosystem's monetary-policy strategy is increasingly urgent' Briefing paper for the Committee on Economic and Monetary Affairs (ECON) of the European Parliament for the quarterly dialogue with the President of the European Central Bank, available online at http://www.princeton.edu/svensson/papers/ep205.pdf

—— (2006). 'The role of science in best-practice monetary policy: in honor of Otmar Issing', paper presnted at 'Monetary Policy: A Journey from Therory to Practice', an ECB Colloquium held in honour of Otmar Issing in Frankfurt, 16–17 March 2006.

—— (2007). 'Optimal Inflation Targeting: Further Developments of Inflation Targeting', in F. Mishkin and K. Schmidt-Hebbel (eds.), *Monetary Policy under Inflation Targeting*. Santiago de Chile: Central Bank of Chile.

Sveriges Riksbank (1999). *Annual Report 1998*. Stockholm: Sveriges Riksbank.

—— (2007). *Annual Report 2006*. Stockholm: Sveriges Riksbank.

Szász, A. (1988). *Monetaire Diplomatie. Nederlands Internationale Monetaire Politiek 1958–1987*. Leiden/Antwerpen: Stenfert Kroese.

—— (2001). *De Euro. Politieke Achtergronden van de Wording van een Munt.* Amsterdam: Mets and Schilt.

Taylor, C. (2000). 'The Role and Status of the European Central Bank: Some Proposals for Accountability and Cooperation', in C. Crouch (ed.), *After the Euro: Shaping Institutions for Governance in the Wake of European Monetary Union.* Oxford: Oxford University Press, pp. 179–202.

Tekin, F. and Wessels, W. (2008). 'Flexibility within the Lisbon Treaty: Trade Mark of Empty Promises?', *EIPASCOPE* 2008/1, 25–31.

The Economist (1997). 'Mr Brown and EMU', November 1: 31.

Tilly, C. (1975). *The Formation of National States in Western Europe.* Princeton: Princeton University Press.

Tinbergen, J. (1952). *On the Theory of Economic Policy.* Amsterdam: North Holland Publishing Co.

Toniolo, G. (2005). *Central Bank Cooperation at the Bank for International Settlements, 1930–1973.* Cambridge: Cambridge University Press.

Townend, J. (1997). 'The UK and the Euro', the Bank of Wales lecture, Pamphlet, Cardiff Business School, 29 October.

Treasury Committee (2008). *House of Commons Treasury Committee: The Run on the Rock. Fifth Report of Session 2007–8: volume 1: Report together with formal minutes.* HC 56–1.

Trichet, J.-C. (2007*a*). *Letter to Manuel Lobo Antunes, President of the Council of the European Union on the Clarification of the Institutional Status of the ECB,* 2 August. Frankfurt: European Central Bank.

—— (2007*b*). 'The role of Research in Central Banks and at the ECB', Award of the Germán Bernácer Prize, Madrid, 21 May.

—— (2008). 'Introductory Statement with Q and A', *Transcript of Press Conference,* 8 February. Frankfurt: European Central Bank.

Tucker, P. (2006). 'Reflections on Operating Inflation Targeting', *Bank of England Quarterly Bulletin,* Summer: 212–24.

Tůma, Z. (2004). 'Speech at CMC Graduation School of Business', December 4.

Valach, V. (2004). '44 Years in Banking, Part 3' *BIATEC,* 12, 12: 19–22.

Valance, G. (1996). *La Legende du franc.* Paris: Flammarion.

Van Apeldoorn, B. (2002). *Transnational Capitalism and the Struggle over European Integration.* London: Routledge.

Vandeputte, R., Abraham, J.-P., and Lempereur, CL. (1981). *Les institutions financières belges, Tome I – Le secteur public.* Namur: Éditions Érasme.

Vanhuysse, P. (2006). *Divide and Pacify: The Political Economy of the Welfare State in Hungary and Poland, 1989–1996.* Budapest: Central European University Press.

Vanthoor, W. (2004). *De Nederlandsche Bank 1814–1998. Van Amsterdamse Kredietinstelling naar Europese Stelselbank.* Amsterdam: Boom.

—— (2005). *The King's Eldest Daughter. A History of the Nederlandsche Bank 1814–1998.* Amsterdam: Boom.

Verdun, A. (1990). 'Naar een Economische en Monetaire Unie (1970–1990): een analyse van de politieke beleidsruimte in Nederland', Mimeo, University of Amsterdam.

—— (1996). 'An "Asymmetrical" Economic and Monetary Union in the EU: Perceptions of Monetary Authorities and Social Partners', *Journal of European Integration,* 20, 1: 59–81.

References

Verdun, A. (1999a). 'The Logic of Giving up National Currencies: Lessons from Europe's Monetary Union', in E. Gilbert and E. Helleiner (eds.), *Nation-States and Currencies*. London: Routledge, pp. 199–214.

—— (1999b). 'The Role of the Delors Committee in Creating EMU: An Epistemic Community?' *Journal of European Public Policy*, 6, 2: 308–28.

—— (2000). *European Responses to Globalization and Financial Market Integration: Perceptions of Economic and Monetary Union in Britain, France and Germany*. Basingstoke: Macmillan/ New York: St. Martin's Press.

—— (2002). 'The Netherlands and EMU: A Small Open Economy in Search of Prosperity', in K. Dyson (ed.), *European States and the Euro. Europeanization, Variation, and Convergence*. Oxford: Oxford University Press, pp. 238–54.

—— (2008). 'The Netherlands and EMU: A Turning Point in Dutch-EU Relations?', in K. Dyson (ed.), *The Euro at Ten*. Oxford: Oxford University Press, pp. 222–42.

Véron, N. (2007). *Is Europe Ready for a New Banking Crisis?* Brussels: Breugel.

Vifell, Å. (2006). *Enklaver i staten. Internationalisering, demokrati och den svenska statsförvaltningen*. Stockholm Studies in Politics 113, Stockholm University: Department of Political Science.

Visser, J. (2005). *Patterns and Variations in European Industrial Relations*. Report Prepared for the European Commission.

Voridis, H., Angelopoulou, E., and Skotida, I. (2003). 'Monetary Policy in Greece 1990–2000 through the Publications of the Bank of Greece', *Economic Bulletin*, Bank of Greece, No. 20, January.

Weber, A. (2005a). 'Bundesbank erfuellt vielseitige Funktionen', *Boersen-Zeitung*, 11 June.

—— (2005b). 'Wirtschaftliche Perspektiven in Deutschland', *Auszuege aus Presseartikeln*, Deutsche Bundesbank, 8 December.

—— (2006a). 'Die Aufgaben und Geschaeftsfelder der Deutschen Bundesbank, *Auszuege aus Presseartikeln*, Deutsche Bundesbank, 47, 8 November: 3–5.

—— (2006b). 'The Role of Interest Rates in Theory and Practice', *Auszuege aus Presseartikeln*, 12, Deutsche Bundesbank, 16 March: 7–13.

—— (2007). 'Wir muessen uns keine neuen Aufgaben suchen', *Auszuege aus Presseartikeln*, Deutsche Bundesbank, 8 August.

—— (2008a). 'The Eurosystem and its Prospects – History in the Making', *Auszuege aus Presseartikeln*, 23, Deutsche Bundesbank, 4 June.

—— (2008b). 'Financial Markets and Monetary Policy', Auszuege aus Presseartikeln, Deutsche Bundesbank, 1 October: 3–6.

Wellink, A. H. E. M. (2008). 'Wim Duisenberg's Legacy as President of De Nederlandsche Bank'. 28 February, Universiteit van Amsterdam.

Werner, P. (1991). *Itinéraires Luxembourgeois et Européens*. Paris: Éditions Saint-Paul.

White, L. (2005). 'The Federal Reserve System's Influence on Research in Monetary Economics', *Economic Journal Watch*, 2, 2: 325–54.

Wood, D. (2005). *Governing Global Banking*. Aldershot: Ashgate.

Woodford, M. (2003). *Interest and Prices*. Princeton: Princeton University Press.

—— (2005). 'Central Bank Communication and Policy Effectiveness'. Paper prepared for the conference on 'Inflation Targeting: Implementation, Communication and Effectiveness'. Sveriges Riskbank, Stockholm, 10–12 June.

—— (2007). 'The Case for Forecast Targeting as a Monetary Policy Strategy', *Journal of Economic Perspectives*, 21, 4: 3–24.

Woods, N. (2002). 'Global Governance and the Role of Institutions', in D. Held and A. McGrew (eds.), *Governing Globalization*. Oxford: Polity Press, pp. 25–45.

Woodward, B. (1997). *Maestro: Greenspan's Fed and the American Boom*. New York: Touchstone.

—— (2001). *Maestro: Alan Greenspan and the American Economy*. New York: Simon and Schuster.

Woolley, J. (1984). *Monetary Politics: The Federal Reserve and the Politics of Monetary Policy*. New York: Cambridge University Press.

—— (1985). 'Central Banks and Inflation', in L. N. Lindberg and C. S. Maier (eds.), *The Politics of Inflation and Economic Stagnation*. Washington, DC: Brookings, pp. 318–51.

—— (1998). 'Exorcising Inflation-Mindedness: Changing the Politics of Macroeconomic Policy in the 1970s', *Journal of Policy History*, 10, 1: 130–52.

—— (2007). 'Institutional Structure and the Politics of Monetary Policy since 1979'. Prepared for delivery at the 2007 Annual Meeting of the American Political Science Association, August 30–September 2.

World Bank (1997a). *Implementation Completion Report, Poland: Enterprise and Financial Sector Adjustment Loan, Report No. 16743*. Washington, DC: World Bank.

World Bank (1997b). *Poland Country Assistance Review, Volume I, Report No. 16495*. Washington, DC: World Bank.

Wrong, D. H. (1970). *Max Weber*. Englewood Cliffs: Prentice Hall, Inc.

Wyplosz, C. (2001). 'The Fed and the ECB', *Briefing Notes to the Committee for Economic and Monetary Affairs of the European Parliament*, May 28.

Zeitler, F.-C. (2007). 'Wir stolzieren nicht wie Dagobert Duck', *Auszuege aus Presseartikeln*, Deutsche Bundesbank, 8 August.

Zubek, R. (2006). 'Poland: Unbalanced Domestic Leadership in Negotiating Fit', in K. Dyson (ed.), *Enlarging the Euro Area: External Empowerment and Domestic Transformation in East Central Europe*. Oxford: Oxford University Press, pp. 197–214.

Zysman, J. (1983). *Governments, Markets and Growth*. Ithaca: Cornell University Press.

Index

ABN Amro 194
accountability:
  and balance of power consideration 391
  and Banca d'Italia 186, 192–3, 195
  and Bank of Greece 176
  and central banks 22
    domestic state traditions 25
  and change in nature of 389
  and consensus on 391
  as contested concept 393
  and definition of 392
    difficulties with 393–4
  and democracy 393
  and European Central Bank 83, 303,
    400–1
    absence of policy debate 404–5
    development of 402
    enhancing democratic image 401
    European Parliament 401–3
    impact of bank's mandate 403–4
    lack of accountability to executive 403
    role of central bankers 404
    self-interested motivations 402–3
  and Federal Reserve System 395–6
    Congressional pressure 398, 400
    development of 396–7
    inflation targeting debate 398–400
    internal pressure for 398
  and political rationale for 393
  and Reserve Bank of Australia 291, 300,
    301
  and Reserve Bank of New Zealand 291, 298,
    300, 301
  and sources of variations in:
    executive policy leadership 395
    legislative oversight power 395
    solidity of central bank independence
    394–5
  and techniques enhancing 392
Adenauer, Konrad 140
Allen, Bill 254
Alphandéry, Edmond 117
Ansiaux, Hubert 92
architecture, and central banks 27
Arthuis, Jean 117, 123

asset prices 31
  and monetary policy 368–9, 372
Australia:
  and economic transformation 287
  and political system 287
  see also Reserve Bank of Australia
Australian Prudential Regulation Authority
  (APRA) 292
Austrian Central Bank, and specialization 43

Balcerowicz, Leszek 227, 232
Balladur, Edouard 117
Baltic States 217
Banca Antonveneta 82, 194
Banca Bilbao Vizcaya Argentaria 194
Banca d'Italia 183–4, 198–9
  and accountability 192–3, 195
    pre-EMU period 186
  and Basel Committee on Banking
    Supervision 197–8
  and central bank cooperation 43
  and convergence 198
  and credibility of:
    'exporting' of 190
    regaining of 195
  and crisis in 42
  and domestic banking system 194–5
  and EMU accession, unpreparedness
    for 188
  and European System of Central Banks 197
  and Europeanization 198–9
  and exchange-rate policy:
    as Eurosystem member 193
    pre-EMU period 187–8
  and financial stability:
    as Eurosystem member 193
    pre-EMU period 188
  and globalization 198
  and governance reforms 191
    adaptation to Eurosystem 192
    appointments 191
    collective decision-making 191–2
    ownership structure 191
  and Governor's power, pre-EMU period
    185

435

Index